D0025022

George of Bohemia

King of Heretics

George of Bohemia
King of Heretics

BY FREDERICK G. HEYMANN

PRINCETON, NEW JERSEY

PRINCETON UNIVERSITY PRESS

1965

Copyright © 1965 by Princeton University Press
All Rights Reserved
L. C. Card No. 64-19821

Publication of this book has been aided by
the Ford Foundation Program to support publication,
through university presses, of works in
the humanities and social sciences and by the
Committee for the Promotion of
Advanced Slavic Cultural Studies, Inc.

✧

Printed in the United States of America
by Vail-Ballou Press, Inc., Binghamton, N.Y.

284.34371

J56w

92092

To Edith

PREFACE

THIS BOOK, in essence, is a sequel to my earlier study: *John Žižka and the Hussite Revolution* (Princeton 1955). There, I had tried to write an up-to-date account and interpretation of the early, militant phases of Hussitism, which I still believe to be the first and thus the most daring and pioneering of the great European revolutions which did so much to change the character and structure of Western society. I had also tried to draw attention to some forms in which Hussitism as a social and religious movement (and even as a phase of military-technological progress) anticipated and pioneered for similar developments of the sixteenth century, notably the German and Swiss Reformations. In concentrating now (without any attempt at chronological completeness) upon the Poděbradian age I hope to present another aspect in the development of the last great and active phase of the history of the Czech people and state in times of transition from the medieval to the modern world.

In Czech historiography of the nineteenth century, especially by Palacký, the Poděbradian age was generally still considered the second act of the historical drama of Hussitism, another wave of militant determination and heroism with which this small nation defended its reformation, thereby playing a European role far beyond its numerical strength. Some special justification for this view seemed to arise out of the fact that these same years witnessed the gestation and birth of one of the most important developments of early Protestantism: the Unitas fratrum or Unity of Czech Brethren. Its growth to real greatness, however, belongs mainly to a later age.

This nineteenth-century view which, with minor exceptions, looked at the Poděbradian age with essentially positive value judgments was not shared by some German Catholic historians but was essentially maintained by Urbánek, the Czech historian who specialized in this field during the last four decades. Some recent Czech interpretations, on the other hand, have taken a less positive view of the Poděbradian age, considering it essentially as the first part of the process of the re-strengthening of feudalism.

While I agree with some of the younger Czech historians that the Poděbradian age can hardly be considered a true continuation of the great revolutionary phase of Hussitism, I cannot help feeling that the characterization of this age as essentially a return to feudalism is an over-simplification. George, indeed, arose from a background of largely feudalist interests and ideas, but he succeeded in freeing himself from them to a remarkable extent, and he used his growing strength to open the way toward a development parallel, in many regards, to Western-European developments, especially to the Tudor phase of English history. This vigorous if short-lived development of "Tudorism" in Bohemia is, as I have tried to show, one of the most important characteristics of the Poděbradian era. It was not because of but in spite of George's life and work (and partly because of his early death) that in the half-century after him that type of late feudalism known as the "ständestaat" prevailed. This destroyed, I think, the chance, still open in George's time, for a monarchy that combined effective central power with constitutionalism and that was able to achieve a form of internal balance among the social forces inside the Czech realm. Therewith, also, disappeared all hope for a sounder development and, as its possible result, for a stronger state than the one which perished in 1620.

This book has been long in the making, for I have had to suspend work on it frequently for periods of many months. This caused some unforeseen difficulties, partly also because new material came out while the work was already in a progressed state. Thus the fourth volume of Rudolf Urbánek's great *Věk poděbradský* appeared (in 1962) at a time when I had already finished that part of this study dealing with the period covered in Urbánek's last volume: the years 1460 to 1464. It did not induce me to undertake any major revisions either of the factual narrative or the interpretation of the developments of that time, but it did bring some materials and facts into focus which had so far been neglected or misunderstood by earlier Czech and German historiography. Thus it certainly asked for another careful review of what I had written on this middle phase of King George's reign, and resulted in a number of minor clarifications and corrections.

The list of my obligations to helpful institutions and individuals is a long one. Much of my initial work for this undertaking was done during a two-year membership at the Institute for Advanced Study at Princeton. I am deeply grateful to its director, Dr. J. Robert Oppenheimer, to its School of Historical Studies and especially to its distinguished medievalist, Ernst Kantorowicz, whose recent death is greatly mourned by his friends and disciples. I also want to mention the help that the librarians of the Institute, just as later those of the University of Alberta, Calgary, gave me in their effort to obtain by inter-library loan works which were not easy to locate. I am greatly obliged to Dr. Francis Wagner, of the Library of Congress, who gave me generous help by drawing my attention to relevant works in Magyar on the problems of Hungarian-Czech relations and developments in the era of George of Poděbrady and Matthias Corvinus and who presented me with a special bibliography containing extended quotations on these topics. I also owe warm thanks to my friend Prof. Peter Glockner of the University of Alberta, Calgary, who translated for me—since I do not read Hungarian—much interpretive writing of recent or contemporary Hungarian historians. (Luckily no original material from Hungarian sources of the fifteenth century is in any language other than Latin.)

Relating to source material my position was, during those last few years, better than it had been when I worked on my *Žižka*. In 1960 a travel and research grant from the Canada Council gave me the chance to spend a substantial part of the summer in Prague and to make use of libraries and archives there and in Moravia. Throughout my stay there I had the support of the Historical Institute of the Czechoslovak Academy of Science, of its director Dr. Josef Macek, and especially of Dr. František Graus, to whom I am very grateful. I am also indebted to Dr. Emma Urbánková, Director of the Manuscript Department of the National (University) Library in Prague. I was glad that I was still able to visit and consult her distinguished father, Prof. Rudolf Urbánek, at the time the greatest authority on the Poděbradian era, whose death, in 1962, has unfortunately deprived us of the hope to see the monumental torso of his great work finished by his own hands. Of high value for me was the chance to meet and discuss issues connected with my work with Dr. F. M. Bartoš, Professor Emeritus at the Comenius Evangelical Theological Faculty in Prague, as well as with Dr. Jiří Kejř of the Institute for Legal History of the Academy of Science. During my visit to several Moravian archives (partly connected with this book) Dr. Ladislav Hosák and Dr. Jaroslav Marek kindly gave me their assistance.

The Bohemian aspects of the Poděbradian story are, of course, so intimately intertwined with developments in Austria and other parts of the Holy Roman Empire that visits to places there in 1960 (and, again financed by the Canada Council, in 1963) were useful. In Vienna Professor Alphons Lhotsky gave me his support. In the German Federal Republic I am obligated to Professor Hermann Heimpel, Director of the Max Planck-Institut für Geschichte in Göttingen, under whose direction the great documentary collection of the *Deutsche Reichstags-akten* is now beginning to fill the large lacuna which had remained in the second half of the fifteenth century. Following his suggestions, three of the editors of volumes due to appear before long made parts of their collections of texts and notes accessible to me in manuscript form. The value of this important source work for studies in this period will fully emerge only when the new volumes are available in print. But even to the extent that I have had access to them I profited much, and shall remain most grateful to Professor Hellmut Weigel in Erlangen, Dr. Irmgard Most in Freiburg, and Dr. Henny Grüneisen in Göttingen, all of whom were generous in their interest and help. Frau Dr. Most in particular went out of her way, at what was for her an especially trying time, to make interesting material available to me and discuss some of it with me in detail.

As with earlier publications my wife has been an indefatigable helper, by providing me with masses of excerpts at the time of research, and by typing and re-typing the manuscript. The dedication of this book to her can only be a small token of my thankfulness.

Calgary, Alberta, April 1964.

BIBLIOGRAPHICAL ABBREVIATIONS

AČ	*Archiv český*
ADB	*Allgemeine Deutsche Biographie*
AÖG	*Archiv für österreichische Geschichte* (till 1864 *Archiv für Kunde österreichischer Geschichtsquellen*)
ČČH	*Český časopis historický*
ČČM	*Časopis Českého Museum* (*Časopis Musea Českého*)
ČMM	*Časopis Matice Moravské*
ČSČH	*Československý časopis historický*
DRTA	*Deutsche Reichstagsakten*
FRA	*Fontes rerum Austriacarum*
HZ	*Historische Zeitschrift*
JČSH	*Jihočeský sborník historický*
KBAA	*Das Kaiserliche Buch des Markgrafen Albrecht Achilles*
LF	*Listy filologické*
MIÖG	*Mitteilungen des Instituts für österreichische Geschichtsforschung*
MVGDB	*Mitteilungen des Vereins für Geschichte der Deutschen in Böhmen*
NDB	*Neue Deutsche Biographie*
RČSAV	*Rozpravy československé akademie věd*
SLČP	*Staří letopisové čeští*, ed. Palacký and re-edited by J. Charvát, in *Dílo F. Palackého* II, Prague, 1941
SLČV	*Staré letopisy ceské z vratislavkého rukopisu*, ed. F. Šimek, Prague, 1937
SLČK	*Staré letopisy ceske z rukopisu křižovnického*, ed. F. Šimek and M. Kaňák, Prague, 1959
SrS	*Scriptores rerum Silesiacarum*
VKČSN	*Věstník královské české společnosti nauk*
ZfGS	*Zeitschrift für Geschichte Schlesiens*
ZVGAS	*Zeitschrift des Vereins für Geschichte und Altertum Schlesiens*
ZVGMS	*Zeitschrift des Vereins für Geschichte Mährens und Schlesiens*

PLACE NAMES IN DIFFERENT LANGUAGES

Czech (or Slovak)	German	Polish	Hungarian
Bratislava (Slovakia) (earlier: Prešporok)	Pressburg		Pozsony
Břeh (Silesia)	Brieg	Brzeg	
Brno (Moravia)	Brünn		
Budějovice (Bohemia)	Budweis		
Budín (Hungary)	Ofen		Buda
Budyšin (Lusatia)	Bautzen	Budziszyn	
Bytom (Silesia)	Beuthen	Bytom	
Cheb (Bohemia)	Eger		
Chotěbuz (Lusatia)	Cottbus		
Duchcov (Bohemia)	Dux		
Hlohov (Silesia)	Glogau	Glogów	
Hodonín (Moravia)	Göding		
Hradec Králové (Bohemia)	Königgrätz		
Hradiště (Moravia)	Radisch		
Ivančice (Moravia)	Eibenschitz		
Jáchymov (Bohemia)	Joachimsthal		
Jager (Hungary)	Erlau		Eger
Javory (Silesia)	Jauer	Jawor	
Jihlava (Moravia)	Iglau		
Jindřichův Hradec (Bohemia)	Neuhaus		
Kadaň (Bohemia)	Kaaden		
Kladsko (Bohemia-Silesia)	Glatz	Kłodzko	
Kološ (Transylvania) (Cluj in Rumanian)	Klausenburg		Kolozsvár
Košice (Slovakia)	Kaschau	Koszyce	Kassa
Czech (or Slovak)	German	Polish	Hungarian
Kroměříž (Moravia)	Kremsier		
Krumlov (Bohemia)	Krummau		
Krumlov (Moravia)	Kromau		

Czech (or Slovak)	German	Polish	Hungarian
Kutná Hora (Bohemia)	Kuttenberg		
Lehnice (Silesia)	Liegnitz	Legnica	
Litoměřice (Bohemia)	Leitmeritz		
Litomyšl (Bohemia)	Leitomischl		
Loket (Bohemia)	Elbogen		
Malbork (Prussia)	Marienburg	Malborg	
Meziříči (Moravia)	Meseritsch		
Most (Bohemia)	Brüx		
Nisa (Silesia)	Neisse	Nysa	
Olomouc (Moravia)	Olmütz		
Olešnice (Silesia)	Öls	Oleśnica	
Opava (Silesia)	Troppau	Opawa	
Opoli (Silesia)	Oppeln	Opole	
Osek (Bohemia)	Riesenburg		
Ostřihom (Hungary)	Gran		Esztergom
Osvětím (Silesia)	Auschwitz	Oświęcim	
Pelhřimov (Bohemia)	Pilgram		
Pětikosteli (Hungary)	Fünfkirchen		Pécs
Plavno (Saxony)	Plauen		
Plzeň (Bohemia)	Pilsen		
Přerov (Moravia)	Prerau		
Prostějov (Moravia)	Prossnitz		
Ratiboř (Silesia)	Ratibor	Racibórz	
Roudnice (Bohemia)	Raudnitz		
Slavkov (Moravia)	Austerlitz		
Svidnice (Silesia)	Schweidnitz	Swidnica	
Špilberk (Moravia)	Spielberg		
Těšín (Silesia)	Teschen	Cieszyn	
Tovačov (Moravia)	Tobitschau		
Trenčín (Slovakia)	Trentschin		Trencśen
Trnava (Slovakia)	Tirnau		Nagyszombat
Uherské Hradiště (Moravia)	Ungarisch Hradisch		
Uherský Brod (Moravia)	Ungarisch Brod		
Czech (or Slovak)	*German*	*Polish*	*Hungarian*
Uničov (Moravia)	Mährisch-Neustadt		
Ustí (Bohemia)	Aussig		
Varadín (Hungary)	Grosswardein		Nagyvárad

(In Rumanian: Oradea Mare)

Vratislav (Silesia)	Breslau	Wrocław
Vysoké Mýto (Bohemia)	Hohenmaut	
Zábřeh (Moravia)	Hohenstadt	
Zaháň (Silesia)	Sagan	Żagań
Zelená Hora (Bohemia)	Grünberg	
Zhořelec (Lusatia)	Görlitz	Zgorzelec
Žitava (Saxony)	Zittau	
Znojmo (Moravia)	Znaim	

CONTENTS

LIST OF ILLUSTRATIONS

Maps

George of Bohemia

King of Heretics

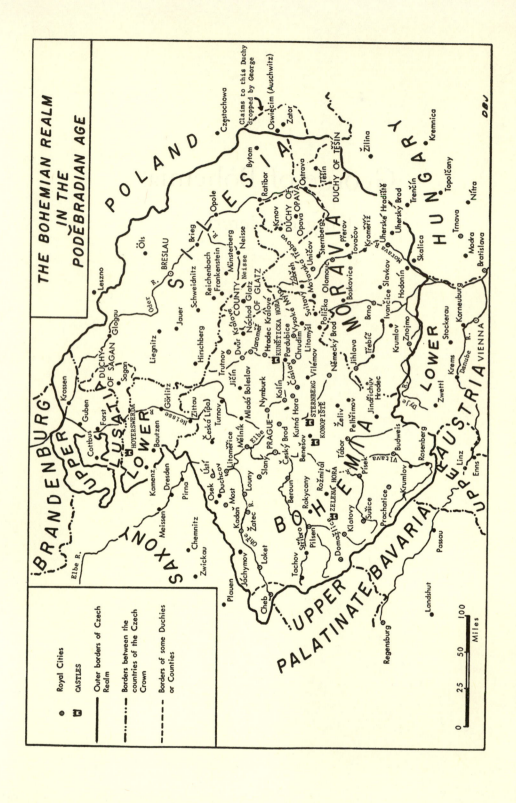

THE BOHEMIAN REALM IN THE PODĚBRADIAN AGE

CHAPTER 1

INTERREGNUM AND ANARCHY

IN THE course of the last five or six centuries there occurred in Europe hundreds of violent upheavals, some within the frame of a city or town, others regional, still others nationwide or even crossing national borderlines. All of them are significant as they usually indicate that processes of longer duration resulted in socio-structural and socio-ideological changes and tensions with which the existing political systems and powers were no longer able to cope successfully by suppression or peaceful adaptation.

Events of this type took place, for instance, when in a medieval city a strengthened urban middle class, reinforced mainly by its craft guilds, rebelled against and overthrew the rule of a resisting but no longer potent patrician oligarchy. Limited but temporarily successful peasant rebellions occurred in many parts of Europe. It is probably a question of semantics whether all, many or a few of such uprisings should be dignified by the term "revolution." But there certainly are a few such events whose significance was extraordinary in that they drew the social fabric of a whole nation into the process of their violent tremors, thereby substantially altering existing power relationships and social structures in that nation, and even spilling over its borders into other regions and to other peoples. These were the truly great revolutions. There were just five or six of them in as many centuries of European history.

It was the extraordinary fate of a small nation of Slav origin, the Czechs, to have experienced, or it may be said achieved, the very first of those great and historically consequential and productive upheavals: the Hussite one.[1] It had been prepared by a mainly spirit-

[1] For the most recent treatment in English see the present author's book, *John Žižka and the Hussite Revolution*, Princeton, 1955 (later cited as Heymann, *Žižka*). This includes a bibliography on primary and secondary sources. Publication of a new work in two volumes, probably to be called *Husitská revoluce*, by the greatest living Czech authority on Hussitism, Prof. F. M. Bartoš, is impending within the framework of the large standard work on Czech history, *České Dějiny* (started by Novotný). It will be a continuation of Bartoš' previous work on the times of Hus (*Čechy v době Husově*, Prague, 1947). On some important aspects of the Hussite revolution, mainly in relation to the Taborite movement, see the works by J. Macek, especially his *Tábor v husitském revolučním hnutí*, 2 vols., Prague, 1955, 1956.

ual rebellion against the strongest single power structure within Bohemia and indeed in most of Europe, the Roman Catholic Church. It
was something of a historical irony that a movement which in itself
had been an attempt at changing and reforming this structure, the
Conciliar Movement, had in its first great and partially successful
effort, at the Council of Constance, put on trial and burned as a
heretic the Prague Master John Hus, and this in spite of a safe conduct given to him by the council's protector and president: the Roman
King (later Emperor) Sigismund.

Hus was probably the greatest in a whole line of reforming religious
minds that had been active in Bohemia in the second half of the
fourteenth and in the beginning fifteenth centuries. But, besides
being a religious and ethical thinker and reformer of great purity
and enormous impact upon his countrymen, Hus had become a national symbol, and his execution in 1415 was felt by people of all
stations, including a considerable part of the high nobility, to be
an insult to the Czech nation. It was largely this common mood of
defiance which led almost the whole nation into resistance against
Sigismund, who was also King of Hungary and a younger brother
of Bohemia's King Wenceslas IV. This resistance took the most
militant forms when, at Wenceslas' death, Sigismund claimed his
right to succeed to the Czech crown. What had begun as a limited
rebellion in Prague, subterraneously connected with provincial and
rural movements and resistance centers, became soon a general revolution against the King and the international Church organization
which backed him and his claims.

The sequence of Hussite victories over King Sigismund and the
other potentates who tried to crush the small nation of supposed
heretics remains one of the amazing epics with which historical
truth occasionally rises above dramatic imagination. But the Czech
nation, which had united in resisting the hated King, did not long
remain united. It could not possibly remain so, for among its motivating, innervating powers of strength were the desires and antagonisms out of which the less privileged parts of the Czech nation
—the peasants, the great majority of the townspeople, and a considerable number of the less well-to-do gentry—reacted against the
pressure inflicted on them by the upper class of society. Above all,
this hostility included the overly wealthy church, but also the—
originally largely German—city aristocracy in Prague and some other
Czech cities, and those members of the Czech baronial class who

came out for the defense of the status quo economically, politically, and, to an increasing extent, religiously.

These antagonisms often resulted in bloody internal struggles, and at least twice the forces of the Right tried to destroy the newly strengthened "lower" elements forming the Center and Left to bring about an outright restoration of much of the previous power structure, at least as far as the dominant position of the baronial class was concerned. In 1424, in the battle of Malešov, Žižka, the old squire who led the "Warriors of God," defeated the army of lords and the Prague Conservatives and thereby helped essentially to stabilize the new, more balanced relation between the major social, political, and religious groups for another decade. But in 1434, at the battle of Lipany, the armies of the brotherhoods, Taborites and Orphans, allied with the majority of the royal cities of Bohemia, were overcome by a coalition of the Right—again lords and Prague patricians, strengthened by some elements of the Center. Thereby the way was paved for a "Thermidor," implying the restoration of the last Luxemburg, the Emperor Sigismund, to the Czech throne as well as for the general acceptance of the compromise essentially worked out even earlier between the Hussites and the Council of Basel.

But if the battle of Lipany was the decisive "Thermidor" of the Hussite Revolution it did not mean, here as in parallel developments, that the revolution had been for nothing, had not worked any changes of real significance. It had, for one thing, largely eliminated the foreign, mainly German, influence in Bohemia and its impact upon the policy of Prague and other royal cities. Far more important, it had decisively weakened the Roman Church by depriving her of the greater part of her enormous land holdings. From now on the Church, earlier the strongest of all the elements in the feudal structure of Bohemia, was limited to a much narrower economic basis and could not even count upon recouping any substantial part of her losses from the Catholic nobility, who had themselves been among the main profiteers. The Church, from now on, was doubly weakened: by the vast defection of the Hussite Utraquists and Sectarians as well as by her lack of sustaining landed estates. She was therefore partly dependent on support from outside, especially from the Holy See, if she hoped to regain a substantial part of her lost position in the fabric of Bohemia's society.

Among those groups that had gained were, as mentioned before, some of the great baronial houses, but their political influence, so

strongly weakened in the years from 1420 to 1434, had not been restored to the high nobility after the end of the Revolution in a measure proportionate to their purely economic gains. This was due to
the fact that all through the revolutionary years the gentry as well
as large parts of the urban middle class had gained positions considerably stronger than those they had ever occupied before. This
was true in economic terms—for they, too, had substantially participated in the confiscation of vast ecclesiastical lands. It was true
politically, for both had participated in the increased influence of
parliamentary institutions—the sněmy or diets—in those prolonged
interregnal periods when the national diets had become virtually the
only sources of authority recognized by the whole country.

The longing for a national authority strong enough to maintain
and protect internal peace was bound to become a very general desire. War, foreign and domestic, had tortured the country too long
to be regarded, by the overwhelming majority of the Czech people,
with anything but loathing. Even those few who would have profited
from the prolonged anarchy would not admit this publicly. But
while the causes for and basic attitudes leading to continued strife
were complex they tended to express themselves in the same terms
that had dominated the period of open war and revolution: the
terms of the religious split. And it seemed obvious that now, and
for as long as anybody could see or plan for, religious peace, the
building and maintenance of stable bridges across the religious
schism, was the precondition of peace in general.

But, under the circumstances, there was only one basis for such
religious peace. It was the agreement between the Czech Estates and
the Council of Basel,[2] culminating in the document called the Compacts, a sort of peace treaty which, after prolonged negotiations, had
been solemnly proclaimed by representatives of both sides (and guaranteed by the Emperor Sigismund) in July 1436 in the Moravian
city of Jihlava.

This agreement, therefore, played a role of extraordinary impor-

[2] The literature on the Council, even regarding only its dealings with the Bohemian heresy,
is tremendous. For the sources see mainly *Monumenta conciliorum generalium seculi decimi
quinti; Concilium Basileense,* vols. I and II, ed. F. Palacký and E. Birk, Vienna, 1857 and
1873; and J. D. Mansi, *Sacrorum Conciliorum nova collectio,* vols. 29 and 30, Venice 1788,
1792. For interpretive treatments see the still lively and useful presentation in Palacký's history
of Bohemia (German or Czech), III, 3 *passim;* Rudolf Urbánek, *Věk Poděbradský (České
dějiny,* ed. Novotný, III, 1, cited later as "Urbánek, *Věk*") vol. I., chapter 2; finally the
valuable sketch by E. F. Jacob "The Bohemians at the Council of Basel," in *Prague Essays,*
ed. R. W. Seton-Watson, Oxford, 1449, pp. 81ff.

tance in the consciousness of the Czech nation as a whole, even more so of its Hussite majority. For them especially the Compacts were the only possible basis for the maintenance of internal and external peace. With the acceptance of the Compacts by Emperor and council the Czech nation had been declared free from the unbearable stain of heresy. Yet the document had never been officially confirmed by the papacy. To achieve this confirmation was one of the foremost goals of Czech official diplomacy in the periods following the end of the great Hussite Wars. When again in 1467 the Hussite-Utraquist majority had to take up arms in another bloody war it was, at least in the minds of most people, again a struggle for the maintenance of the Compacts. It is, indeed, impossible to understand this part of Bohemia's and Central Europe's history without an awareness of the issues connected with this charter.

The Compacts were, in their origin, a weakened version of another great document, the Four Articles of Prague, which had demanded: 1. freedom of preaching; 2. freedom for everyone to receive the Holy Eucharist in both forms ("sub utraque specie," hence the name "Utraquists" for the adherents of this usage); 3. a life of apostolic poverty, without earthly possessions or earthly power, for all priests, and 4. the eradication and punishment of all mortal sins, especially public ones.[3] It was this set of demands which had united all Hussite groups and sects during the long revolutionary war. In the Compacts,[4] the articles about the freedom of preaching and the punishment of mortal sins were accepted in a general way but with more precise definitions of those who should have the right to preach, practically excluding all those not ordained, and of the authorities who should be entitled to proceed against the sinner. The third (now the fourth) article was eventually worded in a way which would make it impossible to use it as a basis for the further confiscation of Church property.

It was the former second article which did, in every respect, take first place in the new charter. No other issue could, in the minds of the Czech people, compare in importance with the question of the Eucharist. No peace could possibly have been achieved without this

---

[3] For the Four Articles see chapter 10 in Heymann, *Žižka*, with bibliographical note on p. 148.

[4] The Compacts (sometimes called Basel Compacts, sometimes Prague and sometimes Jihlava Compacts) together with the large number of connected documents, are printed in *Archiv český*, III (cited hereafter as *AČ*).

concession to the wishes of millions. For this goal, for the Chalice, with all its deep theological, sacramental, and symbolic implications, untold numbers of people had died and were ready to die. And in some parts of the Catholic world, especially in the dependencies of the crown of Bohemia, there were people, mostly men of German origin, who were just as willing to die in their resistance against the Chalice for laymen, which they had come to consider as a heretical practice.

The Roman claim that it was at least an illicit schismatic practice to dispense the Chalice to the laity was of fairly recent origin.[5] The limitation of the use of the cup to priests had been a slow, almost imperceptible change of usage. The Eastern Orthodox Church had never gone along with this change, yet it had never been reproached by Rome for this specific reason. (In later times, e.g. toward the close of the sixteenth century, when Rome accepted the Uniate Church in Eastern Poland as a true Catholic Church, she did not find it difficult to put up with its "Utraquism.") Yet the Council of Constance had ruled strictly against the Chalice, and all through the Hussite Wars a compromise on this issue had seemed well-nigh hopeless.

The Compacts, indeed, had achieved just this compromise, as a result of the desperate longing for peace that in the mid-thirties had animated equally the Czech people and their—mostly German— neighbors. But compromise had not meant a genuine rapprochement of hitherto diverging views—a thing which seemed so rarely attainable in theological disputes—rather was it a successful attempt at finding formulas by which the remaining divergence was, for the time being, skillfully hidden from general view—and especially from the view of the other side.

What was the content of this compromise regarding the Eucharist? The Czechs had demanded first that the communion in both forms be made obligatory for everyone in Bohemia and Moravia, but this was out of the question as it would have required an order from the Council to all Catholics in these countries to submit to a ritual which the Church had only so recently condemned. The representatives of the Council finally agreed that the Chalice be given to those men and women who were used to it and expressly demanded it, as long as otherwise they lived in the faith and the ritual of Christ and the Sacred Church. The priest, however, should never, in giving the

---

[5] See J. Smend, *Kelchspendung und Kelchversagung in der abendländischen Kirche*, Göttingen, 1898.

Chalice, miss reminding the communicant that, in each form, bread and wine, the whole Christ was given to him.

The Czechs reluctantly agreed to this, feeling that at least the substance of their central demand had been granted. They would, so they expected, be left with the right to the Chalice for all time. The important question of whether children would be allowed the Chalice was left open for future negotiations, as were other, seemingly less important details of ritual. The general functioning of the whole arrangement appeared to be safe if the Czechs could elect a trusted clerical leader as the head of the whole Bohemian Church. This right underlay the acceptance of the Compacts by the Bohemian diet, and to this arrangement the Emperor Sigismund gave his official blessing, which appeared to the Czechs as a guaranty, little reason though they had to trust him. The man who, in a rather non-canonical procedure, was elected as Archbishop of Prague by a committee of the Bohemian diet in 1435 was John Rokycana,[6] the Utraquist who had been the leading cleric and theologian of the Hussite center since 1429 and had had a most important role in the long previous negotiations. The struggle over his confirmation by Rome was therefore intimately connected with the general struggle over the Compacts.

But grave difficulties arose only hours after, in July 1436, the formal signing of the Compacts and the conclusion of peace between the Czechs and their former enemies had been joyfully consumed and celebrated in the Moravian city of Jihlava. The legates of the council, Philibert and Palomar, immediately tried to prevent Rokycana and his Utraquist priests from giving the Chalice to some of his Czechs on the grounds that he was not, now, officiating in his own parish.[7] This was just an indication of the policy to be pursued henceforth: this policy tried to establish as narrow as possible an understanding of the Compacts. In the first place the Roman prelates hoped, thereby, to keep the Czechs from widening their special status in a way which could endanger the conception of a unified Church. Yet there was another side to it which the Czechs had not expected: The Church thereby gained a position from which any small deviation from the Roman understanding of the Compacts could be construed as a breach of faith on the side of the Czechs—an act which then could be answered with declaring the Compacts as

---

6 See *AČ*, III, 436f. On Rokycana see my article: "John Rokycana, Church Reformer between Hus and Luther," *Church History*, Sept. 1959, 240–280.

7 See V. V. Tomek, *Dějepis města Prahy*, 2nd ed., IV, Prague, 1899, 708ff.

no longer valid. The Czech Hussites very soon suspected that this was the intention—and felt betrayed by Church and Emperor.

The Hussites were soon to learn that this was not the only subterfuge used by the delegates of the council. There was the limitation of the right to receive the Chalice to those who "had the usage" of the communion in both kinds. This, in the eyes of the Czechs, clearly meant that all Hussites, all Utraquists, would henceforth have this right, free from the danger of again being called and treated as heretics. Essentially the reference to the usage would then merely have been a measure to protect orthodox Catholics from being pressured into the Utraquist practice. This was, of course, what many of the Hussite leaders had hoped to do, as they were as convinced as their opponents that the living together of people with different ritual would probably result in never-ending conflicts. Yet they had made this concession in the sincere hope of obtaining a permanent modus vivendi, and, while it would be wrong to deny that in the years and decades to follow both sides used pressure on each other, the wonder was that this pressure was not any greater, especially on the side of the vast Hussite majority in Bohemia, and that for long stretches of time the religious struggle was kept within narrow limits.

But to the Roman Church the sentence of the "usage" was not meant as the basis of a permanent modus vivendi between the people "sub una" and the people "sub utraque." On the contrary, it was expected to be the basis for the removal of the difference. This could be done simply by understanding this phrase in a limited, personal sense. The Chalice, so Bishop Philibert of Coutances, one of the main legates of the council and one of its most peace-loving representatives, declared in an explanatory instruction,[8] was only to be given "to those who had had the usage at the time of the acceptance of the Compacts." Because children, in the understanding of the Church, were anyhow excluded from taking the communion and thus could not possibly have "the usage," it was only a question of time, just a few decades, till the last man entitled to Utraquist communion would have stopped breathing. And what was the span of a few decades for the Eternal Church! It is easy to see that this argument, which, in the Church's later dealings with the problem of the Compacts, was to play an increasingly important role, impressed the Hussites as a maliciously contrived deceit.

8 *Fontes rerum Austriacarum* II, 20, 477 (hereafter cited as *FRA.*)

This view, easily understandable and almost inevitable as it was, is nevertheless too partisan to be accepted by the historian. The motivations behind this stratagem were more complex. True, among some of the members of the council the old, terrible idea that no faith need ever be kept with heretics had not died out. But others, especially men like Cardinal Giuliano Cesarini, had come to know and appreciate the human qualities of the Czech Utraquist leaders— even of the more radical Taborite priest-general Prokop the Bald— and were impressed by their genuine religious and moral zeal. These prelates, we may assume, did not contrive the scheme just discussed "with malice aforethought." Rather did they feel that those people had been led astray by their over-zealousness for a Church reform the basic necessity of which, especially in regard to the constitution of the Church, they themselves did not deny.

If the prelates hoped that, by this ingenious device, the Hussite deviation would slowly disappear, even though it had, for the time being, ceased to be regarded as heretical, they had, from their ecclesiastical point of view, sound reasons for it. In a sense they, and not the Hussites, were more realistic in their judgment about the ultimate meaning of Hussitism. The Hussites, or at least the more moderate Utraquists, claimed that with their reforms, so strongly based on the Bible and the practice of the earliest Christians, they stayed right in the center of what they understood the Church to mean. Thus it seemed absurd to them to be called schismatics, let alone heretics. But the Roman prelates, with their strong feeling for the historical character and the constitutional structure of the Church, sensed that what was afoot here was much more than the type of reform which they themselves, as advocates of a measure of Conciliar parliamentarism, would have liked to see. Some of them clearly feared that, once on the path of a development as strongly sectarian and apostolic-biblical, as replete with basic deviations as was the theologically fully developed Hussitism of the post-Basel era, the formal reunion with the Church was not going to mend the deep rupture; the union would, at best, remain superficial and in the long run the divergences would prevail. If, then, it was a question of choosing between effective reform and the unity of the Church, they were bound to vote for the latter. The reform, so they might think, could still come later if it did not come now, but the loss of unity might be (and in effect proved to be) irreparable.

If considerations like this make understandable the attitude of the

Roman Church to the Compacts, her deep reluctance to fully confirm and support this peace treaty, they cannot quite justify the
high-handed way in which the Curia continued acting toward the
Czechs, especially if we look at the final, tragically costly and yet
unsuccessful attempt of the Holy See to force the issue by another
armed intervention. But in order to see this policy correctly in its
historical origin we have to consider still another important element.
The very fact that it was the Council of Basel which had concluded
the Compacts with the Czechs made this document not less but more
suspect in the eyes of the Curia. This council, after all, had gone
farther than any of its predecessors in its rebellion against Papal
absolutism and its attempts to establish the quasi-parliamentary institution of the Church Council as the highest ecclesiastical authority.
Thus the steady reminder of the Czechs—in their desire for a full
Papal confirmation of the Compacts—that this document was granted
to the Czech nation by the Fathers of the Holy Council of Basel
was only apt to remind the Popes of the mid-century of the period of
their deepest humiliation which now, luckily, had been completely
overcome.

In Bohemia the years following the peace of 1436, while no longer
a time of all-out war, nevertheless presented a chaotic picture right
up to the mid-century mark. Fate was not kind to the tortured
country. The restoration to the throne of Sigismund, the last of the
Luxemburgs, lasted merely fifteen months: in December he died.
Even in this short period, his policy as Czech King had merely contributed toward sharpening the existing religious and political antagonisms.[9] This was emphasized by threats which forced John
Rokycana, the elected Archbishop, to seek personal safety on a castle
in eastern Bohemia under the protection of some Utraquist nobles.
A majority of the diet which was to elect his successor, following
the lead of some of the great and powerful magnates with Ulrich
of Rosenberg at their head, voted for Sigismund's son-in-law Albert
of Austria (who soon afterwards also became, like Sigismund, King
of the Romans and of Hungary). But a strong minority, consisting
mostly of Utraquists and supported also by Rokycana, after a second election of somewhat doubtful validity, offered the crown to
Casimir, the teen-aged brother of King Władysław III of Poland.
And though Albert, after solemnly promising to hold and protect

[9] On this phase see Tomek, *Dějepis*, VI, ooo.

the Compacts, succeeded in getting himself crowned—which, in the eyes of most Czechs, validated his kingship—he still had to spend most of the time of his short reign in fighting a difficult civil war against the "Polish party." In his second kingdom, Hungary, where he had tried to organize a stronger defense against the Turkish danger, Albert died of a sudden illness in October 1439.[10]

The premature death of this young Habsburg ruler—a man of considerable qualities—left Bohemia and his other realms, Hungary and Austria, in a greatly disorganized state. For the moment there was no "natural heir" in sight. True, the Queen, Sigismund's daughter Elizabeth, was pregnant and four month later, in February 1440, gave birth to a boy, Ladislav, usually called Posthumus. But the Czech estates (unlike the Hungarians who soon had the infant crowned) were wary of electing a King who for a long time to come would be incapable of effective rulership. They tried to get around the "natural" succession by electing as King a German prince, Duke Albert of Bavaria, a man who was well known and liked in the country because he had been raised at the court of King Wenceslas IV and spoke Czech fluently. But he declined.[11]

Only after thirteen years' interregnum was young Ladislav accepted and crowned in Prague in October 1453. The first ten years of this period—1440–1450—were so full of strife and turmoil that eventually the longing of the people—really all the people—for an effective ruler able to preserve peace became overwhelming. The man who was strong and wise enough to fulfill these hopes was sure to gain ascendancy. George of Poděbrady turned out to be this man.

George came from the old baronial family of Kunštát that had its roots in Moravia, where it still held some possessions in the earlier fifteenth century. But already in the fourteenth century it had acquired some important holdings in Bohemia—foremost among them the strong castle and town of Poděbrady on the Elbe river, some thirty-five miles due east of Prague, important because it controlled a much travelled river crossing and by it passed the main road from Prague to the regional center of eastern Bohemia: Hradec Králové. The first of the Kunštáts to hold the castle was George's great-grandfather Boček, a man who expressed his feelings for his nation—the

---

[10] Albert's short reign is the subject of a careful monograph by A. Wostry, *König Albrecht II* (Prager Studien auf dem Gebiet der Geschichtswissenschaften), Prague, 1906–1907. See also Urbánek, *Věk*, I, 227–456.

[11] *Ibid.*, I, 514–542.

lingua Bohemica—by writing letters in Czech instead of the usual Latin.[12] His son, another Boček, George's grandfather, was the first Hussite of the family; he can be found in the first row of Hus's adherents among the high nobility, both before and after the death of the great reformer. Two of his sons, Victorin and Hynek, were among the most active protagonists of the Hussite Revolution. Both of them early became friends, followers, and close allies of the great Žižka, feeling no compunction to put their forces at the disposal—and themselves under the command—of a simple squire.[13] Of the two, Victorin was the more brilliant soldier as well as the more politically consistent. He was at Žižka's side in some of the important battles fought during the Revolution, notably the victorious campaign which in the winter of 1421–1422 drove King Sigismund out of Bohemia, and the great victory won by Žižka at Malešov over the conservative coalition in 1424. He helped Žižka effectively, especially by putting his fairly extensive holdings in eastern Bohemia—among them the towns of Pardubice, Skalice, and Náchod—at Žižka's disposal when the old general reorganized his military and political basis in cooperation with the towns of the Orebite brotherhood—the same religious-military brotherhood and field army that, after Žižka's death, called themselves Orphans. Victorin was one of the men who stayed with Žižka at the time of his death in October 1424, and remained closely allied with the Orphans to his own death—from an illness—in 1427.

Whether Žižka really was the godfather of Victorin's only son, George (or Jiří), will probably never be known with complete certainty. But it is not likely. In view of Žižka's itinerary in April 1420 —the month in which George was born and baptized—he could only have been present at the baptism if the child's first days were lived in Horažd'ovice—one of the number of Bohemian towns which made this claim. It seems more probable that he was born in the castle of Poděbrady, where Victorin could leave his wife—Anna, from the great baronial house of Wartenberg—with some confidence for her safety. Two dates for the birth appear in the sources: the 6th and the 21st of April, but the earlier date appears slightly better docu-

---

[12] This, at least, can be concluded from an agreement concluded with him at Poděbrady in 1370 by a Prague citizen. See *Český listář*, ed. Václavek, Prague, 1949, p. 29.

[13] On their history during the Hussite revolution, see Heymann, *Žižka, passim*, especially 291, 364, 387ff., 409f., 459f.

mented, and it may well be that the second one is really that of the baptism.[14]

At the time his father died the young George was not quite 7 years old. At first his father's oldest brother, Boček, became his warden, then, after his early death (before 1430), one of his father's Moravian cousins, Heralt of Kunštát. Heralt was a zealous Hussite like Victorin, but in 1434, in the great battle of Lipany in which the field armies of the Taborite and Orphan brotherhoods stood against the great majority of the barons and knights and the armies of Prague, Heralt fought on the latter side. With him fought, so we hear, his young ward.[15] Having grown up in times of war, to be ready for war was probably the main goal of his upbringing. Certainly George's participation in this battle, if we take it for a fact as it probably was, had very little significance for the battle or its political consequences. But it must have had some considerable significance for his own development and political outlook. He long continued to look at Tábor as a potential enemy.

George probably had little formal education. He knew, of course, how to read and write, but gave the impression that he was essentially limited to his Czech mother language. He does not seem to have known Latin at all, and his German seemed weak enough to make him, in later times, use an interpreter whenever he had to conduct business of importance with people who did not speak Czech. It was a method which also had its advantages, especially if you had already caught the gist of the other person's arguments. While the interpreter spoke you could consider your answer with care.

As for the rest we know little. Clearly young George grew up very conscious of belonging to partisan groups. He was a Czech at a time when the great majority of all Czechs fought against people of other nations, especially Germans and Hungarians, hardly ever losing a battle in this long and bloody war. He could not fail to be proud of being a man of this warrior-race. He was a Hussite, one

---

14 On the date and place of George's birth see Urbánek, *Věk,* I, 209ff. Also, V. Pinkava, "O rodišti krále Jiřího Poděbradského," *ČMM (Časopis Matice Moravské)*, XXIX, Brno, 1905, 392ff., and A. Sedláček's answer in the same journal, XXX, 1906, 54ff.

15 The fact has been doubted, but seems nevertheless correct. See J. Tenora, "Z mladých let pana Jiřího z Kunštátu," *ČČM (Časopis musea Království českého)*, LXIX, Prague, 1825, 290ff., and Urbánek, *Věk,* I, 218, 219. It is, of course, impossible to consider him, as has occasionally been done, as one of the leaders of the victorious army.

whose father and grandfather had already expressed their belief in the religious reform by taking the communion in both kinds—a symbol of the Law of Christ and Truth of Christ as God had revealed it to His faithful Czechs. It was another strong bond which George would never shake off to the end of his days. Finally he was a baron, one of the great lords of the realm, and he soon, at 21 years, married one of the great heiresses of the kingdom, Kunhuta of Sternberg.

His social standing might have made him proud, yet it failed to make him conceited. He must have learned at an early time that to be a lord did not necessarily mean being a better Czech or a better Utraquist Christian than other people of less lofty origin. He knew that his father had fought with Žižka, nay, under Žižka, and that Žižka had not been a lord but merely a squire. He knew men who, without even the more modest coat of arms of a squire, might wield power by the strength of their personality and of their word. Such a one was John Rokycana, the great Utraquist cleric, a man of his father's generation with whose whole life and work his own became most intimately intertwined. Certainly the times in which George grew up—hard times as years of bitter warfare usually are— were also times that could teach a gifted youngster a great deal; in the first place this experience perhaps emphasized the need to look at the world and his surroundings not merely through the eyes of a narrow caste conception. If he wanted to get along—and this he surely wanted, being ambitious from the beginning—he had to rely on himself and his gifts, had to develop his understanding of society and of people, and had, if possible, to find a good teacher. He found —or was found by—him soon: in the person of Lord Hynce Ptáček of Pirkstein.

During the short reigns of Sigismund and Albert the Czech nation lost some of the most important and effective leaders that the revolution had brought to the fore. The greatest of them was perhaps William Kostka of Postupice, a man whose statesmanship had given him a position of great responsibility as a diplomat and soldier in various places of the war, but who had become even more eminent as the foremost layman among the Czech delegates to the Council of Basel.[16] He died in battle, in the attempt to defeat a separatist rebellion of Hradec Králové, in November 1436. He was followed, in

---

[16] On the early phases of Kostka's life see Heymann, *Žižka, passim*, especially 338, 417f.

January 1438, by Diviš Bořek of Miletínek, a nobleman who had started as a friend and comrade-in-arms of Žižka, had then turned against him in the bloody civil war of 1423–1424, and had finally, as commander in chief of the army of the lords and Praguers, defeated Žižka's heirs, the field armies of the brotherhoods, at Lipany in 1434.[17] During the last phase of his life he had returned to a vigorously Hussite attitude and had taken a strong stand against Sigismund's attempts at undermining the Utraquist position. It was he who took Rokycana under his protection in his castle of Kunětická Hora.

Both of these men, characteristically, had not originally belonged to the baronial class but were knights by birth, though they had risen so high in the councils of the nation that in their case the question of caste was hardly considered, especially as long as the revolutionary tremors had not fully subsided and the social structure had retained a certain measure of mobility. Now, however, as their death coincided with a steady return to more static conditions, it was again members of the baronial class who took over the leadership of the nation, which the once so powerful cities had lost at Lipany. The first among the magnates were three men: Ulrich of Rosenberg, Menhart of Hradec, and Ptáček of Pirkstein. Of these three, only Ptáček had grown up as a thorough Catholic. It is ironical that it was he, eventually, who upheld Hussitism during the years when it seemed rather weak and the Catholic countermovement strong.

Of the leaders of the Catholic magnates, Rosenberg was the greatest, the richest, in some ways the cleverest, and by all odds the most unscrupulous. His changeover from the Hussitism of his adolescent years to sharp antagonism against all Hussite groups had no strong religious foundation. His main motive was the wish for material gains. No other man profited as abundantly and relentlessly from the chance to appropriate the landed estates which the Church had lost as a result of the Revolution. Especially in his private "Kingdom," the southern-most region of Bohemia, he managed to round out his originally scattered possessions to truly princely proportions, and for the purpose of acquiring these huge territories he did not mind forging royal donations and other beneficial documents on quite a large scale.[18]

---

[17] See *ibid.* 363ff., 383ff., 397f., 468f.

[18] On Ulrich of Rosenberg, see Urbánek, *Věk*, I, 175–186; Palacký, *Dějiny národu českého*, 2nd ed., Prague, 1877, IV, 1, 43f. (in German *Geschichte von Böhmen* IV, 1857, 1, 49f., and

Ulrich has, rather fittingly, been compared to the Italian Renaissance princes of his time in his brutal lust for wealth and power which did not stop short of murder, but he could not display it with the same recklessness that was typical for some of the Sforzas or Borgias, partly perhaps because, for all his ambitions, he never had quite the nerve that characterized his Italian peers. Also, in Bohemia, even in the time of troubles that filled the great interregnum after 1439, the moral standards, under the impact of the Hussite reformation, were stricter than in many other European countries. But Rosenberg managed, for a long time, to appear as the true spokesman for the kingdom in its relations with the outer world, especially with the Roman Curia and with Frederick III, the Habsburg prince who in 1440 had followed Albert II as King of the Romans.

Ulrich's main goal thereby was to prevent the establishment of a stable and effective government inside Bohemia which might have limited or stopped the steady aggrandizement of his possessions, his wealth, and his power. It might also, on the basis of a compromise with Rome, have returned to the Church at least some of the rich properties acquired by, among many others, the Rosenbergs. It is for this rather than for religious reasons that he regularly warned the Holy See against any concessions to the Utraquists, especially against the confirmation of the Compacts and of Rokycana's archi-episcopal position. Repeatedly he voted in public, at some of the meetings of the diet, for petitions demanding such recognition; but he followed this up by secret councils to the contrary. In the same way he had openly voted for the election of Albert of Bavaria as King of Bohemia, only to threaten this prince secretly with the most dire warnings against acceptance of his election. Whenever possible Rosenberg boycotted the diets which might establish a more permanent and effective order for the country. But by these tactics he eventually weakened his own influence, at least in the later phases of the interregnum.

Rosenberg was, throughout the time of the interregnum, the undisputed leader of the Catholics. Their actual number was not very imposing, as the great masses of the Czech people—especially among the townsmen and peasants, but also in the main among the lower nobility—still considered themselves as adherents of the reformed

---

passim). On his earlier development see also Heymann, *Žižka,* 170f., and *passim.* His documentary forgeries were proved by V. Schmidt, "Die Fälschung von Kaiser-und Königsurkunden durch Ulrich von Rosenberg," *MVGDB,* vol. 32, 317ff.; vol. 33, 181ff., 1894–1895.

creed. Only two of the leading cities of Bohemia had, throughout the Revolution, been able to maintain their Catholic character under the control of a partly German town aristocracy: Pilsen in the West (with a cluster of smaller places and estates of its region forming the so-called Pilsen Landfrieden), and Budweis, in the South, a place which had always stood directly under the protection of its great neighbor Rosenberg (even though there had frequently been conflicts between them). Indirectly four of the main cities of Moravia, Brno, Olomouc, Jihlava, and Znojmo, could be considered as followers of Rosenberg for the same reasons as Pilsen and Budweis. The baronial families who were—in whole or in parts—strictly Catholic numbered about twelve, foremost among them the lords of Riesenberg, of Švamberg, of Plauen, of Gutstein, of Lobkovice, and of Michalovice. Of the better known, wealthier, and politically active gentry families none stood under Ulrich's immediate "command."

Actually Ulrich's political power was much greater than this list might indicate. A good deal of it came to him indirectly, through his strong personal influence on the second man of this very inofficial triumvirate: Menhart of Hradec.[19]

Menhart was not a strong personality. On the contrary: it was rather his lack of strength, his general mediocrity, which resulted in the power he possessed. When in October 1436 the Emperor Sigismund, after his restoration as King of Bohemia, appointed a new slate of leading court officials, he made Menhart Lord High Burgrave of Prague. This was the highest of all the offices of the kingdom and gave the holder traditionally a position which implied high military command and even a sort of regency in times of the monarch's absence from the country. His special powers included the administration of the two most important castles of the kingdom: the Hradčany, which, with its great fortresses, palaces, and churches formed both symbolically and strategically a stronghold dominating the capital and, therewith, in a sense the country; and the Karlstein, where, among other valuables, some of the most important constitutional documents as well as the crowns and crown jewels of the kingdom were kept—things without whose use, for instance, a valid coronation of a King of Bohemia was impossible. Sigismund, in 1436, would probably have preferred to appoint a Catholic to this supremely important position, but was afraid that such a measure would lead to widespread annoyance and resistance among the Utra-

[19] See Urbánek, *Věk*, I, 201ff., and Palacký IV, I, 40f. (in German, 45f.).

quist majority. Thus he picked Menhart of Hradec, one of the most conservative leaders of the Calixtine aristocracy, who, in his religious tendencies, was influenced by such masters as Christian of Prachatice, Prokop of Pilsen, and John Příbram. All of them had a strong tendency to return to an almost completely orthodox Catholicism— that is to abandon all the reforms with the single exception of the communion in the two kinds. Toward the end of his life Lord Menhart did, indeed, abandon even this last symbol of Hussitism. But Sigismund's choice was not only determined by Menhart's—from the Catholic point of view—relatively innocuous religious position, but by his total lack of color or vigor which would make him a fairly willing tool of the Emperor's policy. Menhart did, indeed, find it difficult ever to make a strong, independent decision. While, in a negative way, he could occasionally be stubborn and headstrong, he always seems to have needed someone to prompt him toward any sort of positive action. This someone, then, during the interregnum, was his friend Ulrich of Rosenberg.

The elements of the nation which, at the beginning of the inter-regnum, recognized Menhart's leadership included, first of all, the city of Prague, as well as a few other royal towns such as Kouřim and Slaný; a very considerable part of the high nobility, which included the great houses of Hasenburg, Wartenberg, Kolovrat, Lichtenburg, and Waldstein; as well as a few of the important leaders of the gentry, in particular John Smiřický, Jakoubek of Vřesovice, and Nicholas Sokol of Lamberg. This was undoubtedly an enormous succor for Rosenberg's policy, though already in the early forties this support began to crumble as more and more people recognized that Menhart's leadership was not what they had expected it to be: the defense of a moderate but determined Utraquism and of a restoration of national strength and unity. The group which profited from this drifting away of the more consciously Hussite elements found its leader in a man whose policy, as late as in 1436, was still not too distinct from that of Menhart of Hradec, but whose stature—alone of the three leading men—grew to be equal to the tasks of reorganizing the nation: Hynce Ptáček of Pirkstein.[20]

Lord Ptáček came from a branch of the baronial house of Lipé and Dubá, a family with great holdings especially in northern Bohemia. He was younger than his two rivals and had not come to

[20] On Ptáček see Urbánek, *Věk* I, 203ff., 901ff., and Palacký, *Dějiny*, IV, 1, 41f., 101f. (German, 46f., 115f.).

the attention of his contemporaries during the Hussite Wars. At Lipany he was one of the many lords who fought the brotherhoods, and the first task in which he occupied a leading position had an equally tragic character. It was he whom Sigismund entrusted, in the summer of 1437, with the conquest of the castle of Sion. In his stronghold John Roháč of Dubá, one of Žižka's most faithful lieutenants and successors, continued his solitary resistance against the hated Emperor with a small group of followers when all others had recognized Sigismund's kingship. Ptáček was successful in his enterprise but could hardly enjoy his victory when Roháč, his own kinsman, was taken to Prague and there, despite strong protests from the Utraquist nobility, tortured and hanged like a common criminal.[21] It may well have been this experience which induced Ptáček to quit the "Austrian party" and to become, after Sigismund's death, a vigorous defender of the Polish candidacy.[22]

Ptáček was a short man, rather fat, and bald at an early age, generally a friendly fellow with a lot of merriness and laughter in him, but with a very keen power of observing and analyzing people and situations, quick and strong in his decisions and soon generally respected. He could play the political game shrewdly, but he used it as a statesman, never for petty, always for important causes. His patriotism was never questioned by anybody, but it would seem that his religious conviction, too, once it was fully developed, was more sincere and less subject to the influence of opportunism than was the case with so many of his peers. Once he had made fully clear his position—and its difference from that of Menhart of Hradec—his appearance on the Bohemian scene acted like a catalyst. From now on the great majority of the people—a considerable part of the high nobility but a much larger proportion of the gentry and the towns—was enclined to follow his leadership. His greatest asset thereby was his close alliance with John Rokycana, the elected archbishop, still and for a long time to come the strongest spiritual influence in Hussite Bohemia. The cooperation between the two men seems to have been complete.

Rokycana, after a short stay on the castle of Kunětická Hora, had taken up his residence at Hradec Králové, the city which had once been the center of Žižka's Orebite brotherhood. This organization had, after the battle of Lipany, disappeared as a political entity (un-

---

21 For Roháč and his end, F. Lupínek, *Jan Roháč z Dubé*, Kutná Hora, 1930, pp. 30–43.
22 See Urbánek, *Věk*, I, 241f.

like their allies, the Taborite brotherhood, which still survived), and its religious adherents, concentrated in eastern Bohemia, had little difficulty in joining the Utraquist center under Rokycana's leadership. Rokycana thereby became the undisputed head of the Hussites of most of eastern Bohemia and indeed of many other Hussite groups all over the country, with the exception only of the dwindling remainders of the Taborite brotherhood.

It was in the East that Ptáček could now more firmly establish his political leadership. This was officially recognized when in March 1440 the district assemblies of four eastern Bohemian districts or "landfrieden," Hradec Králové, Chrudim, Čáslav, and Kouřim, elected him as their head captain. To those four a fifth was soon added, the district of Boleslav, where one of the two local captains was the young George of Poděbrady.

The creation of these landfrieden districts was, in a way, an emergency measure, resulting from the renewed break-down of all central authority.[23] Here, at least, was a way of maintaining law and order in limited areas if not nationally. But by combining their forces the five eastern districts created a nucleus of cohesive political power from which, eventually, a national consolidation would be possible. Here, then, lay the main significance of Ptáček's rather short career as leader of his party.

His first major victory had been achieved even before the formal alliance of the districts when, in January 1440, a diet was called to Prague, in which all the three major groups accepted a "Letter of Pacification" ("list mírný"). This document, which bore the signatures even of Rosenberg and his followers, went very far in proclaiming the basic political principles of the party of Ptáček as those of the whole nation.[24] It demanded full acceptance of, and support for, the Compacts; the confirmation and consecration by the Curia, of John Rokycana as Archbishop of Prague; and finally the annulment of measures which Albert II during his Bohemian kingship had taken against the opposition party, that is mainly against Ptáček and his followers. The only important price Ptáček paid for this victory was his readiness to postpone, for the time being, the election of a King.

The years that followed did bring a few further steps toward con-

---

[23] *Ibid.*, 481–495.
[24] See its text in *AČ*, I, 245ff. Palacký *Dějiny*, (German, IV, 1, 13ff.) somewhat strangely translates it as "Sühnbrief." For Urbánek's comment see *Věk*, I, 468ff.

solidation, but against great obstacles and with many interrupting setbacks. The very next year, 1441, was full of internal struggles, frequently bloody ones that can only be characterized as rather confused civil wars with limited forces and in limited, but changing theaters. What makes the picture so confused is the fact that as often as not the struggle was a triangular one. There was never, it is true, any conflict between Menhart of Hradec and Ulrich of Rosenberg; on the contrary—Menhart's dependence on Ulrich became even closer. The third force, however, which at times fought against one party, at times against the other and occasionally against both of them, was Tabor.[25]

The term "Taborites" had since the early phase of the Hussite Revolution, implied a movement rather than just a city. This movement contained the most dynamic, most radical wing of Hussitism, both in religious and socio-political terms, and had rallied to its views and policies a number of noblemen, a considerable part of the cities of southern and southwestern Bohemia, and much of the politically conscious elements of the peasantry. The Taborite brotherhood had been a theocratic commonwealth dominated by priests, and even its famed and formidable field army, originally found and led by John Žižka, had become the instrument of great priestly leaders such as Prokop the Bald. The settlement of Tabor itself (originally Hradiště), begun as strongly fortified headquarters of the movement, had meantime developed into a city, with a regular town constitution, a middle class, and some small industry. Throughout most of the revolutionary years the Taborite federation was one of the great powers of the country, especially as long as it was closely allied with the other brotherhood—the Orebites or Orphans of eastern Bohemia. The battle of Lipany destroyed much, but not all of this strength. It is characteristic of the awe in which Tabor was still held by most of its former enemies (and especially by its nearest neighbor, Lord Ulrich of Rosenberg) that in the fall of 1436 the Emperor Sigismund found it advisable to conclude a very special arrangement with Tabor which gave the fortress-town some limited guarantee for the unmolested maintenance of its—still strongly deviating—religious

25 On Tabor and the Taborite movement there exists an enormous literature. Much of it can be found in the bibliography of my "Žižka." For newer publications see Josef Macek's above cited work on Tabor, which is rather dogmatic in its Marxian approach but makes profitable use of much new material; and, for the earlier phases of the movement, two articles by Howard Kaminsky, "Hussite Radicalism and the Origins of Tabor," *Medievalia et Humanistica*, X, 1956, and "Chiliasm and the Hussite Revolution," *Church History*, XXVI, 1957, I.

dogma and ritual, and in addition gave it all the rights and freedoms of a royal city.[26]

In the postwar era the influence of Tabor had begun to dwindle. Some of the allied cities which had long followed its leadership fell away. There was political pressure from the two other camps. But there was also the appeal to religious unification from both these camps. For most of the people who had ever belonged to the Taborite federation the orthodox Catholicism of the Rosenberg party held little attraction, but the Utraquist Church under the increasingly firm leadership of Rokycana could present better claims to speak in the name of the Czech-Hussite tradition. In this twofold struggle—the civil war which was rather inconclusive in 1441 but flamed up anew two years later, and the fight over religious issues—Tabor resisted bravely but with slowly weakening power. Eventually she was forced to conclude an armistice and agreed to submit the religious issues to a great synod held at Kutná Hora in July 1443. Here Tabor was represented by two priests who had been her leading clerics for 23 years, indeed since the earliest times of the Taborite commonwealth: Nicholas of Pelhřimov, whom the Taborites, in 1420, had elected as their bishop and who ever since was known under the nickname "Biskupec," a man of great erudition who can be considered as Tabor's leading theologian;[27] and Wenceslas Koranda the Elder, whose gifts, in the first place, were those of a preacher and religious-political propagandist.[28] Against them stood Rokycana, supported, this time, by a man who had only recently been his adversary: John Příbram, for a long time the leader of the most conservative wing of the Utraquist Church.[29] The main issue between the two Hussite groups was the understanding of the Eucharist.[30]

The Taborites had, by this time, accepted the teaching of the group usually called Pikharts, that is they claimed that in the bread and wine Christ was present *"sacramentaliter"* and *"spiritualiter,"* not, however, as Rokycana believed, *"substantialiter"* and *"naturaliter."* The whole disputation about the real presence had a remarkable

---

[26] See *AČ*, III, 450ff.

[27] See Heymann, *"Žižka,"* 172ff.; Bartoš, *Světci a kacíři*, Prague, 1949, 175ff., and Pekař, *Žižka a jeho doba*, I, Prague, 1927, 125ff. See also Z. Nejedlý, *Dějiny husitského zpěvu*, 2nd ed., Prague, 1955, IV, Tabori, 199–203.

[28] See Heymann, *Žižka*, 8off. and *passim*, and Nejedlý, *op.cit.*, 205f.

[29] On Příbram, see J. Prokeš, *M. Prokop z Plzně* (Husitský Archiv, III), Prague, 1927.

[30] About this phase of events and its ideological background, see Z. Nejedlý, *Prameny k synodám strany Pražské a Táborské v letech 1441–1444*, Prague, 1900, and Urbánek, *Věk* I, 812–883.

similarity with the much more famous "Religionsgespräch," which was to take place, eighty-six years later, in Marburg between Zwingli and Luther. The final decision about whose views were to prevail came only through the proceedings of a great diet held in Prague in January 1444. The estates found that Rokycana's teachings were to be accepted as "more reliable, better and securer." [31] The Taborites did not, as had been hoped, submit to this verdict. But it had an important effect on their future and that of the country. Tabor was, from now on, almost completely isolated. The Utraquists, on the other hand, gained enormously in unity and in national influence.

The practical elimination of Tabor as a power which could put a strong weight to either side now left the two main parties face to face for the decisive struggle. Who would retain the upper hand— Ulrich of Rosenberg or Ptáček of Pirkstein? Ptáček seemed to have gained more in the domestic field, but Ulrich had more support outside Bohemia, notably through his close and friendly relationship with the King of the Romans, Frederick III. The King, however, who was having troubles of his own, especially in Austria and in his relationship to his brother Archduke Albert, had no intention of getting too much involved in the thorny Bohemian problems.[32]

The final decisions about Bohemia's fate were clearly due to be taken in the future, and within the country. At this stage it seemed almost certain that Ptáček would be the man to take them, by consolidating and widening his own leadership and thereby restoring political stability essentially on the basis of the Letter of Pacification of 1440. But just now, in August 1444, he was suddenly taken ill and died. It was a grave loss for the country, one that could easily have been considered irreplaceable, another link in the chain of misfortunes which had befallen the country so often in this century. Yet for once things turned out better than expected. For the man who could replace—and more than replace—Lord Ptáček had already made, in a modest way, his appearance on the scene of history. It was George, aged twenty-four, Lord of Kunštát and Poděbrady, and captain of the landfrieden-district of Boleslav.

[31] See the resolution in Nejedlý, *op. cit.* 108ff.
[32] See Urbánek, *Věk,* I, 618–627, 630–648.

CHAPTER 2

THE FIRST GREAT DUEL:

PODĚBRADY VERSUS ROSENBERG

THE LEADER of Bohemia's Catholic party, Lord Ulrich of Rosenberg, had been a representative figure even as a young man in his twenties. Throughout the Hussite Revolution he had been King Sigismund's strongest partisan, and a good deal of the military struggle had been a sort of duel between him and John Žižka.[1] Many of the people who had fought with or against him were now dead, and Tabor, though still extant as a local power and a religious movement, had no longer its former significance. Indeed a good deal of the class character of the original struggle had disappeared with the development that had taken place since the battle of Lipany, and the Hussite side stood, ever since the rise of Ptáček, likewise under the leadership of a magnate. But there was a considerable difference, nevertheless, between the ideas, goals, and methods of Rosenberg and those of the young man who now represented the party of Utraquism: George of Poděbrady.

They had a few things in common. Both came from the same social background, and very likely were relatives.[2] Both were clever politicians and highly interested in strengthening the economic basis of their political position. This indeed, was a practice without which they could hardly have maintained their leading roles. They would need strong and permanent sources of income especially for military purposes.

But this exhausts the similarities. The differences were far more significant. Rosenberg identified the material interests of his class with those of himself and of his family, and saw them in the narrowest sense: any thing he could gain would have to be taken away

---

[1] See Heymann, *Žižka*, 170ff., 183, 408f.

[2] The relationship is not quite undisputed, but Palacký's version (according to which Ulrich's wife, Catherine of Wartenberg, was a sister of George's mother, Anna) is generally accepted. See his *Dějiny*, IV, 1, 104 n. 114 (German, p. 118 n. 115).

from others, and this was in perfect order. To gain as much as possible from others was easiest in times in which the feudal anarchy was virtually unchecked by any strong national organization. This is the real key to all his actions, rather than any religious fanaticism; though it would be convenient enough at times to play the savior of Catholic Christianity against Hussite subversion.

George of Poděbrady, on the other hand, had a remarkable ability —remarkable at least in relation to the time in which he lived— to identify himself with the interests of the larger communities to which he belonged; this not withstanding the careful and successful management of the finances of his family. These communities were, first of all, the Boleslav landfrieden whose leader he had been, together with John Smiřický, for the last few years; the union of the five eastern landfrieden, which had elected him their chief captain, without a dissenting voice, immediately after the death of Ptáček; the Hussite-Utraquist Church, in which he had been born and raised and with whose leader in eastern Bohemia, John Rokycana, he cooperated very closely; but above all the nation—very much in the modern sense of the word, as the community of all the people of the kingdom, especially those of the three estates represented in the diets—barons, gentry, and cities, with the peasants given rather less consideration except, occasionally, in a vague humanitarian way; the nation, then, emphatically including the two main religious parties.

While Rosenberg tried to play the sincere defender of the Catholic faith with an hypocrisy made obvious by his vast acquisition of Church estates which he was most unwilling to return, George was sincere in showing that he was not—and could not be—a religious fanatic. Yet if some historians have tried to characterize him as a man without any real religious beliefs, feelings, and ties, they were clearly mistaken.[3] Indeed it is his greatest antagonist among the Catholic clergy, Aeneas Sylvius, who impressively testifies to the contrary. He tells us in some detail about a conversation, held by George in Breslau around Christmas 1454, with one of the actors or court jesters of King Ladislav's retinue who asked why, against the usage of nearly all nations and princes, he choose to remain in the camp of Rokycana and the Utraquist schismatics. The main part of George's answer, as quoted by Aeneas Sylvius, was: "Everyone celebrates the church ritual according to what he believes. We offer our sacrifice

[3] See e.g. Bachmann, "Ein Jahr böhmischer Geschichte," *AÖG*, LIV, Vienna, 1876, 132., and Voigt, "Georg von Böhmen, der Hussitenkönig," *HZ*, V, Munich, 1861, 429.

and worship as we deem them to be pleasing to God, nor does it stand in our arbitrary choice to believe what we choose. The human mind is, whether we want it or not, subject to the impact of the most powerful arguments, even though according to the nature of the individual one man may be more fully led thereby, another may partly escape this influence. I am fully convinced of the religious truth as it was taught me by my own priests. If I tried to follow yours, I might perhaps manage to deceive men, to the detriment of my soul; but God who looks into the innermost heart I cannot deceive." [4] These words are in many ways characteristic for George. In accordance with them he never claimed any independence of religious judgment based on theological erudition; but he was always ready to listen to arguments. While his religious policy was subject, especially in his later years, to constant and often fierce pressure, and while he could hardly avoid having moments of weakness, he still managed to combine faith in the religious ideas of his grandfather and father, his teacher Ptáček, and his great clerical adviser Rokycana with a serious, responsible attitude of tolerance toward the Catholic minority of his nation, many of whose members, including their bishops, he consulted regularly. We shall, of course, discuss his religious policy in some detail, including his regrettable, yet from his point of view unavoidable, harshness toward the more radical forms of Hussite sectarianism.

The situation into which George had to grow up was so complex that he could never have had any success at all if he had not had a measure of shrewdness. In most phases of history, and quite especially in such very dynamic ones characterized by rapid changes, the statesman has also to be a politician, the lion also to be a fox, to achieve anything worth while. George had this quality. That he could use clever manoeuvres, not entirely devoid of ruse and deception, and occasionally of harshness, has been held against him by those countless enemies who have left a much larger heritage of records than his friends. Even Palacký, the historian who first and most impressively established George's claim to greatness, has found that by the occasional choice of such means he fell somewhat short of the moral stature of Ptáček of Pirkstein.[5] Yet we shall come upon

4 See Aeneas Sylvius, *Historia Bohemica,* ch. 62, p. 157, also almost identically in Eschenloer, G., I, p. 8.
5 Palacký, *Dějiny,* IV, 1, 131 (German, 149). This is perhaps the only instance in Palacký's work where one may wonder whether he has been quite fair to his hero, or rather whether he has not given Ptáček more credit than he deserved.

more than one occasion where we are also struck by opposite traits and attitudes: an unjustified trust in the willingness of other people to keep their word; an aversion against the harsh and brutal war effort, in a struggle forced on him against his wishes; an attitude quite astonishing for one whose initial success was, beside his impressive personality and the clarity and strength of his basic political conceptions, also based on military gifts and successes achieved early in his life.

There is no question that George made a strong impression on the people he met. The very fact that the lords and knights controlling the eastern Bohemian districts, among them some much older men of high standing and considerable prestige, elected him without any hesitation as their leader, proves it sufficiently. Aeneas Sylvius describes him as "a man of short stature, rather stocky frame, white complection, with a strong light in his eyes, and with very pleasant manners. He is infected by the Hussite error, but otherwise devoted to justice and virtue."[6]

The description of George's physical appearance fits in well with the pictorial records that have come down to us, showing him with a roundish face, a rather prominent nose, a wide, but strong chin, expressive eyes and an ample, drooping sort of moustache.[7] Despite his short stature he seems to have impressed people as having great dignity and authority, and at the same time a natural and effective affability. He thus found it easy to win people of all stations over to his side, even men who had first met him reluctantly and with strong reservations regarding his political or religious views and aims. Indeed it seems to have been almost impossible for any of his more important contemporaries to look across to him with cool and distant neutrality. If they were not his followers, if, in particular, they had turned away from him, they tended to become his bitter enemies.

As he was a child of his time so he was prepared to fulfill the needs of his times. In those years, conditions did not yet, in Bohemia, favor the flowering of arts or sciences, great buildings, great teaching. Nor were these things foremost in George's mind. He would hardly have known how to be a Renaissance patron of the Italian variety, (while his Hungarian son-in-law, Matthias, could play this

---

[6] *Historica rerum Friderici III imperatoris,* in Kollar, ed., *Analecta Monumentorum omnis aevi Vindo-bonensia,* Vienna, 1762, II, 181. In later utterances, especially in his Commentaries, this friendly evaluation gives way to harsh judgments.

[7] Urbánek, *Věk,* III, 321 and illustrations in this book.

role to perfection). George's interests were, in the first place, severely practical, as they were concerned with the political and economical recovery and survival of the country. His methods, accordingly, were not based on any general ideas or philosophies but on trial and error. And for a long time these methods served him exceedingly well.

In the first phases of the duel between George and Ulrich, the advantages seemed all to lie with Ulrich. It was much easier to negate and sabotage than to take constructive action. The goal of the Poděbradian party was the reconstruction of a strong, orderly state. As the majority of the nation was Hussite, this would also depend on the construction of a strong, orderly regime for the Utraquist Church. The need, thus, was for a monarch as recognized head of the state—no one seriously dreamed of republicanism on a national level—and for a recognized head of the Church. In the first case it was still a matter of finding the person; in the second, one of having the only possible choice confirmed by Rome. Both tasks, whose solution had repeatedly but unsuccessfully been tried by Ptáček, were now again faced by George with purposive energy. But at first Ulrich found it as easy to cross him as it had been in the case of Ptáček. This play was first acted late in 1444. A diet, called to Český Brod on the insistence of the Poděbradian party, decided unanimously to ask the Pope, Eugene IV, for the confirmation of Rokycana, and to make all necessary preparations for having the boy Ladislav sent to Bohemia so he could be crowned.[8] The chances for the fulfillment of the second demand were none too good as long as Frederick III, the King of the Romans, Ladislav's second cousin once removed, and his guardian, kept the child under strict supervision at his own court. The chances for the confirmation of Rokycana, on the other hand, might have been better at this time than at almost any other time before or after. The reason for this was the renewed papal schism which had come about through the conciliar struggle. Pope Eugene IV had ordered the dissolution of the Council of Basel, which in turn had deposed the Pope and elected Prince Amadeus of Savoy as Felix V. Now, four years after Felix's election, the chances for a victory of the Basel Council over Eugene did not seem very bright. Yet as long as the majority of the German princes maintained a

---

[8] See *AČ*, I, 292f.; *Staří letopisové čeští* (Old Czech Annalists), ed. Palacký and re-edited by J. Charvát in *Dílo F. Palackého*, II, Prague, 1941 (hereafter cited as *SLČP*), 127; Palacký *Dějiny*, IV, 1, 108ff. (German, 124ff.), and Urbánek, *Věk*, II, 33ff.

strict and concerted neutrality, a firm support from the Bohemian estates would have been a valuable help for Eugene for which he might have paid a price. But this would have presupposed that the official policy of the diet was maintained by the dominant power behind it. Instead two secret missions sent to Rome by the Catholic party in 1445 expressly repudiated the support they had given to the resolutions of the diet and solemnly warned the Pope not to confirm the Archbishop-elect. The second message was signed by Ulrich and six other lords, also by three of the leading knights led rather strangely by John Smiřický, once one of the leaders of the Hussite gentry, but now playing a very obscure role.[9]

For Eugene IV these messages were highly welcome. Where, otherwise, he would have stood under a rather effective pressure he was now free to try his own devices. He would, so he assured the Catholics in a message dated May 15, even before he received the second information, soon give the country an archbishop, but one against whom nobody among the people of the kingdom had any objections. He knew, of course, that this was an utter impossibility, but the promise was a way out of an impasse, and the whole exchange of messages showed at least that he was in no immediate danger of a Bohemian recognition for Felix's papacy. To avoid such a danger the Roman diplomacy was anyhow very active at this time, making use especially of the services of a man who had long stood on the side of the Council but who, as King Frederick's secretary, had recently swung over to Eugene's side: Aeneas Sylvius.

Ulrich's success in this phase did not deter George and his party from trying again, this time with a more powerful effort. After preliminary meetings in Pelhřimov a "great diet," representing all countries of the Bohemian crown, was called to Prague in November 1446.[10] This diet had considerable significance for the constitutional development of Bohemia. More clearly than at any previous diet appear the three estates or "curias," lords, knights and cities, as individual entities which would sit and discuss matters separately, trying to reach an understanding within each "curia," before joining with the other two in a common session. While, for the time being, this seemed rather to indicate a strengthening of the two lower groups against the lords, in the long run it was to have the opposite

9 See Palacký, Dějiny, IV, 1, p. 116 n. 126 (German, p. 132 n. 127).
10 AČ, II, 209–217, and SLČP, 132–133.

effect: the time would come when lords and knights would combine to deprive the cities of part of their political rights.

The first indication for this trend were already visible in the discussion of what was, at this stage, the most important political issue submitted to the diet: the appointment of a regent or "gubernator." Both the idea and the term were, at this moment, borrowed from Hungary, where five months earlier, in a basically very similar situation, the estates had elected John Hunyadi as regent with essentially royal prerogatives. That there was just as much need for a strong central power in Bohemia could not be denied by anybody at this stage, even though Ulrich of Rosenberg was firmly determined to prevent any such thing from happening. Thus he was pleased when the matter, despite an acceptance of the principle by the two noble estates, got bogged down in questions of procedure. There was agreement that the regent should be elected for a period of two years and should be bound to cooperate closely with a permanent council or committee to be elected by the estates. But when the knights suggested that this council should consist exclusively of members of the nobility, the cities objected to the whole procedure as endangering their traditional freedoms. They feared that the regent might try to subject them to taxation without their assent and urged the diet to devote its attention first and foremost to the issues of the confirmation of the Archbishop and the introduction of the boy-king into the Bohemian crown lands. The conflict between knight and cities, secretly fanned by Rosenberg, finally served him well. He found sufficient support for a move to adjourn this discussion till after the return of the embassies which the diet had decided to send to the courts of Pope Eugene and King Frederick III.

The hope for a regency had, for the time being, to be buried. Yet the decision to send those two embassies, again arrived at without any visible dissent from the Rosenberg party, seemed at least to indicate a strengthening of the Poděbradian position. There was, so it seemed, no question that the demand for Rokycana's confirmation, as well as that for having young Ladislav taken to Bohemia, expressed the will of the whole nation, at least of such a large majority that it could demand to be regarded as near-unanimous. But Rosenberg had carefully laid his counterplans.

One who would play a central role in these plans was already a leading figure in the Curia, Juan Carvajal, Bishop of the Spanish diocese of Plasencia,[11] whose rapid rise was confirmed by the cardinal's hat which, in 1446, he received from Pope Eugene IV. It was, at the same time, a reward for services rendered to the Roman Pope in his struggle against the Basel party, and a means of strengthening him for the future performance of similar achievement. Carvajal was a man of great perspicacity and ability, a powerful, dynamic personality, deeply convinced of the necessity of Papal absolutism and of a completely unified ritual. The Czech biblicism appeared to him fantastic and dangerous. The claim to retain the communion in the two kinds, based at is was on a literal understanding of the words of Christ, could not be tolerated. The fact that there was a powerful Catholic faction among the high nobility of Bohemia seemed to show the way to liquidate, in good time, the disturbing irregularities. Ulrich of Rosenberg, thus, was his natural ally, and a correspondence between the two men began to design the steps to be taken,[12] with Carvajal assuring Rosenberg that his advice was sure to be followed, though there were people at the Roman court who felt that Rosenberg's constant deceit—openly demanding the confirmation of the Compacts and the Archbishop, while secretly counseling against it— might eventually lead to serious trouble.[13] Yet the success of Rosenberg's plans seemed virtually guaranteed by the fact that, even before the arrival of the official Czech delegation, Carvajal had been choosen to go to Bohemia himself as Papal legate and there to put matters right.

The Czech embassy, which arrived in Rome on May 1st, 1447, had its chances for success sharply curtailed by still another change in the general situation. For by then the uncomfortable "neutrality" of the German princes in the struggle between the two popes had become a thing of the past. On February 7th, only two weeks before his death, the ambassadors of King Frederick as well as some of the foremost princes of the Empire recognized Eugene IV and swore the oath of obedience to him as the true pope. This act, in fact if not yet in form, put an end to the second papal schism of the late

---

[11] See about his life and work the careful and well documented work by L. Gomez Canedo, *Don Juan de Carvajal, Un español al servicio de la Santa Sede,* Madrid, 1945. The older work by Lopez de Barrera (*De rebus gestis Joannis card. Carvajalis commentarius,* Rome, 1752) has little value.

[12] *Monatsschrift des böhm. vaterländ. Museums,* February 1828, Urkundenbuch, pp. 45–51, and Palacký, *Dějiny,* IV, 1, 140 n. 148 (German, 160, n. 149).

[13] See Prokop of Rabstein's letter to Rosenberg, *AČ,* II, 435.

Middle Ages, and essentially ensured the victory of the papal claims over the hopes of a reform in the direction of conciliar parliamentarism. The new Pope, the clever humanist Thomas of Sarzana, who as Nicholas V mounted the throne on March 6th, therefore no longer needed to make concessions to Bohemia in return for her recognition. Also, like Carvajal, Nicholas was a personal acquaintance of Rosenberg, whose guest he had been in his castle of Krumlov.

It took the Czech delegates some time to realize fully how poor their chances for success had become. They were treated politely by Pope and Cardinals, were questioned in some detail about Rokycana, his ideas, his influence, and what his means of substance would be if he were really Archbishop of Prague. But in the end the ambassadors heard, unofficially, that there was very little chance of Rokycana's confirmation unless he was ready to abandon the Chalice. The official answer of the Pope sounded somewhat different: So far there is no true religious peace in the kingdom of Bohemia. Therefore the Pope will send one of his foremost helpers, Cardinal Carvajal, with full power, first to explore the situation, especially the religious beliefs of the kingdom and those of the elected Archbishop —and then, on the basis of a thorough investigation, he will arrange all things that need arranging, including the task of providing the country with ⸱ recognized ecclesiastical head.

This was, as yet, not an unmistakable "No" to the Czech demands. But the Czech ambassadors knew quite well what was meant. Their spokesman, the Utraquist priest Jacob of Jemnice, himself a friend and disciple of Rokycana, answered that the Czechs did not want to widen the breach between themselves and the papal Curia. Yet if confirmation of the Archbishop was not now granted they might be forced to part ways completely with the Roman Church, and they would have to make it known to all the world that this was not their fault. This declaration was not just an empty threat. Even earlier there had been some serious discussion about the possibility of renouncing episcopal ordination and instead giving just priests who had been fully consecrated the right to ordain other priests by laying on hands. As yet, however, the grave step was not taken.[14]

Just as unsuccessful as the embassy to Rome was the one sent to King Frederick. The King, indeed, again largely acting on the advise of Rosenberg, was at first less outspoken in his negative atti-

14 The whole story of the embassy is contained partly in the reports to the diet (*ibid.*, 233ff.), partly in material contained in the Třeboň archives and quoted in excerpts by Palacký, *Dějiny*, IV, 1, pp. 143–148 (German, 164–169).

tude than the Pope. Yet when a large group of men from the three parties assembled late in September 1447 to go to Vienna in the hope of returning with Ladislav, Frederick informed them at the last moment that, if this was their purpose, they should save themselves the trouble, as the boy-king could not be allowed to go till he was of age.[15]

It seems that this was the moment when George decided that his patience was exhausted. The game of calling diets, accepting unanimous resolutions, sending embassies, and having all this secretly counteracted and sabotaged by Rosenberg was, to his mind, played to exhaustion and could no longer offer any hope to the sorely tried country. The only alternative, obviously, was for his own party to oust its adversaries from their seats of power. The plans for such a new strategy were laid at a meeting of the lords and knights of the Poděbradian League at Kutná Hora in October 1447. While complete secrecy prevailed about the decisions taken there,[16] one outcome, nevertheless, became clear: the Poděbradians undertook very considerable military preparations. But at the same time George was resolved to avoid actions that might alert his main adversary: Rosenberg.

Luck, now as often later, came to his assistance. There seemed to be a good cause for those armaments—outside the general development of Bohemian politics. In the course of the year 1447 Duke William of Saxony had hired a rather large army of Czech mercenaries, originally for an attack on his brother, Elector Frederick, with whom he had fallen out over the heritage from their father. When, however, an armistice was concluded between the brothers before the troops had been employed, William induced them to help him in a war which he, together with the Archbishop-Elector Dietrich of Cologne, waged against several places in Westphalia which had rebelled against Dietrich. After considerable initial success the Czech troops failed to conquer the very strong town and castle of Soest and eventually returned home. Throughout most of the campaign the Czechs had been left without the pay or the provisions promised to them by Duke William. In addition, marching through the territories of the Elector Frederick, they had even been attacked and had lost most of what booty they had made before.[17] The fate of

---

[15] *AČ*, II, 219f.

[16] *SLČP*, 137.

[17] See about the whole matter especially J. Hansen, *Westphalen und Rheinland im 15. Jahrhundert, I, Die Soester Fehde* (Publicationen aus dem preussischen Staatsarchiv, vol. 34),

this expedition—most of whose leaders belonged to the Poděbradian party—caused fierce resentment in Bohemia, and by the end of 1447 the possibility of an all-out war between the Bohemian estates and the Saxon princes loomed large. Duke William who had a healthy respect for the military strength that even a disunited Bohemia could mobilize, decided to give in. He submitted the issue to the arbitration of two Czech leaders—George himself and his old friend Aleš Holický of Sternberg. William was let off fairly easily—a fact which helped to lay the basis for a rather consequential friendship between him and George—and eventually paid off most of what he owed. No so, however, his brother Frederick against whom now most of the Czech anger was directed.

The considerable tension which thus prevailed in the winter 1447–1448 was a background against which the consistent preparations of the Poděbradians could continue without arousing too much suspicion. King Frederick, it is true, became somewhat alarmed and asked Rosenberg to explore the situation for him. But Rosenberg, so used to deceiving others, was now strangely ready to be deceived. He wrote the King that there was no danger from this side.[18] George had meantime done what he could to make Rosenberg trust in his good intentions toward him, in particular by taking his side in a minor struggle which Rosenberg had with his old neighbor and adversary, the city of Tabor.[19] Ultimately, the Poděbradian party found itself ready for action when the time was ripe for it.

The next help, however came, albeit indirectly, from a most unexpected side: from Cardinal Carvajal. The papal legate, on his way from Rome, spent a short time at the castle of Krumlov, residence of his friend Rosenberg, who with his three sons, with Menhart of Hradec and other magnates escorted him to Prague. He arrived in the capital on May 1, and was received with jubilation by huge throngs of people who greeted him as if he were their savior. Somehow—despite the most cautious reports of the embassy—strong expectations had risen that he would finally bring from Rome the two things for which the majority of the population had hoped so long: the confirmation of the Compacts and of Rokycana's Archiepiscopate.

Carvajal, however, entirely misunderstood the significance of the

---

Leipzig, 1888, and A. Bachmann, "H. Wilhelm von Sachsen und sein böhmisches Söldnerheer auf dem Zuge vor Soest," *Neues Archiv für sächsische Geschichte*, II, 1881, 97ff.

[18] *Monatsschrift des vaterländischen Museums*, 52.

[19] About this, see Urbánek, *Věk*, II, 149 n. 3, and 150–156.

great popularity which seemed to envelop him wherever he went. He had, so far in his career, been favored by success to an unusual degree. He felt sure that he knew, here as elsewhere, the issues involved and that he could deal with the difficulties simply by a sufficient display of clarity and energy. The extraordinary warmth of his reception made him rely on such a procedure even more. He saw it as a tribute to his personality and to his high office as representative of the Holy See—not, as he should have done, as an expression of the people's belief that he was the bringer of "heavenly presents."[20]

Carvajal, indeed, showed very soon how unfounded their hope was. On the first Sunday of his stay in Prague he publicly demonstrated his annoyance when he found that in the Church of St. George the Holy Communion was given in both kinds. On the day after, May 6th, he met for the first time the lay-leader of the Czech Utraquists, George Poděbrady, in person. Of their discussion—if there was any—we know nothing.[21] It may have served as preparation for the prelate's meeting with the Estates of the kingdom which had been called as a special diet for the occasion.

At this meeting the representatives of the diet—and again we hear of no dissenting voice from Rosenberg or any other Catholics —demanded the confirmation of the Compacts as they were granted by the Council of Basel, emphasizing that this had occurred while the Council was still fully under the authority of Pope Eugene IV. Regarding the archbishop it was pointed out that his election had been permitted to the Estates by Emperor Sigismund. The confirmation of Rokycana, a man "so capable, so worthy and so much needed by the whole Kingdom," would contribute more effectively and more quickly to the renewal of religious faith and ecclesiastical

---

[20] Part of the speech with which he was greeted said: Ingredere, o pater, civitatem nostram cum domis coelestibus: age pacem populo desiderabilem, age sanctam unitatem, age salutem et concordiam salutarem; ut haec inclyta civitas per te, pater, donis repleta coelestibus, decantare possit feliciter illud angelicum canticum vere salutare: et in terra pax et salus bonae voluntatis hominibus." (See the appendix in Gomez Canedo, *Carvajal,* and Palacký, *Dějiny,* IV 1, 162 n. 171 [German, 185 n. 172]).

[21] The main source of the events during the meeting is a diary kept by one of Carvajal's attendants (Viennese Court Library No. 4764, fol. 169–172). The material was fully published only by L. Gomez Canedo, in an appendix (pp. 303–311) to *Carvajal.* There (pp. 112–121) also is a general discussion of the Cardinal's Prague visit. See also Palacký, *Dějiny,* IV, I, 163–167 (German, 184–191), and Urbánek, *Věk,* II, 235–258. Parts of the same material were used literally, others with modification, by J. Cochlaeus, *Historia Hussitarum,* Mainz, 1549, pp. 349–357. A shorter description reflecting the Czech attitude is given by SLČP, pp. 137–139.

order and unity than that of any other man. Finally the estates complained about King Frederick's stubborn refusal to release young Ladislav and ended with the threat, occasionally uttered before, that if Frederick continued in this attitude the Czechs would be forced to elect someone else as their King.

Carvajal answered first that it was of special importance to return the archiepiscopal estates to the hands of the Church, after which the Pope would see to it that Bohemia received again an archbishop in ways fully agreeing with the canonical law. This declaration, of course, constituted a double rebuke to the Czechs. They had offered at least partial restitution of the estates to the Archbishop once he was confirmed. Besides, the method of Rokycana's election had been clearly non-canonical. Carvajal's answer to the issue of Bohemia kingship was that they should have patience and do nothing rash. An attempt to elect anybody but Ladislav would only increase the difficulties of the country. Regarding the Compacts, finally, the Cardinal, somewhat strangely, pleaded ignorance both for himself and for the Pope. He had, so he said, never seen and therefore had never been able to study this document. If given the opportunity he would willingly and carefully examine it and then give the Czechs his own and the Holy See's position to it. Accordingly, on May 9th, George of Poděbrady personally visited the Cardinal, carrying with him the precious document: the original of the Compacts as ratified and signed in Jihlava, on July 5th, 1436, and containing the seals of the representatives of the Council of Basel, of the Czech Estates, and of the Emperor Sigismund. George left the Compacts in Carvajal's hands, together with a new, written declaration about the requests of the Estates. To these voices were added, on behalf of Rokycana's confirmation, those of the three most conservative Masters of the University—men who had gone farthest toward reunion with the Catholic Church: John Příbram, Prokop of Pilsen, and Peter of Mladeňovice. For the next few days the negotiations continued, moving along on almost precisely the same tracks on which they had started. Various groups, such as committees of the diet, the major part of the faculty of the University, and influential individual members of both bodies—including even Rokycana himself—tried to argue with Carvajal and prove to him the justice, fairness, and usefulness of the Czech demands for the sake of peace and religious health of the kingdom, as well as of the Unity of Christendom. In general the Cardinal's tactic was to evade

284.34371
J56 w

the material issues, while at the same time trying to win over as many people as possible—individuals and larger groups—for the attitude of unquestioning obedience to the Curia, implying, of course, the renunciation of the Chalice.

With some individuals, indeed, he was successful. To those whom he could convert—that is induce them to ask for absolution for their deviation and to swear in future to forego the communion in both kinds—belonged one of the better known clerics of the conservative Utraquist group, John Papoušek, priest at the same Týn Church which had, till 1436, been Rokycana's parish, and, even more important, Menhart of Hradec, as Lord High Burgrave the ranking official of the kingdom and, at least in name, still the leader of the more conservative wing among the Utraquist barons.

But if Carvajal thought that he might have a corresponding success with the masses of the people, he was mistaken. On May 12th, in the Utraquist Church of St. James in the Old Town, he took publicly, in the presence of the city councillors, the communion in one kind and gave the order that it be given equally to others. The act, far from impressing the people as an example, outraged them. The event happened to be followed by three days of unusually severe late frost which wrought havock in the vineyards and orchards of the Prague district. The people had little doubt that this was an expression of God's anger about the legate's act.

After this, things quickly drove toward a climax. When the Czechs, in renewed negotiations, pressed for the confirmation of the Compacts, Carvajal confounded them by declaring that the did not even have the power to do this, although, as everybody knew, the Pope had announced that he was sending Carvajal "to arrange everything." At this stage, one of the most conservative among the Utraquist masters, Peter of Mladeňovice, arose and declared: "If you do not confirm us the Compacts and Rokycana's position you will hear strange things about this kingdom even before you get back to Rome." It seems quite likely that this remark hinted at plans which developed only a few years later—the idea of joining up with the Church of Constantinople.

It was only now that the diet received the full, official report from the men who had led the embassy to Rome. They had, as they explained, so far withheld it so as not to prejudice all chances for a success of the present negotiations though they had well known how meager these chances were. From now on the Utraquists saw no

92092

more hope, and if some sort of "negotiations" were still continued for a day or two they were actually conducted by Rosenberg and his friends in the hope of covering up the utter fiasco of Carvajal's mission. This attempt, however, was bound to fail, as the general mood among the people of Prague became more and more bitter. Some people are said to have suggested that the Cardinal deserved to be treated the way Hus was treated at Constance. Thus the legate began seriously to fear for his safety and decided to leave the city early on May 23rd, under the protection of the Rosenberg retinue, through crowds of angry and excited onlookers, some of whom threw stones at the cortege.

At this stage John Příbram, who had long been a near-convert to Rome, alerted the diet that the Cardinal had not yet returned the Compacts. A small troup of horsemen was dispatched to stop the Cardinal and have the precious document returned. Carvajal first tried to get out of this predicament by declaring that the document, which had been entrusted to him by the diet, would only be returned to the diet if and when this body officially requested it. But the Czechs were not fooled that easily, and the Cardinal, pleading that the document was carefully packed in the depth of his coffers, had to promise that he would return it immediately upon reaching his first overnight stay—the town of Benešov. To make sure that he would keep his word the diet sent to Benešov a troop of 400 horse under the command of two noblemen, and here the prelate had to let go of his precious conquest. On the basis of the whole story and of the special importance that the time attributed to the symbolic and legal significance of the physical presence of documents (as e.g. in the case of challenges and safe-conducts) its seems quite impossible to see in Carvajal's behavior anything but a premeditated attempt to deprive the Czechs of the ground they felt they could stand on in their dealings with Rome.[22]

Carvajal's mission was a major turning point in the development of this phase of Bohemian history. Its utter failure illuminated more sharply than any event since 1436 the precarious and artificial structure of the peace, or rather armistice, between Czech Hussitism and

---

[22] See Bachmann's attempt (*Geschichte Böhmens*, II, Gotha, 1905, 413) to excuse Carvajal: "Dass Carvajal inmitten der tumultuarischen Abreise vergessen hatte, das . . . Original der Kompaktaten zurückzustellen, trug ihm noch den schimpflichen Verdacht ein, er habe die wertvolle Urkunde entführen wollen." Against this, see Urbánek, *Věk*, II, 256f. especially n. 3.

the Roman Church. Until now the Church had managed to evade a clear answer to the question of whether or not this armistice was to be maintained. It had been maintained by leaving things alone— to an extent. But the steady pressure that was exerted against them forced the Hussites to press, themselves, for a more explicit recognition and especially for a working arrangement to ordain Utraquist priests. The refusal to do anything of that sort showed that the armistice might be shattered at any time. The situation demanded a stronger effort toward national strength and unity, for an end to the Rosenberg sabotage which divided the nation. Thus the clash of wills of May 1448 seemed to give a clearer mandate to George of Poděbrady. But this clash also illuminated to him the strategy, political and military, to be pursued, and thereby strengthened his chances to pursue it.

The paramount object for the policy of national unification now became the city of Prague. Her role in Czech history is as central as is that of Paris in the history of France. It is hardly an exaggeration to say that whoever, for any sustained period, was lord of Prague was also lord of the kingdom. This was so for reasons of geography, of politics, economics, and communications. It was so, too, for reasons of psychology, for the capital was not only the residence of the King and the seat of the government (as long as there was a King and a national government), it was also the seat of the Archbishop (if there was one) and of the University which, for all the loss it had suffered in international standing during the wars, still held enormous prestige nationally, and even beyond. Finally the city was, by the number of its people which far surpassed that of any other town in the kingdom, the greatest potential recruiting reservoir in the nation and thus of great military significance. As a fortress it was considered impregnable.

Ever since the last Luxemburg King had entered Prague in 1436 the forces of Catholic reaction, the forces of the Rosenberg party, had been at work to strengthen their hold on the capital. They had made considerable progress in this endeavor, and no one had been as useful to them for this purpose as the Lord High-Burgrave, Menhart of Hradec. But all he could do was to make sure that reliable people were in the most important official positions, especially those of the mayors of the three boroughs, of whom only the Old Town and the New Town really counted, as the third one, the Small Side, was still suffering from the destructions inflicted on it during the

Hussite Wars. There was, in addition, the Catholic chapter of the Cathedral of St. Vitus, the paramount ecclesiastical authority of the Roman Church within Bohemia proper. On the other side stood the majority of the people, most especially the lower middle class, that is craftsmen and guildsmen of the New Town. They were determined Utraquists. Thus the city was divided against itself—Catholics and near-Catholics in the seats of power, Hussites dominant among the masses.

For a long time the Utraquist majority had seen little hope of getting rid of their masters, and as long as this mastery was wielded with a combination of strength and caution things seemed bearable. The events during Carvajal's visit, however, had sapped their strength and made caution appear as lack of determination. Thus the internal development in Prague greatly favored the plans which the Poděbradian party began to work out in these days.

CHAPTER 3

THE CONQUEST OF THE REGENCY

THE HUSSITE WARS were among the fiercest and most sustained combats of the late Middle Ages, and brought about enormous changes in warfare. Thus they are of particular interest to the student of military history. In the Poděbradian era this interest is bound to weaken. Not till the open struggle fought in the final years of George's reign against Matthias Corvinus and the League of Zelená Hora does the military development as such again become interesting and significant, and even then it is, as we shall see, only a shadow of the earlier war of survival fought by the Czechs.

In his conquest of Prague George of Poděbrady showed himself a capable leader of an armed expedition, especially in its preparation. Yet the main force which he brought to bear was political and religious propaganda. By its help he eventually succeeded in mobilizing a "fifth column" of devoted adherents, overwhelmingly Utraquist, in the city, and at the same time he frightened the Catholic party into something like inertia, which largely counteracted all attempts at an effective resistance. As a result the attackers, in the night from September 2 to 3, 1448, gained access to the city, mainly through the gates of the Vyšehrad, with hardly any losses, and had the city firmly in their hands before the mass of the defenders had become fully aware of it. The Poděbradians found themselves greeted and fêted by the great majority of the people, while the leaders of the Conservative party were lucky to escape successfully, among them the citys' captain general Hanuš of Kolovrat and the burgomasters of the Old and the New Town. The leading clergy of the Prague archiepiscopal chapter also made good their escape—though for them it was hardly a question of survival, rather one of extreme caution. Most of them, including the renegade, John Papoušek, for the time being established their residence elsewhere, preferably at Pilsen, now as before Bohemia's chief bulwark of Catholic resistance to the Reformation. The conquest of Prague, according to our main source,[1]

[1] *SLČP*, 137ff.; *SLČV*, 111ff. The most detailed modern treatments in Tomek, *Dějepis*, VI, 2nd ed. 147ff., and above all Urbánek, *Věk*, II, 276ff.

also resulted in a considerable exodus of Germans, among them a good many students at the University. For the common people the whole event was one of enjoyment, but one of its nastier expressions was an attack upon the Jewish ghetto, which was thoroughly ransacked.

Among the people who failed to escape only one was of national importance: Menhart of Hradec, lord high-burgrave of Prague, thereby highest official of the kingdom, and leader, in name at least, of what had been the party of the conservative Calixtines. George ordered him to be taken to his castle of Poděbrady and there kept as a prisoner. Menhart, so George declared, would have to answer accusations before a national diet to be called in the near future. It seems possible that George eventually regretted this step, for it created a lot of trouble for him. The prisoner's son, Ulrich of Hradec, immediately interceded for his father in a correspondence which has been preserved and which is rather characteristic for the time.[2] At first he seemed mainly worried whether his father was treated properly, whether, for instance, a jester had been put at his disposal. But as George, with all due respect for father and son, firmly refused to release the father before the diet had met, the son became insistent and angry, claiming the continued confinement to be an insult to the honor of the family. After some time, in January 1449, the old gentleman himself, irate and bitter about his imprisonment, fell ill. At this stage George decided to free him, as he feared the propagandist effects if Menhart were to die as a prisoner in Poděbrady. Menhart was released and taken to Říčany, but the travel was too much for him, and he died a few days later. At the time it was no surprise that murder by poisoning was suspected. In the eyes of Ulrich of Hradec this became very soon an indubitable fact which strengthened his determination to punish and destroy the killer of his father. The group around him—cautiously directed by the Lord of Rosenberg, who was now on his way back from the court of King Frederick— met at the town of Strakonice and there organized itself as a league of Catholic Lords. It included six barons (but by no means all the members of their families among whom at least the Lords of Wartenberg, Riesenberg, Šumburg, and Kolovrat were split) as well as the cities of Pilsen and Budweis.[3] Some sort of negotiations still took place—each side challenging the other to participate in a diet which

2 In the collection of letters of the family of Hradec, *AČ*, IV, 3–33.
3 *AČ*, II, 244ff.; *SLČK*, 209ff.

should decide about the merits of the struggle—but there was now little chance for a peaceful agreement without a trial of strength.

George, by this time, had, for all practical purposes, become the ruler of most of Bohemia, and occasionally used the expression "administrator" or "governor" in some of his pronouncements.[4] If his enemies wanted to prevent him from further reinforcing his position they had to organize and use all their strength, and the renewal of a bitter civil war seemed unavoidable. The lords of the League of Strakonice would have liked, for the sake of national and international support, to present the struggle as a fight against heresy. George, as often in similar situations later on, worked hard to prevent any such interpretation from gaining credence and support. The Catholic element, though a minority, was, especially among the high nobility, too strong to be thus allowed to slip altogether into the camp of his adversaries. To avoid this he had to put some of his Catholic friends into a position of representative influence which could not be overlooked by anybody inside or outside Bohemia. Acting completely as if the regency were his on a firmly legal basis, he appointed Lord Zdeněk of Sternberg as lord high-burgrave to succeed Menhart of Hradec.[5]

The appointment—George's strength appears in the fact that no one questioned its validity—was a step of great significance. Probably Zdeněk was, at this time, already the most prominent, and certainly the most active, member of the great Sternberg clan with whom George himself had become so closely allied by his marriage with Kunhuta of Sternberg. As far as the religious issue was concerned, this noble family, as so many others, had long been split. Among the older members, the dowager Perchta had given strong support to the Hussites as early as 1421, while the oldest among the men still alive, Aleš Holický, originally a follower of the Emperor Sigismund, had after a period of hesitation gone over to the revolution in 1424. Zdeněk himself was and remained a Catholic. He was a proud and intelligent man, calculating and selfish, and therefore generally eager to keep on good terms with those whom he expected to prevail in

---

[4] The term "správce" is somewhat less precise than the two terms used later in non-Czech documents: "gubernator" or, in German, "Landesverweser."

[5] The only monograph on this important figure is by Věra Kosinová, "Zdeněk ze Šternberka a jeho královské ambice" in K dějinám čsl. v období humanismu, Sborník prací věnovaných J. B. Novákovi, Prague, 1932, pp. 206–218. The author assumes that Zdeněk's military experiences and gifts especially recommended him to George. I doubt that this was really decisive. See also below, chapter XVII, n. 8.

the domestic struggles. At this time he rightly expected that this would be the husband of his cousin, George of Poděbrady. Thus he had strongly supported George's policy, and had done nothing to warn his old friend, Ulrich of Rosenberg, in whose house he had spent some of his younger years. Instead he had taken an active part in the conquest of Prague at George's side. As the most prominent Catholic in the Poděbradian camp he did, thus, establish a strong claim to recognition of his merits at the hand of the future regent. It is difficult to decide whether George was under any effective pressure in appointing Zdeněk to this high office. One might wonder why he would not have aspired to it himself. Yet it seems clear that he had more in mind: the officially recognized regency. For it, he needed wide support among the barons, one which would not be limited to the determined Utraquists. (As for the rest of the people represented in the great diets, knights and cities, especially Prague, he had less cause for worry.) This baronial support might depend on the chance of effectively splitting the Catholic part of the high nobility, and this could hardly be achieved without the cooperation of a leading Catholic lord.

The appointment, therefore, was almost certainly the price which George paid, in advance, for the new High Burgrave's help in the future election of a regent. Zdeněk of Sternberg was to play an enormous role in the life of George of Poděbrady and in the history of his rule over Bohemia. It was, for a time, mostly a helpful one, but would become eventually a role of extreme harmfulness to George. Yet no one could have foreseen this at the time of his appointment, when it was merely an appropriate political decision whose advantages seemed greater than the risk involved.

Zdeněk of Sternberg was not the only Catholic to occupy an important position in the new regime headed by George. Even so, the men of the League of Strakonice were far from ready to give in. An armistice concluded between the two groups in April 1449[6] with the goal of opening the way toward a new, all-national diet was breached by the league long before, after one year's duration, it was supposed to end. Soon both sides tried to prepare for the decisive struggle by getting additional support from beyond the Czech borders. Ulrich of Rosenberg's old and friendly connection with Frederick III availed him little at this time. The King, always a cau-

---

[6] *AČ*, II, 250ff. For the resumption of hostilities see George's letter in *ibid.*, V, 268. Also in B. Václavek, *Český listář*, pp. 65–66.

tious man, saw very clearly that Ulrich's chances had suffered greatly by the recent development and could not be expected to recover easily. Thus he wisely held back. But both sides sought and found support in the north where the two Saxon dukes, enemies though brothers, had long been involved in the Czech struggles. Indeed George of Poděbrady, whose military preparations against Prague had been hidden behind the cloak of measures directed against Saxony, had actually followed up the conquest of the capital by a short campaign into Saxony. Now the war was resumed, with Duke Frederick supporting the League of Strakonice, William the Poděbradians.[7]

Yet the participation of the Saxon dukes had only a very minor influence on the outcome of the Czech civil war. Duke Frederick's forces, in particular, partly immobilized by the enmity of his brother William and the Margraves of Brandenburg, came too late to take part in the only important battle, in which, on June 4th, 1450, the Poděbradians, under George's command, suppressed the forces of the League near the little town of Rokycany in western Bohemia.[8] This battle, fought with the arms developed during the Hussite Revolution, had nevertheless little in common with the great and bitter encounters of that tremendous struggle. But then, also, there were none of the sharp national, social, and especially religious issues at stake that had aroused the passions on both sides of that great war. Indeed the Bohemian Civil War of 1450, essentially conducted by two factions of the country's aristocracy and largely limited to their immediate forces and followers, was not unlike the struggle that was to break out, merely five years later, in England, only without its dynastic background and on a much smaller scale.

Though the members of the league had sworn to continue the struggle as a holy fight for the salvation of their faith, now, after the Battle of Rokycany, they felt that their honor, at least, had been saved. As early as June 11th an armistice was concluded at the castle of Wildstein (near Pilsen) in which the members of the League of Strakonice obliged themselves to abide by and support the Compacts and the Letter of Pacification of 1440.[9] The league also agreed to renounce all further cooperation with Frederick of Saxony. On November 25th a national diet was to be held at which all important leaders of the parties involved in the war would appear. Ulrich of

---

[7] Issues and events of the Saxon War are best summarized by Urbánek, *Věk*, II, 382ff.
[8] *SLČP*, 143.
[9] *AČ*, II, 274ff. See its evaluation by Urbánek, *Věk*, II, 454ff.

Rosenberg's oldest son, Henry, guaranteed that, if his father should remain absent, he, Henry, would represent the house and party of Rosenberg. Meantime all pending issues were to be submitted to a committee of arbitrators, two from each side. They were Henry of Rosenberg and William of Riesenberg, both members of great noble families, for the league, and for the Poděbradian party Lord Zdeněk of Sternberg and a man of somewhat lower status, Zdeněk Kostka of Postupice, of a family of knights and son of one of the strongest, most competent leaders of the Utraquist gentry during the Hussite Wars: William Kostka. Like William, his son Zdeněk was to show the qualities of a real statesman, and George trusted him fully. He was the only Hussite among the four arbitrators. They elected as a "neutral" chairman for their group another great Catholic baron: Zbyněk Zajíc of Hasenburg.

Domestic peace thus was restored to most of the kingdom. George of Poděbrady now decided to even accounts with Frederick of Saxony. The military expedition which in September 1450 invaded Frederick's territories answered a feeling of general patriotic enthusiasm with which even fervent Catholics were infected. George, in this campaign, earned more military laurels than the civil war in Bohemia had offered him. His greatest single success was the conquest against considerable opposition of the strong town of Gera. The Czechs returned home with what is called "enormous booty," while one of their allies, Margrave Albert of Brandenburg, undertook the job of mediating between the two warring parties.[10]

On his return George did not yet release his army. As long as he had it ready he was able, without any acts which might be interpreted as unfriendly or threatening gestures, to keep the Strakonice party under a certain degree of pressure. Without this pressure the great diet which did, as arranged, meet in Prague on November 25th, might not have been as productive as it turned out to be. That things were not easy could be seen from the very length of the meeting, which did not adjourn till early in January 1451.[11] But decisive for this success was George's statesmanlike moderation in victory. The members of the League of Strakonice were not asked to acknowledge defeat beyond showing their readiness to accept a lasting peace, and on conditions which were far from onerous. The

---

[10] On the conquest of Gera see the contemporary report of Peter of Sternberg in *AČ*, II, 45, and *SLČV*, 113f.

[11] For the resolution of the diet see *AČ*, II, 287ff.

strongest symbol of this restoration of peace was the mutual forgiveness and friendship expressed between George and Ulrich of Hradec
—based on an arrangement already concluded in the late summer
by the arbitrators appointed at Wildstein. Beyond this, all conquests
of land and property were to be returned by both sides. All agreed
to work, without any subterfuge, for the release of young Ladislav
so he could be brought to Bohemia for his coronation, thereby putting a definite end to the troubles of the interregnum. This goal was
to be achieved by another mission to be sent to King Frederick III,
this time much stronger and more representative than any previous
embassy. It would contain seven or eight members from each of the
two main parties, plus two neutrals. Again it is characteristic of
George's policy that, in contrast to the Strakonice party who, with
five lords, nominated only one member of the gentry, no less than
five knights or squires were appointed by George, together with
only three lords, among them Zdeněk of Sternberg.[12]

The negotiations which were conducted with the King of the
Romans in Wiener-Neustadt, his usual residence, seemed to follow
the pattern that had been experienced so frequently before. The
Czech negotiators asked for Ladislav to be released, otherwise the
Czech estates might decide to elect another King. And the answer,
too, was eventually to sound much like a repetition to Frederick's
previous reactions to the demand of releasing, with Ladislav's person, also his profitable hold upon the administration of part of his
heritage, especially the two duchies of Austria. But this time Frederick expected, with some justification, that his answer would not
necessarily meet any serious opposition in Bohemia. He had, as before, achieved a secret understanding with those in Bohemia who,
as he judged, held the substance of power.[13] Only this time it was
no longer Ulrich of Rosenberg, never more than the leader of a
powerful minority, but George and the Poděbradian League who
could be judged to hold this strong position. It was obvious, at the
moment, that George would, sooner or later, gain not only the substance of regency but also the formal position that went with it.
King Frederick could base this expectation rather easily on what he
had seen happening in Hungary. There John Hunyadi, like George
the gifted leader of a movement for national unification, had been
elected as regent (gubernator) already in 1446, originally very much

12 *Ibid.*, 301.
13 See Palacký, *Dějiny,* 2nd ed., IV, 1, 232 (German, 265).

against Frederick's wishes. But recently, in October 1450, a full understanding had been reached between the King and the regent of Hungary. In the document containing this understanding [14] it was expressly stated that Ladislav was to remain under King Frederick's tutelage till he reached his majority, i.e. became 18 years old. This would give Hunyadi another seven and a half years to consolidate his strength and with it the general situation in the kingdom against all attempt of his fairly numerous enemies to replace him.

The arrangement with Hunyadi created an easy precedent in the eyes of Frederick and George alike. Presumably Frederick found it even easier to come to an understanding with George of Poděbrady than with John Hunyadi. He had always wanted to be King of Hungary, and his attempts to win the crown of St. Stephen were to play a big and at times highly disturbing role in his reign. But the crown of St. Wenceslas never attracted him very seriously, perhaps because he expected it, for religious reasons, to be too troublesome and difficult a position. Thus he came to understand, respect, and support (within measure) the Bohemia nobleman as soon as it became clear that he, and not the head of the Rosenberg clan, was the strongest person in the country. In this situation their interests were clearly similar, and for exactly the same reasons as had been the case in Hungary: to keep the young heir from entering into his royal heritage as long as this could be done without too much difficulty or without infringing too conspicuously upon Ladislav's rights.

Frederick's answer was presented to the Czech Estates at a diet which had originally been called to Prague but which, because of an epidemic of bubonic plague in the capital, was moved to the small town of Benešov. There, on July 18, King Frederick's envoys arrived, at their head the Bishop of Siena, Aeneas Sylvius Piccolomini. The bishop, who, in his earlier years, had served the Council of Basel, had for eight years been one of King Frederick's most skillful clerical servants and advisers. At the moment of the meeting nobody could have foreseen that Aeneas' presence there would become a factor of historical significance—perhaps with the exception of the bishop himself who certainly hoped, if he did not expect with some certainty, that he would rise much higher—indeed to the highest place—in the Roman hierarchy. As the policy of the later Pope Pius II would have decisive influence upon the development of the relation between the Holy See and the Kingdom of Bohemia, and indeed on Bohemian

[14] F. Kurz, *Oesterreich unter Kaiser Friedrich IV*, I, Vienna, 1812, appendix No. VII, 258ff.

and Central European history generally, this mission of his was bound to be of great importance.[15] Aeneas' impressions and judgments were shaped by various factors: first by a meeting, in a city of southern Bohemia, with the former Hussite cleric, now a violent renegade to orthodox Catholicism, John Papoušek, who provided him with material, much of it distorting the truth, about Hussite and especially Taborite religious views; secondly by two short but impressive visits to Tabor itself, during which he had long but rather fruitless discussions with the heads of the religious community of Tabor, and which fortified all the prejudices that he had developed earlier; further by his presence at the diet of Benešov, where he saw members of both religions, Catholic and Hussite-Utraquist, in rather close cooperation; and finally (and most importantly) by a lengthy conference which he had with the leading Utraquist layman: George of Poděbrady. They were introduced to each other by Prokop of Rabstein, himself a friend of both men and present at Benešov not as a member of the diet but, like Aeneas, as the King's ambassador. It was he who acted as interpreter.

The later Cardinal and Pope has left a detailed report on this interview with George, contained in a long letter to Carvajal and styled as if he is giving a literal quotation of his own and George's utterances.[16] While Aeneas tried hard and skillfully to put himself and his behavior as both a statesman and churchman in the best possible light, George, too, appears here as a man of strength and cleverness, even wisdom, whose personal role within the general structure of Bohemia—with her painful divisions and struggles and the heretical infections of her religious mind—he viewed as, at least potentially, highly promising. Not that he tried to hide the differences. He registers George's complaints about Carvajal's negative attitude during his mission to Prague, and his emphatic demand for the recognition of the Compacts. "This is," George says, "the shortest, nay the only way to peace and unity." And he keeps returning to this, as something that cannot be compromised. He is less adamant in relation to the other of the perennial demands made by the Czech estates to Rome:

---

15 On the whole complex history of the meeting see Urbánek, *Věk*, II, 505–533, and the short but highly suggestive and valuable analysis by H. Kaminsky, "Pius Aeneas Among the Taborites," *Church History*, XXVIII, 1959, 287–295. See also A. Císařová-Kolářová, "Návštěva Eney Silvia v Táboře," *JČSH*, No. 20, 1951, 61ff.

16 Most recent publication in Wolkan, *Der Briefwechsel des Aeneas Sylvius, FRA*, 2. Abt. vol. 68, 1918, 22ff. Palacký translated the dialogue into Czech and German in his *Dějiny* (IV, 1, 235–245 and 269–280). See also Urbánek's discussion of it in *Věk*, II, 513–527.

confirmation of Rokycana as Archbishop of Prague, supposedly going so far as indicating that under certain circumstances (one of which would be Rokycana's voluntary resignation which could not very easily be expected) the Czech Estates might consider an alternative solution. The interview ended, somewhat ironically, with Aeneas recommending, as the person who might solve all the problems of Bohemia, the learned Minorite John of Capistrano, and George voicing the hope that this, indeed, might come to pass. (Not too much later it became very clear, even to Aeneas Sylvius, that no one was more apt to exacerbate the struggle between Rome and the Hussites than the future Saint of Capistrano.)

The letter to Carvajal was not merely an intelligence, informing Carvajal about Aeneas's impressions. It contained the seed of a policy which Aeneas, implicitly, suggested to the Curia, in which he hoped to play some role himself, and which for a time he tried to adopt when he had the power to make the decision. And the basis of this policy was a curious mixture of entirely correct and entirely mistaken judgments. Surely he was right when he considered George a man of great ambition to whom political power meant much. But he was wrong if he went so far as to believe that his religious tradition, the Hussite heritage, meant rather little to him and that he would not seriously fight for it. (It was a wrong judgment which he should not have maintained if he took his own information— George's answer to Ladislav's court jester—seriously.) Surely Aeneas was right when he saw that no other man was, at this time, able to win and maintain a strong and faithful following among the Hussite majority of the nation, especially the gentry, and the people of Prague, later also of most other cities. But he was wrong, dangerously so, if he believed that George could lead those people wherever he wanted to have them, even to the abandonment of the Chalice. Aeneas was, from his point of view, quite right—more so than some modern historians of Hussitism—when he considered Rokycana as a man too far gone on the way toward heresy (we might say toward Protestantism) to be trusted by the Roman Curia with the recognized role of archbishop for the Bohemian realm. But he was wrong, again, when he saw this merely as a question of church policy, one which could be solved rather easily by supplanting the man once elected by the Estates, and confirmed by the Emperor Sigismund, with another man of a different religious complexion. Here we may even have some doubt whether George had given him quite as much reason to believe that the Czechs would consider dropping their demand for Rokycana's confirmation as his letter to Carvajal indicates. The strong popular groundswell in favor of the religious attitudes, and the person, of Rokycana was to become more obvious at a later time.

For the moment, however, and for a long time to come, the Czech leader had reason to be satisfied with the impression he had made upon the Italian prelate, just as the latter felt he had made a lasting impression upon George which could be used to good advantage in the future. Aeneas's report to Carvajal was, of course, paralleled by a report to Frederick III.[17] He could inform the King that his refusal to release Ladislav before the boy's having come of age, reiterated in an elaborate address which he, Aeneas, had presented to the Czech diet,[18] had met with little serious protest, owing essentially to the help given by George. Probably he had emphasized his impression that George was a man of growing strength, and not a fanatic but one with whom it would be possible to negotiate. Thus the King was now more ready than before to grant George's factual leadership of the Czech nation his recognition.

At this time, in the fall of 1451, King Frederick III was preparing an expedition to Italy where he expected to meet his fiancee, princess Leonora of Portugal, and where he was to be crowned as Roman Emperor by Pope Nicholas V. He was willing to pronounce his recognition of George as regent ("gubernator"), but some conflicts within the Poděbradian camp and the still active exertions of the Rosenbergs provided him with the opportunity to limit this recognition to the extent that George was to hold his office only "during the King's pleasure." This, of course, would make him, for the time being, rather dependent on the Habsburg ruler's whim. But the recognition by Frederick was anyhow only another step in the direction of a firm, regularized and effective control of the whole Czech realm.[19] The essential act would be to up the Estates of the kingdom. The question was, how and when it would be possible to create a sufficiently favorable political situation for such a nationwide recognition.

The final step, in this case, seemed in some ways the most difficult.

---

[17] Its text is not preserved, but its content emerges clearly from the consequences.

[18] See his *Historia Bohemica*, chapter 60, and J. T. Müller, *Reichstag-Theatrum*, Jena, 1713, I, 517f.

[19] See Urbánek, *Věk*, II, 535.

There was occasional opposition to such a definite legalization of George's power even in his own camp. Zdeněk of Sternberg in particular proved a difficult friend whose support first gained by his appointment as Lord High Burgrave had still to be regained, or at least made more secure, by various concessions whose precise nature was not always evident from the sources but usually resulted in reconciliations after periods of coolness between him and George. But Zdeněk had, at least, basically taken his stand by the side of George as the one most likely to win, with little regard to his religious identification with the Catholic camp. The converse, of course, was true in the case of Ulrich of Rosenberg, who had long ago taken his stand on the opposite side and who felt that any gain for the Poděbradian party—as a gain for the restitution of a strong, organized state—could not possibly be anything but a corresponding loss for the big, near-princely rulers of the largest baronial estates, his own above all others. Here, now, he had to make his last stand or give up. He was not yet ready to give up.

But Rosenberg's last hope of winning the political war, having lost almost all the latest battles, was tied to events outside the Bohemian kingdom. Ulrich of Rosenberg's eyes turned to Austria, and to the relationship between Frederick III and his young ward, Ladislav. Frederick, indeed, was King of the Romans (he was crowned Emperor in March 1452) and head of the house of Habsburg. Yet, of the so-called Austrian crownlands, only a part, mainly Styria and Carinthia, was his by heritage. The Tyrol belonged to Duke Sigismund, some old south-west German holdings to Frederick' brother Albert, and Austria proper to young Ladislav, who had also been acknowledged as King of Hungary and, in a less binding way, of Bohemia. It was not as the head of the Empire but as guardian of Ladislav, and thus as the representative of the bearer of the Bohemian crown, that Frederick could approve and sanction George's regency. Despite the reservations in Frederick's act, everything pointed to his willingness in future to continue his support of George since this seemed to be in his own interest.

But there were strong tendencies in all of Ladislav's countries to get rid of Frederick's guardianship. Throughout the long reign of fifty-two years Frederick, while far from stupid, nevertheless proved himself a rather weak ruler; in some way shrewd and tenacious, he also had little initiative, and was therefore ineffectual not only in the Empire but often also in his own lands. One of his biographers[20]—

[20] Kurz, *Oesterreich unter Friedrich IV*, II, 205.

by no means an especially harsh judge—has described him as peace-
able mainly because of his inclination to live a restful life; dilatory
to the extent that frequently all official business came to a standstill;
often too stubborn to correct obvious mistakes; parsimonious in a
way which created rather than solved financial problems; too willing
to let a few favorites assume and wield much uncontrolled and ill-
used power; and too weak to suppress the lawless violence with which
especially the powerful nobility frequently exploited and ravaged the
country. Even if, at least for his work in his own crown lands, this
judgement would seem to exaggerate, it is still understandable that
there was opposition against Frederick at an early time, and especially in the duchy of Austria where dynastic feelings worked all
in favor of young Ladislav rather than of his guardian. Of such a
character, it seems, was especially the animosity that existed against
him among a large part of the population of Austria's capital, Vienna.
Yet the most dangerous opposition, in Austria as well as in other
territories nominally now under Frederick's rule, came from part of
the nobility. For, they, or at least some of their leaders, were confident that they could easily dominate and use the boy for their
own purposes.

Of these Austrian barons one of the greatest, richest, and most
powerful was Ulrich Eizinger, a man of Bavarian ancestry who had
risen high already under the reign of Ladislav's father Albert II,
(Albert V as Duke of Austria).[21] Eizinger's personal quarrel with
Frederick was ostensibly based on a dispute over a castle in Hungary
which he had tried to buy from the King's brother, Archduke Albert,
and which the King had claimed for himself. In reality he clearly
(and for a time, correctly) expected to increase both his political
power and his wealth far more easily once Austria was officially
ruled by young Ladislav instead of Frederick. Thus Eizinger headed
the group that began to organize itself for action, expecting that
Frederick's prolonged absence in Italy would present them an unusually good opportunity. Frederick, though aware of this plot, was
still unwilling to postpone his departure. He had long looked forward to acquiring the imperial title. But he took the precaution of
having young Ladislav in his retinue during his travels to Rome
and Naples.

While Frederick was on his way the conspiracy—if such it can
be called, for it proceeded with relatively little secrecy—drew ever

21 See *ibid.*, I, 6off., and Max Vancsa, *Geschichte Nieder- und Oberösterreichs*, II, Stuttgart,
1927, 287ff.

wider circles. The most powerful among those who joined up with Ulrich Eizinger was Ulrich, Count of Cilli, a man with huge estates in Carinthia, Styria, Austria, and Croatia.[22] The Emperor Sigismund (whose second wife, Barbara, young Ladislav's grandmother, had been a Countess of Cilli) had raised this family to the rank of imperial princes. Cilli, himself married to a Serbian princess, was a man of almost limitless ambitions, a complete lack of any moral standards or inhibitions, and at the same time a good deal of personal charm. In the later life of his young relative, King Ladislav, he was to play a most important role which brought him into constant conflict with Eizinger.

Yet now, since Ladislav was still under Frederick's guardianship, the two men became allies for the very purpose of "liberating" the youngster, which would open the way to the desired free-for-all. They had friends among some of the great peers of Hungary, even though John Hunyadi remained aloof and stuck to his agreement with Frederick. But now, from Bohemia, a third Ulrich, the head of the house of Rosenberg, joined the coalition of Eizinger, Cilli, and the rest.

For Ulrich of Rosenberg this was, of course, a complete switch of policy. He had long been regarded as the Roman King's most intimate friend and adherent in Bohemia. He had always opposed, sometimes openly but always secretly, the official policy of the Czech Estates which had demanded that Ladislav be released and allowed to establish his court in Prague. As long as there was no power in the country that could effectively and legally check his own strength he preferred to have the interregnum prolonged, the presence even of a boy-king prevented. In addition his friendship with Frederick could open other avenues of partly political, partly financial gains which, as his correspondence with Frederick showed, he had been happy to use.

But now things had changed. A restored central power was in the making and had achieved a most unpleasant progress toward national and even international recognition. The young man who headed it had outwitted Ulrich more than once. And now even Frederick III, the freshly crowned Holy Roman Emperor, was ready to acknowledge and support him in return for keeping young Ladislav under safe tutelage. A complete switch could perhaps save the

[22] For a good short characterization see F. Krones, *Oesterreichische Geschichte für das Volk,* VI (1437–1526), Vienna, 1864, 9f.; in more detail A. G. Supan, *Die vier letzten Lebensjahre des Grafen Ulrich II von Cilli,* Vienna, 1868; and V. Lug, *Das Verhältnis des Grafen Ulrich von Cilli zu König Ladislaus Posthumus,"* Reichenberg 1904.

situation. If he could join the ranks of the Emperor's enemies, then, perhaps, he could also share in the power that would accrue to all those who might gain a decisive influence upon the royal child. The question was only whether all this could be brought about before George of Poděbrady had taken the last, probably decisive step toward national recognition of his regency—formal election by the Estates. Thus, the whole development took, at this stage, almost the form of a race.

Rosenberg, however, had to contend with much graver handicaps than George. The Emperor, even after his marriage and coronation, took his time returning. He enjoyed his stay in Italy and guessed that upon his return home he would be beset by troubles. In vain the conspirators tried to kidnap Ladislav—he was too carefully guarded. The Emperor had not even started on his trip home, when, on the issue of the Bohemian regency, the decision fell.

It was taken at a diet which opened in Prague on April 23, 1452, and thus became known as the St. George's Diet.[23] After four days of preliminaries the members of the Poděbradian party succeeded in convincing the minority—those that stood near the League of Strakonice as well as those who were uncommitted or neutral—that the legalization of George's position was not only inevitable but corresponded to the best interests of the nation. This success was achieved more easily since Ulrich of Rosenberg, his sons, some of his friends, and also the mostly Catholic cities of Pilsen and Budweis and, on the other side, Tabor had remained absent. The election, then, seems to have been unanimous after the majority had agreed to accept two provisions which would tend to make George's power somewhat less unconditional. One was the limitation of the regency arrangement, counted from the present moment, to only two years —a term that could certainly be prolonged, but barring a royal appointment only by the will of the Estates. The other limitation consisted in instituting and electing an advisory council for the regent. It was to consist of twelve members, five from the baronical class, five from the gentry, and only two from the cities, whose position was already considerably weaker than it had been twenty years earlier. The number of Utraquists and Catholics in this body was almost equal, yet there was a clear, if not strong majority of members of the Poděbradian party among the councillors. Its meetings, to be valid, did not generally need a quorum, but for important

[23] *AČ*, II, 309ff.

decisions a majority of all members, plus the sanction of the regent, was needed. The body thus operated more like a privy council than like a cabinet.

Of the five baronial seats in the council only four were filled by election—and there was little question that the one remaining was kept open for a member of the house of Rosenberg, in the hope that eventually this family of magnates would be willing to acknowledge the regency. But this was not simply a hope. Considerable pressure would be put not only on the Rosenbergs but upon all those that so far, by their absence from the diet or in other forms, had refused or would refuse to acknowledge and submit to the new, now fully legalized national government. They would have some time to consider before making a personal or written submission, but August 15 was fixed as the last date after which they would be considered as lawbreakers and be subject to forcible reduction.

On the whole it can be said that the new governmental order tended to reestablish a working constitutional monarchy of the type that, in its basic structure, had been developed a hundred years earlier by Charles IV. The regent's position was limited less by the advisory council—as even the King would always have his council to advise him—than, potentially, by the time limit, since thereby the possibility was kept open that either the Estates or the future King would terminate the present status. There was, however, one other limitation: officially George's power did not immediately reach beyond the borders of Bohemia proper. None of the dependencies—neither the Margraviate of Moravia nor the duchies or principalities of Silesia and Lusatia—were as fully subject to the new administration as was Bohemia proper, since none of their representative bodies ever gave him a special confirmation, and the Prague diet had not included any members from the dependencies. Yet, in fact, George's administration was bound to have a strong influence upon the dependencies. George would act in the name of the King who was also the King of the dependencies. In Moravia, furthermore, the house of Kunštát and Poděbrady still had strong personal influence. In Silesia, too, the active energy of the "gubernator," his quick suppression of brigandage, his success in keeping trade routes open and unmolested, made a deep impression and had direct implication for the country's economy.

Meanwhile the domestic opposition in Bohemia was still determined to hold out against recognition of the regency. Ulrich of Rosenberg did not abandon his hope that the events in Austria might eventually change the whole situation in his favor if only, before too long, young Ladislav would be available. Thus, neglecting the danger that might result from a military action of the regent against him, he sent his son Henry with a considerable force—2,000 infantry and over 300 horse—to join the forces assembled by the Austrian rebels under Eizinger against the Emperor, who had only recently returned from Italy. The strong combined army of the three Ulrichs began an active siege of Wiener-Neustadt on August 24. The Emperor had neglected, partly out of his usual stinginess, to provide himself with the forces needed to fight his enemies and had made very ineffective use of the troops he had at his disposal. Thus he was, after a few days, forced to give in and deliver young Ladislav into the hands of Ulrich of Cilli. The boy was taken to Vienna, where he was greeted and fêted like an angel from heaven.[24]

The Emperor had, during the last phase of the rebellion, tried to secure help from the two regents, John Hunyadi and George of Poděbrady. Both were essentially in sympathy with him, yet neither was willing to expose himself too completely for his cause. In the case of George the reasons are obvious enough. He had a strong army mobilized. But if he used it now in Austria, against the combined forces of the Austrian Estates and their allies, the outcome might be in doubt, and at the same time he was weakening himself dangerously within Bohemia. It might almost be said that to engage all or most of his forces in Austria would be to fall into a trap laid by Ulrich of Rosenberg. But even if, in purely military terms, he should turn out to be successful he would still find himself in a political and moral position which was not easy to defend. For a long time he (as well as his predecessor Ptáček) and his party had demanded publicly that Ladislav take his residence in Prague while the Rosenberg party had sabotaged this policy. If Rosenberg had now made a complete switch this was no reason for George to do likewise. While he was willing, up to a point, to support Frederick's policy, which was in accord with his own interests, he would not go so far as to spoil, in a lasting way, his chances for a good, constructive relationship with the future King. On the other hand, of

---

[24] Main source is Aeneas Sylvius, *Historia Friderici* as well as his *Historia Bohemica,* ch. 60. See also *SLČP* 145f. For Eizinger's policy in this period, see Vancsa, *op.cit.,* II, 307–316. On p. 316, n. 2, also the sources for Ladislav's reception in Vienna.

course, he maintained a positive advantage by his ability to act decisively at home just at the time when his chief adversary had weakened himself by his Austrian enterprise. This, then, became the essential purpose of the next phase of his activities. He did lead his strong forces south,[25] and there was some grumbling when people thought they would have to go to Austria. But the immediate goal was neither Austria nor even the Rosenberg Estates. It was the city of Tabor.

Tabor, as said before, had, with two other cities, refused to participate in the St. George's Diet of Prague. In the case of the other cities—Pilsen and Budweis—the reason was obvious. Both were traditionally strongholds of the conservative Catholic minority. But why should Tabor, of all cities, take a stand against the new regime? In the eyes of the world, in the eyes especially of a man like Aeneas Sylvius, Tabor was still the most Hussite of all Hussite places. From here Žižka had gone forth to beat the "Enemies of the Law of God." His likeness still looked down on the stranger from one of the city's gates. And here two priests were still alive and in positions of influence who had stood at the cradle of the Hussite movement in its militant form: Nicholas of Pelhřimov, once elected bishop of Tabor by the determined sectarians who had first of all Hussite groups cut every tie with Rome, and Wenceslas Koranda the Older, a religious rebel whose personality had been strong enough to maintain the upper hand for his policy in Tabor even against the great Žižka.[26]

The political and socio-economic structure of the city had, of course, undergone a complete change since those revolutionary days of thirty and more years ago. This was no more, and had not been for a long time, the armed camp of a religious and revolutionary community which had defied the old order and tried to establish a completely new, more egalitarian society. Even during the later thirties, when the Emperor Sigismund had been able to establish himself for a short time on the throne of Bohemia, he had raised Tabor to the status of a royal city, and even then it had become a city much like any other, no longer a true theocracy with priests leading and administering every phase of public life including the waging of

---

[25] It seems very unlikely that this army was as strong (16,000) as Aeneas Sylvius claims in his *Historia Bohemica* (Chapter 60). Even in his later great wars, when he had to defend himself and Bohemia against powerful enemies, George rarely commanded forces as strong as these.

[26] See Heymann, *Žižka*, 355f.

war, but a city ruled by a council in which the craft guilds presented the strongest elements.

The priests, indeed, were still there, and, while they no longer governed the city, it would be quite wrong to assume that they had lost all their influence. In general they had been able to maintain, even among the majority of common people, a standard of education, an eagerness to read, understand, and discuss the issues which emerged from the study of the Scripture and their application on the life of this time—in short a religious intensity greater and less diluted than that in Prague and other great cities;[27] a religious intensity which they were, before long, to pass on as their greatest heritage to their spiritual successors, the Czech Brethren. But their influence on political decisions of a general nature had by no means vanished. It was due to them that Tabor had, in 1444, defied the order the Estates had tried to impose on the Utraquist Church throughout the nation.

It seems very likely that Tabor's absence from the St. George's Diet of 1452 had rather similar reasons. Perhaps they were not the only ones. Among Czech cities in general it seems that at this time some fear was rampant lest a new monarchial government would revive taxes which might impose a rather heavy burden upon them. But there remains the question why the resistance to George's election should only have come from such places where there was strong opposition to the Utraquist Church—be it the Catholic opposition in Pilsen and Budweis or the Taborite opposition in Tabor itself and a few towns that had belonged to the old Taborite federation. Perhaps the opposition of both, Catholic and Taborite, was directed less against George of Poděbrady than against another man whose position could be expected to gain some strength and security through the official establishment of George's regency: John Rokycana. At first glance it may seem peculiar that Tabor's resentment against a theologian and churchman who so strongly represented and kept alive the traditions of the Hussite idea, of John Hus himself as well as his great friend and successor Jacobellus of Stříbro, should be so sharp as to make them, in fact, side with the most uncompromising wing of the Catholics against the government of the Utraquist regent. But a moment's reflection will perhaps convince us that this is, indeed, one of the most normal, the most frequent occurrences in the history of religious and near-religious movements and struggles. We have only to think of the way in which, say, Thomas

[27] See Aeneas Sylvius's grudging admission in Wolkan, *FRA,* II, 60, p. 36.

Münzer despised Luther or in which during later phases Lutherans hated Calvinists and vice versa.

This does not mean that the Taborites had permanently shelved their antagonism to Rome or to such of their neighbors as the Rosenbergs. However some sort of modus vivendi had repeatedly been established between those neighbors who had been such fierce enemies three decades earlier, and there were even moments when Lord Ulrich's repeated attempts to include Tabor among his allies against George of Poděbrady seemed not without chances of success. This time—with George's army before the gates of the city—the quest for alliance came from Tabor to Ulrich. And this time it was Ulrich who, probably with some regret, had to refuse, at least for the moment. His troops were far away and he could only hope that the strong city might hold out till succor came.

But when the Taborites saw that they would have nearly no one to help them they gave in—without any serious resistance.[28] Very likely the will to such resistance had from the beginning been limited to only a fraction of the population. On the first of September they promised to put, within a few days, their seal under the declarations of the St. George's Diet. This would also be made binding on the remaining cities of their federation: Písek, Žatec, and Louny. As a result of the capitulation the vast majority of the Taborite clergy declared their adherence to the regulations of the diet of 1444—thereby, for all practical purposes, removing for a while the old schism within the Hussite camp.

Yet not all the Taborite priests were ready to submit in this way. There were a few who would rather suffer than give in, foremost among them the two great old men, Nicholas of Pelhřimov and Wenceslas Koranda. They were held prisoners, first in Prague, then in the castle of Poděbrady, from where they were never released. Whether later claims of one of the historians of the Brethren is true that the Burgrave of Poděbrady starved them to death is difficult to decide.[29] If this is true then it is also possible that George—but by no means Rokycana—was responsible. In any case their disappearance in the dungeons of the castle was a pathetic end to a great and in many ways inspiring story.

The capitulation of Tabor was undoubtedly a shock to all those

[28] *SLČP*, 146.

[29] Tůma Přeloučský, *O původu Jednoty Bratrské a o chudých lidech*, ed. V. Sokol, Prague, 1947, p. 52. It seems certain that Nicholas was in Poděbrady, possible that Koranda was taken to another castle. See Urbánek, *Věk*, II, 677.

in the south and west who had so far tried to maintain their opposition, especially Ulrich of Rosenberg. The grand old man (not actually very old since he was still short of 50), so long the real leader not only of the Catholic minority but of the majority of the country's baronial caste, now was really at the end of his tether. His troops, down in Austria, had achieved their purpose. Yet this did not help him at all since they could not possibly be home in time to make any difference in view of George's overwhelming strength. The meeting that now took place in Budweis between the two men really put an end to their long and at times exceedingly bitter rivalry. The older man had to give in all along the line. He pledged himself to affix his seal to the rulings of the diet by mid-October, together with that of his oldest son, Henry, and representatives of Budweis, and to urge his closest friends to do likewise.[30] Present at the meeting was also Zdeněk of Sternberg, whom George had sent to Austria to observe and if possible mediate and from whom both sides learned about the most recent development there.

The two events—the fall of Tabor and the collapse of Rosenberg's opposition—made George's victory seem complete. When he returned to Prague at the end of September he knew that there was no effective resistance left anywhere. This was most clearly expressed during the "St. Gall Diet," which met in mid-October 1452 in the capital. And again George showed that he was a statesman rather than a party politician when, with his full agreement, Henry of Rosenberg was elected to the still vacant seat on the Regent's Advisory Council.[31] He could now begin with his real task: to bind the nation's wounds and to take her on the way to vigorous reconstruction.

[30] *AČ*, III, 551.
[31] See Tomek, *Dějepis*, VI, 219 n. 10.

CHAPTER 4

AN UNWANTED MISSIONARY:
JOHN OF CAPISTRANO.

WITH THE formalization and universal recognition of George's regency the decisive step toward the construction of a renewed, strong Czech state, the Poděbradian state, had been made. It was a commonwealth that was beset with difficult problems even when it emerged, and few of them were as thorny as the religious one. In our report on George's political victory of these last three or four years we have left these issues aside. But we cannot neglect them.

George had tried hard to make sure that the political party which he led and which had backed his policy was not purely religious, was not limited to the Hussite element. Yet the Utraquist Church had profited greatly from recent developments. During the decade before 1448 this Church had, in various parts of the country, been on the defensive against a Catholic counterreformation which was slowly but effectively gathering strength. This had been especially true in Prague. There the Cathedral Chapter of St. Vitus led by its dean, the capable, energetic Wenceslas of Krumlov, had tried to reestablish the supremacy of the chapter as the highest religious institution of the capital. Progress in this direction had been made easier because the University, still formally a predominantly Hussite-Utraquist institution, had lost most of the strength of her true Hussite (or what might be called her Jacobellian) tradition as a result of the absence from Prague of John Rokycana and most if not all of his more prominent friends and disciples, men such as Martin Lupáč, Jacob of Jemnice, and Wenceslas Koranda the younger of Pilsen. This had, during the first decade after the death of Sigismund, left the field almost completely free to the most conservative men among the old Utraquist masters, men such as Peter of Mladenovice, Prokop of Pilsen, and especially the highly influential John Příbram. They had gone very far in their attempt to remove all religious deviations with the single exception of the Chalice for laymen. The man who went farthest in this direction was Prokop of Pilsen, who cooperated closely with Catholic clergymen in his attack upon Rokycana.[1]

Rockycana's return to Prague in 1448 and his renewed activities in the University as well as on the pulpit of the Týn Church (which by now had assumed the position of a Hussite-Utraquist cathedral) changed this situation thoroughly. It would probably be an exaggeration to give him the entire credit for the recovery by which the Hussite-Utraquist Church in Bohemia, and especially in Prague, regained much of its earlier strength and sense of direction (though not, of course, its original revolutionary fervor). But, to the extent that the leadership of a great personality could revitalize and stabilize a religious reform movement in the shape of an increasingly unified church, Rokycana, in the twenty-two years left to him after his return from exile, did just this. Thus, this may be the proper place to introduce him in more detail.[2]

John of Rokycany (the form "Rokycana" results from the latinizing tendencies of the time) came from the small town of Rokycany, not very far from Pilsen in western Bohemia. He was born in the first half of the last decade of the fourteenth century and received his religious training initially in an Augustinian monastery. Around 1412 he enrolled at the University of Prague, where he seems to have met John Hus but where he soon came under the deep and abiding influence of Hus's friend and successor Jacobellus (Jakoubek) of Stříbro. During the Hussite wars the young cleric emerged only once as an important actor: in September 1424, as representative of the government of Prince Sigismund Korybut in Prague, he persuaded the great Žižka to desist from an attack on the capital.[3] After that, and especially after the death of Jacobellus in 1429, Rokycana, now (since 1430) a master of the University, became ever more the acknowledged leader of the Hussite center. He stood a good deal to the right of the Taborites (though in general he got along quite well with their leader, Prokop the Bald) but far to the left of those for whom the only raison d'être of the Hussite movement was the chalice

---

[1] E.g. the attack on Rokycana's liturgical errors presented by Prokop and the dean of the St. Vitus chapter Wenceslas of Krumlov, as quoted by F. Hrejsa, *Dějiny křest'anství v Československu*, III, Prague, 1948, pp. 114–116. On his whole life, see J. Prokeš, *M. Prokop z Plzně*, Husitský Archiv, III, Prague, 1927.

[2] In English the most substantial treatment, to date, of Rokycana's life and teaching is the present author's article "John Rokycana—Church Reformer between Hus and Luther," in *Church History*, Sept. 1959, pp. 240–280. There also (*passim* and especially p. 275) bibliographical notes as to his writings and writings about him.

[3] See Heymann, *Žižka*, 425ff.

for the laity. As the main clerical leader of the Czech delegation at the Council of Basel he gained, by a remarkable mixture of firmness and understanding for the needs of compromise, the confidence of his own people as well as the respect of the Catholic representatives at the Council.[4] Without this, the peace built around the Compacts would never have been achieved. His election by the Czech Estates to the office of Archbishop of Prague did not only express the acknowledgment of this fact but also the conviction of the majority of the nation that Rokycana alone could give the spiritual leadership around which the Hussite majority of the nation could rally.

It seems remarkable that the demand for Rokycana's confirmation as head of the Church should become such a constant and repeated feature of the meetings of the Czech diets, even in the decade when he resided in Hradec Králové, first for reasons of his personal safety, later also because of his close ties to the predominant religious trends of eastern Bohemia.[5] That these many resolutions were accepted by prominent members of the Catholic as well as the Utraquist Estates does not mean that they were really eager to see him confirmed by Rome—indeed some of them were, as we have seen, careful to make it clear to Rome that their indorsement of Rokycana was not meant seriously. But the act of apparent agreement—even when the Catholic lords had no reason to feel weak—proves their belief that the popular backing for the Utraquist churchman was so strong that, at this time, it was better policy not to challenge it publicly.

Rokycana was eager to receive the confirmation from Rome, which has led some of his detractors to conclude that he was overly ambitious and only interested in his personal aggrandisement. But this is a completely false and unfair conclusion. If Rokycana had merely wanted, at almost any price, to rise within the ranks of the Roman hierarchy he stood a good chance to gain such promotion by sufficient concessions, and he would have shown it in corresponding attempts at compromise. But his church policy, his considerable and increas-

---

[4] For an English treatment see Jacob, "The Bohemians at the Council of Basel," *Prague Essays,* ed. Seton-Watson, Oxford, 1949, pp. 81–123, especially 94ff.

[5] Hradec Králové had, during the Hussite Revolution, been the center of the Orebite movement. In its socio-economic structure and policy fairly similar to Tabor, the Orebite movement did not share its religious ("Pikhart") radicalism, especially in relation to the Eucharist. Thus, while there were conflicts between classes, they were not, in this case, reflected in religious forms. During the reign of a revolutionary group headed by Priest Ambrose, as well as later when his rule had been overthrown by a conservative counterrevolution under Diviš Bořek of Miletínek, relations to the Hussite center under Jacobellus and Rokycana remained close. See Heymann *Žižka* 362ff., 383ff., and Hrejsa, *op.cit.,* III, 22.

ingly "protestant" deviation from orthodox Roman theology as well as from Roman ritual, all these showed that he had very little in common with those clergymen who made a splendid career by brilliant opportunism—men such as his greatest permanent opponent, Aeneas Sylvius.

If, nevertheless, Rokycana badly wanted the Roman confirmation, at least for a considerable time, and was deeply disappointed that he did not receive it, the motive of personal glory had little to do with it. The real reason was that, unlike the Taborites and later the Brethren with their largely spiritualist understanding of the Lord's Supper, Rokycana deeply believed in the real presence of Christ at the sacrament and felt that only an ordained priest could perform the sacred act. Thus the question of apostolic succession was of great importance to him. As long as he was not confirmed, he did not feel that he himself or any other Utraquist clergyman had the right to ordain priests. During the thirty-three years of his administration his church suffered increasingly from the lack of ordained priests (despite the fact that Utraquist clerics frequently succeeded in receiving ordination outside Bohemia, from bishops in Poland, Hungary, and especially in Italy).

The ordination of priests was, in a way, the one great problem for which Rokycana never found a satisfactory solution. But even this, painful as it was, never undermined his belief in his mission. If anything, this disappointment made him, in the long run, somewhat less ready to agree to any compromise or to treat his opponents (or his inferiors among the Utraquist clergy) with diplomatic politeness. His language became harsher and began to sound more characteristically like that of a militant Protestant in the earlier phases of the Reformation. During his later years he also developed a domineering attitude which occasionally brought him into conflicts with his chief protector, George of Poděbrady, then King.

But it was not only disappointment over his shattered hopes that made Rokycana in his later years more sober and more bitter. A crisis, fortelling even graver events of a later period, occurred during the very phase in which George succeeded in getting his position of national leadership formalized and acknowledged. This early crisis was brought about mainly by the fact that the Curia, too, now felt impelled to take some initative in the struggle to reunite the Czechs with the Church of Rome. The Curia could move more freely and with more confidence now, since the second schism was a thing of

the past. Of the Conciliar Movement with its undertones of democratic decision and regional autonomy, not much more than shadows
seemed left.

In a way, of course, Carvajal's mission had already been such a
move. It had failed rather conspicuously, but probably more so in
the eyes of the Czechs (who had looked forward to it with so many
unjustified expectations) than in those of the Holy See. Carvajal had
not, by his rather inglorious retreat from the Bohemian battlefield,
suffered any real loss of either prestige or belief in his own competence. He was still, and perhaps more than before, considered an
expert on the religious and political affairs of Central Europe—a fact
which became especially significant during his long and consequential activity in Hungary. In addition to Carvajal it was Aeneas Sylvius
who would have liked, as soon as possible, to have a hand in the
solution of the difficult Czech problem. But at the moment he was
not given much of a chance, and for a while he was too busy looking
after some side aspects of his career, though, in the long run, his
mastery of German and Central European affairs had much to do
with his fast rise.

At the moment, however, two other men were called upon to try
their hands in this difficult game. Perhaps only one of them, Cardinal
Nicholas of Cusa (more correctly of Kues), was really called upon
by the Roman authorities to shoulder this particular task. The other,
the Minorite friar John of Capistrano, was, at least to some extent,
a self-appointed actor in this important play. Nicholas of Cusa's mission as papal legate to Germany and Bohemia was but a very small
episode in the life of this extraordinary man.[6] He was perhaps the
greatest German of his time, but probably also the greatest philosopher and one of the earliest great mathematical thinkers of the
period of early Humanism. Besides all this he was a remarkably
clear-thinking churchman with a vision of church reform and the
peacefully achieved unity of the Christian world. He lacked only

---

[6] There is, on Cusa, a vast and constantly growing literature, much of it in German. For
his attempt to understand Czech-Utraquist attitudes see the discussion between St. Paul and
the Czech in chapter XVIII of his work "De Pace fidei," in Cusa's selected writings publ. by
J. P. Dolan under the title "Unity and Reform," U. of Notre Dame 1962, pp. 233ff. The
references to his negotiations with the Hussites are generally scarce. There is a slim chapter
(pp. 225–242) in F. A. Scharpff, Nicholaus von Cusa, Mainz, 1843, also a later edition (1871).
Of some importance under this aspect, also because of the considerable documentary annex,
is still, despite its age, the work by J. M. Düx, Der deutsche Cardinal Nicolaus von Cusa und
die Kirche seiner Zeit, 2 vols., Regensburg, 1847. See also E. Vansteenberghe, Le Cardinal
Nicolas de Cues, Paris, 1920, pp. 218ff.

all sense for the political game, and this proved to be a serious handicap. His hope, at least for a time, seems to have been to attack the Czech problem in a spirit of understanding, and therefore he listened with some interest to a proposal which Albert Achilles, Margrave of Brandenburg and younger brother of the Elector Frederick II, submitted to him for a meeting with the Czech Estates, to be held in Cheb in the fall of 1452. The Estates had hoped that the Cardinal-legate would come to hear their own requests and discuss them at a meeting scheduled in Litoměřice, in northern Bohemia. The Cardinal, however, had declined, as he did not want to go there without a prior declaration on the part of the Czech Estates that they would obey his final decisions. This, of course, the Estates refused to do. An exchange of polemical letters took place between the Cardinal and the Hussite cleric Martin Lupáč, elected suffragan bishop, which, however, only hardened the positions of both sides.[7]

The planned meeting of Cheb therefore, never materialized. To whatever extent the legate might have considered the compromise submitted by the Margrave of Brandenburg, he would not have dared to go as far as to accept it, as in the meantime he had come under the critical supervision and very irreverent attack by the other, competing agent, John of Capistrano, who accused him of playing with the dangerous idea of appeasing a horde of heretical criminals. This attack, to which we will return later, was highly effective.[8]

Nicholas of Cusa, as a diplomat and church politician, turned out to be a cautious and even anxious man, too cautious and also politically too rigid to have any chance of success. Yet he was clearly one of the most attractive, admirable figures who ever represented the Church of Rome in her dealing with the Czechs. This is hardly true of his rival, John of Capistrano. It seems rather remarkable that the Church of Rome, generally so careful, so reluctant to bestow the glory of canonization, should have seen fit to make a saint out of this highly gifted but fiercely fanatic and often quite horrifying man. What is most amazing about this is that canonization is what Capistrano had planned for very systematically all through the later years of his life; and he reached this goal quite according to plan, though with the small delay of a few centuries.[9]

[7] On this correspondence see F. M. Bartoš, "Cusanus and the Hussite Bishop M. Lupáč," in *Communio Viatorum*, I, Prague, 1962, 35–46.

[8] See Urbánek, Věk, III, 548ff.

[9] The most recent and thorough study about John Capistrano is Johannes Hofer's voluminous work *Johannes von Capestrano*, Innsbruck, 1936, also in English translation. But this

Friar John was, as were quite a few members of his order, a prominent servant of the Papal Inquisition. He was also an extraordinarily active and successful preacher of penitence whose effect upon his hearers, as described by his contemporaries, sounds much like that of Savonarola. After Capistrano's invariably long, exciting, dramatic, and truly overwhelming sermons people, often by the hundreds, came to burn their clothes, their jewelry, and what ever "vanities" they possessed. His hypnotic fascination upon his hearers is revealed also in the fact that in Germany, Moravia, or Silesia the people, by the thousands, would stand listening to sermons lasting for two or three hours of which they did not understand one word since they were given in Latin. Capistrano never permitted his interpreters to start the translation until he himself had finished speaking.

But the most striking fact, testifying to a psychological power of exceptional strength, was the frequency and the unusually large number of miracles that he was supposed to have wrought, most of them miracle healings. "Miracles" of this sort were, of course, not too unusual at the time, given the proper psychological atmosphere. We know, for instance, that they occurred with fair regularity during those ceremonies during which Kings of England would "touch" people, even in ages a good deal later and a little more enlightened than the mid-fifteenth century. But there is perhaps no other figure in Europe's religious history whose miracles became as much of a mass phenomenon as John of Capistrano. With systematic care and foresight the later saint saw to it that as many as possible of these miracles were written down, confirmed by witnesses, and thus documented and notarized for eternity. Probably a good many people, whether their sufferings were of a hysterical or any other psychosomatic origin, experienced some real help or relief as a result of Capistrano's ministrations. But there is no lack of evidence from con-

book, while now indispensable for a study of the life and work of Capistrano, is exceedingly biased, indeed, it is an enormous apology for him. This may be tolerable in other fields, and simply amusing when for instance, in discussing the great duel between Capistrano and Rokycana, he charges Rokycana with demagoguery but does not see any such attitude in the case of Capistrano. The apology becomes painful and ludicrous when it tries to defend, or at least to make appear defensible, Capistrano's treatment of the Breslau Jews (and the Jews altogether, see later). Other works, combining part biography with source collections, are A. Hermann, *Capistrano triumphans*, Cologne, 1700; F. Walouch (in modern Czech quotations: Valouch), *Žiwotopis swatého Jana Kapistrana*, Brno, 1858; C. Jacob, *Johannes von Capistrano*, Breslau, 1903–1911; Z. Nejedlý, *Česká missie Jana Kapistrana*, in bookform or in *ČČM.*, LXXIV, Prague, 1900; and G. Voigt, "Johannes von Capistrano, ein Heiliger des 15. Jahrhunderts," *HZ.*, X, Munich, 1863. Besides the source material published by Walouch and Jacob a good deal of the correspondence is to be found in L. Wadding, *Annales Minorum*, XII, 3rd ed., Florence, 1932, mainly 92–166.

temporary sources that people who had been declared or had declared themselves as healed by Friar John, cripples who could walk, blind men who could see again, were just as crippled or blind when the brother had left town.[10]

The Minorite preacher had received his commission from the Pope partly upon requests of Frederick III, who may have hoped that Capistrano's views—especially his extreme absolutist views regarding the powers and rights of authority and the duty of subjects to obey —would be useful in expelling the devilish mood of rebellion from the minds of his people. It even seems that Frederick's friend Aeneas Sylvius had been in favor of the mission—at least he later mentioned this, and he announced the preacher's impending arrival to George as something that would be of the greatest help. Whether Aeneas really believed at the time that Capistrano's methods would be useful it is difficult to determine, but, if so, it would provide additional proof for the incompleteness of his understanding of the Czech scene, perhaps also for a lack of sufficient acquaintance with the real Capistrano.

Capistrano's own view of his task was very peculiar. He looked upon Bohemia as a sort of jungle in which the poor Czechs, seduced and misled by a small group of criminal heretics, had lost their way. As he had an almost limitless admiration for himself, for his own gifts, his understanding of theological issues, and especially for the task given to him by divine providence, he felt that there was simply nothing he could not achieve in order to change this unfortunate situation—given the opportunity. This opportunity, however, would consist in offering to him the free use of pulpits—or, since no church would be able to hold the number of his listeners—of the public squares of Prague and other cities of Bohemia and Moravia. The question was only whether the powers in control of the country would be willing to grant him this freedom. He did think it possible that there might be difficulties—indeed there are early utterances of his which seem to welcome even the harshest resistance as it might lead to the martyr's crown.[11] Later, on the other hand, he was very careful to avoid any serious trouble that might result in harm to his person. He made sure to be well protected by friends, and only travelled with strong armed guards.[12]

[10] See the very sobering and sarcastic remarks of another Catholic cleric, M. Döring, in F. Riedel, *Codex diplomaticus Brandenburgensis,* Berlin, 1848 and later, IV, 1, 225f.

[11] See MS Codex I 3855, f.105, in Vienna National Library.

[12] See Riedel, *loc.cit.* Taking notice of this does not imply any doubts in his personal courage, At the time of the defense of Belgrade he was to show that he had plenty of it.

If Capistrano had been somewhat less cautious—and on the other hand less inclined to violent invective—he might indeed have started in Bohemia, and perhaps even in Prague. But not really willing to undergo any great risk, he entered the countries of the crown of St. Wenceslas by going from Austria to the city of Brno in Moravia. Brno, like Olomouc, Znojmo, and Jihlava, was still a predominantly Catholic city, and he did not anticipate any danger there. On the other hand he could hope that the fame that preceded him would attract a sufficiently large crowd, including Hussites, from the surrounding countryside. In this expectation he was not disappointed. He could also, right at the beginning, boast the successful conversion of one of Moravia's leading nobleman, the sub-chamberlain Beneš of Boskovice. This man proclaimed his break with the Chalice, a wonderful liberation from grave errors, before masses of listeners on one of Brno's public squares, and Capistrano felt sure that his example would lead untold numbers of men of every station in the same direction.[13]

Yet all was not easy sailing. Resistance came from Moravia's Hussite centers, where his activity was viewed with growing concern and annoyance. Especially incensed were the people of Kroměříž, where the Utraquist clergy, through its priest Stephen, protested Capistrano's activity in sharpest terms. Perhaps as a result a crowd of Hussites from Kroměříž put themselves in the way of forty pilgrims who had intended to hear Capistrano, and imprisoned them.[14]

Meanwhile, however, Capistrano's arguments became better known to the people in Prague, especially to George of Poděbrady and to Rokycana. Capistrano, it turned out, took the most radical stand imaginable against the Utraquist Church. He made not the slightest distinction between schismatics and heretics. The mere use of the Chalice by laymen was, in his eyes, a mortal sin; though later he denied having said that all laymen who had ever taken the Chalice had irrevocably lost their souls. The literary understanding, by the Hussites, of the famous passage in John 6:53, was in his view absurdly false (though it had often been understood in this way by orthodox Catholics). The Compacts had never been valid because Bishop Philibert, when signing then in the name of the Basel Council, had acted without instructions or had gone far beyond what they would have permitted him.[15]

---

[13] Walouch, *Žiwotopis Kapistrana,* 787f.
[14] See the sources for the role of Kroměříž in Urbánek, *Věk,* 11, 565.
[15] Thereby Capistrano went far beyond what at the time the Curia (and such of its repre-

If Capistrano had ever had a chance of proceeding to Prague and of addressing (and, as he expected, convincing) the Utraquist leaders and George of Poděbrady, then this chance was killed by his angry, spiteful attack upon the Compacts. In the eyes of George the Minorite preacher thereby became immediately an odious and highly unwelcome stranger, subversive and dangerous to the still young and precarious peace of the country. It seems indeed possible that George, in this case, made up his mind even faster than Rokycana. For the statesman who bore the responsibility for the country's peace, any resumption of the great religious dispute under such conditions was unbearable. But Rokycana on his side felt rather tempted to react to the challenge. This, so he thought, was a worthwhile opportunity to subject the issue of the Chalice and the Compacts to a public disputation. In a couple of letters (the friendly and civil tone of which was acknowledged even by Capistrano) the Utraquist churchman suggested this to Capistrano. Specifically he proposed, in his second letter, to hold the meeting in one of three towns within easy reach of Brno, where Capistrano still dwelt: in Moravská Třebova or in the Bohemian border towns Německý Brod or Pelhřimov.[16]

But Rokycana first felt the need to investigate the growing unrest in Moravia. Thus he decided to participate in a meeting held by the Moravian estates in the royal city of Uničov, in the north of the margravate. There he read the text of the Compacts to the assembled noblemen of both religious groups and defended them against Capistrano's attacks. The estates thereupon recommended a disputation, if possible to be held in Moravský Krumlov under the auspices, and presumably in the castle, of Lord Henry of Lipé, Marshall and Governor of Moravia. Armed with this additional proposal Rokycana travelled south, hoping that in this way he might catch Capistrano in Brno. But Capistrano left the city as soon as he heard of Rokycana's intention to meet him, supposedly warned by some of his friends that he was no longer safe in Moravia.[17] Via Austria he now entered Bohemia—the place where he went (just across the border) was the great castle of Krumlov, where he stayed as guest of Ulrich of Rosenberg and his three sons. From there he wrote letters of the

---

sentatives as Cusa and Aeneas Sylvius) would hold. Even Hofer registers slight doubts in the wisdom of such argumentation (*Johannes von Capestrano*, 381 f.)

[16] See Wadding, *Annales Minorum*, 106–108 (older edition 91–93.

[17] See Rokycana's letter to him in Walouch, *op.cit.*, 711.

warmest recommendation for Ulrich and his house to several powerful men, including the Pope and the King of France.[18]

From Krumlov he finally answered Rokycana's invitation to a disputation which so far he had so successfully evaded. (He was quite
aware of the fact that it would not be easy to "beat" a man of Rokycana's erudition, especially in the theology of the sacrament.) He had
to maintain the pretense of being only too keen on meeting the
"heresiarch" on his own ground. In a jeering letter he declined
contemptuously the "villages" suggested by Rokycana as places for
the disputation. He who had been so desperately eager to preach and
speak publicly in the very center of Bohemia now offered as counter-
proposals almost all the capitals and great cities of the continent,
including such places as Naples and Toulouse. The only place he
named, as a last concession, nearer his own goal was Cheb.[19] But he
sharply declined to use the "Cheb judge" which had been considered
as the basis for rapprochement during the negotiations, fifteen years
ago, between the Czechs and the Council of Basel. Instead he demanded that the Kings of Europe—of England and France, Castile
and Aragon, Portugal and Navarre, Poland and Cyprus—be judges.
(He also mentioned the "Kings" of Hungary and Bohemia, well
knowing that they were one and the same: a little boy, at present in
the retinue of Emperor Frederick on the latter's procession through
Italy.) In short, almost every line of his letter shows that Capistrano
was quite resolved not to have a disputation but intended to give the
impression that it was not his but Rokycana's fault when the disputation never materialized. He tried to uphold this impression even in
later communications, though in one of them, which he felt sure
would never reach the public, he had no qualms to give his real intentions away.[20]

During his stay in Krumlov, Capistrano received an answer from
Rokycana in which the latter, this time in much less friendly terms,
reacted mainly to Capistrano's reproach that he stubbornly resisted
the truth as accepted by the vast majority of people. This, indeed,
was the last time that Rokycana wrote to him, and his silence was
certainly in complete agreement with the wishes of George of Poděbrady not to prolong so fruitless and even dangerous a discussion.

[18] See the correspondence between Capistrano and Ulrich of Rosenberg and the letter of
recommendation in Ryněsová-Pelikán, *Listář a listinář Oldřicha z Rožmberka*, IV., Prague,
1954, 323–331.
[19] Walouch, *op.cit.*, 711.
[20] See the letter to Cusa in Wadding, *Annales Minorum*, 149–152 (older edition, 128ff.)

George himself, to the intense annoyance of Capistrano, kept many of his urgent and at the beginning quite ingratiating messages and petitions unanswered. Instead (backed up at the time by Frederick's recognition of his regency) George wrote to Ulrich of Rosenberg, requesting in strong terms that he no longer permit the friar to stay in his castle and under his protection.[21] Nevertheless Capistrano stayed there for another few weeks, till about mid-November. Then he went to Germany, and now (without officially giving up his plans for reconverting the Hussites by the power of his word) he began an activity based on his often expressed conviction that heretics must be destroyed and not parlayed with. He wrote to Pope Nicholas, demanding greater powers for himself, a more vigorous condemnation of the communion in both kinds, and a solemn abrogation of the Compacts. The Pope fulfilled his first two demands but not the last one, as he did not consider it wise to burn all the bridges that had been built, since the end of the Hussite Wars, between the Church and the Czechs.[22]

Burning those bridges, of course, was exactly what Capistrano was aiming at. He revealed this, especially by the sermons he gave in Germany where he talked his listeners into a white-hot fury till they asked for nothing better than a renewed crusade against the heretics. His personal attacks against Rokycana now became poisonous. He accused him absurdly of having a whole harem of concubines and of having bought himself a castle. And he went so far as to use the famous "joke" about Hus, the fat goose who had been fried at the stake in Constance.[23]

Capistrano's violent assaults, in his sermons as well as in his widely publicized tractates, finally provoked a strong counter-demonstration, contained in a long letter in justification of the Compacts which all the important members of the Poděbradian party, including such Catholics as Zdeněk of Sternberg and Henry of Michalovice, directed to a number of German princes who had assembled, during February 1452, in the Franconian town of Lauf. The message also protested against the Papal bulls which had characterized the communion in both kinds as heretical.[24]

A further step was taken by the St. George Diet, the same

21 Walouch, *op.cit.*, 716.

22 See Urbánek, *Věk*, II, 574f.

23 Walouch, *op.cit.*, 840. This is, of course, a pun since the Czech word "husa" means goose.

24 Wadding, *Annales Minorum*, 142 ff. (older ed. 122 ff.)

whose most important achievement was the official establishment of George's regency. Together with directions laid down for the Utraquist clergy (which, it seems, led to some opposition on the part of Rokycana) and for the prosecution of heresy (presumably meant to apply to Tabor), the diet approved suggestions for a meeting in Regensburg with the papal legate Nicholas of Cusa. A Czech delegation, led by Zdeněk of Sternberg and John Smiřický, did indeed go to Regensburg, where again hopes seemed to rise for at least a beginning of serious negotiations. When, however, rumors about possible concessions reached Capistrano he immediately expressed his extreme displeasure to the cardinal legate.[25] This intimidated the great Cusa to the extent that he politely asked the Minorite friar to come to Regensburg himself—an invitation, in fact, to control procedures and make sure nothing would occur of which he did not approve. And once in Regensburg, despite attempts of Zdeněk of Sternberg to gain his confidence, Capistrano destroyed all hopes for even a provisional understanding about procedures by the harsh conditions which Cusa, under the steady pressure of his rival, felt obliged to impose upon the Czechs.

The Czechs themselves, and especially the Utraquist Estates, had no intention of welcoming either of the two Roman emissaries into Bohemia on the basis of a guarantee of unconditional surrender. Nor had they any need, in their own view, to go that far. For already a different way to solve the difficult issue of priest ordination seemed to open up. Communion in the two kinds, after all, had never been abolished by the Eastern, the Greek Church, and the thought of contacting Constantinople for a closer relationship had been "in the air" for some time. It now was taken up with real determination, owing, it may be assumed, largely to the entirely negative results of the missions of Cusa and Capistrano.

The Czech mission to Constantinople was, in its eventual shape and outcome, hardly more than a chimera which can be dealt with briefly here. Some of it, for all the research that has been devoted to the subject,[26] is still doubtful. Thus we have little information about

---

[25] See above, n. 20.

[26] For the most up-to-date treatment see M. Paulová, "L'Empire Byzantin et les Tchèques avant la chute de Constantinople," *Byzantinoslavica,* XIV, Prague, 1953, 158–225. F. M. Bartoš originally agreed with an attempt to identify "Constantine Anglicus" with Master Payne (Magister English). See his *M. Petr Payne, diplomat husitské revoluce,* Prague, 1956, pp. 41–44. Meanwhile further research has convinced him that this diplomat was not the Englishman Payne but a Czech clergyman and graduate of Prague University whose name

the identity and national origin of the chief negotiator for the Utraquist Church, Constantine Anglicus, as he was called. We know that he made two trips to the imperial city, the first one starting as early as 1450. His activities in Constantinople resulted early in the following year in a message sent to the Czech Estates by the Greek Church. In it the Greeks welcomed the Czech wish to go to the sources of the true faith. The man responsible for this attitude was the Patriarch Gennadius, the leading opponent of the recent (but quite ineffectual) union of the Eastern and Western Churches concluded at the Council of Florence in 1439. Indeed it may be said that acceptance of the Czech schismatics by Constantinople was dependent on the survival of the great schism between East and West. The advocates of firmness against Rome were inclined to accept the Czech accession as a symbol of their equal status to Rome, and only in the second place as a possible accretion of strength, even perhaps in military terms, against the overwhelming Turkish danger. But to the extent that the Emperor Constantine XI—who tried to gain a more general western support by religious unity—tended to prevail, the chances for the Czechs were correspondingly weakened. This was the situation which the Utraquist ambassador encountered upon arriving again in the city by the Bosphorus in 1452. The negotiations got stalled, and were never to be resolved properly till the city's and empire's fall in 1453 put an end to all such hopes.

Even if this whole thread of events had not been cut short by the tragic fate of the imperial city the difficulties, clearly, would have been considerable, as the Czechs, and especially Rokycana, were scarcely willing to give up all their hard-gained autonomy in exchange for another dependency, this time from a Church which, while itself "Utraquist," was in other ways far more tightly smothered in conservative ritualism than Rome. Thus the question arises whether the idea of union with the Greeks had ever been taken with complete seriousness in Prague or whether it was meant only as a manoeuvre which would put pressure on Rome and impell the Curia to concessions which otherwise had seemed unobtainable, especially the confirmation of the Compacts. It seems to me that these two pos-

---

was Matthew of Hnatice, later called Matthew English. See the first part of his article (the second has not yet become available to me): "A delegate of the Hussite Church to Constantinople in 1451–1452," *Byzantinoslavica*, XXIV, 2, Prague, 1963, 287–292. There also are bibliographical notes.

sibilities do not exclude each other.[27] The leadership of the Utraquist Church may well have hoped for a positive effect of such pressure on Rome. If, on the other hand, the Greeks had really, as they promised, sent one of their bishops to Prague, the advantage in having a permanent and reliable source for the ordination of Utraquist priests might well have seemed of overwhelming importance to Prague. Nor would this step necessarily have been considered a declaration of war by Rome. But all this belongs to the realm of mere historical speculation.

We are on much safer ground by returning, from the wanderings of Constantine Anglicus, to those of John of Capistrano. We find him still in Germany, though for a short while he even succeeded in entering Bohemia again—staying at the city of Most, which was accessible to him since it was, at this time, under lease to the ducal house of Saxony. From there he renewed his urgent requests to be allowed safe-conduct to Prague, but when at one point such safe-conduct was offered to him he refused it. From there he also wrote the fiercest of all his slanderous attacks on Rokycana. It was in a lengthy tractate, called an "apology," and was meant to influence the Czech Estates assembled at the St. George's Diet, which elected George as regent.[28] It cannot be said to have been successful.

If Capistrano resumed at all his attempts to undertake his planned "mission to the Hussites" it was because the release of Ladislas Posthumus, the young ruler who had recently become the hope of many Czech enemies of Hussitism, had made him, too, hopeful for a change. This, he guessed, might either take the form of the removal of George of Poděbrady from his position of regent or pressure being put upon the regent to cut his own ties with the heretical church. It was not long till Capistrano saw his mistake. The capitulation of the Rosenbergs, their official acceptance of the settlement of the St. George's Diet, made him furious and resentful, and he bitterly reproached Lord Ulrich, who, as he claimed, had given up when victory was already almost in his hands. How little he knew or could judge the situation in the Kingdom of Bohemia.[29]

But even though Capistrano's hopes to defeat and destroy the Hussites in Bohemia and Moravia were all bound to fail, he was by no

---

[27] I find myself here in some disagreement with Urbánek (*Věk*, II, 612ff.), who does not admit of any other interpretation of the Czech action than that of merely trying to influence and pressure Rome by flirting (this is mine, not his term) with Constantinople.

[28] Hermann, *Capistranus*, 371ff.

[29] For this letter, written from Magdeburg, see Rynešová, *Listář*, IV, 355–358.

means finished as an adversary. Indeed he was still capable of doing considerable harm to "his friends, the Hussites," and especially to their leader George of Poděbrady. And the place where he did this most successfully was Breslau.[30]

The policy of Breslau was, at this time, of great significance. The city government of Breslau—as was usual at the time—was dominated by a city council which, in the main, represented the great trading interests; but the "little people," too, had influence—a great deal of it in times of crisis—through the "commune," which consisted of all men holding citizenship. A special influence, in addition, was wielded by the clergy, which was divided between the men of the cathedral chapter and the parish priests. The latter were much less dependent on the views and wishes of the bishop. The local situation in Breslau will occupy us later.

The people of Breslau had tried for some time to induce Capistrano to come to them, and as a special lure had promised to finance the building of a new Franciscan-Minorite monastery and church. He did, indeed, arrive in mid-February 1453, greeted by jubilant masses and conducted in solemn procession to the cathedral. His closest adherent and friend in the city became Dr. Nicholas Tempelfeld, a man who (as the only one) combined the position of a canon of the Cathedral chapter with that of a preacher extremely popular with the masses of people. He was one of the bitterest enemies of Hussitism and was to play a prominent role in the later resistance movement of Breslau against George of Poděbrady. He immediately put his pulpit in the Church of St. Elizabeth at Capistrano's disposal.

Capistrano's agitation in Breslau against the Czech Hussites did not differ very much from his activities before, nor did his general preaching activity. Despite his previous failures, he sent still more petitions to the young King Ladislav as well as to the Czech regent with the request for another safe conduct to Prague. It seems likely that at this stage he did not really expect the request to be granted; thus he could demand it without fear of how he might be treated in Prague. He could a least claim that he had tried his utmost, and could attempt to show how the young King had become the prisoner of the regent, against whom he now let loose a stream of abuse. He certainly laid the basis, among the people of Breslau, for a mood of wild hatred not only toward the Hussites in general but toward

---

[30] On the topic of Capistrano's activities in Breslau see mainly H. Markgraf, "Geschichte Schlesiens und Breslau unter König Ladislaus," in *ZVGAS*, XI Breslau, 1872, 235–274, especially 240–246; Jacob, *op.cit.*, I, 77f., 89f.

George in particular. At the time George did not particularly mind this activity, but its consequences were to become very serious for him a few years later.

But the act that was perhaps most instrumental in making Capistrano's stay in Breslau noteworthy and memorable through the ages was the way in which he helped to bring about and to direct the great persecution of the local Jewish community.[31] Fierce attacks against the Jews were a standard element of his sermons. It was in this atmosphere of a boundless religious antisemitism largely created or at least whipped up by Capistrano that accusations of repeated debasement of hosts (which began to bleed when wounded, or jumped out of the fire into which they had been thrown) as well as charges of ritual murder were laid to several members of the old and well-established Jewish community of the city. The ensuing trial was largely master-minded by Capistrano, who even instructed the hangman how most effectively to torture the "criminals." As a result of confessions thus obtained, forty-one Jews were burned at the stake, while the rest of the members of the Jewish community had to leave Breslau. This was clearly a "final solution" within the framework of one city, all the more so as Breslau requested and obtained, soon afterwards, the special permission from King Ladislav not to have to suffer any Jews within the city walls ever again. Here, indeed, we find the Minorite preacher in his special role as inquisitor. There is no reason to assume that he would have shown himself more humane toward Hussite heretics, provided he would ever have had the opportunity and the power to deal with them.

[31] The main source here is Peter Eschenloer. See his *Geschichten der Stadt Breslau,* ed. Kunisch, I, Breslau, 1827. It is Eschenloer, an admirer of Capistrano, who reports on p. 13, that he "war selbst dabei, da der Nachrichter die Juden marterte; er selbst ihm Unterweisung gab, wie man sie martern sollte." See Hofer's strangely apologetic treatment, presenting the reports about ritual murder and other Jewish crimes as if, while doubtful, they might still conceivably have been true, *Johannes von Capestrano,* 485–504.

GEORG: PODIEB:
RAD: CORONAT:
REX · BOH · ĀNO ·
M · CCCCLVIII ·
MORTVVS · ET ·
SEPVLTVS · ĀNO ·
M · CCCCLXXI ·
DIE · XXII · MARTii

1. Tomb Portrait of George of Bohemia, St. Vitus Cathedral, Prague
(photo: Vratislav Tachezy)

3. Matthias Corvinus of Hungary (from Imre Lukinich, ed., *Mátyás király emlékkönyv*, 1, Budapest 1940)

2. Frederick III, after a painting in Kloster Lankowitz (from Max Mell, *Enea Silvio Piccolomini Briefe*, Jena 1911, opp. 236)

CHAPTER 5

THE BOY-KING AND THE REGENT

AMONG THE many rulers in history who inherited a crown before they came of age, none had a position more peculiar and difficult to define than Ladislav Posthumus. The possibility of difficulties and frictions between a young ruler and a regent who, usually by will of the former King, is to hold the reins of government during the son's minority, is a frequent occurrence and one which almost seems inherent in the situation. But in the case of Ladislav confusion was confounded by the weakness and incompetence of his guardian, Frederick III, who by rights should have been regent for Ladislav in all his realms but in effect never was—with the partial and doubtful exception of the duchy of Austria. And things became still more complicated by the fact that Ladislav was to be the legitimate bearer not of one but of three crowns, ruler over three countries which had no cohesion, no common tradition [1] but which had each recently experienced grave internal conflicts amounting to prolonged civil war, and in one of them, Bohemia, even to a tremendous revolution.

This basic situation immediately opened up a whole range of problems. Until his release from the supervision of the Emperor, Ladislav, just 12 years of age, had been merely a name. The men who held power in his three realms would have liked this state of affairs to continue, and in this they had considerable support in their countries. But only in the Kingdoms of Hungary and Bohemia was there a clear constitutional basis for their position, and a somewhat tenuous one at that, since both "gubernators" had to face a still considerable opposition. In both countries it was taken for granted that the regents, to continue to govern, needed a confirmation from the young King as soon as he ceased to be Frederick's ward and legally became ruler. Such a confirmation only the King could give, and this very fact lifted him now, in terms of potential influence, somewhat above the level of a mere figurehead.

---

[1] All instances of a union between Bohemia and Austria (under Přemysl Otakar II) or Bohemia and Hungary (under Sigismund) or all three (under Albert II) were extremely short-lived and had not established any tradition.

But his position was a different one in each of the three countries. In Hungary as well as in Austria he was already the acknowledged sovereign whose right of inheritance had been accepted long ago. In Hungary, however, he was well aware of strong countercurrents against his rule, while on the other hand he could rely on strong forces, led by an exceedingly able leader of Czech origin, John Jiskra of Brandýs,[2] which enabled him at least partially to balance out such opposition. This situation which we shall discuss in more detail clearly favored any attempt on his side to strengthen his position.

In Bohemia, as we know, a somewhat similar situation—an uneasy balance of forces—had existed until recently. But George of Poděbrady's victory over his political adversaries had been more substantial and in a sense more final than the success that John Hunyadi had achieved over his enemies. In addition Ladislav's own constitutional position was weaker in the Czech countries than in Hungary because his hereditary rights were under dispute, especially in the kingdom of Bohemia proper, and because his rule could not be considered legally valid till he had been crowned. In the dependencies —the margraviate of Moravia, the duchies and principalities of Silesia, and in the two Lusatias—he was more generally recognized as a hereditary King, a fact which indirectly strengthened his position vis-à-vis the estates of Bohemia. Nevertheless, on the whole, his position in Bohemia was relatively the weakest.

Strongest, on the face of it, was the young ruler in Austria. (It has always to be remembered that the term refers only to the duchy of Austria—the provinces of Upper and Lower Austria with the city of Vienna—not to Styria and Carynthia, not to the Tyrol, where the Emperor Frederick and Duke Sigismund were the respective hereditary rulers, nor, of course, to Albert's western lands or to the large archiepiscopate of Salzburg.) In Austria the boy-king had no need at all to prove his legitimacy or to doubt his popularity which could be measured in terms of the strong dislike in which many Austrians held the man who had ruled them until recently. (Again, this was true only for Austria proper; in Styria Frederick was fairly popular.) In Austria too, as we know, there were two factions: one, often identified with the estates but mainly consisting of the gentry and the people in control of the cities led by Ulrich Eizinger and his friends, the other mainly limited to the magnates under the leader-

2 See Urbánek, *Konec Ladislava Pohrobka* (Rozpravy české akademie věd, I, 67), Prague, 1924, 93ff.

ship of the Count of Cilli. Of the two, Eizinger alone, on the basis
of resolutions passed by the Estates at the beginning of their rebellion against the Emperor, had a claim in any way comparable with
that which Hunyadi held in Hungary or the Lord of Poděbrady in
Bohemia.[3] In reality it was much weaker, and had hardly been meant
to give Eizinger much authority beyond the date of the King's release.

Naturally, the King, even if he was—as he turned out to be—unusually mature for his age, would need a man who was really in
control, one who was something more than a first minister. The
question, in Austria, was whether and how the youngster would
be able to choose this man himself.

Now it was obvious from the beginning that there would be no
really free choice. Of the two men who had concluded the temporary
alliance with one another to force the King's release against the
Emperor's wishes, one or the other, Eizinger or Cilli, had to be the
man in charge. No one else could muster the backing, politically
and militarily, which would make his leadership effective. And those
two did not really have equal chances. Eizinger, it is true, had led
the Austrian estates, had a wider support among the people, and
could claim that during the last phase of the struggle no one else
had fought as hard for the King's release than he. Yet Cilli's position was stronger. As an imperial prince he far outranked Eizinger
and had more support among the other princes of the Empire. As
an "uncle" (in reality a first cousin, once removed) of Ladislav he
could claim the right to stand by the orphaned child as his nearest and strongest male relative, just as he had once helped Queen
Dowager Elizabeth to get the infant crowned as King of Hungary
when he was only a few months old.[4] Rather naturally the boy
preferred the relative to the stranger. Before long it was clear that
Cilli had gained Ladislav's complete confidence, that every step
taken by the King was decided by Cilli as surely as if he had been
given the official mandate as the King's new guardian and as the
new regent of Austria. Thus Eizinger's influence, seemingly guaranteed in the written agreement concluded between the two before
the enterprise against the Emperor, had essentially waned.

It is not easy to evaluate the direct impact of Cilli's personality
upon Ladislav. Cilli himself lived a life of debauchery, and it was
widely believed that he tried to spoil the young boy to make him

3 See Aeneas Sylvius, *Historia Bohemica*, chapter 60.
4 Aeneas Sylvius, *Historia Frederici*, 113.

all the more dependent on himself.[5] To what extent this is true, and, if so, whether and to what extent such an "education" was successful, it is difficult to say. Later, at the time of Ladislav's death, there was a tendency to glorify, almost sanctify him, and nothing was allowed to be said about him that would make him appear as anything but the noblest human being. This, clearly, was far from a true picture. Yet we have no reason to think of him as depraved or especially inclined to a licentious life.

Perhaps of greater importance was what we might call Ladislav's political education. And here we may well assume that the King's amazing ability to dissemble, to hide his feelings and deceive others about his intentions—certainly amazing in one so young—may partly have been the result of Cilli's influence, though the long and frustrating time at the court of his unloved guardian Frederick may already have laid the ground for this development in Ladislav's mind.

In the period immediately after his release, however, Ladislav's policy, clearly determined by Cilli, did not reveal the caution of the would-be deceiver but, on the contrary, the assumption that, being the King, he could expect his orders to be obeyed in all three of his realms. If this was naïve, it was Cilli's naïveté.[6] He may have thought that he could bluff his way into a position which would make him the real power behind the throne not only in Austria but also in Hungary and Bohemia. In the latter country the period between the King's release and the political capitulation of the Rosenberg's permitted Cilli to harbor such illusions. He had not rid himself of them when, in November 1452, delegations of the estates of Ladislav's countries arrived upon the official invitation of the King.

The Czech delegation arrived in Vienna with 400 horse but with little additional splendor. George himself did not go along; he was, it seems, the sender rather than one of those who were sent. The envoys, however, were representative enough, since among them were Zdeněk and Aleš of Sternberg, Henry of Rosenberg, and a number of other barons from the most powerful houses of Bohemia. Whether it was due to the regent or to other influences among the Estates, the two former groups—those of Strakonice and of Poděbrady— were about equally represented, which resulted in a majority of Catholic over Utraquist lords. This may well have been intended, as

---

[5] This is especially the view of Aeneas Sylvius, who disliked the count heartily. See *ibid.,* 396ff.

[6] *Ibid.,* 447.

it might have seemed better to present especially those demands that had to do with the religious peace of the country through men not suspected of heresy. The religious requests led off a whole set of clauses which were, to all intends and purposes, the conditions under which the Czech Estates were willing to accept and acknowledge Ladislav as their King.[7]

This strictly conditional acceptance did not imply a new policy. The right of the estates to elect a King had been emphasized repeatedly during the last decades. It had been used in the case of the election (though it had not been accepted) of the Bavarian Duke Albert (and to some extent also of the earlier election by part of the estates of Casimir Jagiello in competition with King Albert II, Ladislav's father). "Until now," so the transcript says in an article (No. 9) which demands the revision of acts by Frederick III, "King Ladislav is not yet our crowned King." The implications were clear. Nor was it merely incidental that among statements mentioning Czech Kings from the time of Charles IV, Albert II was conspicuously missing.

In this framework the estates demanded that the King acknowledge, maintain, and protect the Compacts, that he should do all in his power to have Rokycana confirmed, because he rather than anybody else could bring about unity and mutual understanding; he should recognize acts of transfer of royal or Church property into private hands during the reigns of Charles IV, Wenceslas IV, and Sigismund; should renounce the right of escheat of estates whose owners died without direct heir; should bring about the return to Bohemia of territories or fiefs lost to neighbors during the recent troubles; should join his duchy of Austria to the Bohemian crown; should take his residence in Bohemia; should restore Bohemia's mining industry, mainly that of Kutná Hora, to its old prosperity; and should use no one but Czechs as officials, burgraves, advisers, and deputies, especially in times when he should be out of the country.

It is worth noticing that there was no word in these demands about the confirmation of the regent. Yet all of them reflect so clearly the wishes of George that we cannot draw any conclusions from this, except perhaps that he intended to leave this issue to a later, more intimate form of understanding with whoever would then have most influence over the King.

Count Cilli, of course, was by no means pleased with these demands. As far as Bohemia was concerned, they would prevent all

[7] See *AČ*, IV, 413–415.

chances of establishing a strong reign over Ladislav's territories in which he, Cilli, would remain the real power. And it was perhaps not only Cilli's influence but also Ladislav's earlier upbringing which made the young King angry at the religious requests from Bohemia. "If the Czechs," he is supposed to have said, "want me for their King they will also have to accept my religion." [8] The Czech delegates, a few of whom, especially Henry of Rosenberg, were themselves somewhat less than enthusiastic about the demands they had presented, tried to work out a compromise in which Aeneas Sylvius, the Emperor's observer in Vienna, also had a hand. From what Aeneas reports, it appears that this agreement had changed only a small number of the original demands. Yet Cilli and the King seem at least to have insisted on a wording which would restore to some extent the hereditary character of Ladislav's kingship, especially by repeated mention of his father, King Albert II, whose obligations to the Czech nation Ladislav promised to safeguard as well as those of his grandfather Sigismund. In addition Cilli and the King balked at the demand for the union of Austria with the crown of St. Wenceslas (a clause which may have been merely a *ballon d'essai*) and, more seriously, were unwilling to do much for Rokycana.[9]

Whatever the major stumbling block—and it is difficult to believe that it was not the issue of heredity—the compromise agreement, concluded in Vienna sometime early in December 1452, was not accepted by the Czech estates when the negotiators returned to Prague. Consequently Ladislav was as distant as before from being "a crowned King of Bohemia," and the decision whether and how he could attain this aim was still safely in the strong hands of George of Poděbrady.

George's Hungarian counterpart, John Hunyadi, was more accessible to Cilli's influence. He knew his own strength and weakness, and though there had been much antagonism between him and the powerful count in the past he was prepared to meet him half-way. Around Christmas he arrived in Vienna, where he was welcomed with the greatest honors. In the ensuing negotiations he was induced to sacrifice the title of "gubernator" but retained much of the substance of regency, for he was confirmed as the King's captain general

---

[8] *Ibid.*, 406f.

[9] Our sources on the reaction of Cilli (and Ladislav, if he counts) are rather scanty and essentially limited to the hints of Aeneas Sylvius in his *Historia Friderici*. If, among modern historians, Bachmann pretends to know a good deal more (such as an express refusal of the King to recognize George's regency) he simply voices his guesses which in this case are not too convincing. (See his *Geschichte Böhmens*, II, 432ff.)

for all of Hungary and given charge of the King's income.[10] Nevertheless Cilli could consider this as a success. He had, at least, made Hunyadi partly dependent on the King's (and his) good will, and, though for the moment he maintained an outwardly friendly relationship, he was to show very soon that he had by no means given up his design of removing altogether this popular figure from the Hungarian scene.

Cilli had not convinced himself that the Czech regent was unassailable. He was fully aware, probably through his Rosenberg contacts, that resistance to the regent, though much weakened, had not completely ceased. It seems likely that he had his hands in the wave of intrigue and agitation against George which suddenly swept Bohemia and especially the capital in the early weeks of 1453.[11] From the trial of one of the agents we learn that among the people who backed this resistance was John Smiřický, prominent leader of the Utraquist gentry who, for a while, had shared with George the captaincy of the landfrieden of Boleslav but who had meantime (without changing his religion) changed from his original cooperation with the Poděbradian party to a close friendship with the leaders of the League of Strakonice. He was one of the few knights who were members of the regent's advisory council.

It may be that the very quick and definite suppression of this unrest, effected by the city council of the Old Town of Prague, convinced Cilli that at least for the present any such manoeuvres were futile and that he had better seek an understanding with George if he wanted to avoid the danger that Ladislav might altogether lose his chance of gaining the Bohemian crown. But the decision to seek a direct understanding with George was perhaps made even easier for Cilli and his royal disciple by a letter which, clearly basing his views on the information and judgments passed on to him by Aeneas Sylvius, Pope Nicholas himself wrote to Ladislav.[12] It is a remarkable letter in that it expressed for the first time the view that George, and George alone, could and would lead the Czech people away from their religious errors to true Catholic orthodoxy. (It is also remarkable in that it voices none of the strong reservations which the Curia had so often uttered toward the Compacts.) It shows that, in what must have been a sort of duel of views between John of Capistrano and Aeneas Sylvius,

---

10 *Ibid.*, 437; and Stephen Katona, *Historia critica regum Hungariae*, XII, Pest, 1790 833.
11 See Tomek, *Dějepis*, VI, 222ff.
12 Quoted by Urbánek, *Věk*, II, 706f., from Mareš, *Prokopa písaře . . . praxis cancellaria*, 107.

it was the latter who had prevailed in the highest circles of the Roman hierarchy. And it was a view which was to dominate papal policy for the next nine years, though not always with equal conviction.

The letter can hardly have failed to make some impression in Vienna, and as a result a meeting was arranged which might lead to a final understanding. Cilli did not go to Prague for it, nor was George, as yet, ready to go to Vienna. Instead they met halfway, in the Moravian city of Znojmo, toward the end of April. Which of the Czech leaders went with George is unknown,[13] but it may have been at the regent's wish that Cilli invited Eizinger to be present—a fact which gave the arrangement a more solid basis in case Cilli should have to step down. (George's caution proved to be thoroughly justified, though Cilli immediately afterwards, and perhaps unwisely, removed Eizinger from all public activities.) The official outcome of the meeting in Znojmo was a treaty of mutual consultation and support between the two men,[14] supposed to be maintained in the service of God and the Church, and especially of Ladislav who already was titled King of Hungary and Bohemia. It is very clear that this treaty, soon to receive the King's sanction,[15] was only concluded after a substantial and complete understanding had been achieved about all issues which had so far stood in the way of Ladislav's official recognition and coronation in Prague. Only now was George ready to accompany Count Cilli on his return to Vienna and to meet the young King, to whom he gave his personal homage. During the three days he stayed in Vienna he remained almost constantly in the King's presence, and the ground for a warm personal relationship was laid which was to survive later phases of considerable political disagreements.

The document[16] in which the King now gave his official answer to the previous requests of the Czech estates shows that George's policy prevailed in all essentials. Only the Czech demand for the union of the Duchy of Austria with the Bohemian crown received a polite refusal by the King's declaration that this issue could only be dealt with at a later date. It seems most doubtful that George was really very eager to increase the number and power of the larger depend-

---

[13] *SLČP*, mentions that "George of Poděbrady, the regent of the land of Bohemia, and other Czech lords and cities held discussion in Znojmo about King Ladislav, so he would be an elected King of Bohemia." (p. 147) The last emphasis seems important.

[14] See Kurz, *Oesterreich unter Friedrich IV*, App. XIV, I, 276.

[15] In the document giving the King's final answer to the Czech requests. See note 16.

[16] *AČ*, IV, 416–419.

encies and therewith of the Catholic population of the realm. The issue of elective versus hereditary kingship was not expressly mentioned, but the royal declaration contained none of those attempts made previously to get the hereditary principle recognized by implication. Finally the King, after promising not only protection for the Compacts but the most serious efforts in behalf of John Rokycana, declared that in case it was still not possible to obtain his confirmation he would only further act in this matter on the advise and with the consent of George of Poděbrady.

George's own position was clarified in three documents issued by King Ladislav.[17] The first confirmed his election as regent by the Czech estates. The second, to be kept secret for the time being, prolonged the term of the regency by six years. The third was a declaration ordering all officials in Bohemia to obey George, confirming his power to appoint and depose them, and putting all taxation and crown income into his hands. He was now, indeed, as unassailable as any man could be in his position, and the Count of Cilli had been forced to help him to achieve just that. The count's dream of a strong rule over the three realms—a dream not without prophetic quality in view of later Habsburg achievements—was shattered as far as Bohemia was concerned. There still seemed a possibility for Cilli to regain a position of power in Hungary, and to this task he immediately began to devote his considerable gifts.

George's strengthened position is perhaps most clearly reflected in the changing views, among the political groups in Bohemia, about the King's coronation. Until recently George's enemies had pinned considerable hopes to this event. The King, so they thought, would come, and all those who stood against the Chalice and, therefore, against George, would rally around him. Now, however, it became obvious that no such development could be expected, that on the contrary Ladislav, once in Prague, might come under the lasting influence of George's strong personality and thereby might strengthen him still further. Thus, far from working for Ladislav's early arrival in Prague, George's enemies did what they could to postpone it or have it cancelled altogether till a time when conditions would favor them again.

This situation must explain a peculiar action undertaken by one

17 *Ibid.*, XV, 211–212, 213; Lichnowsky, Prince E. M., *Geschichte des Hauses Habsburg*, VI, Vienna, 1842, Regesten No. 1782, and full text in Czech (poorly edited) on pp. CCXXIIf.

of George's personal enemies, John Smiřický.[18] He wrote a letter to King Ladislav in which he tried to warn the King against coming to Prague. He would be in danger there unless he came at the head of strong military forces which would insure his capacity to enforce his will on everybody (meaning, of course, on George). Count Cilli himself passed this letter on to George, presumably to make quite sure that the regent, whose help he felt he might need soon, would not suspect him once the matter became known.

The regent reacted dramatically. He presented the content of the letter to his council and asked its members what they felt would be the right way to deal with the man responsible. All of them, including Smiřický himself, declared that whoever wrote such a letter had committed high treason and would have to pay with his life. Only then did George show them the letter itself with Smiřický's signature and seal. The council which, like any true privy council, combined judicial with advisory functions, sentenced Smiřický to death. On the following day, September 7, he was decapitated.

Smiřický's action has puzzled historians, especially in view of his early record as a vigorous fighter for the Chalice. The explanation given by Aeneas Sylvius (who just at this moment happened to be less inclined to George) was that Smiřický was a pious Catholic and, in a way, a martyr of his faith.[19] This version has been accepted also by some modern writers. In reality Smiřický remained an Utraquist to the end. Whether his hatred of George dated from their common captaincy in the Boleslav landfrieden or from later events will always remain unknown. Perhaps his own ambition could not accept the fact that the far younger man had outstripped him in a career the beginnings of which had been so similar to his own. On the other hand it seems possible that the die-hards of the old Strakonice League, in their last attempt to weaken George, might make use of one of George's co-religionists rather than a Catholic. In this way the implied accusation would seem more credible, since religious prejudice could not have played a role. In the outcome, of course, this was again one of those actions which had the opposite effect from that intended. Far from weakening George it strengthened him further.

---

[18] Main sources: Aeneas Sylvius, *Historici Friderici*, 446; *SLČP*, 147; for the most thorough treatment with additional references see Urbánek, *Věk*, II, 721–723, 727–732.

[19] Aeneas Sylvius, *Historia Friderici*, went so far as to claim that Smiřický had "never been infected by the Hussite plague." This statement proves again how full of gaps and errors was his much-boasted knowledge of recent Czech history. Smiřický, now in his fifties, had in his young years played a not inconspicuous role as a Hussite military leader. See Heymann, *Žižka*, 371, 379f.

If considerations like those expressed in Smiřický's letter were in any way responsible for the considerable delay in Ladislav's arrival in Bohemia, the trip was certainly expedited once the situation had been brought into the open. In reality this issue may have had little to do with the delay. Probably far greater importance was a different problem—that of Ladislav's position as the ruler of the margraviate of Moravia. The Moravians—part of the nobility as well as some of the cities with their still strongly German population—had never quite shared the determination of the Bohemian estates to recognize Ladislav merely as an elected King. (The same was true for the other dependencies.) In Moravia, in particular, the feeling for Ladislav's line was very different from the one prevailing in Bohemia because the Margraviate had already in 1422, during the early phase of the Hussite Revolution, been turned over as a fief by King Sigismund to his son-in-law Albert, Ladislav's father, with the result that for the next seventeen years a considerable part of the country remained under Albert's effective control. Now, too, the dynastic feeling was strong enough in Moravia to make the Moravian estates far more ready to fulfill Cilli's (and in this case undoubtedly Ladislav's also) wishes for a recognition of their ruler as their hereditary lord. The negotiations about this had been conducted all through June, and on July 6 Ladislav, accompanied by Cilli, had arrived in Brno, where he received from the assembled estates the solemn oath of allegiance and homage as their hereditary lord.[20] The matter had caused considerable annoyance and very bitter comments in Prague and remained an open issue even when, in October of the same year, the King finally started on his way from Vienna via Jihlava to Prague. Indeed, it was not settled till after the coronation in Prague.

The date for this solemn procession had been arranged between Cilli and George, but Cilli found himself in severe trouble before its start. He had long attempted to get along without ever calling the Austrian estates, but he was not able to finance the King's ride to Prague in proper style without new taxes, which only the estates would grant. This, now, became their opportunity to force the King to dismiss his powerful relative.[21] With little success Cilli tried to

[20] For the dates see Lichnovsky, *Geschichte des Hauses Habsburg*, VI, Regesten 1809 and 1812. For the whole issue of the Moravian attitude regarding hereditary as against elective kingship, see the book called *Kniha Tovačovská*, written by Stibor Tovačovský z Cimburka, later Moravia's highest official and a remarkable man with strong Humanistic leanings (ed. Brandl, Brno, 1868, chapters 6 and 7).

[21] See Kurz, *Oesterreich unter Friedrich IV*, I, 155ff., largely based on Aeneas Sylvius, *Historia Friderici*, 450ff; also Supan, *Ulrich von Cilli*, 8off. and Vancsa, *Geschichte Nieder- und Oberösterreichs*, II, 320f.

change his allegiance over to the side of the Emperor. But Frederick III was not interested; he had not forgiven the count his activity in freeing Ladislav from his (the Emperor's) guardianship. Finally, angry but hopeful that before long he would make a comeback, Cilli retired to his vast estates in northern Croatia.[22]

The royal procession which began to assemble in Jihlava during the last days of September was one of the most brilliant seen for a long time. Besides the King himself there were a number of imperial princes, among them Archduke Albert of Austria and Margrave Albert Achilles of Brandenburg. The Czechs, with 3,000 horse, came led by George; the Hungarians, with half that strength, under Hunyadi and the chancellor Bishop John Vitéz; Eizinger led the Austrians. On October 19th Ladislav crossed the border between Moravia and Bohemia and there, on Bohemian ground, he dismounted and solemnly swore his oath as the country's new ruler.[23] His arrival in Prague, on October 24, was a triumph. Four days later he was crowned in the Cathedral of St. Vitus at Hradčany Castle. As there was no confirmed Archbishop of Prague, John Haz, Bishop of Olomouc, put the crown on his head.

In legal terms Ladislav was now truly the King, for all the narrow limits that his age, the constitutional "rights and freedoms" of the estates, and particularly the position and personality of the Czech "gubernator" and the leading personalities in his two other countries imposed upon him. These limitations were bound to grow even tighter if, and as long as, those three men and their chief assistants were able to work in harmony. It would be to their interest to prevent, by mutual help, the recurrence of internal difficulties which the King, eventually, might use to strengthen his own position. This especially if he should ever again revive his friendship with and his reliance upon the Count of Cilli.

The man most sensitive to such danger at this moment was John Hunyadi, and it seems that it was upon his initiative that a treaty of mutual help and service to the King was concluded between him, the Czech regent and the leader of the Austrian estates.[24] Beside those three "heads of government" there were additional signatories from all three countries: the Hungarian chancellor, Bishop John Vitéz of

[22] Supan, *Ulrich von Cilli*, 84ff. There also is given (p. 108) a list of his astonishingly large holdings.

[23] The text in Palacký, *Dějiny*, IV, 1, 294f. n. 282.

[24] Kurz, *Oesterreich unter Friedrich IV*, I, Appendix XV, 277–279.

Nagyvarád; Aleš and Zdeněk of Sternberg, the Lord Chamberlain and the Lord High Burgrave of Prague; also Ulrich Eizinger's two brothers and one of his cousins. The King could not possibly claim that he saw anything wrong in the promise of his leading helpers and servants to work together for him in devotion and harmony. He endorsed the contract which was concluded for six years, that is to the end of his minority, as being concluded by his own will. He may not even have fully understood the implications, though more likely he did realize that this tended to limit his freedom of choice, especially in Austria.

We cannot be sure whether or how badly the King missed his friend, the Count of Cilli. It is obvious that Eizinger could never replace him. The man who, it seems, truly took the count's position as somebody Ladislav could trust and feel close to, a substitute for the father he had never known, was George. The only man whom the youngster ever called "father," George developed a program for his education very different from the dry instruction given to him by the narrow, bigotted official whom Frederick III had charged with this task, or the program of self-indulgence that seems to have been the leading principle of Cilli's guidance. George's first consideration in planning for Ladislav's education was to induce and enable the youngster to identify himself as fully as possible with his role as King of Bohemia. Here he had to struggle with other, older influences. Ladislav had grown up mostly in German-speaking lands, in Austria and especially in Styria. Thus German was his mother language. Cilli, for political reasons, had encouraged him to emphasize his identification with Hungary,[25] and during his short visits there, in a country where Latin was for centuries to remain the official language, he had no trouble understanding and being understood. If he was to do justice to his task as King of Bohemia, he had to learn Czech, which, especially since the Hussite Revolution, had gone far in replacing Latin and German as the language of government (on the national as well as the local level), as it was also the language of the courts and of Czech culture in general. But for personal reasons, too, it was important for the regent that Ladislav should learn to be easy and fluent in his use of Czech since George himself was none too good in foreign languages, spoke and understood German only with some difficulty and Latin hardly at all.

The man whom George choose as Ladislav's teacher was John

25 See Aeneas Sylvius, *Historia Friderici*, 401.

Holubář of Nachod, author, it seems, of a well thought-of Latin-German-Czech dictionary.[26] Under this tutor, and encouraged by an entourage which, on George's urging, was no longer as exclusively German as it had been at the time of Ladislav's arrival, the young King before long became proficient in the Slavic tongue.[27] Nor would his Czech friends and teachers have much difficulty, by appealing to Ladislav's sense of history, in strengthening his identification with the role played by the great rulers of the houses of Přemysl and Luxemburg.

If George was successful, during the King's Prague sojourn in 1453 and 1454, in somewhat weakening the German and strengthening the Czech in Ladislav, there was from the beginning not the slightest chance that the King could be drawn to the Utraquist religion. Here, he had been most thoroughly and effectually immunized. Not only had he been educated from his early childhood as a pious and fervent Catholic, but he had, as soon as this would mean anything to him, been forewarned that heresy was rampant among the Czechs and that he would have to take the greatest care not to be infected by it once he went to live in Prague. As yet he was rather naïve about it, as we can see from his utterance quoted above: "If the Czechs want me for their King they should also share my religion." But beyond this there is little doubt that he was soon instructed by his ecclesiastical advisers in a way which forced him to act somewhat deceitfully. For in order to gain this kingdom he had not only had to promise to protect the Compacts—a policy with which a large proportion of Czech Catholics would thoroughly agree—but also to do his very best to get Rokycana confirmed. Yet it is obvious from his actions that he was not eager to fulfill this promise. Rokycana, to him, was nothing but the great, sinister heresiarch, the seducer and spoiler of Christian people. Indeed he would not even talk to him, nor would he ever visit one of Prague's Utraquist churches or witness the service in which laymen were permitted to drink from the Chalice.[28]

It is on this account that the youngster, whose good looks, fine stature, and general friendliness had at first made him the very idol of the Prague people, including the strong Utraquist majority, began to lose some of his popularity. And for this very reason, but also in

---

[26] About him see Urbánek, *Věk*, II, 759–761.
[27] See N. Tempelfeld, "Tractatus," in *AÖG*, LXI, 168.
[28] For this whole issue see Urbánek, *Věk*, II, 806–811.

order to avoid future trouble, George of Poděbrady must have tried
to influence him in the direction of a less rigid attitude toward the
religion of the majority. Yet here, it seems, he was completely unsuccessful. Very soon George felt that any attempt to overcome Ladislav's deep-seated prejudice against Utraquism would only result in
making him suspicious and hostile and in destroying the relationship
of warmth, trust, and understanding which he had been able to establish between himself and the King. If, in the eyes of the King, he
were to appear as too zealous a partisan of the reformed Church,
then indeed there was danger that eventually the King, shaking off
George's strong influence, would become the rallying center of all
the elements that tried to fight him under the banner of Catholic
orthodoxy. George did not intend, himself, to abandon the Chalice
in which he truly believed. He never left any doubt about this even
in Ladislav's mind.[29] But between such an abandonment, in other
words a return to Catholic ritual, and a zealously active struggle for
the Utraquist Church and against the Catholics, there was a middle
position, one which would try to minimize the conflicts between the
two religious camps, which would permit each side to live in peace
with the other. It was the policy of toleration on the basis of the Compacts. Any other way, so George felt, would lead to the renewal of
religious and political war. Only by maintaining this toleration—which
to the zealots on either side might easily look like a lukewarm attitude of religious indifference—could such a renewed outbreak be
prevented, could the terrible wounds of revolution, civil war, and international isolation be healed. This, he felt, was his central task from
which nothing must deflect him.

---

[29] For a proof see an utterance in another, shorter tractate by Tempelfeld printed by Jordan,
Das Königsthum Georgs von Poděbrad, Leipzig, 1861, p. 375f.

CHAPTER 6

THE WORK OF RECONSTRUCTION

SINCE 1444, when, as a young man of 24, he had followed Lord Ptáček as leader of the Utraquist party, George of Poděbrady had widened and strengthened his influence as well as his field of responsibility, and had even taken the first measures in a program of national reconstruction and consolidation. The conquest of Prague in 1448, the Peace of Wildstein after the victorious civil war of 1450, his election as regent by the St. George's Diet, his subjection of Tabor, and his final victory over Ulrich of Rosenberg had all been vital steps in this direction. Now the final acceptance and coronation of Ladislav and his prolonged residence in Prague—all originally expected by George's enemies to become instruments of his destruction—had given his position of national paramountcy, at least for the next few years, an even stronger and more reliable sanction. In his earlier years the constant party struggle, the incessant need to fight, to defend himself against and to counterattack his domestic enemies by political and military means, had absorbed much of his time and and strength, leaving little for the great task of reconstruction that was expected of him. But now that his position was fairly secure he could devote himself to an increasing extent to those positive tasks, and even his enemies acknowledged that he did this with extraordinary strength, skill, and certainty of purpose.

It is quite true that, while the regent looked after the strengthening of his nation and the realm which it had built up, he never neglected his own interests and those of his family. But as long as he did this without damage for the community at large there is very little justification in blaming him for it. This, after all, was not a society ruled over by a modern civil service where unselfish work, rewarded merely by a moderate but secure income and the feeling of duty handsomely done, should be aimed at even if it cannot be taken for granted. In the Bohemia (as in most of the Europe) of the fifteenth century the only man who could expect to be an effective national leader, even a leader toward peaceful national growth, was

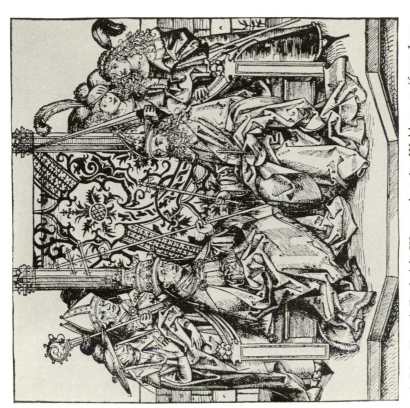

5. Pius II and Frederick III, woodcut by Wohlgemut (from Imre Lukinich, ed., *Mátyás király emlékkönyv*, I, Budapest 1940)

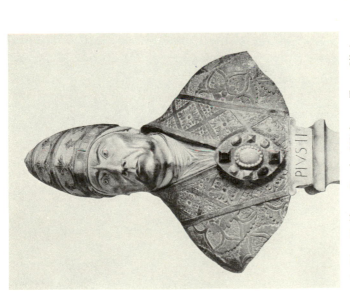

4. Pius II (from Berthe Widmer, *Enea Silvio Piccolomini, Papst Pius II*, Basel 1960, fig. 8)

6. Utraquist Leader Presenting His Book to King George (woodcut from *The Struggle between Truth and Lie* by Ctibor Tovačovský of Cimburk)

that one who was able, if necessary, to mobilize strong forces, be it of vassals or of mercenaries. This he could only do if he was wealthy, mostly in terms of land owned. Thus we cannot be surprised when we see that George was eager to add to his own holdings as well as to those of the crown of Bohemia. At least he did not employ that sort of glorified highway robbery, often supported by blatant forgery, that had been so characteristic of Ulrich of Rosenberg.

More important to George were the national tasks that he had to face. Among them were the rebuilding of the country's administrative and legal machinery; the restoration of safe travelling and safe trading on roads and rivers; the improvement of monetary conditions; the restrengthening of the dangerously loosened ties of the kingdom of Bohemia proper with her dependencies—Moravia, Silesia, the two Lusatias; the recovery of lands and cities which previous rulers (especially Sigismund during the Hussite Wars) had pawned away to neighboring rulers and which were in real danger of being or becoming lost forever; and finally a foreign policy aiming at the general restoration of Bohemia's international position—once strong but now rather weakened by her reputation as an outlaw among nations—especially with regard to the states and princes of Central Europe. But every single item in this formidable list of needs did presuppose a strong royal government. And here we are faced with an interesting and difficult problem that was to play a key role in the whole history of George's rule.

George had grown up as a prominent member of the baronial caste. Even while he was the leader of one of the two great parties, which included strong sections of the gentry and the urban middle class in Prague as well as in other cities, his natural element was the relatively small number of leading magnates who had weathered the Hussite Revolution and had returned to full social prominence after the battle of Lipany. It was in the circles of the high nobility that George found some of his closer friends (though there were among them also members of the gentry), and it was there that he picked his spouses—first the fine, gentle, much loved Kunhuta of Sternberg, Zdeněk's cousin and the mother of most of his children, who died in 1449; and then the strong, energetic Johanna of Rožmitál, whom he married a year later and to whose political understanding and loyal support the later King George was to become much indebted.

If this whole situation did not make it easy—even for a man who had as little caste arrogance as George—to free himself from the ties that tended to bind him to his peers, there were, in addition, very specific reasons which induced him, and his peers, to identify the rights of the nobility with the welfare of the nation. It was not only the comfortable justification and rationalization of their economic and political class interest, though that, of course, played its considerable role. The struggle of the feudal nobility against any attempts of the crown to establish absolutist power was age-old in Bohemia as elsewhere. It had played its role in the tragedy of the great King Přemysl Otakar II. It had caused some difficulties to Charles IV, whose far-reaching law reform, the Maiestas Carolina, never became, in its complete form, the law of the land because it met with the opposition of the baronial class. The same struggle had caused much misery to his less capable son, Wenceslas IV.

But with the tremors of the Hussite Revolution this old, we may say classical, antagonism had taken on a new and somewhat different color. At a time when an imposing majority of the nation had rallied behind the religious reform ideas of Hussitism and behind its symbol, the Chalice, the worst enemy of this movement was just the man who claimed to be the hereditary King of Bohemia, Sigismund of Luxemburg. It was against him that a united revolutionary nation operated, at the National Assembly of Čáslav,[1] with the weapon of solemn deposition. It was against him that they looked for an elected King in neighboring Poland.[2] In a similar mood, though no longer as strong and united as they had been fifteen of sixteen years earlier, the Utraquist estates opposed the succession of Albert II, Sigismund's son-in-law, and tried to put Casimir Jagiello, as a purely elective King, in his place.[3] And in the same way, finally, the young boy who now became King had been recognized only as an elected King who had to buy his election by all the concessions and guarantees which would prevent him from destroying the Compacts and the freedom of the Chalice.

Thus it was largely because of his adherence to the Chalice that George's policy, in essential agreement with that of Ptáček, had emphasized the electoral character of the crown—a kingship which would therefore be limited in its power and dependent on the sup-

---

[1] See Heymann, "The National Assembly of Čáslav," *Medievalia et Humanistica*, fasc., VIII, 1954, 32ff.; also *Žižka*, Chapter 14.
[2] *Ibid.*, 269ff., 319ff., and *passim*.
[3] See Tomek, *Dějepis*, VI, 48ff.

port and good will of the estates, especially of course of the lords
and knights, since the cities had, since Lipany, lost some of their
temporary strength. In a way, therefore, no one had done more
than George for the limitation of the royal prerogative and the
strengthening of the power of the estates, for the establishment of
what German historiographical terminology, with a word hardly
translatable into English, has called the "ständestaat."

But once George had achieved this goal, once he, as the highest
representative of the Estates, had made the King dependent on himself and the Estates, he realized almost immediately that he had to
stop, perhaps even to reverse this process. Limitation of a royal power
which otherwise might be able and willing to suppress and destroy
the Chalice, together with the traditional strength of the nobility—
this might be one thing; another was to permit this royal power
to be weakened beyond a point where it would still be able to hold
the nation together, to keep the dependencies in line with the Bohemian center, to keep the whole realm from breaking out into
renewed civil war. And it seems easy to see that George would be
dominated by the second rather than the first consideration from
the moment in which his relation to the King—below him in legal
terms, far above him in terms of power to direct and decide—had
been clearly established. From now on—rather than looking at himself as the King's subject and potential antagonist—George could
and did identify himself with the King, his functions and interests,
at least as far as they were the functions and interests of a Bohemian
King. Any disagreements that were to arise in later phases of Ladislav's reign between him and his Czech regent rarely developed from
their deviating interests, but almost invariably from the fact that
George's view of what should, in a particular situation, be the right
understanding and the right action of the King of Bohemia somehow
deviated from that of the King, (who, after all, neither would nor
could quite forget that he was also King of Hungary and Duke of
Austria).

No such disagreements arose in the early phase of Ladislav's reign,
and during the remainder of 1453 and the long year to follow the
two men, or rather the man and the boy, never lost sight of each
other for more than a few hours. We have every reason to think
that on the whole this was a happy time for both of them, for the
boy, because besides finding a fatherly friend he could not have found
a better, more serious and more rational teacher of the art of govern-

ment; for the man, because he could soon feel rewarded by the sense of satisfaction resulting from solid achievements.

George's first measures, in this period devoted both to national reconstruction and to strengthening of the royal position, are reflected in the work done by the diet called to Prague immediately following the King's coronation and thus conveniently called the Coronation Diet.[4]

George's first endeavor had to be to put the finances of the royal government into proper shape. This was done in a rather radical way, by granting to the King a special tax to the amount of one half of the yearly income of any baron or knight as he normally received it from his dependent farmers and workers. A fairly heavy tax was also to be paid by each freeholder. The tax to be paid by city dwellers owning some form of business was to be fixed by an executive rule of the King (i.e. the regent) and its amount remains unknown. The justification for the tax (which had been promised earlier in expectation of the King's coronation) was expressly to give the King the chance to establish his residence properly in the country. At the same time the King was asked to promise that he would never again demand a tax of this sort; and that the list of payments which the land registers acquired on the basis of their receipts would be burned—a suggestion or order, however, which was not followed.[5]

Of great significance for the reestablishment of orderly and definite property relations was another law passed by the diet. According to it all people who had, since the death of King Wenceslas IV (in other words since the beginning of the Hussite Revolution), acquired land of other property from Church or royal possessions, had to submit the documents authorizing such transactions to a commission of five men, among them, beside two barons, the Mint Master of Kutná Hora, John Čabelický of Soutice, whose position was much like that of a Secretary of the Treasury, and the man whom George had just appointed as sub-chamberlain, the official responsible for the supervision of royal towns: Vaněk Valečovský of Kněžmost. Another committee, also consisting of two barons and two knights, was to look into all disputed private property relations with the task of bringing the court registers (Zemské desky) up to date and revert-

---

[4] See *AČ*, IV, 419–423.

[5] See Hasselhold-Stockheim, *Urkunden* . . . , as quoted by Urbánek, *Věk*, II, 781 n. 2 and 4.

ing them to their normal usage. They had been closed to the public for the last thirteen years.

While both procedures were of great importance for the normalization of economic, social, and legal conditions in the country, the more important issue, historically speaking, was the first one. Here, in fact, the attempt was made to limit and, to some extent, undo the enormous changes in the ownership of landed property that had taken place during the Revolution.

It was not exactly the first such effort. Another had been made during the short restoration, in 1436, of the rule of Sigismund. At that time, however, the quick return of unsettled conditions during the reign of Albert II and the long interregnum had prevented any such measures from becoming truly effective. Now, seventeen years later, things were even more difficult. The bulk of the lands and properties which had changed hands during the revolutionary times had belonged to the Church, a lesser part to the crown and to private owners. The gainers had mainly been members of the nobility, both the high and the low, though some cities also had gained. It may be suspected that some of the greatest profiteers, among them such noble Catholic families as the Rosenbergs, had been able to procure (and in some cases manufacture) the documents showing some form of legal transfer which would leave them in possession of their acquisitions. Thus the shift of property, whatever its size, would almost certainly, in socio-economic terms, benefit or at least favor the rich and the strong and thus have a reactionary character. On the other hand, however, it must not be assumed that the partial recovery of former Church property would benefit the Catholic Church itself and its bishoprics, chapters, monasteries. The properties to be thus taken away from illegitimate occupants were not earmarked (despite certain hopes entertained in Rome and elsewhere) for immediate return to the clerical authorities but were to go to the King —to be used by him as he (or rather his regent) found appropriate. Thus the measure meant, beside the special tax, another considerable financial and thereby political strengthening of the crown— how considerable we cannot say, as the records in question, regrettably, have not come down to us.

Neither of the two committees mentioned before was to operate as a court. Yet a thorough reform of the judicial system was just as necessary as—and perhaps more difficult than—the reestablishment of a working court register. And, here, too, George had to reverse the trend which had gone rather too far in favor of the high nobility. During the periods of revolution and civil war the State Supreme Court (Great Court of the land—Velký soud zemský) had ceased to function for long periods, as had also the royal court chamber (Nejvyšší soud dvorský), whose functions were more limited. In the place of these courts much of the essential judicial functions, of civil and, even more, of criminal jurisprudence, had reverted to the regional "landfrieden," which had been organized on a basis of fairly balanced representation of high and low nobility with some participation also of the towns. (For internal legal action the royal cities had of course their own municipal courts.)

But in the period immediately following George's victory over the League of Strakonice, specifically during the long diet held from November 1450 to January 1451, he had to conciliate his baronial adversaries (and incidentally also please his baronial friends and adherents) by agreeing, however reluctantly, to the reintroduction of the old baronial jurisdiction on the local level (the office of popravci, somewhat comparable with, though probably more independent and powerful than, English justices of the peace under the Tudors and early Stuarts) which had been practically abolished in the time of the Hussite Revolution.[6] While the legal power of the landfrieden continued to exist side by side with that of the lords, the change nevertheless weakened all other elements in favor of the high nobility. There was only one way, now, to restore a measure of balance: through the full restoration of the power of the State Supreme Court.[7] True, in this institution the lords held still a number of the more important positions, such as the office of lord high chamberlain, which was, from Sigismund's time in the hands of Aleš Holický of Sternberg; of lord chief justice, which, for just as long, had been held by Nicholas Zajíc of Hasenburg; and of the Lord High Burgrave, since 1448 in the hands of Zdeněk of Sternberg—all of which were now reconfirmed by Ladislav. On the other hand, George, through the King, could at this moment appoint knights to two other positions within the state court: Ernest of Leskovec, formerly a friend of the Lords of Hradec but one who had contributed to the rapprochement between them and George, as lord secretary; and

---

[6] See AČ, II, 294f., and Urbánek's comment in Věk, II, 490ff.

[7] About the court, its functions, and its members at the time, see Tomek, Dějepis Prahy, IX, 3ff., 253ff; also Urbánek, Věk, III, 114–120.

the Prague citizen later knighted, Vaněk Valečovský of Kněžmost, as sub-chamberlain. As the Supreme Court met with the King present and presiding—George, as regent, was by his side and later, after the King had left Prague, took his place—the effective reactivation of the Supreme Court was one of the most important steps of consolidation resulting from the Coronation Diet, even if this development was mentioned in its transcripts only by a short announcement of the date of reconvening the court and by the demand that there, and nowhere else, people should seek justice for themselves.[8]

What was spelled out in considerable detail was, on the other hand, a whole set of ordinances and rules concerning public safety. They concern, among other things, the measures to be taken by the local authorities to supress banditry; the freedom of the royal highways, including those leading into and out of the kingdom; the abolition of illicit tolls both on roads and on waterways, and of illicit dams or weirs on navigable water; the suppression of the issue of forged coins; the prohibition of the establishment, without concession, of new breweries and taverns; and the suppression and persecution of the trade with stolen goods.

Clearly, most of these measures were aimed at the restoration of the internal peace, security, and freedom from banditry for which, under Charles IV and, to a lesser degree, even under the early reign of Wenceslas IV, Bohemia had been famed, in impressive contradistinction to many of its neighbors. And it must have been a matter of gratification to George and his friends that they proved effective—not completely and not at once, but before long to a remarkable extent.

One clause in the transcript of the resolution of the Coronation Diet, while ostensibly aiming at the same goal of public safety, had essentially a different and less creditable purpose. It declared that workers or serving fellows should have a master and serve and work for him. Whoever of such people had no master, did not serve or work or who loafed in taverns or elsewhere, should be brought to the nearest judge to show what work he did and how he made a living. And if he could not prove this satisfactorily he should be ordered to work for a master to be found for him within two weeks, and if he did not comply he was to be treated as a vagrant criminal.

---

[8] For George's activity in presiding at sessions of the court during his regency as well as his early kingship see some of the entries in the registers in J. Emler, *Reliquiae tabularum terrae regni Bohemiae*, Prague, 1870–1872, I, 113–145; II, 245, 274–276, 281ff., 291ff.

This measure, apart from the existence of a truly vagrant element, arose out of the lack of workers, both in agriculture and in the towns. (Characteristically the eventuality that no master might be found willing to employ the man was not even considered.) But it also showed the tendency of the ruling groups of the nation to limit the free movement of those who might want to leave, perhaps for good reason, their present employment. It was a policy which was followed, during the long reign of Vladislav II, George of Poděbrady's successor on the Czech throne, by a number of similar but more severe laws which finally, in the sixteenth century, were to reduce the peasants of Bohemia, like those of Poland and Hungary, to a state of real serfdom.

As long as George ruled the countries of the Czech crown this process did not progress beyond those first cautious attempts of the nobility to limit the freedom of movement of the peasantry. At the time of his regency, in particular, and under the influence of the finally and firmly established internal peace, all parts of the kingdom's society tended to profit, especially economically, to an extent which would in turn tend to strengthen that internal peace and to restrict, at least for a time, antagonistic tendencies and to soften conflicts of class interest. In the eyes of the masses of the people, especially those in the cities, nothing could be of greater importance than the availability of goods, especially food, at far lower prices than those which had prevailed in times of permanent internal crisis. In the most important collection of (anonymous) chronicals during the fifteenth century, named by Palacký the "Old Annalists," we find, between the story of King Ladislav's arrival and reception in Prague and the report on the conquest of Constantinople by the Turks, a chapter wholly devoted to such economic facts.[9] In this time, so the report says, when the country was wholly pacified, merchants came from all places bringing with them goods to satisfy the demands of the Czech people. Also, everything was cheap. The "Annalists" give a long list of the prices then paid for all sorts of things, such as corn (rye and oats), eggs, herrings, various types of beer, cider and all sorts of imported and domestic wine, cows, sheep, and large and small birds—including partridges—peas, salt; but also wool and several sorts of cloth and fur. In Litoměřice, so we hear, two large cans of wine were no more than one heller (or farthing), and in Prague a can of the very best Bohemian wine (probably the wine

[9] See *SLČP*, No. 498, p. 148.

grown around Mělník) was also only a single heller. "And this state, when everything was so cheap, lasted throughout the regency of the Lord George, supreme governor of the Czech Kingdom, and also during the time when King George was King things were like that in Prague for some more years."

Besides the legislative work and the reform of the judiciary, the job of reconstruction also included the further strengthening of the administration, largely in terms of added appointments to royal offices. One of these appointments, already made earlier, was a peculiar one: it gave George, besides his position as regent (in Czech, "správce," in Latin, "gubernator") also the title and office of "hofmistr" (master of the court, meaning, of course, the royal court). There is, it seems, no proper equivalent to the title in western languages except the title and office of chamberlain, and this (komorník, camerarius) existed in addition to that of court master. The latter office, historically, was not always occupied, and in a later period (during the reign of King Vladislav II) it was held in common with the office of chancellor. In George's case it seems simply to have indicated the close relationship of regent and king, and to have given George the chance to organize the King's court and household essentially as he thought best.[10] (According to one report, his closeness to the King went so far that the two, for some time, shared a bedroom in the King's town residence.) [11]

Among other appointments, so far not mentioned, by far the most important was that of the new chancellor.[12] He was the member of a richly gifted family of Czech knights, one of three brothers who were later raised by George, when he was King, to the baronial rank and each of whom made a respected name of himself: the Rabsteins. Prokop of Rabstein had long been in the service of the emperor. There he had gained the respect and soon the friendship of Aeneas Sylvius, and he accompanied the Italian prelate during the latter's visit to the great Diet of Benešov in 1451. He had introduced Aeneas to George of Poděbrady and had interpreted the interview between the two men. Prokop's close relation with the Emperor and the later Pope made him a valuable acquisition for the actual ruler of Bohemia, and it seems that George had made considerable efforts to gain Prokop's services for his own country.[13] As head of the royal

10 See Tomek, *Dějepis*, IX, 20ff.
11 See Aeneas Sylvius, *"149 bisher ungedruckte Briefe,"* ed. A. Weiss, Graz, 1897, p. 219.
12 Tomek, *Dějepis*, IX, 22f.
13 See Aeneas Sylvius' letter to Carvajal of June 7 in *FRA*, II, 20, p. 58.

chancery, and as supervisor and adviser on all issues needing Latin documentation—and this was practically the whole of Bohemia's foreign policy—Prokop rather than the man titled lord secretary held a position corresponding to a secretary of state. While a strict Roman Catholic, he was and remained intensely loyal to the man who had trusted him with this task.

The same was essentially true of his brother, John the Younger, whom George, soon afterwards, appointed to another highly important and newly created office. It was the position of royal procurator whose main task was to look after the King's properties as well as his income from estates falling to the crown.[14]

At the next diet, called the Lent Diet, it became clear that the "honeymoon" between the government of King and regent on the one hand and some groups of the estates on the other could not last forever. The most dramatic, and at the same time perhaps most ominous, event arose out of a speech made there by one of the veterans of the Hussite Revolution, a man who, in his youth, had actually fought under Žižka and was one of the signatories of his famous "Military Ordinance," Beneš Mokrovouský of Hustiřany.[15] Beneš started with an expression of appreciation addressed to the King and the regent —both of whom were present—for the excellent work done recently in restoring peace, order, and effective government in the kingdom. Yet, so he said, the main task had not even been touched upon: the religious issue. It was high time for the Compacts to be properly fulfilled. All parishes in the kingdom should be administered by priests who were ready to dispense the communion in both kinds, and all clerics ordained as priests in Bohemia should induce the people to communicate in the Utraquist way. He went on, emphatically, to remind the diet of the many previous occasions when they had demanded and sworn that Rokycana, and no one else, should be Archbishop of Prague and should receive confirmation; yet of this there had not even been any mention recently.[16]

[14] About the office of royal procurator see the detailed description in J. Demel, *Geschichte des Fiskalamtes in den Böhmischen Ländern* (Forschungen zur inneren Geschichte Oesterreichs, ed. Dopsch, 5, I), Innsbruck, 1909, 41ff., 67ff., 97f, 244ff. John of Rabstein was succeeded in the following year (but not, as Demel thinks, because of his death, see Urbánek, *Věk* II, 804, n. 1) by Čeněk of Klinstein, who proved to be an excellent choice of George's and who maintained his position, against some resistance from the high nobility, for 26 years.

[15] See Heymann, *Žižka*, 311, 364, 470.

[16] The story is preserved in the report of a diplomatic mission of 1454. The last (and only correct) edition of the report is called "De factis regni Bohemie," by Loserth in *MVGDB*, XVIII, 299–306.

While Beneš was strongly supported by exclamations of agreement from his more zealous Utraquist friends, he immediately met with a strong verbal opposition not only from Catholics but also from a few of the more cautious adherents of the Chalice. Some of the lords, among them the two Sternbergs, seem to have felt that the speech was not only disturbing but unbecoming a mere knight. But even one of the prominent members of the Utraquist gentry, the mintmaster of Kutná Hora, John Čabelický of Soutice, took sides against Beneš when he stated that Beneš had obviously misunderstood the meaning of the Compacts, from which no such conclusions could be drawn as those he presented. All speakers on this side declared that not the open public meeting of the diet but the King's council was the proper place to vent such criticism. This, finally, was the decision which prevailed after a strong appeal to the same purpose had been directed to the diet by the regent.

In evaluating the significance of this debate it first must be admitted that those arguing against Beneš, notably John Čabelický, were materially more correct than the old soldier.[17] The Compacts, as shown by their wording, had been accepted by the Council and the Czechs as a protection of the status quo, as a solemn permission for Utraquists to continue in their form of worship. But there is not a word in the Compacts that could be understood as encouraging or justifying any proselytizing activity of the Utraquist Church among Czech Catholics, let alone exerting any pressure upon ordained priests (and especially the Catholics among them) to dispense, and to induce people to take, the communion in both kinds.

The one issue on which, in logical terms, Beneš was perfectly right was the complaint that so little had been done or even attempted regarding the confirmation of Rokycana. And here, indeed, is one of the more obvious blind alleys into which the whole religious issue had run.

There was, by now, a long tradition, approaching two decades, of the demand for Rokycana's confirmation, always officially supported by united appeals and resolutions of the diets, recently even by the young King's promise prior to his acceptance. Yet it seems obvious that among the people holding the important positions in the country's government no one seriously believed any longer that Rokycana would ever be confirmed by the Curia (quite apart from the fact that the more zealous Catholics, among them the King, did not

---

[17] Here I must disagree with Urbánek, who, in *Věk*, II 797, claims, especially in regard to Čabelický, that it was impossible for Beneš' critics to disprove the justification of his attacks.

truly want him to be confirmed, though they did not dare to say so openly).[18]

But once things had got to this point, something like a vicious circle began operating. As time progressed and the chances for Rokycana's confirmation (and for the better supply of ordained Utraquist priests) became ever dimmer, he had less and less cause to moderate or hide his strong (and, from the Roman point of view, indeed largely heretical) religious views, also expressed in much of his ritual and liturgical practice.[19] And even though Rokycana, presumably, was aware of the political difficulties which might be caused by activated Hussite propaganda, by a great resurgence of the reform movement of which the Chalice was but a symbol, such political considerations could not always dominate his thinking. True, he knew and watched the domestic and to a lesser extent the international scene, and was not inaccessible to political arguments which the leaders of the nation, and especially George, would present to him on such issues.[20] But he also saw the danger that too much political caution might leave the Utraquist Church strangled, lifeless, forced to give in all along the line. Nothing, in this regard, could be more disturbing to those for whom their Hussite religion was all-important than the silent—and sometimes not so silent—contempt and aversion with which the young King treated them. (In addition, the hope which had recently been held for some cooperation or affiliation with the Eastern Church had just been finally shattered with the fall of Constantinople to the Turks.)

It seems very likely, then, that Beneš Mokrovouský's vigorous action was the direct or indirect result of Rokycana's views and worries. Even if Rokycana did not put him up to acting publicly in this way, Beneš quite certainly expressed the feelings of that large group of active Hussites who regarded Rokycana as their leader and spokesman. Those who, in Bohemia or outside the country, considered such

[18] On George's attitude and his waning hopes for Rokycana's confirmation, see e.g. Urbánek, *Věk*, II, 934f. On the other hand, the King, by confirming Rokycana as administrator of the Utraquist Church on occasion of the synod of both churches, held in June 1454, went one step farther than the Catholic clergy found acceptable. See Hrejsa, *Dějiny*, 95ff., and Urbánek, *Věk*, III, 25ff.

[19] I think it is true to say that from a strictly orthodox Catholic view, much of Rokycana's thought and teaching has rightly to be considered as heretical. This is true even though much of what his Catholic accusers said about him and about his supposed moral failings tended to be wrong and fiercely prejudiced. See the arguments put forward by Wenceslas of Krumlov and Prokop of Pilsen, in Hrejsa, *op.cit.*, III, 114ff.; Urbánek, *Věk* III, 59ff., and my own article on Rokycana in *Church History*, September 1959.

[20] About their relation at this time see Urbánek, *Věk*, II, 580ff., and III, 23f.

feelings as a thing that could be neglected, or imagined that a great man like George would be able, now or later, to eliminate or redirect this great force if he but willed, were much mistaken. Yet it was just this view which was presented, at this very time, in a letter of Aeneas Sylvius, written on the eve of his expected move from the Emperor's court to Rome.[21] It was, to say the least, a dangerous illusion.

The religious issue was not the only internal rift which, after the impressive unity dominating the Coronation Diet, came to the fore during the Lent Diet. Another one concerned the relationship between the three estates—barons, knights, and cities. The knights were dissatisfied that, in the newly reorganized State Supreme Court, they were allotted only eight members against twelve of the barons. They specifically objected to the fact that sentences were pronounced "in the name of the Lords." Eventually George, who tried his best to pacify feelings, solved at least the second problem by himself announcing sentences "in the name of the King."[22]

The resistance of the gentry to the overweening attitudes and claims of the high nobility was based to a large extent upon their important role during the Hussite Revolution, when the military leadership of the national forces—the brotherhoods as well as the cities—had as a rule been in their hands and when politically, too, they had been far stronger than in pre-Hussite times.[23] As so many of these historical successes were based on the cooperation between gentry and cities, it would perhaps have been logical if now, too, the gentry had allied themselves with the cities against the barons. But in fact the opposite happened, the gentry fought a sort of two-front war against the other estates, and at a later stage came out on the side of the barons rather than the cities.

The friction between gentry and cities was, in the first place, the result of what both sides considered to be encroachments upon their territories from the other estate. In some of the royal cities, and especially in Prague, a number of well-to-do knights had purchased houses and taken up residence. To this the Praguers objected and an ordinance passed on March 1454, just before the meeting of the "Lent Diet," by the commune of the Old Town forbade the sale of real estate to anybody who was not a citizen, and especially to

21 See *Briefe*, ed. Weiss, 259ff.

22 See the entries in the "land tables" (court registers) in J. Emler, *Reliquiae tabularum terrae regni Bohemiae*, I, 117ff.

23 See Heymann, *Žižka*, 40f., 479.

members of the nobility, without the express permission of the city council, to be granted only in exceptional cases.[24]

The gentry hit back fast and in almost exactly parallel terms. Referring to the fact that, not infrequently wealthy townspeople, especially citizens of the capital, had acquired landed estates from the gentry, they demanded that no such sales be allowed in future, and no landed property owned by the gentry be entered into the land register.[25] The issue was brought before the State Supreme Court, which rendered the decision that new sales of this sort needed the King's permission, but that purchases already concluded could be entered into the land register and thus legalized.[26] It was clearly a compromise decision. Since the cities were represented in the Supreme Court only by the sub-chamberlain it seems likely that it was due to the regent that the decision did not turn out to be more thoroughly in favor of the nobility.

George, indeed, was aware of the importance of the cities, and he became increasingly willing to protect them in the interest of that balance of forces without which there could be no strong and effective royal government. And it was just around this time that he was taught a very impressive lesson about this issue, which for him was especially complicated since, in this case, it involved his relationship to the greatest of the baronial clans.

We have seen how carefully George, after his victory over Ulrich of Rosenberg, tried, in the interest of domestic peace, to regain some measure of friendship and cooperation with this powerful family. This had become much easier when, in 1451, Ulrich had surrendered his position as head of the family, with most of its political and economic implications, to his sons, especially to his oldest son, Henry.[27] With Henry, a man of George's own generation who was not so deeply involved in the old enmity, George could get along, provided he treated him well enough. At the same time Henry could hope to be regarded with special friendship by the young King since he, as leader of the Czech troops that had joined Eizinger and Cilli, had contributed to Ladislav's release from the hated Emperor's wardship. Thus, at the time of the King's coronation, Henry of Rosenberg had approached him with the request for a fitting reward. He

[24] Tomek, *Dějepis*, VI, 236.

[25] *AČ*, III, 311, Urbánek assumes (*Věk*, II, 800 n. 2) that the Praguers were exempt from this disability.

[26] Emler, *Reliquiae*, II, 247.

[27] *AČ*, XI, 258.

had asked for possession during his lifetime (with possible renewal for his heirs) of the royal city of Budweis, the greatest, richest, and strongest urban center of southern Bohemia.

A peculiar relationship had long existed between the Rosenbergs and Budweis. Most of the time it was one of strong antagonism, based on the general dislike which the baronial class had for the rising urban class, and conversely on the anger of the Budweis people over the many big and little wrongs done to them especially by Ulrich of Rosenberg. Yet during the Hussite Wars the great Catholic baron and the city—second biggest of Catholic urban centers after Pilsen—were forced to cooperate rather closely, especially as long as both were under the relentless pressure of the great militant power of southern Bohemia: Tabor.[28]

By now, however, little if anything was left of this temporary alliance, and memories of old frictions grew sharper and were frequently renewed on a small scale. If this made rule over Budweis highly desirable to the Lord of Rosenberg, it made the idea just as deeply repulsive to the people of Budweis.

Henry's demand, as he expected, was received by Ladislav in the friendliest spirit, but the King could hardly take a step of such consequence without the agreement of the regent. George now found himself in a difficult position. The real interests of the King and the country would impel him to refuse, but at the same time this would clearly lead to a renewed outbreak of the old, highly dangerous, and undesirable hatred and open conflict between himself and the House of Rosenberg.

George tried a compromise. The King did grant to the Lord of Rosenberg the possession (not the ownership) of Budweis for life. Yet he must not impose any undue and unusual taxation upon the citizens, nor shorten any of the King's specific rights within the city, including that of free entry.[29]

But if either George or the King had thought that they could thereby gain the city's submission to its transfer from the King's into Rosenberg's hands, they were mistaken. There had always been a very great difference in status between royal towns and those dependent on a lord or bishop. The citizens of Budweis, led by their mayor, Andrew Puklice, a man of unusual courage and vision who represented the Czech craft guilds rather than the German mer-

28 See e.g. Heymann, *Žižka*, 277, 282.
29 See Palacký, *FRA*, XX, 68–69.

chants, simply declared that they would resist by force any attempt of the Rosenberg officials to enter to town, and that they would rather burn every house in the city than submit to the lord's rule.[30] Neither Rosenberg's threats nor repeated royal letters demanding compliance had any effect. Conquest of the city by force of arms would have been a long, difficult and very costly undertaking for which Henry on his own was not strong enough and for which George was not willing to commit the power of the kingdom. George's personal involvement was much reduced when in 1457, before he himself became King, Henry of Rosenberg died and his brothers and heirs no longer pursued the hopeless quest with the same urgency.

But the Rosenberg clan might still have borne a grudge against George for the fiasco of Budweis if they had not received ample compensation elsewhere, mainly in Silesia. And in this George showed the hand of the brilliant statesman-politician in an impressive fashion. In this way, he not only satisfied the ambitions and expectations of some of the greatest baronial houses—especially the Rosenbergs and Sternbergs—without upsetting the domestic balance of power within the Kingdom of Bohemia, he also restored the ties which bound the dependent countries, especially Silesia and Lusatia, to the Bohemian crown—ties which, for more than three decades, had been weakened until they sometimes seemed to be near the breaking point.

Of the dependencies, Moravia had always been most closely integrated into the greater realm, by the age-old history of the union, by the complete ethnic identity of the Slavic majority in both countries, and, more recently, by the strength of its Hussite-Utraquist Church. But even among Moravian Catholics the tie was close, since the bishopric of Olomouc belonged to the archdiocese of Prague, whereas Silesia, with the bishopric of Breslau, belonged to the Polish archdiocese of Gniezno. Nevertheless, even here tensions had risen which we have mentioned earlier, based especially on the unwillingness of the Moravian estates to let those of Bohemia decide about their relationship to their margrave, now King Ladislav, whom they preferred to consider as their hereditary ruler rather than an elective and elected prince.

---

[30] See the material on the struggle in *ČČM*, 1831, 284–289, and Erben's article on Puklice in the same journal, 1846, 176ff.

The issue that had led to mutual incriminations at the time of King Ladislav's visit to Brno prior to his coronation had meanwhile been peacefully resolved on the basis of declarations somewhat paradoxically admitting that both sides had been right,[31] and thus the danger of a further weakening of Moravia's ties with Bohemia was removed, as was shown very clearly a few years later, at the time of George's succession to the throne. Much more difficult, however, was the situation in the two northern dependencies.

Silesia's case was especially complex, in view of the utter lack of unity between its various duchies and principalities—almost a reflection, in miniature, of the political structure of the Holy Roman Empire to which Silesia, indeed, had closer ties of sentiment than did Bohemia or Moravia. The country's northwest, later usually identified as Lower Silesia, was predominantly German, especially in the towns where the Slavic minority, most of it Polish, had been much weakened. In Upper Silesia, on the other hand, both Polish and Czech elements were strong, and there, too, the Hussite movement had gained more influence than it had been able to achieve in Lower Silesia. (During the Revolution one of the Upper Silesian princes, Duke Bolek of Oppeln or Opole, had even joined the Hussite camp.)

But the specific reason for Silesia's staying within the Bohemian realm arose from the possibility that her strong neighbors might nibble off bits of her loose federation, if such it can be called, and that, especially in times of a severe crisis of the Czech state, some of the small principalities might succumb to such temptation.[32] This danger came from three sides: from Poland, where many people still looked nostalgically back to the time, only a century and a quarter ago, when their King had considered Silesia as part of his own territory; and from the two leading east-German princes, Frederick of Saxony and Frederick (II) of Brandenburg. Also interested in Silesian affairs was Elector Frederick's brother, Margrave Albert Achilles (thus titled, for all times, by Aeneas Sylvius), who, in 1439, had occupied, by appointment of his namesake, King Albert II, the

---

[31] See the discussion of the issue (with repeated references to the *Kniha Tovačovská*, ch. 6) in Bachmann's, *Geschichte Böhmens*, II, 440ff., where however his polemic against Palacký's view on the matter (p. 442, n.1) is neither clear nor entirely justified.

[32] This, actually, did occur in the case of the Duchy of Auschwitz (Oswiecim), which under its Duke John turned back to Poland. See Grünhagen-Markgraf, *Lehns und Besitzurkunden Schlesiens*, II (Publ. aus d. preuss. Staatsarchiven XVI), Leipzig, 1883, 594–613. (later cited as "Grünhagen-Markgraf").

office of captain of the "duchy of Silesia," that is specifically those
principalities that owed their fealty immediately to the crown of
Bohemia such as Breslau, Schweidnitz, Jauer, and Neisse.[33]

It was precisely this office to which, early in 1454, King Ladislav
appointed Henry of Rosenberg, who was also made royal governor
of the so-called "Sixtowns" of Upper Lusatia.[34] In other ways, too,
the Rosenbergs were encouraged to strengthen their position in
Silesia. Henry's younger brother John—who in those years began to
look up to George as a national leader and a personal friend—soon
became the son-in-law of one of Silesia's princes, Duke Henry of
Glogau, which made it easier for him to take his older brother's
place in 1457. And before very long even the third of the three
brothers, Jost, was to become a highly important figure in Silesian
politics—as Bishop of Breslau.

What the Rosenbergs (and, as we shall see, George himself) were
to do in Silesia, the Sternbergs were to do in Lower Lusatia. This was
the northern part of the country, as against the Sixtowns of the South,
whose contact with Bohemia, for geographic and even ethnic reasons,
was closer. Lower Lusatia had, during the forties, the time of Bohemia's greatest weakness, attracted both neighboring princes, Frederick of Saxony and Frederick of Brandenburg, in a struggle in which
King Frederick III was also involved and which almost had led to
war between the two northern German electoral principalities. In
the outcome Brandenburg had been more successful. Its margrave-
elector had been able to acquire, through considerable financial in-
vestments, a good many holdings, among them the "Vogtei" or
government of the so-called Lusatian March—the northern border
region of Lusatia nearest to Brandenburg—as well as, farther south,
part of the domain and city of Kottbus. Altogether, Lower Lusatia
seemed to be on the point of getting quite firmly into Brandenburg
hands.[35] Here, perhaps even more than in Silesia, existed the serious
possibility that a territory that had been part of the Bohemian crown
for a century would be lost, a danger which George felt he had to
ward off. He had scarcely established his legal position through his
visit in Vienna and his confirmation by Ladislav in May 1453 when

[33] In Neisse, however, the Bishop of Breslau had special rights beyond those he held in
Breslau.

[34] For the significance of this appointment, especially in terms of Henry's actual function
and powers, as well as the sources, see Urbánek, *Věk*, II, 859–862, notably 861 n. 1.

[35] About this see J. G. Droysen, *Geschichte der preussischen Politik*, 2 ed., II, 1, p. 141.

he devoted himself to this difficult problem. He informed Elector Frederick of Brandenburg that he had taken the necessary steps to repay the money by which Frederick had acquired the rule over the Lusatian March. And now, in January 1454, King Ladislav, upon George's recommendation, authorized the two Lords of Sternberg, Aleš and Zdeněk, to recover the domain of Kottbus from the Brandenberg ruler.[36] Frederick certainly was not happy to see these territories slip out of his hands again. But he had to be careful, since he as much as any other of the princes of eastern and southern Germany was unwilling to challenge the power of a united Bohemia—after the bitter experience of Frederick of Saxony, in 1450, in the war in which, of this power, only the Poděbradian League had been committed. The transaction would take time—there was always the possibility of diplomatic postponements. For the Sternbergs, already prominent by occupying the offices of lord chamberlain and lord high burgrave, this nevertheless contained the hope for important acquisitions, especially in view of the extraordinary energy and almost boundless ambition of Zdeněk.

There was one more reason, presumably, for George's readiness to reward and strengthen these two great families: in this way he had less to fear from their jealousy or ill will when he, now, went about strengthening his own economic (and therewith also political) position.

Just as for the Rosenbergs, so for his own house, the family of Kunštát-Poděbrady, George sought wider holdings in Silesia and in the border regions between Bohemia and Silesia. To some extent this was territory adjacent to older Kunštát family possessions, especially in the region of Náchod. The most important purchase which George made, with permission (and some limited monetary help) from the King, concerned the county of Glatz and the principalities of Münsterberg and Frankenstein.[37]

The county of Glatz, at this time, was still part of the kingdom of Bohemia proper, while later it became more closely attached to Silesia (and with it, in the eighteenth century, was conquered and retained by Frederick II of Prussia). It was a sort of natural fortress, surrounded by mountains, and could function as such during the time when Silesia became a theater of war. The principalities of Münsterberg and Frankenstein were in central Silesia, not too far from Bres-

---

[36] FRA, XX, 71ff.
[37] See Grünhagen-Markgraf, II, 150ff., 180f.

lau. With them George's family acquired a position that later enabled it to maintain princely rank far beyond George's lifetime.

In addition, George also hoped to achieve a strong position in the duchy of Liegnitz. Here opportunities seemed to arise, originally, from the drawn-out struggle over the inheritance of this small state,[38] one of the many Silesian principalities which were fiefs of the crown of Bohemia by virtue of the feudal vassalage of their duke to the Czech King. The struggle had begun in 1449, when, upon the death of its Duchess Elizabeth without direct heir, the wealthier merchant aristocracy of the city of Liegnitz had attempted to achieve a status immediately under the Czech crown. These attempts, originally, had seemed to be successful, but just as in other parts of Silesia and Lusatia, the rulers of Saxony and Brandenburg tried to use the opportunity to gain a foothold here. In the case of Liegnitz the Margraves of Brandenburg seemed to have a special reason to interfere, since the nearest claimant, the Duchess-Dowager Hedwig, was herself a Hohenzollern princess. With great bravery and stubbornness she defended the rights of her son Frederick, still a minor, even after she had been forced to leave the city and duchy. For a while, besides the help of her own family, she was supported by the majority of the other Silesian princes, while two other Fredericks, the Saxon and the Emperor, stood against her. The Emperor had tried to turn the duchy over to Saxony, since the strengthening of the friendly house of Wettin would mean a corresponding weakening of the potentially enormous power of Ladislav. But the release of Ladislav enabled George and the Czech estates to act more decisively. George felt that it was time to defend Bohemia's legitimate interests as the suzerain of all Silesia, and in the process also to further his own cause. The King, upon George's suggestion, appointed the regent's cousin, Procek of Kunštát, as captain of Liegnitz, and in December 1453 Procek went there to receive the city's homage to the King. But George was aware of the strong resistance among the majority of the people of Liegnitz against the merchant aristocracy as well as against those whom the masses, under the influence of John of Capistrano, had recently learned to regard as the terrible Czech heretics. He felt that it would be difficult and perhaps politically unwise to keep the Duchess and her son permanently from returning to Liegnitz. Through the mediation of the Elector of Brandenburg's younger brother, Albert Achilles,

---

[38] See *ibid*, I., 400–451, for most of the source material. For the most thorough treatment see Markgraf, *Der Liegnitzer Lehnstreit 1449-1469, Abhandlungen der schles. Gesellschaft für vaterländ. Cultur 1869*, Phil.-Hist. Abt., I, 25–70.

the possibility of a compromise was vented and was approved by the King. The agreement now concluded, approved the return of Duchess Hedwig and her son to Liegnitz. At the same time the young duke would be affianced to George's daughter Zdeňka. George would take over the government of the Duchy in Frederick's name until the young prince reached the age of 16.[39]

The agreement was never put into force. In June 1454 a popular rebellion broke out in Liegnitz which resulted in the overthrow of the existing government. The Czech captain and his small garrison were forced to evacuate the castle, and the Duchess returned with her son without permission from Prague. Though the King, at first, seemed to be angry and willing to take strong measures, and though George can hardly have been less perturbed, the princely rebellion remained unpunished and successful.

There were good reasons for this: King and regent had meantime become involved in a rather perplexing and at the same time somewhat dangerous question of Silesian politics which put the Liegnitz quarrel in the shade: a bitter struggle with the great city of Breslau about whether, and if so how, she was to do homage to King Ladislav. (George's diplomatic caution in regard to Liegnitz actually proved to be very wise. Before too long Frederick of Liegnitz became one of George's supporters in Silesia, and much later even the marriage project materialized, though it was not George's daughter Zdeňka—she was to make a better match—but her younger sister Ludmila who eventually became Duchess of Liegnitz).

Not only was the struggle over Breslau's homage of some importance at the time but it was the prelude to a later struggle that assumed truly epic proportions. We must therefore devote some attention to even this early phase of what was to be the fight between a city and a man, as well as, to some extent, a conflict between some of the basic currents and principles dominating the history of this part of the world in the third quarter of the fifteenth century.[40]

Within Silesia, Breslau, the largest city, the seat of the bishop, and the trading center of the whole country, had assumed the position of an unofficial capital. Together with the surrounding countryside

---

[39] Grünhagen-Markgraf, I, 442f.

[40] See on the whole struggle the careful and on the whole excellent monograph by R. Koebner, *Der Widerstand Breslau's gegen Georg von Podiebrad* (Darstellungen und Quellen zur schles. Geschichte, vol. 23), Breslau, 1916, with an appendix containing important documents, as well as the present author's article "City Rebellions in 15th Century Bohemia and their Ideological and Sociological Background," *Slavonic and East European Review*, London, June 1962, pp. 324–340.

and the smaller town of Neumarkt it formed the principality of Breslau, but there was no prince. Instead the city, that is in fact the city council, governed the principality directly under the crown of Bohemia. In previous times the captaincy, that is the military and police power over the principality, had at times been entrusted to captains appointed by the King; at other times it had been left in the hands of the city council. At the present, as we have seen, the captaincy (at least over all parts of Silesia directly under the crown) had been given to Henry of Rosenberg, but he had as yet not been able to turn his legal position into effective power.

In her claim to be Silesia's capital, and thereby to have an influence larger at least than any one of the many small dukes and princes (for all their distinguished descent, through sidelines, from the great royal houses of Piast and Přemysl)[41] Breslau had to emphasize her very special relationship to the King, and this, indeed, had been answered in the past by considerable interest (and, at times, special favors) at the hands of the four Luxemburg Kings of Bohemia. During the more than hundred years they ruled over Silesia the usage had developed that not only the council and the "Mannen" (knights owing feudal vassalage and military service) but also all the princes of Silesia themselves did homage in one great and spectacular collective act staged in Breslau on occasion of the King's first visit to the city after his coronation. This, in addition to being an honor for Breslau, was also practically the only demonstration of Silesia's otherwise highly doubtful political cohesion. It was far from astonishing —it was even natural that the people of Breslau, proud of such a role and such traditions, would expect and hope that this usage would be maintained in the case of King Ladislav.[42] This, in addition, would give the representatives of Breslau as well as the princes an opportunity to emphasize that their fealty to the King (like that of the Moravians) was based on his being their hereditary ruler, rather than on his election or confirmation by a diet of the Czech estates in which they had not been represented. It may even be that the King's demand to send representatives to Prague for the act of homage, which reached the city in January 1454, was due to the wish of the regent and the estates to prevent just this sort of a demonstration of the hereditary principle, at least at this moment. There was then nothing very strange or surprising in the fact that the city was at first reluctant to

41 See e.g. Grünhagen, "Breslau und die Landesfürsten während des Mittelalters," *Zeitschrift f. Geschichte Schlesiens*, XXXVI, 1901, 1–28.

42 This is a point to which Urbánek, in his otherwise thorough treatment, hardly pays sufficient attention (*Věk*, II, 835–849, 901–912). See Koebner, *Der Widerstand*, 9ff.

comply. What made it strange and resulted in a real conflict was the way it expressed this reluctance. And this reflected, besides the arguments just stated, the internal situation and the mood of the masses of the "little people" of Breslau.

The social structure of the city of Breslau was not remarkably different from that of other major central-European towns of the time. It was perhaps wealthier than many other cities its size; it had adopted capitalist methods of trade and banking early and successfully; and its "patricians," its great merchant families, had acquired an especially strong economic position not only in the city itself but also by the purchase of large landed estates outside its walls and even beyond the borders of the principality.[43] As elsewhere they, in the main, ran the city council much like a closed corporation, and, as elsewhere, the social group just below them, the craftsmen organized in their guilds, and the large number of apprentices and day laborers, were not very happy about this and were frequently in a quite rebellious mood. Once, in 1418, this had led to a bloody revolt which replaced the merchant-aristocrats in the city council by guildsmen. This revolution had been followed, three years later, by a just as bloody counter-revolution staged and supervised by King Sigismund himself.[44] After that the guildsmen and their adherents had, it seems, lost every inclination to take over responsibility for the city's government. But this did not imply that they had lost their appetite for loudly criticizing the city council and, at times, by making the life of their members miserable. The framework of their activities was the city commune, which, in the years after 1453, stood under the strong direct influence of some gifted agitators among the city's parochial priests.[45]

To say, therefore, that in Breslau there was a situation of fairly permanent (but not always equally vehement) class struggle is hardly much of an exaggeration. And this potentially explosive and ever-present tension was given a new sense of justification, dignity, and direction by the man who a short time before had intended to extirpate, by the mere power of his personality, the whole Hussite heresy, and who thought that it was merely the lack of a safe, well-protected sojourn in Prague which had prevented him from achieving this miracle.

In two long stays in Breslau, in 1453 and 1454, John of Capistrano

---

[43] See G. Pfeiffer, *Das Breslauer Patriziat im Mittelalter* (Darst. und Quellen z. schles. Gesch. vol. 30). Breslau, 1929.

[44] See H. Aschbach, *Geschichte Kaiser Sigmunds*, Hamburg, 1844 ff., III, 45ff.

[45] See the details partly in Koebner and in Heymann, "City Rebellions," *Slavonic and East European Review*, 1962.

had steadily increased his influence on the masses of the people. We have already mentioned his role in the destruction of Breslau's Jewish community. Less spectacular was his steady preaching about the danger that threatened the good, Christ-loving and God-fearing people of Breslau from the bestial depravity of the Czech Hussites. This agitation went so far that King Ladislav, in two letters, urged him (through the bishop of Breslau) to stop those violent attacks since they might only result in making the return of the schismatics to the Roman Church more difficult.[46] (While perhaps the initiative to the letters could have been George's, their trend of argument must have been either the King's own or must have originated from one of his Catholic friends and advisers.) The King even tried to make the friar leave Breslau, and eventually he complied, though only after leaving behind him, firmly rooted, fears, hatreds, and prejudices against the Hussite Czechs in general and George in particular. We shall see later how the masses, in an orgy of sentiment in which nationalism, crusading zeal, and class hatred were oddly mixed, forced the more rational city council to a policy entirely in conflict with the true interests of the city as a whole, and especially of its important mercantile development. This emotional hostility was to be dangerous for Breslau, but not for Breslau alone. In the last resort it proved a most dangerous seed also for Bohemia and for George, one by which Capistrano's hatred survived his own life, a posthumous revenge on the man who had kept him out of Prague and most of Bohemia.

For the people of Breslau, then, things had been remarkably clarified. They had heard from Capistrano, and would hear for many years from his disciples such as Nicholas Tempelfeld and other popular preachers that the Hussites, and especially Rokycana and George, were enemies of Christ and God. They were deeply sorry for the young King who was now in the power of the heretics and might never escape from it. They did, however, set themselves the task, if at all possible, to deliver the boy-king from this mortal danger. One way to do this was to force him to come to Breslau to receive their homage.

This view was not shared in its entirety by the more diplomatic, less fanaticized members of the council. While they, too, would have preferred the ceremony to take place in Breslau, they were yet willing to obey the King's order, even if it might be inspired by "the

---

[46] Wadding, *Annales Minorum,* XII, 208f.

heretics." They dispatched their representatives rather early, but when the priests around Tempelfeld got wind of this, the commune was alarmed and the council was forced to send express messengers to Prague with changed instructions for the city's representatives. They had to express their regret that they could not obey the King's request since to do homage outside the city was against their laws. While they recognized the King as their lord, they would do homage only as soon as he came to Breslau.[47]

The situation was difficult for Prague. Breslau had openly flouted the King's order, yet George was not, or not yet, willing to go to any extreme in his answer. Especially he wanted to give the Silesian princes an opportunity to do homage, thus obviating the argument of the need for a collective ceremony in Breslau, and isolating the city. In this he was at least politically successful, in that before long some of the princess did their homage singly. It was perhaps partly on the basis of this development that the city council found itself ready for a compromise arrangement for which, it seems, the first suggestions came from the council itself.[48] On this basis, then, the King appointed a delegation of men in high position who would go to Breslau to receive the city's homage in his name. An embassy of considerable splendor, led by Bohemia's constitutionally highest official, the Lord High Burgrave Zdeněk of Sternberg, and several other high noblemen, all of them well known Catholics, arrived in Breslau early in May for the intended ceremony.[49] But again the city council found out that it could not make policy decisions like this one without the prior knowledge and express agreement of the commune and its alert watchdogs, the city preachers. The council (two of whose members had from the beginning stood on the side of the preachers) had to confront the King's ambassadors with the declaration that they had come in vain. They expressed this decision in a memorandum[50] that was meant to explain their attitude to the King but that was, in reality, apt to infuriate not only the members of the delegation but even Ladislav himself by treating him like a child. He would, so they said, better understand and approve their attitude once he grew to a

---

[47] Koebner, *Der Widerstand*, 28, 146ff., 163.

[48] This question is discussed in almost extreme detail *ibid.*, 146ff., and 155ff., with special regard to the main source, the town secretary Peter Eschenloer.

[49] *Ibid.*, 163f., and P. Eschenloer, in German, *Geschichten der Stadt Breslau*, ed. J. G. Kunisch, Breslau, 1827–1828, I, 17. (Later, in distinction from the Latin version, cited as Eschenloer, G.).

[50] See Markgraf ed., *Politische Correspondenz Breslaus, Scriptores rerum Silesiacarum*, VIII, Breslau, 1873–1874 pp. 1ff. (later cited as *SrS*). See also Koebner, *Der Widerstand*, 31f.

more mature age. The King was so angry that he wanted immediately to proceed against the city with military measures. It would appear that George, far from goading him on, rather tried to restrain him. He knew how difficult it would be to conquer by purely military means a city of Breslau's size, and he had already to cope with the Liegnitz controversy. Yet some preparations for a campaign were allowed to proceed.[51] They would at least impress those princes who had so far hesitated with their own homage. Indeed, on June 28, in a highly solemn celebration on the Old Town Square of Prague, a number of princes—we do not know which ones—payed their homage to the King.[52] Breslau, by now, was rather isolated in her stand. Still, under the influence of the priests (even Capistrano paid a last, short visit) the city did not budge. The final scene of this prelude to a greater drama had to wait till the end of the year.

George had tried to keep the King in Prague as long as possible, and especially until his "Czech education" was finished. But now, after a stay of a year and a quarter, he probably felt that he had achieved all that he could expect, and that he could not really, with sufficiently sound reasons, stand in the way of Ladislav's taking his residence, for a time, in his other realms. It was but fitting that the King, before leaving his Bohemian lands for a longer period, should visit those provinces that he had not yet seen, Silesia and Lusatia. He went to Lusatia first, where, in Görlitz, the representatives of the Sixtowns repeated the homage that they, unlike Breslau, had paid to the King in Prague a year earlier.[53] On December 6th the King, accompanied by George and with magnificent retinue, including 2,000 horse, arrived in Breslau. Five days later the city paid homage to Ladislav as their hereditary King and lord, in the presence also of Elector Frederick II and Margrave Albert Achilles of Brandenburg, two of the Dukes of Bavaria, and nearly all the Silesian princes.[54] For the people of the city it was a grand spectacle, and they could claim that, in this struggle, their constancy had prevailed. It gave them a somewhat exaggerated idea of their strength.

Yet there was a taste of gall in this heady wine. The King had come, it is true—he had been removed from the snake pit—yet the terrible George was still with him, and, obviously, was making all the important decisions. Nor could they prevent the leader of heretics,

---

[51] *Ibid.*, 163f., and *SrS*, VIII, 4.
[52] See Z. Theobald, *Hussiten-Krieg*, Nuremberg, 1621, II, 279.
[53] Palacký, FRA, II, 20, p. 87.
[54] *SrS*, VIII, 5, and Grünhagen-Markgraf, I, 83, 287f.

together with other Czechs, from participating in (and, as they felt, desecrating) the many religious celebrations connected with the King's presence. The city's captaincy had now really to be yielded to a Czech, Henry of Rosenberg.[55] Further, the presence of the royal court, for two months, was a heavy financial burden. And in addition they had now to take their punishment. George himself, in a jovial mood, informed them that they had gravely insulted the King's majesty and must now pay for it. Thirty thousand ducats would be the fine. The councillors, horrified, implored the regent to relent. George, pleasant but tough, eventually let them get away with half this sum.[56] While well within the city's means, it was still a harsh tax. Only two-thirds of it had been paid when, in February 1455, the King and his retinue left Silesia to go to Vienna. The remaining third, 5,000 ducats, George was allowed by the King to cash in for himself.[57] It was one more reason—but surely only one of many, as they saw it—for the people of Breslau to hate the regent. They soon expressed their feelings in pamphlets and songs.

With Ladislav's arrival in Austria there ended perhaps the happiest period in the life of the young King. It had been, on the whole, most fruitful and thus happy also for George. It was to be a fairly long time, two and a half years, before Ladislav returned to his Kingdom of Bohemia. By then the pleasant, happy youngster of former days had experienced much, and little of it had been pleasant or happy.

[55] *AČ*, VII, 208.
[56] Eschenloer, G., I, 22, and in Latin (*Historia Wratislaviensis, SrS*, VII, Breslau, 1872) p. 7.
[57] See Urbánek, *Věk*, II, 904 n.2.

CHAPTER 7

THE TURKS, HUNGARY AND TRAGEDY

The royal visit to Breslau had not only been intended as an opportunity for the city's long delayed homage. It was also hoped that some important international business would be settled. The two Margraves of Brandenburg had come with very specific wishes. A revolution had broken out in Prussia, the semi-ecclesiastical state of the Order of the Teutonic Knights, where the local nobility and towns had risen against the oligarchy of the order. The rebels, though all German, had sought and received the support of the King of Poland, whereas the Hohenzollern princes, and to some extent the Emperor, rather ineffectually tried to uphold and protect the much weakened Teutonic Knights.[1] The issue had even earlier been brought before Ladislav and George during a visit paid to them in April 1454 by Margrave Albert Achilles. Albert had made, in the name of the knights, a handsome offer of 300,000 ducats for Czech military help, and the King, clearly with George's agreement or upon his suggestion, had declared himself ready to accept it. But in fact no such help was ever given. (The problem was to come before George again at a much later time during the drawn-out war when he, then already King, was asked to mediate or even arbitrate.) Now, however, the matter remained in abeyance. Nor did the hope materialize that King Casimir of Poland, who by his recent marriage to Princess Elizabeth of Habsburg had become Ladislav's brother-in-law, might himself come to Breslau.

Another issue brought before King and regent by the Brandenburg Margraves arose from the Czech demand for a return to Bohemia of several towns, castles, and estates, on Bohemian and Lusatian as well as on Saxon-Meissen soil, which had been pawned out to the Saxon

---

[1] For the general background of the rising, also in relation to Bohemia and Poland, see the corresponding chapters in Joh. Voigt, *Geschichte Preussens,* VIII, and J. Goll, *Čechy a Prusy ve středověku,* Prague, 1897, pp. 259ff. As to documentary sources see the correspondence between the order and Elector Frederick of Brandenburg in Joachim-Hubatsch, *Regesta Ordinis S. Mariae Theutonicorum,* I. Göttingen, 1950, and now also vol. XIX, part 1, of *Deutsche Reichstagsakten.*

dukes during the long time of troubles, as well as demands arising out of Czech armed help during the war between the hostile Saxon brothers.[2] Here, again, nothing was achieved, and here, for the first time, a distinct difference in attitude developed between the regent, whose demands were those of the Czech patriot, and the King, for whom the patriotic aspects seemed of lesser importance than his dynastic tie to a related prince. It is ironical that George acted in a much more energetic way than the King in pressing accusations over the ill-treatment that Princess Anne, Ladislav's older sister, had received from her somewhat dissolute husband, Duke William of Saxony.[3]

The conflict between Bohemia and Saxony was to engage the attention of both King and regent at a later time. Yet none of the problems which were so inconclusively discussed at Breslau could compare in seriousness with events much farther afield—events of truly world-shaking importance, which were to form the solemn and sinister background to almost all of Europe's history at the time, and especially of the history of Central Europe: the steady, victorious approach of the Ottoman power across the Balkans and into the Danubian plains.

It was now, in the spring of 1455, just two years since Constantinople had fallen and the once great empire of the Greeks had ceased to exist. The event neither started nor concluded but merely highlighted in a dramatic fashion the seemingly irresistable progress of the Turks. Two Kings of Hungary, Sigismund of Luxemburg at Nicopolis in 1398 and Władysław Jagiello at Varna in 1444, had tried in vain to stop the movement before the Imperial City had gone down. At Varna even the presence of John Hunyadi, the one man who—beside the Albanian Skanderbeg—had occasionally defeated the Turks, had not been able to save Władysław's life and reign.

Yet all along everyone talked of the Turkish danger, but nobody seemed willing to do anything about it: "nobody," especially, among the rulers and princess of the Empire, beginning with the Emperor. The one great exception was the Holy See. The three Popes of this period, Nicholas V, Calixtus III, and Pius II, all made consistent and often extraordinary efforts to initiate and organize a strong, concerted military action which would not merely stem the Turkish advance but drive the invading infidels out of Europe altogether. If, in

---

[2] See e.g. Palacký, *Dějiny*, IV, 1, 320ff.
[3] Palacký, *FRA*, II, 20, 69–70.

the end, so little was achieved it was certainly not the fault of the Curia.

Whose fault was it then? To a considerable extent it was because there was almost everywhere plain lack of understanding of the need, lack of willingness to sacrifice, in particular to sacrifice the money which was needed to build up armies able to do the job. There was also—again with the exception of John Hunyadi—little capable leadership in places from where immediate action could be taken. And there was, finally, the frequency, not to say permanence, of struggles between those rulers who might have made a significant contribution to a strong, concerted action.

But none of these conflicts had as important a bearing on the question of mobilization against the Turks as had the struggle between the young King of Bohemia and Hungary and the Holy Roman Emperor. Combined, the two ruled, or were supposed to rule, a territory roughly identical with that of the Dual Alliance between Germany and Austria-Hungary in the era of Bismark and William II. Granted that neither Frederick III nor Ladislav could operate with true authority within their realms, because the strength of the Emperors had long faded and had reached a very nadir under this first Habsburg ever to bear the imperial crown and title,[4] and because Ladislav had to contend, in both of his kingdoms, with powerful estates and even more powerful national leaders. Even so, something could have been achieved, at least in terms of a limited support for Hungary's possible military effort, if the relationship between the King and the Emperor had been tolerably cooperative. But instead it was one of outright hostility.

The reasons for this hostility are obvious. Ladislav never forgave his former guardian for his long "imprisonment." In addition the Emperor still kept in his possession the Holy Crown of St. Stephen (though Ladislav had already been crowned with it) and also still held a number of strong castles in Hungary as well as in Austria. Various attempts at a compromise, especially in the form of payments to be made to the Emperor in return for the crown and the castles, had so far had no success. While the Emperor, probably, did not hate the young King as fiercely as he was hated, his attitude, too, was partly determined by his feelings. His dislike was directed not

---

[4] The three earlier Habsburgs often called Emperors, Rudolf I, Albert I, and Albert II, were all elected by the electoral princes as "Reges Romanorum," but none of them was crowned as "Imperator."

only against Ladislav himself but at least as much against the man who had once been one of Frederick's favorites and whose defection to his enemies had been decisive in Ladislav's release from his wardship: the Count of Cilli.

Cilli, again, heartily returned the Emperor's dislike. He did not easily forgive the way he was snubbed when, having lost his powerful position with his young cousin, he had offered his services to the Emperor. During the time when he was in disgrace (at least officially so, though Ladislav seems never have ceased to think of him as a friend), and especially during Ladislav's long stay in Bohemia George's influence had at least been able to keep the young King's belligerence toward the Emperor within limits. But now things began to change.

The man who had replaced Count Cilli as the leading statesman of Austria, Ulrich Eizinger, had lost much of his popularity in Vienna by his nepotism—he had a large family—and some of his greedy financial practices, and had had to defend himself against attacks before the estates. Ladislav, who had never really cared for Eizinger, thus found it easy to get rid of him and to replace him with his friend Cilli. The great count splendidly re-entered Vienna (at the head of a thousand horse) in late February 1455, only a couple of weeks after the King, with George of Poděbrady, had arrived there from Breslau.[5] The King's quick action, incidentally, shows that, once on Austrian soil, George's influence could not remain as strong as it had been, for Eizinger had always been (and was to remain) one of George's most devoted and most reliable friends.

But this created a new situation for George. At first he tried, but it seems without success, to bring about an understanding between Cilli and Eizinger. He knew that, in the near future, not he but Cilli would, simply by being present, have the King's ear most of the time. Little as he welcomed the change he could not risk alienating the King through an open hostility against Cilli. For his part, the count could be expected to tread cautiously in his relations to George lest he weaken his whole international position. He had learned from experience that George's strength in Bohemia was much too firm to be challenged at this stage. Thus all conditions were given for a renewal of the agreement concluded between both men two years earlier in Znojmo.

---

[5] See Aeneas Sylvius, *Historia Friderici*, 457, and for the general background e.g. Kurz, *Oesterreich unter Friedrich* IV, I, 163ff.

We do not know whether this was done officially. We do know, however, that George continued his attempt to mediate between Cilli and the Hunyadi party. And since it was clear that with Cilli's return his friends in Hungary would also gain influence, it seemed sensible for George to strengthen whatever ties he had with them, without thereby giving up his friendship with Hunyadi. The outcome was a betrothal between George's son Henry and Jeronyma, daughter of Lord Nicholas Ujlaki,[6] one of Hungary's leading magnates and, with Laszlo Gara and the Czech general John Jiskra of Brandýs, one of the pillars of Cilli's and King Ladislav's strength in Hungary.

It is not likely that George's policy, aimed at peace and cooperation between all main groups in Ladislav's three countries, was misinterpreted or criticized by Hunyadi and the men around him. The regent's inclination for mediation and compromise, which was to make him later a much sought-after diplomatic mediator and arbitrator, was here as in most other cases not the outcome of selfless idealism but rather the feeling that more often than not such a peacable approach was in the best interests of his own country. (If he thought it necessary he could also strike, with arms in hand, quickly and decisively.) But just as he felt that an outbreak of open conflict in Hungary should be avoided, so he looked with little favor at the steadily worsening relationship between Ladislav and Frederick III. In a war between the two it would be well-nigh impossible to keep Bohemia out, as the King could expect to receive help from his Czech subjects. Thus mediation between Ladislav and Frederick was surely his foremost though by no means his only purpose when, in the second half of March, George, accompanied by some of the leading Czech noblemen and by the royal Chancellor Prokop of Rabstein, travelled from Vienna to the Emperor's favorite residence: Wiener-Neustadt.

How George's prestige had risen in the meantime could be seen from his reception. The Emperor himself, accompanied by several princes and prelates, among them the Elector of Trier, Archbishop James, Margrave Albert Achilles of Brandenburg, and Margrave Charles of Baden, greeted him before the gates of the city. The Emperor, it seems, was at this moment more inclined toward a compromise with Ladislav than vice versa, and hoped that George would be in a sufficiently strong and influential position to prevent the outbreak of war. We hear later that, on the basis of his discussions with the Czech regent, Frederick proposed to King Ladislav an arbitra-

[6] *AČ*, III, 560f.

tion of all their differences, with George of Poděbrady and Margrave Albert Achilles as arbitrators. It would, indeed, have been difficult to find two other prominent men who, to an equal degree, could have been considered true friends of both antagonists, the King and the Emperor. But the King—or, we should say, the unforgiving Count Cilli—rejected the proposal.[7]

In the months to follow, the King did indeed make considerable preparations for war, and some of his Austrian vassals actually started small-scale military actions in the neighborhood of Wiener-Neustadt. The King also tried hard to get the Czech estates to do what he considered their duty, but they evaded, by another attempt at mediation, such unpleasant involvement in a war in which Bohemia had little or nothing to gain.[8] Cilli's hopes thus were frustrated, and he can hardly have felt warmly toward the man whom, quite rightly, he considered primarily responsible for this evasion: the Lord of Poděbrady.

We have pointed out before that a reconciliation between King and Emperor seemed especially necessary against the background of the Turkish danger and the need to organize a strong counteraction. It is for this reason that George's repeated attempts at mediation must have seemed especially meritorious to the one institution that wanted action most urgently—the Curia. In Wiener-Neustadt he had no chance to talk to an official representative of Rome, yet a discussion of Bohemia's perennial religious demands—the confirmation of the Compacts and of Rokycana's office—had been on his program. He had intended to ask the Emperor for a strong intercession, and the Emperor obliged him, though he delegated for this purpose a man who would anyhow be the logical choice to express the Emperor's wishes to the Holy See: Aeneas Sylvius. Again, as in Benešov, Prokop of Rabstein functioned as interpreter. Aeneas Sylvius could flatter himself that the almost four years which had passed since that earlier meeting had amply justified his judgment of George. He was a man of strength but a man of peace, a man able to steer the Czech ship of state wherever he wanted, a man, therefore—and the only man— who could really reconcile and reunite the Czech people with the Roman Church, which needed them to help fight the Turks.[9] Yet

[7] *AČ*, IV, 429.
[8] *Ibid.*, 424ff. 432f.
[9] About the hope for and the presumed value of Czech participation in the war against the Turks at this time, see Urbánek, *Dvě studie o době poděbradské* (Spísy filos. fakulty Masarykovy University v Brně, 27) Brno, 1929, 113ff.

Aeneas realized at this time—and was later to plead strongly before the Pope himself—that George could not be expected to walk rough-shod over the sentiments and what to Aeneas were the prejudices of the Czechs. This might mean confirming, either expressly or implicitly, the Compacts.

This (together with the continued determination not to recommend confirmation of the real heresiarch, John Rokycana), was clearly Aeneas' understanding of the situation and what it called for, at and after the meeting of Wiener-Neustadt. And without doubt he permitted George (and also, of course, Prokop of Rabstein) to know or at least to think they knew that this was his understanding. It must have made George hopeful and optimistic. But even more important—it colored and determined for a long time the regent's understanding of what sort of a man this clever clerical diplomat was, what he thought and what he wanted.[10]

King Ladislav, under the strong influence of Cilli, had set his heart on the war with the Emperor. If the Czechs were unwilling to participate perhaps it was still possible to set the Hungarians in motion. There, at least, the King could argue that, with the crown of St. Stephen and a number of castles, Hungarian interests and Hungary's honor were at stake. These arguments, however, were rudely answered by the fact that the Turkish danger had not just been an empty threat. It materialized in the form of a renewed attack upon Serbia, of which the Sultan, after a preparatory invasion in 1454, now occupied the whole southwest. Thus Serbia's ruler, George Branković, Count Cilli's father-in-law and princely vassal of the Hungarian crown, asked urgently for the King's help.

The King and Cilli had intended anyhow to devote increased attention to Hungary. But their, and especially Cilli's, real aim had been, and still was, to destroy Hunyadi. The great soldier's position in Hungary had grown considerably stronger during the time when Cilli was in disgrace and when he, allied to George of Poděbrady and Ulrich Eizinger, clearly had the upper hand over his adversaries —Gara, Ujlaki, Jiskra. The duel of wits and strength that was staged between John Hunyadi and the Count of Cilli cannot be dealt with here in any detail. Both, of course, were driven by ambition and lust for power, and neither of them was squeamish in his means. Yet it is difficult not to feel more sympathy with Hunyadi, who could claim

10 See G. Voigt, *Enea Silvo de Piccolomini*, II, Berlin, 1856–63, 165–170; also H. Kaminsky "Pius Aeneas among the Taborites," *Church History*, September 1959, 281–309, especially 296–300.

that he really stood for a strong, healthy Hungarian kingdom, who had fought more than one battle in the defense of his country, and who even now was ready, with all due precautions, to conclude a peace or at least an armistice in the political struggle with Cilli in order to be free for the war that really counted. Cilli could not refuse openly, especially since Cardinal Carvajal, the Pope's special legate, was a most careful and well-informed observer who was able to see through many of Cilli's intrigues and who kept reminding the King of the need to concentrate forces against the Turks. The attempt was made to fortify the armistice by the exchange of hostages. Cilli agreed to the marriage of his daughter Elizabeth with John Hunyadi's younger son Matthias, and while Matthias was made a page to the King, who was the same age, his young bride was welcomed to the household of the Hunyadi family. Unfortunately for the Hunyadis the girl died before the end of 1455, and the King—that is Cilli—now had his hostage without a reverse.[11]

During the second half of 1455 the King and Cilli had spent very little time in Hungary—their main hope was still that the Turks might stop in Serbia and that it might be possible, after all, to wage an all-out war against the Emperor. It was in the hope of gaining Czech support against the Emperor, not the Turks, that Ladislav, who had finally gone to Buda in February 1456, granted, over the heads of George and the Czech estates, an armistice to two ambassadors of Saxony—at a time when the direct negotiations between Bohemia and both the Saxon dukes had largely broken down. George, in a sort of protest action, sent in March a renewed challenge to Frederick of Saxony. Only after he had, by a quick action, gained the strong fortress and castle of Most, was he ready to resume negotiations, more or less on the basis of the armistice concluded by Ladislav.[12] It was, so far, the most obvious clash between the national interests of Bohemia and the dynastic desires (and supposed interests) of the King. But before long events in Hungary, and especially the growing Turkish danger, were bound to absorb even Ladislav's attention. Thus he gave George full powers to deal on his own with Frederick of Saxony.[13]

Early in 1456 it was learned that Mohammed II was making vast

11 See Chmel, *Materialien zur Oesterreichischen Geschichte*, Vienna, 1838, II, 105f., and Urbánek, *Konec Ladislava Pohrobka*, Prague, 1924, 40f. For Carvajal's role see also W. Fraknoi, "Cardinal Carvajal's Legationen in Ungarn," *Ungarische Revue*, X, 1890, 7ff., 124ff.

12 See Urbánek, *Věk*, II, 950–962.

13 *AČ*, XV, 219ff.

preparations for the conquest of Belgrade, the border fortress which provided the key to southern Hungary. In March Hunyadi—with safe conduct, but also at the head of considerable forces—visited the King at Buda, and now, at least on the surface, a full conciliation took place, largely upon the urging of Carvajal. John Hunyadi ceded to the King the direct control of a considerable number of royal castles, while the King gave Hunyadi full charge of Belgrade and some castles in its neighborhood as well as in Transylvania.[14] The garrison of Belgrade was under the command of Hunyadi's friend and brother-in-law, Szilagyi.

But even now Ladislav's and Cilli's policy appeared uncertain. Their sudden and unannounced departure from Buda in May left the capital and its castle without military cover and seemed to contradict the King's later claims that he had gone to collect troops to bring succor to Hunyadi. Whether or not suspicions are justified that he—or at least Cilli—would have been perfectly happy to see Hunyadi beaten by the Turks and that the strong forces now raised were meant for a different purpose altogether—the fact remains that in the decisive hour the military forces available to Hunyadi were far weaker than, in view of available resources (even in Hungary alone), they should have been. The only effective reinforcement that Hunyadi received consisted of the masses of so-called crusaders mobilized and led by the fiery John of Capistrano, men who came from many parts of Europe, few of whom were properly armed or trained, but whose fervent and passionate faith proved, in the decisive hour, an astonishingly effective substitute for better arms or training.

The story of the epic battle for Belgrade, won on July 22, 1456, has often been told and can be left untold here.[15] Nor need we go into the old question whether this victory was due more to Hunyadi's military genius or to the inspiration which Capistrano gave to his crusaders.[16] The death of both men of the plague so soon after their hour of triumph—in August and October—only added to their glory. But to Cilli the situation appeared as a great stroke of luck. With the strong international army that he now led he was not really forced to fight the Turks who, for the moment, seemed to lose much of their

[14] See the King's declaration in J. Teleki, *Hunyadiak kora Magyarorszagon*, Budapest, 1855, X, 495ff., 506ff., 519ff.
[15] The most recent account is by F. Babinger, *Mehmed der Eroberer und seine Zeit*, Munich, 1953, pp. 145–154.
[16] Treated in great detail by Hofer, *Johannes von Capestrano*, 610–650.

terror.[17] (This, indeed, was one of the unfortunate consequences of the great victory: far from destroying Ottoman military power at the source, it yet removed all the sense of urgency which, for a short moment, seemed to have inspired at least some of the people and statesmen in the countries not too far from the danger zone, including those of Bohemia.)

But with the army free to use as he saw fit, Cilli could make sure that this time he would gain the hoped-for power without having to contend any longer with the "national party" that had earlier, especially from the circles of the gentry, formed itself around first John Hunyadi and now his son Laszlo, a young man of 23. Once such unlimited power, officially in the King's name, was achieved by Cilli in Hungary, he had a much better chance to gain an equally unassailable position in Bohemia and Austria.

During various phases of the King's Hungarian sojourns members of the Czech high nobility had attended the King, especially Henry of Rosenberg and Zdeněk of Sternberg. Yet Cilli could not feel confident of having his rear secured until he made sure that the real power in Bohemia, George of Poděbrady, would not counteract his plans before they had begun to mature. Thus he asked George to meet him, and while the King went on his way, returning from Vienna to Buda, his two chief advisers and representatives met at the little town of Troskotovice in southern Moravia. This time the agreement of Znojmo of 1452 was indeed renewed, though, upon George's wish, with the clause that all rights and freedoms of the King's lands would remain untouched.[18]

The agreement does not reveal much about what was behind it. It is conceivable that Cilli had offered to use his influence upon the King to remove the difficulties or disagreements which had arisen between Ladislav and the Czech regent, especially concerning Saxony, and that in return he asked George not to support the Hunyadi party against him. But while this is perhaps the most plausible guess, it is still a guess. And it is just as plausible that George gave Cilli no guarantees that he would henceforth completely sacrifice his old ties with the Hunyadis and support Cilli's every step against them. At least the sentence about the rights and freedoms of the King's lands would

---

[17] See Aeneas Sylvius, *Historia Friderici*, 463, or, among modern discussions, Babinger, *Mehmed der Eroberer*, 160.

[18] See Chmel, *Materialien z. ö. Gesch.*, II, 111f.

remain as an escape clause by which George could recover his freedom of action in case Cilli tried in Hungary (and elsewhere) to establish, in Ladislav's name, an essentially absolutist regime.

Yet this was exactly what Cilli now intended. In a national diet, held at Futak,[19] the King solemnly appointed the count as regent of Hungary, while his friend Nicholas Ujlaki was made captain general of all the King's forces in the country. With considerable difficulty and after long delay Laszlo Hunyadi was induced to come to Futak, having received, as had his father a year earlier, a safe conduct, but also, as his father before, keeping a very strong body guard. Cilli wanted primarily to induce him to give up the great castles he held as his father had held them before him, above all that of Belgrade. Laszlo eventually agreed to turn Belgrade over to the King after Ladislav had promised that an investigation of John Hunyadi's handling of the royal finances would be suppressed.

The real intentions with which Laszlo now sped to Belgrade, ostensibly to prepare the great fortress for the King's arrival, may have been very different. Both sides were determined to settle the issues quickly, Cilli because he believed that he now had the strength and the opportunity to remove what he considered the greatest obstacle on his way to unlimited power, Laszlo because he suspected this and did not want to become the victim. Laszlo's suspicion seems to have become certainty when his uncle Szilagyi, the commandant of Belgrade, came into the possession of a letter which Cilli had intended for his father-in-law George Branković, the Prince of Serbia. In this letter Cilli announced that he would soon have two unique balls to play with—the heads of Laszlo and Matthias Hunyadi.[20]

On November 8th, 1456, the King and his relative, at the head of a strong army, arrived before Belgrade Castle. Both entered, with them the van of their forces, but, when only a few of them had got inside, the drawbridge was pulled up and the gate locked. Both men found themselves to be virtually Laszlo's prisoners, though he politely explained that to let in a larger number was against the laws of the country valid for border fortresses. On the next day, while the King, after Mass, stayed in another part of the castle, Hunyadi and his friends engaged Count Cilli in a discussion, suddenly confronted him with his letter to Branković, and denounced him as a traitor. In

---

[19] For the history and the source material on the Futak diet see Urbánek, *Konec Ladislava*, 58ff.

[20] See Urbánek, *Konec Ladislava*, 61 n.5.

the ensuing melee, the count's own attendants fled, and he was slain. The princely house of the Cilli's had ceased to exist.[21]

The young King thus found himself in a rather terrifying position. He had lost the man in whose guidance he had trusted, and he could not be sure whether he himself was safe. But he showed extraordinary presence of mind and mastery of his emotions. The young Hunyadi, suddenly, as it seems, himself shocked by what had happened, explained to the King that Cilli had attacked him and that he and his friends had killed him only in self-defense. The King accepted this, declared that the count alone was to be blamed for what had occurred, and smilingly promised complete forgiveness. This promise the King renewed a little later, when he went, upon Laszlo's urging, to Temesvar, the residence of Elizabeth, John Hunyadi's widow. There he even went so far as to swear by the sacrament that never in his life would he make either of her two sons responsible for what had happened at Belgrade but would always consider both of them as his brothers. These assurances, as well as those given by the Palatin Gara, who had recently become Laszlo Hunyadi's father-in-law, seem to have calmed his suspicion completely,[22] even though Gara was Cilli's first cousin and thus, besides the King himself, the count's nearest surviving relative. For a time, indeed, it was Gara who took over the role of Ladislav's chief adviser, around whom the group of Cilli's former friends and supporters crystalized again. The King, however, at a sparsely visited diet, proclaimed that forthwith he would keep the conduct of the kingdom's government in his own hands. That with all these happenings no one—neither Ladislav nor Laszlo nor Szilagyi—thought any longer of taking the offensive against the Turks can hardly be surprising, all the less since the King, with his mind fixed on his personal enemy the Emperor, had never had much heart for it.

At this time—in the winter 1456-57—some people in the circle around Hunyadi may have seen the first shadows of danger from Ladislav. This, at least, may have been behind some attempts they made to give the Hunyadi party a firmer cohesion by a "treaty" or "alliance," in substance not unlike that which had been concluded

---

21 Most of the sources (with the important exception of Aeneas Sylvius) tell the story from the point of view of the King. Thus e.g. the "Chronica der edlen Grafen von Cilli," in Simon Friedrich Hahn's *Collectio monumentorum veterum et recentium*, II, Braunschweig, 1725–1726; or the "Anonymi Chronicon Austriacum," in H. C. Senckenberg, *Selecta Iuris et Historiarum*, V, Frankfurt, 1739, 18–29. See also the bibliographical notes in Urbánek *Konec Ladislava*, 64–70.

22 Aeneas Sylvius, *Historia Friderici*, 464ff.

at the time of Ladislav's Prague coronation between the leading statesmen of his three countries. The actual character of the arrangement
or the names of the participants are unknown. Nor do we know,
whether among the people implicated or at least approached, were
men not now in Hungary, such as Ulrich Eizinger or George of
Poděbrady. That the alliance included a conspiracy against the King
himself—as one source claims with simply absurd details[23]—is extremely unlikely, especially since we hear that among the participants
were two men who essentially belonged to what might be called "The
King's party"—Nicholas Ujlaki, who had never abandoned Ladislav
but who clearly disliked the ever-growing strength of his old friend
Gara, and the Austrian "Hubmeister" (treasurer) Conrad Hölzler.
The latter, probably, was the source through whom the King was
informed of a plot. But even in the ensuing trial no attempt was
made to prove a real conspiracy, let alone, as was alleged by Hunyadi's
enemies, a planned attempt on the King's life.

The claim that a crime was here discovered did, however, make it
possible for Ladislav to have his revenge, probably planned long in
advance, ostensibly without breaking his solemn oath to Laszlo and
his mother. The surprise arrest of the Hunyadi brothers on March
14, 1457, was made after they had joined the King in Buda. In a
summary court procedure Laszlo was sentenced to death, his young
brother Matthias, with others, to permanent imprisonment. Laszlo's
decapitation is movingly described, after eye witnesses, by Aeneas
Sylvius.[24] The main motive for the bloody act was the King's wish
to punish the man (and his family) who had caused Cilli's death.
This emerges very clearly from Ladislav's own letters at the time.
They breathe a feeling of triumphant strength, based on the belief
that now no one will dare to oppose him.[25] Only later would he

---

[23] This source, under the title "Hofmär von Ungern," was published by E. Birk in his
"Beiträge zur Geschichte der Königin Elizabeth von Ungern und ihres Sohnes K. Ladislaus,"
in *Quellen und Forschungen zur vaterländischen Geschichte, Literatur und Kunst*, Vienna,
1849, p. 253f. Among the details referred to is the claim that the conspirators intended to
capture Ladislav and then deliver him as a present to the Sultan of Turkey! Further, all
Germans, but also all Czechs in Buda were to be killed. Another near-contemporary source
of a similar character is the "Historia seu epistola de miserabili morte ser. regis Ungarie," in
SrS, XII, 86ff., which tries to incriminate the Czech regent (of course without the assumption
that all Czechs were to be killed) and seems to belong to the propaganda war waged by
Hölzler against George. The claim that George played a role becomes far more definite in
later attacks on George which were part of the general hate campaign waged especially in
connection with Breslau's struggle against him (see later pp. 148f.). The lack of substance in
the King's accusations become very clear from his letter, justifying his action, in *Quellen und
Forschungen* (Birk), 254–258.

[24] *Historia Bohemica*, chapter 68.

[25] See Palacký, *FRA*, XX, 105, 107.

claim that it was "the barons" (meaning Gara) who had forced him to do what, in the event, destroyed his position in Hungary instead of strengthening it.

King Ladislav's belief that now, having just reached the age of 17, he could really be his own first minister soon turned out to be an illusion. True, he did not permit Gara, for all the political strength that he now had among the Hungarian magnates, to gain the position of personal closeness and trust that so far only two men had ever achieved: Cilli and, to a somewhat lesser extent, George of Poděbrady. While, partly, this may have been due to Gara's personality, it was also very clearly connected with his being a Hungarian. Indeed, the King—who on his release from the Emperor had flattered the Hungarians by declaring himself one of them—had by this time acquired a distinct dislike of this nation which had begun to be mutual—the execution of the popular Hunyadi had caused a wave of furor and revulsion. This feeling is strongly reflected in the semi-poetical accounts of one of Ladislav's most devoted and faithful courtiers,[26] which not only described this dislike, but even contrast it to his much warmer feelings for the Germans and for the Czechs. And indeed at this moment the men on whom Ladislav most strongly relied were a Czech and a German. The Czech was John Jiskra of Brandýs; the German (or Austrian) was the former Austrian treasurer, Conrad Hölzler.

Jiskra was a brilliant soldier who, as a young man, had gained his military training and experience in the Hussite Wars,[27] though at a later period he was no longer, if he had ever been, a Hussite himself. In the late 1430's, after some successful flings as a condottiere in Italy and elsewhere, he became attached to the Habsburg family, fought for King Albert II and, with equal fervor, for Queen-Dowager Elizabeth of Luxemburg, who anxiously tried to retain her husband's thrones for her son Ladislav. Jiskra did very well in these wars and even succeeded in defeating the numerically superior army of the great John Hunyadi.[28] Therefore, Queen Elizabeth, in 1440, made

[26] The poet is Michael Beheim, who was in Ladislav's retinue during the King's stay in Hungary and also during the sinister days in Belgrade Castle. See his poem with the characteristic headline "Von der Beham trew und von der Unger untrew," in Th. G. v. Karajan ed., "Zehn Gedichte . . . . zur Geschichte Oesterreichs und Ungerns," in *Quellen u. Forschungen*, 1–65, esp. 50 f.

[27] See Palacký, *Dějiny*, IV, 1, 445ff.; further, Urbánek, "K historii doby Jiskrovy na Slovensku," in *Věstník král. č. společnosti nauk*, Prague, 1940. Perhaps the most up-to-date bibliography about Jiskra and the Slovak brotherhood armies in Ladislav Hoffmann, *Bratřici*, Prague, 1959, pp. 79–84.

[28] See about this another poem by Michael Beheim, in *Quellen und Forschungen*, 46ff.

him governor of what was then called Upper Hungary, the wide-spread, mountainous regions of the kingdom's north. This area was inhabited mostly by Slovaks, whose language was close to Czech and many of whom, especially among the lower nobility and the peasants, were conscious of kinship with the Czechs in neighboring Moravia and Bohemia. For a considerable time, thus, Slovakia (which once had been a part of the early Bohemian state) regained a status of virtual autonomy under the protection of Jiskra and his Czech troops. Not all of the troops, in the long run, were maintained by Jiskra, and in time an increasing number, both Czechs no longer in the army and Slovaks who may have been locally hired, formed military brotherhoods of their own, much as those originally formed in Tabor and in eastern Bohemia by Žižka and his friends. We shall meet them again as an important and disturbing element of Czech-Hungarian relations.

But at the moment it was not those guerilla fighters but the strong regular army, still mostly Czech in origin, that Jiskra commanded in northern Hungary. It had long been, and still was, the only military force in Hungary on which the King could depend. Thus, at the time of the planned action against Laszlo Hunyadi, Ladislav had ordered Jiskra himself with most of his troops to Buda. Jiskra had, indeed, helped him directly when he made the arrest. While the King dealt with Laszlo, Jiskra had seized young Matthias.[29]

But if Jiskra, essentially in military terms, was the strongest and soon the only pillar of strength left to Ladislav in Hungary, it was the German, Hölzler, who now, speaking his mother language with the soft Viennese accent, gained Ladislav's confidence to the extent that the King was soon quite dependent on the man's advice, help, and direction.[30] He may, in this case, have been less conscious of such dependence than in the cases of George of Poděbrady or Ulrich of Cilli. Hölzler, as a man of low origins whose knighthood even was of quite recent date, was presumably more modest and assumed less in his personal attitude to the King, and thus made him believe that here he had, for the first time, not a man trying to dominate him but a true and faithful servant. But Hölzler (who may or may not have seen his tasks mainly in such loyal terms) was soon engaged in a policy basically little different from that pursued by Count Cilli.

There was then a short period—in later March and in April 1457 —when not only the King and Hölzler but even some observers out-

29 "Hofmär von Ungern," *Ibid.*, 254.
30 See Urbánek, *Konec Ladislava*, 106f.

side Hungary had begun to believe that the King was really master
of his fate, that he had utterly smashed the Hunyadi party and with
it the opposition of the Hungarian estates, and that a similar fate
now awaited all those who had ever played a corresponding role in
Ladislav's other two countries—that is certainly Ulrich Eizinger and
his brothers and friends in Austria, and quite possibly also George
of Poděbrady and his friends in Bohemia.

It would have been naïve to expect this to happen, especially in
Bohemia where the regent's power had long become more solidly
entrenched than John Hunyadi's had ever been. Yet even so it could
not be denied that a good deal of mischief could be done were the
King to appeal to those elements who potentially stood in opposition
to George. Rumors did, indeed, circulate that George had been implicated in the supposed Hunyadi conspiracy, and that he would
have to answer for it.[31] One of the noblemen in the regent's service,
Beneš of Veitmil (or Weitmühl), whom George had sent to Buda
for information, retorted angrily to these rumors and was thereupon
warned to leave lest he be arrested himself.[32] But more important,
and perhaps more indicative of the general mood, was the fact that
one of the great figures of the Czech political scene, Zdeněk of Sternberg, just at this time got into an open quarrel with the regent. The
issue itself had nothing to do with the Hungarian events,[33] but it
seems that the timing did. The lord high burgrave always watched
with the utmost care the trend of events and the balance of forces
to be quite sure that he would never be on the losing side. For that
very reason Zdeněk shortly made his peace with George, even though
this meant that, in a cautious way, he had to admit a minor defeat.

But the time during which the King's power had seemed so firmly
established was to be short indeed. The hostile mood of the strong
majority of the Hungarian people soon turned to action. The Hunyadi party showed, only a few weeks after the death of its young
leader, that it was far from smashed or dead. Organized, with skill
and grim determination, by John Hunyadi's widow and her brother,
Michael Szilagyi, the rebellion was soon widespread, engulfing whole
provinces and conquering a growing number of the King's castles.[34]

31 See above, n.23.

32 See the report of Hans Kuchaym, the representative of the city council of Pressburg
(Bratislava), in Birk's "Beiträge," *Quellen und Forschungen*, 258.

33 It had to do with Zdeněks understanding of his rights and duties as a guardian of
orphans, in this case of the sons of Smiřický. See Urbánek, *Konec Ladislava*, 107–109.

34 See among standard histories of Hungary: Ignaz Fessler, *Geschichte von Ungarn*, Revised
Edition, ed. Klein, vol. II, Leipzig, 1869, 572ff., also W. Fraknói, *Mathias Corvinus*, Freiburg,
1891, pp. 33ff.

Even in the north Jiskra had no easy time holding his own. In May, in Buda itself, a crowd of fighters, by a bold stroke, succeeded in freeing most of the men whom the King had imprisoned in March. Even in his capital, the King clearly was no longer safe. He left—it might better be said he fled—and went to his beloved Vienna. Along with him went his one precious hostage—Matthias Hunyadi—in chains and guarded by Conrad Hölzler. The task—a most difficult and unenviable one—of recovering those large parts of Hungary now under the control of the Hunyadi party was left to Jiskra and Gara.

Back in Vienna the conflict with the Emperor again occupied the minds of the King and Hölzler. Far from losing its edge, the antagonism had been intensified by the death of the Count of Cilli, whose enormous possessions were claimed by Ladislav as his nearest relative and by the Emperor on the basis that, with the extinction of the line of a prince of the empire, his lands reverted to the empire. The struggle, as before, tended to impair the relationship between the King on the one hand, Eizinger and George of Poděbrady on the other. This had become obvious in January when George had called to Znojmo a diet of the estates of the Bohemian crown, including also an invitation to the estates of Austria, at which the struggle with the Emperor would have to play an important role. It was probably just for this reason (though perhaps also to emphasize his own constitutional rights) that Ladislav, on Hölzler's advise, had cancelled the diet.[35] Hölzler continued his attempts to sow distrust between George and the King by spreading rumors about George's friendship with Laszlo Hunyadi, to the extent that in June, soon after Ladislav's arrival in Vienna, George directly complained both to the King himself and to the Czech diet. The diet, as could have been expected, backed him fully, and even Ladislav was sufficiently cautious and informed about the situation in Bohemia to declare that he neither knew of nor believed in any such complicity.[36] At the same time, however, he invited the regent to come to Vienna for a general discussion of outstanding questions. George, upon the official advice of the diet, accepted the invitation.

There were two main issues which he knew would have to be discussed between himself and the King. One, ostensibly the most difficult one, concerned the struggle with the Emperor, still characterized by Ladislav's hope for Czech support in an open war, and by

[35] See Bachmann, *FRA*, XLII, 197f., and Kuchaym's report, *Quellen und Forschungen*, 232.
[36] Palacký, *FRA*, II, 20, 113.

George's wish for mediation leading to the maintenance of peace at this time. In reality, however, it was the second question which occupied the center of the stage: where was the young King to celebrate his impending wedding. This question had much greater significance than appeared on the surface.

The King's wedding plans had been under consideration for some time, possibly since the later part of 1456. It would surely be of political importance for his countries if the ties between Ladislav and the royal house of France could be strengthened. Then, for instance, France might help to defeat the attempts of Duke Philip the Good of Burgundy to absorb the duchy of Luxemburg, the only important fief that the crown of Bohemia, ever since the early fourteenth century, had held in Western Europe.[37] Such a marriage, therefore, would benefit Bohemia most of Ladislav's three countries. Thus George of Poděbrady had, from the beginning, had a hand in these plans, and one of the diplomats of his circle had actively participated in the negotiations conducted with Charles VII in Lyons sometime in the spring of 1457.[38] As a result it was arranged that Ladislav would marry, early in 1458, King Charles' daughter Madelaine.

But where would the wedding take place? Buda, capital of a country now rent by rebellion, was hardly considered. The King himself would have preferred Vienna, where he felt most at home. For the Czechs, on the other hand, Prague had to be the place. Prague was the "head of the Kingdom," Vienna only the head of a rather small duchy. The element of prestige in this issue should not be underrated.

Yet it is clear that for George himself, who now began to fight for Prague with grim and almost reckless determination, prestige was only a secondary consideration. The main thought behind George's demand was that he wanted to have the King in Prague—as soon as possible and for as long as possible.

The reasons are obvious. George could feel that he had got along well with the boy-king who had been his young friend and "son" in 1453 and 1454. Ever since then the King had been in the hands of men who were far from being George's friends. Cilli, indeed, might have become very dangerous if he had been successful. With

---

[37] About this complex issue see best Urbánek, *Dvě studie*, 26–34, 84–90.
[38] He was Frederick of Donim (or Dohna, from an originally Saxon family). See the letter of Charles VII to George in *FRA*, XX, 123.

Hölzler, however, a man had got hold of this immensely powerful position who was, for all we know, a more decent human being than the Count of Cilli, but who was more direct, clumsier, and possessed of a much more limited horizon. George, of course, was a Czech first and foremost, but he could also understand the wider interests and needs of the three crowns to the extent that he would want to avoid or compromise potential clashes. Hölzler, hardly looking beyond the interests of Austria, was willing to challenge these issues head-on. Trusting the support he had from the people of Vienna he had already made an enemy of the estates among whom Eizinger's leadership was still essentially unquestioned. In the further process he might bring about clashes in Austria and Bohemia not unlike those that were now torturing Hungary. In the end it was the King who would suffer most, and thus George, in trying to free him from this influence, could really feel that what he did was in the King's best interest. Yet we may assume that, in his mind, even this was secondary compared to those interests with which he had long identified himself most completely—the Czech nation and state. A renewal of the bitter internal fight, happily buried by his purposive blending of strength and moderation, had to be avoided at all costs, so that the reconstruction and reformation of the state, started so auspiciously, could continue.

But could he really hope to regain the King's confidence and cooperation after the years during which Ladislav had been under strong, strange, and in the end even openly hostile influences? The King, still a child when George had released him from his tutelage early in 1455, was now a young man who had shown his cold blood and his capacity for quick and ruthless action. Would he now bend to the older man's stronger hand and greater experience? And what, especially, if the regent's appointed term was completed and, in view of the King's having reached his majority, would no longer be renewed? Could George still count on remaining, after the King, the first man of the kingdom and thus finish his great task?

The answer to these questions, George must have thought, was yes. If there was one thing about which he was free of doubt it was his ability to win, persuade, influence, and direct people, even those very reluctant to be thus won and influenced. Again and again he showed this capacity to an often amazing degree. Most of the time it would serve him splendidly. In a few cases he would be mistaken, in that the influence had not worked, and he would have to suffer the consequences. In this case he was hardly mistaken.

But before he could even try to regain the King's confidence and friendship he had to regain the King himself. This proved to be a difficult task indeed, all the more difficult for the extreme distrust between George and Hölzler. Thus when George, accompanied by Eizinger, arrived near Vienna with a strong cavalry escort he refused to enter the city and asked the King to meet him before the gates. The memory of things that had recently happened on both sides—first to Cilli and later to Laszlo Hunyadi—could not easily be erased, not even by letters of safe conduct. The long negotiations which then took place, starting at the beginning of August, first on a bridge across the Danube, later at Klosterneuburg,[39] were also attended by Archduke Albert of Austria and two Bavarian dukes. The presence of the Emperor's brother indicated that the struggle between Ladislav and Frederick III was among the issues discussed. All three princes, just as the King's Czech councillors, among them Zdeněk of Sternberg, now reconciled with George, and Prokop of Rabstein, urged Ladislav to accept George's demand and go to Prague. But only in the second half of August, after George had angrily left his quarters, did the King finally promise to George his early departure for Prague. There he arrived, accompanied by Eizinger and Hölzler (who thereby showed more courage than wisdom) on September 29th, and was solemnly greeted by George, the heads of the nobility, and those of the two churches.[40] (He barely acknowledged Rokycana's greetings, even that only upon George's urging.)

Hölzler's fate as the King's chief adviser was sealed as soon as the plans were worked out for the great embassy which should solemnly conduct Princess Madelaine to Prague. Zdeněk of Sternberg was to lead it, with several members of the high nobility and high clergy representing Bohemia, Hungary, Austria, and also Luxemburg. Earlier, in Vienna, Hölzler, as the King's treasurer, had declared that the cost of the mission had all been taken care of. Now, however, he admitted that the money was not there, because royal income expected by him had not materialized. He could not have put himself into a worse position, and when he tried to offer very unconvincing apologies before the royal council not even Ladislav tried to save him.

[39] See Urbánek, *Konec Ladislava*, 111–113.
[40] See *SLČP*, 150f.

He was sentenced to prison, and his large estates, gained in a long and profitable service as Austrian treasurer, were confiscated in favor of the King. His great career and historical role was over, though after some months he was allowed by George—generally not a vindictive man—to return to Austria.[41]

The confiscation of Hölzler's estates had an indirect bearing on the fate of Matthias Hunyadi, who had lately been kept, by one of Hölzler's burgraves, at his castle of Lengbach. The King, no longer able to make Hölzler responsible for the fate of his most valuable hostage, ordered the young prisoner to be brought to Prague.[42]

One of the immediate consequences of Hölzler's fall was a change in Ladislav's policy toward the Emperor. It is hardly likely that his feelings had changed, but by this time he must have been aware of the weakness of his position as revealed by his inability to get support for his warlike policy from the estates of any of his countries. As a result Ulrich Eizinger was permitted to go to Austria and resume negotiations for a settlement of the various issues pending between the two rulers, including that of Cilli's heritage. Early in November he achieved a compromise which the Emperor approved and which, it was hoped, the King, once again with George as his chief adviser, would accept. The arrangement, in any case, was expected to make it possible for the Emperor, together with many other kings and princes, to attend King Ladislav's wedding.[43]

Preparations for this great occasion occupied much of the King's time in the following weeks. Meantime the relationship between him and the regent assumed, at least in the eyes of foreign observers, much if not all of the old warmth and friendship. George, as in the past, used great caution as soon as religious issues came to the fore. He tried to calm down popular discontent when King Ladislav gave the appearance of a great Catholic and perhaps anti-Hussite demonstration to the introduction of John Rabstein, the Chancellor's younger brother, as Provost of Vyšehrad. George, as Master of the Royal Court, introduced some Czechs again into the King's service,

---

[41] Urbánek, *op. cit.*, 116f., and Tomek, *Děiepis*, VI 262. For a mention of the quite modest role played by him later see Vancsa, *Geschichte Nieder- und Oberösterreichs*, II, 492.

[42] It seems rather improbable (as was later assumed by critics of George) that this decision was much influenced by the Czech regent. It is much more likely that Ladislav was very eager to retain full control of this prisoner who, in view of the Hungarian situation, must have seemed to him an invaluable hostage. Matthias' arrival in Prague just on the day of Ladislav's death can hardly have been anything but incidental. About the King's order to fetch Matthias from Lengbach Castle see Urbánek, *Konec Ladislava*, 136 n. 3.

[43] About the negotiations, see Aeneas Sylvius, *Historia Friderici*, 469.

since Ladislav had come to Prague only with German-Austrian chamberlains and attendants.

One of our more important sources for these days is Peter Eschenloer, Breslau's town secretary and member of an embassy which the city council of that town had sent to Prague to represent her in a lawsuit over tolls or customs against the Lusatian city of Görlitz (Zhořelec). He reports that George, whose influence upon Ladislav appears to him immensely strong,[44] tried to prevent the young King from showing to the Breslau delegation his gracious feelings.[45] That George's own feelings toward the city were anything but gracious cannot be doubted. Ever since the end of the struggle over the homage to Ladislav, the city had shown its hostility to George in the most insulting ways. When he had asked them for war material to help destroy one of the most dangerous brigands of the region they had denied it to him even though it would have been in their own interest. They repudiated a treaty about mutual acceptance of coins which they had concluded with him. And they alone of all his Silesians neighbors had refused to pay him the usual neighborly visit of welcome when he came first to his county of Glatz.[46]

The city, aware that under the present conditions Ladislav might not protect them effectively against George's anger, now tried to make up with the regent. They offered him a special present—a number of oxen. It was, probably, less the present than his wish to avoid any unnecessary tension that made George agree to a reconciliation. But, as Eschenloer said, "the friendship did not last long."[47]

It was on November 19 that the King and George gave the audience to the Breslau delegation. On the day after the King began to show symptoms of illness:[48] a severe headache (though a strongly

[44] "Miser adislaus," so he says in his Latin version (SrS, VII, 5), "amabat Georgium ad suum interitum, surgit inter ambos mutua relacio: Ladislaus patrem Georgium, Georgius Ladislaum appellat filium." (But, so he says, George, under this semblance of love, harbored treacherous intentions."

[45] Ibid., VII, 15.

[46] Ibid., VII, 9.

[47] Eschenloer, G., I., 41.

[48] The sickness and death of Ladislav, and the question whether his death was natural or not, soon became what must be called a cause célèbre. Instead of giving here a bibliography of the sources, contemporary and near-contemporary, and the later discussions, which would have to be unduly long, I limit this to mentioning those books or articles concentrating on the issue and, most of them, giving a bibliographic survey. They are in chronological order:

a. Palacký, Zeugenverhör über den Tod König Ladislaws, Abhandl. d. Kgl. Böhm. Gesellschaft d. Wissenschaften, Prague, 1856.

b. E. W. Kanter, Die Ermordung König Ladislaws, Munich, 1906 (a highly biased pamphlet, not a serious historical investigation).

melancholy mood, reported even for preceding days, may well have
been such a symptom too). On the following day, a Monday, the
King still went to preside at a meeting of the State Supreme Court,
but complained that he could not bear ordinary clothing on his body
which seems to have begun to swell. In the evening, if not earlier,
two bubonic boils appeared in his groins. Of the two Austrian
physicians who belonged to his court, one did not think the King to
be in any danger. The other took a more serious view, without, however, diagnosing bubonic plague. Their treatment with purgatives,
emetics, and bloodletting was not of any help. Throughout Tuesday
and early Wednesday the King fought his constantly worsening illness. Eventually, convinced that he was about to die, he called the
regent and, before many witnesses, put the care for his subjects into
his hands. He also asked him to permit his Austrian courtiers free
return to their country. He died toward four o'clock in the afternoon,
just three days after the beginning of the illness, 17 years and 9
months old. His death was sincerely mourned, even by the Utraquist majority of the Prague population. It was a shock, too, for his
many subjects outside the capital. And the circumstances as well as
the consequences of his death seemed so extraordinary, in particular
so extraordinarily favorable to a few men, that soon many people
had no doubts at all: King Ladislav of Bohemia and Hungary could
not have died a natural death. He must have been murdered.

c. V. Novotný, "Ueber den Tod des Königs Ladislaus Posthumus," *Věstnik k. č. společnosti
nauk,* Prague, 1906, X.
d. R. Urbánek, *Konec Ladislava Pohrobka,* Rozpravy č. akademie věd, I, 67, Prague, 1924,
pp. 128–188.
e. G. Gellner, "Nemoc Ladislava Pohrobka," *Český časopis historický,* 1934.
f. F. G. Heymann, "The Death of King Ladislav," *Report of the Canadian Historical Association,* Ottawa, 1961, 96–111.

CHAPTER 8

GEORGIUS, DEI GRATIA BOHEMIAE REX

FOR THE last hundred years no serious historian who has studied the history of George of Poděbrady has come to the conclusion that he was a regicide. Yet if we consider the events that proceded and followed Ladislav's death, and the highly unusual role that George, all through these times, played both in reality and especially in the view of his contemporaries—then we can hardly be astonished that the story of the killing of King Ladislav was first invented, and then so widely believed.

The logic that created this story was this:

1. Healthy young Kings like Ladislav do not easily die a natural death after so short an illness.

2. Bubonic plague did not, at the time, appear in Bohemia in epidemic form (as it had, only a few months before, in neighboring Hungary). Why, then, should only Ladislav have become a victim of it?

3. The Austrian doctors, not having been able to make a proper diagnosis or to help the King, uttered, upon their return to Vienna, suspicions that he had been poisoned.

These three considerations seemed, by themselves, sufficient reason to assume a violent death, at least to those many people who were prejudiced from the beginning and who either could not or would not study the available medical evidence. And those sufficiently well informed about the pre-history of the King's death could and would consider it as additionally incriminating that the King had been induced, against his original wishes, to come to Prague in the fall of 1457.

But this was only the beginning. The next step was to ask whether anybody had profited from Ladislav's death, and the answer could be (and can still be) only in the affirmative. For it is obvious that, if King Ladislav had lived to a ripe age (and especially if he had had children) the following things could hardly have happened:

1. George could not have become King, his wife Johanna not become Queen of Bohemia.

2. Matthias Hunyadi, Ladislav's prisoner, could not have become King of Hungary—and his first wife Catherine, George's daughter, Queen—certainly not without further violent civil war.

3. The Emperor, Frederick III, would not have inherited the duchy of Austria from his young cousin who in time might have resumed a policy of unforgiving hostility toward him.

4. Ulrich Eizinger could not have continued his political activity in Austria in the ways that he did, that is in close cooperation with and under the strong protection of a powerful King of Bohemia.

5. The Hussite-Utraquist Church, led by John Rokycana, could not easily, under a devoutly Catholic King, have experienced the period of resurging strength, resuming even the offensive after a time of mostly defensive survival, that was granted to it during the reign of an Utraquist King.

In this list of events made possible only by Ladislav's death, we have mentioned the names of seven persons. All of them, with the exception only of the later Queen Catherine of Hungary, who was at the moment still only a child, were, more or less circumstantially, accused by contemporary antagonists of having, directly or indirectly, caused the death of the young ruler.

This accusation was not heard frequently against the Emperor, and Matthias Hunyadi himself could hardly have been very effective in poisoning or otherwise killing the King since, to the end of Ladislav's days, Hunyadi had been his prisoner. But Matthias was simply taken as representative of the Hunyadi party, and many remembered the claim that his older brother had tried to seize, possibly even kill the King. (Also it was now, after Ladislav's death, that rumors about George's part in the supposed Hunyadi conspiracy became much more positive.) Ulrich Eizinger, like the Emperor, with whom he had been negotiating at the critical time, had been far away and could, at worst, have been only an accessory. He, however, was the only man against whom steps were ever taken (by Archduke Albert) which were later, in defense of this arbitrary step (really directed against the Emperor by his brother), claimed to have been prompted by Ladislav's death.

The other three people—George and his wife ("der Girsik und die Girsikinne") and John Rokycana ("der Rockenzahn")—were all considered the real murders, not only singly but collectively. The stories spread around, especially in Vienna and Breslau, where Hölzler's and Capistrano's influence was still alive, and often took the melodramatic form of poems recited by street singers, poems in which the good and pure young Christian Prince and King was killed (but not necessarily always poisoned, as throttling, for instance, seemed more dramatic) by the sinister heretics, perhaps with Rokycana in the lead. If, however, poisoning was the cause, then George's wife was a good guess, since supposedly murder by poison is usually committed by women. The basic guilt still rested on him who became King, on George of Poděbrady.[1]

Two additional elements, probably, contributed most of the deep prejudice that in itself was the fertile soil in which rumors hostile to George could grow and strike root. They were nationalism and religious hate, both intimately interconnected: both "feelings against" rather than "for" something, and both, in their present vigor, going back to the Hussite Wars. Ever since then many of the German neighbors of the Czechs had identified "Czech" and "heretic," and thereby excluded both from what was assumed to be the community of good Christian men. Here, indeed, was the source for one of the worst misapprehensions operating against the Czech regent (as well as his friends and relatives): being a heretic, any crime could be expected of him. As a heretic he constantly betrayed God and Christ, and thus was sure also to betray his fellow man.

In reality, moral standards were very strict among the Hussite "heretics." There was still a good deal of the old Hussite puritanism alive. A man like Rokycana, while perhaps relieved that God had eliminated, at this moment, the danger of a strongly anti-Hussite ruler, would constitutionally and on the grounds of his religious philosophy have been quite unable to condone, let alone abet or commit a crime as heinous as regicide. Indeed I believe we can say that, for all his own religious prejudices and his strong convictions that George, by God's will, was the right man to rule his nation, Rokycana would not have made the tremendous and highly effective effort in favor of his election if he had known, or suspected, that the path to such an election had been cleared by murder. But if then, in historical reality, the suspects' religion is one more element contro-

---

[1] See again the works quoted in Chapter VII, n. 48, with their bibliographical material. About the works of popular poetry dealing with these events see also H. Kraus, *Husitství v literatuře, zejména německé*, I, Prague, 1917, 106ff. For an especially dramatic versification see the poem quoted (but not taken seriously) by the "Anonymi Chronicon Austriacum," Senckenberg, *Selecta*, V, 42–49.

verting the suspicion, in the minds of many of their Catholic contemporaries it was the strongest of all incriminating circumstances.
(And to some extent it continued, together with a more clearly developing nationalism, to play this role in studies right down into the
nineteenth century.)[2]

The popular rumors, songs, and tales, especially in Austria, had
by the year's end assumed such proportion that George decided to
launch an official protest with the Austrian estates through one of
his principal diplomatic aides, Jost of Einsiedel, accompanied by Beneš
of Veitmil. Einsiedel declared that a bishop, several councillors,
chamberlains, and physicians had been in the King's presence and
could bear witness against this rumor, added a reference to the
Czech's love for their King, and demanded that steps be taken to
stop the spread of such rumors. The estates, emphasizing that they
had no doubt about the natural causes of the King's death, asked
the Czech embassy not to pay too much attention to attacks from
such low quarters which it was difficult to stop. Actually some measures were taken by the Viennese city council to silence the street
singers, but we know little about their effectiveness.[3] In any case
this was the only time that George made any attempt to counteract
this sort of propaganda by official denial. From now on, it seems,
the rumors were consistently disregarded.[4]

In the unsettled situation that arose after Ladislav's death George's
first concern was to make sure of continued domestic peace and
order. For this purpose he immediately called a meeting of the country's high officials, members of the nobility, and the city councillors
of Prague to inform them that he was going to call a diet for mid-
December and that meanwhile he would continue to act as regent.[5]
On the basis of previous arrangements his term would have lasted
for another two and a half years, till spring 1460. But with the King's
death it might be considered that these arrangements, though confirmed by the estates, were no longer valid.[6] A similar conference

[2] As an example, in addition to those quoted in my monograph "The death of King
Ladislav," see e.g. the attitude of Prince E. M. Lichnowsky in his *Geschichte des Hauses
Habsburg*, VI, Vienna, 1842, 187.

[3] About the Czech demarche and Einsiedel's speech see Palacký, *Zeugenverhör*, 9ff.

[4] Presumably upon George's order. See *ibid.*, 15.

[5] For his action at this stage see especially Urbánek, *Volba Jiřího z Poděbrad za krále
českého* (Sborník přispěvku k dějinám hl. města Prahy, vol. V,) Prague, 1932, pp. 642ff.
(Later cited as Urbánek, *Volba*.)

[6] The documents giving the terms for which George received confirmations of his regency
by the estates and the King seem somewhat contradictory. See e.g. Urbánek, *Věk*, II, 710 and
795f., and *AČ*, XV, 212.

was called by the regent soon after the solemn funeral, also with those representatives of the dependent countries who happened to be in Prague, among them those of Breslau.

But the great issue, obviously, was the succession. And there is little doubt that George, almost immediately, considered himself a candidate for this high office. He was an ambitious man, and one who had every reason to look upon his career and his achievements with a good deal of pride. But he knew that there was still much left to be done, and that it all might be endangered by a foreign king who would try to rule without his (George's) guidance and without his broad basis of popular support, especially among the Hussite majority. George was a brilliant and strong man who could make up his mind quickly. Thus, there is nothing surprising in his quick understanding of the situation, the implication of which were obvious, or of the necessity for quick action if he was to be successful.[7]

This is especially true of his actions in regard to Hungary. It was even his duty—from a purely constitutional and diplomatic point of view—immediately to inform the estates of Ladislav's other great kingdom of the death of their King. He knew also that in Hungary Ladislav had retained little of that popularity that he had, largely by George's help, maintained in Bohemia even among a considerable part of the Utraquists. (Indeed the King's death was, in Hungary, frequently interpreted as God's punishment for the judicial murder of Laszlo Hunyadi.)

It was also easy to see that the Hunyadi party, comprising men who had all along been good friends to George and whose interests had paralleled his own more closely than the King's and Gara's party, was sure to gain in influence by the fact that the throne had become vacant. Clearly the Hunyadi party would not retreat just when their chances—which had almost constantly improved since the execution of Laszlo—were now so vastly improved.

Thus it was almost a matter of course that George—who had all along disapproved of the way in which Ladislav had treated the sons of his old friend John Hunyadi—would not continue to treat young Matthias as a prisoner. He was, indeed, immediately received into George's house as an honored guest. And at an early time George broached the question of a future marriage between his daughter

---

[7] This has to be emphasized in view of the tendencies of some historians to find this swift reaction "surprising." See e.g. Bachmann "Ein Jahr böhmischer Geschichte," in *AÖG*, LIV, Vienna, 1876, 77f., and using these passages as another proof for George's supposed criminal guilt: Kanter, *Die Ermordung K. Ladislavs*, 49ff.

Catherine and young Matthias. Clearly it was the future King of Hungary whom George desired as his son-in-law. That this splendid future was "in the cards" for Matthias was confirmed to the Czech regent when, three weeks after George's first communication was sent to Buda, Bishop John Vitéz of Nagyvarád (Oradea), long the main friend of the Hunyadis among the high clergy of Hungary, arrived in Prague to discuss the question of George's help for young Matthias' election.[8] The bishop could, incidentally, point to a support even weightier than his own: that of Cardinal Carvajal, still the Pope's legate in Hungary.[9]

It is hardly exaggeration to say that George, more than any other individual, "made" Matthias King of Hungary. True, it was not within his power to provide the broad popular support without which "the young gubernator"—as he was still called after his father—could not have obtained his election or maintained his rule. But in the first place Matthias was in his hands, and if there had been ill-will, he could have stayed there for a long time. In the second place George gave him a considerable and, in the outcome, perhaps decisive support in the weeks before his election. The very fact that this powerful man stood behind Matthias heartened his supporters and tended to discourage his adversaries. But there were at least two strong and important potential adversaries with whom George wielded some personal influence. The first of these was Ujlaki, with whom George had maintained some contact since they had sealed their friendship by promising each other the marriage of one of George's sons with Ujlaki's daughter.[10] The second, no less important, was John Jiskra, long now a Hungarian magnate with considerable landed property in the north, yet even now retaining some of the pride in his Czech ancestry and on good terms with the leading Czech statesman. George was not able to induce either of the two men to come all out for Matthias, and this, surely, would have been asked too much especially in the case of Jiskra. But both stayed away from the diet that, later in January 1458, was to elect Matthias, thereby depriving what had once been the legitimist party of Count Cilli of two of their three strongest pillars.[11] The third,

---

[8] See Urbánek, *Věk*, III, 249f.

[9] See W. Fraknoi, "Cardinal Carvajal's Legationen in Ungarn," in *Ungarische Revue*, X, 1890, 1–18, 124–143, 399–425, and about this specific phase, p. 139ff.

[10] Urbánek, *Věk*, III, 250.

[11] For a detailed discussion of Matthias' election see Urbánek, *Volba*, 674ff. George's letter to Jiskra in favor of Matthias published V. Chaloupecký, *Středověké listy ze Slovenska*, Prague-Bratislava, 1937, pp. 90f.

the Palatin Gara (whose position paralleled that of the lord high burgrave in Bohemia), had himself hoped for the crown but soon discovered that he lacked the needed support, and was finally won over by the leaders of the Hunyadi party—John Hunyadi's widow and her brother Szilagyi—who offered the hand of the future King to Gara's daughter. This arrangement was solemnly sworn to by the Hunyadis, and thus created renewed bitterness and hatred when it was later repudiated by the young King himself who, for good reasons, preferred to honor the promise he had given himself: to marry the daughter of the man about to become King of Bohemia.

While not quite as crucial as for Matthias, the gains for George were nevertheless highly important, though not all of them could have been foreseen at the time. The most obvious, perhaps, was the basic fact that Ladislav's death, in one of his two kingdoms, resulted in the free election of a young nobleman of far from princely origin, without the least regard to the hereditary claims either of the Habsburg dukes (with the Emperor in the lead) or of Ladislav's two sisters and their husbands, of whom at least one, King Casimir IV of Poland, tried in vain to reverse the trend that had begun to run in Matthias' favor. The constitutional situation in Hungary was extraordinarily similar to that in Bohemia, and a free election in one of the two countries might well foreshadow and facilitate the same event in the other.

The whole issue of the succession to Ladislav in the light of the development of the Czech constitution is rather complex.[12] Those in favor of a hereditary succession as well as those claiming for the Czech estates the right or electing a new King could both refer to the order of succession established in 1348 by Charles IV and confirmed by the estates at that time. According to it, the succession belonged to the men—or, if none survived, the women—of the royal house of Luxemburg. If neither of them survived, a diet of the whole crown (that is including the dependencies) was to elect a new King. But in addition to this Charles had, in 1364, concluded with Duke Rudolf IV a mutual agreement of inheritance between the houses of Luxemburg and Habsburg which had also been recognized by the Czech estates.

The latter, perhaps, was less doubtful in its implication than the former and might have been pursued with greater determination

---

[12] See Urbánek, *Volba*, 642–674, and in less detail Bachmann, *Geschichte Böhmens*, II, 466ff., and *Ein Jahr böhmischer Geschichte*, 59ff.

by a more vigorous head of the Habsburg family than was the Emperor. In fact, he limited his claims to Austria, to which certainly no one but the Habsburg family had any really valid claims, but even there Frederick III had severe troubles through the disagreements which broke out immediately between himself and the other male princes of his house: his brother, Archduke Albert, and his cousin, Duke Sigismund.[13]

Far more determined and active was Duke William of Saxony.[14] His claim was based on that of his wife, Anne, the older of King Ladislav's two sisters. (Weaker, for that reason, was the claim of the younger sister Elizabeth, only recently married to King Casimir IV of Poland.) While Ladislav's sisters were Habsburgs through their father, they could, through their mother, who was the only offspring of the Emperor Sigismund, claim descent from the house of Luxemburg. For a while it did, indeed, look as if William, as Anne's husband, had a better chance than anybody else to achieve recognition of his claims, at least by the other potential or real hereditary candidates. In particular he was supported by his brother, Elector Frederick, with whom he was now fully reconciled, and by the Margraves of Brandenburg. But he also had support in parts of Lusatia and in Silesia, and there especially he soon began to solicit support with great energy. When, late in December, he also wrote to George with the request for his support he received a rather cool answer. The decision, the regent declared, was not his but rested with the estates, who would soon be called together, and to this diet the duke was also free to send his ambassadors. He should, however, refrain from trying to gain special influence with the Silesian cities and princes who had long supported the crown of Bohemia.[15]

George's declaration, referring the duke to the decision of the estates, could conceivably have meant it was up to them to decide who among the candidates had the strongest hereditary claims. But in reality, of course, George meant the opposite: the crown of Bo-

[13] See H. v. Zeissberg, "Der österreichische Erbfolgestreit nach dem Tode des Königs Ladislaus," *AÖG*, LXVIII, Vienna, 1879, 69ff.

[14] William's position and policy are the subjects of an extraordinary detailed study by Urbánek. See his "Kandidatura Viléma Saského na český trůn," in his *Dvě studie o době poděbradské* (Spisy filos. fakulty Masarykovy university v Brně, No. 27), Brno, 1929 (generally cited as *Dvě studie*). The work is, however, wider than its title indicates and treats with great precision the whole struggle for the recognition of George's kingship.

[15] See *FRA* II, 20, 120.

hemia, at this stage, was open to free election by the Estates of the kingdom.

The constitutional development which served as the basis for this view had revolutionary origin, but had received the sanction of factual recognition by later Kings of Bohemia. The revolutionary origin can be traced first to the Diet (or, as I have called it previously, the National Assembly) of Čáslav of June 1421, where the estates of Bohemia and Moravia saw fit solemnly to depose King Sigismund of Luxemburg as an enemy of the Czech people.[16] The right to depose, there so emphatically assumed by the estates, had to be correlated to the right freely to elect, and this, too, was exercised, some months later, by a diet held in Kutná Hora, which chose Grand-Duke Witold of Lithuania as King of Bohemia. The election was accepted, though the grand-duke was never crowned and ruled only vicariously and temporarily through his relative Prince Korybut.[17] From then on no one, including Sigismund himself, had been able to assume the kingship without accepting specific conditions put by the estates to the King, and twice, in the cases of Casimir Jagiello and Albert of Bavaria, men without any hereditary claims had been elected, though eventually they had failed to exercise kingship. Altogether, then, there was a sequence of seven different acts essentially presupposing the right of free election, only one of them having been passed by a minority of the estates. In the other six cases the act itself, or the conditions imposed on the ruler, were backed by a majority—and not as a matter of historical accident.

This late medieval parliament reflected the strong majority which the adherents of the Hussite-Utraquist Church represented in Bohemia as well as in Moravia (though not in the other dependencies). It was this Utraquist majority, then, which was now determined not to give in either to the estates of the dependencies or to the small minority of the Bohemian estates proper who would have liked to cling to the hereditary principle. As had been shown during the negotiations with Ladislav (or Cilli) after the King's release this minority did by no means include all the great Catholic magnates. Not a few of them, headed by the Lords of Sternberg, had been just

---

[16] See my article "The National Assembly of Čáslav," in *Medievalia et Humanistica*, fasc. VIII, Boulder, 1954, also in a somewhat shorter version in my *Žižka*.

[17] See the most up-to-date treatment of Korybut's role in F. M. Bartoš, "Kníže Zikmund Korybutovič v Čechách," in *Sborník historický*, VI, Prague, 1959, also the chapter called "The Prince from Lithuania," in my *Žižka*.

as emphatic in backing the right of free election [18] as the late Lord
Ptáček of Pirkstein or, following his lead, George of Poděbrady
himself. The supporters of the hereditary principle, on the other
hand, were not in accord among themselves. Some of them were
ready to back William of Saxony, whereas others, led by the Lords
of Rosenberg, felt themselves bound by their old friendship to the
House of Habsburg. (Since the recent death of Henry of Rosenberg
the leadership had passed to his second brother, John, even though
their retired father, Ulrich, tried at this important moment to raise
his voice once more against his long-time enemy, George of Poděbrady.) [19]

Against this divided and thus weakened legitimate minority stood
a national majority which, at this moment, was united as it had
rarely been since the Hussite Wars. True there were Catholics among
its ranks, since George had always tried to avoid a national division
along strictly religious lines. Nevertheless the bulk of this national
party which was now demanding the renewal of a national, ethnically Czech kingdom, was provided by the Utraquist, and there was
now no other religious reform party or sect able to compete with
their strong and well-led organization. For them this was the great
opportunity. For the first time they could hope to elevate to the
highest rank a man who was both a Czech and a Utraquist. It is
said that at one time Rokycana played with the idea of having,
instead of a King, a rule of judges like ancient Israel.[20] If so, this
might have been a harking back to the epic radicalism of Old Tabor,
though Rokycana, a radical of a different type, had never had much
in common with Tabor. Conceivably it might also have been a hint
to George not to take the support of the Utraquist Church and the
masses behind it too much for granted. But Rokycana, even though
he may have been dissatisfied with the less than zealous support
which his claim for recognition as Archbishop of Prague had lately
found from George, was too much of churchman and statesman not
to see that only George could hope, as a Utraquist, to reign over the
kingdom of Bohemia.

It was mostly through the activities of Rokycana and his chief
helpers (among whom was Martin Lupáč, the author of a highly
effective pamphlet in favor of George's election [21]) that the whole

---

[18] See Urbánek, *Věk*, III, 217, 240.

[19] *AČ*, VII, 234. See also Urbánek, *Dvě studie*, 162f.

[20] See Urbánek, *Volba*, 721. There (pp. 701–723) is the detailed history of the election
campaign.

[21] See the text in N. Tempelfeld's "Tractatus," ed. Loserth, *AÖG*. LXI (also special print,

campaign assumed, in its forms and implications, a truly democratic and thereby strangely modern aspect. There was a slowly but steadily growing "ground swell" in favor of George among the masses both in Prague and in the smaller cities and rural districts, and while this could directly, that is by way of future elections, influence only the members of the third curia—the representatives of the cities—there was nevertheless a strong psychological pressure also upon the other two curias. Among these, however, the gentry hardly needed such nudging because it had a Utraquist majority probably at least as strong as the cities. That the pressure was felt also among the lords is indicated by some of the reports of the events of the electoral diet which met in Prague on February 27, 1458, after the earlier diet in December had only dealt with some preliminaries.[22]

The character of this diet was not very clearly determined. It had not been officially designated as an electoral diet, though, in fact, few people could have doubted that this was its main if not only purpose. It was a general diet of the Bohemian crown to the extent that participation in it had been open to representatives of the dependent countries. Yet very few of them made any use of the opportunity; in the end only two Lusatian cities had sent representatives, and even they did not take part in the election itself but left before it began. It was not even certain whether they would have been permitted to vote if hey had stayed, since some of the members of the diet seem to have taken the somewhat strange stand that the succession law of Charles IV permitted the dependent countries to be formally represented by their presence but not by the voting of their delegations. (In the dependent countries themselves, on the other hand, and especially in Silesia, one would soon hear the view that an election performed only by the Czech estates was not valid or binding on the other parts of the Bohemian realm.) [23]

But the election itself could not take place without a struggle. Normally it was assumed that minorities would, in such cases, submit to the will of the majority and thus help to bring about a unanimous decision. Yet in a situation so novel and in certain respects so controversial, it could not be expected that opponents would yield too easily. This was especially true for the baronial estate. Once a

---

Vienna, 1880), 169 ff., and, in Czech, with introduction by the editor, in Urbánek's collection (partly translated into Czech) of all sources on George's election, publ. by the Čsl. Academy of Science, (*O volbě Jiřího z Poděbrad za krále českeho*, Prague, 1958), pp. 42–45.

22 See e.g. Bachmann, *FRA*, II, 42, 212f.

23 For the composition of the election diet see Urbánek, *Volba*, 725ff.

positive decision had been reached by the lords—of whom there were about thirty, a rather large representation of their caste—there was no doubt that the other two estates, with their much stronger majority belonging to the Poděbradian party, would follow suit. The task thus was to win over the die-hards among the lords adhering to the hereditary principle.

As said before not all the Catholic lords belonged to this group. Zdeněk of Sternberg, especially, was a resolute adherent to the principle of free election, which, he felt, might one day result in his own elevation to the throne. He had long been George's most important but by no means his most faithful adherent. He was usually willing to work with and for George as long as he thought that George had the best chance of coming out on top, and that, furthermore, cooperation would be handsomely rewarded.

Zdeněk had, only a few days before, returned from his great mission to France. On receiving the news of Ladislav's death he had suggested to King Charles VII that he offer one of his two sons as candidates for the Bohemian throne. While this, even more than the marriage of a French princess to a Czech King, might conceivably have served to help Bohemia retain the duchy of Luxemburg, now threatened by the expansion of Burgundy, Zdeněk's primary motive was probably different. Having invited another candidate to enter the field he could now demand an additional payment for switching back to George if this seemed necessary or convenient. Otherwise he, not George, would become and remain the king-maker, even if George, with another boy-king on the throne, might for the time being retain the regency.[24]

Charles VII had agreed to the plan, offering his son Charles as candidate, after Zdeněk had assured him that Ladislav's two sisters had no rights and that the election was entirely free. Once in Prague and present at the diet, the French ambassadors had to be heard, and heard first. Their offer was handsome, especially in financial terms, yet even so their chances were never great, since they could neither attract the adherents of strictly hereditary kingship, nor the Utraquist majority. The ambassadors of the Polish King and the Habsburg princes followed. Last were the ambassadors of Duke William. They felt that they had the best claim and they, too, were not stingy in their promises. In particular they could hold out the chance of a

[24] *Ibid.,* 727.

full return to Bohemia of the many towns, castles, and estates temporarily lost by her on both sides of the border. The Saxon delegates were, however, well enough informed to realize that their hopes were weak if they could not gain the support of the regent. Repeatedly but in vain they tried to obtain a personal interview with George. The diet listened to them and questioned them politely.[25]

After these unavoidable preludes, which also included the reading of the essential constitutional documents fetched from their safe-keeping in Karlstein Castle, the main problem was merely when and how it would be possible to gain the agreement of the small but by no means powerless minority to the choice already made by the great majority. The large and vocal crowds milling around the Old Town City Hall—whose great ceremonial chamber served the diet for its plenary meetings—must have impressed (and occasionally perhaps worried) the representatives. Yet the strong police measures taken by the regent in cooperation with the city council of the Old Town were certainly meant to provide protection for the diet rather than (as assumed later by some of George's adversaries) a threat to those not willing to vote for George.[26] On the other hand there can be little doubt that other attempts were made to overcome their resistance, especially promises of financial and political rewards which were presumably not very far from bribes. Of a different character and less open to criticism (though not less modern) was a list of assurances and guarantees for the freedom of their religion which the Catholic lords submitted to the regent and which the latter did not find too difficult to accept.[27]

The last barrier was almost a personal one. John of Rosenberg, now head of the great clan and generally a sincere, decent, but rather stubborn man, claimed to be bound by his honor to keep his promises to the Habsburg dynasty. Zdeněk of Sternberg finally, with con-

---

[25] See their reports home in *FRA*, II, 20, 129ff.

[26] Against reports or interpretations indicating a policy of intimidation by the Poděbradian party (see e.g. Bachmann, *Geschichte Böhmens*, II, 480f.) we have the testimony of Eschenloer, certainly far from a friend of George's and very unhappy about his election, who says (in his German *Geschichten*, I, 47) "Viel Reden entstunden aus dieser Kure, wie sie durch Gewalt geschehen were . . . Oder man konnte es nicht darnach erkennen, sondern alle Behmen. . . . beide unter dem Gehorsam des römischen Stuls und unter Rokiczans Secta, waren eintrechtig und frei in dieser Kur."

[27] See Urbánek, *Volba*, 738ff., on the inducements or promises given. Immediately following this is the detailed presentation of the events of the election. See Urbánek's source collection cited above in n. 21, and the entry into the city register of the Old Town of Prague as reproduced in B. Kut's edition: *Ceskoslovenské dějiny v archivních dokumentech*, I, Prague, 1961, p. XXXIXff.

siderable effort, overcame John's reluctance. Once he had given in all other resistance crumbled fast.

It was again the lord high burgrave who, on the afternoon of March 2nd, pronounced the decision of the assembly with the words "The Lord Regent shall be our King," and who then, kneeling before George, called the words, immediately taken up by the assembly: "Long live George, King of the Czechs." All those present then followed Sternberg's example and vowed that they would be faithful subjects, while George, in a short speech of acceptance and thanks, asked the men of the diet to grant him their advice and help for this task.

Greeted by wildly enthusiastic crowds, the new King was now taken, amidst the ringing of bells, to the Týn Church—the "Hussite Cathedral"—where the *Te deum* was sung and where Rokycana gave thanks to God for this happy choice. Then, with the sword of the kingdom carried before him by the lord marshal, King George was taken to the royal palace in the Old Town of Prague. A new chapter in Czech history had begun.

Yet the election did not, by itself, establish the King's position in a fully valid form. This could only be done by the coronation. Only its mystical power elevated the ordinary human to the superhuman rank of a true King. Therefore an early coronation was of the greatest importance to George, who would not feel secure on his throne without it. Those who had fought his election as enemies or competitors could still see some hope if a valid coronation could be prevented. Thus the question of the coronation was intimately interconnected with that of George's recognition at home and abroad.

In Bohemia itself, of course, there was no longer any problem of recognition since he had received the votes even of those who had at first been most reluctant to take that step. John of Rosenberg especially, once he had pledged his support to George, proved to be a reliable friend even though he was harshly reproached by his father Ulrich for not having sought the crown for himself and his great house.[28]

Not so simple, however, was the question of recognition in the case of the dependent countries. In all of them there was at least some resentment that the election had taken place without their having been represented at all. In Silesia and the two Lusatias, where

[28] Urbánek, *Dvě studie*, 162f.

sentiment for William of Saxony had been strong, things were much worse, and there could, at the moment, be no certainty that this conflict might not lead to their secession from the mother country. Finally, outside the Bohemian realm there was, with the exception of Hungary under its young King Matthias, hardly any place where it looked as if George could hope for a friendly or even only a neutral reception. It was a chilling situation which might well have frightened a weaker man.

George, far from frightened, immediately took the initiative. Announcements about the election, together with the request for recognition, went out from George himself as well as from the Czech estates, to the princes, estates, and cities in the dependent countries. In Silesia and Lusatia, the success of such steps was at first anything but promising. In mid-April most of the princes and estates of Lower Silesia, (but not those of Upper Silesia) having listened to the arguments of the embassies of the King as well as those of William of Saxony and the Habsburg princes, concluded an agreement with one another according to which they would "not recognize or accept anybody as King, until they have learned from the proper authorities whom they should under God, and with regard to honor and law, accept as a true Christian Lord and King." [29] In Breslau, where George had sent an especially splendid embassy in the hope of thereby strengthening the elements less hostile to him, the Czech noblemen had to be heavily guarded by the city council to protect them from the fury of the people to whom they (all of them Catholics) were nothing but heretics and regicides. This was the beginning of the grim, prolonged struggle which later will occupy our attention in some detail.

Even in Moravia, so near to Bohemia in its general structure, there was some resistance. True, the country's largely Utraquist barons and gentry, at a diet held in Brno in April—after a protest against the fact that the election had taken place without them and a request for confirmaion of their rights and freedoms—acknowledged George as King and declared him officially elected as margrave of Moravia. [30] There was, however, some substantial resistance against George from four of the larger cities, Brno itself, Olomouc, Znojmo, and Jihlava. All of these were predominantly German and Catholic, and in all of them the Habsburg tradition had already taken root in the time of

---

[29] See *SrS.*, VII, 25.
[30] Concerning the Brno diet where this occurred see Urbánek *Věk*, III, 332ff.

the Hussite Wars. The Emperor's brother, Archduke Albert, now tried by all means at his disposal, including the dispatch of troops, to strengthen his chances in Moravia and especially in those four cities. His chances ever to become King of Bohemia had, by this time, certainly become extremely weak. But it seems that he underrated the cohesion between the margraviate and the kingdom, and in view of the events during the Hussite Wars, when large parts of southern Moravia had frequently been under the control of an older Albert, Sigismund's son-in-law, he hoped to be able to separate Moravia from Bohemia. This, of course, was a serious challenge and could not fail to provoke sharp counterstrokes by George.

But possibly the military preparations or actions of Archduke Albert of Austria were less dangerous to George than the diplomatic activities of his namesake of Brandenburg, the Margrave Albert Achilles.[31] His strong interest in the matter was probably based less on his friendship for William of Saxony than on his correct understanding of what George's general recognition (nearly unavoidable as it would be after a canonical coronation) would mean for the future role of this King and his Bohemia in all of Central Europe and especially in the Holy Roman Empire. Margrave Albert had met George and, it seems, had not disliked him as a person, but he did not want to have this huge energy let loose in the most strategic corner of his own world if he could help it. It would have just as much influence on such issues as Brandenburg's hold over Lower Lusatia as it would on the position of his own territories in Franconia. Thus he argues, in letters to the Saxon dukes, that above all it was necessary to prevent such men as the new Bishop Jost of Breslau, one of the Rosenbergs and a good Catholic but also a good Czech, or Bishop John Vitéz of Nagyvárad, the foremost cleric of the Hunyadi party in Hungary, from crowning the supposed usurper of the Czech throne. If all this was not successful, the attempt could still be made to deny George recognition as the ranking electoral prince of the empire.[32]

Margrave Albert's demarche, immediately followed up by a diplomatic step of Frederick of Saxony, shows his shrewd understanding for the real difficulties faced by George. At the moment, the archbishopric of Prague and the bishopric of Litomyšl were both offi-

---

[31] Concerning his relation to Bohemia, see *ibid.*, 413ff., also Droysen, *Geschichte der preussishen Politik*, 2nd ed., II, Leipzig, 1868, 113ff.

[32] See the documents in M. Jordan, *Das Königthum Georg's von Poděbrad*, Leipzig, 1861, pp. 429ff.

cially vacant (since Rokycana's position and those of his suffragan bishops had not been confirmed). The Bishop of Olomouc, Tas (or Prothassius) of Boskovice, had only recently been elected and had not yet received his consecration. If, therefore, it was possible to prevent Jost of Breslau and the Hungarian bishops from crowning George, he certainly would be in a highly difficult position, since it was obvious that coronation by Utraquist bishops, Rokycana or Lupáč, would never be considered outside Bohemia as anything but a piece of presumptuous and invalid heretical play-acting.

Only in one thing were Margrave Albert and his friends mistaken: in regarding Bishop Vitéz as the only Hungarian prelate who might go to Prague. And this mistake was based upon their insufficient understanding of the specific and peculiar stage which had been reached in the relationship between George and the Roman Curia. For its clarification we have to go back to earlier times.

We have discussed and tried to characterize the Basel Compacts at the very beginning of our account. We have pointed out that it was a compromise whose chance of success had largely depended on the vagueness and, in a sense, ambiguity of its terms, especially those referring to the Chalice. We have shown the reservations carefully built-in by the negotiators of the Council, and based on them the ever-present danger that either side might try to press its own understanding upon the other. This danger, however, was from the beginning far greater on the Catholic side, which would always feel tempted, if it could, or if it underrated the dangers inherent in such an action, to proceed toward a completely rigid and narrow interpretation of this peace instrument which would thereby destroy its very capacity to function as such.

While, in the first quarter-century after the conclusion of the Compacts, no serious attempt was made by Rome to challenge this precarious peace, the papacy had nevertheless consistently refused the Czech demand for a full recognition of the Compacts as the basis for mutual relations, and there had been no lack of utterances referring to acts or attitudes by which the Czech Utraquists themselves had supposedly infringed upon the Compacts. In general it might be said that all along there existed in the leadership of the Church the fear, not unjustified, that already the existing degree of ritual separation tended to make the split between the Utraquist Czechs and the Catholic world deeper and more permanent. It is perhaps characteristic that in Bohemia herself this pessimism was shown almost exclusively, but strongly, by part of the Catholic clergy, mainly among the Prague Cathedral Chapter, and there again with special vigor among some men who had begun their clerical careers as Utraquists.[33]

The Utraquist clergy, too, probably had a stronger feeling of belonging to a separate tradition from the Catholics than had the masses of laymen. Not that the feeling of separation was absent in thoughtful and intelligent Utraquist laymen. George's famous answer to Ladislav's court jester, related to us by Aeneas Sylvius, shows that he, too, was conscious of a significant difference.[34]

But in George's case as in that of many of the leading Utraquist laymen, this difference did not necessarily imply (as it did in the case of the clergy) a feeling of severe disapproval or even of hatred of the other side, just as it did not imply necessarily a belief in a permanent and unhealable schism. There was in him none of that who-is-not-for-me-is-against-me attitude which had characterized the man who, a generation earlier, had dominated the Czech scene, John Žižka; or later, but with equal hate-filled intolerance, George's and Rokycana's fiercest enemy, John of Capistrano. In George's special case it was perhaps his lively interest in and understanding for individual human beings which made him, not at all a religiously indifferent, yet truly a religiously tolerant man. It was the tolerance of someone who could still believe that even the person on the other side of the fence might be a good man and in that sense a Christian. This important humane attitude was indeed felt and warmly appreciated by some of his Catholic friends and adherents, people such as the man whom George had made the kingdom's chancellor, Prokop of Rabstein.

In view of the long-range development it was probably unfortunate that George's basic religious attitude was misunderstood and misinterpreted by the other of Prokop's two main friends and protectors, Aeneas Sylvius. George's obvious reasonableness made Aeneas think that the Czech leader was not a true Hussite, that his heterodoxy was superficial and based on political rather than religious grounds. This misunderstanding led to wrong expectations and, in the end, to unjustified and fateful disappointments on the side of the prelate. But at the present moment such expectations proved to be a great help for George.

Aeneas' estimate of George had, of course, been based on the meet-

---

[33] Above all Václav of Krumlov, who had become administrator of the Prague Cathedral Chapter. About him and his attitudes, among others, see Hrejsa, *Dějiny*, III, 95f., and Urbánek, *Věk*, III, 463ff.

[34] See above, chapter II, pp. 27, 28.

ing at Benešov in 1451, but at least as important for both men was
the renewal of their acquaintance at Wiener-Neustadt in 1455. It was
there that the all-important Turkish issue was introduced into their
relationship. From this moment on George figured in Aeneas'
thought as the man who not only could, if and when he wanted,
lead back his people to essential orthodoxy, but who also was much
needed, at the head of these strong, soldierly people, to help throw
the Turks out of Europe. George was not a man to overlook the
implications of Aeneas' attitude. The ambitious prelate, whether as
bishop, as cardinal or eventually as Pope, was as likely to need George
as George might need Aeneas' help. It can also be assumed that
Aeneas' own argumentation, presented in impressive detail to Pope
Calixtus III, did not remain a secret to George, since Aeneas, in his
role as mediator between the Czechs and the Holy See, would want
to win George's approval as well as that of the Pope.

This great speech,[35] in some ways a masterpiece of intelligent persuasion, went farther in recommending concessions to the Czechs
than had ever before been considered by the Church of Rome. Having surveyed the many reasons that coercing the Czechs toward full
unity had failed and was bound to fail again (how prophetically right
Aeneas here argued against his own later policy and that of his successor) he came to the conclusion, with the use of many of the arguments previously employed by the Czechs themselves in defense of
the Chalice, that a confirmation of the Compacts was the wisest policy and the one most likely to lead to true reunification.

The policy recommended by Aeneas Sylvius was not fully adopted.
There was no confirmation of the Compacts. It is tempting to speculate about what would have happened if Rome had taken this step.
Would it have prevented the new, bitter clash that occurred in the
later years of George's rule? Would it have led to a renewed split
within the Utraquist camp, between those who followed Rokycana's
substantial reformatory policy and those to whom reunion with Rome
was more important than most reforms as long as the Chalice itself
was granted? We can only know surely that at no time before or
after was there so much optimism for a permanent settlement on
both sides, in Rome and in Prague, than in the years following the
meeting of Wiener-Neustadt and Aeneas' great speech to Calixtus III,
and especially in the years 1457-1458. Calixtus himself, a less militant

---

[35] See the text in Mansi, *Pii II orationes politicae*, I, 352ff., and substantial summaries in
G. Voigt, *Enea Silvio*, II, 165–170, and H. Kaminsky, "Pius Aeneas among the Taborites,"
Church History, pp. 297–300.

character than some of his predecessors and successors, probably also held fewer prejudices against the Czechs than had his predecessors, partly because he was no longer so seriously concerned with the papal struggle against the Conciliar Movement, and partly because Aeneas Sylvius' arguments had impressed him sufficiently to make him hope for an effective Czech participation in the expected struggle with the Turks, about which he, like his successor, felt very strongly. Also, by the end of 1456, the most rabid and probably most influential enemy of any solution of the Czech church problem short of unconditional surrender, John of Capistrano, had left the scene. (Not before he had launched vigorous protests against what he assumed to be a probable betrayal of the principles of Catholicism in favor of the heretics.)[36]

The strength of the optimism now prevailing in Rome is perhaps best expressed in the letter which in late February 1458, just a few days before the election in Prague which he may well have anticipated as a serious and by no means disagreeable possibility, Pope Calixtus wrote to George of Poděbrady, welcoming enthusiastically the regent's announced willingness soon to send an embassy to Rome, assuring him of the warmest possible reception, and urging especially the inclusion of his "beloved son Johannes de Rokyczano" among the Czech ambassadors.[37]

This suggestion, incidentally, was not without piquancy at a time when in Austria, a country through which Rokycana would have to pass, the Utraquist churchman was just being castigated as a devilish regicide. Nor did the suggestion imply a readiness of the Holy See to confirm him as archbishop and, thereby, implicitly, give him authority over Czech Catholics. Rather was there still some hope in Rome that Rokycana might be satisfied with a substitute honor (possibly the cardinal's hat) and thereby free the way for the installation of a Catholic archbishop. (Aeneas Sylvius' own candidate was none other than Prokop of Rabstein.)

George, indeed, had known for a long time that there was practically no chance for Rokycana's confirmation. But he had every reason to hope that now, if ever, the long desired confirmation of the Compacts would be achieved. He knew that Aeneas Sylvius had recommended this. He knew that, harboring such welcome views about the solution of the Czech problem, the Bishop of Siena had recently been elevated to the exalted rank of cardinal. And why

---

[36] See Hofer, *Capestrano*, p. 550, and n. 65, 67.
[37] *FRA*, II, 20, 127f.

should the Pope look forward with such joy to the coming of a Czech embassy which, he could be sure, would ask for the confirmation of the Compacts, if he did not even consider such a measure as a way toward effective reunion? Indeed we find, in this spring of 1458, both the Curia and the newly elected King acting as if an understanding had already been reached—an understanding which George expected, in the main, to be the confirmation of the Compacts, and which the Curia, in the main, expected to be a visible approach by the Czechs toward Catholic orthodoxy under George's leadership. Only if we keep this peculiar situation in mind can we fully understand and correctly interpret the events that happened now.

In the difficult search for a bishop to officiate in his coronation, George, as correctly foreseen by Albert Achilles, turned to Hungary. He asked King Matthias (whose own coronation, incidentally, had met with difficulties because the holy crown of St. Stephen was still in the Emperor's hands) to help him in this matter. For the young King this was a welcome opportunity to show his future father-in-law both his good will and his power. He did, however, discuss the matter with Cardinal Carvajal, the papal legate, who had been a good friend to him and his family, who was vaguely (and somewhat unpleasantly) familiar with conditions in Bohemia, and who could also be expected to know the intentions and views of the Holy See. The fact that he was one of the very first prominent churchmen to congratulate George upon his election [38] seems to indicate that his views about George did not then deviate much from those of Aeneas Sylvius, though, in contrast to Aeneas, he never considered, let alone advocated, official recognition of the Compacts. Carvajal, indeed, did not object to Matthias' complying with George's wishes, though he also refrained from an explicit endorsement. But he recommended to the two bishops whom Matthias had in mind—Augustine of Rab and Vincent of Vacz—not to proceed with the coronation unless the King had solemnly forsworn all heresy and promised complete obedience to the Pope. This the bishops undertook to do. [39] It was to be a step of great consequences.

Even before the two bishops arrived in Prague early in May, the issue of the relations between the two churches and especially between the King and the Catholic Church had been taken up again by the Catholic barons. The discussion was somewhat protracted

[38] *Ibid.*, 140.
[39] See Fraknoi, 401ff.

since the barons tried to get specific guarantees which would not only have protected the freedom of Catholic worships (and of free accession of Catholic teachers and students to the University of Prague) but would even have tended to limit the Utraquists in their religious domain. The lords, eventually, had to be satisfied with a much more general promise of the King to protect them within the framework of the present status.[40]

But the real difficulty arose for George when, on one of the first days of May, the two bishops arrived in Prague and informed him of the conditional character of their mission. It is clear—especially from later comments of Cardinal Carvajal from whom the bishops had received their instructions—that they tried to induce George to make a declaration, which, at least implicitly, would have amounted to a definite abandonment of the Compacts, an act by which he would practically renege his whole religious past. Specifically he was asked to declare that he was renouncing all errors in favor of the true Catholic creed. But George vigorously refused to do this. He was not going to confess to any errors or heresies of his own (or, for that matter, of the Utraquist Church), especially in regard to the Compacts in general and to the communion in the two kinds in particular. To do this would not only have been an impossibility on the grounds of his own religious feelings—it would have destroyed the broad basis of his influence with the large Utraquist majority of his nation. He saw this clearly and tried his best to make the Hungarian bishops understand it too.

Yet he was sorely dependent on them. It can almost be said that they had him in their power, in this difficult and dangerous moment, and both sides knew it well enough. For if they had left with the public declaration that they could not crown him after all, since he was an unreformed heretic, he would still be backed by the Utraquists of Bohemia, but much less by his Catholic subjects. He would never find any recognition abroad, and would immediately and probably forever lose all the chances—which until recently had seemed so excellent—for a confirmation of the Compacts. Indeed it is difficult to imagine a worse collapse of all chances for a constructive solution of Bohemia's difficult domestic and foreign problems. His whole work, those ten successful years since his conquest of Prague, would probably have been for nothing. It was an outcome he had to avoid at almost any cost.[41]

---

[40] *FRA*, II, 42, 241. See also Urbánek, *Věk*, III, 347ff.

[41] The extraordinary power that, in this moment, the bishops had over George is, strangely,

Thus, while he remained adamant in his decision not to confess or condemn any supposed heresy of his own, George was willing, on the other hand, to go far in promising obedience to the Pope and conformity, in the way of other Christian Kings, with the teachings and rites of the Roman Church. He also agreed to the demand of the bishops that he promise to lead his people away from any errors, sectarian deviations, or heresies existing among them, and turn them back to true conformity and union with the Roman Church. A solemn oath embodying these points was worked out as a result of this precarious compromise.[42]

What did this oath signify? It certainly did not imply, as has often been alleged, that George had "converted."[43] He had not recanted anything, and, in particular, had strictly refused to renounce the Compacts without which religious peace in Bohemia was a lost cause. Neither the errors nor the sectarian deviations and heresies could have been identified with the content of the Compacts or the use of the Chalice by laymen. It was too obvious, and had only recently been argued by Aeneas Sylvius himself, that this had once been general Catholic usage, and that the Greek Church had never been reproached for this specific deviation. If one had to look for heresies in Bohemia

---

not fully realized in any of the fairly numerous discussions of George's coronation oath, such as Markgraf, *Das Verhältnis des K. Georg zu Pius II 1458–1462*, Breslau 1867, or the various works of Bachmann and Urbánek, or finally in Zdeněk Tobolka's monograph, *O volbě a korunování Jiřího z Poděbrad*, Prague, 1896.

[42] In view of the special importance of the oath I am quoting here the main part of it in its official Latin form as given by Raynaldus, *Annales Ecclesiasticae*, ed. J. D. Mansi, X, Luca, 1753, 147f.: "Ego Georgius, electus Rex Bohemiae inproximo coronandus, promitto . . . atque juro, . . . quod ab hinc et in antea et deinceps fidelis et obediens ero sacrosanctae Romanae et catholicae ecclesiae, ac sanctissimo domino nostro Callisto div. prov. Papae III ejusque successoribus . . . et eis obedientiam et conformitatem, more aliorum, catholicorum et Christianorum Regum, in unitate orthodoxae fidei, quam ipsa, s. Romana . . . ecclesia confitetur, praedicat et tenet fideliter observabo, ipsamque catholicam et orthodoxam fidem protegere, tueri, et defendere volo toto posse, populumque mihi subjectum secundum prudentiam a Deo mihi datam ab omnibus erroribus, sectis, et haeresibus, et ab aliis articulis s. Romanae ecclesiae et fidei catholicae contrariis, revocare et ad verae . . . fidei observationem ac obedientiam, conformitatem et unionem, ac ritum cultumque s. Romanae ecclesiae reducere et restituere volo. . . ."

[43] Such a conversion, occasionally assumed even by contemporaries (see *FRA*, II, 20, 151), was later claimed by several authors, notably by Bachmann (see "Ein Jahr böhm. Geschichte," 128, and *Geschichte Böhmens*, II, 488f.), who concludes from it that the King "lacked the force of religious conviction." Bachmann's view, surely mistaken, was also based on the equally mistaken assumption that George did, after all, expressly forswear "his heresy," though only orally and without written deposition. This he thought he could conclude from Carvajal's report to the Pope saying: "Abjuratio erroris non est scripta in juramento." But this simply states that the oath, contrary to his (Carvajal's) hopes, did not contain a passage forswearing the King's former error, not, however, anything to prove an oral forswearing of such errors (see *SrS*, VIII, 7f., Bachmann, *Reichsgeschichte*, I, 88, and *Geschichte Böhmens*, II, 486f). See further about this Tobolka, *O volbě*, 32, and Urbánek, *Věk*, III, 356.

or even for sectarian deviations, then it was easy enough to remember the Pikharts of Tabor and their denial of the real presence of Christ in the Eucharist, or any of the smaller sects related to them. George could tell himself and others that he would do his best to fight such heresies wherever and whenever he came across them, and would sternly lead such schismatics back to what to him was true orthodoxy.

If, to this extent, George could feel that he had, by his promises, not put any blame on his own religious past or that of his Utraquist teachers and friends, it must be admitted that the part of his oath referring to the future was, to say the least, highly ambiguous. True, as long as the Compacts existed and were, de facto, recognized by both sides as the binding basic law for the maintenance of religious peace in Bohemia, George could always argue that his own religious attitudes were at any time essentially as orthodox as those of any other Christian King, and that thus he was keeping his solemn oath. This all the more as he had also publicly sworn to uphold the Compacts together with all other privileges and freedoms of his people.

But George could by no means assume that this interpretation would be shared by others. If there was, especially, the promise to "lead back the people who are my subjects" to the "observation, obedience, conformity and union with the true Catholic and orthodox faith" and to "restitute among them the ritual and cult of the Holy Roman Church" then, even though this promise was tempered by the clause "according to the wisdom given to me by God," it was difficult to see why the Church of Rome should not, if and when this seemed possible and advantageous, interpret this obligation in a very literal sense which left the other side little freedom of evasive action or inaction. It cannot be denied: in order to win the crown—which, until the moment of coronation, was really not his by full rights—George was now paying a very high price, was weakening, in effect, the firm basis of his previous stand on the Compacts.

And for the moment he was clearly worried. He did not fear what the Church might do to him later, for with this he believed he could deal. At the time, after all, he had still reason to hope that the Holy See itself and such of its servants as the highly influential Cardinal Aeneas Sylvius would be willing in the end to grant confirmation of the Compacts. Nor did George, in his dealings with the two bishops, make any secret of his intention to renew, through an early embassy to Rome, his request for the confirmation of the Compacts.

But he was truly concerned about how the Hussite people of Bohemia and Moravia and the Utraquist Church would understand and react to his oath once it became known. And so, in this quandary, he took the step which, more than the oath itself, was later to lead to the accusation that from the beginning he acted with the intention of deceiving the Church of Rome and of breaking a solemn oath: he demanded and obtained the permission from the bishops to swear this oath in secret, before the bishops and a very few witnesses in high position.[44]

It is difficult to say whether George thus made a mistake. I am inclined to think so. For the very secrecy of the oath seemed to indicate that his action was not straightforward. If it were true that what he had done would severely shock the Utraquist people, and could not be explained by him in a way acceptable to them and if it were true, as he probably argued, that he could only stand up to such difficulties later when his position had been more solidly fortified, then this would all the more support an understanding of the oath as an "abjuration of heresy." If, on the other hand, the oath could have been offered publicly and above all explained publicly (in the way in which this was done later, at the time the crisis broke), if, in addition to this, a vigorous action for the confirmation of the Compacts had followed immediately—perhaps George would still have had to face some unpleasant altercations with some of his people (for instance Rokycana), but the oath itself could not so easily have been understood and described as a "conversion," and thus he might not have come so soon under the prolonged and growing pressure of the Church of Rome and of those of his own subjects to whom this pressure was, for their selfish purposes, only too welcome.

But here, I believe, we encounter one of George's principal weaknesses: an inclination to deal with difficult problems by what seemed, at the moment, the easiest way out, usually based on the confidence that thus a crisis could be postponed again and again till it had (or so he hoped) evaporated. This tendency to buy relief from a difficult pressure by what seemed to be expedient at the moment led, more than once in his life, to consequences which later he had cause to regret. But if we want to be fair in our judgment of him at this time, we must never forget the enormous weight of the pressure to which he had, rather unexpectedly, become subject by the action of the Hun-

---

[44] For the list of men present see Urbánek, *Věk*, III, 357. The most important ones were (besides the Hungarian clerics and the leaders of their retinue) Bishop Tas of Olomouc, Lord Chief Justice Zbyněk Zajíc of Hasenburg, and the Chancellor Prokop of Rabstein.

garian bishops, and his strong reasons for hoping for an early and real understanding with the Holy See.

Once this barrier had been overcome and the secret oath administered, the path was finally free for the coronation itself. George had requested that the ceremony be conducted as faithfully as possible according to the coronation order of Charles IV. On May 7th, in the presence of a very full representation of the estates of Bohemia and those of Moravia (but not of the northern dependencies) the King was led up to the Cathedral of St. Vitus by the bishops, while the great dignitaries of the kingdom carried before him the regalia. In the cathedral the oldest of the bishops present, Augustine of Rab, anointed the sixteenth King of Bohemia, while the Bishop of Vacz and Bishop Tas of Olomouc assisted. On the following day Queen Johanna was crowned with similar ceremonies.

But the coronation order of the great King-Emperor Charles, so carefully observed wherever possible, contained one clause which, under the circumstances, was of rather special significance. It said that, during or immediately after the solemn mass, the King, here as in other ways following the still older coronation order of France, was to be conducted by the chief magnates of the realm to the high altar and there was to receive, from the hands of the Archbishops of Prague, the holy communion in both kinds, bread and wine.[45] It may seem odd that this part of the ceremony is nowhere specially mentioned. There is yet little doubt that it was performed, exactly as prescribed, as its omission in this particular case would have been far more conspicuous and would have aroused far more attention and even shock among the majority of the nation. Even so the act, time-honored and regular though it was, presents an ironical commentary to the voices of those who, soon after, were eager to call George a heretic because he was not willing to forego this ceremony in the self-same form for all future days.

This, indeed, he was not willing to do. If he tried strongly for compromise, and if he may have gone rather far in this endeavor at this fateful moment, he could claim later that never in his life had he accepted the Lord's supper in any other form but that in the two kinds. Thus it was, especially in the eyes of the Hussite majority of the people, still as a Hussite King that he had had the crown put on his head.

---

[45] See the material edited and discussed by J. Loserth, "Die Krönungsordnung der Könige von Böhmen," *AÖG*, LIV, 36. Also Karl Fürst Schwarzenberg, *Die Sankt Wenzels-Krone und die böhmischen Insignien*, Vienna, 1960, pp. 47-51.

CHAPTER 9

FOREIGN POLICY AND GENERAL RECOGNITION

THE CORONATION of May 7th had enormously strengthened
George's position in Bohemia, so much so, indeed, that all later attempts to shake his hold over the main land of the crown were bound
to fail. But the same was not yet true for the dependencies. And,
among them, it was Moravia where the King meant to act first.
Moravia, an essentially Czech country, was anyhow much closer to
Bohemia than the northern dependencies, and the job to be done in
reducing the few men or places still resisting seemed much less difficult here than in the north. They have been mentioned before: Baron
Hynek Bítovský of Lichtenburg on Zornstein and four cities largely
inhabited (and above all ruled over) by Germans: Brno, Olomouc,
Znojmo, and Jihlava.

The elimination of such resistance would have been an easy enough
task if the cities had had only their own strength on which to rely.
However, behind the resistance of the Lord of Lichtenburg and some
of the Moravian cities stood the Habsburgs. Among them, again, no
one was as active as Archduke Albert, the Emperor's younger brother,
a lively, energetic, imaginative, somewhat spendthrift and extremely
ambitious young man who chafed under a situation in which the
power over—and the income from—the majority of the alpine duchies
of the Habsburg dynasty belonged to his cautious, stingy, and phleg-
matic brother, Frederick III.[1] The death of his cousin Ladislav had
anyhow opened up a whole range of difficult inheritance problems
in relation to the duchies of Austria proper where the Emperor would
have somehow to share his part of the estate with his brother Albert
and possibly his cousin Sigismund.[2] Otherwise, however, Albert's
claims were negligible compared to the Emperor's direct holdings in
Styria and Carinthia, or Sigismund's in the Tyrol and the Vorarlberg.

---

[1] As to Archduke Albert's character see Urbánek, *Věk*, III, 385f., and for a much less favorable judgment, Kurz, *Oesterreich unter Kaiser Friedrich IV*, II, 58–65.

[2] See for this and some of the following, including the Czech invasion of Austria, the
rather detailed monograph (with all documentary references) by H. R. von Zeissberg, *AÖG*,
XLVIII, pp. 1–170.

True, Albert still had rights in the original Habsburg lands, in Switzerland and along the upper Rhine (where he founded the University of Freiburg in Breisgau). Moravia, however, would have been a different matter. Here, he would have had a sizable and rich country to rule over, which might give him the strongly desired status of a ruling prince with some wealth and power of his own.

While, from the point of view of legitimate heredity, Albert's claim to Moravia was not any stronger than to any other part of Ladislav's Bohemian (or, for that matter, Hungarian) heritage, he could, in more sentimental terms, always refer to the fact that another Habsburg Albert, Ladislav's father, had been enfeoffed by the Emperor Sigismund with Moravia alone, long before this same Habsburg prince was elected King of Bohemia and Hungary. Whatever his legal rights, Archduke Albert was determined to use all his strength in his quest for Moravia. King George's measures to obtain secure possession of the margraviate thus became almost immediately and to the same extent a struggle with the Habsburg claims, and especially with Archduke Albert. In this fight it was very much to George's advantage that the archduke received rather little support from his imperial brother.

George left Prague for Moravia in the month of his coronation, late in May 1458. A direct way into the margraviate would have led him via Jihlava, near the Bohemian-Moravian border, but he went straight for Znojmo, in the very south of the margraviate, sending meanwhile a smaller detachment of troops to Jihlava. The city council of Jihlava, under this urging, promised to do homage to the King by early July. It would seem that this offer was meant seriously, but the men who made it almost immediately lost all power to implement it. There was, sometime early in June, a revolution in the city which, in its basis and its implications, throws an interesting light upon the general antagonism that arose between a few of the German-speaking Catholic urban centers of the Bohemian realm and their new King.[3]

The old city council of Jihlava was dominated traditionally by a relatively small number of families of the merchant aristocracy. If

---

[3] The somewhat scanty documentary material on Jihlava's resistance, including however a number of important entries into the town books or archives of the city, is used fully and intelligently by J. Wallner in his article "Iglaus Widerstand gegen die Anerkennung Georgs von Podiebrad," *MVGDB*, XXII, 103–120. I have largely relied on his account. See also my article "City Rebellions in 15th Century Bohemia and their Ideological and Sociological Background," *Slavonic and East European Review*, XL—95, June 1962, 324–340. For the general background see also C. d' Elvert, *Geschichte der Stadt Iglau*, Brno, 1850.

there was a change in the composition of the council it took place normally through new members being appointed or co-opted by old ones. There was thus no influence, let alone control, or the council and its policy by the people of the city, especially by its craft guilds. It seems that, for some time prior to the election and coronation of George, considerable class tension had developed between the city aristocracy and the lower classes. The latter's revolutionary tendencies had been activated especially by one or two popular preachers who came originally from the Premonstratension monastery of Želiv in eastern Bohemia. This fact gains some importance if we remember that the greatest popular leader of the radicals of Prague during the early years of the Hussite Revolution was Priest John, also originally from the monastery of Želiv and historically better known as Jan Želivský.[4] We find thus that the same monastery served as the point of departure of a radical social-revolutionary attitude either in the form of heretical protest against the power structure of the Roman Church or, less than a generation later, of orthodox Catholic protest (combined with ideas of hereditary legitimacy) against the newly established power of a supposedly heretical King. We shall find exactly the same attitude in the contemporary struggle of Breslau against the same "heretical King," only it seems that in the case of Jihlava the lines between a merchant aristocracy ready for compromise and a revolutionary lower middle class bent on a die-hard policy of resistance were still more clearly and decisively drawn. Jihlava, after all, did have an internal revolution before embarking on its challenge to the King—Breslau did not.

The revolution in Jihlava broke out because, of the people involved —all German Catholics—the "little people" were unwilling to permit the patricians to submit the city to the King's rule. The rebels threw out every member of the old city council and threatened the "patrician" families who had held the power before: in fear of their lives most or all of them left the city and sought refuge across the border in Bohemia proper.[5] The new council then sent an urgent call for additional help to Archduke Albert, as they felt they needed stronger support than the few hundred men whom Albert had sent earlier in the year under the command of his captain, Wolfgang Kadauer. Albert, though anxious not to lose the strategically valuable basis he held in Jihlava, was hardly able to comply since he was still

---

4 See the numerous references to him in my *Žižka*.
5 Report in the town book as quoted by Wallner, *MVGDB*, 22, 110 n. 2.

busy preparing himself for what threatened to become a major war between himself and the Czech King.

By mid-July Jihlava was besieged and isolated, not only in military but also in political terms.[6] For of the other three cities which had at first been unwilling to follow the barons and knights in their acknowledgment of King George, Znojmo had greeted George as King as soon as he arrived. Olomouc did the same on July 5th. Brno had put up only a very brief token resistance. Early in July two other Moravian royal towns, Uničov and Uherské Hradiště, sent their envoys to do homage. Jihlava alone remained.[7]

But George now shifted the struggle to the country of the really dangerous adversary, Albert of Austria, who had already started a small-scale invasion of Moravia. Another and, in George's eyes, very serious complaint was that the archduke, very soon after George's election, had seized Ulrich Eizinger under vague accusations, making him, among other things, responsible for the death of King Ladislav.[8] In reality Albert was trying to reduce thereby the considerable power of the leader of the Austrian estates, whom he also knew to be an old ally and supporter of the new King of Bohemia. Eizinger was held captive in Vienna, and to the Viennese city government both George and Matthias protested, demanding his immediate release.[9]

Czech arms, eventually, decided the issue. As not only Albert's but also Frederick's territories were hit,[10] the two brothers offered to negotiate. In September George was received near Vienna by the Emperor[11] who promised to "act toward him as to a King of Bohemia," thereby essentially recognizing his rank. Albert, too, gave up his claims on Moravia.[12] Jihlava, the only remaining opponent in Moravia, had to capitulate after a heroic but senseless resistance of three months. George treated the rebels (except for a few of their leaders) leniently and repeated his promise to safeguard their religious freedom.[13]

These events had a considerable impact also upon the development

---

[6] *Ibid.*, 112.

[7] Much of the source material on the subjection of the Moravian cities in Palacký, *FRA*, II, 20, 150–158.

[8] See material on this affair in K. Schalk, *Aus der Geschichte des oesterreichischen Faustrechts* (Abhandlungen zur Geschichte und Quellenkunde der Stadt Wien III), Vienna, 1919, 142ff. See also Vancsa, *Geschichte Nieder- und Oberösterreichs*, II, 332.

[9] See H. J. Zeibig, ed., *Copey-Buch der gemainen stat Wien*, FRA, II, 7, 115f.

[10] See Zeissberg *AÖG*, XLVIII, 154ff, also Vancsa *Geschichte*, II, 338–343.

[11] *Ibid.*; the treaties also in Kurz, *Oesterreich unter K. Friedrich IV*, I, 279–288.

[12] See Chmel, *Materialien z. öst. Geschichte*, II, 161ff., also Zeibig, *FRA*, II, 7, 164ff.

[13] See Wallner, *op.cit.*, 117–119, and Heymann, "City Rebellions," 324–340.

in Silesia.[14] Most of the princes—with the exception of Duke Balthasar of Sagan—now found themselves ready to negotiate with George about early recognition, but the city of Breslau declared firmly that George should never get its acknowledgment, and a solemn covenant to that effect was concluded by all voting members of the community.[15] In fact it was the commune (gemeine) which, under the influence of some popular priests, was most directly responsible for the worsening of the relationship with the King. Repeatedly this large group succeeded in frightening the city council away from compromises which it would have been glad to accept under other circumstances.[16]

But the hope that Breslau would lead the whole of Silesia against King George soon proved an illusion. Unity broke up at three meetings that the League of Silesian princes and towns held in the course of the summer. When Breslau asked recognition of Duke William as King, the majority declined and instead suggested negotiations directly with George, who had just come to Glatz. Finally, in September, in a communication directed to the Bohemian estates, the same majority promised submission if and when George's election found the approval of the Holy See.[17]

Some doubt about this question might have been justified. For only recently Pope Calixtus III had died, and in his place stood now a new Pope. Cardinal Aeneas Sylvius, under the name of Pius II, had mounted the papal throne on August 19. To learn his views Bishop Jost of Breslau had gone to Rome. But before he returned the situation became somewhat more tense. The Czech estates answered the Silesian League in a curt way, demanding recognition for George by mid-December. This ultimatum had rather the opposite effect, and the League, egged on by Breslau, asked William for a common meeting early in 1459.[18]

The negotiations, however, went on, and the Czech estates felt confident enough of the support which George would receive from Rome to threaten the Silesian League with complaints to be lodged by the Pope, the Emperor, and the electoral princes.[19]

---

[14] For the Silesian development as touched on in this chapter see, among the sources, above all Eschenloer and Markgraf's collection in *SrS*, VIII. Of modern treatments see Urbánek, *Dvě studie*, 177–200, 247–255, 269–279 and 312–328; Köbner, *Der Widerstand Breslaus*, 41–53, and Heymann, *loc. cit.*

[15] See *Breslauer Stadtbuch*, ed. H. Markgraf in *Codex diplomaticus Silesiae*, XI, Breslau, 1882, 189.

[16] See Eschenloer, L., *SrS*, VII, 27ff.

[17] *Ibid.*, 30ff., and Eschenloer, G., I, 69f.

[18] Eschenloer, L., *SrS.*, VII, 33f.

[19] *Ibid.*, 35.

It seems doubtful whether it was really in George's best interests to make the Holy See the judge between him and his subjects. Yet this was exactly what happened now. Both sides sent their representatives to Italy, where they arrived in February 1459, first the royal ambassadors, led by John of Rabstein the Younger, Provost of Vyšehrad, well known to the Pope as the brother of his old friend Prokop of Rabstein, chancellor of the kingdom. John, one of the foremost Czech humanists of his time, had the task of presenting the King's obedience to Pope Pius and thereby establishing a firm working relationship between the two men. The subjection of Silesia was, in this framework, only a side issue. The whole question of the relation between King and Pope was, indeed, of such fundamental importance (also for George's general recognition), that we shall discuss it in some detail.[20]

Almost certainly George's personal act of obedience had been preceded by a letter of congratulations sent to Pope Pius as soon as George learned of his election. But the declaration of obedience itself was presented merely as a private gesture of the King. It did not include the obedience of the estates and people of Bohemia, as would have been the normal procedure if Bohemia had still been fully part of the Catholic world. The official reason given by George's ambassador was the newness and relative weakness of the King's position and the possible resistance such a public act might arouse among many of his subjects. The Pope, who would have much preferred the public act, somewhat reluctantly accepted this excuse.

In reality, there were probably weightier reasons behind this limitation. If George had presented the obedience as a public act in the name of the whole Czech nation, there would have been, at least in the field of religious reunification, very little left for him to offer to the Holy See. He never seriously considered giving up the Basel Compacts, without which the precious domestic peace in the kingdom could not be preserved. The general act of obedience would have to function as the main price he would pay, one day in the future, for Rome's official recognition of the Compacts. Without such a quid-pro-quo the general obedience might even turn out to be dangerous since it might strengthen the Curia in her demands for a more thorough unification than the majority of the Czech people would be ready to accept.

---

[20] A valuable monograph on the relation between them at this stage is H. Markgraf's *Das Verhältnis des Königs Georg von Böhmen zu Papst Pius II*. See also Bachmann, *Böhmen und seine Nachbarländer*, 76ff., and Urbánek, *Dvě studie*, 283ff., 328ff.

Even in the face of all these considerations there seems little doubt that George, when he learned about the election of Aeneas to the See of St. Peter, felt that he was fortunate. When Pius later, in his memoirs written at the time of his open conflict with the King, claimed that George had regretted his elevation as that of a man who knew him and saw through his deceitful plans, then this was, of course, one of the many imaginative inventions which this gifted author was fond of presenting as the truth.[21] George knew enough about the Pope's very flattering views of himself and his constructive role in Bohemia's political life as well as of the policy which the former bishop and cardinal had advocated for the solution of the Bohemian ecclesiastical problems, to feel strengthened in what might be called his constitutional optimism. Calixtus, so it seemed, had very nearly confirmed the Compacts. Was there not some reason to hope that Pius, who had so strongly urged his predecessor to take this step, could eventually be induced to take it himself?

George probably could not do much more, at this stage, than to ask this question and hope for the best. One might wonder why he did not immediately take the initative in this direction, by sending, as soon as possible, a great embassy for the official purpose of gaining confirmation of the Compacts, all the more so as he had already announced such an intention at the time of his coronation. He tended to postpone difficult decisions, and in this case especially his political instinct might have told him to proceed slowly. As long as the Compacts could retain their de facto validity as an integral part of the Bohemian constitutional set-up he might just as well not disturb this situation unless circumstances forced him to do it or he was quite sure of success. (Failure, on the other hand, would be most painful.) But at this moment neither condition had developed. There was no particularly urgent reason to force the issue now, since religious peace in Bohemia had not recently been disturbed. But neither could George be as sure of success as he may have been when he announced his intention to send the embassy to Rome. For between that time and the present lay the secret oath and its impact upon the Curia.

George knew well enough that his secret coronation oath, even if interpreted in the way in which he alone was willing to interpret

---

21 *Commentarii rerum memorabilium*, Frankfurt, 1614, p. 32. See also p. 107 in the English edition (*The Commentaries of Pius II*) by Gragg and Gabel, Smith College Studies in History, XX, 2, Northhampton, 1937, very valuable because it is far more complete than the Frankfurt edition.

it, would oblige him to take measures which would be unpopular with many of his people and which might cause resistance among the Utraquist clergy. Tabor, indeed, had ceased to exist as a center of political, let alone military power, but many of its ideas had lived on, and some of them, clearly heretical in Roman Catholic terms, had been preserved and revived in a new sectarian movement, still small but fast growing, the Unity of the Brethren. No less a man than Rokycana had interceded with George in favor of this group, asking the King—almost immediately after his election in March 1458—to grant them a sort of asylum in the village or small town of Kunwald, on one of George's own estates. The King, perhaps remembering how much he owed to Rokycana's help in the election campaign, had agreed.[22] But there were also other groups of the Brethren, such as those of Krčín near Litice and another, larger one which had originated in Moravia and had now settled in Klatovy.[23] George's personal inclination was clearly not to subject these people to a persecution on purely religious grounds, yet he must have realized that they were in no way covered by the Compacts and that, by leaving them alone, he was already violating his secret oath. He might not be able always to evade such unpleasant duties, but at present he could at least ask for time until he had fortified his position all-around. (This, indeed, was to become a favored formula of his for the next few years.)

What, however, were the attitudes and views to these problems of Pope Pius II? He could not have been any further from "looking through" George and discovering in him, as he was to claim later, the incorrigible heretic. As at any time since he first met George he saw in him a fine politician, mainly and almost exclusively motivated (as he was himself) by a strong ambition. The problem was how to use him best.

One way which Pius could have chosen—to think of George and treat him as a heretical usurper and fight him and his kingship all the way from the beginning—clearly never even seriously occurred to the Pope, even though this was precisely what George's enemies in Germany and Silesia would have liked him to do. It would, of course, have marked a complete reversal of his previous attitudes and politics. It would have led (as it did at a much later date) to the renewal of the Hussite Wars with all the unfortunate implications

---

[22] See Müller, *Geschichte der böhmischen Brüder*, Herrnhut, 1922, I, 70 n. 177.
[23] *Ibid.*, 72f.

and results that Aeneas had pointed out so impressively in his great oration before his predecessor in 1455. Above all, in the one great cause which, following the example of his predecessor, Pope Pius immediately made his own—the crusade against the Turks—a Czech King (and a Czech people) actively treated as an outlaw would change from a potentially strong helper to an equally strong hindrance. Pius II was not going to start his reign with so foolish and futile an act.

But should he take a course which to him would have seemed the opposite extreme? Should he now go to the length which he had once recommended to Calixtus and actually confirm the Compacts? There were very good reasons why he would not now take the advice that he had once given. He would meet with considerable resistance within the Church itself.[24] As influential a churchman (and as close a friend of his) as Cardinal Carvajal was dead set against it, and there were numbers of others, both high clergy and princes, especially in Germany, who might be alienated by a policy so helpful to the "Czech heretics."[25] In addition he could tell himself that the situation had changed a good deal since 1455. George had been strong then as a regent, but he was far stronger now as crowned and anointed King. If the general goal was to enable him to force his people to a maximum of religious conformity, then he did not now need as much help as he might have needed a few years earlier.

But above all the situation had changed by the existence of George's secret coronation oath. During the years of his regency he had owed little to Rome—neither a debt of gratitude nor a solemn obligation solemnly sworn to. The oath had altered this, and Pius was perspicacious enough to see the hold this gave him over George. The Church, indeed, had already paid what Pius may have thought of as a fairly high price for George's cooperation, by permitting and granting him the canonical coronation. She would not now pay another, equally high price to get from the King the services which he had already promised. Pius might now at least consider Carjaval's argument that the royal oath had by itself obviated the Compacts.

But all this did not mean that Pius was unwilling to give some support to the man whose climb to the summit of power and influence had almost equalled his own. For if George was to assist the Pope in his great plans for an eastern crusade, and if he was to help

---

[24] See Urbánek, *Věk*, III, 460f.
[25] As claimed by Pius later, in 1462. See *AČ*, VIII, 352.

in creating the political and military organization which could put such a vast enterprise in motion, then George had to have a respectable and respected strength which would not be jeopardized or sapped by the constant need to fight for the recognition of his kingship. And even in terms of his domestic position, George had to remain strong if he was to perform the great act of unification, liquidating the Bohemian schism, which meant, for all practical purposes, killing the Utraquist Church as an essentially independent, living religious body. (That Pius, with so many other members of the Roman hierarchy, thought this at all possible and considered George the man who, under sufficient pressure or for a sufficiently high price, might be willing and able to perform such an execution—this assumption was, of course, his greatest mistake and error of judgment in relation to Bohemia.)

Pius thus was going to maintain a nicely balanced attitude toward the new King, a policy of limited support, effective enough to prevent any serious damage to his strength, yet always conditional, always with reminders to the King of his obligations toward the Church.[26] And the very first measure Pius took in regard to Bohemia, only three weeks after his elevation, could hardly be especially welcome to George. It was the appointment of Wenceslas of Krumlov as sole administrator of the archdiocesis of Prague.

Wenceslas, a very capable and highly learned man, holding the degree of doctor of canon law from the University of Padua, and politically a protégé of the house of Rosenberg, had long occupied the foremost place among Bohemia's Catholic clergy,[27] though for much of this time he had to share the office of administrator with others. In 1448, when George conquered Prague, Wenceslas had, with the whole Cathedral Chapter, moved to Pilsen, but had returned to Prague upon King Ladislav's inauguration in 1453. Since then he had been the most important antagonist of Rokycana. In cooperation with Prokop of Pilsen, once a leader of the conservatives among the Hussite masters of the University but now reconverted to Catholicism, he was the author of seventy articles intended to prove that Rokycana could not even qualify as a proper Catholic priest, all the less as an archbishop. While some of those articles relating to Rokycana's (in truth exemplary) personal life were merely bits of slander,

---

[26] That he was not too happy about some very rapid successes of George is shown by his reaction to the King's triumph at Cheb (see later in this chapter, n. 62).

[27] See Urbánek, *Věk*, III, 56ff.

others referring to his unorthodox views and ritual practices contained a good deal of truth.[28] By proving that the "elected archbishop" was far from an orthodox Catholic, Wenceslas effectively helped to destroy all hopes of Rokycana's confirmation and consecration by the Pope, even though he had not been able to prevent the official confirmation (on George's urging) of Rokycana's position as Utraquist administrator by King Ladislav.

Wenceslas of Krumlov had already gone to Rome during the summer and had been there during the electoral meeting of the College of Cardinals. Upon his return he claimed that the term "sole administrator" gave him the right to be regarded as the head not only of the Catholic clergy but of all priests within the area of the archdiocese, thus also of the Utraquist clergy of Bohemia and Moravia.[29] Whether this claim, at this moment, was really planned and backed by Pope Pius or not—it was in line with the idea of complete ecclesiastical unification envisaged by the phraseology of George's secret oath (the gist of which at least was probably familiar to Wenceslas by this time). But while the claim might have had some logic—it was yet an utter impossibility. This was shown very clearly by the extremely angry reaction of the people of Prague, whose main spokesman was the first burgomaster of the Old Town, Samuel Velvarský of Hradek. He countered the claims of the Catholic administrator not only by heated attacks in public but also by bitter complaints before the King at a meeting of the diet in December 1458, in tones very similar to those once before uttered by Beneš Mokrovouský.[30] Just as then the speech drew an angry reply from Zdeněk of Sternberg, who reminded the King of his promise to protect the freedom of Catholic worship. The King answered immediately, confirming this promise, but emphasizing that he had given the same guarantees of free worship also to the Utraquists. It was a programmatic statement and, as the realists even in the Catholic camp knew well, it was the only policy that could preserve peace and cooperation in Bohemia. For the time being neither Wenceslas of Krumlov nor the Holy See took any steps to upset this peace.

[28] Hrejsa, *Dějiny*, III, 114ff., and for an English summary, Heymann, "John Rokycana," *Church History*, September 1959, 271f.

[29] See the material for this (and the rest of this paragraph) mostly in the "Tractatus" of Nicholas Tempelfeld, ed. Loserth, in *AÖG*, LXI, 142f., 152f., also the discussion in Urbánek, *Věk*, III, 463 (especially n. 2.), 465. On the specific issue of Wenceslas' appointment see also Thomas Pešina, *Phosphorus Septicornis*, Prague, 1673, pp. 241–243.

[30] See above, chapter 6, pp. 106ff.

If Pope Pius, at this moment, was unwilling to press this issue, if, in actuality, he was willing to help King George's quest for universal acknowledgment of his kingship, the main reason was that he had meanwhile launched what he hoped was the first stage in the organization of the great crusade against the Turks.[31] On October 12 he had announced his intention to call together an international congress which would prepare all the necessary measures. So as to make it easier for princes or their ambassadors from other parts of Europe he would himself cross the Apennines and the Po. The final invitation, sent out soon afterwards, called kings and rulers from all over Europe to meet at the beginning of June 1459 in the town of Mantua. Among them was the King of Bohemia, and as Pius was very anxious to obtain George's active participation he could hardly style the breve inviting him in any way but that giving him his full title and calling him, as was the usage, "his beloved son in Christ." [32] The invitation (followed in January by a bull of similar content) was one of the matters which John of Rabstein, leader of the Czech embassy George sent to the Pope, was to take up with him.

Sometime in late February or early March, Rabstein arrived in Siena, where the Pope, on his slow travel north, had established his residence for a number of weeks and where he also received many embassies from other princes bearing the usual messages of obedience. Rabstein had with him, and introduced to the Pope, a man whom the King, probably upon the recommendation of his brother Prokop of Rabstein, had selected as Czech procurator (diplomatic representative) at the papal court. The new procurator, Dr. Fantino de Valle, was a native of Trogir in Dalmatia and was to prove himself a capable and valuable spokesman of George, able soon to gain the whole confidence of the Pope.[33] He considered his main task to make the Pope equally confident that the great hopes and expectations he had of George's willingness and ability to achieve ecclesiastical unity would, before long, be strictly fulfilled. George did not think it politic or even possible, at this stage, to dampen such sanguine beliefs by any direct reservations.

In indirect forms, nevertheless, George tried repeatedly to warn the Pope not to expect any quick action by showing him the strength

---

[31] See L. Pastor, *Geschichte der Päpste,* 3rd ed., II, Freiburg, 1904, 18f.

[32] Pastor (*ibid.,* 168) calls it a breve while other historians (e.g. Urbánek, *Věk,* III, 462) talk of a bull sent to George in October 1458. The text (not quoted by either of them) in Goldast, *Commentarii de Bohemiae iuribus ac privilegiis,* Frankfurt, 1627, Appendix, p. 102f.

[33] See Urbánek *Dvě studie,* 330f., 342f.

of the feelings that existed among the masses of Hussite Czechs against any policy of complete fusion with the Roman Church. He did this, as explained before, even in the way in which he ordered John of Rabstein to present his declaration of obedience: only in the name of the King himself, and only in camera, in the presence of the cardinals, not in a great public ceremony. The Pope, though disappointed, showed Rabstein his personal affection by appointing him papal protonotary.

It was about a month after Rabstein's reception (in the beginning of April) that the Silesian embassy arrived at the Papal court, still in Siena. The embassy consisted of the Breslau canon Dr. Wartenberg and Matthias von Unruhe, one of the knights of Duke Balthasar of Sagan, the only passionate and consistent enemy whom King George had among the Silesian princes. Thus the embassy represented less the moderate majority of members of the Silesian League than its radical minority led by Breslau. This was also very clearly expressed in the memorandum which the two envoys submitted to the Pope. Its author, or at least the man who was responsible for much of its general argument, had inspired the Breslau resistance movement against George before and was to become, in the further course of events, its very soul: it was Nicholas Tempelfeld, himself a canon of the Breslau chapter, yet a far from willing subordinate of the bishop, since he crossed his policy freely and operated mostly through his effective and enormously popular sermons which successfully kept the ideas and passions of John of Capistrano alive.

In this memorandum [34] the Pope was asked to declare invalid the election and coronation of George, to free the Silesians from any duty of obedience toward him, to repudiate the demands made upon them by the Czech estates, and above all to take the Silesians under his specific protection against any attempts of forcible subjection by the Czech ruler. The demands were based upon the dangers of the Czech heresy and the merits of the Silesians in having resisted it since the time of the Hussite Revolution.

The Silesian envoys finally complained about the wording of Pius' invitation to Mantua, in which George had been granted the title King. The Pope tried to calm the two envoys by claiming that this address did not constitute a final recognition, but it seems quite clear that George's procurator, Fantino, was right—at least for the moment

---

[34] The text in Markgraf, *SrS*, VIII, 16–20, a summary in Koebner, *Der Widerstand Breslaus*, 49.

—when he reported to George that the Silesians had achieved "little or nothing." [35] The King could derive even greater reassurance from a letter in which Jost of Rosenberg, Bishop of Breslau—whose visit to Rome had served the very purpose of getting the decisive instructions from Pope Pius—promised him all compliance and support.[36] This clearly showed the Pope's ideas and intentions, and in addition promised George increased support in Silesia, if not in the city from which the bishop held his title.

Meanwhile William of Saxony still found it difficult to give up his dream of kingship, and there were moments late in 1458 when he might have dared to challenge George's military strength—despite the caution that the King's Austrian victory should have instilled in him—if only he could have found some strong allies in Germany. Yet the general situation in the Empire was none too favorable to him, and it became less so in the course of the late fall and the winter of 1458-1459.

The Empire, at this time as so often in the past, was badly divided. Essentially there were two main parties. One of them consisted of the two princely houses of Wettin and Hohenzollern—the Dukes of Saxony and the Margraves of Brandenburg—and its unofficial leader and spiritus rector was the younger brother of Elector Frederick II of Brandenburg, Margrave Albert Achilles, whose own main holdings were not in Brandenburg proper but in Franconia (the region of Ansbach) and included the burgraviate of Nürnberg.[37] Albert had long and rather successfully posed as the Emperor's most faithful partisan and had held the rank of master of the imperial court and imperial captain general. He had defended the Emperor against recurring waves of antagonism among the electoral princes and especially against attempts, which appeared early in Frederick's III rule, to replace him by a more capable man or at least to put such a man at his side. The main service that Albert expected in return from the Emperor was support in raising the Nürnberg Landgericht, orig-

---

[35] Palacký, *FRA,* II, 20, 180f.

[36] See Urbánek, *Věk,* III, 500 n. 2.

[37] There is strangely no proper monograph on this highly interesting prince. E. W. Kanter's book (*Markgraf Albrecht Achilles v. Brandenburg,* Berlin, 1911), apart from being incomplete, is confused to the point of being unreadable. There are suggestive passages in the great standard works on Brandenburg-Prussian history, so in Droysen *Geschichte der Preussischen Politik,* 2nd ed., II, 1, 113, in R. Koser, *Geschichte der brandenburgisch-preussischen Politik,* I, 137, and in Höfler's introduction to vol. I, of *Das Kaiserliche Buch des Markgrafen Albrecht Achilles,* Bayreuth, 1850. See also Urbánek, *Věk,* III, 413ff.

inally one of several regional courts, to the rank of the only Court of Appeal for all of central and southern Germany. The general acknowledgment of this claim would have given Albert a far stronger position in Germany in political as well as in economic terms.

This claim, especially, brought Albert into an extended conflict with the princes of the house of Wittelsbach and the ecclesiastical princes of the region. Most aggravated was Duke Louis "the Rich" of Bavaria-Landshut, who proved to be a strong and capable adversary,[38] though his figure, among German princes, was eclipsed by that of his cousin and friend, the Count Palatine Frederick "the Victorious," a violent but highly gifted and truly powerful personality, who, acting first as guardian of his nephew, had usurped the position of Palsgrave and Elector.[39] There had been short lived attempts to bury the struggle between Wittelsbach and Wettin-Hohenzollern sufficiently to enable both sides to cooperate against the newly arrived nobleman on the throne of Bohemia. This, and this alone, would have given Duke William a truly promising chance of destroying the rival who had gained all the advantages of a strong local following and of fast and determined action. But the struggle was not buried. At best William could hope that his party, recently strengthened by the accretion of princes hostile to the quick and reckless way in which Frederick of the Palatinate had usurped the position of Elector—notably the Margraves of Baden, the Counts of Württemberg, and the Archbishop-Elector of Mainz—would prevent the Wittelsbachs from attacking. Indeed the war that had threatened was therefore prevented (or rather postponed), and at Bamberg in January 1459 all the leading German princes—the two great Wittelsbachs, Albert Achilles and his brother John of Brandenburg, and William of Saxony—met to see what could be done to achieve a more solid and permanent understanding. For William it seemed the last chance to gain wider support for his plans, but his friend Albert Achilles warned him that the calm was only ostensible and the danger of a German civil war as great as ever.[40] Having been the first to attempt to block George's kingship, Albert was now one of the first to recognize the futility of such endeavors and to act accordingly. He got in touch with the King of Bohemia, indeed he

---

[38] His biography by August Kluckhohn, *Ludwig der Reiche, Herzog von Bayern*, Nördlingen, 1865 (later cited as Kluckhohn). There (pp. 55–69) material on the relationship between Louis and Albert Achilles, with special discussion of the Nürnberg Landgericht, 59–66, and of the struggle between Louis and the Emperor over the city of Donauwörth, 90ff., 104ff.

[39] See C. J. Kremer, *Geschichte des Kurfürsten Friedrichs I von der Pfalz*, Frankfurt, 1765.

[40] Kluckhohn, 83ff., 100.

had done so even before the meeting of Bamberg.[41] The outcome was a preliminary meeting of the Saxon-Brandenburg party with Czech representatives held at Wunsiedel early in February.[42]

This meeting, at which, of the princes themselves, only Albert Achilles was present, had as yet a mainly exploratory nature. There were envoys from the other Wettin and Hohenzollern princes, and George was represented by the Lord Chief Justice Zbyněk Zajíc of Hasenburg as head of the mission and two or three other noblemen. They were assisted by some of George's experienced diplomats, among them his personal chaplain, John Špán of Barnstein, who accompanied Zajíc at several privately held discussions,[43] and Jost of Einsiedel, in whom George had special trust.

The main result of the rather protracted meeting—it lasted through and beyond the first half of February—was the decision to arrange for a meeting of the principals of the struggle, the King of Bohemia and the ruling princes of Saxony and Brandenburg, in early spring at the city of Cheb. The place of the meeting was, in itself, of considerable importance. Cheb, while as an old imperial city holding on to an autonomous status, had on the basis of an old security pledge long been under the Bohemian crown, and George would be the host.[44] In addition, largely due to Albert's skillful and persistent mediation, some hopeful tentative agreements had been concluded for the solution of the many difficult questions still outstanding between Bohemia and Saxony.

What the Saxon-Brandenburg negotiators may not have known was that their party was not the only one to establish contact with George. The same was soon true also for the Wittelsbach princes.[45]

[41] The basis for these first contacts was, so it seems, the fact that the city of Lübeck, as the leader of the Hanseatic League, had sought help from George against the aggressive policy of Hohenzollern absolutism directed especially also against the Hanseatic towns in Brandenburg. George, so it seems, let some information about this seep through to Margrave Albert. See *FRA*, II, 42, 255 f., also Bachmann, *Böhmen u. seine Nachbarländer*, 16f., the article by Walter Stein, "Über den angeblichen Plan eines Bündnisses . . ." in *Hansische Geschichtsblätter*, 1897, 239ff., and finally Urbánek, *Dvě studie*, 212 (esp. n. 2), and 213. On still earlier contacts see Urbánek, *Věk*, II, 495–498.

[42] See Palacký, *FRA*, II, 20, 173f.; also Urbánek, *Dvě studie*, 306, 311.

[43] We encounter this man here for the first time. While he was not much in the limelight of history he seems to have belonged to George's most intimate circle. At one time, it appears, he had been an abbot, but was now an Utraquist. Later he served not only as a successful diplomat, especially on missions to France, but also in a judicial capacity (see Tomek, *Dějepis*, IX, 256, 257.) Otherwise see Urbánek, *Dvě studie*, 306 n. 1.

[44] For all the exterior aspects of the Congress of Cheb, see the article by Karl Siegl, "Zur Geschichte der Fürstentage Georgs von Podiebrad in Eger," *MVGDB*, XLII, Prague, 1904, 203–226.

[45] See Bachmann, *Böhmen u. seine Nachbarländer*, 44 n. 4.

It enabled George to invite them, or at least Palsgrave Frederick, also to Cheb, thus raising even further the significance of this great meeting.

But before the meeting took place, indeed immediately after the conclusion of the meeting of Wunsiedel at which he himself had not taken part, Duke William met the representatives of the Silesian League and of the Sixtowns of Upper Lusatia at Kottbus in Lower Lusatia. He arrived with considerable military power, and obviously did not yet feel bound by the agreements of Wunsiedel to the extent which would prevent him from making a last attempt in his long and ever more hopeless quest.[46] He asked the princes, cities, and estates of the northern dependencies to recognize him unconditionally as their hereditary lord, in which case he would protect them with all his strength and (a rather daring claim) that of his relatives and friends of Wettin and Hohenzollern.

The answer, however, was negative. The Silesians, no longer seriously in doubt about the Pope's attitude and aware of the negotiations that had gone on at Wunsiedel, had every reason to suspect that William was neither strong enough nor any longer seriously willing to risk war with George, but that he merely hoped, with such additions to his strength, to increase his bargaining power. To avoid the impression of a complete failure the two sides concluded (but left open for later signature) a purely defensive alliance just for the contingency that either side was militarily attacked by George. In view of later events this alliance had very little if any significance.

The meeting of Kottbus was also the beginning of the end of the Silesian League. Barely three months later it was dissolved. By that time or soon afterwards all the Silesian dukes and principalities— with the exception of Breslau and Balthasar of Sagan—had done homage to George, King of Bohemia.[47]

The Congress of Cheb,[48] carefully prepared mainly by Jost of Einsiedel, got under way on April 7th when King George arrived

---

[46] See Eschenloer, L., *SrS*, VII, 36ff., and Eschenloer, G., I, 73, further Rosicz, *SrS*, XII, 74, and for modern treatments Koebner, *Widerstand*, 51f., and Urbánek, *Dvě studie*, 312f.

[47] See Volkmer-Hohaus, *Urkunden und Regesten zur Geschichte der Grafschaft Glatz* (Glatzer Geschichtsquellen II), Habelschwerdt, 1888, pp. 252f., 255.

[48] For the Congress of Cheb, and especially for the treaties concluded there, see the following sources: Johann Joachim Müller, *Reichstags-Theatrum*, Jena, 1713, pp. 537–545; C. J. Kremer, *Geschichte des Kurfürsten Friedrich I von der Pfalz*, Frankfurt, 1765, pp. 175–177; K. Menzel, *Regesten zur Geschichte Friedrichs des Siegreichen* (Quellen u. Erörterungen z. bayr. u. deutsch. Geschichte II), Munich, 1862, pp. 306–311; A. F. Riedel, *Codex*, II, 5, 47–50,

in the city with an escort containing 900 horse and 100 battle wagons and accompanied by his son Victorin and all the leading men of the country's nobility. On the day after he greeted the first of his guests: Albert Achilles, whose official role was again to mediate or even arbitrate between his friends, the two Saxon rulers, and the King of Bohemia. Albert was surprised and rather angry when, on April 9th, Frederick, the Elector of the Palatinate, arrived in Cheb. He was received with great honors, which he returned with confessions of friendship and admiration for George. His immediate purpose, of course, was to make sure that the Saxon-Brandenburg party did not gain too much strength, and he proposed a one-sided and close alliance "to the death," which George was glad to accept. Things became more difficult, however, when Frederick tried to enclose in this alliance Duke Louis of Bavaria. The Duke, as George knew, had only recently been quite hostile to him, and George wanted more concrete expressions of his change of heart than merely the word of his relative. He was, however, eventually willing to have him exempted, that is named as one against whom the alliance would not operate.[49] In addition George, in a milder mood which was probably due to the influence of Frederick's chief adviser, the well-known lawyer and diplomat Dr. Martin Mair, agreed to meet Duke Louis in Prague toward the end of May, when all questions pending between Bohemia and Bavaria-Landshut would be taken up to be settled.

The negotiations with Palsgrave Frederick—the first member of the electoral college with whom George achieved close contact—were much easier than those with the Saxons. Margrave Albert Achilles, though always emphasizing his role as mediator rather than as partisan, nevertheless turned out to be a good advocate of the Saxon cause, always armed with all the documents he might be able to use. There were, in fact, two great issues: William's claim to be the true "natural" heir of the Bohemian crown, and the old territorial demands pending between the two countries, all based in some way

---

also Supplement, 1865, 80–82; Palacký *FRA*, II, 20, 177–180; V. Hasseholdt-Stockheim, *Herzog Albrecht IV von Baiern*, Leipzig, 1865, Beil. IV, 74–78; see also M. Stieber, *Böhmische Staatsverträge* (Forsch. zur inn. Gesch. Oesterreichs 8), Innsbruck, 1912, pp. 188f. For interpretative discussions see Palacký, *Dějiny*, IV, 2, 76–85; Bachmann, *Böhmen und seine Nachbarländer*, 45–58; Kluckhohn, 122–125; Urbánek, *Dvě studie*, 345–366 (and *Věk*, III, 502ff.).

[49] See Kremer, *Geschichte des Kurfürsten Friedrichs I von der Pfalz*, 178. This shows that Bachmann is mistaken in his presentation of this issue in *Geschichte Böhmens*, II, 497, where he seems to have mixed up Louis' exemption (agreed to) with his inclusion into the alliance (refused by George).

or another upon enfeoffments, subinfeudations or securities taken and given in relation to castles, towns, and estates, some of them of rather large size.

There is little need here to go into the protracted yet already entirely outdated discussion over the succession. The Saxon interest here, as Albert understood it, was essentially to make George acknowledge the greatness of William's sacrifice if he withdrew his claims and thus to exact as high a price for such withdrawal as possible. George's interest, of course, was precisely the opposite, and so he argued that, ever since the time of Sigismund, Bohemian Kings had become Kings on the basis of an entirely free election.[50] It was of little significance that this claim went rather beyond the historical truth, since obviously there was, on this count, no posssibility of compromise. George either was or was not King of Bohemia. At this time he clearly was, as he said himself, not only the elected and crowned but the only possible King of Bohemia, and he could have no real peace with William and his friends and allies unless they acknowledged his kingship without reservations.

The situation was different in regard to the territorial wishes of both sides. Here indeed George, too, could make concessions. This he did, and to an extent which was later criticized by many patriotic Czechs. But it would be wrong to assume that he gave way on some of these issues only as payment for Saxon acquiescence with his kingship. While in some details the settlement was the result of shrewd negotiating by two very clever and determined men, the over-all outcome reflected a realistic understanding of the ways in which, under the changing conditions of the time, it became possible to adapt personal ownership of lands, castles, and cities more nearly to national borders and international power relationships.[51] In a sense this was a great cleaning-up process. To George, of course, it mattered most to recover full possession of places within the borders of the Czech kingdom to which the Saxons had acquired rights. Of these by far the most important was the city of Most (in German Brüx) with its great castle, as well as the smaller town of Duchcov (Dux) and the strong fortress of Osek (Riesenburg). Against this stood a larger number of fiefs which were held by the Bohemian crown on the other side of the mountains in Thuringia or in Saxony-

---

[50] See Urbánek, *Dvě studie,* 353f.

[51] For a list of the castles, towns, etc., officially held as fiefs by the Bohemian crown see J. C. Lünig, *Teutsches Reichsarchiv,* Pars Specialis, VI, Leipzig, 1711, 469–471.

Meissen but had got lost to her during the last decades. Of these some magnates, notably the Counts of Schwarzburg-Rudolstadt and the Lords of Plauen, Reuss, and Gera were, with all their possessions, to return fully into their original position as vassals of the Bohemian crown. A much larger number of former Bohemian fiefs in the same regions, however (altogether some sixty castles and estates) were settled by George upon Albert of Meissen, the younger son of Elector Frederick of Saxony, who was to hold it all from the Bohemian crown as tenant-in-chief, with the right to dispose freely of parts of it by way of subinfeudation. While, in this way, Bohemian feudal suzerainty was nominally maintained (as was also the case with the town and castle of Pirna, sold to Meissen for a substantial sum), the actual possession and economic use of all these holdings now beloged in permanence to the Saxons. It was a peace settlement that did away with old conflicts arising from claims and counter-claims, that reflected the spirit of neighborly reasonableness, and that stood the test of time remarkably well.

The settlement, the result of two weeks of hard work, was pronounced as the content of his arbitration award by Albert Achilles on April 25. For the last stages of the negotiations nearly all the Saxon and Hohenzollern princes, including the two electors Frederick, had arrived in Cheb. Duke William, who had waited in a small town on the Saxon side of the border, was finally prevailed upon by Margrave Albert Achilles to join the congress and, in order not to look too insignificant, had borrowed for his entry 150 horsemen from his brother Frederick. George treated his stubborn rival with the greatest distinction, and thus succeeded in making the reluctant and disappointed man feel somewhat more cheerful,[52] even in the face of the great withdrawal of succession claims which was pronounced, as part of the general settlement, on the same April 25.

This statement said that Duke William, also in the names of his wife (King Ladislav's sister) and of their descendants, renounced all claims to the Bohemian crown and all that belonged to it, and ceded those claims "to the most serene Prince, the Lord George, King of Bohemia, our dear Lord and Brother, and to his heirs and successors, Kings of Bohemia, and to the Bohemian Crown."[53] William also renounced all connection with any of George's subjects who should not be willing to submit freely to the King, and would, in common with his brother the elector and the princes of Brandenburg,

---

[52] See his letter to his brother Elector Frederick in *FRA*, II, 20, 178.
[53] See *ibid.*, 42, 274f.

support the King in his attempts to gain their free and peaceful submission. George, on his side, would not punish the princes, cities, and estates of Silesia for the "good will and affection" which they had shown to William, but would retain them in all their honors, dignities, and customs, provided they now willingly submit. If, on the other hand, it should be necessary to lead them forcibly toward obedience, the Saxon princes will help the King (a passage which did not cause much rejoicing in some quarters in Silesia, especially in Breslau).

But the peace arrangement went beyond the elimination of the actual causes of dissent. It was accompanied by solemn "hereditary unions" between the King of Bohemia and the Saxon princes as well as those of Brandenburg. These "unions" were really treaties of alliance, and to make them, in the case of Bohemia and Saxony, especially firm, solemn, and lasting, the union was buttressed by an agreement involving a double marriage. George's daughter, Princess Zdeňka (in German, Sidonia), was to wed Duke Albert, son of Elector Frederick of Saxony,[54] while Catherine, Duke William's daughter, was affianced to Hynek, George's youngest son. Zdeňka's and Albert's solemn wedding was to take place in November of the same year. For Duke William the union with the house of Poděbrady provided a curious face-saving satisfaction. He now claimed in public that he had given his claims to the Czech crown as dowry to his daughter.[55]

But George gained most by this marriage arrangement. For the many people who, in Germany and elsewhere, had scoffed at the "man of low origin," at the heretic who now claimed to be a King, the marriage which now connected his house with two of the oldest and greatest of German dynasties—the mothers of both Albert and Catherine were Habsburg princesses, in Albert's case the Emperor's own sister—must have made a deep impression, even though the Saxon dukes themselves were attacked for it by zealous Catholics,[56] and found it necessary to justify their policy in public. And, while in some circles in Bohemia the connection of the house of Kunštát-Poděbrady with the houses of Wettin and Habsburg—later to be followed by a similar intermarriage with the Hohenzollern—gave George added prestige, in the eyes of some zealous Hussites the

[54] A most detailed discussion of the background and significance of this marriage in F. A. von Langenn, *Herzog Albrecht der Beherzte*, Leipzig, 1838, pp. 36–41.

[55] Eschenloer, L., *SrS*, VII, 44.

[56] *Ibid.*, 42

German-Catholic connection smelled of betrayal.[57] Finally we hear that even Pope Pius thought that the marriage contracts went rather far, but received a cool answer from the Saxon dukes.[58]

The success of the Congress of Cheb bore fruit in one other way: it established and secured the King of Bohemia's standing as the foremost prince in the College of Electors, still the most influential political body in the Holy Roman Empire. The three temporal electors beside the King of Bohemia (the senior princes of the Palatinate, Saxony, and Brandenburg, curiously all of them named Frederick) were now his allies, and while still in Cheb he received intimations from the Archbishop-Electors of Mainz (through the mediation of the Bishop of Würzburg) and of Trier that both men wished to recognize and take up friendly relations with the new King of Bohemia.[59] Thus, with the single exception of the Archbishop of Cologne, all the electoral princes were ready to consider George as one of them. They realized that no one among them could match his power.

The Congress of Cheb of April 1459 is in many ways a high point in George's life. With truly lightning speed, within little more than a year, he had achieved a recognition which seemed but little marred by the continuing resistance of one city and one small princeling in Silesia. He had acted with determination and moderation and had hardly made a wrong step. He had tried the way of peace wherever he could, had used his sword only in Moravia, the land of his ancestors, where he had felt himself attacked by Archduke Albert, and had even there made the conclusion of peace as easy as possible. If he now was, beyond question, the most powerful figure in all of Central Europe, he owed it to some good luck, more so to the support of the Czech people of both creeds, but most of all to his own skill, his own healthy combination of caution and daring, and to his great confidence in himself, which he was able to implant quickly in those people with whom he came in contact. Since, however, so many deeds, and deeds so difficult if not impossible to achieve, were now expected from him by men of great consequence, he would not find it easy to hold all that he had gained so fast. Yet before long he was driven to try to climb still higher.

[57] This seems to have been true even of Rokycana and Lupáč, the two leading spirits of the Utraquist Church. See Tanner, *Historia Heroum de Stellis*, MS XIII D 160 in Prague University Library, 463, also Urbánek, *Dvě studie*, 367f.

[58] Droysen, *Geschichte der preussischen Politik*, II, 1, 219f.

[59] *FRA*, II, 20, 182f.

CHAPTER 10

WIDER HORIZONS?

IF SOME historians, referring to the Holy Roman Empire, have called the middle period of the fifteenth century the "Age of Imperial Reform," then this was certainly a strong euphemism.[1] No real reform took place in Germany at this time, not even the very limited and ultimately ineffectual sort that was achieved somewhat later during the age of the Emperor Maximilian I. During the long reign of his father, the Emperor Frederick III, the chaotic conditions of German politics and the Reich's inability to defend itself against the steadily increasing exploitation by the Curia were "gravamina" which did not really find any cure or even mitigation. The Emperor, well aware that he himself was not a reforming prince, had begun his rule with a slight to the more reform-minded electors by giving up the policy of "neutrality" which, during the later phases of the Council of Basel, had put pressure on the Roman Pope. He had, as Gregory Heimburg said later, "sold his obedience for 221,000 ducats." Also later, usually unwilling to leave Gratz or his beloved Wiener-Neustadt to bother to come "up into the Reich," even less to tackle the strenuous job of reform, Frederick continued, in return for some papal support, to let well enough alone, making sure only that no one touched his legal claims and titles and his dynastic heritage.

The papacy, on the other hand, was extremely unwilling to let anything like reform happen. This does not imply that limited attempts at reform were not made, by various pontiffs as well as by prelates who had not quite forgotten their conciliarist past. Such men as Cardinal Nicholas of Cusa continued to combat, especially on a local or regional level, the moral decay that had long been spread among laymen and clergy, notably among the inmates of monasteries, whether men or women. But such "reform," if at all effective, was and remained invariably patchwork. Cardinal Cusa's main writings touching the issue of reform were highly significant

[1] For this terminology, see e.g. the work by E. Ziehen, *Mittelrhein und Reich im Zeitalter der Reichsreform,* 1934.

contributions to the development of the history of ideas, especially of political theology. Yet in the realm of political realities they remained ineffective.[2] None of them successfully attacked the central problem, none resulted in any changes and improvements in the basic structure of Church or Empire or in the Empire's relation to the Church of Rome. Imperial reform, in particular, would tend to endanger the strong economic position which the Curia held in Germany. A strong, or even merely strengthened, central political power in the Empire might result in developments similar to those of France where the Ecclesia Gallica, under the skillful direction of King Charles VII, had, through the implementation of the Pragmatic Sanction of Bourges, achieved considerable political, organizational, and economic autonomy from Rome in which the Curia, at times, saw something much like a schism. In any case imperial reform, to the extent that it would lend more strength and cohesion to the political fabric of Germany and would establish at least a sort of working federalism out of the anarchic competition of territorial princes—including the powerful ecclesiastical rulers of the Rhine region—would thus work against the absolutist power structure of the Roman Church. It would endanger the recent recovery of this absolutism from the encroachments of the conciliar movement.

It must be remembered that this movement, while pretty thoroughly defeated during the late forties and not fated ever to regain the strength it had had during the early decades of the century, was not really dead and forgotten. The hope for strong councils—which would meet regularly every ten years as resolved at Constance—would still be expressed every time that the policy of the Curia, in Germany as elsewhere, came under criticism. How much Pope Pius II, himself originally a partisan of conciliarism, still feared and detested this threat to his present absolute position became especially clear during the great Congress of Mantua. In its historical significance this Congress was less consequential by what it did for the struggle against the Turks—for that was, despite Pius' intense and devoted efforts, precious little—than by the pronouncement of the bull "Execrabilis" of January 18, 1460. In the bull the Pope condemned, and threatened with the most severe punishment, any appeals from a papal decision

---

[2] See e.g. E. Molitor, *Die Reichsreformbestrebungen des 15. Jahrhunderts* (vol. 132 of Untersuchungen zur deutschen Staats-und Rechtsgeschichte, ed. Gierke) Breslau, 1921, pp. 52ff. On Cusa's reform ideas, see the most recent treatment in Paul E. Sigmund, *Nicholas of Cusa and Medieval Political Thought*, Cambridge, Mass., 1963, especially chs. V to VII.

to a general church council.[3] At the time, the measure—in itself only moderately effective—was meant to quell any new outbreak of the "deadly poison" of conciliarism especially in France, where such appeals had originated most recently, and in Germany, where they were imminent. But the time was not far when the situation in Bohemia, too, would be understood by Pius and his successor as a challenge to the sacred principles of papal absolutism and would be answered accordingly.

A peculiar and rather ironical situation existed, with regard to the reform idea, between Pope and Emperor. Pius II was, of course, an old clerical servant and close friend of the Emperor, who had helped him much in his brilliant career.[4] In personal terms it would therefore seem natural that the two men should be friends. Historically, however, an originally close personal relationship between the two highest dignitaries of western Christendom had in the past frequently and just as naturally turned into bitter hostility if and when the Emperor began to act like an Emperor.

Frederick III, of course, rarely acted like a strong Emperor, and one might say that it was just this that made him such a good and safe ally of the papacy. On paper, indeed, Pope Pius II, or at least Aeneas Sylvius, had glorified great men, among them great Emperors, and in relation to Frederick III he had indulged in maintaining the fiction of the medieval world in which Emperor and Pope, to rule this world, would have to stand side by side rather than against each other, even though the Pope was just one step higher than the temporal lord of the world.[5] In reality this was more the exercise of an elegant literary gift shaping romantic memories than political theory taken seriously.[6] A truly powerful Emperor—even if his power was based on his dynastic holdings and his cleverness in playing the German princes against one another—would necessarily reduce the Curia's chances of interfering in the affairs of the Empire, and would himself be tempted to exert influence upon the Church. This truth—even at times when the old grandeur of the Roman Emperors had long vanished—would be proved again in the two fol-

---

[3] For the text in English see *The Commentaries of Pius II* (transl. Gragg, ed. Gabel), book III, pp. 276f.

[4] See *ibid.*, 107.

[5] E.g. *ibid.*, 62. See also J. B. Toews, "Dream and Reality in the Imperial Ideology of Pope Pius II," *Medievalia et Humanistica*, Fasc. XVI, Boulder, 1964.

[6] See the description of Frederick's coronation, quoted from the *Historia Friderici* (with German translation) in Bertha Widmer's *Enea Silvio Piccolomini*, Basel, 1960, pp. 216–221.

lowing reigns, under Maximilian I and even more under Charles V.

But Frederick III was not to be feared. He had, by his inactivity regarding matters outside his hereditary lands, become the object of incessant attacks from many circles in the Empire, especially those that thought—or at least talked—in terms of reform. Thus he needed all the support he could get, especially that of the papacy. He could be sure of this support as long as he did not cross the policy of the Holy See in any essential point.

But papal support did not, at all times, suffice to ward off the attacks to which the Emperor was exposed, especially those schemes of reform which were connected with the replacing the Emperor himself, or at least with making his position a purely nominal one. Only two generations ago, in 1400, one of Frederick's predecessors, Wenceslas IV of Luxemburg, had been deposed by the Electors for reasons very similar to those which were now brought forward against Frederick. This had not led to any real reform, at least not any imperial reform, yet Wenceslas' younger brother and successor Sigismund had helped to terminate the Great Schism, and his name, at least, had been given to one of the most daring, most radical schemes of reform ever to be conceived for the peoples of the Empire in the late Middle Ages.

Remembering these facts, men of some stature and daring began at a fairly early time to think either of others or—if they were princes—of themselves as able to replace the Emperor, if not in name, then in his essential functions. The Emperor, so the idea was, would remain Emperor, but just as it had been possible in previous times to elect, during his lifetime, the Emperor's son as King of the Romans, so now some other person would be elected to this dignity by the princes-electors, without having to go through the painful procedure of deposing the Emperor first.[7]

The idea itself, while not entirely without precedent, was peculiar enough. Far stranger, however, was the way in which the Emperor himself reacted to those frequent attempts to make him a purely titular head of the Empire. Repeatedly his attitude was clearly designed to give the impression that he was not really averse to such a scheme, that at least he would very seriously consider it if the right man came along and if his dynastic rights, his formal position, and

[7] For the following discussion of the early attempts at putting a stronger ruler at Frederick's side, see A. Bachmann, "Die ersten Versuche zu einer römischen Königswahl unter Friedrich III," *Forschungen zur deutschen Geschichte*, 1877, pp. 277–330; K. Menzel, *Diether von Isenburg, Erlangen*, 1868, pp. 75ff.; G. Voigt, *Enea Silvio de Piccolomini*, II, 234ff.

his financial status were fully safeguarded. Maybe Frederick III felt that in this way he would bring to the surface trends and groups eager for such action and thus could defeat them better than otherwise. If so, the Emperor's tactic proved, in the long run, remarkably successful.

Such a scheme was first vented some years earlier, in 1454. As was often the case in later years the urge for imperial reform was, at this moment, intimately connected with the idea of driving the Turks out of Europe—a task which appeared especially urgent so recently after the loss of Constantinople.

And, as later, the man most active, most interested in furthering the scheme was one of that strange and interesting group of international lawyer-diplomats who, for a good salary, were willing to serve anyone who might want to employ them, whether Emperor or prince, bishop or city. This did not exactly make for constant and reliable loyalty. It was not unusual that one of these men would be lured from the service of one potentate by the higher offers of another—one whose interests, in many respects, might be diametrically opposed to those of the previous employer. It was not even unknown for a lawyer-diplomat to serve two, perhaps even three lords at the same time—usually with, occasionally without their knowledge, but rarely without a certain measure of conflicting interests and duties.

We shall, in the course of our story, meet a few of those men. The most famous were probably Gregory Heimburg and Martin Mair, and it is the last-named whose political career was most intimately connected with the idea of imperial reform.[8] Several times it was he who took the initiative, which resulted repeatedly in profitable employments for him. Nevertheless one would probably do him less than justice to assume that he was motivated by nothing but the wish to make money. If he was not (as Palacký thought) the very model of a German patriot striving for imperial reform, he can still be believed to have had a sincere interest in the schemes he proposed, and a real hope for their implementation and usefulness. There is a consistency and urgency in his operations that is not fully explained by the assumption that his craving for wealth and power, strong as it was, was his only motive.

[8] See Bachmann, *Böhmen und seine Nachbarländer 1458–1461*, 60ff; A. Kluckhohn, 155ff., K. Menzel, *op. cit.*, 76ff., Urbánek *Věk*, III, 521ff, and Sigmund Riezler, *Geschichte Baierns*, III, Gotha, 390ff. (Riezler also wrote the article on Mair in *ADB*). The only monograph on him (G. Schrötter, "Dr. Martin Mair," Dist., Munich, 1896) treats only the earlier part of his career.

Of the princes who, partly upon Martin Mair's suggestion, became interested in this matter, the first was Duke Philip the Good of Burgundy. It was the lethargy and reserve that Frederick showed in 1454 at the Regensburg Congress of Princes (intended to take the needed measures for the crusade) which, it seems, turned Mair against the Emperor. From that moment on he—as well as his friend and colleague Gregory Heimburg—considered the Emperor the worst hindrance to any improvement in the internal conditions of the Empire.

Mair's scheme, in this case, did not get much beyond its earliest phases. Among the electors—upon whose support, after all, the whole plan depended—none but James, Archbishop of Trier, was willing to endorse it, and even he only as long as there seemed to be some hope that the Emperor himself might agree. Thus the chance of somehow shouldering the Emperor aside collapsed in the face of Frederick's passive resistance.

Somewhat more hopeful seemed an attempt to raise the Emperor's own brother, Archduke Albert, to the rank of King of the Romans. Thereby, it might be thought, effective power as well as nominal headship remained with the Habsburgs. This time, Mair's initiative seemed to carry the scheme a good deal farther than his original plan. The connection with the Turkish question is as clear as before: in February 1456 the Reichstag of Frankfurt had just reduced very considerably the figures of those armed forces that the Reich was supposed to send, as help against the Turks, to the combined forces of Hungary and Bohemia. In this sad state Albert, ambitious from the beginning, was only too glad to take up Mair's suggestions. In his name the diplomat approached the electors, beginning with the three ecclesiastical ones and the Palsgrave, all of whom seemed to be willing to give the matter a friendly consideration. Fairly favorable was, at first, also Frederick II of Brandenburg.[9] The next step —which might conceivably have gained the plan a working majority —was to approach King Ladislav. Since his rank as an elector was based only on his Bohemian Kingship the last word would probably have been with the kingdom's regent George of Poděbrady. But before it came to such a decision the plan faltered again, mainly because the German prince closest to the Emperor, Margrave Albert Achilles of Brandenburg, used his considerable influence with his

[9] See the detailed discussion of this phase in J. P. v. Gundling, *Leben und Thaten Friderichs des Anderen, Churfürsten zu Brandenburg,* Potsdam, 1725, pp. 399–405, 422–424.

brother the elector and with the latter's namesake, Frederick II of Saxony, which was sufficient to put an end to any thought of Archduke Albert's elevation. It now seemed that Albert's blood relationship to the Emperor, far from being a help, was rather a hindrance. Certainly the feelings between the brothers, never good, became rather more hostile as a result of this attempt.

Mair now tried a different approach. If, so far, the candidates had failed to gain sufficient support within the small group of electoral princes, then perhaps it was better to induce one of the electors themselves to become a candidate. While, at times, Mair hoped to win for this plan the Elector of Brandenburg, Frederick II—who might have been the only one to overcome the resistance of his brother Margrave Albert, the Emperor's "faithful Eckehard"—Mair's choice finally fell upon a stronger and more ambitious man: Frederick I of the Palatinate, even though he could almost be sure to run up against the resistance not only of the Emperor himself but also of the electors of Brandenburg and Saxony. This time all would depend on gaining the support of the three ecclesiastical electors and, if possible, of the King of Bohemia. Frederick, highly interested and immediately active, tried to gain the needed support at a Diet at Nürnberg in the fall of 1456. He could count on Mainz, had good hopes for Cologne, and expected the archiepiscopal see of Trier—at the moment vacant—to go to his Wittelsbach cousin and friend, Rupert of Bavaria. Ladislav, it is true, was then away in Hungary, but his dislike of the Emperor had become so universally known that much could be hoped from his cooperation. The Chapter of Trier, however, did not elect Rupert but John of Baden, a close friend of the Emperor's. John's resistance, combined with that of the two Fredericks of Saxony and Brandenburg, would be too difficult to overcome. This, at least for the moment, seemed to kill all chances for the Palsgrave.

Dr. Martin Mair, however, was, if anything, a tenacious man and did not easily resign himself to defeat in a matter as important and as needful as this one. It was probably at the great Congress of Cheb —where he had still appeared as adviser to the Palsgrave—that Mair thought he had at last found the right man to take over the effective rule of the Empire: the new King of Bohemia.

This was not Mair's first acquaintance with George. He had met him five years before, in Wiener-Neustadt, when the then regent had tried to build a bridge between his young King and the Emperor. At the time George had appeared as a clear-thinking man, sure of his goals, a true statesman, yet one of a few of perhaps similar stature. Now he was victor in a difficult struggle for recognition—and, as a result, clearly the most powerful, the most truly respected man in all of Central Europe.

True, he was not a German, and this was bound to cause doubts among Germans. He was, so some thought, hardly an orthodox adherent of the Roman Church but "infected by the Hussite poison," and this again was bound to cause doubts about his suitability, especially among the archbishop-electors. But then he would not be the first Bohemian King to become King of the Romans, and his orthodoxy was not, so it seemed, any longer seriously doubted by the Pope himself. In almost every other way George seemed to Mair far more suited to fill this important position than any other man alive. First of all he was himself an elector, indeed the first in rank of all electors, and in an election the Bohemian voice was his alone. He had just now been befriended by the other three lay electors, among them Mair's own employer the Palsgrave, and Mair was well aware that at least two of the Rhenish archbishop-electors had sought his friendship. Thus his chances for securing the election seemed far better than in the previous cases.

Mair could not ignore the fact that, as long as there was an "imperial party" among the electors, including, at the time, Saxony, Brandenburg, and Trier, the Emperor himself had still considerable influence in the matter. For the time being he hoped that it might be possible to gain his agreement.

Dr. Mair spoke of his dream to King George while the Congress of Cheb was still underway. George was highly skeptical. The most important consideration for him was still the attitude of the Emperor himself. He felt, as a later witness (indeed, not a friend of Mair) reported, that "no advantage but only great trouble would result from this." But Mair made a strong effort to convince him that the Emperor was by no means disinclined to such an agreement. It seems doubtful that George believed him right away. More had to happen to convert him to Mair's views.[10]

The relationship between George and the Emperor was not a sim-

---

[10] Our source is a detailed report made, by Duke Wolfgang of Bavaria, to the Emperor, directed against his relative Duke Albert of Bavaria and against Martin Mair of June 1, 1471. It goes on to say that Mair had never worked sincerely for George, but had always hoped to fish in muddied waters by getting King and Emperor into trouble with each other. See the document in Ulm St. B. Ulmensia 5557–5574, to be printed in *DRTA, XXII*, partly already published by Kluckhohn, 370–371.

ple one and not easy to circumscribe. During the earlier part of his career George was able to look at Frederick III with a sort of patient forbearance of his weakness combined with some understanding of the enormous difficulties in which the Emperor found himself. He had previously, with great effort and not without some risk for his own position, prevented the outbreak of an all-out war between King Ladislav and the Emperor. In his collision with the Habsburgs in 1458 he had struck hard, but merely in answering the offensive action of Archduke Albert and with some consideration for the Emperor's special position. But since the conclusion of the peace based upon the Habsburg princes' recognition of George's kingship, the issue which increasingly determined the relationship between George and Frederick was the Hungarian situation. This situation, however, was soon dominated by the strong antagonism between the young King Matthias and the Emperor.

Though up to his liberation by George Matthias had been the victim of the hate and distrust of his predecessor, Ladislav, he nevertheless inherited from Ladislav the latter's difficulties with Frederick III. It was like a symbol of this unpleasant inheritance that the Emperor still held the sacred crown of St. Stephen. This had been a cause of deep annoyance to Ladislav even though he himself had been crowned with it as an infant and there was no danger that, on that account, his kingship might fail to be recognized. But in Matthias' case the situation was different. Nowhere, not even in Bohemia, was so much authority attributed to the crown as in Hungary. The mystic force of the holy crown of St. Stephen, and almost this alone, truly made the King. The fact that it had, so far, not been possible to put this crown on his head was a serious set-back for Matthias and was soon used by his adversaries inside and outside Hungary to challenge his right to call himself King of Hungary.

We have to glance at Matthias' early reign, the challenges to his kingship, and especially the positions taken by his two great western neighbors, the Emperor and the King of Bohemia. These events were important enough in their effect beyond the borders of Hungary.

The relation between George and Matthias had started with the help which George gave to Matthias' elevation, and the equally important help George himself received when he was crowned by the two Hungarian bishops. For a while the situations of the two men who had, rather unexpectedly, recreated a national monarchy after a period of at least nominal Habsburg rule continued to be similar.

Both had to contend with foreign challengers, including the Habsburg princes. Of the late King Ladislav's brothers-in-law it was, in Matthias' case, Casimir of Poland rather than William of Saxony who hoped to gain the Hungarian crown. But Casimir was a far greater, more powerful ruler than the Saxon duke, and thus potentially more dangerous to the young King. Whether Casimir—or perhaps any other claimant—would gain the support of a weighty part of the Hungarian opposition remained a crucial question. In the case of Bohemia it had become clear—at the latest by the beginning of 1459—that such opposition was doomed, even in the northern dependencies. But Matthias, at the same time, was yet far from having achieved a similar strength and security.

At the time of his election the leading members of what may be termed the Habsburg party—the former adherents of Ladislav, with Gara in the lead—had been partly cowed by the wave of feeling against Ladislav and for the Hunyadis, while others, notably Ujlaky and Jiskra, had abstained from active opposition against Matthias upon the urging of George of Poděbrady. George had even tried to make Jiskra participate in the solemn embassy which had greeted the newly elected King in Strážnice in Moravia—the place to which George had accompanied Matthias before the latter's entry into Hungary in February 1458. Jiskra had not come—showing that George's influence on him was limited—yet it seems that he had given George, and thus indirectly Matthias, promises which indicated his willingness to give the young ruler a chance. The later correspondence between the two Kings shows that Matthias, to some extent, felt that he could make George responsible for the attitude of Jiskra, and even of those "Bratříci" who were not, or no longer, under Jiskra's command. This, too, is understandable, since those Czech and Slovak guerilla fighters had never quite given up their contact with Bohemia and even with George. For George they were simultaneously a possible instrument of pressure and a source of embarrassment.

There is no clear indication why he should have turned against Matthias as early as the spring 1458.[11] At that time he left Slovakia in March 1458 and went to Poland, where he offered his services to King Casimir. His purpose was clearly to support Casimir's candidacy for the Hungarian throne, expecting that, as a Hungarian King, Casimir would back his own position in Slovakia. Since there Jiskra

---

[11] For the sources to the following see Urbánek, *Věk*, III, 446–454; Hoffmann, *Bratříci*, 53f., Josef Spirko, *Husiti, jiskrovci a bratríci*, Spišska Kapitula, 1937, pp. 102ff.

dominated the very region through which the Polish ruler would want to enter Hungary, this offer was of great significance for Casimir. There was, on the other hand, little hope for a successful Polish invasion as long as Poland was still involved in her war with the Prussian knights. The enormous respect in which Jiskra was held is shown by the fact that he was trusted by Casimir with the task of arranging an armistice with the Prussians, and that he eventually succeeded, though only in October. For the duration (to July 1459), the fortress of Marienburg was given into his custody.

Jiskra's prolonged absence, however, gave Matthias a chance to strengthen his position in the north. He sent one of his most reliable adherents, Sebastian Rozgonyi, into Slovakia, having given him the official position of "Captain of the upper region of the Kingdom," which until then Jiskra had held himself.

Above all he could now deal with those Czech and Slovak partisans who has established themselves as an independent force in the Slovak mountains. They were officered by men who had originally served under Jiskra and who sometimes returned to his service, first among whom was the highly gifted and attractive Peter Aksamit. Under the name "little brothers" (bratříci), but by their enemies nicknamed "beggars" (žebráci), they considered themselves as Czechs, most of them as Hussites, and at times they waged a vigorous guerilla struggle against the Magyar nobility.

In May 1458 Rozgonyi succeeded in trapping, near Sarospatak, a strong force of "bratříci," some 2,000 men led by their most successful captains, Peter Aksamit and John Talafús, both of them born Czechs. While Talafús, at the head of a few hundred cavalry, among them many Czechs and Poles, succeeded in breaking through the vastly superior enemy forces and to escape, Aksamit fell in battle, and with him about 600 of his soldiers, a smaller number being taken prisoner. Rozgonyi's victory significantly weakened the movement of the "bratříci" in Slokavia. While Jiskra himself was not directly involved in this defeat—indeed, there are reports indicating that on a short return to Hungary in late June he managed on his part to inflict a defeat on Rozgonyi—the permanent result of this campaign strongly favored Matthias against the Czech-led movement of the Slavic brotherhood in Slovakia. But if this was the beginning of the end, the end was still far away. There is no doubt that the destruction of his largely Czech force was taken as an unfortunate event in many Bohemian circles, surely also at the court of King George.

But the news from Hungary at this time was far from giving the impression that King Matthias' position had become generally stronger. The old Habsburg party was as hostile as ever, and in addition the young King had experienced a severe set-back through the defection of his closest and strongest supporter, his mother's brother Michael Szilagyi. Szilagyi had not expected his teen-age nephew really to rule when he helped to make him King, but had hoped to retain the position as "gubernator" that his brother-in-law John Hunyadi had held so long and that he had, as it were, inherited at the death of Laszlo Hunyadi.[12] Matthias, however, had removed him from the center of governmental power by giving him the command of an army intended to campaign against the Turks. Szilagyi had used his absence from Buda to conspire with Gara and Ujlaki. In this highly dangerous situation Matthias acted with extraordinary energy and self-confidence. Szilagyi was arrested and strict measures also taken against his associates. Matthias' enemies therefore tried to gain stronger support outside the country, and the man whom they approached first was the King of Bohemia, using the personal bonds between him and Ujlaki as a basis for these negotiations.

George was then, during the earliest weeks of 1459, in Moravia. He spent some time in Znojmo and in Uherské Hradiště and, later in January, he was present at a diet of the Moravian estates held in Olomouc. Somewhere during this time the Hungarian representatives got in touch with him to offer him the Hungarian crown. But he refused without much consideration. He said no, again, when Ujlaki suggested that George's gifted and promising third son, Henry, though only eleven at the time, might replace Matthias on the throne of Hungary.[13]

Only now, having ascertained that the Czech King was not available, the Hungarian magnates turned to the Emperor. He had repeatedly informed them of his intention to secure his succession to the Hungarian throne, and he held one important trump: the crown of St. Stephen, sacred symbol of Hungarian royalty, was in his hands, and he as well as his Hungarian partisans could believe that this crown, kept out of Matthias' grasp and put on his own head, would clinch the issue in his favor. With this encouragement, on February 17, at the town of Nemet-Ujvár, twenty magnates of Hungary elected

12 See W. Fraknói, *Matthias Corvinus*, 67ff.

13 See Palacký, *Dějiny*, IV, 2, 67f., with the sources listed in n. 46. There seems little reason to doubt (as Bachmann does in *Geschichte Böhmens*, II, 502) the substance of these reports. See further Urbánek, *Věk*, III, 479–481.

Frederick of Habsburg, Archduke of Austria and Emperor of the Romans, to be also King of Hungary.[14] In March Frederick solemnly accepted the new dignity and soon after had himself crowned with the crown of St. Stephen by the Archbishop of Salzburg. From now on he regularly carried the Hungarian Kingship among his other titles.

It is against this whole background that George's attitude has to be understood and judged. That his feelings for Matthias, and with them the relationship between the two courts in Prague and Buda, had undergone a considerable cooling off lately can hardly be doubted. This was, in all likelihood, due less to the destruction of the Czech brotherhood in Slovakia than to the persistent rumor which, at this time, was making the rounds of Central Europe: that Matthias was no longer interested in his engagement to George's daughter Catherine and did not intend to go through with the marriage. One variant of this story was that the young King considered strengthening his hand and dividing his enemies by re-negotiating the marriage—once already contracted by his family—with the daughter of Gara. Perhaps it was more likely that he, like George, considered ties with an older ruling house. In any case, at a time when personal ties like this seemed of the utmost importance, even the mere rumor of Matthias repudiating the marriage to his daughter may well have hurt deeply George's sense of honor and dignity.[15]

But essentially the issue now was how the Bohemian King should behave toward the Emperor, who at a very early date tried to gain not only George's acquiescence but his active support and cooperation in the imminent efforts to make the possession of the Hungarian crown more than an empty title. Is it so astonishing that George, in this situation, did not act like Matthias' father and friend? Matthias had been helpful to him, but he had at best balanced accounts. On the basis of a sober calculation—which was not without a measure of cynicism—the young man's political survival and success seemed highly doubtful. Would it be wise, now, to play his protector and thereby to endanger the valuable friendship with the Roman Emperor that had been the outcome of the peace treaty of October 1458? Or could George, in this conjunction, simply retire into neutrality?

There was now more involved than merely an issue of friendship with the Emperor, as against friendship with Matthias. For, at the

---

[14] See S. Katona, *Historia critica regum Hungarie*, VII (ordine XIV), Cluj, 1792 196ff.
[15] See Urbánek, *Věk*, III, 479f.

time that the question, with its rather unpleasant choice, really became acute, a few more events had occurred. The Emperor (or rather his captain) had actually won a battle against Matthias, though he could not maintain his advantage for long. Rumors spread that the young King, beset by so many troubles, was willing to step down in return for a generous financial offer. And finally the Congress of Cheb had taken place, with the tempting suggestion, presented by Dr. Martin Mair, that George was the right man to take over the government of the whole, vast Holy Roman Empire. George, at first, had been skeptical, but slowly his interest had been awakened. If he were to succeed where others had failed, if in particular he could achieve this goal with the consent of Frederick, then his international position, especially in relation to the papacy, would be well-nigh unassailable—or so he thought.

His early skepticism had been largely based on his doubts that the Emperor would give his consent. But Frederick's recent policy, in particular his demand for George's support of his Hungarian claims, seemed to put things in a new and much more hopeful light. Clearly Frederick's weakness had been his apparent lack of interest and his inactivity in the Empire. By spreading his rule still wider and thinner, and still farther away from the center of the Empire, the need would grow for adding a stronger, more effective head of government to the essentially titular head of the Empire. Would not Frederick, so George could ask himself, be conscious of such needs? In this light his request for help may well have appeared to George like a sign from heaven.

Yet George was not unaware of the less attractive aspects of this whole business. He was far from eager to turn his whole strength against the young man whose fate was so much like his own and whom, until recently, he had considered as his future son-in-law. This is shown not only by his refusal to consider the offer of the Ujlaki party but also by his later attitudes: that is the way in which he persistently evaded the fulfillment of all the obligations which he had undertaken toward the Emperor. And here, indeed, the position of the Holy See and of its legate in Hungary, Cardinal Carvajal, may well have played a role. If at the beginning George had thought (or had believed the Emperor's assurance) that Rome, especially Pius II, would support Frederick III in this struggle for Hungary, he must soon have realized that this was not so; that the Church, indeed, did its best to prevent an open clash between the Emperor and Matthias, a policy dominated by the interest in western unification against the Turks and in accordance with its desire for conciliation in the older struggle between the same Emperor and the previous King of Hungary, Ladislav.[16] At that time George's own policy had been in complete agreement with that of the Curia. And it was, very likely, the memory of the peace policy of the then regent of Bohemia which caused Cardinal Carvajal to suggest that George was the man to restore peace between the Emperor and Matthias—a suggestion accepted in Rome as well as in Buda. It seems that the legate hit upon this idea during or after a visit to the Emperor's residence in Wiener-Neustadt in late April 1459. The Emperor, indeed, was then quite unwilling to give up his claims to the Hungarian crown, but Carvajal was probably not fully informed about the intensity with which the Emperor had wooed George.[17]

Yet the first negotiations between the two courts took place almost simultaneously, at a meeting of the Emperor's envoys with those of the Czech King at Znojmo in Moravia. (It was also the time of the Congress of Cheb.) George's embassy consisted mainly of Moravian noblemen and was led by Bishop Tas of Olomouc, in whom the King put increasing trust during the years to follow. Here the Hungarian issue, it seems, came up only as a side issue, with the imperial councillors expressing Frederick's hope that George would not permit his daughter to marry a man whose claim to be King of Hungary was invalid. These first contacts—in which the initiative was still exclusively on the Emperor's side—were followed by a second meeting in which George, as it were, showed his own growing interest in the matter by agreeing to send his envoys to Baden near the Emperor's residence in Wiener-Neustadt. As a result a far-reaching and somewhat complex arrangement, expressed in two main parts, was concluded between the rulers. After a draft agreement, contained in a transcript of the King, dated June 15, the first official document followed a month later and expressed the Emperor's willingness to give the fullest recognition to George's position as King and electoral prince, to support him liberally, and above all "to direct our own affairs, whether in the Empire, in Hungary or in our other territories fully on the basis of [the King's] advice, and to keep all these prom-

---

[16] See Pius' letter to Frederick in I. Kaprinai, *Hungaria Diplomatica temporibus Mathiae de Hunyad*, Vienna, 1767, II, 288.

[17] See the last paragraph in Urbánek, *Věk*, III, 518ff., and Bachmann, *Böhmen und seine Nachbarländer*, 93ff., both with detailed source references.

ises to him."[18] This peculiar assurance that he would consider George's advice, especially in the empire, as binding upon his actions, could certainly be understood—and was quoted by Martin Mair, meanwhile hired by George as one of his chief councillors in legal and foreign policy matters—as an indication of the Emperor's willingness to go even farther, to make formal the King's position as the Emperor's foremost (and presumably only) princely adviser and deputy. The King, in turn, promised his help to achieve, either by negotiations or by force, recognition of Frederick's lordship in Hungary.

The second set of treaties was to have a much more solemn character, based on a personal meeting of both monarchs, significantly not at the Emperor's court but in the King's lands, in Brno. The Emperor arrived there on July 30 with a most magnificent escort, at the same time that an embassy from Matthias made its entry. For George the first and the most important immediate result of the meeting was his solemn enfeoffment by the Emperor with all the countries of the Bohemian crown, made even more gratifying for the King when the Emperor elevated his son Victorin, a young man in his seventeenth year, as Duke of Münsterberg and Count of Glatz, to the rank of an imperial prince.[19] For the first time, evidently, George could hope that beyond his personal rise he might establish his family as a new, fully Czech dynasty—the first one for a century and a half, since the extinction of the male line of the Přemyslides in 1306. For some time to come Victorin was to appear in a role which seems to indicate that George considered him as crown prince or heir apparent. (George's oldest son, Boček, was, so it seems, retarded in his mental development and was never allowed to play any role in public. Later, the third of George's sons, Henry, began to emerge as an equal to Victorin and eventually as the more likely successor to his father.)

But in return for these concessions, which eliminated the last possible doubts about George's legitimate position at the head of the Bohemian realm and as the ranking member of the college of electors within the Empire, the Emperor insisted on a more solemn repetition of the arrangements previously concluded by correspondence. Among the documents signed there,[20] one constituted a permanent

---

[18] See J. Chmel, *Materialien zur österreichischen Geschichte*, II, 173, and F. Kurz, *Oesterreich unter Friedrich IV*, I, 232f. See further Urbánek, *Věk*, III, 525ff., Bachmann, *Böhmen und seine Nachbarländer*, 99ff.

[19] See the report in *SLČV*, 126, George's letter to Prague in *AČ*, V, 279, and Victorin's elevation in Grünhagen-Markgraf, II, 153.

[20] The documents in Kurz, *Oesterreich unter Friedrich IV*, I, appendices XX to XXII, 288ff.

alliance, including a clause which obliged either party to help the other to suppress any conspiracies, conventicles, and other disturbances against their rule in their realms. George could use this clause immediately in asking the Emperor's support against his still refractory Breslau subjects, and it was to play an important role later when the Emperor himself was in extreme danger. In another document George obliged himself, as he had done before, to try to gain Matthias' peaceful abdication, but, in case this proved unattainable, he promised military assistance to Frederick. In the first case George was to receive 8,000 ducats for his services, but no less than 60,000 (paid out of the income from the Hungarian salt monopoly) for three years in case Hungary had to be conquered by force.

Perhaps the most important of the documents contained an addition to the previous promises made by the Emperor in a handwritten letter: not only would he govern his empire and realm according to George's advice but he would even organize his court, and make appointments for this court, and the imperial offices according to George's advice.[21] This, surely, appeared an important step toward the acceptance of George as a co-regent, which would mean as the man who would really rule the Empire.

But if George put substantial hopes in such ill-defined promises and assurances he was due for disappointment. Nor did the Emperor have reason to expect too much from George's declaration of support for his Hungarian plans, at least not in a form which would force the King to carry, virtually alone, the burden of a military conquest of Hungary with Bohemian arms. Indeed the very first thing that George did, while still in Brno, was to arrange with Matthias' envoys and those of the Emperor an armistice between the two rulers[22] to be in force till July 24, 1460, during which time friendly negotiations were to be taken up in Olomouc by January 20 at the latest. The armistice went into force and actually was of considerable help to Matthias in further consolidating his position in Hungary, including the Slovakian North. Thus it might well be said that the only obligation that George really took seriously was the one essentially put on him by Cardinal Carvajal and the Curia—to end by arbitration what might otherwise have been a drawn-out, damaging, and bloody war between Frederick and Matthias. (Indeed he emphasized, in his pro-

---

[21] The document itself is not preserved but is quoted in some detail in the instructions presumably formulated by M. Mair, in *FRA*, II, 20, 244.

[22] See Kaprinai, *Hungaria Diplomatica*, II, 341.

nouncement, that in war victory or defeat are always uncertain, general suffering, however, is certain—a truth which he rarely if ever forgot.) Matthias himself, therefore, had rather little to suffer under all these proceedings. Nor do the sources yield any proof whatever for the claim that he "rightfully resented (George's) policy as vile treachery and never really forgot it." [23] This judgment is based on no other evidence than Matthias' much later actions against George. These actions, however, are fully in character with Matthias' general mentality and his understanding of his own best interests. While some lingering resentment on Matthias' part cannot be excluded, there were then plenty of immediate, manifest motivations other than a wish of revenge.

If any man had a right to complain about George's actions it was Frederick III, not so much because Frederick was a victim of the King's deceit—for his own promises, or half-promises, which he never seriously intended to keep were hardly less deceitful—but because, in the process of such mutual double-dealing, he had clearly paid much the higher price than George. Indeed, George received a great deal: the enfeoffment, the final and full recognition with all that it implied, the elevation of his son, the support of his claims against Breslau, even the very fact that the Emperor, for all this, had come "after him" all the way to Brno. It can hardly surprise us that there were some astonished and indignant commentaries on the Roman Emperor's self-effacement.[24] And what price did the King of Bohemia pay? Promises, some of which he did not keep at all, while, for some of those that he did keep, he later expected and received additional payment. Yet he was not only disappointed but even very angry when eventually he found out that the Emperor, too, had engaged in double-dealing. Altogether George was clearly determined to make hay while the sun shone. To a considerable extent this was a successful operation. It was far less successful as soon as he tried to cash in on what he thought was the Emperor's main promise, and what, for a while at least, now became the main goal of his foreign policy: his election as King of the Romans.

At the time—in the fall of 1459—the King's high hopes seemed to have a sound enough basis. The friendship with most of the German electors combined with the Emperor's assurances justified expectations that the hoped-for elevation would be achieved with relatively

---

[23] Thus Bachmann, *Geschichte Böhmens*, II, 503.
[24] See "Anonymi Chronicon Austriacum," in Senckenberg, *Selecta*, V, 82.

minor difficulties. In particular there seemed now little reason to worry about the two electors who, last spring, had concluded with him such far-going "hereditary union," soon to be cemented by inter-marriage—Saxony and Brandenburg. Somewhat less close was the relation between George and the Rhenanian princes, and there was still considerable uneasiness regarding Duke Louis ("the Rich") of Bavaria-Landshut, himself not an elector but a powerful figure of great influence with the princes of the "reforming" party, especially his cousin Frederick of the Palatinate. The duke, however, who was engaged in a difficult struggle with the Emperor over his attempt to annex to his duchy the imperial city of Donauwörth, had recently manoeuvered himself into an impossible position. He had finally been left with the choice of waging an all-out war against the Emperor and all the princes of the "imperial party," perhaps even against King George (without any hope of retaining those Bohemian mercenaries on whom he had relied before), or of seeking the support and protection of the King of Bohemia on terms rather similar to those which had created a stable relationship between Bohemia and Saxony. For this endeavor he had two excellent mediators: Palsgrave Frederick himself and Frederick's former legal adviser who had now taken service with him—Louis—as well as with King George: Dr. Martin Mair.[25]

After a preliminary meeting of negotiators at Domažlice in mid-September, had laid the groundwork for the understanding, the principals met a month later in Pilsen: George with his chief advisers, including John of Rosenberg and Zdeněk of Sternberg, the two Wittelsbach princes, the bishop of Worms, and other leading figures of southern and western Germany. Here, again, mutual claims regarding fiefs across the borders were cleaned up. In general they were declared to stay dormant during the life of the King and the Duke of Bavaria, but Louis assured himself of possession of eight important castles by nominally lending to the King the sum of 30,000 Rhenanian guilders for which the castles were to serve as security. In fact they were thus sold to Bavaria. There was, in addition, the usual treaty of friendship and alliance. Yet George was careful not to tie himself to the Wittelsbachs so closely that he would thereby spoil his relationship to the "imperial party"—the Emperor himself, and the Wettin and Hohenzollern princes.[26] Thus, as King of Bohemia, he acknowl-

---

25 For the following the best source is A. Kluckhohn, 126ff., with most of the documentary sources derived from *FRA*, II, 20, 190ff., 198ff. See also K. Menzel, *Diether von Isenburg*, 55ff.

26 See Bachmann, *Böhmen und seine Nachbarländer*, 130.

edged Palsgrave Frederick's "arrogation" of electoral dignity, but as electoral prince of the Empire he made the very same concession dependent on the agreement of the Emperor. On the other hand he tried to show his interest in the issues of imperial reform by inviting the Wittelsbach princes to send representatives to a conference intended to stop further debasement of coinage and to improve the safety of road and river travel and trade in the Empire. It was to be held during the impending meeting of princes and their representatives at Cheb.

Whether and in what way the problem of George's elevation to the Roman kingship was vented at Pilsen is not clear. But this issue certainly assumed a far greater weight when, in November, the wedding between the house of Poděbrady and Wettin was to be celebrated in the old city of Cheb.[27] The wedding itself—between Zdenka and Albert—took place with great pomp in the presence of King and Queen, the Saxon dukes and Brandenburg margraves (including both electors), Duke Otto of Bavaria, and the Archbishop of Magdeburg. At the same time, Catherine of Wettin, at the tender age of six, was turned over to her future parents-in-law. Zdenka, known in Saxon history as Duchess Sidonia, was to become an influential and popular princess, considered as the co-foundress of the Albertinian (Saxony-Meissen) line of the house of Wettin, which is still extant and through whom (as well as through others among King George's children) the blood line of the Poděbradys contributed to all major European dynasties.

The days immediately following the wedding were devoted to political discussions, largely concerned with the old and stubborn struggles between the two German princely parties, among whom the Wittelsbachs were represented by Duke Louis' chief chamberlain, William Truchtlinger, and above all by Dr. Mair, while Margrave Albert Achilles did most of the arguing for the other side.

George, at this stage, did his best to achieve a rapprochement between the princes. This was not only in his interest—since his hopes for the Roman kingship depended largely on an understanding between the majority of the electors—but also corresponded to his natural feelings, as a man to whom war was not an enjoyable game but at best an unpleasant if not always avoidable means to an end. George's success in this direction, however, was anything but promising. Nor did the efforts for an imperial reform make any progress. And if

---

[27] *Ibid.*, 131f., and F. A. von Langenn, *Herzog Albrecht der Beherzte*, 39f.

these facts were disappointing to the Czech King, another sobering experience was in store for him as soon as he began discussing the idea of his role as King of the Romans with the virtual leader of the imperial party, Margrave Albert Achilles. The margrave, more familiar than George with the somewhat devious mind of the Emperor, gave vaguely positive but generally evasive answers. When George assured him that he had excellent reasons to expect Frederick's consent, Albert countered this clearly honest expression of the King's over-optimistic belief with the knowing remark: "If your Grace would give me a little slip of paper from our Lord the Emperor— were it only as long as a finger—in which his Grace were to ask me to work in this matter with the electors or elsewhere, I should do so faithfully and industriously." [28]

While, seemingly, this meant only a postponement of such action on the Margrave's part, George may well have realized that Albert himself did not really expect ever to receive such directions from Wiener-Neustadt. It was probably this disappointment which began to drive him toward a closer association with his erstwhile adversary, Duke Louis of Bavaria. Indeed it was during these days (on November 20th) that George concluded an additional treaty of friendship with the Munich line of the Bavarian dukes,[29] and at the same time it seems that the first steps were taken, by Louis himself, to reconcile George with the Emperor's brother—and by no means his friend— Archduke Albert of Austria.[30]

Meanwhile Dr. Mair continued to discuss with George the tactics to be employed to gain support for the scheme. One of the prime considerations seemed to be the procurement of sufficient money, as electoral votes were rarely given without some financial advantage for the voter. George, while by now far from poor, was still not nearly as rich as many other European rulers of even much smaller countries. But Mair had what seemed a brilliant idea. He was aware of the urgent wish of Francesco Sforza, since 1450 the actual ruler of Milan, to have his position as Duke of Milan recognized and himself formally enfeoffed with the duchy. Why should the duke's craving

---

28 For this whole phase see *Das Kaiserliche Buch des Markgrafen Albrecht Achilles*, ed. C. Höfler, I, Berlin, 1850, 72–75 and 82ff. (henceforth cited as *KBAA.*). Also Vienna H.H.St.A., Allg. Urk. Reihe A B 387 c, sog. Sextern. See finally the material in the forthcoming *DRTA*, presumably XX.

29 See G. V. Hasselholdt-Stockheim, *Herzog Albrecht IV von Baiern und seine Zeit*, II, Documentary appendix pp. 135f.

30 See the treaty concluded between George and the archduke in December 1459, text in Kurz, *Oesterreich unter Friedrich IV*, II, 211–214.

for his legitimatization not be turned into money? [31] Mair himself would go to Milan and explain to the duke that he would certainly receive the official title and fief as soon as George was installed as King of the Romans, but that to help in bringing this about, and in recognition of such favor, he was to pay the King 70,000 ducats. Also offered was the usual treaty of friendship and alliance, and a possible marriage between both houses.

Mair did cross the Alps in the depth of winter, returning to Landshut in February 1460. But the outcome of this trip was again rather disappointing. Francesco Sforza was willing indeed to take the investiture from any King of the Romans, whether his name was Frederick or George, and he did not refuse to pay the handsome reward. But it was to be a reward, to be paid only after or at the investiture, not before. Future negotiations might decide about alliance or marriage plans. Nevertheless Mair was far from discouraged. The letter in which he reported the meager results of this trip to King George was full of good advice for the future which, according to him, still very nearly guaranteed success.[32] At the next reichstag, supposed to meet in Nürnberg in March, the King should, with the Emperor's support, be appointed as *"conservator pacis per totum imperium"* and, at the same time, as commander-in-chief, in the Emperor's place, of the hoped-for crusade against the Turks. If George agreed to this, Mair himself would pave the way to these appointments which in turn would put him far ahead on the road toward the goal: the throne of the King of the Romans.

In reality things did not go at all smoothly in the desired direction. Soon it became clearer than ever that the Emperor, for all his vagueness and indolence, still held the key to any important changes in the government of the Reich. George had to acknowledge this basic fact, and throughout the year 1460 he tried to act accordingly, first by gaining the Emperor's voluntary agreement through appeals to his friendship and his given word, later by attempts to put him under pressure and thus force him to acquiesce. In any event both methods failed. But the course of these attempts was largely determined also by the turn of events in Germany herself, in particular by the extreme worsening of the relationship between the two dominant princely parties.

This old struggle, especially sharp between Louis of Bavaria and

---

[31] For the following see *FRA*, II, 20, 198–200.
[32] *Ibid.*, 201–216.

Margrave Albert Achilles, apparently came to a head with Louis' declaration of war in March 1460.[33] It was prompted by Albert's continued attempts to impose the jurisdiction of his "Landgericht" upon Wittelsbach subjects. Now it became clear how consequential and advantageous the rapprochement between King George and Duke Louis had been for the latter. For now Louis, with his proverbial wealth, could hire the famous, feared Czech mercenaries who had not been available to him as George's adversary, but whom George had no reason to withhold from a friend.[34] Some 4,000 Czechs and a smaller but still substantial number of Swiss mercenaries gave Louis a superiority sufficient for the conquest of the bishopric of Eichstaedt as well as of a number of castles and smaller towns in Albert's Franconian lands. Before long the margrave saw himself forced to sue for peace—a course which he was strongly urged to take also by his Saxon friends. In the armistice of Roth, soon followed by a peace concluded at Nürnberg (June 29) Albert renounced all claims to cite Bavarian subjects before the court.[35] But he did not mean to abide by this, as his immediate appeal to the Emperor showed. The struggle had merely been interrupted. And while it lasted it had become clear that George—for all his striving to appear as a friend of both sides and as the most suitable arbitrator—was nevertheless now a good deal closer to the Wittelsbachs than to the Hohenzollerns. It was, after all, only through the Wittelsbachs and their allies that he could identify himself with the demand for imperial reform which, as he hoped, would result in a more general pressure upon the Emperor to permit his own election as King of the Romans. And since his first intimations to Frederick III in this direction had met with no response at all he now tried to increase pressure on him by a further rapprochement with Frederick's enemies, among them his highly dissatisfied subjects in Lower Austria.

It is difficult to imagine a stranger relationship than that which had developed, in this period, between the Emperor and his most immediate subjects, those men who considered him as the senior Duke of Austria, directly responsible for their government and their well-being. It was, of course, not unusual for a nobleman to send a letter of challenge to his prince and wage war against him if he could claim that the prince had done him wrong and was unwilling to grant him justice. But rarely have the estates of a country—including,

[33] For this development see Kluckhohn, 136ff.
[34] See *FRA*, II, 20, 224f.
[35] Kluckhohn, 149f.

with its nobility, also its capital city—gone to such lengths in trying to "educate," to guide and shake and push their ruler toward what they considered his sacred duty. And rarely had the ruler reacted with such utter inertia.[36]

Just as in the rest of the Empire so in Austria Frederick did far too little to safeguard the free use of roads and waterways. In his anxiety to strengthen himself financially, however, he increased, in a rather arbitrary way, the tolls on roads and rivers. Worse by far were his enormous issues of inferior coins—the so-called "black pennies" or "schinderlinge"—which drove all the better money out of circulation and caused, by their inflationary pressure, a ruinous rise in prices not only in Austria but also in neighboring countries, among them Bohemia. The fiercely annoyed estates of Lower Austria continued to protest and accuse the Emperor, but the most effective militant attack to which he was exposed was conducted by one of the barons of the duchy, one Gamaret Fronauer. The Emperor had started a legally very dubious campaign aimed at driving Fronauer out of the strong castle of Orth, which he claimed, probably rightly, to have inherited from his brother Gerhart. Fronauer became a truly formidable enemy of the Emperor, but the victims most to be pitied were the peasants of Lower Austria. They were pillaged by the angry soldiers of both sides. These men—with a good many Czech mercenaries fighting on both sides—tried thus to compensate themselves for receiving their pay in worthless coins.[37]

In view of these chaotic conditions the Austrian estates looked longingly across the border to Bohemia, where for the last ten years a strong government had maintained that peace which seemed forever to pass Austria by. The political turn, of course, suggested itself most easily to the man whom the estates of Lower Austria still considered their uncontested leader, Ulrich Eizinger. For him George was both a model ruler and an old and proven friend to whom he owed his freedom and therewith the restoration of his strength and influence in Austria. And King George himself thereby got into a

[36] For the following paragraph see Bachmann, *Böhmen und seine Nachbarländer*, 169–178; Kurz, *Oesterreich unter Friedrich IV*, II, 3ff., Appendix 230–232; O. Brunner, *Land und Herrschaft*, 4th ed., Vienna, 1959, pp. 44f. For documentary evidence see esp. "Anonymi Chronicon Austriac," ed. Senckenberg, *Selecta*, V, 92ff., *SLČP*, 157. On the influx of the debased coinage into Bohemia see K. Castelin, *Česká drobná mince doby předhusitské a husitské, 1300–1471*, Prague, 1953, 223–229, and on the monetary situation in Austria itself, Vancsa, *Geschichte Nieder- und Oberösterreichs*, II, 348ff.

[37] See Vancsa, *op.cit.*, 357ff., also Schalk, *Aus der Geschichte des österreichischen Faustrechts 1440–1463*, 149ff.

position which was at the same time awkward and tempting. It was awkward since he himself had always (e.g. in the case of Duke William of Saxony and the Silesians) sharply resisted any attempt of a foreign ruler to meddle into what he considered, in a very modern sense, the sovereign rights and prerogatives of the Bohemian crown —an act which soon afterwards seemed to him a good enough reason for declaring war upon the offender. Yet it was also tempting because it seemed an excellent opportunity to put the Emperor under effective pressure, without, however turning him into an outright enemy —an outcome which would have to be avoided also because of its possible effect on the attitude of the Holy See.

Thus George, in order to achieve the desired results, would have to do a good deal of tight-rope walking. This, however, flustered him now no more than at other times. Thus he answered the urgent request of the Austrian estates for help and protection with what seemed a highly evasive letter, telling them that there were, after all, besides the Emperor himself, two other Austrian princes—Archduke Albert and Duke Sigismund—and that one of these surely would be able to help them to safeguard their liberties and rights.[38] Since he was now in good contact with the archduke—another former enemy with whom, at the end of 1459, he had concluded a treaty of friendship and alliance—the King's position was at best that of a doubtful "neutrality" between the Emperor and his subjects in Lower Austria. As a result, the Emperor—probably with little relish—accepted George, at this stage, as mediator between himself and the estates.[39] To this point, then, George's calculation proved entirely correct. The Austrian estates received new assurances from the Emperor that he would deal with the issues about which they had complained. Indeed there even resulted a moderate measure of restriction in the issuing of debased coin—a fact which was welcome also to Bohemia, where the "schinderlinge" had wrought considerable damage.

But this was about the extent of the King's success. While the Austrian estates continued, in their official and unofficial correspondence with Emperor and King, to claim and proclaim their own right to appeal to George and George's right to intervene in Austrian affairs,[40] the Emperor, very understandably, angrily denied any such

---

38 See "Anonymi chronicon," Senckenberg, *Selecta,* V, 124ff.

39 See Bachmann, *Böhmen und seine Nachbarländer,* 180f., largely based in the Ebendorfer von Hasselbach, "Chronicon Austriacum," ed. H. Pez, in *Scriptores rerum Austriacarum,* II, Leipzig, 1725, 898ff. Further Vancsa, *Geschichte Nieder- und Oberösterreichs,* 362ff.

40 See J. Chmel, *Materialien zur öesterreichischen Geschichte,* II, 211ff.

right, and, it seems, reminded the King that he had so far neglected several promises given during the Brno meeting.[41] George answered with both excuses and attacks. He, like the Austrian estates, claimed that he had received the right to look after the Austrians by the oral testament of King Ladislav. He also claimed that he had only taken the Austrians under his protection to calm them down and prevent them from more hostile acts against their lord the Emperor, a claim which, as later events showed, was at least partially true. He warned the Emperor that the situation in the Empire was desperate and urgently needed a strong hand—another statement which surely was far from exaggerated. He also drew the Emperor's attention to the dangerous situation of Jiskra, a common friend, after all, of himself and Frederick, and to the need of defending him against further attacks by Matthias. And he finally urged the Emperor to send his envoys to Olomouc, where, for December 6, he had invited Matthias or his ambassadors for a renewal of peace negotiations.[42]

This message, taken to the Emperor sometime in the fall of 1460 by two of George's highest dignitaries, the Lord High Burgrave Zdeněk of Sternberg and the Chancellor Prokop of Rabstein, did not bring the two principals any nearer. The Emperor's answer[43] was outright unfriendly, and any illusions that he could possibly be induced to tolerate, more or less willingly, the Czech King as a coregent seemed completely shattered. The only hope left to George at this stage was to win over the electors even against the Emperor's will. Perhaps he should have realized at this point that the chances for such a manoeuvre were slim. But he had experienced too often that consistence and perseverance led, in the end, to success even if the chances had first appeared poor. He decided to persevere again.

This, clearly, was also the advice that came to him from Dr. Martin Mair. Mair accompanied his other employer, Duke Louis of Bavaria, on a visit to Prague in the autumn of 1460 which served to tie the two princes together in a truly firm alliance for mutual benefit.[44] The duke obliged himself to work with the greatest urgency to win over all the electoral princes, especially the Archbishops of Mainz and Cologne and the Palsgrave, to achieve George's elevation to the

---

[41] Ebendorfer, *"Chronicon Austriacum,"* 904ff.

[42] *Ibid.,* 919.

[43] Chmel, *Materialien zur öesterreichischen Geschichte,* 257f. As to the answer's dating and background see Bachmann, *Böhmen und seine Nachbarländer,* 205f.

[44] *FRA,* II, 20, 226f., 232f., and *KBAA,* I, 66ff. See also the detailed summary in Bachmann, *op. cit.,* 220–223.

Roman kingship "by whatever means seemed most suitable." For this effort the duke would be given the position of Supreme Master of the Royal Court of the Roman Empire with a yearly income of 8,000 Hungarian ducats, and in addition, as security, the city of Donauwörth, the very place over which he had struggled so doggedly with the Emperor and which, at the time of his political isolation, he had been forced to give up. Very specific arrangements were drawn up according to which the duke, with his cousin the Palsgrave as a possible alternate, would act as regent in the Empire during periods in which the King himself should be forced to be "absent." Among the main motivations for the whole set-up figured, beside the general troubles of the Empire, the permanent dangers of a Turkish attack.

The pact, dated October 8, was partially implemented when the principals gave full power to Dr. Mair to negotiate with the Rhenish electors. It was not too difficult for him to obtain a provisional agreement with his former master, the Palsgrave, although the latter's conditions were rather stiff and, even so, his consent was still far from a definite promise of support against other electors.[45] Somewhat more complicated was the acquiring of similar promises from the Archbishop of Mainz, Diether of Isenburg, with whom Mair negotiated in the later part of November. Yet even here Mair was optimistic and seemed to have good enough reasons. For Diether, more than any of the other electors, was becoming a strong protagonist, in a sense even a symbol, of the general dissatisfaction of the German princes and of other large groups of Germans with the two paramount authorities, Emperor and Pope. In Mair's eyes this was an excellent basis from which to work for George's elevation. All that was needed, so it seemed, was for George to identify himself and his great power unmistakably with the call for reform—a reform which, if meant seriously, would have to be achieved by a determined struggle against both Emperor and Pope.[46]

Diether's role in this struggle had emerged at the time when, soon after his election, he had tried to achieve papal confirmation through an embassy sent to Mantua. The negotiation conducted there centered around two issues: the attempt of Pope Pius to obtain from the new archbishop—as imperial chancellor, the ranking ecclesiastical prince-elector—assurances which would have given the Pope an enormous

---

[45] *KBAA*, I, 52–58; Bachmann, *op. cit.*, 234–238.
[46] See for this and the following the generally excellent monograph by K. Menzel, *Diether von Isenburg*, esp. pp. 69ff., 84f., 88ff.

influence on the electoral college and its policy within the Empire; and financial demands in the form of Annates which were a good deal higher than those paid by Diether's predecessors. Though, before long, the Pope dropped some of his purely political requests (such as the demand that the archbishop never summon the electoral princes without the Pope's prior agreement), both issues seemed highly typical of the oppressive and exploitative power wielded by the Curia in Germany, against which the reform movement had managed to mobilize the general opinion of the politically informed or interested German circles.

The archbishop—himself an impatient and short-tempered man—thus managed to gather considerable support for his resistance against the Pope in terms which, in the political field, recalled the attitudes and actions of the German high clergy and electoral princes during the days of Rense and Frankfurt in 1338. This became especially obvious during a bitter struggle, to be discussed in a different context, between the Pope (acting for his friend Cardinal Nicholas of Cusa) and Duke Sigismund of Habsburg, the ruler of the Tyrol. At this time, the two other archbishops-electors and many other princes joined Diether of Mainz in protest against the excommunication of Sigismund by Pope Pius. The Pope's most recent legate to Germany, the famous Greek Cardinal Bessarion, did not improve matters by the over-temperamental way in which he tried to hector the German princes into a more active participation in the Pope's crusading plans. The general annoyance among the German princes went so far that for a while it seemed as if even the struggle between the two main parties—the Wittelsbachs with their allies on the one hand, the Wettins and Hohenzollerns on the other hand—could be overcome and all the leading German princes would unite in the cause of reform—this word now implying essentially resistance against papal infringements, political and economical, upon their princely rights and freedoms. Diether did, indeed, get considerable support also from the princes of the "imperial" party.

The question was now: would this common front, at this moment allied much more solidly against the Pope than against his friend the Emperor, ever present a platform from which George could realize his hopes for German kingship? Dr. Mair thought so. This was clearly shown by the way he negotiated on George's behalf with the Archbishop of Mainz. Diether's conditions were no less demanding than those of the Palsgrave, combining requests for personal and family gains with those for real reform measures, including the calling of a "parliament" and of a General Council to Mainz.[47]

But besides all this, it seems that Diether demanded additional proofs for George's orthodoxy, such as his taking, in public, the communion in one kind. This, indeed, was only to be expected. The more acrimonious the struggle between archbishop and Pope became, the more the Elector of Mainz had to show that, if he was a rebel or at least the leader of a resistance movement against the Curia in the field of imperial policy and church policy, his orthodoxy in terms of dogma and ritual was above suspicion. He simply could not afford to be allied with, let alone to promote to Roman kingship, a man suspected of heresy. This would impair his own cause in the eyes of his fellow princes as well as of the Mainz Cathedral Chapter, without whose support he could not possibly maintain himself against the sustained pressure from Rome.[48]

It was characteristic of the intricacy and the uncertain character of George's international position that, when Mair happily accepted this like the bulk of Diether's other conditions, the King could not disavow him. He would not only have discredited himself for the hoped-for dignity of Roman King, but beyond that would immediately have endangered his friendship with the Pope, which at this time seemed rather secure and had—as will be discussed—born fruit especially in relation to Breslau's position within the kingdom. But this was only one aspect of George's peculiar situation at this moment: the newly strengthened reform front—a boon in the eagerly dreaming eyes of Martin Mair—brought no real improvement but, if anything, a worsening of George's chances for the powerful position. What he would have needed was a strong and concerted action against the Emperor—not against the Pope. George, in all his utterances, was extremely careful not to appear as the Pope's enemy. At a meeting in Bamberg, held in mid-December, the King's envoys (as well as those of Duke Louis of Bavaria) had therefore refused to join in Archbishop Diether's appeal against the Pope's supposed encroachments on the freedoms of the Empire.[49] And if this did

---

[47] *KBAA,* I, 59–65.

[48] See Menzel, *Diether von Isenburg,* 89, 90.

[49] The documentation in *KBAA,* I, 81. For its evaluation see Bachmann (*Böhmen u.s. Nachbarländer,* 250ff., especially 252 n. 2.) and, on the other hand, Menzel (*Diether von Isenburg,* 94–96). Menzel is quite right in his emphasis on George's determination not to antagonize the Pope under any circumstances. On the other hand, Bachmann is certainly right in pointing out that the course and outcome of the Bamberg meeting cannot possibly have been welcome to the King.

not bode well for the idea of the common front, neither did the refusal of Saxony and Brandenburg to sign the general resolutions for reform endorsed by the other princes.

Yet George, unwaveringly, went ahead with his plan. He called another conference of princes to Cheb for the beginning of February 1461. There, on his own soil and under the impression of his brilliance and power, he hoped that the Electors of Brandenburg and Saxony would feel impelled to go along with his requests. With their support in addition to the votes of Mainz and the Palatinate as well as his own, he would have five of the seven electoral votes. Once he got as far as this the rest, surely would be easy.

This third meeting of imperial princes in Cheb was no less spectacular than its two predecessors.[50] Among the princes present were the Margraves of Brandenburg and Baden, the Saxon and Bavarian dukes, the Landgrave of Hessen, the Archbishop of Salzburg, five other bishops and all the important cities represented by diplomatic envoys. In the beginning, George's direction of events seemed purposeful, clear-minded, and successful. He postponed the discussion and arbitration—originally intended as one of the main topics of the congress—of the old and never fully pacified struggle between Duke Louis of Landshut and Margrave Albert Achilles. Instead he put the idea of imperial reform in the foreground, and this in a way which would show how large and serious this issue loomed in his mind. At the same time George's procedure would deflect all essential criticism from the Pope—whose hopes for energetic action against the Turks, rather, would be revived—and concentrate it against the Emperor. The main points of the discussion as he directed it were, first, the question of financing the planned crusade by sufficient taxes; second, the organization of the army to be built up by these means; and, third, the securing of peace in Germany, clearly a precondition for the dispatch of a strong army, by the establishment of a comprehensive landfrieden throughout the Empire.

As long as this discussion moved in more or less general terms things seemed to go exactly according to George's wishes. And when, in connection with the issue of the person of the prospective commander-in-chief, the possibility of electing a Roman King was men-

---

[50] A detailed account of the congress is in Bachmann, *Böhmen u.s. Nachbarländer*, 258–268. There also (260 n.2) appears a list of the sources among which the most important are *FRA*, II, 44, Vienna, 1885, 68ff.; *KBAA*, I, 80–91, J. J. Müller's *Reichstags-Theatrum*, II, 4–14, and Th. Pešina, *Mars Moravicus*, Prague, 1677, pp. 721f. See also Menzel, *Diether von Isenburg*, 97–102.

tioned, it looked for a short while as if George's hopes were going to be fulfilled. Several of the princes seemed inclined to support his candidacy. But the Elector Frederick II of Brandenburg pointed out that Cheb was not the place for an imperial election, and in view of his obvious opposition the debate ground to a halt.

George finally decided to take the bull by the horns. He approached, first, the Elector of Brandenburg, trying to gain his collaboration by offers in which Brandenburg's hold over lower Lusatia —still open to a radical revision in case Bohemia offered to redeem the territory—seems to have played some role.[51] But Frederick did not rise to the bait. As a member of the Union of Electors, he declared, he could do nothing without the agreement of its other members. On George's reference to the arrangements made with the Electors of Mainz and the Palatinate, Frederick declared that this could not have much influence since, as yet, neither of the two had been acknowledged as members of the Electoral Union.

George, clearly annoyed, tried to use the influence that Albert Achilles was known to have upon his brother, and the margrave considered it the best diplomacy to hold out considerable hopes to George in case the two new electors could be received into the Union during the Nürnberg diet in late February 1461.

This—a small enough gain for so great an effort—now appeared as the last possible opportunity for the realization of George's dream. But it was perhaps an indication of the skepticism which, at this time, must have replaced his former optimism that the King decided, against the advice of his guests of Brandenburg, not to go to Nürnberg himself.[52] Since it seemed increasingly doubtful whether things could still work out there in a favorable way, at least he would avoid suffering such a defeat in person. He did not even send his chief representatives. Neither Zdeněk of Sternberg nor the Chancellor Prokop of Rabstein were present. The Czech delegation was led by the chief justice, Zybněk Zajíc of Hasenburg, and by Jost, Bishop of Breslau. Besides them, the most important member was presumably

[51] See Gundling, *Leben und Thaten Friderichs des Andern*, 512.

[52] At this stage Bachmann's otherwise clear and consistent account begins to flag. In particular his assumption (pp. 266f.) that, in preparation for the meeting at Nürnberg, George solemnly promised ("gab . . . bündige Versprechungen") to abolish the communion *sub utraque* in Bohemia is highly unlikely. None of the contemporary sources know anything of this. Against the far from contemporary and politically and religiously prejudiced presentation by Dubravius and Hajek and a contradictory account by Zacharias Theobald, in his *Hussiten-Krieg*, III, 70, stands the far more likely report of Thomas Pešina (*Mars Moravicus*, 722) that the King only promised to proceed against the radical sects in Bohemia—a promise which he did, indeed, keep soon after.

Martin Mair, to whose activity—of doubtful value, thus far—the King was still willing to give another chance.

But they achieved nothing.[53] The Electors of Mainz and the Palatinate—both present in person, as was Frederick of Brandenburg—were indeed received into the Union of the Electoral princes, largely as a result of Bohemian pressure. But once in, neither prince made any attempts to follow through in his promises to work for George's elevation. For Archbishop Diether, in particular, the whole meeting had only the purpose to gather support for his ever more desperate struggle with the Pope. He seemed to be fairly successful when a majority of delegates joined him in protesting against papal taxation demands and against the bull "Execrabilis," which had outlawed appeals to church councils. But Diether's success remained short-lived, and the Czech delegates refrained from supporting him at any stage. In view of this, we cannot be surprised that Diether, on his side, was not really interested in the project of the Czechs.

This was not only a question of quid pro quo. George, with his non-German background and his need to tread carefully in his relation with Pius II, was, in the eyes of men like Diether and those following him at this time, simply not the right man for the job. But if this was true for the most active among the electors of the reform party, it was just as true for those of the other camp. Or rather could it be said that for them there was no legitimate need at all for such a position. The Emperor had, meanwhile, been very fully informed about the whole development by his faithful friend and servant Albert Achilles.[54] But the margrave found it difficult to convince the Czech envoys that he was, as he claimed to be, equally the friend and servant of their King. All their attempts to get any action on the project of George's elevation met with a cool and rigid resistance, which usually took the form of putting things off for a possible later opportunity. In George's eyes—and he based his judgment largely on the reports of his envoys, especially Mair—the man most to blame for the blocking of all their efforts was Albert Achilles. His anger was not quickly nor easily appeased.

It seems that now, finally, he was ready to bury the dream of

[53] By far the best and most detailed account of the meeting at Nürnberg is in Menzel, *Diether von Isenburg,* 103–127. (There, on pp. 125–127, is the text of the official "Abschied" of Nürnberg.) The sources are essentially the same as those about Cheb, especially *FRA,* II, 44, 70–75, *KBAA,* I, 83, 86–91, Müller's *Reichstag-Theatrum,* II, 5ff., 10ff., to which has to be added Janssen, *Frankfurts Reichskorrespondenz,* II, Freiburg, 1866, 148f.

[54] See Hasselhold-Stockheim, *Herzog Albrecht IV,* 232ff.

his Roman kingship. From now on, at least, no more steps were taken to influence the electors, and if pressure upon the Emperor did not cease entirely, it was for other reasons and for different goals. We have, it is true, the undated draft for a note which indicates that somewhere in Prague court circles an entirely new approach was considered: to ask Pope Pius for his support in this matter. Some historians have paid undeserved attention to this draft. It is fairly certain that this was merely another, final essay issuing from Dr. Mair's ever fertile brain. The King himself may not even have seen it, and certainly he never permitted it to be dispatched.[55] For if it had reached Rome, there would have been a reaction, and certainly not a favorable one.

Thus, by the spring of 1461, another phase had ended in the extraordinary career of George of Poděbrady. For the first time it had brought little or no profit to the King himself or to his country. And for once the question remains whether the whole concept had really made sense from the very point of view which, so far, much to his credit, had dominated George's attitudes and actions: the needs of a successful national policy for the Czech nation and the Bohemian realm. It is clear that George, in his endeavors for the Roman kingship, not only collided with foreign interests but had also to contend with skepticism, in some circles even with outright opposition, among his own people. True, they could have remembered the time

---

[55] The original document, originally in the Haupstaatsarchiv in Munich, was later in the Bamberg Kreisarchiv under Rt. A. 1414–93, fol. 88–97, but it is now no longer in Bamberg. The material can be expected to be fully available in vol. XX of the *Deutsche Reichstags-Akten.* See further Höfler, *Urkunden z. Geschichte Böhmens,* Abh. der. K. böhm. *Gesellschaft d. Wissenschaften,* 1865, pp. 53ff., and Hasseloldt-Stockheim, *Urkunden* I, 1, 301–316; also partially *FRA,* II, 20, 244, and the detailed abstract in Bachmann, *Böhmen u.s. Nachbarländer,* 292ff. It seems astonishing that this fragmentary draft which, as Bachmann himself admits, the Pope never saw, and which is important mainly as a source for prior events (see above, n.22), should have inspired this historian to the far-reaching conclusions and considerations concerning George's lack of religious conviction which supposedly led to the King's resolve (*Entschluss*) to reach his goal with the Pope's help. The draft, so he says, "corresponds to the wishes and intentions of the King. He had the will to act accordingly, and this alone suffices to throw an ugly shadow upon the King's memory" (*ibid.,* 281f.) This "ugly shadow" (*hässlicher Flecken*) is based, according to Bachmann's view, on George's (highly doubtful) intention to let the Pope decide about the occupant of the Roman throne, without any regard to George's "duties toward the Empire whose elector he was, toward the defense of the sovereignty (*Selbstständigkeit*) of the German crown, toward the sacred rights of the whole German nation . . ." This is a most peculiar standard, based on an odd mixture of a somewhat anachronistic German nationalism with other prejudices against the King, whose history owes much to the research of this gifted and hard-working historian. In few places does his prejudiced attitude appear as clearly as here. As in other cases, Bachmann finds a faithful and uncritical follower in B. Bretholz, *Geschichte Böhmens und Mährens,* II, Reichenberg-Liberec, 1922, 112–115. See also Urbánek, *Věk,* IV, 396ff.

of Charles IV, when the personal union of the Roman with the Bohemian kingship had been accompanied by a period of prosperity and glory for the Czechs. There is no question that for George himself—history-conscious as he was—such memories had considerable weight. And while he must have been just as aware of the fate of Wenceslas IV, which showed how uncomfortable a seat the Roman-German throne could be, he still expected that its glory would provide that final, crowning security which would safeguard not only himself but also his nation against new explosions triggered by the ever-present religious tension. It is perhaps understandable that, for this very reason, the Catholic bishops and prelates of the realm were most willing to help him in the endeavor. Bishop Jost of Breslau, for instance, had not only supported but partly conducted the negotiations between Prague and Mainz, and if eventually Diether had not fulfilled his promises it was certainly not Jost's fault. He and his friends clearly felt that George's becoming King of the Romans was bound to strengthen the Catholic influence in Bohemia, since in this position he would be even less inclined and able to expose himself to the reproach of heresy.

But for this very same reason, coupled with nationalistic sentiments, the project was looked upon with little favor by the leaders of the Utraquist Church, among them Rokycana.[56] They suspected that, to achieve his goal, George might be induced to make undesirable concessions to the Catholics. Before long this fear, together with the total development of the religious question in Bohemia, was to lead to real tension between the King and influential representatives of the Hussite majority which had made him King.

In the final analysis the impression remains that, in pursuing this dream, George showed less of the sound judgment and the generally fine instinct that so far had distinguished him. After his initial reluctance he had allowed himself to be convinced by Dr. Mair and had put a great effort into a scheme whose chances had always been highly doubtful and which, even in the case of success, was far from certain to yield the hoped-for advantages, especially in view of the strong resistance he was to encounter at home. Perhaps the one justification that can be found for this phase of his policy was, besides his undeniable but generally not unreasonable ambition, his worry over the increasing pressure of the religious issues, and his assumption that

---

[56] See the allusion to priestly (meaning the Utraquist leadership) attitudes in Židek's *Spravovna,* ed. Tobolka, Prague, 1908, Section 11, p. 11. line 42–44.

the King of the Romans would have far better hopes of obtaining from Rome a confirmation of the Compacts than a mere King of Bohemia. Papal pressure, indeed, had become noticeable already in 1460, and much more so in 1461. The time, George must have guessed, was running short in which peace and prosperity alone could form the happy keynote of his reign.

CHAPTER 11

THE RELIGIOUS STRUGGLE REOPENED

IF POPE PIUS had, in the early spring of 1459, voiced his reservations in regard to the intimate relations created at Cheb between King George and the ducal house of Saxony, there seemed nothing but friendship left in the Pope's relation to the King in the following months. It was the time of the Congress of Mantua. The Pope was still hopeful that he might induce the powerful Czech ruler to come personally to the Italian city and thus to give a strong impulse to the mobilization of all Christian forces against the Turks. In this hope Pius II was not only most careful to treat the King, in his correspondence, with all imaginable respect as a true Christian King but even showed his impatience to the one small power within the Bohemian realm that still dared to defy the King: the Silesian city and principality of Breslau.[1]

In reflecting upon the relation between George and Pius—a truly central question for George's and Central Europe's history—one is tempted to speculate what consequences might have arisen if George had followed this urgent invitation to Mantua. He would have been by far the greatest of the temporal rulers present, and his very presence would have given the assembly a significance far beyond that which it really attained. Thus George would have spared the pontiff a disappointment he felt rather keenly, and Pius might well have been inclined to show George his gratitude. In addition George, once in Mantua, would probably have been able, at least to some extent, to name his price for a serious military effort against the Turks. This, conceivably, might have been the long sought-for confirmation of the Compacts, a policy which Pius had recommended only a relatively short time before his elevation to the papal dignity.

All this, of course—like every discussion of "missed opportunities" in history—is pure speculation, and it seems likely if not certain that George never seriously contemplated such a course. He was not altogether fond of travels that took him far away from the Czech lands.

---

[1] See Eschenloer, L., *SrS*, VII, 46f.

But there were more important reasons why, at least at this time, George's interest in actually fighting the Turks was rather lukewarm (though we have no reason to assume that his often repeated hope for a joint action against the Turks was merely a pretense). But this, after all, was the time when the King of Bohemia had begun to identify himself with Dr. Mair's idea of adding to his titles that of "King of the Romans." This undertaking made him look west instead of east. (The same was later to be true, in a rather similar but more striking fashion, for George's son-in-law and future enemy, Matthias Corvinus, with far more dangerous long-term consequences for his own country.) In discussing the future course of events we shall have to express our doubts in the wisdom of Pope Pius's policy. But at this stage it seems that he had a better understanding of the urgency of the threat presented by further Ottoman expansion than either one of the two great "national Kings" of Central Europe.

However, during the summer of 1459—a time to which we have to go back in our quest for the understanding of the relations between George and Pius—the Pope's attitude toward him was as friendly as the Czech King could wish. The attempt of Breslau to denounce his orthodoxy and to prove to the Pope his utter unworthiness to bear the crown was, for the time being, completely unsuccessful. With the Pope the Emperor, too, following his visit in Brno, informed the city of George's enfeoffment and in consequence demanded recognition for him.[2]

In the city itself the internal struggle—the "gemeine," led by the popular preachers, against the much less war-minded, far more cautious majority of the city councillors—became acute. The popular party succeeded in sabotaging every attempt of the city government to find a modus vivendi, and in August this conflict very nearly led to a bloody revolution of the sort which had taken place, more than a year before, in Jihlava. As a consequence two of the members of the council, among them the head councillor, had to flee to save their lives, and were replaced by two men who were friends of Nicholas Tempelfeld and frequent supporters of his radical policy.

The parallel to the development in Jihlava did, indeed, become ever more striking. George, strengthened by his general recognition, began to lose patience with the stubborn city and decided to use force. During September 1459 the city received letters of challenge not only from the representatives of the Bohemian estates, without

[2] *Ibid.*, 50.

regard to their religion, but also from an increasing number of Silesian princes and cities.[3] Bishop Jost, upon his return from Mantua, made a very strong effort to prove to the people of Breslau how unjustified was their attitude, by reading to the assembled members of the "gemeine" the Pope's latest, rather impatient letters to the city as well as those to King George, in both of which Pius took the stand that there should be no further delay in Breslau's homage to their rightful King.[4]

Breslau, at this time, was actually at war with the whole Bohemian realm, including most of the Silesians. If the city, nevertheless, did not suffer the fate of Jihlava, if indeed there was nothing but a very weak and short-lived attempt at a military showdown, then this was due entirely to the King's reluctance to use violent means in a struggle in which the city had already succeeded in involving the Pope himself. This became especially clear in September, when the Pope took the important step of sending two high prelates as his legates to Breslau to achieve by peaceful means the city's submission to George.

Late in October the legates, Jerome Lando, Archbishop of Crete, and Dr. Francis of Toledo, Arch-Deacon of Seville, spent some time in Prague, where they had a very friendly reception from the King. On November 11 they arrived in Breslau. Now began a peculiar struggle between the two Roman Catholic prelates acting as personal representatives of the Pope and the commune of Breslau, led by equally Roman Catholic preachers, over the question whether the city should or should not submit to the King of Bohemia,[5] a struggle in which the real government of the city, the council, still frightened by the threat of a revolution, at first only acted as a cautious onlooker. The legates, in repeated addresses, tried to convince the people of Breslau that their attempt to stand up, in their present isolation, to the full power of the Bohemian crown, was utter madness; that they had no right to doubt the true Christian character of the King as long as the Holy Father himself had no such doubts; that George, in all his undertakings, had been exceedingly lucky and successful—a fact which presumably showed God's blessing; that his help and that of his kingdom was of the greatest importance to all of Christian Europe, which was in deadly peril from the Turks; and that finally,

[3] Eschenloer, G., I., pp. 90f.

[4] SrS, VII, 59, 60.

[5] A thorough account of the action of the legates and its consequences, based essentially on SrS, VII, 65ff., can be found in R. Koebner, Der Widerstand Breslaus, 69–84.

even if George were not (as it was assumed he was) a good, orthodox Christian, it was still the duty of subjects to obey the King, since
a crowned and annointed King had received his dignity from God.

The arguments of the papal legates, at first, made little impression
upon the Breslau crowds, and even less on those popular preachers
whose whole political and religious leadership seemed thereby put
in question. The preachers, especially Nicholas Templefeld and his
friend and assistant Bartholomaeus, tried their best not only to refute
the arguments of the legates but also to make them, as men and
clerics, suspect in the eyes of the masses. They were, so the people
heard, not the well-informed, orthodox and learned churchmen they
claimed to be, but badly confused men, obfuscated by the general
corruption of the times and probably even personally corrupted
through money given to them during their Prague sojourn by the
heretical King.[6] As a result of this agitation the masses became ever
more suspicious of and hostile to the prelates. Thus the legates requested that the council take steps to silence the agitators, and especially to put Bartholomaeus into prison. The council did not feel
nearly strong enough for so energetic a procedure. It answered the
legates by presenting a memorandum which, while on the whole
trying to defend the policy pursued by the city up to now, did contain an element of possible compromise: they expressed the hope
that the Pope would not attempt to force them at the present
moment to do homage to the King, but would rather induce the
King to leave them in peace for a period during which he could
prove that he was really a faithful son of the Church. It was a shrewd
move, since it would seem to refute the charge of a blindly stubborn
defiance on the side of the city and yet would lay the burden for
reaching any recognition upon the King himself. But at least it implied that the old stand—expressed in the solemn convenant of 1458
—was abandoned: that never under any circumstances would the
city submit to the King.

Yet before any rapprochement could take place, a last crisis had
to be overcome. The commune seemed far from ready to tolerate
even the cautious compromise indicated by the council, and the
legates eventually threatened to put the city under an interdict unless
their demands were obeyed. When the news became known, together
with rumors about an impending arrest of the popular preachers, a
new explosion of popular fury seemed imminent, sufficiently so to

[6] See Eschenloer, G., I., p. 149.

make the legates accept on their part a more concrete compromise solution suggested by the council and formulated, in most of its details, by Peter Eschenloer, the town secretary. This compromise was then presented also to the commune. As it removed the danger of excommunication and as one of its features was the statement that, for the coming year, 1460, no act of homage was yet demanded, it was received with jubilation by the people of Breslau.

Yet the agreement could hardly have been claimed to correspond to the previous demands of preachers and commune. On the whole, at least for the time being, it was a victory for George, and was regarded by him as a fully satisfactory result. This is what it contained:[7]

The city promised to obey and be subject to George, as requested by Pope Pius. George, on his part, promised to terminate all hostilities and not to punish the city but to confirm its old rights and privileges, the freedoms of Breslau as a principality (including its right to elect its council), its judicial independence, its right to appoint a captain for the principality as well as its tolls and customs. The formal act of homage remains in abeyance for the next three years. After this the people of Breslau will do him homage as the true and indubitable Christian and Catholic King of Bohemia.

George's certainty of his essential victory is shown by the fact that he agreed not only to the delay of three years—he could certainly, without much difficulty, have shortened the term to at most two years—but that, in a jocular vein, he even added an extra month to it.

And now, for a short while, a veritable "honeymoon" seemed to break out between the King and his bitterest enemies within his realm. This feeling, at least, emerges from the more than obsequious speech in which the Breslau ambassadors, sent to Prague sometime around New Year 1460 to complete the agreement, celebrated George as the greatest and best of all rulers and told him that they would "worship his very footmarks." [8] The secretary-chronicler from whom we derive more knowledge about Breslau's policy than from any other source informs us that in the following three years, strongly protected and furthered in their trade and their rights by King George, the people of Breslau even began to love him.[9] We may well wonder how justified this generalization was. The people who

---

[7] *SrS*, VII, 95f.
[8] See the document in the appendix of Jordan, *Das Königtum Georg Podiebrads*, 388.
[9] Eschenloer, G., I., 169.

now "began to love him" were, in all likelihood, the very people who had never hated him very much and who, good Catholics and good Germans as most of them were, had never intended to go to extremes in this struggle: the patricians, whose trading interests could only suffer from an open conflict with the King. In alliance with the papal legates they had finally prevailed, or so it seemed. The clerical agitators, at this time, were forced to keep quiet, but not forever. The spirit of John of Capistrano was now mute, but far from dead.

Breslau's submission, undoubtedly, was a great advantage for King George, and he owed much of it to the Pope. This substantial help was given in addition to previous services which Pius had rendered him—all of them relating to the general recognition of George's royal office. Clearly George was deeply obligated to the Curia, and he knew it. He also knew what Rome expected in return: substantial steps in the direction of religious unification—and an equally substantial contribution to the hoped-for crusade against the Turks. It is impossible to know or even guess what George's long-range intentions were in regard to the struggle against the Turks, if he had, at all, tried to make up his mind on this matter. That he did not expect to do much about this in the immediate future was shown by his inactivity in relation to the Congress of Mantua—probably a tactical mistake since it disappointed some of the Pope's fondest hopes. But in this he did not act differently from any other European ruler of the time. The real issue was the demand of the Church of Rome for reunification of the Churches in Bohemia.

Before long, however, the Pope slowly began to lose patience. Early in 1460, when Breslau had just concluded her peace treaty with George, the Pope had firmly believed that a full reunification, in the way in which he understood George's secret oath, was only a question of rather limited time. But the year itself was mostly used by George in the pursuing of his dream of Roman kingship, a policy which was largely meant to strengthen his position with regard to the Curia. It was, however, also a policy too closely tied up with the idea of general reform (and with the "reform party" in Germany) to please the Pope. Even though George had carefully tried to avoid being identified with the harsh attacks which Diether of Mainz and his friends had launched against the Holy See, Pius' relation with Frederick III was too close to consider the growing political and at times even military advance of the reform party against the imperial party as anything but unfortunate and reprehensible. True, it would

have been impossible to hold George alone or in the first place responsible for those struggles—on the contrary he had, at least until
recently, tried to maintain a fairly neutral position between the two
groups which would correspond to his general preference for peaceful procedures and would add to his stature in relation to those
fairly evenly matched groups of potential adversaries. Yet during
1461 his attitude became ever more hostile especially to Margrave
Albert. It was clear that he had not forgiven him what he considered
a sabotage of his plans for the Roman kingship. He was determined
to show the margrave that he could not twist the tail of the Bohemian
lion without paying a penalty.[10] Thereby, however, George's prestige
as the peacemaker and peace preserver of Central Europe was bound
to suffer, in the eyes of the imperial party as well as in those of the
Pope, quite apart from the fact that Pius, to whom Albert owed his
classical epithet, had always looked upon the Hohenzollern prince
with special fondness.

But the main reason for Pius' growing impatience and irritation
with George was, of course, the fact that, since he had mounted the
papal throne, nothing had happened that could be interpreted as a
real step forward in the religious reunification of the Czech people.
Nor had the King sent the solemn embassy that should have brought
the general obedience of the people of the kingdom and that he had
promised repeatedly. The only convincing explanation for his slow-
ness in sending this embassy is his hope that meanwhile he would
be able to strengthen his position—possibly through the acquisition
of the Roman kingship—to an extent where he could hope to receive
in turn the confirmation of the Compacts. Actually, however, the
postponement had, if anything, the opposite result. The embassy was
sent, as we shall see, at the most unpropitious moment for any such
papal concessions.

Yet the pressure kept growing. The first serious expression of Pius'
impatience and annoyance was carried to Prague, so it seems, in
the late summer of 1460 by George's own envoy at the papal court,
the procurator, Fantino de Valle. The King's answer—in a letter
of September 12—emphasized his firm resolution to keep and fulfill
the "due reverence, subjection and obedience vowed to Your Holiness and to the Holy Roman Church at the assumption of Your
office." If this had not been done before, then it was because of do-

---

[10] See e.g. Chmel, *Materialien zur österreichischen Geschichte*, II, 252; Lichnowsky, *Habsburg*, VII, Regesten 599, 606.

mestic difficulties such as the struggles between the barons and the gentry over their participation and role in the country's judicial system. To safeguard the sacred faith George expected "to meet the malice of people and of times not so much by the use of arms but by wise counselling and prudence." He finally promised to send his embassy to submit his country's obedience in February 1461.[11] This date is reaffirmed in a letter of November which names as his ambassadors Bishop Protas of Olomouc and his chancellor Prokop of Rabstein.[12]

The Pope's answer to this last message was more than cool, and criticized sharply the King's policy in relation to Germany. Yet George could hardly expect that Pius would be satisfied with the little or nothing he had, so far, to offer, or that on this basis he could obtain the confirmation of the Compacts. Thus he decided once more to ask for delay—and he employed as his agent a man whom he considered a particularly capable and clever diplomat: the Frenchman Antoine Marini, a native of Grenoble (though of originally Italian descent) who had begun to replace Dr. Martin Mair as one of the King's foremost advisors on foreign policy. Marini, a gifted and versatile man, had entered the King's service sometime in 1460 and had, in a short time, achieved a sufficient knowledge of Czech to be able not only to converse but even to write, in this language, some memoranda requested by the King. While a few of the memoranda (including the only one that has been preserved) are concerned with problems of economic policy, one—the very first the King requested—dealt with the present issue: George asked him how a Bohemian state governed by the principles of the Compacts could, without any weakening of their legal validity, be reconciled with the Roman Church. Unfortunately Marini's answer is not known to us.[13]

---

11 *SrS*, VIII, 47.

12 *Ibid.*, 49.

13 Marini probably deserves a more thorough treatment than the rather short monographs existing. The longest but also oldest is contained in Ernest Denis's "De Antonio Marini," his Latin thesis submitted to the Faculty of Letters of the University of Paris, 1878. The Roumanian historian Nicola Jorga devoted an essay to him: "Antoine Marini," in *Études d'histoire du moyen âge, dédiées a Monod*, Paris, 1896, pp. 445ff. For Palacký's views see vol. IV, part 2 in the second ed. of his *Dějiny národu českého*, pp. 114–117. Palacký has also published the only remaining memorandum which Marini wrote for King George: "Rada králi Jiřímu o zlepšení kupectví v Čechách," *ČČM*, II, 3, Prague, 1828, pp. 3–24. German historians have been rather hostile in their treatment of him, least so perhaps Markgraf in "Über Georgs v. Podiebrad Plan eines christlichen Fürstenbundes," *HZ*, XXI, 264ff. Bachmann hardly ever mentions him without expressions of distaste, calling him an "adventurer" even in his index (*Geschichte Böhmens*, II, 833) but more frequently a "notorious liar" or "impostor" or "a lying Frenchman" (*ibid.*, 525, 568, further in *Deutsche Reichsgeschichte*, I, 142,

Marini did not have an easy time in Rome, especially since George's permanent ambassador, Fantino de Valle, was not happy about this interference in what he considered his proper business.[14] Yet in his immediate task Marini was successful. The Pope granted, on June 30, the King of Bohemia an eight-month extension of the safe conduct for his embassy.[15] But it was clear to George that he could hardly expect another postponement and that, whatever he could do to improve his position vis-a-vis the Curia, had to be done in the immediate future.

Apart from the obedience itself there were two issues where concessions seemed possible and substantial enough, perhaps, to impress the Holy See. One was the attempt to restore to the Church of Rome at least a part of the enormous landed wealth which it had possessed before the Hussite Revolution and of which so much had been secularized. The profiteers from this great change of poverty were by no means merely Hussites—on the contrary (as pointed out earlier) some of the leading Catholic baronial houses, with the Rosenbergs in the lead, had uninhibitedly enriched themselves by the acquisition of Church estates. During the spring of 1461 the King tried to induce some of these barons to release part of this property to be returned to the Church. As far as we know this attempt was entirely unsuccessful.[16] The lords, so we hear, "are by no means willing to cede any of this property."

The second step, however, had a more direct relationship to his coronation oath and to the impending negotiations with the Pope. Sometime in late March 1461 the King ordered a renewal of the anti-heretical decrees of his predecessor Charles IV. They were directed against all groups outside the two Churches covered by the Compacts: Catholics and Utraquists. The main victim of this action, however, was the Unity of Brethren, the group that later, in ideological and theological terms, was to become the most important and culturally most productive of all movements growing out of the Czech Reformation of the fifteenth century.[17]

---

195). We shall hear much more of him in connection with George's foreign policy in the years 1462 to 1464, and especially with the King's plan of a European League of Princes.

[14] See his letter to George in *FRA*, II, 20, 243ff.

[15] See *AČ*, XV, 236f., also L. Pastor, *Geschichte der Päpste*, 3rd ed., II, Freiburg, 1904, 172 n. 3.

[16] See Bachmann, *Reichsgeschichte*, I, 93 n.1, also, for the growing opposition among the high nobility, *FRA*, II, 44, Vienna, 1885, 127–131.

[17] See below, n. 24.

But the purpose of these steps were overrated or misunderstood by some of the leading Catholics of Bohemia, including possibly even Jost of Rosenberg, Bishop of Breslau. On the Thursday before Easter of 1461 Jost gave a sermon in St. Vitus Cathedral of Prague in which he openly demanded that the people of Bohemia renounce and abandon the communion in both kinds. There was, subsequently, a great uproar in Prague "against that fat Bishop"; the King was then in Kutná Hora and the bishop thereupon went to see him.[18] The final outcome of this "uproar," however, was that the King was induced to give very solemn assurances to the estates as well as to the people of Prague that he would stay and fall with the Compacts.[19]

This, surely, was an important, clarifying, and consequential event. The King's action, as well as the whole development leading to it, faces us with one of the most difficult problems of interpretation inherent in the history of this time, largely reflecting the deep misunderstanding that already separated the main actors of the time itself.

One interpretation [20] is as follows: King George had promised, in his secret oath, to lead back his nation to Catholic orthodoxy, that is to complete conformity with the Roman creed and liturgy. By an (assumed) oral declaration abjuring former heresies he had actually taken the fateful step of "re-conversion to Catholicism." He had, however, kept his oath secret and had so far held back on any measures directed against the Hussite-Utraquist Church because he had not felt strong enough to challenge, by this undertaking, the heterodox majority of his nation. This school of thought generally interprets his attempt at gaining the Roman crown as at least partially meant to gain him additional strength for his expected counterreformatory task (rather than for the actual task which soon faced him: the inevitable struggle with Rome). Nor would he, so the argument goes on, ever have embarked on this ambitious scheme, which depended so much on the good will of the three ecclesiastical electors, if he had not been serious about his own conversion and that of his nation.

---

[18] *SLČP*, 158.

[19] See the statement, with sources, in Palacký, *Dějiny*, IV, 2, 165 (and n. 131). His assumption, on p. 166, that George only now gave up the attempt to gain the crown of King of the Romans, hardly seems tenable, as no serious steps in this direction had been taken by the King after the diet of Nürnberg. But other historians (including Bachmann) agree.

[20] It is presented with most emphasis and most coherently by Bachmann, in his *Geschichte Böhmens*, II, 520–524, and *Reichsgeschichte* I, 88–94. But it is taken over also by other, mainly German historians. See e.g. B. Bretholz, *Geschichte Böhmens und Mährens*, II, 115f; Pastor, *Geschichte der Päpste*, II, 170–172; or, in almost literary adherence to Bachmann's version, Koebner, *Der Widerstand Breslaus*, p. 87.

He expected to fulfill his promise as soon as his kingship would be strongly established. As further support for this interpretation its advocates refer to the activities of Bishop Jost of Breslau: first his participation in the negotiations with the Elector-Archbishop of Mainz about George's elevation to the Roman kingship, then, as the supposedly decisive step, the sermon preached in April 1461 in St. Vitus and his subsequent visit with the King in Kutná Hora. If it is assumed that George did, indeed, plan to eliminate Utraquism altogether, then these single facts may well seem to fall into place. The King, so it would then appear, had prearranged everything with Jost of Rosenberg. He knew that he had reached whatever domestic and international strength he could hope for, and that further procrastination in the fulfillment of his promises would merely increase his future troubles, especially with Rome. Thus the bishop's sermon was to initiate the great action—the reconversion of a whole nation, led or, if necessary, enforced by its popular and powerful King. Only the violent reaction of the Prague population made it clear to the King that this way was barred.

This interpretation, emphatically presented as the only one possible by some influential historical writers of the later nineteenth century, does not sound implausible and may in some points correspond to the basic understanding of the situation to be found, at the time the conflict began to become acute, among some of the principal representatives of the Catholic side. But even by the Catholics this interpretation would not have been fully accepted—even less so by the Utraquists. For, as presented, this interpretation suffers from one of the most dangerous sources of historiographical distortion: anachronism. It is essentially an understanding of the religious split of the time based on the experience of and equalization with that long-lasting schism, unhealed and deemed unhealable, between Catholics and Protestants. This experience did not dominate the thinking of the time. In consequence the use of such terms as "creed," "denomination," "conversion," even of the term "Catholic" as something constitutionally different from the Utraquist Church, has to be limited, if not eliminated, simply because they result in historical associations not valid at the time. While, for instance, the East-West schism had been going on for centuries and was fully present in the consciousness of most educated people, its character, for all its deep implications, did not cause radical doubt in the Christian character of the Eastern Church. The Hussites, in the mind of the Catholic-Western World, were more or less badly infected by the heretical "disease" or "poison," but the very fact that it was considered possible, even easy, for a strong ruler to lead them back to full orthodoxy shows clearly how little the idea of a separate Hussite religion—one from which a proper "reconversion" could and must take place—had as yet taken root. In the Hussite camp, on the other hand, especially among the leaders and followers of the established Utraquist Church which had not taken the separatist steps characteristic for Tabor and the Brethren, the idea of more than one true Christian Church was considered impossible, even though differing organizations and centers (such as Constantinople) had long existed. There was, all would agree, only one religious truth and essentially one proper and fitting religious ritual, though there was dissent on its true and proper form. While the old revolutionary optimism of the preceding decades, which expected a general and thorough regeneration of all Christendom as a result of the Czech reform, had given way to a much more sober attitude of self-defense and slow, logical development, there was certainly no willingness among the Utraquist clergy and leading laymen—least of all Rokycana himself—to give up the claim to be truly Catholic, that is to stand in the center of a well-understood Christen orthodoxy. While in substance the Utraquist Church—in dogma as well as in ritual—had developed in a direction rather more "Protestant" and farther away from that Roman Catholicism that would find its final form at Trent, there was so little clarity among its ranks about this nearly inescapable trend that its attitude toward the papacy was, a least in certain periods, less antagonistic than that of many perfectly orthodox Catholic people, including such prelates as the Archbishop of Mainz. The real inability, even and especially among the advocates of a thorough and radical reform, to envisage the religious split as something definite, permanent, which forced one to belong to one side or the other, will perhaps be better and more easily appreciated if we remember how long it took Western Christianity to think of Luther's rebellion against Rome as creating a final and unbridgeable break. After all, the very purpose of the Augsburg Confession was to show the possibility of an understanding between both sides, and as late as 1541 Charles V could call the diet of Regensburg in the hope of leading both sides to compromise and reunion—this following all the radical steps of separation and non-recognition of papal power on the side of the Lutherans, in many aspects far more radical and definitive than any taken by Rokycana and his disciples.

Thus, with all due recognition for the high degree to which Hus-

sitism anticipated and prepared the religious revolution of the sixteenth century, we should be most careful and reluctant in applying
the terms and standards of the later, more permanent and, in its
significance, more obvious religious split to the events of the 1460's,
and to the particular views and actions of George. The often-heard
claim that George was basically unconcerned about religion, that this
struggle was to him merely a question of political expediency, is
clearly a gross over-simplification. But it is true, indeed, that it was
impossible for him to separate the basic religious issue from its
political aspects, that is from the relationship of the Utraquist majority to the Catholic minority in Bohemia and to the vast and overwhelming Catholic world surrounding his own realm. This relationship was to him—and this cannot be emphasized too strongly—
subject to the law of the Compacts, not, indeed, to all their intricacies
but to the Compacts as a living and working arrangement. As such
they had, with all their defects, functioned remarkably well in maintaining the status quo against expansionist attempts from both sides,
and on their basis alone it had been possible for the Utraquist Church,
its officials and adherents, to consider themselves essentially as "members in good standing" of the Christian World of Western and Central Europe. This emphatically included George himself. He had
never doubted that he belonged to this community as clearly as any
Catholic, indeed, he felt that, as a believing and faithful Utraquist, he
was, on the strength of the Compacts, ipso facto also a believing and
faithful Catholic Christian in the original sense of that term. Thus
he did not, in his own understanding, need a conversion in order to
become a Catholic. He had always been one.

This, of course, did not mean that George was not conscious of
the difference between the two churches. His whole career as the
political leader of the Utraquist party of Bohemia was bound to have
made him constantly aware of it, and he had taken his stand on the
question how far he, his friends, and his party should go in defending this separate character. His had always been a compromise position, compromise not only with the Catholics but also with the "hard
core" of Utraquism—Rokycana and the group around him—whom
with caution and skill he had to prevent from endangering, by too
uncompromising a stand, the religious peace. He had always watched
with extreme alertness over this need, had always tried to stop what
seemed to him dangerous manifestations of over-zealous partisan-

ship, and if he ever seemed to lose control over his anger, it was almost always over one of these incidents.

Yet George's historical claim to have been a religiously tolerant man has been challenged just on account of his actions at this time: specifically the persecution, beginning in the spring of 1461, of the Unity of Brethren. In "objective" historical perspective this will always remain one of the darker aspects of George's rule. He, the "Hussite King," was the first to use the means of forcible suppression against this clean and noble reformatory movement. It gave him a sinister fame especially in the historiography of the Brethren themselves, and understandably so.[21]

And again we have to beware of over-simplification in our judgment of George. Neither his nature nor his upbringing nor the particular circumstances and needs of a strong and viable Czech-Utraquist state within the Catholic Europe of his time could possibly make it easy for him to achieve a liberal and tolerant understanding of the newly rising movement of the Brethren. In the first place it could not really appear to him new—nor was it entirely new in its genesis. For him it was, and not without some reason, a continuation of the Pikhart heresy, itself widely considered one of the "worst" aspects of the Taborite movement because of its spiritual understanding of the Eucharist and the implied doubt in the real, physical presence of Christ in the sacrament. But this was not only a theological question. Even in his teens, at the time of the battle of Lipany, George had been taught to see in Taboritism a challenge to all hopes for a reconsolidation of that society that was desired by the majority of the members of his own, the baronial, caste as well as much of the gentry and of the patriciate of Prague. When he became regent, one of his first steps was the conquest of Tabor and the destruction, for political rather than religious reasons, of what had remained of the old theocracy of this strange and fascinating city state—a sort of mixture of Sparta and later Geneva. George knew that in 1452 the spirit of Tabor had not died in its entirety. If its fanatically militant aspects had been buried, the same was certainly not true of those trends which Tabor largely shared with (and partly may even have derived from) the Waldensians.

<hr>

[21] See as one of the earliest examples (dating from 1502) the apologetic tractate of Tůma Přeloučský, *O původu Jednoty Bratrské a o chudých lidech,* ed. V. Sokol, Prague, 1947, pp. 50–54.

To do justice to the Czech Brethren in terms of its general history, its ideology, and its church policy would require a considerable part of this study. Yet the reign of King George, though it witnessed the birth and infancy of this impressive, highly creative, and consequential religious movement, closed before the group had developed beyond the framework of a small and rather esoteric sect. If it had not survived and developed so powerfully in the period after George's death its existence, from 1458 to 1471, could hardly be rated as one of the more notable events of his reign.[22]

Even so it will be necessary to point out here some of the salient facts about the movement of the Brethren, especially as far as it reacted to and influenced the religious situation and the policy of King George as well as of the Utraquist leaders at the time. (A more thorough treatment will, I hope, emerge in the context of future work.)

The genesis of the movement has much to do with the deep general ferment which had been such a powerful force in the history of the Husite Revolution as such. Many of the ideas developed by the most uncompromising representatives of the Brethren can be found already in Taborite (or Pikhart) teachings. The most radical difference here is the emphatic insistence by the Brethren upon non-violence, as opposed to the highly militant attitudes of Taboritism. But it would probably be wrong to see in the Brethren's war-hating and war-condemning attitude a completely new development. In fact the principle of non-violence, based on the literal interpretation of the fifth commandment, was present in the heretical movements preceding the Hussite Revolution, especially in Waldensianism, but also, it seems, in part of the early "Pikhart" trends including the "Brethren and Sisters of the Free Spirit," though another development from the same stem, the Adamites, was extremely militant. The cataclysmic storms of the revolution, among them the hope of the peasantry to improve their social positions, had helped to

---

[22] Characteristically King George's most recent and most important Czech biographer, Urbánek, has in his last published volume presented a careful treatment of the early history of the Brethern which, however, very frequently refers to developments which occurred after, sometimes quite long after the end of George's reign. As Urbánek's volumes were supposed to be only part of a greater work on the whole of Czech history, his procedure was fully justified. For the interested reader unable to go to Czech sources there are now, fortunately, some detailed and up-to-date treatments available in Western languages. See J. T. Müller, *Geschichte der Böhmischen Brüder*, I (1400–1528), Herrnhut, 1922; R. Říčan, *Die Böhmischen Brüder*, Berlin, 1961; and Peter Brock, *The Political and Social Doctrines of the Unity of Czech Brethren*, The Hague, 1957, in all cases the early chapters.

strengthen the militant element especially in the form of the fighting brotherhoods of Tabor and Oreb under the leadership of soldiers and priests, eventually under priest-soldiers. But the pacifist trend, while muted and of little public influence, had never completely died. Even during the war years, but still more distinctly during the decades following immediately upon the revolution, it had found its outstanding spokesman in the person of Peter Chelčický. Eventually it was the combined influence—brought about through a very unusual and remarkable relationship—of Chelčický and Rokycana, which resulted in the birth of the Unity of Brethren as an independent religious community.

The earliest members of the community had known Rokycana first. It was his sharp social criticism, his harsh moral judgment about Bohemia's priesthood—Roman as well as Utraquist—and his positive puritanism, all this presented in a moving and persuasive way, which induced a number of his most devout disciples and listeners to form what they seem to have considered at first as an inner circle, determined fully and uncompromisingly to live a pure Christian life which would correspond to their teacher's pleas. Rokycana himself, feeling that in view of his wide responsibilities as head of the national Utraquist Church his leadership could not concentrate sufficiently upon this small number, brought those people into contact with Chelčický, recommending that they read Chelčický's works and take his personal advice. It was a remarkable step, showing how far the Hussite archbishop was from that selfish vanity and ambition with which his enemies and critics tended to charge him. For Rokycana was at this time fully aware not only of the views he and Chelčický held in common but also of those about which they disagreed. They had discussed these matters personally and in a correspondence whose surviving fragments are of great value.[23] The two men differed relatively little on purely theological issues, both being under the influence of Matthew of Janov and Wyclyf as well as Huss. (Both, on the issue of the Eucharist, arrived at some point which may well be described as co-substantiation.) But of the two, Chelčický, never thinking in terms of church policy as part of the policy of the nation, was much the more independent thinker, less burdened by the traditions not only of office but also of any great bulk of scholastic erudition. If both of them were devoted to a thorough biblicism, only Chelčický went much farther in depreciating the Old and concen-

---

[23] See Chelčický, 'Replika proti Rokycanovi," *LF*, XXV, 1898.

trating on the New Testament. If both were critics of the social disgraces of the time, only Chelčický, in one of his main works, went so far as to abandon and refute the medieval assumption of the three kinds of people. If both took the fifth commandment very seriously, only Chelčický went to the length of disapproving even of all weapons and methods of self-defense (thus, e.g., severely condemning his Taborite friends for their militancy). Finally, and above all, if both abhorred the corruption of the Christian churches everywhere, only Chelčický saw in the existence of the medieval ties between Church and State the very root of all evils, and drew from this view the consequence of demanding a Christian community radically divorced from all the activities of worldly power and organization.

Chelčický's thoughts made a powerful impression upon the original group out of which the Brethren were to grow, and most of them were adopted, with the consequence that the group sought a retreat where they could practice what they believed. Again it was Rokycana whom they approached, and it was the churchman's influence with George of Poděbrady, probably soon after his election as King of Bohemia, which enabled the most important among the small groups influenced by both Rokycana and Chelčický to settle on the King's estate of Litice near the village of Kunvald.

During the years that immediately followed, the movement grew considerably, both in Kunvald and neighboring districts and in the region of Klatovy, where a more radical group of people had sought refuge after they had been driven out of Moravia. Among the Unity's leaders Rokycana's nephew, generally known as Brother Gregory (Řehoř) was the most important, but there were others of some erudition, men such as Prokop of Hradec, Martin of Krčín, and the man who later became the Unity's first historian, Tůma Přeloučský. The larger number of adherents, however, seems to have come from the peasantry and the poorer people of the cities.

Hand in hand with the growth, in the process of a more conscious and determined development of their religious thoughts and practices closely following the ideas of Chelčický, the Brethren visibly parted ways from the greater body of the Utraquist Church. They still hoped that this was a path in which Rokycana, who had so long been their first leader, would follow, as they felt that he must understand that there could be no salvation within the badly corrupted body of the existing Church. And it is from this stand that the originally close relationship between the early Brethren and the Hussite Archbishop was to break apart. They could not understand his reluctance and interpreted it as lack of courage and consistency. He, on his side, had thought of them as an elite who would help him in his desire to heal some of the sicknesses of the Church. By leaving it and going their own way they could not possibly function in this way. Thus both sides were aggrieved and disappointed. Yet both were bound to act as they did. The Brethren could never have grown into the clean and rich reformatory movement inside the Utraquist Church. The period of withdrawal was a necessary stage of their development. The Hussite archbishop, on his side, could not possibly follow them, as they asked him to do, into this self-imposed withdrawal from "the world," into that rural seclusion where only the small number of those would gather who refused all compromise with world, state and magistracy. For him there still remained the task of saving a far larger number of souls—and of keeping, with its autonomous church, a whole nation, his own nation, as near as possible to the right path.

Yet for all the alienation that eventually took place between Rokycana and some of the most intensely pious among his disciples, nothing would ever have induced him to direct or even to sanction an actual persecution in the forms so familiar from the workings of the Inquisition. Wherever he could, he tried to make things easier for the Brethren by interceding directly for them with the King and by intervening skillfully in the proceedings against them, eventually by devising formulas of recantation so general and so innocuous that most of them could accept them without sacrificing any essential part even of those teachings which clearly deviated from the basic creed of the Utraquist Church. Yet even Rokycana could not prevent the action as such.[24]

King George, at this conjunction, believed he could no longer avoid the procedure against the Brethren. He had, it is clear, by no means rushed into this policy. On the contrary, it was quite easy to charge him on this account with considerable procrastination. Nearly three years had passed since he had promised, in his secret oath sworn at his coronation, to turn away the people subject to him "from all errors, sects and heresies and from other articles contrary to the Holy Roman Church and the Catholic faith." If he could—as he most surely did—consider the Utraquist Church, its dogma and ritual

---

24 See Heymann, "John Rokycana, Church Reformer between Hus and Luther," in *Church History*, September 1959, pp. 269–271, with reference to other literature.

sufficiently sanctioned by the Compacts to be safe from any such characterization as errors and heresies, the same could not possibly be said about the movement of the Brethren, nor could it be doubted that it was, in the terminology of the time (and of later times) a typical "sect." If he permitted its further undisturbed growth and development (especially on his own estates), then surely he would expose himself to the accusation that thereby, if by nothing else, he was breaking his solemn if secret oath.[25]

Thus started the first of the many persecutions which the Church of the Brethren had to undergo in its long history down into the seventeenth century, to the Thirty Years War and to the administration of its last great bishop or "senior," John Amos Comenius (who himself was to write the story of those and earlier persecutions in an important work published in 1648).[26] There were many arrests, and a number of people, among them university students, were subjected to torture. This first wave of persecutions did not last very long, partly because of the attempts made by some influential friends of the King to obtain a milder treatment—among them, so it seems, was George's own, much liked court jester, John Paleček, himself very near in his thinking to the Brethren and possibly even a member of their community. Many had a very hard time, which resulted in some of them, or their families, going into hiding. The harshest treatment was meted out to a few of the arrested students. Five of these are known to have been tortured, and two of them who refused to revoke remained imprisoned for several years. The majority of the arrested men, however, were released after a confinement of about three months.[27]

Altogether then, it seems, the persecution was just harsh enough to create the martyrs whose images would strengthen the further growth of the movement, but too weak to check it effectively or even to drive it underground for any length of time. It is clear now

[25] For George's motives in his persecution of the Brethren (to be discussed later in some detail), see also the little monograph by A. Molnar, "O příčinách pronásledování Jednoty králem Jiříkem," in *Křest'anska revue, teologická příloha*, 1960.

[26] *Historia persecutionum ecclesiae Bohemica . . . ad annum usque* 1632, published in Latin first in Leyden in 1647, later also in other languages. A recent critical edition in Czech (by M. Kaňák and F. Šimek) under the title *Historie o těžkých protivenstvích církve české*, Prague, 1952.

[27] The most detailed and best documented presentation of the first persecution in J. T. Müller, *Geschichte der Böhmischen Brüder*, I, 77–95, and Urbánek, *Věk*, IV, 450ff. See also R. Říčan, *Die Böhmischen Brüder, ihr Ursprung und ihre Geschichte*, 21–24, and J. Goll, "Jednota bratrská v 15: století," *ČČM*, LVIII, 1884, pp. 449ff. About Paleček see Urbánek, "Jan Paleček, šašek krále Jiřího," in *Příspěvky k dějinám starší české literatury*, Prague, 1958.

that some of the later historiography of the Brethren—which even tried to make Rokycana partly responsible for this phase of their sufferings—contains considerable distortions of the truth. The only person in high position within the Utraquist camp who was and remained active in pushing for an effective persecution was Queen Johanna. The King himself seems soon to have lost whatever zeal he had displayed at the beginning. His heart—this is rather obvious —never was in this action. He simply was not a religious zealot, and once it became clear from the earliest questionings that these sectarians, for whatever they thought or taught about the Eucharist, were not the harbingers of a reviving Taboritism endangering the state, the action no longer appealed to him.

We must now ask whether, as has been assumed, the persecution of the Brethren can be considered, on the side of George, as a step preparatory to an intended liquidation of the Basel Compacts, of the Chalice for laymen, of the organization headed by Rokycana, in short to a total reduction of the Utraquist Church in full compliance with the wishes of the most uncompromising unification demands of the Curia. Was this really ever George's intention and plan, thwarted only in the end by popular resistance?

The persecution of the Brethren, if it can prove anything in this context, can only prove the opposite. For if George had really intended to give up, or to destroy with one stroke, all the achievements, dogmatic, ritual and organizational, of the Czech reformation, then there was little need to deal separately with a religious group which at this time counted hardly more than several hundreds, that is a tiny fraction of the mass of people adhering to the Chalice. To single out, as was done, the "Pikharts" for a highly conspicuous action, and to put the implementation of this action to a considerable extent into the hands of the Utraquist, not the Catholic, clergy of the kingdom[28]—this clearly indicates how George interpreted the assurances which he had given in his secret oath, and how he wanted them understood also by others, in particular by the Catholics of his kingdom and by the Roman Curia itself: There were, so he in fact admitted, still some errors and heresies rampant in Bohemia, though on a rather small scale. Against these he, George, Christian ruler of a Christian people, was now proceeding. Thereby he was fulfilling his promises and his oath. And if the action indicates anything much in addition, then it is that he neither would nor could go much beyond this—except, of

---

[28] J. T. Müller, *Geschichte der Böhmischen Brüder*, 82f.

course, for the general act of obedience promised in 1459. It is to underestimate the political judgment of this ruler—whose political acumen is generally acclaimed even by his critics—to assume that until April 1461 George had not been aware of the tremendous and indeed insurmountable resistance that any attempt to liquidate Utraquism would encounter among the masses of the Czech people. The persecution of the Brethren was, then, indeed an action in fulfillment of his secret oath with its promise of eradicating schismatic and heretical tendencies. It was not, if we may use this term, a "downpayment" indicating his readiness eventually to go much farther in enforcing religious conformity, but rather as the one important action needed and appropriate to discharge the obligations toward the Church of Rome which he had entered at the moment of his coronation.

But how, then, can we explain the action of Bishop Jost of Breslau? This is not too difficult if we only get away from the preconception that every step taken by the prelate, including an Easter sermon, was necessarily done in detailed agreement with, or even upon the specific request of King George, if we realize that in fact he also acted in line with the expectations of Rome—the only mistake being his hope that at this time there was no serious difference between the policies of Rome and of the King. It is true that during the preceding months Jost's relationship to the King had been rather close, that he had been employed by George for important diplomatic missions, and that he enjoyed, to a considerable extent, his ruler's good will. This policy of using prominent Catholics among his most important advisers was, of course, a continuous feature of George's policy of national integration. Jost's own warm feelings for George were, at least partly, a result of his patriotism and his pride in his Czech nationality.[29] Though originally he may have inherited his father's antagonism against George, he could not help admiring the man who had done so much to restore the greatness and international prestige of the Czech state. His admiration and friendship for him even survived, in some measure, all the pressures which were later, during the open conflict with Rome, exerted upon him by the Curia. Though for a time he could not help taking the side of George's adversaries he never did so with much conviction or happiness and for the last months of his life—he died in December 1467—he made his peace with the King and strictly refused to take any further part in what was to him an

---

[29] See his letter to his brother John, then captain (or royal governor) of Silesia, in *SrS,* VIII, 206.

unnecessary and hopeless struggle. Perhaps it was the very experience made on this Maundy Thursday of 1461 which even then proved to him convincingly the hopelessness of making the Utraquist masses give up their special form of Christian worship. This may well have been the message which he took to the King when he visited him in Kutná Hora after the event.

George can hardly have been as surprised by it as Jost and his Catholic friends seem to have been. But even George found it necessary to take notice of and act upon the strong expressions of anxiety and anger among the Utraquist masses of the capital. He had to return to them the feeling of security which had suffered for some time, first under the influence of the disagreement of leading Utraquists, among them Rokycana, with his attempts at achieving the rank of King of the Romans, and more recently by the growing hopes of Catholic circles that the old, precarious balance between the two religious bodies could be decisively revised in their own favor. The increased pressures exerted upon the King by the Curia was, after all, no longer a secret, and both sides tried to draw their conclusions from it.

Thus George's freedom to manoeuver between the two factions had become greatly restricted. The loudly proclaimed optimism of some leading Catholics,[30] the corresponding fears and protests by the Utraquists, especially Rokycana, made it ever more difficult for the King to remain "above the parties," as he would have liked to do. He tried, as far as possible, to clarify his position without disappointing or antagonizing the Catholics. In this, so it seems, he was successful when he met the estates on May 15 at a diet in Prague. His declaration, given in the form of a solemn confirmation of the old rights and freedoms of the people of Bohemia as organized in the estates,[31] did not cause any protests, even though its emphasis on the Compacts as one of those freedoms would probably no longer be received with special satisfaction by the Catholic representatives who, while forming small minorities among the gentry and the cities, included rather more than half of the barons. Soon afterwards, however, on the day of Corpus Christi the increasing tension between the two religious groups expressed itself more distinctly. There were two great competing

---

[30] To this time, presumably, belongs the letter of Czech Catholics asking George "ut Catholicam fidem in regno stabilisat et errantes reducat." See fol. 28 and 29 of the *"Cancellaria regis Georgii,"* XXIII, D 163, ("Lobkovice MS") in the Ms-Collection of the University Library in Prague.

[31] See for the main part of the text Bretholz, *Geschichte Böhmens und Mährens,* II, 253 n. 32.

processions: one, led by Rokycana, started from the "Hussite Cathedral," the Týn Church, in which the King and Queen marched; the other, including the chief members of the Catholic nobility, and with the Lord High Burgrave Zdeněk of Sternberg leading, started in the immediate proximity from the Church of St. James. Many of the people in the procession, so we hear, carried hidden arms, and only with some effort was a bloody collision averted. It seemed an ill omen for the further maintenance of religious peace in the country.[32]

There was one place where the return of religious tension in the country was watched with pure glee: among the irreconciled radicals of Breslau.[33] It was not immediately the preachers who again became vocal. The two councillors elected at the height of the old tension, who had all along taken their cues from Tempelfeld or his friends, now displayed a much livelier activity than they had been able to do during 1460. It was probably largely due to their clever agitation that the council, in August 1461, decided to establish the office of a permanent envoy at the Papal Court. The new procurator, John Kitzing,[34] was an unusually able man, fanatically devoted to what he considered his foremost task: to open the eyes of the Pope and his court to the true, treacherous character of the great heretic and, above all, to prevent the Curia from confirming the Compacts. This diplomatic agitation of Breslau, supported by frequent letters, would have had little or no success in 1460. In the later part of 1461 this had ceased to be true. The longer Kitzing's agitation at the Curia lasted, the more deeply he impressed those who had expected a spectacular change in Bohemia. And while Kitzing gained more credence in Rome he was almost as effective in the propaganda directed back to Breslau itself,[35] constantly urging his friends in the council to remain steadfast, to remember the dangers threatening Breslau from the King (dangers quite imaginary, derived from floating rumors which he presented

---

[32] See Bachmann, *Reichsgeschichte*, I, 94.

[33] Koebner's claim in his *Widerstand Breslaus*, 90, that this time Breslau's new campaign against George resulted from the united determination of the whole city ("aus dem einmütigen Wollen der Stadt hervorgegangen") is contradicted by the sources he quotes himself in notes 1 and 2 on the following page (91), which indicate the pressure exerted, at this stage of the development, by the "radical" councillors Haunolt and Hornig, close friends and disciples of Tempelfeld. Eschenloer's attempt, in this case, to let things appear in a rather harmonious way is also amply contradicted by his own information, incl. for this time the fact that much of the almost hysterical fear of George's "sinister plans" derived from the agitators in the commune. (See his German edition, I., 168, 177.)

[34] See about him Koebner, *Widerstand Breslaus*, 85-87, 100–102, 104–108.

[35] See e.g. his messages to Breslau in *SrS*, VIII, 69f., 71–74, 79, 105f., 117–121, 131f.

to them in frightening colors [36] and to understand that nothing short of the complete destruction of the great heretic could render their city secure. It was, indeed, the spirit of John of Capistrano which now walked the earth again.

George, in reality, had no thoughts of any sinister action against Breslau. Since the beginning of 1460 his attitude toward the city had never ceased to be that of a benevolent prince and protector. He would not now confirm, by violent action, all the prejudices of his enemies. Besides he had good reason to present himself as a force for peace within the Christian world—that peace without which the Pope's dream for a strong concerted action against the Turks could not possibly be realized.

This image of the "Prince of Peace," as Palacký called George [37] with some degree of idealization, seemed, however, somewhat tarnished by his stand, during the summer of 1461, in the struggle between the German princes.[38] While he did not directly interfere in the war that had broken out between the Emperor on the one hand and his brother Archduke Albert and King Matthias of Hungary on the other, he did permit one of his friends among the baronial class, Albert Kostka of Postupice, to send a challenge to the Emperor. Soon after, however, he agreed to the latter's request to mediate between him and his brother. He was, at first, unwilling to include Margrave Albert Achilles in this action of conciliation. The margrave's recent attitude at Cheb and Nürnberg—concerning the Roman kingship—was clearly not yet forgotten nor forgiven, but the reason George gave for joining the Wittelsbach party in the war against Margrave Albert was different.[39] The margrave, imperial captain, had sent out in the Emperor's name (though not clearly on his orders) letters demanding military service against the Emperor's enemies, specifically against George's ally Duke Louis of Bavaria. He had sent many of these letters, without asking for George's permission, to the

[36] George, supposedly, was building a gigantic movable bridge which would enable his troops to cross over, above the walls, into the city. See *SrS*, VIII, 79.

[37] He was, so Palacký said, "praised by contemporary orators as a prince of peace, as a sort of Numa Pompilius who, hating war, everywhere tried to awaken the faculties of peaceful arts and industries," (*Dějiny*, IV, 2, 184).

[38] For the (extremely complex) background of events in the empire see Bachmann, *Reichsgeschichte*, I, 73–87, 95–137, bibliography also in Riezler, *Geschichte Baierns*, III, 409 n. 2, and the corresponding passages in *DRTA*.

[39] See the King's letter of challenge to Albert, *FRA*, II, 20, 247, and Albert's answers *ibid.*, 247–248, and *SrS*, VIII, 63–66. For further sources see above n. 10, and Bachmann, *Reichsgeschichte*, I. 122.

King's subjects in Silesia and Lusatia and also to some in Bohemia, including the University of Prague and John Rokycana as the official head of the Czech Utraquist Church. The King considered these letters a direct interference in the affairs of the Bohemian crown as well as a breach of the treaties of friendship and mutual support concluded between himself and Albert during the first great Cheb conference. Almost at the same time (September 6) that he had mediated —it might almost be said "imposed"—the Peace of Laxenburg between the Emperor and his enemies [40]—an act which neither Archduke Albert nor George's son-in-law Matthias appreciated nearly as much as Frederick III—he still sent reinforcements to Duke Louis of Bavaria, Albert Achilles' most determined enemy, with unfortunate results for the margrave's military situation in his Frankish territories. But Albert was by no means helpless. He had the full support of his brother, Elector Frederick of Brandenburg, who saw himself in trouble through George's attempts at restoring all of Lower Lusatia to the Bohemian crown.[41] In addition he tried, directly and through the Emperor, to mobilize the papal diplomacy against George, going so far as to demand excommunication of the King.[42] This was, at this moment, a strategy rather dangerous for George who had to think of his impending negotiations in Rome and the climate in which they would be conducted. His political realism—as well as the fact that by now Albert's trespass seemed to have been sufficiently punished— led the King to a rapid change of policy. He decided, at short notice, for an all-out "peace offensive." Specifically he called, for early November, a great conference to Prague which was to end all the wars in Germany.

It was an extraordinarily difficult task, since George's allies, especially Duke Louis, were as unwilling to make any concessions as were his enemies. Again and again the ambassadors of the two sides—the princes themselves had not been invited, presumably because they were thought to be in too emotional a frame of mind—were about to break the negotiations off. If, at any time, George proved his ability as a mediator it was now. He supported the demand for ending the war by pulling his own troops out of the Frankish region and calling back Zdeněk of Sternberg, who had begun to besiege Kottbus. By

---

[40] The text in the appendix (No. 29) to F. Kurz, *Oesterreich unter Friedrich IV*, II, 224–227.

[41] See *FRA*, II, 20, 253, and for the background Bachmann, "Die Wiedervereinigung der Lausitz mit Böhmen, 1462," in *AÖG*, LXIV, I, 254ff.

[42] See *FRA*, II, 20, 250–25.

December his efforts began to pay dividends. While it was obvious that a final settlement of the material issues, whether in Austria or in Franconia, could not immediately be achieved, especially in view of the extensive demands of the Emperor against Duke Louis, both sides finally agreed, on December 16, to an armistice. It should, at least, end all the bloodshed and suffering which seemed to exhaust almost all concerned—least of all, indeed, Bohemia—and would furthermore present the chance, at a later meeting of the princes to be held in Znojmo, in Moravia, in early February 1462, to deal with the substantial issues. In order to leave sufficient time for their proper solution the armistice was to last till April 24th.[43]

For a while it looked as if the war was really ended. During the last weeks of the old and the beginning of the new year the arms were at rest. Already the Wittelsbach party, more subject than their enemies to the direct pressure of the King on whose support they depended so strongly, assumed that this was truly peace and acted accordingly. So, after the signing of the documents, did King George himself.

And so, convinced that peace, thanks to his vigorous efforts, was finally assured, George decided to prepare the Pope for the arrival of his embassy. He sent the Pope copies of all the peace arrangements arrived at during the recent Prague negotiations, and accompanied them with a letter [44] in which he said that his own hard work for peace had now clearly been blessed by the Lord. Besides the long and bloody struggles in Germany, the war between Poland and the Order of the Teutonic Knights seemed especially unwelcome in view of the need for united action against the Turks. George informed Pope Pius that he had submitted suggestions for a peaceful solution to both these powers, that the Grand Master of the Prussian Order had already accepted him as mediator, and that a similar acceptance could be expected very soon on the part of King Casimir.[45] All this, so George said, he had done for the honor and glory of God and the Church, and to strengthen the hands of the Pope and the Emperor so both could the more successfully fight the Turks and preserve Christendom against this danger. Finally he pointed out that, because of all these tasks, he had not been able to spare his chief diplomatic advisers, especially his chancellor, Prokop of Rabstein. Now, however, Prokop and other ambassadors could be released for their urgent trip to Rome,

---

[43] See G. v. Hasselholdt-Stockheim, *Herzog Albrecht IV*, II, (Urkunden und Beilagen), 588–599, and Müller, *Reichstags-Theatrum*, 89–92.

[44] *SrS*, VIII, 67.

[45] See about the background Joh. Voigt, *Geschichte Preussens*, VIII, 624–626.

taking along all the necessary instructions for the creation of permanent peace and unity in the kingdom.

When this letter was dispatched, on December 11, 1461, George's expectations did not seem to be unreasonably optimistic. Yet the picture would change greatly by the time the announced embassy got under way in mid-January. New fighting had already broken out, before the start of 1462, in the Rhineland, where Archbishop Diether of Mainz—who had only recently signed a treaty submitting to the papal demands for his resignation—renewed the war against his successor, Adolf of Nassau, and the Margrave of Baden, having been encouraged by the help promised and generously given to him by Elector Frederick of the Palatinate.[46] The hoped-for armistice between Poland and the Prussian Order, too, failed to materialize. But by far the worst thing was that the Armistice of Prague, George's greatest apparent success, was suddenly undermined by the policy of Albert Achilles.[47]

The margrave's position, at this time, was strong. He had not gone nearly as far as most of his adversaries in demobilizing and had already regained much ground in November by a short campaign against the Bishop of Würzburg, the greatest of the ecclesiastical princes in the Franconian region. At first he was inclined, nevertheless, to ratify the agreements of Prague. He ordered the bells to ring and the *Te-deum* to be sung. He had also been asked by the Emperor's envoys, returning from Prague, to stick by the peace treaty.

But the Emperor himself had let George know that his own decision for or against ratification would largely depend on Albert's. And Albert's most vigorous ally among the German princes, Ulrich of Württemberg, was quite hostile to the agreements of Prague, since peace in southeastern Germany would give Palsgrave Frederick, allied with Diether of Mainz, a better chance in his struggle against Württemberg and Baden. Also some of Albert's friends among the imperial cities, notably Augsburg and Ulm, only now entered the struggle. Thus Albert Achilles decided against general ratification. He was willing, so he told King George, to conclude and keep peace with Bohemia and the Bishops of Würzburg and Bamberg, not, however, with Duke Louis of Bavaria, who had proved himself the Empire's worst enemy. Various efforts of George to persuade him, in the most friendly forms, to change his mind failed completely.

[46] See Menzel, *Diether von Isenburg,* 150–168.
[47] For the following two paragraphs see Bachmann, *Reichsgeschichte,* I, 170–173, with the source material mostly derived from Hasselholdt-Stockheim, *op.cit.,* 600–618.

For George the situation was doubly awkward. If he left Louis—now his most important ally in Germany—to his fate, he would not only lose the Duke's friendship but his whole reputation in Germany as a reliable ally, would suffer irreparable harm. If, on the other hand, he re-entered the war on the side of Louis against the margrave, his position in regard to Frederick III was again compromised, and this at a time when he needed the Emperor's help to an unusual degree. For George had asked him—and Frederick had agreed—to strengthen his position in relation to the Pope by sending either a special embassy or at least one ambassador to accompany the Czech delegation and support their requests.

The refusal of Margrave Albert Achilles to abide by the treaty of Prague had destroyed the hopes attached to a conference of princes to be held in Znojmo in early February, and it was cancelled. At the suggestion of the sorely pressed Duke Louis, George did, however, ask his friends and allies, notably those of the Wittelsbach party but also Archduke Albert of Austria, to meet him early in March in Budweis [48] in order to decide how to meet the renewed emergency. The military threat was one aspect which George could not neglect. Thus he did permit his own subjects, especially some of the noblemen of the southwest, to be taken into Louis's service, but as yet he himself did not move against the Hohenzollern rulers. In fact it seemed for a while as if new hopes for peace could be discovered, especially when the Emperor sent a message asking Duke Louis to send his councillors to him for negotiations, and when a visit in Budweis of the papal legate Jerome Lando, Archbishop of Crete, one of the mediators in the struggle over Breslau, made it appear that perhaps the Pope himself would take steps which would help effectively in easing tensions in Germany.[49] Thus the meeting at Budweis ended with plans for another peace congress, this time to include all the princes engaged in the struggle, to be held in Prague in April. It actually was not held until much later.

But meanwhile the center of gravity of Central European events had moved south. It had followed the little group of men, King George's long promised embassy to Pope Pius II, who had left Prague in mid-January 1462 and reached Rome, after a journey of seven weeks, on March 10.

---

[48] See besides Bachmann (*Reichsgeschichte*, 185–187) and Palacký (*op. cit.* 177–179) also Max Vancsa, *Geschichte Nieder- und Oberösterreichs*, II, 382.

[49] *FRA* II, 20, 263f.

CHAPTER 12

ROME AND PRAGUE:

THE FIRST OPEN CLASH

KING GEORGE's policy of the maintenance of internal peace, of a full political reintegration of the Hussite majority and the Catholic minority, could not succeed without constant regard to the actions and reactions of the outer world—a world which was still inclined to look at the Czech religious peculiarities with deep distrust. Indeed the two relationships—the internal one between the adherents of the Czech reformation and those of the orthodox creed, and the external one between Bohemia and the outer world—were interconnected and constantly reacted upon one another. In few other societies or ages was this interconnection between domestic and foreign policy closer than in Poděbradian Bohemia. This very closeness made both policies especially difficult to conduct, and thus made heavy demands upon George's understanding and statecraft. Indeed the situation, frequently, was of such unusual difficulty that it seemed to demand unusual measures, measures which were far from routine and repeatedly turned out to go beyond what in George's time and world was possible of realization. On the other hand just such a policy—which, in other lands, might be considered as a reckless or irresponsible adventure—could under less than favorable circumstances turn against George. To some extent this had happened with the effects of George's striving for the Roman crown. This, at least as much as religious issues, had contributed to the deterioration of George's relationship with the Pope in 1461.

If for George religion and politics could hardly be separated, because all conflicts, internal and external, either resulted from religious issues, tended to be expressed in religious terms, or at least were covered with a religious cloak, for Pope Pius the two were equally inseparable, but for different reasons. Like George, he, too, thought in terms of integration, but on a far larger scale. Where George worked for an integrated nation in a strong monarchy, trying to lead his country essentially in the direction which was to become dominant in western Europe in the late fifteenth and sixteenth centuries, Pius II, romantically taking his cue from the past, tried to reestablish a more clearly united Europe under papal, that is under his own, leadership. There was one political fact which gave this policy of reunification, this attempt at the reawakening of an essentially antiquated idea a measure of realistic urgency. This was the Turkish danger, the fact that not one of the nations now exposed to the growing pressure of the Ottoman Empire, neither Venice nor Hungary nor Poland, could be expected individually to defeat the formidable enemy in the Southeast. There was, perhaps, a measure of vanity and seeking for glory among the motives for Pius' policy of recreating the spirit of the Crusades. Yet it cannot be denied that he correctly appraised the reality of that danger which was strongly underrated by other European powers, even those most immediately threatened such as the Venetians or King Matthias of Hungary.[1]

But if Pius' aim to create a united front against the Ottomans was essentially sound and even urgent, the way in which he tried to go about it was not. As had many Popes before him, he tried to combine the office of the spiritual leader of the Christian world with that of the leading prince and statesman of Italy. As head of the Church he tried to maintain and strengthen the paramount position that the Papacy, as an autocratically monarchial institution, had regained by its victory over the Council of Basel, the very Council which the young Enea Silvio de' Piccolomini had served. The act that had most emphatically underlined this decision—the determination to have done for all times with councilar parliamentarism or constitutionalism—was the bull "Execrabilis," pronounced by Pius at the time of the Mantuan Congress and designating all attempts at appeal from the Pope to a Council as crimes leading automatically to excommunication.

Nowhere in Europe had the "Execrabilis" found more vigorous criticism and opposition than in France. There, the Pragmatic Sanction of Bourges, largely a product of the spirit of the Conciliarism of Basel, was staunchly defended by its original protector: King

---

[1] For the general background see the passages in vol. II of Pastor, *Geschichte der Päpste*, (used here 3rd ed., Freiburg, 1904), cited hereafter as "Pastor," especially chapters 2, 7, and 8, and the monograph by Else Hocks, *Pius II und der Halbmomd*, Freiburg, 1941, both without any attempt to criticism of this policy. For a critical treatment see G. Voigt, *Enea Silvio de' Piccolomoni*, III, 674f., 694f., Among the most peculiar actions of Pius in regard to the Turks was his attempt, in 1462, to persuade the Ottoman Emperor Mohamed II in a long letter, almost a learned dissertation, to convert to Christianity, with promises to recognize him on this basis as the "Emperor of the East and Lord of most of the world." See Pastor, II, 231f., with bibliography, and Voigt, III, 658ff. The original in Raynaldus-Mansi, *Annales ecclesiastici*, X, 44-112.

Charles VII. The Pragmatic Sanction had given him much power over the French episcopate and clergy, while at the same time severely restricting the flow of money from France into the treasury of the Curia. He was quite unwilling to give up such important advantages, and he had the support of the great majority of the French Catholic hierarchy as well as the University of Paris.[2]

Besides the defense of the "Pragmatique" against Pius' bull the French court had another complaint against the Pope: it was his attitude in relation to the throne of the kingdom of Naples. His predecessor, Calixtus III, had, upon the death of his bitter enemy King Alfonso of the house of Aragon, refused to recognize Alfonso's illegitimate son Ferrante as King of Naples. He had in fact, if not deliberately, thereby awakened the hope of the French dynasty that the choice of one of their own candidates as King of Naples, either of King Charles's brother-in-law Duke Rene of Anjou-Provence or of his son, Duke John of Calabria, would make southern Italy again a French sphere of influence.[3] But Calixtus had died soon after Alfonso, and Pius II had taken his place. On this issue the Italian prince in Pius was stronger than the Pontiff. He hated the French in general and the French clergy in particular—he never forgave the French members of the Holy College for their opposition to his election as Pope.[4] But he also feared French power over Italy, which more than once had proved able to restrict papal freedom of movement and decision. In close understanding with Francesco Sforza, Duke of Milan, and Cosimo de' Medici, the uncrowned ruler of Florence, Pius therefore decided to acknowledge and enfeoff Ferrante, not indeed, without forcing the young King to pay a considerable price. Ferrante had to give the hand of his daughter to Pius' nephew, Antonio de' Piccolomini, whom sometime later he made Duke of Amalfi. It was quite in line with the Pope's uninhibited nepotism, but it also tied him down to the continued support of Ferrante.[5]

Nevertheless the French did not give up the hope of eventually winning the Pope over to their side. They based this hope on the activities of Jean Jouffroy, Bishop of Arras, who had cautiously medi-

[2] See Pastor, II, 103–106. For Charles's position as formulated by his "general procurator," Dauvet, see Pierre Danou, *Essai historique sur la puissance temporelle des papes,* 4th ed., Paris 1818, I, 274.

[3] Pastor, I, 738–742, 772–776.

[4] Pius' *Commentaries* abound with expressions of this sentiment. See e.g., in the Smith College edition, Book I, 14ff., especially 99, or Book X, 675; the passages in italics often are of importance because they had for political reasons been purged from previous editions.

[5] See Pastor, II, 20ff.

ated between Pius and the Dauphin Louis. As a result, Louis, who, consumed by deep hatred of his royal father, lived in exile in Burgundy, promised to abolish the Pragmatic Sanction as soon as he would become King. Thus when Charles VII died in July 1461, the negotiations between Pius and Louis XI were intensified, with the Bishop of Arras acting now as the official representative of the Pope. By the end of 1461 Pius learned that Louis was indeed willing to keep his promise.[6] But the King assumed that this act would only be part of a bargain: that in return the Pope would drop his support for Ferrante. It is impossible to say whether Bishop Jouffroy had planted this belief in the King's mind on his own or whether he had received some slight encouragement for such tactical procedure from Rome.[7]

One fact, however, is clear: right up to the moment of the official abolition of the Pragmatic Sanction there had been very little real hope in Roman Catholic circles that such a step could be achieved so easily and without any real sacrifice.[8] It seemed an extraordinary success for the Pope, measured against the danger of a wide split in the Church of Western Europe. That this was no mere chimera could be seen from the contacts that had existed between the "reform party" in Germany, specifically between Diether of Mainz and his ally Frederick of the Palatinate, and the court of Paris. While the end of the "Pragmatique" did not necessarily mean that henceforth there would be friendship between the Pope and the King of France—this, of course, would depend on their future policy and especially on Pius' attitude in the Neapolitan dispute—at least the threatening picture of Europe's most powerful nation living largely outside the organizational framework of the Roman Church would be removed. The King could not too easily restore the act whose abolition he had begun to force, against stiff resistance of Parlement, University, and clergy, with such unyielding determination. This, at least, was also the Pope's reaction when, in January 1462, he received a report from Jouffroy —who, on Louis's request, had been raised to the rank of cardinal— that Louis would surely implement his decision regarding the Pragmatic Sanction only if he received satisfaction in his demand for papal support in the issue of Naples.[9] While, only a short time before,

---

[6] *Ibid.*, II, 110ff. (For the role of Jouffroy see in much detail A. Varillas, *Histoire de Louis XI*, Paris, 1689, I, 89ff.)

[7] Pastor, II, 108f.

[8] Pius, *Commentaries*, VII, 511.

[9] Pastor, II, 111.

the mood in Rome regarding the relations to France had been distinctly gloomy, the arrival of the French embassy, on March 13, 1462, abruptly changed this feeling into one of nearly triumphant happiness. The signing of the official act, unconditionally revoking the Pragmatic Sanction, was one of the greatest moments of Pius' generally so eventful and personally successful life.[10] The Pope considered himself as victor in a difficult struggle, he speaks with contemptuous sarcasm of the French bishops who "burst into tears and returned passionate thanks to God who had at last dragged them from the darkness of the Pragmatic Sanction and brought them to the pure light of Apostolic truth." Soon afterwards, so he says, "they reverted . . . as dogs to their vomit, to their baying against the Apostolic See."[11] Indeed the triumph proved to be short lived, the gain in terms of French concessions would melt away fast under the impression of Pius' stubborn support for Ferrante.[12]

But for this very moment the psychological effect of the triumph could not have been more profound. A victory of such magnitude over schismatic tendencies in Europe's strongest realm could not possibly induce the Pope—or the leading officials among the members of his court—to condone what seemed similar schismatic tendencies in a far smaller nation, tendencies, moreover, which had taken a more drastic, more clearly deviating form. This was the moment to do away with all those drives for a special national status that were, in Pius' much transformed view, the evil bequests of the Council of Basel. Where, against all expectations, King Louis had bent his proud neck, King George would have to follow suit.

No time, therefore, could have been less propitious for the hopes and requests of the Prague court than March 1462; no day more hopeless than March 13, the occasion when the Pope, with the trumpet sounds of the great ceremony still filling his ears, decided to give a first audience to the two noblemen leading the Czech mission.[13]

---

[10] Quoted in *ibid.*, 119.

[11] *Commentaries*, VII, 512.

[12] *Ibid.*, VIII, 549f. For the French background see also J. Combet, *Louis XI et le Saint Siege*, Paris, 1903, and C. Lucius, *Pius II, und Ludwig XI von Frankreich* (Heidelberger Abhandlungen z. mittl. und neueren Geschichte, vol. 41), Heidelberg, 1913.

[13] There is a considerable amount of source material from both sides on the Czech embassy in Rome and its failure. The longest, most detailed report was written in Czech by Wencelas Koranda the Younger, one of the two Utraquist priests belonging to the embassy. It is very obvious from the precision of the quotations and their thorough conformity with other sources, including Catholic ones, that Koranda made his notes on the proceedings and speeches during or immediately following the proceedings. Palacký used them widely. One Ms version was published by its discoverer Adolf Patera in *AČ*, VIII, 321–364. A later critical edition

Even the embassy itself looked less impressive than had the French, with its cardinals and bishops, its noblemen and guards of honor. Yet it was well selected. George, as long before announced, had sent his chancellor, Prokop of Rabstein, eminently suitable as a Roman Catholic of liberal views, an experienced diplomat and statesman familiar with his King's thoughts and intentions, and an old friend of the Pope from the time when both had been in the service of Emperor Frederick III. From the Utraquist side, with at least equal standing, came Lord Zdeněk Kostka of Postupice, son of William Kostka, who had played such a distinguished role as leader of the Hussite gentry and of the administration of Prague, but also as Czech ambassador at Basel, through long periods of the Hussite Revolution.[14] Zdeněk and his brother Albert were among the King's closest friends from the time of his regency. In recognition for their many services the two men—whose family had long been leading among the class of knights —had been elevated by George to the barony, a reward conferring high distinction by its very infrequency. Zdeněk was a faithful Utraquist but not a hothead, a man who could be expected to present George's views soberly, but with due emphasis. To support the laymen in their demand for the confirmation of the Compacts two Utraquist clergymen had been sent, Wenceslas Vrbenský, Dean of St. Appolinaris in Prague, and Wenceslas Koranda the Younger, Master of Arts of Prague University. Only the latter was to play an important role during the negotiations with the Curia as well as later in the history of Czech Utraquism.[15] His report on the Roman nego-

---

in *Staré letopisy české z rukopisu křižovnického* (SLČK), ed. F. Šimek and M. Kaňák, Prague, 1959, pp. 232–271. A much shorter report is contained in Pope Pius' *Commentaries*, VII, 512–515. Breslau's procurator Kitzing gave some details in his reports, published by H. Markgraf together with some other news from Rome, in *SrS*, VIII, 78–90. Kitzing's reports were one of the sources for Eschenloer; see his German ed., I, 181–187. An anonymus report from Rome, giving especially Pius' denunciation of the Compacts in some detail, was published by Palacký in *FRA*, II, 20, 268–271. The same ground is covered in a diplomatic report published in Müller's *Reichstags-Theatrum*, II, 238–240. Further Ammanati (Jacobus Cardinal Piccolomini), *Commentarii*, published in a common edition with Pope Pius' autobiography, Frankfurt, 1641, 432–434. Among secondary sources see Palacký, *Dějiny*, IV, 2, 215–237 in the German ed. (1860), 191–209 in the second Czech edition (1878); further M. Jordan, *Das Königthum Georg's von Poděbrad*, 48–73; G. Voigt, *Enea Silvio*, III, 458–468; Pastor, II, 172–177; Bachmann, *Reichsgeschichte*, I, 196–209; Tomek, *Dějepis*, VII, 35–45; E. Denis, ed. Vančura, *Konec samostatnosti české*, 3rd ed., I, Prague, 1921, 105–111, finally Urbánek, *Věk*, IV, 520–538.

14 See Heymann, *Žižka*, and 338 *passim*, 417f. More details on these and other members of the Czech embassy in Urbánek, *Věk*, IV, 522 n. 7.

15 He has been the subject of a monograph by K. Krofta: "V. Koranda mladší z Nové Plzně a jeho názory náboženské" in *Listy z náboženských dějin českých*, Prague, 1936, pp. 240–287. See also Hrejsa, *Dějiny* IV, 16–18. In English see Heymann, "The Hussite-

tiations, very detailed and specific, belongs to our most important sources on their course. In addition to those four individuals, the King had also accredited his "roving ambassador," Antoine Marini, but had left out his regular envoy in Rome, the royal procurator, Fantino de Valle—a sign that Fantino's frequent and impatient urging had already put the relationship between him and his royal employer under a strain.

The first audience given by the Pope to the two noblemen immediately showed up all the basic difficulties. Rabstein was personally received by the Pope with a warmth which seemed natural among old friends but which could also be expected to make him, the faithful Catholic, receptive to the arguments of the Pope. When the Czech chancellor announced as the first and foremost task of the embassy the conveying of the obedience as done by the King's predecessors, the Pope answered that he could not easily accept this as a normal procedure since the kingdom was not now in union with the Church. King George, he continued, had not yet taken any steps to fulfill the promises given in his coronation oath—on the contrary he still gave freedom of preaching "to that bad man Rokycana" and had only recently, on the day of Corpus Christi, abandoned the regular procession for the procession of the heretics. If no better guarantees could be given that the King's obedience would really be implemented, he, the Pope, would not be able to accept it.

When the two ambassadors answered that they had no additional guarantees to give except the solemn act of obedience, the Pope told them that he would appoint a committee of four cardinals to deal with the issues posed by the presence of the embassy, and suggested that the ambassadors should, before the actual ceremony, try to achieve an understanding with those four men. Three members of the committee were: the famous Greek Patriarch of Nicaea, Cardinal Bessarion; the Spaniard Juan Carvajal, Cardinal of Sant' Angelo; and Nicholas of Cusa, Cardinal of St. Petrus in vinculis. All three had served the Pope as legates north of the Alps, and the two last-named, especially, were considered as experts on the problems of Bohemia. The fourth, much less interested and playing only a minor role, was Guillaume Cardinal d'Estouteville, Archbishop of Rouen.[16]

Discussions did take place between the Czech ambassadors and the

Utraquist Church in the Fifteenth and Sixteenth Centuries," *Archiv für Reformationsgeschichte,* 1961, I, 9f.

[16] See Voigt, *Enea Silvio,* III, 460, and Bachmann, *Reichsgeschichte,* I, 206 n. 1.

cardinals, first of all, on March 14, with Carvajal, then two days later with Bessarion. In these talks the two sides found themselves essentially at cross-purposes. The prelates tried to convince the Czech envoys that their king had firmly sworn to lead his people to religious unity. He would, they said, certainly have had the power to do so if only he had had the will. Instead, so declared Carvajal, he and the Queen had continuously maintained the erroneous usage of the communion in the two kinds. The King had said that he wanted to lead his people away from errors not with the sword but with wisdom, but "we here have not yet perceived any such wisdom." Finally Carvajal asked the ambassadors to accept in advance, and with binding force for the kingdom, any solution decided on by Pope Pius, a suggestion which, Rabstein tried to explain, he and his companions had no authority to follow.

The Czechs, and especially Rabstein, then made a stronger effort on March 16 to give the Curia, this time represented by Cardinal Bessarion, a more realistic picture of the general conditions in Bohemia. Rabstein started out by mentioning the Pope's reproach that the King had participated in the Utraquist Corpus Christi procession. "The King," he stated, "does not always take part in the same processions, but sometimes joins one, sometimes the other. On the highest holidays especially he is often up in the Castle [with the Catholic clergy]. After all you know that there are two kinds of people in Bohemia, and our King is the ruler over both of them and must tolerate both. For if he were to hold with one side only and tried to impose it on the others, there would be the danger that the other side would rise in rebellion against him." Here, indeed, George's Catholic friend and adviser spoke with complete sincerity out of his experience and his realistic appraisal of the situation in his country.[17] And Bessarion's answer made it obvious how much the apparent submission of France had reduced the Curia's ability and willingness to listen to any voice presenting such unwelcome truth. He emphasized the harshness and strictness with which King Louis had enforced his willingness to renounce the Pragmatic Sanction. "And you must know," so he continued, "that in France there are 101 bishops, and many abbeys and great prelatures, and the clergy did not want at all to suffer that this royal act be put in force, but resisted with all their strength. But

---

[17] See *AČ*, VIII, 324. It is characteristic for the bias that more or (often) less subtly colors the presentation of Bachmann that in his otherwise so detailed account of this discussion no mention is made of this striking utterance.

when the King firmly wanted it, see what happened in spite of the large number of the prelates and their helpers. So also, if only your King really wanted it, he could soon achieve it, especially since all the important men, the wise and powerful ones, also the doctors and the men of great learning stand in the unity of the Roman Church and do not commit those errors, but those who do and take the communion in the two kinds are the flighty and unserious ones, and their priests are without any learning and stature." [18] Finally, after this display of wishful thinking and wrong judgment, the great cardinal tried to win the delegates by depicting the glorious and magnificent honors that, like King Louis's, George's act of unification was sure to receive. In the face of such firm, if mistaken conviction, the Czech chancellor could achieve little when another two days later, he once more tried to impress the reality of the situation on Bessarion by referring to the awsome and relatively balanced strength of the two religious parties in his country.

On the following day, March 19th, Pope Pius himself entered the fray again, this time by inviting only Zdeněk Kostka, whom he rightly assumed to be, of all members, nearest to King George. [19] Besides the Pope, Cardinal Cusa and some less known bishops were also present. This time the Pope tried, above all, to prove to Lord Zdeněk—and if possible to make him admit—that the Compacts were without validity and without value. He omitted none of the many arguments which had previously been collected and presented, including the tricky one that, by limiting the right to the Chalice to those "who had had the usage," only those who had been adults at the time of the conclusion of the Compacts could still possibly claim such privilege, and that there were few of those left alive. He claimed (and here he was, legally, on firmer ground) that according to the Compacts only those should receive the Chalice who expressly asked for it, while in practice the Utraquist clergy gave it to all, even children, without having received such request. The Council had granted the Compacts only to overcome the particular hardheadedness of the Czechs, who at the time would otherwise not have been pacified, but if, in the name of the Church, the Council had had the power to grant the Compacts, then he, the Pope, had now the power to withdraw them in favor of something better.

Kostka tried to warn the Pope against such a step. "If," he argued,

<hr>

[18] See *AČ*, VIII, 325.
[19] *Ibid.*, 326–329.

"the Compacts were to be abrogated by papal order without giving the Czech people an understandable and plausible reason for it, we have to fear the outbreak of grave unrest. The Czechs will not let go so easily of the Chalice unless it can be truly proved to them that they are in error." The Pope's answer was: "God is in heaven, we on earth. We have to seek God's honor and glory, not our own. God wants you to be obedient rather than to think of your own honor, just as he destroyed Saul and his house when he sought his own honor more than that of God. If you do not obey, then King and Kingdom together will be disowned and destroyed. And you know well," so the Pope concluded this sinister warning, "that I have the power to do just this."

If the Pope had expected to see the Czech nobleman soften up under the impact of this harsh threat, he was mistaken. "The Czech people say," Kostka answered, "that just by possessing and keeping the Compacts they have always been in the obedience and unity of the Holy Church, for whatever they do here they do on the basis of the agreement, the permission and the will of the Basel Council."

This discussion was followed by a historical discourse presented by Cardinal Cusa, pointing out that in the early Church one priest had given the bread, another the wine, whereas, in Bohemia both are now given by the same priest. Kostka quickly saw a chance to establish his position. "Then," so he asked, "there is no religious error contained in taking the Holy Communion in both kinds?" Cusa, far more honest than some of his colleagues, admitted: "Whoever says that this is a religious error is himself a fool. But it is indeed an error to claim that there is more divine grace in taking both kinds, as people think in your country." Kostka did not let loose: "Then, if it is not a religious error, I shall stand with the communion in the two kinds."

It may well be that the obvious failure of Pope Pius and his chief advisers to impress or convert Kostka (or even to find much support for their demands in the attitude of Rabstein) resulted in a change of tactics on the side of the Pope. Whereas so far he had tried to make the acceptance of the act of obedience dependent on guarantees for complete ritual unification, he now decided to accept the obedience and then use it as a means of renewed and greatly intensified pressure. It was this procedure that determined the course of events of the following day, March 20th, which was now given over to the first public reception of the embassy.

The great meeting was held in one of the largest halls of Rome, which was filled to capacity, with seats provided only for the twenty-four cardinals present. The first man called to talk was the Emperor's special envoy, Dr. Wolfgang Forchtenauer. He spoke with great warmth, emphasizing the old and close friendship between Frederick III and Pope Pius. The Emperor, he said, strongly supported King George's plea, not only because the King had asked him for it but because he was convinced that, if the Pope could fulfill King George's request, this would help to strengthen the Christian religion and to establish harmony within the Church. Clearly this was as far as Frederick could go in George's support.[20]

The next act was the presentation of the obedience. Prokop of Rabstein offered it to the Pope in the name of George, King of Bohemia, but the Pope immediately inquired why the obedience was not presented also in the name of the people of George's realm. The chancellor was unsure whether he could do this in the name of all the people, including the Utraquists. He consulted with Kostka, who encouraged him to speak for all the people, as the people would go along with the King. Thus Rabstein presented the obedience for a second time, now expressly including the people of the kingdom of Bohemia.

Pope Pius then asked whether the members of the embassy had any other matter to bring before him. In answer to this request, Wenceslas Koranda arose to argue for papal recognition of the Compacts. And now, for the first time, the Pope and the dignitaries of the Curia were faced by one who truly represented the vigorous and dynamic spirit of a great reform movement, not in the politically refined and mellowed form in which it had entered into the diplomatic game between Prague and Rome, but with much of its original power, freshness, and conviction. The young master—he was still in his early thirties—did not consciously try to challenge and shock the Pope and the great prelates; on the contrary, he tried to be as polite, even as humble, as possible, and his most urgent request was for the maintenance of peace. But he was a fast and fiery speaker, almost breathless in his diction, deeply serious and firm in his conviction of the righteousness of his cause and of God's blessing upon it. And with this he probably shocked the other side more than he or his friends had either expected or intended. Clearly this was not a man who could be bought by clever politics, and in the eyes of some of his listeners he filled much more clearly the picture of the religious rebel and heretic that had been so

[20] *Ibid.*, 355f., also Kitzing in *SrS*, VIII, 85.

firmly connected with the Hussite movement in its early days of greatness.[21]

Koranda began by apologizing that he, with his weak mind and gifts, had been charged with the awesome task of presenting this plea to the Vicar of Christ. He then described the Hussite movement as a great light that had come to the Czech nation by the grace of God and the Holy Spirit through the study of the Scriptures and the Fathers by Czech masters and priests. "And this holy truth was preached and received with joy by the great nobles and knights of the kingdom, by the great city of Prague and other cities and towns, and by the other people of the country, not recklessly or thoughtlessly but out of a deep care for true religion and sincere urge for the salvation of their souls. Then, however, the enemies of this truth arose and assaulted and persecuted its adherents." Koranda then described, in vivid colors, the terrible sufferings of the Hussite Wars, but also proudly pointed to the many victories which God had given the Czechs against the far greater numbers of their enemies. Yet for all these victories the Czechs had not become arrogant but had stretched out their hands in the negotiations for peace at Cheb and Basel, which led to the granting of the Compacts by the Council. They had also been approved and their protection solemnly sworn to by the Emperor Sigismund, and when he was accepted as King he had declared "that for the communion in the two kinds and the other three articles no one should henceforth attack the Bohemians and Moravians or call them heretics, but on the basis of these Compacts should recognize them as faithful, true and good sons of the Holy Church and thus treat them with respect and friendship." Equally, the Kings, Albert and Ladislav had sworn to protect and observe the Compacts. Finally "by the goodness of God and the wise, circumspect leadership of King George, all those sufferings and storms have finally ceased and such blessed peace has returned as not the oldest people of the kingdom and the margraviate can remember. This peace the King has brought not only to his own lands, but he has worked to spread it even to the lands of neighboring kings, princes and lords, as he knows that where there is strife and hatred there is also instability and misery, but where there is peace and concord there also the land is blessed with every happiness."

---

[21] *AČ*, VIII, 328–336. The Pope (see *Commentaries*, book VII, 513) noted his "sonorous voice" and his "headlong delivery." On the strong impression see Ammanati, *Commentarii*, 433.

Perhaps to show the great humanist on the papal throne that he and his like were not without classical education, Koranda, on confirming this last passage, quoted from Seneca and Cato.[22] Then, however, he turned to the present. There are now again people, both inside and outside the Bohemian realm, who attack the Compacts and slander the Czechs as schismatics and heretics. "Some of them" (clearly with reference to Breslau) "even claim that they are supported by the Pope's Holiness himself. But it would seem absurd to assume that from such a fountain of love there could ever issue acts of such a harsh and ungracious nature." So far, following the precepts of the Compacts, the Czechs had simply ignored such attacks. But they hoped with confidence that the Holy Father in his mercy would take those unjustly attacked under his protection, would punish those guilty of slander, and would establish lasting friendship between the Bohemians and Moravians and the other Christians on the basis of the Compacts. Once this was achieved it would also be possible for the Czechs to give much help in the struggle against the Turks. Koranda ended with a passionate appeal to the Pope, by confirming the Compacts to heal completely all the wounds of the past, thus gaining immortal fame and gratitude.

It is perhaps a testimony to the effectiveness of Koranda's speech that Pope Pius considered it necessary to answer immediately.[23] He first referred in a highly laudatory way to the Emperor and his message, then complained in slightly ironical terms about the lateness of the Bohemian obedience, though acknowledging that some of the reasons given for this by Prokop of Rabstein were justified. Then, in a discourse lasting two hours, he discussed in detail Bohemian history. First he extolled the glories and beauties of the country and its magnificent cities and emphasized that its people used to be faithful, economical, religious, but also strong and handsome, men who could defend themselves against all enemies with their own strength. Then, in a detailed survey of the history of the Czech Kings from the earliest times, he especially praised Charles IV and his piety. "Wyclyf's appearance," he continued, "was the beginning of all ills. From him Hus took his errors like this one, that priests must have no worldly possessions and laymen not be forced to pay tithe. After him came Jacobellus of Stříbro, a little school teacher of no judgment and not much learn-

---

[22] See Urbánek, *Věk*, IV, 528 n. 28.

[23] *Ibid.*, 336–342. The report again appears completely factual and essentially literal, especially if compared with the (shorter) version given by Pius himself, *Commentaries*, book VII, 513, 514.

ing,[24] who one day came across St. John 6:53, 'Except ye eat the flesh of the Son of man, and drink his blood, ye have no life in you.' So he called the priests in Prague and said: 'What are we doing? The priests mock us! They close the gates of paradise when they keep the blood from us. Make sure that the words of our Savior be followed and that the communion be taken in both kinds by all, under danger of eternal perdition.' Thus he took all these words in the Scriptures literally. But in reality they have to be understood merely in a spiritual way, as the Doctors and the Church have always known. This Jacobellus, therefore, fell in error with all his disciples. But the misfortune was that the simple people, religious as they were and devoted to all that was good and Christian, believed these priests and accepted their teaching, not out of any wickedness or impertinence, but out of true religiousness and the wish for the salvation of their souls. In Bohemia it was the ordinary people who believed them and the lords and the distinguished people stayed in union with the Roman Church, but in Moravia some lords and gentry turned away from the Church whereas the ordinary people in the cities stayed with the Church." [25]

Then the Pope gave his own version of the Hussite Wars, very different, of course, from the glorifying one given by the Hussite Koranda, and generally in agreement with the presentation in his *Historia Bohemica*. He referred to his impressions at the time of his visit to Benešov, when he had seen the terrible devastation of this war with his own eyes, and to the "blind rogue" Žižka, the cruelty of his warfare, and the great number of his victims. The Czechs, so he continued, should not boast of their deeds and victories in this war—these had only been possible because God had wanted to punish others for their sins. Finally, after having discussed in some detail the Four Articles of Prague and their significance, the Pope came to the negotiations in Cheb, Basel, and Prague and their result, the Compacts. He treated them in an altogether negative way, as a concession made under the pressure of circumstances, meant only for the then living generation of Hussites "who had practiced it before and still desired it. Of these,

---

[24] It was an old habit of Aeneas Sylvius to belittle Jacobellus as a nobody and an ignoramus —in fact an extremely inaccurate judgment. See Heymann, *Žižka*, 151ff.

[25] This detail, supposed to show Pius' comprehensive and specific knowledge of conditions in the Czech realm, was at best a half-truth. In both countries those cities where the population was mostly German remained Catholic. Not only in Moravia but also in Bohemia originally the majority of barons and knights had turned Hussite in the 1420's. Since then a number of the baronial houses, but very few of the gentry had returned to the Roman ritual. In translating this part of Pius' speech I have closely followed Koranda's text (*AČ*, VIII, 338), but have occasionally used terms or expressions recorded by the speaker himself in his *Commentaries*, book VII, 514.

however, only few are left. The Council, thus, did not grant the Compacts as a permanent measure but only for a limited time, so as to give the Czechs a chance to calm down from the excitement of the war, to reconsider errors and return to the unity of the Church." All this had been said before, but now the Pope added an essentially new legalistic argument against the Compacts. The understanding, so he said, was that if the Czechs wanted to continue under these rules they had to ask the Council for renewed permission. "This, however, the Czechs failed to do, and thus the Council did not give them such a permission. Therefore the Compacts were automatically repealed and can have no more force." This argument was clearly presented ad hoc and has no basis in the sources on the genesis of the Compacts.

"Now, however," the Pope went on to say, "we expressly declare that the Compacts have no validity. From now on the Czechs can no longer stand up and say: we have the Compacts from the Council."

The Pope then returned to the King's obedience and chided him for not having sufficiently fulfilled those promises and oaths without which he would not have been crowned. "The communion in the two kinds," he said, "still goes on as before, nor has he even ordered the people to desist from it. The priests of his side insult true Christians, and do not bury their dead, and all those things the King lets pass.... He must now finally fulfill what he has sworn."

Pius II concluded by saying: "We, too, want nothing better than peace, but we cannot accept the way in which you seek it, for what you demand disagrees with the unity of the Church. But since you ask for bread we shall not give you scorpions, since you ask for fish we will not give you a serpent. We and our brethren the cardinals are the fathers, you are the sons. The fathers cannot want anything but the well-being of their sons. We shall call our brethren to consult with them, and having carefully considered the matter shall give you an answer such as will best agree with our honor."

The great meeting, thus, ended on a rather dismal note for the Czech embassy. It had now little if any success to hope for. The members had presented the full obedience in the name of their nation, but, far from gaining confirmation of the Compacts, there was now little doubt that the Curia would use the obedience as an additional instrument of diplomatic pressure.

This, indeed, became even more obvious when, on March 22, the Utraquists of the Czech delegation, led by Kostka, were invited to meet with the committee of cardinals in the house of Bessarion. Cardinal Carvajal greeted the Czechs with an expression of great joy about the act of obedience. This, he said, would finally lead the Czechs to do away with all their differences and, after the extinction of all errors, to join in the full unity of Church. The Czech answer to this was that even before the pronouncement of obedience they had stood, and would always stand, in the unity of the Church, since already the Compacts, far from being in the way, had established that unity. There are furthermore, they said, very few people in the country misled by errors or heresy, but wherever they may appear the King sees to it that they are punished and their errors prevented from spreading.

Cardinal Cusa answered with an appeal to the Czechs to obey the orders of the Pope and Church rather than the recommendations of the ignorant Jacobellus, and not to make a joke of the very word obedience. They should put all their trust in the decision of the Holy Father, who would do what would be best for them. The Czechs asked for time to consider, and four days later the negotiations met again with most of the same people present, but also Rabstein and Forchtenauer as well as the Bishop of Ferrara, Lorenzo Roverella, and the old Spanish Cardinal Torquemada.[26] This conference gave the last and final proof that there was no hope for understanding. Above all the cardinals tried again to persuade the ambassadors to give their own, firm guarantees that the Czechs, on the basis of the obedience, would forego the Chalice. Cardinal Carvajal made a special attempt to convince the Czechs that their inhibitions and fears over renouncing the Compacts, and with them the Chalice, were unwarranted and from the point of view of Bohemian national politics quite unnecessary. He tried to buttress his arguments by telling his listeners what he claimed had been his experiences during his stay in Prague fourteen years earlier, in 1448. At that time, he claimed, Rokycana had admitted to him that the Compacts could never lead to internal peace in the country since the Catholics would not adhere to the Chalice. Rokycana had also conceded, according to Carvajal, that if he had but wanted he could have led the people away from the Chalice and back to religious union. This, however, he could no longer do, merely because too long

---

[26] Lorenzo Roverella, Bishop of Ferrara, was later to play a significant and passionate role as papal legate in the struggle against Hussite Bohemia. He must not be confused with Cardinal Bartolomeo Roverella, Archbishop of Ravenna, an important contemporary figure in the administration of the papal states (see Pastor, II, 208). Cardinal Torquemada, on the other hand, is not the famous grand inquisitor who was only promoted to that office in 1483, long after the death of the old cardinal. The latter one, however, survived Pius II and was even, shortly before his own death, considered as Pius' possible successor (see Pastor, II, 296).

and too eagerly had he preached the need for communion in both kinds, and so the people would not take him seriously if he now changed his tune. Master Příbram, too, had seen and admitted to Carvajal that Utraquism was an error, and had himself died in the full union with the Church. Upon his reporting all this to Rome, Cardinal Carvajal concluded, Pope Nicholas V had therefore refused to confirm the Compacts.[27]

In view of this astonishing discourse—a mixture of misunderstandings, distortions, and wishful thinking—it must have been difficult for the Czechs to remain patient and polite listeners. Kostka, now clearly functioning as the actual head of the embassy, eventually tried, for a last time, to lead the debate back to the political realities of Bohemia.

He first reacted to the cardinals' demands for personal guarantees for complete ritual conformity. They had, Kostka said, no authority whatever for such an undertaking, and even if they were to give guarantees, it would only lead to their complete and angry disavowal by the majority of the Czech people. If it were really true—which Kostka was far from accepting—that the Compacts had no longer any value and validity, then the only way to make the Czechs understand such a change would be "for the Holy father to send one man or several men to Bohemia who are wiser and better educated and suited than I. They would have to give to the Czech people the full trend of thought of the Holy Father, and all the reasons why he thinks that the Compacts are no longer valid so they can understand this. And all that I can do for the glory of God and the welfare of the Church, and for the honor of the Kingdom and the Margravate, I shall be glad to do."

This sounded like a concluding statement, and the suggestion it contained was indeed to assume importance. Yet the Czech baron felt the need once more to warn the men of the Curia of the dangerous consequences of their present policy. "It seems to me," he said, "that unless you fulfill our request [for the confirmation of the Compacts], there is little hope in Bohemia for the obedient compliance that the Holy Father wants to see. Rather do I expect internal storms and upheavals

---

[27] Rokycana's supposed admission is absurd. He took his creed far too seriously to think of it as something he might have dropped if this had not damaged his prestige. (See my monograph on him in *Church History* September 1959, pp. 240–280). Příbram, far from being won over to Catholicism by Carvajal, was responsible for the steps by which the cardinal was deprived of the original of the Compacts, which he had tried to take away with him. In the last phase of his life Příbram, while still a Hussite conservative, made his peace with Rokycana and died, contrary to Carvajal's claim, as a convinced adherent of the Chalice. See Hrejsa, *op.cit.*, III, 70, and Palacký, *Dějiny*, IV, 1, p. 229 n. 220.

which might well make the King angry against such sort of an 'obedience' and may result in bitter enmity between the two religious parties. And if you get the people into a mood of storm and defiance, who, then, can succeed in ordering them back to any obedience, except by the power of the sword, which would be extremely dangerous." These, to some extent, were prophetic words. It is perhaps not strange that a man as fully conversant with the conditions in his country as Kostka should have felt correctly that the present course of events was inexorably heading toward crisis and bloodshed. But Kostka was not the first to utter, as a warning, such somber prophecy. He had been preceded, seven years before, by none other than the bishop Aeneas Silvius.[28]

But the policy of Pius II was different from that of Aenas Sylvius. This, considering his position as Pope, and the strong resistance which a confirmation of the Compacts would have found among the College of Cardinals, is not difficult to understand. The very hesitation with which King George decided to ask for the confirmation of the Compacts shows that he himself had, in the years since his coronation, not been too confident that he would receive it. Yet neither George nor other influential figures such as Emperor Frederick or the leading German princes had been prepared for the course now taken by the Pope. (The one exception was the city of Breslau, whose envoy Kitzing had done his best to impress upon the Pope the heretical character and implication of the Compacts such as they were now used by the Utraquists.[29]) Pope Pius—and this was the decisive change—was now no longer satisfied with refusing to confirm the Compacts, which would, by itself, only have left things where they had stood before. Instead he now struck a resounding blow at the tolerance and "coexistence" of which the Compacts had been the symbol and basis.

It was on March 31 that the Pope called a special consistory where he gave his decision in the presence of about 4,000 people. In another long speech [30] he brought forward once more all the arguments which he and the cardinals had previously employed against the Compacts. Then he continued: "We have, with our brethren, the Cardinals, carefully studied the copies of the Compacts, and we have found, as we also now declare publicly, that they have no force or validity."

---

[28] See Voigt, *Enea Silvio*, II, 165–171, and Kaminsky, 'Pius Aeneas among the Taborites," *Church History*, September 1959, p. 298.

[29] See e.g., *SrS*, VIII, 76–78.

[30] Besides the sources mentioned earlier (such as Koranda and Ammanati), see also *SrS*, VIII, 82–83, *FRA*, II, 20, 268–271.

Then he named five main reasons why the continuance of the Compacts, and with it the right to dispense the communion in the two kinds, could not be granted:

"1. because of the danger of heresy, since people might think that the first element does not contain Christ whole;

2. because of the danger that in dispensing the sacrament the blood of Christ, as has frequently happened, might be spilled on the ground;

3. for the sake of unity and peace in your kingdom. For you know that each realm divided against itself is doomed to perdition, and therefore it is necessary that one of the two parties give in. This, however, cannot be expected of those who continue in the way of their ancestors, but of those only who are eager to embrace innovations;

4. for the sake of peace between yourselves and your neighbors, the Germans, Hungarians and Poles, so you can have trade, intermarriage and friendship with them. For if we were to grant you your special status they would never cease their repugnance against you because of your difference; and

5. finally for the sake of your humility. For we do not want to give you what might induce pride and arrogance in you, as if you were wiser than your fathers and better than other Christians. Do not assume in yourself more wisdom than you really possess. The Roman See, supreme guardian of divine mysteries, has carefully considered your demands and found that they are not necessary, not salutary and not proper.... Therefore join up with the Holy Mother Church who never errs, and obey her call. Then the old glory and peace will return to your realm, and God's grace and blessing will rule where too long, unfortunately, the land had been darkened by execration and ruination."

As soon as the Pope had ended, Antonio da Gubbio, papal Advocate of the Faith, rose and read these words: "I hereby testify publicly before the assembly of the most reverent lords the cardinals, archbishops, bishops and others present that the Holy Father has revoked and annihilated the Compacts granted by the Council of Basel to the Bohemians; that he has put under a ban and strictly forbidden the communion in two kinds of lay people; and that he will not accept the obedience of the King of Bohemia unless said King will forego all errors, will enter into the union of the Roman Church and establish, for himself and his whole realm, complete conformity with the Church in each and every regard without exceptions." [31]

Insofar as the Compacts had been a basic instrument of peace, their solemn destruction at the hand of the Pope was, in fact, very nearly a declaration of war. The only question still open was perhaps: whose war and against whom? If George were to bow to the Pope's command, then it would have to be his war against the Hussite people of all estates—including a minority of the barons, but a large majority of the knights and the burghers in the cities, not to mention (and indeed they were hardly ever mentioned) the little people in the towns and in the rural regions, few of them truly independent, yet again most of them Utraquists. It was difficult to imagine King George willing to wage a war against them to force them by the sword to abandon the Chalice. And if he was not willing to do this, if he remained true to his own religious upbringing and his repeated oaths to preserve the Compacts—then, indeed, sooner or later, the papal abrogation of the Compacts, if maintained and taken seriously, would probably mean war between the Church of Rome and Utraquist Bohemia, indeed a second series of Hussite Wars.

The Pope, therefore, who had once seen quite clearly that such was the situation, now tried hard to convince himself and his Czech guests that this was not true, that indeed the King could easily bow to his command without provoking a bloody conflict with the majority of his own subjects. All that George had to do, so Pius told the Czech ambassadors when they took their leave from him, on April 1st, was to "try to take publicly the communion in one kind, and to make sure that the Queen and also his children and the whole court do likewise. Then the Czech people who, as we know well, have much love for this their present King, will follow him without much resistance. Nor will the clergy be able to oppose him effectively. For the people everywhere usually like to follow the example of their ruler, and especially of such a one whom they love." The Pope closed with a special appeal to the two Utraquist masters, Koranda and Vrbenský, to educate the members of their Church to obedience so as to make it unnecessary for Rome to use force, and with another appeal to King George to be

---

[31] For the text of the official declaration of the Advocate (or Procurator) of the Faith see *ibid.*, 269, and the bibliographical remark of Bachmann in his footnote on p. 198 in *Reichsgeschichte*, I. Yet the text as published later (on p. 208, and taken over from him by Pastor, II, 176) is incomplete and somewhat distorted. For translation of the more complete version, see Palacký, *Dějiny*, IV, 1, 204, in German, IV, 1, 232.

especially careful to keep on friendly terms with the Emperor who was his, the Pope's, close friend. This was the one advice given by the Pope to King George at this time that, in the ensuing phase of events, the King followed. On the whole the Pope's last address to the embassy, despite some friendly phrases at the beginning, went far in firmly closing the door on any hope for a compromise between Rome and Prague.

It is obvious that the Pope's fateful decision, for all the extensive knowledge of Bohemia's conditions which he and his chief advisers flattered themselves that they possessed, was based on a totally wrong judgment about the nature and strength of Utraquism as a movement and a church, and of the depth of feeling that millions of people attached to the Chalice not only as the one true form of the sacrament but also as the symbol of their being, and having always been, true Christians. The Pope's utter misconception of Utraquism as a mixture of unsophisticated religious primitivism and arrogant hardheadedness—as an essentially superficial phenomenon easily exterminated if there was a will to it—led him and his advisers to believe that George's unwillingness to act in the expected direction could be overcome by a papal policy of rigid and consistent strictness. This, so it was hoped, would make George see how much more he had to lose, how much worse he would fare by antagonizing Rome than by merely antagonizing Rokycana and a few of his underlings, and would thus push him toward the action desired by Rome.

There was only one concession which, at least in his own eyes, the Pope had made: he had accepted the suggestion of Kostka and Rabstein to send a special legate to Prague to discuss with the King ways of implementing the wishes of the Curia. Unfortunately even this decision, supposedly meant to make things easier, in the end only served to exacerbate the conflict. For the man on whom the Czech ambassadors and the Curia agreed as the papal legate to follow them back to Bohemia was none other than Fantino de Valle, the Dalmatian-Slavonic Doctor of Law who, for the last three years, had been King George's procurator or ambassador in Rome. It was assumed, apparently by both sides, that Fantino would be better able than any other man to make himself understood by the King whose language he spoke and whom he had represented at the Curia. At least we do not hear of any protest from the Czech ambassadors, though later the Utraquists among them sharply accused him of having been disloyal to the King. It seems very possible that the one Czech envoy with whom the matter was seriously discussed by the Curia was Prokop of Rabstein.[32] At the time he was probably not aware of the motives which prompted Fantino to accept the papal appointment even though he had neither asked for nor been given his release as the King's servant.

Fantino hardly believed that his task was one of compromise, nor would the instructions he received from the Holy See have encouraged or even permitted him to be less strict in his demands for full ritual confirmity than the Pope had been himself. But apart from such instructions it is obvious, from his actions in Bohemia, that this had also become a personal issue for him. He had long persisted in his assurances to the Pope that King George was not only a good Christian but would also establish complete religious unity. During the last few months before the arrival of the embassy his attitude toward the King's policy had, however, become increasingly critical and possibly even antagonistic. Of the extraordinary problems existing in Bohemia his specific knowledge was at best limited, incomplete, and partly distorted. As he now felt that he had also to reestablish his own personal prestige as an orthodox Catholic, he entered Bohemia with a prejudice as strong or stronger than that of other people in the diplomatic service of the Curia. In King George's eyes, however, he was still his servant, even though, just because of his changed relation to the King, he had not been included among the official members of the embassy to Rome.

Pius II put Fantino in an even more difficult position by adding to the task originally envisaged that of being the Pope's spokesman in the discussions with George about the steps to be taken in Bohemia in view of the decisions of Rome. As Pius believed that the success of his general policy depended on the degree of pressure he could bring to bear upon the King, he authorized Fantinus to contact immediately those groups from whom support of the papal policy could be anticipated, such as the great Catholic barons—especially the Rosenbergs—but more importantly the new Catholic administrator of the Prague

---

[32] This surmise, it is true, would have to be rejected if we could fully trust Pius II, who writes in his *Commentaries* (VII, 515): "When the ambassadors asked that this man be sent, the Pope thought it impossible to refuse their request." This version seems to indicate that the choice of Fantino was entirely due to a request by the Czechs, and not only by one of them. This seems extremely unlikely. That the Pope's decision was not just kindness without any ulterior motives is made obvious by the following sentence: "Fantinus was therefore despatched to inform not only the King but the loyal barons of Bohemia of what had taken place at Rome, in case the envoys might leave out something." This already contains some hints about the special tasks given to Fantino in regard to the "loyal" barons, though these went far beyond mere "informing." See also Urbánek, *Věk,* IV, 535 n. 48.

Chapter, Fantino's old friend Hilarius of Litoměřice [33] and finally the one outspoken enemy which George had in his realm: the city of Breslau. The Czech embassy to the Pope, of course, had had ample opportunity to learn about the feverish activity which the Breslau procurator, John Kitzing, had displayed against King George prior to and during their presence in Rome. Prague was probably aware that Kitzing intensified his agitation, and with better hopes for success, after the essentially negative results of the Roman negotiations between the Czechs and the Pope. If now Fantino, while still in the service of both the Pope and the King, began to send encouraging messages to Breslau,[34] then this was a case of divided and partially betrayed loyalty going a good deal beyond the measure of such betrayals considered usual among Renaissance diplomats. Breslau, incidentally, was also one of the first places to be informed by her hard-working Roman ambassador that the Pope had ordered the publication of the secret oath sworn by George at the time of his coronation.[35]

King George does not seem to have been in any hurry to bring about a showdown. If the Pope could try to increase the pressure, he himself could apply counterpressure in various forms, and above all in the field of international policy. If he did so he believed that time would be working for rather than against him—a confidence he tended to show throughout his life. In this particular situation he was, at first, not very wrong, as we shall see later from a discussion of his foreign policy in the years 1462–1464. But for this reason, too, he avoided for the time being all personal contact with Fantino.[36] He spent a considerable part of the later spring and early summer in diplomatic negotiations with such foreign princes as King Casimir of Poland and Elector Frederick II of Brandenburg, making sure, so it seems, that Fantino would not follow him to the places where those negotiations were held. It was not till the middle of June that George was back in Prague, just in time to take part, with the Queen, in the Utraquist Corpus-Christi procession, in a fashion perhaps even more demonstrative than the year before. Yet this time precautions were made to prevent any collision with the Catholic procession.[37]

[33] *Ibid.*, IV, 538, 549.

[34] See *SrS*, VIII, 103–104, 106–107.

[35] *Ibid.*, 93–96.

[36] Bachmann's assumption that the King, until the Diet of August, carefully avoided to meet Fantino personally (*Reichsgeschichte*, I, 232 n. 1) is doubtlessly correct. No trace of such a meeting can be found in any of the sources.

[37] I conclude this from the fact that the sources, especially the "Old Annalists" (*SLČ*) who had reported the untoward events of June 1461 in excited detail, have not a word

Fantino was informed that the issue which ostensibly had brought him to Bohemia was to be treated at a special grand diet of the whole realm, a solemn "royal court day," as it was called, to be held in Prague beginning on August 9th, almost three months after his arrival from Rome. In preparation for the diet Fantino submitted to the King a lengthy memorandum accompanied by letters from the Pope.[38] In this document he urged the King to start his reunion with the Roman Church by taking, without delay, the communion in one kind publicly with his family, in the Cathedral of St. Vitus, and to release all Utraquist priests from his service. (The legate also uttered his severe misgivings about George's participation in the Corpus Christi procession as an unfortunate portent.) The memorandum further contained a detailed and rather emotional description of the policy of Louis XI, as a model to be followed by George. What had in reality been an act of cold political speculation appears in Fantino's words as a marvelous triumph of the piety of a deeply religious young King, conscious above all of his duties toward the Holy See, over all the fierce domestic resistance. One wonders whether this interpretation, too, had been in the Pope's instructions. King George would have had to be a good deal more naïve and less well informed than he was to take such arguments seriously, at a time when the King of France had already switched back to a policy of severe hostility toward the Holy See and had begun to reinstate much of the substance, if not the letter, of the Pragmatic Sanction of Bourges.[39]

While most of this first communication of Fantino dwelt in generalities, the legate some time later submitted a second memorandum which, it seems, answered the request of the King's advisers for a far more concrete presentation of how he thought the demanded unification could be implemented.[40] He did, indeed, put forward no less than eleven statements and demands, some still rather general, others quite specific. Of some interest are the following: the masters of the University of Prague will forthwith cease to dispute issues of the Catholic faith (No. 5); those scholars and masters of the University who have

---

on any such events in the following year; and also on the obvious and strongly expressed wish of the King not to provoke unnecessarily the outbreak of religious antagonism. Also, if there had been such an outbreak our source for the King's participation in Rokycana's procession, Fantino's own memorandum, would have mentioned it.

[38] See *SrS*, VIII, 107–110.

[39] See Louis's declarations and actions of the summer of 1562 as described by Pius himself in his *Commentaries*, VIII, 549–551.

[40] *SrS*, VIII, 112–113.

not shown themselves to be rebels against Rome shall ask for and achieve free and complete readmission to the offices of the University and the Church (No. 6); there must be an immediate end to all church songs in the Czech language, as well as to such songs which are sung to spread confusion about or deride the Holy Roman Church or the Supreme Pontiff (7); only good Roman Catholics shall be permitted to be elected or appointed as burgomasters, city councillors, and city judges (8); everywhere in the kingdom there must be complete freedom for true Catholics in relation to burials, masses, and other religious functions. People trying to limit such freedoms should be severely punished (9); John Rokycana was to be deprived of all rights of spiritual jurisdiction over any part of the Czech clergy, especially since he has no true faculty to bind and loose (10); finally, in view of the papal decision, the King was to warn all people in Bohemia and Moravia severely against taking the communion in two kinds as a practice detrimental to the salvation of their souls (11). Once these rules and commands are all followed and implemented Pope Pius will appoint a legate *de latere* who will finish this work, will give Bohemia a Catholic archbishop, and will reward the King with the highest favors and honors. He, Fantino, will be willing to explain and interpret any doubtful passages and solve any difficulties which may still remain.[41] Fantino's pleas were seconded by two letters sent by Hilarius of Litoměřice, containing harsh attacks against Rokycana and other "bad counsellors" and demanding, above all, a right for him to control all teaching, freedom for Catholics to buy houses and become members of guilds in Prague, full freedom for them to teach according to their creed at the University, and to take everywhere publicly the communion *"sub una."* [42]

Nobody could, at this time, seriously expect that Fantino's and Hilarius' pleas could lead to an understanding between King George

[41] In view of a program which demands the immediate and complete destruction of the Utraquist Church as an institution, the termination of the ministry of all those priests who were not willing to submit in every regard to the Roman ritual, the commentary of a historian as influential as was Bachmann seems little short of amazing. "Notice," he says (*Reichsgeschichte*, I, 234), "how the official of the Curia puts all emphasis on the personal relationship between the King and the Church and *how carefully the latter avoided to put the Hussite people before the question of faith* out of which the civil war, ended less than a generation ago, might burst into flames again. If now, *merely because the King did not keep his promises,* war broke out nevertheless, was not he alone then the cause of it?" (Italics are mine.) Not even the majority of Czech Catholics were at that time willing to see things in this strange light.

[42] One of these letters was published by Jordan, *Das Königthum,* 467–474; the second by Podlaha, *Editiones archiv. et bibl. capit. prag.,* XXIII, Prague, 1931, as quoted by Urbánek *Věk,* IV, 551–554.

and the Curia. If published they would only have led to an outbreak of fierce excitement among the Utraquist clergy—whom Fantino in consonance with the papal policy simply wanted to annihilate, if not physically then at least as a spiritual power in the land—and in the further process also among the Utraquist gentry and the masses of people in the cities. The memoranda, of course, were not published at that time, and at the great "court day" of Prague which actually did not open officially until August 12, the first proceedings took place in the absence of the legate.[43]

At the diet itself not only the Bohemian kingdom but also the dependencies were represented, and while a few of the Catholic barons kept away, the majority of the great families as well as of the gentry and cities were represented. The bishops of Breslau and Olomouc were both present. The King, who presided, was accompanied by the Queen and his sons.

The first day was used for reports of the men who had belonged to the Czech embassy to Rome. Especially detailed accounts were given by Prokop of Rabstein and Wenceslas Koranda. After they had finished, the King spoke himself. "We wonder," he said, "what the Pope means to do. When this Kingdom has just been reunited by the Compacts and peace reestablished therein, does he now intend to revive the old troubles, to divide us again and to goad us into new civil strife? How can he take away and destroy what the Holy Council of Basel and his predecessor Pope Eugenius have given to us, considering that the Council is above the Pope? If at all times Popes wanted to undo and destroy what their predecessors have granted and given—who could ever be secure in the possession of his rights?

"We are accused by the Pope of not fulfilling the oath we have sworn at our coronation. We shall read to you this very oath." And after he had read this oath in Czech, the King continued: "You hear that we have sworn to destroy and extinguish heresy in our realm.

---

[43] On the Prague diet the most detailed reports have come down to us through correspondents of the city council of Breslau. The council passed this material on to the Pope in a message printed by Markgraf in *SrS*, VIII, 123–127. Essentially the same material in German is contained in Eschenloer's *Geschichten*, I, 196–201. Pius himself used this material in his *Commentaries*, X, 621–625. See a similar but less prejudiced Latin report also in *FRA* II, XX, 272–277. A German diplomatic report, quite detailed and destined presumably for Duke William of Saxony, was published from the Weimer princely archives by Müller in *Reichstag-Theatrum*, II, 244–247. Finally a short but interesting report, called "De rege Bohemie Georgio," in Goll, *FRB*, vol. V, XXXVII n.8. For secondary treatments see Palacký, *Dějiny*, IV, 1, German 241–252, Czech 212–221; Tomek, *Dějepis*, VII, 47–53; Bachmann *Reichsgeschichte*, I, 234–242; Jordan, *Das Königsthum Georg's*, 110–115; Voigt, II, 471–477; Pastor, II, 179–181; and Urbánek, *Věk*, IV, 560–568.

Truly I want you to know that we do not love heretics but that we despise them and are their enemy. But that the Pope could call a heresy or make appear as heresy the Communion in the two kinds, and our Compacts, this has never been our understanding. For these are grounded in the Holy Gospel, in the acts of Christ and of the primitive Church. And it was granted to us by the Council as a privilege, as it were, in recognition of our virtues and our devotion. These we should have forsworn? Truly, this be far from us. For you should know for certain that, since we were born and brought up in this communion, and, standing by it, were by the will of God raised to this royal dignity, we will also hold it and defend it and with it live and die. And so the Queen our wife, sitting at our right, and our children, and all those who want to act from their love for us, should live with us within the Compacts."

Up to this point the King's speech seems fairly well documented. But in the report which the Breslau city council immediately sent to the Pope, these words appear: "Nor do we believe that there is any other way toward the salvation of our souls than to die within the Compacts, and to use the communion in the two kinds according to the way in which our Savior has instituted it." Later King George himself denied categorically that he had ever said this, but his curial enemies always ascribed this utterance to him and used it to demonstrate that he was not merely a schismatic but, by denying the salutary force of the communion "sub una," a heretic as well.[44]

King George's purpose at this moment was complex: he had to establish again, as securely as possible, harmony with the Utraquist majority on whose agreement his position depended. But he also had to prevent, if that was still possible, a widening of the gap between

---

[44] The question whether George did or did not say this has long been under dispute. Palacký (*Dějiny,* IV, 1, 215, n. 163, *Geschichte,* IV, 1, 244, n. 163) expressed his doubts that George would have been rash enough to use these words which, as he could have foreseen, would be used against him. Bachmann (*Reichsgeschichte,* I, 236 n. 1) declares that he has "no scruples" about including the passage in his text, since it was the ordinary Utraquist doctrine ("die gewöhnliche Lehrmeinung der Utraquisten"). This is not completely exact, at least not in the way in which Pius II interpreted Hussite thinking. Rockycana, for instance, did not deny that the communion in one kind did contain the whole Christ, nor did he insist (as some other Utraquists did) that those who had been denied the Chalice could therefore not attain salvation, but only that each of the elements supported salvation in a different way. (See Heymann, "Rokycana," *Church History,* September 1959, p. 261.) To me the most important fact supporting Palacký's view is that the sentence, striking as it is, is completely missing in the otherwise very detailed report from the Weimar Archives (Müller's *Reichstags-Theatrum,* where the neighboring passages are to be found II, on p. 244, bottom). A good point is also Markgraf's suggestion (*Forschungen zur Deutschen Geschichte,* IX, 220) that the Czech bishops would not have listened to this phrase without protest.

the two religious groups. If only he could now retain that measure of consent with the basic principles of the Compacts that the Czech Catholic minority had generally been ready to provide throughout the last decades, then the papal attack would lose much of its strength and danger. It is for this reason that George had postponed facing Fantino. Now, while the assembly still stood under the emotional impression of his words, he ordered a public reading not only of the Compacts themselves but also of the letters in which the Kings Sigismund, Albert II, and Ladislav, albeit all of them orthodox Catholics, had solemnly acknowledged and promised to hold and protect the Compacts. He could have quoted as well many resolutions of the Czech estates in which the Catholics, together with the Utraquists, had backed up the Compacts (even though some of them, like the late Ulrich of Rosenberg, might have secretly informed the Curia that this support should not be taken too seriously in Rome).

After the preparatory statements the King declared that, as in the past, he would faithfully protect both religious parties in the free exercise of their religious rights, but that he could successfully do that only on the basis of the Compacts. He then asked the members of the diet whether they would be ready to support him if, from any side, he and the realm should be attacked for the sake of the Compacts.

It was not a very good sign that the two groups, Utraquists and Catholics, went to discuss this matter in two separate caucuses. The Utraquists' answer was then given by Lord Zdeněk Kostka, who expressed the enthusiasm and gratitude of his party for the King's declaration and promised to support him and his policy in defense of the Compacts with their lives and possessions. After him Zdeněk of Sternberg spoke for the Catholics: he and his party, having always been faithful and obedient to the Papal See, had never had anything to do with the Compacts. If the King now decided to maintain the protection of the Compacts, then he should rely on the help of those upon whose advice he had so decided. Just as the King himself they, too, intended to live and die in the faith in which they had been brought up. But they would continue to serve and dutifully defend the honor and well being of the kingdom.

Sternberg's declaration, an uncomprising refusal to the King's request, was essentially, though perhaps in a less abrupt form, supported by the two bishops, with Jost of Breslau urging the King especially to consider that an open collision between him and the Pope could be a great danger for the lands of the crown of St. Wenceslas. Nor was

George successful when he tried, on this day and the day after, to convince the Catholics that it was in their own interest to maintain the Compacts since they as well as the Utraquists were protected by them and possessed those rights and freedoms which all members of the Czech estates had the duty to defend. The Catholic answer was that they would defend all these rights as long as they were not expected to turn against the Church. George's hope for a united reaction of the representatives of the nation to the papal challenge thus was bitterly disappointed. He ended the debate by saying that he expected all the members of the diet would do their duty to him and the country, and that he would see to it that no internal strife would break out over religion. These were strong words, but they could hardly conceal the fact that in his main attempt at gaining support from both sides the King had been defeated. It cannot have made this hot tempered if generally well-controlled man feel more lenient toward the representative of that Pope who, in older times, had understood the significance of the Compacts for the internal peace in Bohemia and who was now willing to risk and possibly smash this peace.

Nevertheless King George, when he had Fantino called before the diet, was wise enough to order that he be given a free and uninterrupted hearing—this even before the legate himself asked for such freedom of speech after entering the hall. It was granted immediately.

Fantino presented all the well-known arguments for the papal claim that the Compacts had long been invalid. They had now been expressly abrogated by the Pope, therefore no Christian layman any longer had the right to receive the communion in both kinds. He then solemnly charged the King, in the name of the Pope, to fulfill his coronation oath as well as his promise of obedience in the following way; henceforth he was to take, with his family, the Lord's supper only upon the Castle of St. Wenceslas (that is in the St. Vitus Cathedral, which was in the hands of the Catholic clergy); to dismiss all Utraquist chaplains as wicked teachers of errors and deliver them for their deserved punishment to the administrator of the Prague archbishopric, Hilarius of Litoměřice; and to make sure that all communion in the two kinds was everywhere thoroughly suppressed. If this was not done the King could not escape the judgment of perjury. When the King interjected that he had never perjured himself, as his good conscience proved to him sufficiently, Fantino answered that it was not up to him to interpret his own oath but to those who had imposed the oath upon him. Finally, in a state of considerable excitement, Fantino declared that those who disobeyed the Pope would be subject to excommunication, and that, since the royal dignity like all other dignities came from and was subject to the will of the Pope, the Pope could also take this dignity away.

Fantino's threat, together with the accusation of perjury, was just enough to sting the King into fierce anger, and according to one report he barely contained his wish to kill the legate on the spot.[45] However, in accordance with the promise given him earlier, Fantino was permitted to leave. He was summoned again on the following day, August 14, this time no longer as papal legate but to answer for his activities as the King's ambassador. This hearing was not held before the full diet but only before the members of the royal council acting as a court. Before this body the diplomat was accused by members of the embassy which had been in Rome for the negotiations with the Pope, though it seems that only the Utraquists among them took part. They submitted writs claiming that all through their stay in Rome Fantino, far from serving King George as had been his duty, had actually agitated against the King. Probably Fantino's activities since his arrival, including his correspondence with Breslau, were also mentioned. Fantino defended himself by declaring that he had served the King faithfully as his procurator as long as he could hope that the King intended to fulfill his oaths and promises. When, however, it had become clear to him that the King's actions belied his words and that he was not willing to stand by his oath, he, Fantino, had not felt any longer the duty or the possibility of serving him. The King and the majority of the council saw in this declaration both another insult and a confession of guilt.

While some of the Catholics present, including, it seems, the Chancellor Prokop of Rabstein, tried to mitigate the judgment, the actual sentence was that Fantino, by acting faithlessly and betraying the trust of the King, had really forfeited his life. Only the King's personal regard for the Pope induced him, as Fantino was told, to be merciful and to reduce the sentence to imprisonment.[46] He was taken to the Old Town city hall under heavy guard—a precaution necessitated by the great excitement that the news about his attitude at the diet (with added rumors about a Catholic rebellion) had caused among the Utraquist masses of Prague. Some time afterward Fantino was re-

---

[45] *SrS* VIII, 125.

[46] Some parts of Bachmann's detailed report on this part of the proceedings are clearly products of his lively imagination (*Reichsgeschichte,* I, 241f.) See also Urbánek, *Věk,* IV, 567 n. 104.

moved to the castle of Poděbrady—where before him some of the Taborite priests had suffered for their faith.

Whether it was due to his attempt to defend Fantino or some suspicions about his activities during his recent stay in Rome—Chancellor Prokop of Rabstein, too, fell into disgrace with King George. He was deprived of his office and at first ordered to remain, until further notice, at his Prague residence. For a short time he, too, was detained at Poděbrady.[47] George, however, soon convinced himself that Rabstein did not deserve this rebuke—it seems that the Queen also interceded for him—and after only a few weeks his office and rank were restored to him and he was fully received back into the King's grace. Soon afterward, in October, Fantino too was released from prison and allowed to travel to Regensburg under safe conduct, not, however, until his arrest had itself become a cause célèbre in the international life of Europe.

This had, indeed, been a moment of dramatic greatness for both men. George, the King who, in his own eyes and those of his Utraquist subjects and followers, had stood manfully for his religion against the awe-inspiring, world-wide, and tradition-hallowed, yet also religiously depraved and worldly-corrupt power of the papacy; and the papal legate who, in his own eyes and those of many good Catholics, had stood against the great and barbaric power of a self-confessed and deeply depraved heretic and King of heretics, manfully ready for martyrdom in the service of the one true creed, the one true church, and the one Pope. In personal terms and in the long run this juxtaposition of the two protagonists did more for Fantino than it could for George. The King, as long as he stood by the Chalice, was sure of the support of its adherents even without the great drama of the "Diet of St. Lawrence," as the August meeting became known. But for Fantino it did everything: from a little known procurator he rose, as a near-martyr, to the status of a great curial diplomat and prosecutor, not only with Pope Pius II, who upon Fantino's return rewarded him with the proceeds of a Dalmation bishopric,[48] but also and even more with Pius' successor Paul II, who delighted in giving Fantino the opportunity to take revenge for the days of August 1462.

But the immediate effect seemed threatening. Among the Utraquist masses of Bohemia, and especially of the capital, the news of the events at the diet itself, coming as it were on top of the events in

---

[47] See Urbánek, *Věk*, IV, 567 and 568, n. 105–108.
[48] Pius II, *Commentaries*, X, 628 and n. 12, and Urbánek, *Věk*, IV, 523 n. 126.

Rome, had created a mood of real and deep excitement. While George had certainly meant Fantino's imprisonment to be a punitive measure, he was not merely seeking excuses when he explained, in an apologetic statement to his friend Louis of Bavaria, that this step had been necessary to protect his former envoy from the furious anger of the Prague population.[49]

This angry mood, much of it surely spontaneous, did not lack some direction from above. There is nothing in our sources about Rokycana's attitude at the time, and Koranda, prior to the diet, was presumably busy preparing his report to this body. But one prominent leader of the Utraquist Church, Martin Lupáč, had reacted strongly and, one can assume, publicly to the events in Rome.[50] Lupáč, who three decades before had taken part in the negotiations about the Compacts in Cheb, Basel, and Prague, had after that been elected suffragan bishop of Prague at the time of Rokycana's election as archbishop. He had always been the most radical among the prominent clerical leaders of the Utraquist Church, and this came through very clearly also in his contemporary writings.[51] There were two of them, one of a more clearly theological character correcting the Papal statements about the origin and significance of the Compacts in his own light, the other a direct and rather uninhibited attack upon the Pope. Both were answers not only to the Pope but in a sense also to Fantino and to Hilarius of Litoměřice.

In the first pamphlet Lupáč took the stand that the Compacts, based upon the holiest sources of the Christian religion, never needed a papal confirmation. In the second one the Pope is, as in the times of the revolution in which Lupáč still had his roots, called "Anti-Christ." The Hussite Czechs are for Lupáč, according to Mathew 20:16, the few chosen among the many called. Lupáč finally came out in favor of that complete separation from the Church of Rome which was, during the Hussite Revolution as well as in the later fifteenth century, gen-

---

[49] See Dlugosz, *Opera omnia*, ed. Przezdziecki, V, 348, and Eschenloer, German I, 259. In Bachmann's view (*Reichsgeschichte*, I, 242) "the joy of the mob (Pöbel) and the insolence of Rokycana's priests knew no bounds," and "in addition to the King's acts there came the savage outbreaks of Utraquist arrogance among the populace."

[50] See F. M. Bartoš, "Martin Lupáč a jeho spisovatelské dílo," in *Reformační sborník*, VII, Prague, 1939, 115–140, containing (137ff.) a survey of all of Lupáč's fairly numerous preserved writings (though the major part of his literary work seems to be lost). See also Bartoš's sketch "Biskup Martin Lupáč" in *Bojovníci a mučedníci*, Prague, 1939, p. 39–43.

[51] The first part of the first pamphlet "Super responsis Pii pape" was published by Beda Dudík in his *Forschungen in Schweden für Mährens Geschichte*, Brno, 1852, pp. 458–466. The remainder and the main content of the second tractate "Contra papam" are presented by Bartoš, *Reformační sborník*, VII, 123–126, and again by Urbánek, *Věk*, IV, 557–560.

erally openly advocated by the more radical sects, such as Tabor and the Czech Brethren—the very groups whom King George, and to some extent also Rokycana, considered as heretical.

All this, clearly, was a reaction which King George had not hoped for, of which he had never approved, and which could only damage his political position, nationally as well as internationally. Thus he had to intervene in order to prevent a further radicalization on both sides of the religious split. He decided that his declaration—he would under no circumstances tolerate a new outbreak of religious unrest in Bohemia—would be implemented especially by impressing his determination upon the clergy of both parties. Accordingly he ordered the members of the Bohemian Utraquist and Catholic hierarchy, with Rokycana and the administrator Hilarius of Litoměřice at their lead, to appear without fail for a general synod at the Castle of Prague in the second half of September. To make sure that everyone would appear, the heads of all church districts had to obtain, and pass on to the King's chancery, signed notes from all priests proving that they had received the summons.[52] In the general excitement of the time this act was interpreted by some of the Catholic priests as a sign that the King would destroy them all, and even after their arrival in Prague, when it should have been easier to discern truth from rumor, not a few of the Catholics considered martyrdom as their possible if not probable fate.

In reality, of course, nothing was farther from George's mind. On the contrary, much more than in August, when he had still been under some compulsion to prove that he did not plan a counter-reformation, George now presented himself, as Rabstein had characterized him in Rome, as the "lord of both kinds of people." His stern countenance and his severe criticism was not specifically directed at the Catholics but at all the Czech clergy present, altogether some 714 men (more than two-thirds of them Utraquist, the rest Catholic).[53] He chided them, without much distinction, for their tendency to engage in dogmatic squabbles and mutual incrimination, their reluc-

[52] See Hilarius' order in FRA, II, 20, 278, also the information contained in the consistorial acts, ibid., 279, which refutes the claim that Fantino was subjected to the torture in his imprisonment.

[53] Our sources on the course of events during the synod are scanty. Much of what we know is derived again from a report to Breslau. See SrS, VIII, 133–135. This, together with reports from Hilarius, may have been the basis for the report given by the Pope Pius, in his Commentaries, X, 626–628, and largely also for Pešina's report in Phosphorus Septicornis, 249–252. For modern discussions see Palacký, in both editions on the last three pages of chapter 4 in IV, 2. Better in this case Tomek, Dějepis, VII, 55–57. Bachmann has it in his Reichsgeschichte, I, 243–246, and Urbánek in Věk, IV, 570–573.

tance to grant one another access to churches and the right to burial, but also for the frequent occurrence of immorality and for their propensity to gambling. If the churches themselves did not stop such abuses he, the King, would have to interfere directly. Finally he demanded that the Compacts, as the one basis on which it had been possible to maintain religious peace within the kingdom, be strictly respected by both sides.

The King's speech, for all its sternness, must have caused evident relief among those who had thought it possible that they would all be martyred.

After some short discussion in separate groups the two sides gave their answers through their leaders. It was an easier task for Rokycana, for whom at least the principle of the Compacts—in whose origin he had had such a notable part—was all welcome. When he tried to establish that the Utraquist clergy had not gone beyond the religious deviations clearly permitted by the Compacts he certainly was on doubtful ground. Nor was his claim that the moral lapses criticized by the King were only to be found on the side of the Catholics quite incontestable (as appears from his own writings). Yet it was probably true to the extent that in general a stronger will to reform in the moral behavior of the clergy had survived in the Utraquist Church than among the Catholic hierarchy of the time.[54]

Hilarius, referring to the issue of wanting morality among priests, declared that there were bad people in every large group, but that all crimes or misdemeanors that came to the knowledge of the Prague archiepiscopal chapter were always strictly punished. Then, regarding the Compacts, he followed the example of Lord Sternberg and the bishops by stating that the men who stood in the obedience of Rome had never had any real need for the Compacts. As far, however, as internal peace was derived therefrom, the Catholic clergy was, so he said, grateful and would do everything to strengthen it.

On the whole it can probably be said that the September synod was less a disappointment and a failure for George's policy than the preceding diet. He could hardly have expected the Catholic clergy to give his policy more direct support than he had received from the bishops of the realm or from the leading Catholic barons. On the other hand the energetic, severely critical stand he had taken toward the clergy of both sides did, at least for a time, have the desired effect of quelling

[54] See e.g. his orders to his clergy in *FRA*, II, 20, 267f.

the waves of mutual hatred and active disturbance of the religious peace. Thereby the King also gained more freedom of action in his attempt to counter the great and dangerous offensive which, though as yet only in its beginnings, was now to be conducted by Rome against him.

CHAPTER 13

A "GRAND DESIGN"

THE FAILURE of the Czech mission to Rome and the events during the great Prague diet of August 1462 clearly marked a turning point in King George's European position and in the foreign policy this position demanded. The Pope, from a phase of definite support for George (though lately it had more looked like neutrality), switched to a phase of distinct hostility, ending in a life-and-death struggle. The highly critical character of this situation perhaps became visible in all its danger at the moment of the imprisonment of Fantino. The news was received with real glee in Breslau where the party of the King-haters felt that the Pope, deeply insulted by what had been done to his legate, was now sure to understand the depraved character of George and to act accordingly.[1] The view was shared by a very small minority of Czech Catholics.

Also among the fervent Utraquists in Prague and other Czech cities gladness was the predominant note. Finally, so it was believed, George would put an end to all ambiguities and come out with full force against the domestic Catholics and their influence.[2] But both groups were disappointed in their hopes, the Utraquists even more so than the zealots of Breslau.

In view of these prevailing radical moods, it would have been easy for George, at this stage, to start the civil war which, as it turned out, was unavoidable anyhow. It might have had advantages for him in that he would have caught his domestic foes unprepared. But it would have alienated large numbers of Catholics to whom the recent estrangement between Prague and Rome was a matter of concern and unhappiness since it would force them to chose between competing claims to their loyalty. It would also, and perhaps more importantly, have alienated those foreign powers upon whose friendship, or at least

---

[1] This was the time when the Pope freed the city from the obligation of doing homage to the King as had been arranged in the peace agreement of 1460. See *SrS*, VIII, 127, and Eschenloer, G., I, 200ff.

[2] See the discussion of the activity of Martin Lupáč in chapter 12.

friendly neutrality, the survival of the Czech state in its present form depended. And it was altogether an idea quite alien to George.

In reality his policy was directed toward keeping the conflict from becoming more embittered and less open to a compromise solution. The imprisonment of Fantino, while understandable as reaction to an unusual provocation, and perhaps not quite without legal justification from his point of view as a King betrayed by his servant, was essentially a mistake. George himself soon understood this, as shown by the steps that he took to make it look less bad in the eyes of others—including the Pope himself.[3] What is perhaps more remarkable is that he succeeded so well—that indeed his international position, during 1462, did not only not deteriorate but actually improved.

This showed itself even before the Prague diet of August. Indeed this diet, presumably, was called so late by the King to make it possible for some of his diplomatic actions to show results. Not all of these can be considered as George's answer to the action of the Holy See, yet most of them resulted in either temporary or lasting improvements for him without which he could hardly have weathered the impending storm.

This was true, first of all, of the development of the war in the Empire. Margrave Albert Achilles who, early in the year, had stubbornly refused to ratify the peace agreements of the previous November, was to have reason to regret it, as were his principal allies Charles of Baden and Ulrich of Württemberg. These two, together with Charles's brother George Bishop of Metz, were surprised at Seckenheim, south of Heidelberg, on June 30th by an army led by Elector Frederick of the Palatinate. Not only was their army completely destroyed but all three princes became the prisoners of the Elector (whose later surname "the Victorious" mainly dates from the battle of Seckenheim).[4] The margrave had hardly recovered from this blow to his allies when he himself suffered a defeat of even larger proportions. The "imperial" army under his command, some 7,000 men with strong contingents of battle waggons and artillery, on July 19th met the army of Duke Louis of Bavaria—supposedly about 10,000 men, including considerable numbers of Czech mercenaries—near the old Suabian imperial city of

[3] A list of George's letters and their places of publication is given in Bachmann's *Reichsgeschichte*, 1, 243 n. 1–3. The most important seems to be the one to the people of Cheb (*FRA*, II, 42, 351) in which he emphasizes that he would leave them, as before, free to maintain the customs and rituals of the Roman Church, and would protect them against anyone trying to force them to change. Bachmann rightly assumes that George wrote in a similar vein to other predominantly Catholic cities.

[4] See Menzel, *Diether von Isenburg*, 179–183.

Giengen. Again the imperial party lost, and, while Margrave Albert Achilles himself managed to escape, his army was sorely battered, with most of his battle waggons (he himself says 284), many guns, and other valuable material lost to the Bavarians.[5] Thus, in less than three weeks, the Wittelsbach party in Germany, strengthened by its alliance with Bohemia, had achieved two largely decisive military victories over the imperial party and Albert Achilles as the captain general of the imperial forces. It was a strong reminder, especially for the Hohenzollern margrave, that he had no real chance to win an all-out struggle within Germany as long as the other side was supported by the King of Bohemia. The Emperor was so disturbed and angry about the development—for which he himself was largely responsible [6]—that he treated the Czech Chancellor Rabstein, when he visited him on his return from Rome to Prague, with unusual coolness.[7] But the outcome of the two battles was essentially what George had hoped for: peace negotiations were resumed at a Reichstag meeting at Nürnberg, in the presence of the papal legate Archbishop Jerome Lando of Crete. He urgently requested King George's representatives not to leave for the Prague Diet but to stay for the conclusion of an armistice.[8] It was finally signed on August 22, to last till Michaelmas 1463, with further negotiations for a definite peace to be conducted later in the fall at Regensburg.[9]

Long before this date George had achieved a more important success by putting his relationship to Poland on a new basis. He transformed a tense and nearly hostile relation into one of friendship—though, of course, not without selfish motives on both sides.

The uneasy relationship between the two Kings, George and Casimir IV, was originally partly determined by issues of dynastic rights.[10] After the death of Ladislav Posthumus his two older sisters had claimed Ladislav's crowns as their heritage, and in their names their husbands, Duke William of Saxony and King Casimir, appeared

---

[5] See Gundling, *Leben und Thaten Friderichs des Anderen*, 555–557, and Kluckhohn, 215–221 (includes the political results of the battle).

[6] By encouraging the war-mindedness in Albert Achilles and his allies at the time after the Peace of Prague, i.e. in the beginning of 1462. See Bachmann, *Reichsgeschichte*, I, 174ff.

[7] *Ibid.*, 289.

[8] *Ibid.*, 292.

[9] See Chmel, *Regesten* II, Appendix CXLVII–CXLVIII.

[10] The relation between the two rulers has been the subject of a monograph by Zd. Tobolka, "Styky krále Jiřího z Poděbrad s králem polským Kazimírem," in *ČMM*, No. 22, Brno, 1898, pp. 70–76, 163–175, 300–310, 373–384. See also F. Papée, "Zabiegi o czeską koronę (1466–1471)" in *Studya i szkice z czasów Kazimierza Jagiellończyka*, Warsaw, 1907, pp. 51–140.

among the candidates for the vacant throne of Bohemia. In contrast to William, however, Casimir was far more interested in the Hungarian kingdom upon which he believed to have claims not only through his wife, Queen Elizabeth, but also through his older brother Władysław Jagiello, who for a few years, till his death at Varna in 1444, had held the two crowns in personal union. Yet King George, too, was at first regarded by some Polish circles—and especially by the Queen—as an usurper. If nevertheless no serious efforts were made by Casimir to stand up for his claim, this was due primarily to a realistic evaluation of his chances in political as well as in military terms. Ever since 1454 Poland had been at war with the Order of the Teutonic Knights, a war in which the knights had proved stronger than had been anticipated, partly owing to the support they received from the empire and from King Christian I of Denmark and Norway. To provoke now another military clash in the south would clearly have been unwise. Thus when George, in November 1458, had sent an embassy to the Polish diet—it was led by Albert Kostka of Postupice—the Polish answer had not been unfavorable and Breslau's attempt, in 1459, to gain Polish support against George had remained unsuccessful.[11] Nevertheless the relationship between the two Kings, apparently mostly under the influence of Queen Elizabeth, remained cool. In 1460, it even seemed to explode into a peculiar crisis. Rumors swept Bohemia that, upon special orders from the King and Queen of Poland, Poles in many parts of Bohemia, especially in the district of Žatec, had committed arson. The same source that reports this supposed Polish crime wave goes on to say that thereupon King George had ordered all Poles to be kept out of the Czech cities or banished from them. Later it was assumed that the incendiaries had been instigated by the Prussian Order.[12]

It is not impossible that George deliberately used this odd incident in order to break the ice between himself and Casimir. If so he was certainly successful. For the King of Poland sent two of his diplomats to Prague to lodge a protest. They even offered to meet in a duel anyone who maintained the claim of their King's responsibility for these fires. King George thereupon assured them that he had never believed such rumors, and their negotiations led to the calling of a meeting, at Beuthen or Bytom in Upper Silesia, of leading noblemen and diplomats from both countries—including Zdeněk of Sternberg

[11] See Tobolka, op.cit., 72f.
[12] See SLČV, 127, 128, and Długosz, Opera omnia, V, 304–306. For other sources and their evaluation see Urbánek, Věk, IV, 356f., nn. 92–97, and Tobolka, op.cit., 74f.

and the famous Polish historian Długosz—which resulted in the first concrete steps toward a rapprochement between the two countries.[13] They included permission for Poland to hire Czech mercenaries for the Prussian war as well as other mutual assurances of freedom of trading and general mutual assistance. Abeove all, the two Kings were to meet personally, in the spring of 1462, in the Silesian city of Glogau (Głogów). There was also mention of the possibility that King George would be acknowledged as an arbitrator in the Prussian struggle, and for a while it looked as if both parties would accept him in the role. This hope, incidentally, had been at the basis of King George's optimistic letter to Pope Pius of December 1461.

The long-planned meeting of the two Kings did indeed take place in Glogau on May 18 and lasted for two weeks.[14] Both Kings had come with all the splendor at their disposal: George with 2,000, Casimir allegedly with 5,000 horses, George surrounded by two of his sons, several Silesian princes, the bishops of Breslau and Olomouc and the greatest of his noblemen; Casimir with a retinue which, Jan Długosz proudly relates, was even more splendid. The negotiations themselves eliminated all outstanding problems between the two kingdoms. In particular George agreed to forego, during his lifetime, all demands for the return of the Upper Silesian holdings now in Polish hands, especially the principalities of Oświęcim (Auschwitz) and Zator, while Casimir would do the same with claims on Queen Elizabeth's dowry based on the Bohemian inheritance from her mother. There was nothing unusual in the majority of the other clauses relating to the maintenance of peace: the promise not to help the other party's enemies; an end to private feuding (with causes to be submitted to courts, if necessary, to a special commission to meet in January 1463); the safeguarding of freedom and security of roads; and the prohibition of the issue of false and debased coins. But the most important issue was contained in the introduction to the agreement, which emphasizes that, on the suggestion of King George, both rulers resolved to help one another with all their power in case one of them should be threatened by the Turks. This, it is true, sounds rather vague and general, especially if it is realized that for geographical

13 The text of the agreement in *FRA*, II, 20, 236–238. See also Tobolka, *op.cit.*, 75, 76, and Urbánek, *Věk*, IV, 384, 385.
14 About the meeting see Długosz, *Opera omnia*, 343–345; Eschenloer, G., I, 188–190; *SrS*, X, 15 (Chronicle of Glogau); and *SrS*, XII, 78; finally M. Toeppen, *Acten der Ständetage Preussens*, V, Leipzig, 1886, 62–65. Modern treatments: Bachmann, *Reichsgeschichte*, I, 222–225; Tobolka, *op.cit.*, 163–165; and Urbánek *Věk*, IV, 540–544.

reasons alone the two realms were not—or not yet—exposed to an immediate attack by Ottoman forces, and that at the time in question, the spring of 1462, the immediate threat was still to the principality of Wallachia and the kingdom of Bosnia. Thus, among the three important eastern European powers, Hungary alone was left under substantial pressure from the southeast.

But the clause in question was not really meant as a reaction to an immediate military threat. Its purpose—clearly envisaged by George— was twofold. It was to establish a new, close relationship between the two West-Slav nations. But it was also to prepare the way for an unusual and daring scheme of international organization, one whose very daring, whose advanced concept, reveals its historical interest as well as its main weakness: it was sure to shock and it was likely to fail. But at the time King George was not aware of its long-range hopelessness, and, even if he had been, he might still, for other reasons, have chosen this course.

The first purpose—close cooperation in the terms of a truly functioning, reliable, and lasting non-aggression pact, was the most important direct gain that resulted from the Glogau meeting for George and his Utraquist commonwealth in the tense situation in which he now had to operate. It seems astonishing that the value of this achievement should have been doubted or denied by any historian looking objectively at this meeting.[15] This value must be measured in the terms of the strong and, for a while, quite relentless pressure that was later put on Casimir to renew his claim to the Bohemian crown which Pius, and even more his successor Paul II, would have been only too happy to bestow on the Polish ruler. It must be measured, furthermore, in terms of the impression which a falling out of the greatest power of Eastern Europe with the Czech King would have made, especially among those German princes who for a while would sit on the fence in the great and prolonged struggle between Prague and Rome. Under such circumstances, the attempt of the Curia again to concentrate overwhelmingly strong forces against Hussite Bohemia might well have had far greater success than it actually attained.

In emphasizing this we are, of course, anticipating. Yet this "negative" success—the prevention, by the firmly cemented friendship with Poland, of a future catastrophe—must weigh heavier than many a

---

[15] All that Bachmann admits is an effective "diplomatischer Schachzug" on the side of George, but otherwise he judges: "Es war materiell wenig, was Podiebrad in Glogau erreicht hatte." (*Reichsgeschichte*, I, 224.)

"positive" success which George's diplomacy could have had at this time. And it is all the more remarkable as it was achieved against considerable resistance from some Polish circles, which included the Queen and a considerable part of the Polish clergy, as well as the historian Jan Długosz himself, to whom we owe much of our knowledge about this whole development. It is probably due largely to George's personal impact and his effective arguing in a situation where language difficulties would not hamper him. In the face of these successes it mattered less that the absence of the representatives of the Prussian Order prevented George from functioning—as he had expected—as arbitrator in the war between Poland and the knights.[16]

There remains the question: why was it necessary for a treaty of friendship like the one concluded at Glogau to refer to the Turkish danger? The answer to this question reveals also the second purpose of the meeting—far more striking and, as such, less successful than the first. For behind it stands the great plan for an organization of European princes and their states which is indeed an attempt by George to answer in a positive form the attack of the Curia against him.

It is clear that the plan for a League of Princes,[17] intended to maintain and guarantee the internal peace of Christian Europe and thus to enable the participants to stand up to the Turkish danger, was not, in all its complex details, a brain child of George alone. Usually Antoine Marini has been credited with the draft. He, more than any other of King George's advisers or diplomats, was later charged with

---

[16] An apology of the Grand Master of the Order, sent to King George, in Toeppen, *Acten der Ständetage*, V, 64.

[17] The plan has been treated by a large number of historians, political scientists, and students of law, in the framework of larger works as well as in monographs. Among the latter are: H. Markgraf, "Uber Georgs von Podiebrad Project eines christlichen Fürstenbundes," *HZ*, 21, München, 1869, 257–304; E. Schwitzky, *Der europäische Fürstenbund Georgs von Podiebrad* (Abhandlungen aus dem juristisch-staatswissen-schaftlichen Seminar der Universität Marburg, ed. Schücking, vol. 6, Marburg, 1907); W. Weizsäcker, "Fürstenbund und Völkerbund," in *Prager juristische Zeitschrift*, X, 1930, 234–245; J. Kapras, *The Peace League of George Poděbrad, King of Bohemia* (The Czecho-Slovak Republic vol. II, part 5), Prague, 1919; J. Kliment, *Svaz národů Jiřího z Poděbrad a idea jediné světovlády*, Prague, 1935; F. M. Bartoš, "Návrh Krále Jiřího na utvoření svazu evropských států," *JČSH*, XII, Tabor, 1939, 65–82; J. Polišenský, "Problémy zahraniční politky Jiřího z Poděbrad," *Acta Universitatis Palackianae Olomucensis*, Historica I, Olomouc, 1960, 107–125. Polish contributions to the topic are J. Pogonowski's *Projekt związku wlaców króla Jerzego z Podiebrad*, Warsaw, 1932, and Roman Heck, "Czeski plan związku wladców europejskich z lat 1462–1464 i Polska," in *Studia z dziejów polskich i czeskoslowackich*, I, Wrocław 1950. The project is also discussed in some detail by Jacob ter Meulen in *Der Gedanke der internationalen Organization in seiner Entwickelung 1300–1800*, The Hague, 1917. Of the more important standard works, the plan is treated by Palacký, IV, 2, 209–212 (German, 237–240), Bachmann, *Reichsgeschichte*, I, 214–218, and above all, Urbánek, *Věk* IV, 580–599.

the presentation of the plan to various European courts, and we find several important similarities in a memorandum [18] which he had prepared some time before the Glogau conference to be submitted there to both Kings. Thus it would seem most unlikely that he was not also, to a considerable extent, responsible for and instrumental in helping to draft the plan. Yet it seems doubtful, as has recently been pointed out,[19] that he had the legal training to work out by himself a plan like this in all its aspects. Nor is there reason to assume that for an undertaking of such importance, once he had decided upon it, George would not have drawn on the talent of two or more of the gifted minds at his disposal. With this in mind, the suggestion that

[18] The memorandum, as yet unprinted, had already been mentioned by Jorga in his sketch on Marini in *Études d'histoire du moyen âge dediées a G. Monod*, pp. 451–453. Urbánek, in *Věk*, IV, 585–589, gives an extended presentation of its content (details about the Ms on p. 583, n. 25). Among the striking similarities between the memorandum and the final plan as we know it is a jeremiad about the decline of the Christian World that forms the introduction in both documents. Marini sees three possibilities for future development: either a return to the old status of a Christian Europe led by two powerful heads—Pope and Emperor—in purposive strength and unity; an alliance of all the great Christian lay princes; or the final destruction of Christianity. Despite a very sharp criticism of the errors and omissions of the lay princes who are so divided that the people have lost confidence, he sees real hope only in their alliance. But he goes into considerable detail in his criticism of the sins of clergy, of princes and lawyers, of the corruption in ecclesiastical administration, and the sophisms and errors of the university teachers. He sharply castigates, among other things, the criminal selfishness which has induced Western people and traders, blinded by monetary gains, to help the Turks by supplying them with ships, guns, and other war material. He finally names five great nations which should form the backbone of the resistance to the Turks: Greeks, Germans, French, Italians, and Spaniards. Despite the somewhat odd inclusion of the Greeks a decade after the fall of Constantinople and the absence of the English, this point of Marini's memorandum, like the final plan, distinctly shows its model: the Council of Constance. Here, indeed, appears now a strange inconsistency: while no Slavic power is mentioned, Marini nevertheless appeals to the two Slavic rulers to organize the needed cooperation of the princes of the Christian nations of Europe. And he justifies his belief in their great European role with a prophecy which he claims he heard from Flavio Biondo, apostolic secretary since the time of Eugene IV and a close friend of Pope Pius, who mentions him in his *Commentaries* (XI, 76f.). Marini ends with the suggestion that the Kings should invite the rulers of France, Burgundy, Venice, and Bavaria (perhaps meaning all Wittelsbachs) to a common meeting in Venice, where Marini himself was soon to travel. The inclusion of the Duke or Dukes of Bavaria, a rather small power in comparison with the others, makes one wonder whether Dr. Martin Mair, Duke Louis of Landshut's chief counsellor, had not already had some influence on the redaction of the memorandum (see later).

[19] See F. M. Bartoš, whose article in *JČSH*, XII, 1939, 65ff., quoted above, is mainly devoted to proving that the real author of the plan was Mair rather than Marini. Beside contributing to the general discussion of the project and helping to clarify its genesis, Bartoš has also, in an appendix to his article (pp. 74–81), presented a text of the project, superior to the older publications by Schwitzky and Kliment. (See the editorial notes by Bartoš, *op. cit.* 81–82, and Urbánek, *Věk*, IV 580, n. 16.) Still another text, until quite recently unknown and clearly the oldest and most authentic, has been discovered in the archives of the Royal Polish Chancery, called "Metryka koronna," XI, 578–587. A publication of this text is imminent in Prague. I am much indebted to Dr. Jiří Kejř for making it accessible to me. The difference between it and the majority of the other texts (especially Bartoš's) are, however, essentially of philological rather than historical interest.

Martin Mair had something to do with developing and writing the plan has much to recommend itself, though not to the extent that Mair alone could be considered the author. Documents of such length and such wealth of ideas and constructive conception are rarely produced by only one mind. In this case, in particular, several of the guiding ideas most likely came from George himself, whose helpers, probably Mair at least as much as Marini, would then have provided most of the legal-historical knowledge, the sophisticated organization, and the Latin diction.[20]

As far as the pre-history of this earlier "grand design" is concerned certain similarities to the much older plan of Pierre Dubois [21] are probably accidental, though the possibility cannot be completely excluded that the Frenchman Marini had some knowledge of it. One of the elements of the plan—the reorganization of Christian Europe for the task of an anti-Turkish crusade—was, of course, very much "in the air" at the time. We have only to recall Pope Pius' initiative in calling, quite early in his reign, the congress of princes to Mantua, as well as the many Reichstage called to deal with the same problem. The Mantuan Congress as well as the Reichstage were notoriously unsuccessful, and this in itself could well have taught a critical observer like George that the old conception of the defense of Christian Europe against the Unbelievers, under the common leadership of Pope and Emperor, was now even less promising than it had been in times past and should be replaced by something more effective. Modern commentators have mostly emphasized that George's plan put forward the idea of an organization of the temporal power in the form of national states, as against the previous expectation of ecclesiastical leadership. There is much truth in this, and to that extent the project is certainly far closer to the one developed by Sully a century and a half later than to Dubois' scheme presented a century and a half before. Yet the "secularization" of the idea of European organization in George's project is not yet complete, and the role of the Holy See in it not quite as negligible as is often claimed. (This, at least, is true for the draft text that has come down to us in a number of slightly different versions.) Even so the draft clearly expresses a political trend directed largely against the papacy and its leadership claims, since it contains important elements which the papacy had all along

20 In a personal discussion which I have had with Prof. Bartoš he seems to have found this assumption quite acceptable.

21 Pierre Dubois, *De recuperatione terrae sanctae*, ed. Langlois, Paris, 1891. See also ter Meulen's evaluation in *Der Gedanke der internationalen Organization*, 101ff.

resented, and no one more (despite his own past) than Pius II. These elements are derived from the church councils, especially those of Constance and Basel. While their main emphasis is organizational, this is enough to make the plan appear to belong to the very policy fought with such energy by Pope Pius in his bull "Execrabilis." And for the same reasons it would make the plan appear attractive in the eyes of all those opposed to that bull, first of all, presumably, the King of France, Louis XI, whose disappointment with Pius' policy had long made him regret his concessions regarding the Pragmatic Sanction of Bourges.

It is difficult to date with precision the genesis of the plan. There are only a few clues, such as a letter from Marini to King George[22] in which he, as early as August 1461, thus before the outbreak of the crisis, pointed to Godfrey of Bouillon as a model for George's policy, and, more important, the memorandum mentioned above. Other than this we have no clear indications of how the idea materialized. Yet it is almost certain that the substance had taken shape before the great meeting of the Kings at Glogau. The earliest and most authentic text of the plan has (recently) been found in the royal archives of Poland—in a version which was never substantially revised in the other preserved texts, including those found in France. This seems to indicate that by the time that King George (and with him Marini) left Glogau, the plan was finished in all details.[23] Soon thereafter Antoine Marini went on to present the draft, in the form in which we know it now, to Venice. From our records, which include the text of a letter from the Doge to King George dated August 9, 1462, it seems clear that in Venice Marini's diplomatic work, based on the program of close cooperation of the rulers of Bohemia, Hungary, France, Burgundy, and the Republic of Venice, had made a good impression and would be supported.[24] The Venetians did, however, suggest that the Curia be given a more influential role. They did not believe, or pretended they did not believe that, merely because of the participation and expected leading role of the King of Bohemia, Pope Pius II would be reluctant to cooperate.

It is not clear whether Marini, after his preliminary and highly qualified success in Venice, returned to Prague and stayed there through the autumn. In any case he took the plan westward around

---

[22] See Palacký's publication in *Časopis českého Museum*, 1828, III, 21–24.
[23] See above n. 19.
[24] See *FRA*, II, 20, 289f.

the turn of the year [25] visiting first the court of the Duke of Burgundy in Brussels, where, however, he seems to have found little encouragement. The fact that Duke Philip was included in Marini's itinerary has been presented as proof of the poor judgment of King George's diplomats, since the duke was just then the object of lively wooing from the two princely parties in the Empire and would thus not be accessible to the Bohemian advances.[26] But is is difficult to see why a scheme of which the Wittelsbach party was at least well informed, and in which it might even have had a hand through Mair, should not include an attempt to gain the support of Burgundy, especially at a moment when the relationship between Burgundy and France seemed on the point of being mended. True, the court of Burgundy could not be expected to keep the matter hidden from the Curia, but at this time the Pope would have heard of it anyhow, if from no other sources than his intelligence service in Venice.[27]

In any case Brussels was only a stop on the way to Paris, and there Marini's reception was, by his own evaluation, as warm as that in Burgundy had been cool. King Louis found the plan worthy of energetic support, and the only regret the French uttered at this stage was that Marini did not have the full power to conclude a formal treaty embodying all the points put forward by the Czech King's ambassador.[28] Whether, and to what extent, French suggestions for further changes of the scheme were advanced and to what extent they were considered by King George's ambassador is a matter of conjecture.[29] In any case Marini went once more to Venice with his plan,

[25] It is generally taken for granted that, at this stage of the negotiations, King Matthias of Hungary was entirely disregarded—a neglect which would reflect also on George's general treatment of his son-in-law. There is, however, one source which makes it appear possible that, before his great western trip, Marini had also visited Matthias, though perhaps without presenting the scheme to him in detail. See the letter of Otto de Carretto, ambassador of the Duke of Milan at the papal court, written from Rome to Duke Francesco Sforza on January 13, 1463, concerning recent discussions with the Pope. In it Carretto mentions Marini as a French national who has not only recently been in Hungary as well as in Bohemia, but is now in France as an envoy of the King of Bohemia as well as of the Kings of Hungary and Poland. See Pastor, II, documentary appendix pp. 736, 737. See also Urbánek, *Věk*, IV, 592 n. 45.

[26] See Bachmann, *Reichsgeschichte*, I, 404, 405; Markgraf, *op. cit.*, 279, and Urbánek, *Věk*, IV, 593.

[27] Possibly Theodore de Lelli Bishop of Feltre, who later became a prominent diplomat under Paul II. For information about his stay in Venice see Joachimsohn, *Gregor Heimburg*, Bamberg, 1891, p. 243.

[28] See the Venetian answer to the lost letter of Louis XI, in *FRA*, II, 20, 290–291.

[29] Bachmann (*Reichsgeschichte* I, 406 and 407) sees strong French influence upon the project, and assumes that it was, by the clever Frenchmen, "noch weiter zu ihrem Vorteile umgemodelt . . ." Details which are supposed to prove this are to be found in the footnotes on both pages. Urbánek clearly does not share this view, nor does he see the reaction of Louis

strengthened, as he must have thought by the French support, but otherwise, as we may assume, unchanged.

What, then, was the scheme? The document, over 4,000 words long, begins with a long preamble describing the misery to which the Turkish conquests have reduced the Christian world. Once, this world had embraced 117 flourishing realms and had included even the tomb of the Savior. Of these realms barely 16 are left since Mahomet has seduced the Arab people, and his followers have overrun large parts of Africa and Asia. Even Greece and Constantinople have fallen. This dreadful collapse, the preamble says, is difficult to grasp, and is probably God's punishment for our sins.

Nothing could please the Lord better than the urge to create peace and concord within, and to defend the Christian world on this earth against all its enemies, and especially against the Infidels. But since it seems hopeless for any single nation to resist the Turkish power, all the Christian nations of Europe will have to unite in a perpetual union, in order to work with combined strength to drive the Turks from the soil of Europe. Such a union, however, can only be achieved if it is possible to establish a true Christian peace within the union and with other Christian nations.

This preamble—whose rather passionate language clearly tries to appeal to the emotions of those to whom it was addressed—is followed by what might be called the constitution of the intended League of Princes, for despite the important role that the Republic of Venice is expected to play, even there it is the prince, the Doge, who is referred to as one of the regional leaders of the League.[30] This constitution is organized in about 23 or 24 paragraphs of which the first four are actually numbered.[31] The following extract attempts to adhere to the logic rather than to the literal sequence of the draft.

---

in as positive a light as Bachmann, since he assumes, probably correctly, that under the influence of some of his clerical advisors the King was somewhat hesitant to assume a leading role in the scheme. (pp. 599–600). The recent discovery of the most authentic text in Poland (which was presumably deposited in the royal chancery during or after the meeting of the two Kings at Glogau) also makes Bachmann's assumption rather improbable, since the text found in France shows no changes other than a very few minor verbal deviations.

[30] In reference to Italy, however, alone of all nations or regions, there is also mention (in § 20) of the city states (*communitates*) especially necessary in view of the official structure of the Florentine state where the factual rule of the Medici had not yet been recognized in any formal way.

[31] The original has no paragraph numbers beyond those first four, but all modern editors have, for good practical reasons, continued the numbering throughout. Naturally there are differences, as the numbering is bound to be somewhat arbitrary. Thus Schwitzky counts only

The constitution, following the example of the Council of Constance (but also the much older examples of some great universities such as Bologna, Paris, and pre-Hussite Prague), divides Christian Europe into a small number of large *nationes,* a term by no means identical with the modern usage of the word. This difference is most obvious from the fact that the King of France appears "together with the other Kings and Princes of Gaul"; that no mention is made of the Holy Roman Emperor, but there are several "Kings and princes of Germany," among these presumably all rulers of Central and East Central Europe, not only of Bohemia, but also of Poland and Hungary neither of whom is expressly mentioned anywhere. In this sense it would be correct to speak of a regional rather than a national division of Europe. Besides the two regions mentioned before, there was the Italian, which was supposed to be under the political leadership of Venice, and finally, planned as a future addition, the kings and princes of Spain, which clearly meant the whole peninsula, under the leadership of the King of Castile rather than Aragon which, with its great Mediterranean empire and its strong navy, would probably have been better able to play a role in a common war against the Ottomans. This is perhaps accounted for by a desire to consider French interests which, as we know, were in sharp opposition to the Aragonese rule in southern Italy.[32] Why the authors of this constitution neglected England is difficult to say, though it would not be overly surprising to see the English kingdom included in either "Gallia" or even in "Germania." The latter region seems likely to have included Scandinavia, all the more since its ruler, Christian I, was in any case, as Count of Holstein, a prince of the Empire. A clear delineation between the member "nations" is not recognizable, and the position of a border state as important as Burgundy (probably within "Gallia") can only be guessed.

The three or four "nations" or regions—the term *provinciae* is also occasionally used—would operate as units within the league. The main organ of the league would be a council of representatives or ambas-

---

21 whereas Kliment counts 24. Bartoš follows Kliment. I have therefore quoted on the basis of these two publications. For readers to whom Schwitzky rather than Kliment and Bartoš may be accessible I might mention that paragraphs 9–11 are listed as one paragraph and paragraphs 17 and 18 again as only one by Schwitzky, so that from 10 on, his count lags by two figures, from 19 on, by three figures behind the count used here. Markgraf, too, incidentally, used 24 paragraphs, but differs in detail from those of Kliment and Bartoš. The newly discovered earliest text, about to be published, has 23 paragraphs.

32 See the remarks of Bachmann, *Reichsgeschichte,* 407, and Urbánek, *Věk* IV, 598 n. 66.

sadors of the princes who are members. This council is variously called "congregation," "collegium," "corpus" or even "universitas," each "nation" or region holding but one vote in it (§ 20). This arrangement might well have caused difficulties if and when the total number of "nations" in the league reached four. However, there are no attempts to solve this problem on the international level, which is the more noticeable because the same problem is faced and at least partially solved in relation to those decisions within one nation or region upon which the vote on the international level is based. Normally, each king or prince, whatever his general status and whatever the number of his representatives, is supposed to have but one vote, and if no unanimity can be achieved, simple majority decides. If however, the vote is evenly split, the voices of the rulers shall be weighed and those of the more important members (such as kings as against dukes or princes) shall prevail. But when the two sides remain numerically even, then the "nation" to which they belong loses, on the issue in question, its voice as against those of the other "nations."

The fact that, measured by the thinking of the time, considerable care is given to the voting procedure shows that the author or authors of the constitution intended to develop a congressional mechanism which could really function. This, indeed, was of central importance, since there was no other, higher central organ, and since the functions and powers of the only other body, the international court, were naturally more specialized and more limited than those of the general council.

What were these functions and powers? They went very far indeed in determining the actions of the league and, therewith, of every one of its members. In some ways those powers went farther in the direction of world government than any of the two great modern experiments of international organization. It was, above all, up to the general assembly to maintain the peace between and within all the members of the league, a duty based on those rights which it derived from the solemn obligation of each member never under any circumstances to resort to the use of force against any other member (§§ 1 and 2). The league, again upon the decision of the assembly, would protect any of its members against attacks from outside after first having made attempts at reconciliation through its own diplomats (§ 4). Since wars even between non-members were considered dangerous, the council offered its services as arbitrator for settling major quarrels, but if this procedure should be unsuccessful, it would eventually use its own military power on the side of the power that had refrained from aggression and has been prepared to accept arbitration (§ 5). The power of the league, in an age in which the line between private feuds and international wars was still so fluid, was also supposed to include the quenching of such feuds. While acts of aggression in the form of feuds were, in the first place, to be punished severely by the local ruler, the latter was also responsible for the maintenance of peace and order to the extent that he himself would be punished by the league for tolerating disturbance of the peace with the same punishments normally meted out to the delinquent (§§ 6–8).

Since the waging of individual wars or military actions of any size was completely outlawed as a result of the basic obligations undertaken by any member (including new members whose accession had to be agreed to by the council) (§ 12), the question remained how and in what form the league would and could build up its own supranational military forces. This problem, of course, has plagued modern international bodies down to the United Nations. The constitution of the league devoted a number of paragraphs (§ 13–18) to this difficult problem, and from them it appears (though it is not spelled out expressly) that the instrument of feudal levies, especially for the purpose of anti-Turkish crusaders, is meant to be discarded. At least the fact that much emphasis is put on the financial aspects seems to indicate that the army to operate in the name of the league would consist essentially of mercenaries. Herein, as in so many other aspects of the plan, we can see the attempt to move away from older time-worn patterns and to accept instead the needs and trends of an economically and socially changing world.[33] A common tax rate would be applied for war, especially the war against the Turks, by all members of the league, and it would be allocated in a way which would fully consider each member's ability to pay. In all member states the clergy would be taxed one tenth of its income, and other subjects three days of income as long as needed (§ 13). The league, furthermore, would have the right to coin its own currency (§ 16) to pay the armed forces to be hired, according to orders given by the council, in the individual member states. The council would also determine the place and date of military action, the type and strength of the forces to be employed (§ 14), and the ways in which they were to be provisioned (§ 15). Finally it would be up to the council to decide about

---

[33] Here, in a field in which he was considered an expert and authority, Marini's ideas and suggestions must have prevailed against any competing ones.

and to administer territories conquered in a common war, the permanent security of the Christian world being the predominant consideration.

The second and only other organ [34] of the league was the international court. It is called variously "parlamentum" [35] and "consistorium" (both terms sometimes used together), occasionally also "judicium." Its foremost tasks were judicial decisions on issues arising between member states (§ 3) and in connection with actions considered crimes against the peace of the land (§ 4). There is also a remarkable paragraph (§ 9) giving something like the philosophical basis for this new and—outside the ecclesiastical jurisdiction—unheard-of conception. It points out that there can be no international peace without justice, and its justification for introducing a new law (*de naturae gremio nova jura producere*) [36] essentially anticipates the Grotian conception of a natural law of the nations.

The international court would consist of one chief justice (judex) and an indefinite number of associate judges (assessores), all of them appointed by the council, but there was no indication of how they were to be selected. Some emphasis is put on the need to give punitive sentences which were clear, easily understandable, and, in their implementation, do not permit any subterfuges or prolonged and frustrating ligitations (§ 10). The following paragraph (§ 11) reconfirms the emphasis on the complete authority of the court in all quarrels or differences between the member states.

It is toward its conclusion that this document, thus far essentially devoted to the principles and the structure of the planned organization, becomes more concrete in the political and topical sense. And it is here that we find important historical clues as well.

The council of the league, says paragraph 17, will meet for the first time on the Sunday Reminiscere (February 26) 1464 in the city of Basel, within the territory of the German nation, where it will reside for five years. After that, in 1469, it will move to a city in France, and five years later to a city in Italy.

[34] Urbánek (*Věk*, IV, 599) assumes that besides the general assembly there was provision also for a narrower body of the greater princes, somewhat akin to the Security Council of the U.N. There is, however, only one reference, in § 16, to justify this assumption.

[35] As far as I can see, the term *parlamentum,* in accordance, of course, with French medieval and modern pre-revolutionary terminology, is used only in relation to the international law court. Thus I am somewhat puzzled by Urbánek's consistent usage of the term for the league as such, the chapter in question being called *Plan o "parlamentu."* (See *Věk*, IV, 576–608). (Palacký had also used the term, but only occasionally.)

[36] P. 62 in Kliment's, p. 78 in Bartoš' text.

The council, as we see in the same context, is considered essentially a judicial person, with its own coat of arms, its own seal, archives, and treasury. It also has its own syndics, fiscal officers, and other officials. This sounds similar to the modern development of an international civil service, a conception, indeed, which was not alien to the time, having been approached both in the papal Curia and to a lesser extent in the organizations of the great church councils. The following paragraph (18), however, states that the council of the league, during the five-year period it resides in one "nation," should appoint or elect most of its officials from the people within that "nation." This, of course, would tend to reduce the international character of the staff of the league in favor of a "national" character expected to change every five years.

The question arises how far this clause would reach toward the top of the chain of command? Paragraph 17, which in many ways gives us the best historical clues, establishes the position of the head of the league (unus praesidens pater et caput), and with virtual unanimity it has been assumed by the historians and political scientists who, following Palacký and Markgraf, have so far studied the document, that King Louis XI was meant immediately to fill this position.[37] But there may be some justification for disagreeing with this assumption, which is based merely on guesswork and on what might be called the political logic of the situation, especially in its subsequent development. On the basis of paragraph 18 one would, indeed, expect that the position of head of the league would, during the five-year period in which the league would reside in a city in "Gallia," fall to the French King as the leader and most powerful ruler of that region or nation. Similarly the Doge of Venice would take over the presidency of the league during the third period. But what of the first period? In this phase the league was supposed to have its headquarters in Basel, still a German imperial city made famous by the long years of the church council and by the very recent establishment there (1460) of a university. Thus it would seem logical to make the leader of the "natio Germaniae" the head and "presiding father" of the league. But who was the leader? Under normal circumstances it would naturally be the Emperor of the Romans. Yet he is not even men-

---

[37] In view of the historical importance that the negotiations with Louis XI necessarily assumed in this connection, and on the basis of the decisive role he would have had to play in it simply in terms of political and military strength, this assumption easily appeared plausible. See Markgraf, *op. cit.*, 285, Bachmann, Reichsgeschichte, 405, Urbánek, *Věk,* IV, 597.

tioned. Where the draft says "nos, rex Franciae, una cum ceteris regibus et principibus Galliae" and nos, Dux Venetiarum, una cum princibus et communitatibus Italiae," it says in the case of Central Europe only "nos vero reges et principes Germaniae." What conclusion can we draw from this striking omission and especially from the use of the plural of the term "kings"?

On the basis of what we know about his activities immediately preceding this period, as well as some intentions later expressed, of the man essentially responsible for the whole bold scheme, the answer is not too difficult to find. King George had made considerable efforts to become King of the Romans—an elevation which would have given him the leading position in the Empire formally as well as factually. The recent events in the Empire (including the battles of Seckenheim and Giengen) had made George's political dominance in Central Europe clearer than ever before. All this might have made him feel that the leading role in the league during the first phase of its existence by rights belonged to him. This position, if it really could be created, would serve him as well as the Roman kingship would have served him. It would indeed check effectively the attempts of the Pope to isolate him and, if he did not capitulate, to destroy him. If we accept the astute surmise that much of the structure and diction of the draft can be ascribed to Martin Mair, then the logic of this answer becomes even more forceful. It fits in well with the advice to King George by Mair upon the latter's return from Milan, as well as with his later plans for George's role in a contemplated crusade against the Turks.[38] And if George expected or at least hoped, at the time of the conception of the scheme, that he himself would be the president of the league during the decisive five years in question, then this easily explains why the draft only discusses the "reges Germaniae" without so much as mentioning the Emperor as one of them, and this at a time when, in general, George had reason to maintain friendly relations with Frederick III and when, indeed, he was soon going to save him from a situation of deadly peril. (This assumption does not preclude the possibility that, if necessary for political reasons, George would eventually, perhaps even soon, be ready to cede the priority for the presidency of the league to Louis XI. This, indeed, is what George did

[38] See e.g. Mair's approaches to King George as summarized by Bartoš, *op. cit.,* 69–71. It seems to me that the very arguments Bartoš used for Mair's role in the scheme also support my thesis that, in the view of its author, no one but George himself was originally supposed to be the natural leader of the league in its decisive early years.

when, in the summer of 1464, he sent Marini and the Utraquist Lord Albert Kostka of Postupice to France for further negotiations about the league.[39]

There is still another small riddle which can probably be solved more easily by the assumption that George expected to become the first head of the league: the fact that of the two greater powers then in steady contact with the Turks only one, Venice, figures importantly in the draft, whereas the other, Hungary, is not mentioned. George, it seems, did not want to jeopardize his own role, in what would have been his own creation, by allowing his young and ambitious son-in-law, Matthias Corvinus, to compete with him. Venice, of course, was another matter, since her contribution was bound to be primarily that of a naval power. Though himself the ruler of a landlocked kingdom, George was clearly aware of the great role that naval power would have to play in any attempt at a really powerful undertaking of the Christian world against the explosive strength of the Crescent.

And here, then, is one of the roles which the draft allotted to the figure against whom, in other ways, the scheme is directed: the Pope. The references to him are essentially limited to one paragraph, if a very long one (§ 22). In it only two tasks are assigned to the Pope. First he should, by the issue of "authentic bulls" and under the threat of "formidable punishments," enforce the prompt payment of the taxes without which the league could not possibly fulfill its function of defending the Christian world against the Turks, or for that matter any other function. Second, the Pope should call together a conference of the princes and cities of Italy and, again under the threat of heavy punishment, induce them to employ all their available naval strength to help the league in the struggle against the Turks.

The language used in relation to the Pope is full of those expressions of extreme devotion and veneration which were the style of the time. This is by no means astonishing since George himself still claimed to stand in the full unity of the Church. Also most of his advisers, chief diplomats, and secretaries (except for the brothers Kostka of Postupice and a few others) and, of course, all those princes who were supposed to join the league, were Catholics like the overwhelming majority of their subjects. Yet in spite of all these utterances of respect and veneration for the person and office of the Supreme Pontiff, the essentially anti-curial character of the document is clear. Of the dominant role that the papacy, and especially Pius II, had tried to play

[39] See Urbánek, *Ve službách Jiříka Krále*, Prague, 1940.

in facing the Turkish threat, only little is left in the project. The task allotted to the Pope is strictly auxiliary. What Pius II had tried to do with conspicuous lack of success, during the months at Mantua—to rally around himself all the important princes of Christian Europe—King George's plan now tried to do on a permanent basis, without any direction from the Holy See, simply as the decision of the allied princes, based on clear reasoning and high resolve, to abolish war and organize perpetual peace between themselves as the only healthy basis for survival. And he expected to start this action in Basel, in a city whose very name in this situation had a symbolic sound, recalling the days when great assemblies of Christian statesmen and churchmen defied the papal claim to absolutist rule over the Christian world.

Though the need for defense, eventually even for the crusading offensive, against the Turks provided the strong motivating force for princes and nations to join together, the vision behind the plan is not limited to an organization against anyone. Rather is it rooted in the great human hope for peace on earth, based on justice for everyone and organized by those who would combine a genuine will for peace with the strength and power to maintain it. While, in the five centuries that have elapsed since the great plan was conceived, the whole idea has often been thought to be utterly utopian, today we are perhaps more than ever ready for the understanding that pure, anarchic power struggle must lead to catastrophe. In this sense, then, George's league, as a bold image shaped in an early pioneering effort, merits a place of high honor in the history of the idea of organized peace, even though its actual historical role for his reign and his struggle with Rome was—except for the resulting friendship between King George and the Kings of Poland and France—of minor importance and though at the time it achieved nothing at all for Christian Europe's struggle with the Turks.

The exception—George's friendship with France and Poland—was, however, far from unimportant. It gave him considerable support in Western Europe and certainly diminished the chances for the papacy to push the German princes out of the neutrality that most of them would keep throughout the struggle. The development of a closer Franco-Bohemian relationship continued to be an important object of George's foreign policy, and we shall later devote more attention to it.

Although the plan as a political potential gradually disappeared from the international scene (see chapter XIV), there remains the need to gauge George's part in evolving the plan, and its significance for his historical role. We might, of course, be satisfied with the knowledge that the plan was evolved and presented under his name and under his authority, and this judgment, with the limited credit remaining for George, would fit the earlier assumption that the whole project was originally conceived, fully elaborated and brought to its final stage of presentation by one man only: Antoine Marini. As soon as we introduce one additional participant—Martin Mair—into our assumption about the genesis of the plan, however, we also have to assume some over-all direction in its development for which no one can be credited except the King himself.

But perhaps we can be even more specific about George's part. At least one important element in the draft rather distinctly shows his way of thinking. It is the emphasis on mediation and arbitration in international conflicts. George was often attacked, by contemporaries as well as by later historians, for his supposed faithlessness, for the fact that he usually did not go all-out in his support of an ally but left him, as it were, in mid-air just before that ally could achieve a decisive victory over his enemies. The claim as such is not without some measure of truth, and it may well be admitted that "Nibelungentreue," the willingness to stand and fall (especially to fall) with one's ally was not in George's program. We may go further and state that he may have preferred, in that sphere of Europe's political geography which had much influence upon his own political status, the existence of princes and states none of whom would be too strong. It is a principle of politics honored by the term "balance of power." Yet it would probably be a mistake to see in this policy nothing but the "selfish" seeking of strength for his own nation and throne at the cost of other states.[40] It is certainly true—and eventually admitted even by his critics—that George really disliked war, used it only reluctantly as a last resort in what seemed a political emergency, and above all never expected to wage it, or have to wage it, as an instrument of total destruction of the enemy. Rather was war, more than once, for him a quick way to nudge or push the opponent toward certain limited political concessions, or to deter him from going too far in certain political demands. In consequence most of the wars in which he was

---

[40] See e.g. Bachmann, *Geschichte Böhmens* II, 535: "nicht heiliger Eifer für den Glauben. . . .", or, more pronounced, Weizsäcker, "Fürstenbund und Völkerbund," 237. See the opposite view in Kliment, *Svaz národů Jiřího z Poděbrad,* 38f., and Urbánek *Věk* IV, 594 n. 51.

involved were really "little wars," often ended by armistice before any real military action had properly started, except, of course, for the last period of his reign when war on a large scale was forced on him by his enemies. While he admitted by his actions that recourse to arms could not always be avoided, he was usually at his best in manoeuvering toward rapprochement, and most in his element when peace was within reach and became the object of his political operations. This genuine appreciation of peace as the most desirable state of affairs between people and between states did, indeed, impress his contemporaries to the extent that even in the mid-sixties, already an object of papal hostility and persecution, he was, as we shall see, still the most acceptable international mediator and arbitrator in Central Europe. And it is this whole mentality that so clearly finds its expression in the great plan for a League of Princes.

Surely the desire of peace is age-old and had found many an expression deeper and more unconditional in some of the great literature of the earlier Middle Ages, for instance, in the nineteenth book of St. Augustine's *City of God*. Yet outside the spheres of theology and philosophy, outside the moribund conception of a universal Roman Empire allied with a universal Roman Church, it would be difficult to find any previous document which not only expresses with such clear determination the need for peace on the widest possible scale, but also looks with such sober clarity for ways to achieve and maintain it at first within the Christendom and hopefully, after the Turkish drive has been defeated, all over the known world.[41] It is extremely difficult to decide whether and to what extent George's sponsorship and direction of the great peace plan contains conscious elements of the idea of ideological and political progress against the essentially hopeless muddle which at his time dominated all other attempts at restoring to the Western world any sense of unity and concerted purpose. It remains remarkable, that pressed to the wall by the Pope's action, his most ambitious countering step took the form of so constructive and imaginative a project. To recognize and acknowledge this fact, it seems to me, disposes also of the reproach of insincerity or hypocrisy in this instance or in George's policy in general. It would be absurd to expect that he could have presented a project like this (or

---

[41] Among the great men of later times who were impressed by this great plan was also Goethe, who, on this basis, called George a man of great thoughts and wide perspectives ("ein grossdenkender und überschauender Mann"). Goethe's judgment, expressed in the draft to a review of an early publication of Palacký, was published in *Jahrbücher für Wissensch. Kritik*, Berlin, 1830. I owe this information to my friend Johannes Urzidil.

any other in later times) if it were not also in the interest of the Czech realm. No attempt at strengthening the cooperative element in international relations was ever made by any statesman of rank in any age who could not hope and assume that such a policy was also in the interest of his own people. But here as elsewhere we perceive again King George's ability to identify himself and his immediate interests with those of a wider, greater community, wider and greater at this time than even the nation which he directed and served.

CHAPTER 14

TO SAVE AN EMPEROR

GEORGE'S PLAN for a League of Princes, while important in the history of ideas and not without influence upon Bohemia's relation to Poland and France, had no influence at all on the great struggle between Christian Europe and the Ottoman Empire. In the realm of political realities, indeed, it might be said that the Curia—which George's plan had intended largely to eliminate for the European organization of resistance to the Turks—was more realistic and more successful than the King. While this success was to be short lived, it nevertheless looked like an impressive riposte dealt to the King of Bohemia by the Pope. What it amounted to, above all, was an alliance of the Pope, in October 1463, with two of the very powers with whom Marini had negotiated about the League of Princes: Burgundy and Venice.

The question arises whether and to what extent this alliance can really be considered, as has been done repeatedly,[1] primarily as a countermove to the diplomatic activities of King George and especially to the ideological schemes which were to dominate it. And here we meet with the somewhat astonishing fact, rather neglected so far, that Pius II, in his own historical record, does not mention either King George's plan for the League of Princes or Marini's activities, of which he was aware soon after they had started, while on the other hand he describes in considerable detail his own motives and goals in planning for an attack upon the Turks in close alliance with Burgundy and Venice. It might be argued that Pius' silence on this phase of George's activity just shows the sovereign contempt of the superior strategist

---

[1] Palacký was the first: Dějiny IV, 2, 240 (in German, 274); in Bachmann's eyes the action of the Curia, whom George had tried to beat by a surprise action, "had already begun its own action against him, only more unified and more far-reaching and effective because based on safe foundations and calculating on the basis of the actual situation" (*Geschichte Böhmens*, II, 535). Urbánek, less careful than he usually is, goes even farther, saying that "at this time [mid-1463] Venice had already become involved in the diplomatic action which Pope Pius, having been informed about George's negotiations regarding the parliament, had started against him" (*Věk*, IV, 601).

for the blunderings of an inferior foe. But this is hardly the true explanation. For one thing Pius, in his autobiography, did not tire of showing the King of Bohemia in the unflattering light in which— in distinction to earlier views—he saw him now, and he would have had no difficulty in depicting the King's recent steps in the same light, if this had been sufficiently in the foreground of his mind. (He had time enough, since the "Commentaries" reach to January 1464.)

In reality, according to Pius himself, and on this issue it is difficult to doubt him, the basic planning that led to Pius' alliance with Burgundy and Venice—and later paved the way for an alliance between Venice and Hungary—was begun by the Pope during or probably even before the stay of the Czech embassy in Rome, in the late winter or early spring of 1462, when the plan of the League of Princes, as far as we can judge, was only in its first stages of planning, of which Pius could hardly, as yet, have been aware.[2] If Pius' own subsequent steps look like an answer to George's actions, then this was, to him, at best a secondary significance. Primarily they flow from the Pope's traditional dream of mobilizing Europe against the Turks, but also from his own vivid recognition of the futility of his previous efforts, especially of the great Congress of Mantua. In the speech in which he presented his whole new plan for a crusade under his own leadership to the six "most loyal and wise" members of the Sacred College[3] he confessed to be in despair for his lack of success in repulsing the Turks. Only power, not the good will, he declared, had been lacking. He then expounded his new plan by which he finally hoped to overcome the inertia and avarice of both princes and clergy which so far had frustrated his best efforts. (There are, indeed, in this speech some critical remarks about these two groups of men which actually remind one of corresponding passages in Marini's memorandum.) But, by putting himself, physically, at the head of the crusade, Pius was now going to force Duke Philip of Burgundy finally to make good on the solemn oath he had sworn in the year of the conquest of Constantinople: that if but one of the great rulers of Europe should take the cross he would immediately, with all his strength, follow his summons. Philip's participation, on the other hand, would morally force the French to come in, too, perhaps not with the 70,000 men once

---

[2] *See Commentaries*, VII, 515–519. For the dating see the emphasis (on p. 519) that this occurred before Holy Week, and the decision, after the discussion with the cardinals, to send Roverella on his mission to France, again just about Easter. (See also Pastor, II, 241f., 246.)

[3] See above n. 2.

promised by King Louis, but at least with 10,000. Above all, however, neither the Hungarians nor the Venetians could, for reasons of self-preservation, stay out of an undertaking thus set in motion.

Once the Pope felt that he had achieved sufficient support for this plan in the College of Cardinals—though the official sanction was not given by a consistory of the sacred College till September 1463 [4]— there began intense diplomatic activity, especially in France, Burgundy, and Venice.[5] In France, where around Easter 1462 the Bishop of Ferrara Lorenzo Roverella had already tried to win Louis XI over for Pius' plan, the papal diplomacy was entirely unsuccessful. Eventually it was perhaps unavoidable that the Curia would associate, to some extent, the French King's openly hostile criticism of Pope Pius' scheme with the activities of the King of Bohemia, especially when Louis, in one of his many rather unfriendly communications, listed among the Pope's main misdeeds that of having called King George a heretic.[6] Only in the fall of 1463 did another papal diplomat, Teodoro Lelli, Bishop of Feltre, make another major effort which now, it seems, included specific attacks against the King of Bohemia.[7] It is difficult to say whether Lelli's activities had anything to do with the position, very unfriendly to King George, later taken by Jean Balue, Cardinal of Angers, who, after some years of considerable influence on King Louis, eventually exchanged it for complete disgrace and prolonged imprisonment.[8] But though Balue, as we shall see, restricted the scope of the alliance sought by King George and generally favored by King Louis, he did not even try to overcome Louis's extreme unwillingness to support the crusading plans of the Curia. Pope Pius, on his side, could never be induced by all this pressure to drop his support for Ferrante of Naples. Louis's determination to punish the Pope for what he considered his treachery went far enough not only to make him refuse all help for the crusade on his own account, but also to do all in his power, especially his position as Philip's liege lord, to prevent the duke from making good on his repeated promises to help in this undertaking. Philip, it seems, was not too unhappy to be thus prevented. This was a disappointment which the Pope felt keenly and expressed strongly in his memoirs.[9]

[4] *Commentaries*, XII, 817–828.
[5] See Pastor, II, 246ff.
[6] *Commentaries*, XII, 794.
[7] See Urbánek, *Věk*, IV, 604ff.
[8] See Pastor, II, 372ff., and Comines, *Memoires*, ed. Godefroy, Book VI, chapter 6.
[9] *Commentaries*, XII, 852–856.

But if France refused, and Burgundy, despite the treaty concluded with the Pope and Venice, broke his solemn promise and the treaty of October 1463, Venice was less untractable. There, of course, just as in Hungary, the question whether or not to wage war against the Turks was a much more real issue than it appeared in those parts of the world less immediately exposed to the Ottoman menace. For Venice the question of war or peace with the Turks was dominated by considerations of the gains and losses which either course of action would yield. Ruling an extensive empire in the eastern Mediterranean, the great city state's interest might well demand a policy of vigorous defense of her outlying possessions, necessitating in many cases an offensive strategy which would anticipate and prevent further Turkish expansion. As a great commercial community on the other hand, she might eye such a policy of war with extreme misgivings, not only because it would be costly and risky but also because a peaceful relationship with the Ottoman power—which at times seemed not so impossible—might permit the continuation of her highly profitable oriental trade, and perhaps would even enable her to inherit the Black-Sea trade which the Genoese had managed to retain.[10] Under the influence of these conflicting hopes and fears two parties had formed, one in favor of war, the other of peace. For a considerable time, following the conquest of Constantinople, the peace party had prevailed, basing its strength on the treaty of 1454, which was supposed to normalize, to mutual benefit, the relations between the Republic of San Marco and the Porte. If the latter had refrained from further expansion southward into the Morea and westward along the hinterland of the Adriatic Sea, there would have been little chance for the war party to prevail. But Mohammed II was not satisfied with his present gains.

Yet a turn of Venetian policy toward war seemed unlikely as long as Prospero Malipiero, a strict adherent of the policy of compromise, was Doge. His death and the election, on May 12, 1462, of Christoforo Moro opened the way for a change.[11] This became a certainty after the conquest, in September 1462, of Lesbos, an island principality which had been thought to be a strong bulwark and which above all had tried hard to maintain some degree of freedom by steadily raised tribute payments. There was now little doubt that the rapidly growing naval power of the Ottomans would sooner or later attack the remaining Venetian possessions in the Morea and the islands, including the

---

[10] See also for the following, J. W. Zinkeisen, *Geschichte des osmanischen Reiches in Europa*, II, Gotha, 1854, 18–39.

[11] Pastor, II, 242f.

largest: Negroponte (Euboea), a Venetian possession since the early fourteenth century.[12] The final decision was taken, partly at least, due to vigorous prodding by Cardinal Bessarion, who went to Venice in July 1463 and could, after a few days, report that the declaration of war had definitely been decided upon.

Just as Lesbos and the Morea determined Venice's decision for war, so the fall of Bosnia decided the attitude of Hungary. The conquest, in 1463, of that country, whose King, Stephen Tomašević, had been a vassal of the Hungarian crown, made it clear that Hungary was by no means safe from attack.[13]

The question remained, however, whether Venice and Hungary would be able to bury their age-old hostility over Dalmatia.[14] Some preparatory work, highly valuable for the Curia, had been done in this direction by Cardinal Carvajal during his prolonged stay at the court of Matthias. Now the combination of the military threat from the Ottomans with the friendly pressure exerted by Rome was successful, the more so as the Holy See, recently much enriched by the discovery of abundant alum ores within the borders of the Papal States, could now promise considerable subsidies.[15] On September 12, 1463, a treaty of alliance was signed between Venice and Hungary at Nagyvárad.[16] Thus, despite the complete lack of cooperation in the West, despite the meagerness of the response of the Italian states, whom Pius addressed at the same time,[17] something like a real hope for action seemed to arise in the fall of 1463, especially when Skanderbeg, Prince of Albania, long one of Sultan Mohammed's most hardy and dangerous enemies, joined the coalition.[18] These hopes, at the time, were substantial enough to make Pope Pius' insistence in personally leading the crusade appear less fantastic and less theatrical than it might otherwise be judged to have been.[19]

[12] For the conquest of Lesbos see Zinkeisen, op.cit., II, 238–246; for the defense and loss of Negroponte, ibid., II, 319–326, also the corresponding passages in Babinger, Mehmed der Eroberer, 224–229, 299–305. Zinkeisen, incidentally, though not yet in possession of all the sources, has a lively and generally very good description of the policy of Pope Pius toward the Turks on pp. 248–295.

[13] Ibid., 150–158.

[14] For the origins of their struggle, See B. Homan, Geschichte des ungarischen Mittelalters, Berlin, 1940, I, 368–374. The same struggle in a later period, the reign of Sigismund of Luxemburg, is treated by Aschbach, Geschichte Kaiser Sigmunds, I, Hamburg, 1838, 213–224; II, 1839, 406–411; IV, 1845, 48-55.

[15] See Pius II, Commentaries, VII, 505–507. See also Pastor, II, 259–262.

[16] See the treaty in A. Theiner, Vetera monumenta historica Hungariam sacram illustrantia, II, Rome 1860, 380–382.

[17] Note especially the violent resistance of Florence, Pius' Commentaries XII, 812–817.

[18] Zinkeisen, op.cit., II, 388ff.

[19] See e.g. Hocks, Pius II und der Halbmond, 178–192.

Even before the treaty between Matthias and Venice was concluded, the Curia had had some part in another detente by which the King of Hungary had strengthened his position: a treaty of peace concluded with Emperor Frederick at Wiener-Neustadt in July 1463.[20] It was a development which King George had neither helped nor hindered, but which, in terms of the balance of power, was bound to weaken him. Both these great neighbors now needed his support or at least his friendly neutrality much less than they had as long as they had been at each other's throats. (We shall observe the consequences later.)

Indeed the Emperor, shortly before his final decision to settle his difficulties with Hungary, had been in truly desperate need of King George's support, and this he received in ample measures. In the total course of George's reign this action for Frederick III will figure essentially as an important episode which might well have been more than that if George had not himself later thrown away some of the fruits of his own actions.

The near-catastrophe from which George had to save the Emperor had its origin in those inner-Austrian struggles which have engaged our attention before. The open warfare in which Archduke Albert, supported by Hungarian troops and confident also of Czech help, had engaged against his brother had been ended by the treaty of Laxenburg (September 6, 1461).[21] It was essentially an armistice which King George had forced upon the two sides, notwithstanding the unwillingness of his own allies, Matthias and Albert. Whether the archduke assumed that the King of Bohemia had not really meant the war to cease altogether or whether he merely felt that he was not bound by the agreement, he certainly did not keep it even in the period immediately following. The very structure of the armistice of Laxenburg made it rather easy for him; it had tried to end the fighting between the Habsburg brothers on the basis of the status quo reached as a result of the fighting, without any clear delimitation of which area, especially in Lower Austria, was to belong to whom. It was even worse that the hostile brothers had released their mercenaries, often without having paid them off, in the more or less correct expectation that they would recoup themselves for those demands by attacks on the territories and villages of the other side. Sufferings of the people, especially the peasants, of Lower Austria increased considerably when this land (as subsequently most of Central Europe) was hit in 1461

---

[20] See Voigt, *Enea Silvia*, III, 681ff., and Bachmann, *Reichsgeschichte*, I, 389–391.
[21] The text in Kurz, *Oesterreich unter K. Friedrich IV*, II, Docum. appendix XXIX, 224–227. See its discussion by Bachmann, *Reichsgeschichte*, I, 108ff.

and 1462 by a severe epidemic of the bubonic plague.[22] This again induced the Emperor to cancel a long awaited travel to Vienna, where he had been expected to attend a general diet and also meet King George of Bohemia in an effort to turn the armistice of Laxenburg into a real peace. The Emperor's decision to call off the diet was received with great disappointment and anger everywhere, even in Vienna, which had so far kept faith with Frederick but was now suffering almost as badly from the general chaos and economic distress as the rural areas of Austria. But the Emperor also forbade the meeting of another diet which Archduke Albert had called to Melk, and before long the war between the brothers was again in full swing, with the Emperor's old Czech general, John Jiskra, waging the usual fight of devastation in the region of St. Pölten, while the archduke's condottieri, in the foreground the notorious lansquenet leader with the romantic name Nabuchodonossor Nanckenreutter, established in the name of the archduke a number of strongholds in the immediate surroundings of Vienna.[23]

When, despite Vienna's ever-repeated call for help, the Emperor maintained his complete inactivity regarding Lower Austria, the city decided, for the first time without the Emperor's permission, to take part in a diet of nobility and cities held at Städteldorf in May 1462 which tried to force an effective armistice upon the two warring Habsburg rulers.[24] The Emperor, when officially informed, agreed and again promised soon to come to Vienna, where the Empress and his little son, Maximilian, had already taken residence.

For all his lethargic ways of government the Emperor's position was still far from hopeless when, in June 1462, at the time the armistice of Laxenburg expired, Archduke Albert sent a new declaration of war to his brother. Not only Vienna but also several other cities and above all an assembly of the estates decided to support the Emperor, basing their attitude upon Frederick's promise to appear in Vienna at the earliest time with a strong army and there to settle all grievances. If he had now finally fulfilled this promise, his adherents in Vienna, among them the old burgomaster Brenner [25] and the great majority of

---

[22] See the source references in *ibid.*, I, 262f.

[23] See *ibid.*, 264f., with the main source used the *Copey-Buch der gemeinen Stat Wienn*, ed. Zeibig, *FRA*, II 7, 1853, 277ff.

[24] *Copey-Buch*, 312f.

[25] Thus based on the *Copey-Buch*, Bachmann, *Reichsgeschichte*, I 299. In our other important source: "Anonymi Chronicon Austriacum," in Senckenberg, *Selecta iuris et historiarum*, V, he is called Prauner. (This work henceforth cited as "Anonymus.")

the city council, might have prevailed. His extreme penchant to procrastination weakened his friends and strengthened his enemies in the
city. It is difficult to analyze the division among the two parties—for
and against the Emperor, and implicitly against and for Archduke
Albert—in terms of class structure or the socio-economic background
of the main actors. This could be of some importance, as we shall see,
for the understanding of King George's later intervention. Though
there might have been a bias for the Emperor among the well-to-do
circles of the population, it was by no means obvious or strong, and not
a few of the members of the high nobility outside Vienna stood by
the archduke.[26] It is, in any case, interesting that the university, with
the majority of its masters, in a declaration of neutrality, turned practically against the Emperor,[27] and that the movement to overthrow
the present loyalist city government was headed by a university professor, John Kirchheim, then considered one of the leading physicians
of Austria. In August, Dr. Kirchheim organized the rebellion and with
sixty accomplices[28] arrested by a surprise coup the mayor and the
councillors. But the new burgomaster now elected did not come from
an academic background. It was Wolfgang Holzer, a wealthy former
cattle dealer who owed his rise to considerable power (temporarily as
treasurer of Lower Austria) to Ulrich Eizinger (who late in 1460 had
died of the plague). A capable, unscrupulous, and highly ambitious
man with fine oratorical gifts, Holzer was quite willing to lead the city
on her new way of opposition to the Emperor and to accept, in the
process, any financial and military support which the Emperor's
brother might be willing to provide.[29]

But the news of the overthrow of the city government in Vienna
achieved what all the humble but urgent petitions of the overthrown

---

26 " . . . Khirchaimb und andere . . . zugen die bürger unziemblicher und unbilligen
handlungen, darums der Rath und gemain gegen ainander in zwitracht khamen, und die
gemain hielt sich des Rhömischen Khaisers" ("Anonymus," 158).

27 See Bachmann, *Reichsgeschichte*, I, 296f.

28 "Anonymus," 158–160.

29 Holzer is an interesting, if not particularly attractive character, who might well deserve a monographic study which so far, to my knowledge, he has not received. Among the
contemporary sources—the majority of whom tended to take the Emperor's side—he is
treated with considerable dislike as nothing but an ambitious and utterly unscrupulous
demagogue. This is true for Ebendorfer, Hinderbach, Beheim and the "Anonymus." (for the
latter, see pp. 161f.) Among later historians, Kurz (*Oesterreich unter Friedrich IV*) treats
him with special loathing, both in introducing him (II, 33f.) and in discussing his horrible
death a few months later (*ibid.*, 57f.) Somewhat less biased is Krones (*Oesterreichische
Geschichte für das Volk*, VI, 1437–1526), 124, 125, 129. Bachmann, (*Reichsgeschichte*, I,
300) limits himself to a few words of characterization and later tries to let the facts speak
for themselves (chapters 13 and 14, *passim*).

council had failed to achieve: the Emperor realized that his whole position in his hereditary lands was in danger, and he finally bestirred
himself.[30] Already by August 15 an imperial army of considerable size,
including the feudal levies from Styria and Carinthia, Frederick's
faithful home duchies, as well as sizable mercenary troops (including
some of the Czech bratříci) had assembled at Wiener-Neustadt, to
which place additional levies from the faithful in Lower Austria itself
were also summoned. But before he could move there arrived at
Wiener-Neustadt a delegation of the new Vienna council, led by Dr.
Kirchheim, who tried to explain that the old council had only been
removed because of misconduct, and that the new one was as faithful
to His Imperial Majesty as any of its predecessors. They asked the Emperor to be gracious to them as he had been in the past.

Behind the humble petition, however, stood a threat: the Viennese
had within their reach the most valuable hostages imaginable: Empress
Leonora and the little crown prince, Maximilian. The Emperor,
warned that things might get out of hand in Vienna if he did not
arrive soon, promised the envoys that there would be no punishment
provided that no further unrest took place in the city. When, however,
Frederick with his army arrived before the city he found that the
council, frightened by rumors about an impending attack, had bar-

---

[30] The sources for the following narrative, up to and including the Emperor's arrival in
Vienna, the siege of the Hofburg (Castle), the appeal to King George and his actions, are
quite rich. Two of the contemporary witnesses, Johann Hinderbach (*Historiae Austriacae
Aeneae Silvii Continuatio,* ed. A. F. Kollar, *Analecta Monumentorum omnis aevi Vindo-
bonensia,* II, Vienna, 1762), and Michael Beheim, author of the long verse chronicle called
Buch von den Wienern, were personally engaged in these events and thus direct eye witnesses. The latter was published twice, first in Hormayr's *Taschenbuch für die Vaterländische
Geschichte,* vols. 6 to 8, Vienna, 1825ff., and then again in an approach to a critical edition
by the same title by Th. G. von Karajan, Vienna, 1843. (See also the important details to
be found in the works of Thomas Ebendorfer of Haselbach, both in his *Chronicon Austriacum,* ed. H. Pez, SRA II, Leipzig, 1725, 959ff., and in his *Chronica regum Romanorum,*
MIÖG, Vienna, 1890, Ergänzungsband, III, 197ff. Also Ebendorfer, being a university man,
was not biased in favor of the Emperor whom, on the contrary, he now began to judge
highly critically. (See on this Alphons Lhotsky, *Thomas Ebendorfer,* Stuttgart, 1957, 53f.)
The author of the *"Anonymus,"* (see especially pp. 147–187), also was a contemporary
observer, being rather near the events in question. Pope Pius' *Commentaries,* (X, 628–633),
while doubtlessly contemporary, are second-hand and in this case replete with wrong facts
and distorted judgments. (On his special evaluation of George's policy see later.) Among
Czech sources see SLČP 159f., and T. Pešina (of course, no longer a contemporary but
often in possession of contemporary sources otherwise lost), *Mars Moravicus,* 729ff. Among
modern narratives see Palacký, *Dějiny,* IV, 2, 225–234 (German, 256–267); the most
detailed and all-round best account is probably still Bachmann's in *Reichsgeschichte,* I, 294–
352. (He also published some pertinent correspondence in FRA II 44, 456–475). His account seems superior to that by Huber in *Geschichte Oesterreichs,* III, 151ff., or even the
much more recent Vancsa, *Geschichte Nieder- und Oberösterreichs,* II, 385–405. See finally
Urbánek, *Věk,* IV 617–630.

ricaded the gates. The Emperor with his court had to camp outside while at the same time Holzer secretly admitted, through the western gates, a troop of 400 cavalry sent to him by Archduke Albert. Only four days later, and after further negotiations in which Holzer himself took a hand, was the Emperor, together with a small part of his troops, admitted into the city, but only because he had agreed to the demand of Holzer and his followers to dismiss the mercenaries in his service.

This concession proved to be a fateful mistake. The Emperor did not have the money, at this stage, to pay off the mercenaries, and Holzer, in the name of the city, refused to make any contribution to this and even protested the Emperor's attempt to get money through mortgages on some of his castles. When the Emperor tried to replace Holzer's government by a city council of his own choice the result was new uproar. It ended with a second election of Holzer whom, to show his good will, the Emperor now confirmed. But the break was already unavoidable, especially when late in September the leaders of the dismissed and unpaid mercenaries sent a letter of challenge to the Emperor and immediately began waging war against the city and its surroundings, an event for which the city made the Emperor alone responsible.

Eventually, after a meeting of the commune, to which the Emperor, almost like an accused man, had been summoned but had of course not appeared, the city government sent him, on October 5, a letter declaring that, after all the damage Vienna had sustained through the Emperor's fault, the city was now forced to join those working for peace (that is, the group of cities and nobles now in alliance with Archduke Albert.) They declared themselves no longer bound by the oaths of loyalty and obedience sworn to the Emperor previously, and would no longer pay any taxes to him.[31] It was very nearly a declaration of war, and this was confirmed by the arrest, on Holzer's order, of several of the Emperor's councillors who happened to have gone out from the castle into the city, as well as of Viennese citizens known as being on Frederick's side. As a result of these arrests a number of loyalist citizens, fearing for their freedom, fled into the Hofburg, the old, very strong ducal castle which had only recently (in 1444 and 1447) been considerably enlarged and strengthened. It was now, as fast as possible, put into a state of readiness against the expected onslaught.[32] The total

31 See the text in "Anonymus," 169–177.

32 See T. G. v. Karajan, *Die alte Kaiserburg zu Wien*, Vienna, 1863, p. 11, as quoted by Bachmann, *Reichsgeschichte*, I, 320, n. 4.

number of defenders—less than 300 men, about half of them mercenaries [33]—was small but, since they had plenty of firearms and other weapons, able to put up a good defensive fight. It was worse that there was at least an equal number of noncombatants in the castle which would shorten the period during which food and other provisions could last. Nevertheless, when the Viennese city council offered safe conduct for the Empress and the little prince, the Emperor declined.

The actual fight between the castle and the city began by mid-October, but letters of challenge were not sent to the Emperor until October 19th. About the same time large numbers of challenges were received by the city from those members of the nobility who were on the Emperor's side. The struggle itself was essentially a prolonged artillery duel between the castle and the city houses in the neighborhood, some of which had been turned into forts. In this duel the castle clearly held the advantage, since many of those houses were soon reduced to rubble. What the defenders of the castle had to fear was starvation. Thus both sides tried to strengthen for a showdown. Holzer, impatient of the long and so far ineffectual attacks on the castle, sent a call for help to Archduke Albert, who soon arrived in Vienna with troops and heavy siege artillery. He, together with the council, offered the Emperor free egress from castle and city, provided that he cede the government of Lower Austria to a regency council which was to govern the duchy in the name of young Maximilian. As expected and presumably intended, the Emperor declined, having good reasons to doubt that the offer would be fully kept. Altogether Frederick showed both courage and tenacity in a situation in which the main task was to hold on to what he had, not to display any far-reaching activity.

This task, indeed, had to be left to others. There was only one side from which fast, substantial help could be hoped for: the King of Bohemia. George, until last March still allied with Archduke Albert, had meanwhile taken steps to overcome the remaining coolness which the Emperor had displayed to him after the double victory of the Wittelsbachs. In September he had sent Prokop of Rabstein, released from detention and fully restored to grace and office, to the Emperor. Through him he had assured the Emperor that, in case of serious difficulties, he could count upon Bohemia's help. The Emperor on his side had promised to use his influence on Pius II to prevent rash and dangerous actions by the Holy See. A strong letter with this purpose in mind was indeed sent to the Pope on October 1st.[34]

[33] Main source here is Behaim, *Buch von den Wienern*, ed. Karajan, 62, 64.
[34] See *FRA* II, 20, 280.

George, on his part, tried to warn the people of Vienna immediately upon hearing about the last changes in the city government and the growing hostility among the Viennese people. When the Vienna city council neither answered nor permitted a letter from the King to be passed through to the castle, George did not even wait for an official call from Frederick but sent, at the end of October, his letter of challenge to the city.[35]

But this step alone would hardly have saved the defenders of the castle in their steadily worsening plight. In those days of slow communication the time element was crucial. Extraordinary measures were needed, and they were provided by a man who was then one of the Emperor's most faithful adherents. Andrew Baumkircher was a member of the nobility of the mostly German districts of Western Hungary (called Burgenland today) who had served as captain of Bratislava and had taken some part in the negotiations leading to the armistice of Laxenburg. He was thus known quite well to King George. His dash from Wiener-Neustadt to Prague, a distance of over 200 miles, was one of those epic rides which tended to become famous in history, and it even found its contemporary bard in Frederick's court poet, Michael Beheim. Beheim, for all his use of poetical license, was present in the castle during the siege and got his information on the fighting as well as on Baumkircher's mission to Prague at first hand. Thus even if we discount some of the more suspiciously romantic elements [36] he remains an important witness. According to the poet, Baumkircher set out at nightfall on October 26 with a cavalcade of forty people, went on without rest day and night, and arrived with only four riders in the evening of October 29, the rest having been unable to maintain the furious pace. He was immediately received by George, who promised him the most speedy action and agreed that Baumkircher, on his return trip, be accompanied by Prince Victorin and Lord Zdeněk of Sternberg with 600 horse.

The early days of November saw the little army grow as it was joined by Czech and Austrian troops while the King had ordered a general levy with horse and infantry to move via Znojmo into Austria. At the same time George called on the diet of German princes just meeting at Regensburg as well as other courts to contribute to the action. By mid-November Czech forces, amounting to some 20,000 men,

35 See George's report in his letter to John of Rosenberg, A.C., V, 288.
36 As when he lets Baumkircher, upon his arrival in Prague, offer his wife and children as hostages and his possessions in western Hungary as security, while King George, with almost equal generosity, promises him immediate help without any expectations of reward (pp. 145ff.)

in conjunctions with Austrians had begun to draw a circle around the Austrian capital. The situation, now, was a strange one: Here was a castle besieged by a great city and its allies, but these in turn were nearly, and increasingly surrounded and besieged by an army which, in the terms of the time, was truly formidable.

Of the two, at this stage, the castle was in greater immediate peril. There, provisions had fallen to a dangerously low state while there was, as yet, no immediate shortage of food and other provisions in Vienna. This, presumably, was the main reason why the King, from the beginning, contemplated a direct assault. When, however, Archduke Albert, until so recently his friend and ally, requested negotiations George agreed to a short armistice of two days, stipulating that, during the same period, all bombardment of the Hofburg had to cease as well. The two princes met on November 16th on a boat on the Danube, half-way between Korneuburg, on the left bank, where the Czechs had established their headquarters, and Klosterneuburg, on the right bank, occupied by Albert's strongest contingents, commanded by his captain Nebuchodonossor Nanckenreutter. The negotiations—though the armistice was prolonged by another two days—remained fruitless, and the archduke angrily returned to Vienna.[37] King George now decided upon immediate offensive action. The plan was for the main Czech army to force the Danube from the North, while the smaller Czech contingents under Prince Victorin—which had crossed early and taken up positions in the South—would, in conjunction with the Austrian imperialist troops standing in the southwest below the Wienerwald hills, start the main assault as soon as fire signals showed that the Viennese were occupied with defending the northern approaches. The scheme misfired. The Viennese had succeeded in burning the northern bridges before the Czechs had taken them, and when, on November 19th, the troops in the south, seeing a fire burning, believed this to be the signal for their advance they found the ramparts fully manned and were beaten back.[38] For the moment the Viennese considered themselves the victors, and Holzer did his best to maintain this feeling.

In reality their situation was anything but hopeful. They could possibly force, before long, the castle's inhabitants to surrender, but they also knew that whatever they did to them would be paid back with interest. In the long run Vienna could not prevail, and there were too

[37] See Hinderbach, *Historiae Austriacae,* 642; "Anonymus" 181.
[38] On these developments see, beside the sources mentioned in the previous note, the detailed report in *FRA* II 44, 469–472, and Ebendorfer, *Chronic. regum Rom.,* 199.

many people in the city who, after the first triumphal mood had evaporated, were not only conscious of the hopelessness of permanent resistance but even eager, against the wishes of Holzer, to seek a
compromise. Thus when Archduke Albert and his advisers learned
that King George was willing once more to try negotiations they were
more than ready for it. During the last days of November a real peace
conference began in Korneuburg, with prominent representatives from
all sides taking part.[39] Besides King George himself and a number of
the most prominent Czech leaders, they included the archduke with
some of his baronial adherents, Frederick's chief counsellor, George of
Volkensdorff, Andrew Baumkircher as representative of the imperial
army, and finally representatives of the city of Vienna, including the
burgomaster. After long and difficult negotiations in which George
repeatedly had to overcome strong resistance from both sides, an agreement was signed on December 2nd which, on the same day, was taken
to the castle by a delegation consisting mostly of Czech barons led by
John of Rosenberg. The Emperor, informed that some further discussions on details would be conducted in his presence, set his seal under
the document.

After a preamble declaring all causes and all forms of the war to be
ended, the peace treaty [40] returned to the Emperor, as his rightful property, "all castles, cities, lands, people and estates which he has gained
recently and in past wars" in the duchy of Lower Austria. The Emperor, on the other hand, entrusted, for the next eight years, the
government of the duchy to his brother "as a ruling lord and prince."
At the end of this period, or at the death of the archduke—if this
should occur earlier—the rule of the duchy would revert to the Emperor or his heir. As long as the archduke administered the duchy he
would pay, out of his income, 4,000 Hungarian ducats annually to the
Emperor. All prisoners, especially those arrested because of their
loyalty to the Emperor, were to be freed, and all material damages
suffered during the siege and bombardment of the castle by the
Emperor, the Empress and members of their court or their followers
to be fully repaired or compensation given.

The treaty, one of the most important pieces of arbitration achieved
by George,[41] could not possibly make both sides happy; yet it was as
satisfactory a compromise as could gain acceptance. It tried to safe-

[39] The Text in Kurz, *Oesterreich unter Friedrich IV*, II, docum. appendix XXXXI,
232–236.
[40] See Hinderbach, *Historiae Austriacae*, 657f.
[41] See the letter to Elector Frederick of Saxony, *FRA*, II, 44, 471f.

guard all the basic legal prerogatives which the Emperor, in all phases of his long reign, was anixous to defend. On the other hand the arch-duke—at this time surely the choice of the majority of the people of Lower Austria including Vienna—was to gain the substance of his demand that the actual government of both Austrias, Upper and Lower, were to be united in his hands, if only as a sort of limited and temporary enfeoffment by his brother. The limitations—such as the demand for the previous surrender of the castles and for the regular payment of a considerable part of the tax income, but also for the liberation of the prisoners in the hands of the Viennese city council— all met strong resistance from Holzer, who, at a meeting of the commune in the Cathedral of St. Stephen on December 3, tried once more to whip up popular resistance against the Emperor and therewith also against the treaty. He lost out when the archduke, worried by the threat of a renewed and this time perhaps ruinous war with the Czechs, defended the agreement and asked for a show of hands in its favor.[42] Holzer, as a last (but rather profitable) gesture of defiance, during the night after the agreement was made, organized a great common action of his adherents pilfering all the houses belonging to those whom he knew or suspected of sympathies for the Emperor.[43]

At about the same time the Emperor and his family left the castle, at whose gates they were received by Duke Victorin and a number of prominent Czech nobles. He met King George at Korneuburg, where the two rulers spent a week together.[44]

King George, during this time, made a real effort to achieve a re-conciliation between the Habsburg brothers. With some difficulty he overcame the reluctance of Archduke Albert to go to the King's head-quarters at Korneuburg.[45] Yet the success of the meeting was extremely limited.[46] The Emperor, still full of hatred, refused to speak to his ever-rebellious brother when the latter attempted to address him, and the archduke could achieve any exchange of views only through the Emperor's chief adviser, Volkensdorff, acting, as it were, as interpreter. The main material stumbling block arose around competing claims to the cities and castles of Lower Austria. The archduke even de-manded that King George, beyond his work of arbitration, go to the length of providing special guarantees for his installment as the de

[42] Hinderbach, *Historiae Austriacae*, 657f. and 663.

[43] "Anonymus", V, 183f.

[44] Hinderbach, *Historiae Austriacae*, 665f.

[45] See the sources in Bachmann, *Reichsgeschichte*, I, 346 n.l.

[46] "Anonymus," 184.

facto ruler of Lower Austria, a request which the King somewhat angrily refused. The only issue which was positively settled was arrangements about the release, according to the treaty, of all prisoners. The other questions, especially those regarding the cities and castles, remained unsolved and soon provided enough friction for the struggle between the Habsburg princes to break out again in the old, militant forms.

The two brothers, indeed, separated on the following day, still without having spoken to one another. Albert went to Vienna, where he immediately demanded—and obtained—an act of homage.[47] The Emperor, accompanied by the King of Bohemia and his army, went eastward to Enzersdorf, where the two rulers stayed together till December 16th. From there Frederick went to Wiener-Neustadt, George to Brno on his way back to Prague. They separated as the closest of friends.

From the beginning of George's involvement in the Emperor's dramatic conflict with Vienna, it was clear that the Czech King had substantially switched his friendship from Albert to Frederick, a change already anticipated by the armistice of Laxenburg. This was true even though, during the negotiations at Korneuburg, he had been rather careful to maintain the attitude of essential neutrality which would make his arbitration acceptable to Albert as well as to Frederick. Thus he had sent his declaration of war only to the city of Vienna, never to the archduke.

There was presumably more than one motive for George's energetic and on the whole—despite the temporary setback—successful action, which at the time created a real sensation all over Europe. Obviously he was not just embarking on a selfless and romantic adventure of liberation, though this is exactly the light in which Michael Beheim would have liked to make his action appear. Nor was it, as George's enemies, including the Pope, claimed, a devilish design meant to keep the Habsburgs as weak as possible by never allowing their struggle to abate.[48] On the contrary George did what was in his power to consolidate the situation in Central Europe, which he considered a benefit to himself and his country.

But to suggest that he acted as a Sir Galahad is almost as absurd as to blame him for not having acted in this way. For one thing this was

[47] *Ibid.*, 186.
[48] See Pius II, *Commentaries*, X, 631f. See also his letter to the Emperor in *FRA* II, 20, 287–289, discussed later in this chapter.

a costly expedition, and George was far too parsimonious a ruler to spend so much money if he could not have hoped for some worthwhile gains.[49] It was almost a matter of course that the Emperor would make arrangements to indemnify the King for those financial outlays: he was to receive, in permanence, one-half of the income from the wine- and the salt-tax of the duchy of Lower Austria. Frederick did this, however, on the spur of the moment and regretted it later. Other proofs of his largesse came easier to him. He did not have to be pressed to show his gratitude in forms which would not later appear as a mortgage. Beside such presents as a new golden crown for Queen Johanna and a golden chain for the King, George's sons Henry and Hynek (Ignatius) were, as previously had been Prince Victorin, raised to the rank of princes of the Empire, dukes of Münsterberg, and imperial counts of Glatz. In case of the Emperor's premature death King George was to be the chief guardian of his son Maximilian with a yearly income of 10,000 ducats, and in case his son as well as the Emperor should die without heirs, King George should have the right to follow him in his hereditary duchies, a claim which would be redeemable only by other members of the house of Habsburg through payment of 100,000 ducats. The special privileges of the kingdom of Bohemia, defined first by the Emperor Frederick II in the Golden Bull of 1212, were improved. For example the Czech contribution to the Roman crowning expedition of the Emperor—anyhow merely an insignificant formality—were reduced to one-half. More important was the Emperor's decree that in the future no King or Emperor of the Romans should, directly or through one or several of his captains, give orders to or make demands on subjects of the King of Bohemia which in any way would infringe on the "liberties of the Kingdom." Here, clearly, George's interpretation of the full sovereignty of the kingdom —an interpretation which had previously led to his declaration of war against Margrave Albert Achilles of Brandenburg—was acknowledged and confirmed. This concession should make it easier, also, to bridge the gap which still separated George and Albert. In this regard a special agreement[50] said that the Emperor was to reconcile the King with the Margrave, while the King was to reconcile Duke Louis of

---

[49] For all the following rewards and concessions by the Emperor, see Ebendorfer, *Chronicon Austr.*, 964, and Chmel, *Regesta chronologica diplomatica Friderici III*, II, 397–398. See also Lünig, *Reichsarchiv*, VI, 2, 84, as quoted by Bachmann, *Reichsgeschichte*, I, 349, n.2. Besides King George and his family, the Czech nobles who had participated in the action, with Zdeněk of Sternberg in the lead, also received substantial rewards. See the sources in *ibid.*, V. 351f.

[50] See *FRA*, II, 20, 284f.

Bavaria with the Emperor. Finally both rulers would support a rapprochement between the two princes, the Emperor particularly by
supporting, and sending his envoys to, a great congress of intra-im-
perial pacification to be held in Prague in the near future. Another
assurance of cooperation consisted in the King's promise to help in the future, as in the past, to maintain the Emperor's claims in his hereditary
lands, while the Emperor promised to see that the internal peace in
Bohemia should not be disturbed by actions of the Pope.[51]

The political gains that now developed, and which George had quite
justifiably anticipated, were clearly the main factors which induced
him to put all this effort into his actions in the Emperor's favor. Frederick's continued, and indeed intensified, intercession with his old
friend and secretary who was now Pope was surely one of these
political gains—though it may be doubtful whether one should consider this intercession, temporarily successful as it proved to be, as
necessarily the most important of these gains. Perhaps it was even more
crucial for George's political position, especially in the long run, that
the Viennese campaign with all that it entailed gave him an excellent
opportunity to mend his relations with all the German princes of the
so-called imperial party—in particular the princes of Hohenzollern
and Wettin—without thereby losing his contacts and too much of his
influence with the Wittelsbachs. Nobody could, at the time, quite fore-
see how long the effects of this powerful reorientation would last, how
deeply they would implant, especially in Germany, the image of the
King's apparently unbeatable strength, but also of his superior understanding of the quarrels of the time and his unique suitability as the
arbiter of the whole Central European world. From this point of view
George's intervention in the Viennese incident was indeed far more
than an episode, and he achieved pretty much what he expected.

But one other aspect, one other motive remains to be discussed. We
have mentioned previously that George sent a letter of challenge—a
declaration of war—to the city of Vienna even before receiving the request of the Emperor for military support. From some of the communications that came from his side during and immediately after
the campaign, it seems that the King felt rather strongly the need to
put the rebellious city in its place, to punish those impudent people
who had the temerity not only to endanger but even to humiliate
their royal master.[52] This, then, might reflect in some way upon

[51] *Ibid.*, 287ff.

[52] See e.g. his letter to Elector Frederick of Saxony from Korneuburg of December 8 in
FRA, II, 44, 468f., also the letter to the same prince from an anonymous person of George's
entourage, December 16, *ibid.*, 469–472.

George's whole attitude toward the cities and especially to those groups among their people who were, in this as in some other cases, made responsible for the rebellion.

Any attempt at a more complete evaluation of George's views and his role in the socio-economic tensions and shifts of the time will have to wait until our narrative has reached the great crisis of his relationship to the other layers of Bohemia's society, notably of course to the high nobility from which he himself had emerged but from which he had become increasingly separated. It is in the framework of his attempt to put his royal position on a partially new and potentially stabler basis that we have, I believe, eventually also to evaluate his relations to the cities. Yet a glance at this question seems appropriate even at this stage.

At first sight it appears that George was inconsistent. We find him, in the earliest phase of his regency, engaged in destroying the remaining autonomy of the city-theocracy of Tabor. We see him in a short but dramatic conflict with Jihlava, later to be renewed, and in a long and fateful struggle with Breslau, which lasted, except for a relatively short armistice, throughout his whole reign. Eventually Pilsen, too, was to enter the ranks of his more permanent antagonists. On the other hand he was, as we shall see, not only a "gracious lord" but an effective promoter of the legal and economic interests of the majority of the cities, Prague above all, but also Kutná Hora and the great majority of the cities of Bohemia proper. That this favor was not limited to ethnically Czech cities is seen by the special warmth of his relation with the predominantly German people of Cheb. Among the great cities of Moravia, Brno enjoyed his favor, and a fair number of towns in Silesia and Lusatia had reason to appreciate his friendly, and for them profitable, proto-mercantilism. (This was, during the peace or at least armistice existing in 1460 and 1461, even true for and acknowledged by Breslau.)

We can hardly go wrong in assuming that, in principle, George's policy was friendly to the cities, that he considered them, financially as well as politically, one of the mainstays of the strong kingship which he had built and was trying to consolidate, and that his collisions with the first-named cities had some special reasons—exceptions then, rather than the rule. Again the names of these cities seem to indicate that the main issue creating hostility was a religious one. Hussite radicalism in the case of Tabor, irreconcilably anti-Hussite radicalism in the cases of Jihlava, Breslau, and Pilsen. While this is obviously true, we must look closer. There were many good Catholic cities in the realm—Cheb was by no means the only one essentially untouched by the "poison" of Hussitism—whose relation with George was friendly and close, until the combined pressure of Rome and the League of the Lords forced them to at least an outward compliance with Church policy. Finally we must not forget that in all the cases mentioned above, with the partial exception of Tabor, it was the cities rather than George on whose side the antagonism first appeared. In the case of Jihlava and Breslau the situation is especially clear. Here the religiously—and in Breslau partially also nationally—motivated rebellion against the heretical King received its main impulse from the lower stratum of urban society, especially the craftsmen organized in the guilds and led by popular preachers, not unlike the rebellion of Prague against King Sigismund in the early years of the Hussite Revolution.

It would, thus, not be astonishing to find George distrustful of, even hostile to urban rebellions resulting in the overthrow of an older, senatorial regime by popular leaders of the commune. The real socio-economic background of the Vienna rebellion of late 1462 is far from clear, and far from properly investigated. The question whether and to what extent this can be considered a true parallel to the rebellion of Prague against Sigismund, of Jihlava and Breslau against George, must therefore as yet remain unanswered. But that the general appearance of events seemed to indicate such a parallel can hardly be doubted. It seems almost certain that George must have seen the situation in this light, and this gives his action a certain emotional quality which it would otherwise not possess. He might even have had Breslau in mind in a more distinct way. This was, after all, the time at which, according to the treaty of January 1460, the city should finally have done homage to King George as a Christian King. In view of the recent and violent deterioration of his relationship with the Curia, and of the way in which Pope Pius had already officially encouraged the city's challenging attitude toward its King, an early showdown with Breslau was clearly a very real possibility. For this George would need understanding and what might be called "moral support" not only in his own country and in Silesia—where he could as yet be fairly sure of it—but also in other lands and especially in the Empire. If he now had so effectively supported the Emperor against his rebellious city of Vienna, then he could expect, if not a real support, then at the very least a benevolent neutrality of the Emperor toward his own action against the rebellious city of Breslau.

That such an action might be imminent was clear to the people of Breslau as well as to the Pope himself. Two years earlier Pope Pius, in the case of such a conflict, would still have taken George's side. Now even George's action against Vienna, though Pius could not help approving of its result, appeared to him in the worst possible light. In a long letter to the Emperor [53] he thanks God for his delivery. He acknowledges the fact that the Emperor "had no other hope for salvation than the King of Bohemia, as the only one who was able to curb the impudent Viennese and to restore your freedom to you." Therefore he understands that the Emperor now wants him to stop the proceedings against King George. "Oh unfortunate age," the Pope continues, "oh poor Germany, oh unhappy Christianity, whose Emperor can be saved only by a heretical King." Thus, since he, the Pope, could not save the Emperor himself, and since all his attempts to make other princes come to his help proved of no avail, "we now bowed our head and for your sake suspended all the censures planned against the Bohemian." Finally, however, he states that the Emperor's liberation was not of the sort that he, the Pope, had hoped for. "The Bohemian has used all his artful tricks. He did not want you to perish, but neither did he want you to come out victorious. He wants the Austrians to be locked in perpetual hate and war, so that, playing the role of arbiter, he may end up as their master." This interpretation, as were so many other statements and views of Aeneas Sylvius, was later echoed by a few lesser lights.[54] But it was so clearly refuted by the ample facts that among those modern historians who had access to all or most of the sources even those who otherwise were most inclined to look at George through sharply critical eyes would reject it.[55] Perhaps the facts by which even the skeptics among them were bound to be most impressed are the arrangements and treaties made in Prague, under George's sponsorship and presidency, during the summer of 1463, by which at least some of the vicious circles which had held the Holy Roman Empire in perpetual and exhausting tension and warfare were broken.

[53] See above, n. 48.

[54] Characteristic here is Kurz, *Oesterreich unter Friedrich IV*, II, 51–53.

[55] See especially Bachmann, who in this case does full justice to George's action and motives. See his remarks in *Reichsgeschichte*, I, 346, n. l.

CHAPTER 15

PEACE AND REFORM FOR THE EMPIRE

DURING THE years following the events discussed so far, an enormous effort was made by both King George and the Roman Curia to win over to their sides the leaders—and with them eventually the masses—of the Catholics of the Bohemian realm. These leaders, so the principal actors felt, would in the long run decide the issues. If the King could again persuade them to consider the Compacts as an institution which protected them as well as the Utraquists, and which therefore should not be challenged or destroyed, then the attack of the Curia must be hopeless and its failure sure. If, on the other hand, it was possible to induce the whole of the Catholic minority in Bohemia and Moravia—perhaps almost half of the population, if Silesia and the Lusatias were included—to follow the lead and the orders of Rome up to the last bitter consequences, then the chances for a survival of the Utraquist commonwealth, and with it the Utraquist Church, were dim indeed. Yet for a considerable time both sides manoeuvered rather than trying any direct attack. This was especially true of George, partly because he enjoyed political manoeuvering—his enemies or critics might call it intrigues—and by gaining time, he also hoped to gain strength. Finally, of course, and perhaps most importantly—he was essentially on the defensive, which made it easier for the other side to gain and maintain the initiative. As George did not want all-out war, especially not in military terms, political manoeuvering was indeed a policy which the general situation almost unavoidably imposed on him.

But the various steps which he took merely to maintain the status quo, against an antagonist who demanded change which was no less radical for being a change in a historically backward direction, these various steps would, to historians, not look exactly imposing or heroic. The George who stood before the estates of the realm with the vow to live and die within the Compacts might appear a heroic figure. There is clearly greatness, if less practical value in his scheme of a league of princes, and with this he continued to operate in 1463 and the year after. When, however, he tried again and again to obtain from the Curia a deferment of the threatening measures against him with the assurance that, if only the Pope sent a legate *a latere* to Bohemia to whom he could explain his attitude, everything would be all right and all the doubts about his being a true Christian King would disappear, it is perhaps understandable if neither his contemporaries nor many later historians were impressed.

It is indeed somewhat difficult to imagine that he himself quite believed this possible. He could tell any member of the Curia, any papal legate, no more than what Pius II himself had been told with so much effort and conviction by the Czech ambassadors in March 1462, or what Aeneas Silvius had told Pope Calixtus in 1455. If the present Pope had so thoroughly changed his mind on the possibility of guiding the Czechs back to orthodoxy by pressure or force, then it was partly because George, the successful King, had seemed to be so much better able to do away with the Czech schism than either George the regent, or the earlier Kings since Sigismund. In its attempt to force, by steadily increasing pressure, the Czech King to use his strength against the Utraquist majority of Bohemia, the Curia had put itself in a position where it seemed increasingly difficult for it to compromise, at least on any matters of substance. Rome had taken final success so much for granted—and for a long time George had done rather too little to undeceive her—that all she was ready to grant now, and even that with rapidly decreasing willingness, were short delays of the great process of liquidating Utraquism. It gradually became clear, from George's reaction to the formal repudiation of the Compacts, that his earlier demand for time had not signified his willingness to liquidate the "heresy" but only his readiness to get rid of sectarian excesses, to restore some church properties, and to stabilize ever so firmly the status quo. The Curia, and especially Pope Pius himself, felt to have been the victim of a deliberate deception—although the deception had, to a decisive extent, been the self-deception of Pius II (and to a lesser extent of Cardinal Carvajal). Since George, in his attempts to continue his direct contact with Rome and thus escape Rome's worst weapon, excommunication, could hardly find any other approaches than the ones used for so long, the Roman interpretation that he was a dishonest schemer became ever more firmly established. The propaganda of the city of Breslau greatly stimulated this image of the King.

The radical elements in Breslau could now triumphantly say to the Pope and his court: "We have always told you so!"[1] When Pope Pius

[1] See the memorandum of Breslau's envoy in Jordan, *Königthum*, 389ff.

had urged them to recognize the King, when he had sent his legates to convince them of George's essential orthodoxy, they, and they alone, had insisted that George, as a Hussite, was a heretic who never could nor ever would truly reform! After the arrangement which had allowed them to postpone the act of homage by three years and one month, this propaganda had temporarily ceased, but had been resumed when, in August 1461, the city council had sent a permanent procurator, John Kitzing, to Rome. Kitzing's instructions came mainly from councillors Haunolt and Hornig, close friends of Tempelfeld and the other radical preachers. While initially he had had little success, this changed greatly during and after the Roman sojourn of King George's embassy, and radically after the St. Lawrence Diet of Prague and the arrest of Fantino. Already in late September the Pope declared, in a special bull, that the treaty of January 1460 was, until further notice, to be considered invalid,[2] and in December the Pope also took under his protection the one Silesian prince who, alone among the many, had defied the King: Duke Balthasar, whose small duchy of Sagan had therefore been taken away from him and bestowed by George on his younger brother, Duke John.[3] In January, however, the sanguine hopes of the Breslau agitators for an immediate and effective action, preferably implying George's deposition and replacement, were sharply disappointed: George's successful campaign for the Emperor brought all curial actions against him to an abrupt halt. In Silesia it became especially noticeable when Jerome of Crete, sent by the Pope to look at the situation in Breslau and also to help in settling the war between Poland and the Prussian Order, received the latest news from Austria. New Year 1463 he wrote a letter to the King which was so full of congratulation and admiration, of friendship and of optimism regarding the future relationship between George and the Curia that it sounded as if the critical events of the last spring and summer had never taken place.[4] Breslau's new procurator in Rome, Nicholas Merboth—Kitzing had died in the previous autumn[5]—could, during the early weeks of his service in Rome, report very little that could have cheered his employers. When they heard that early in March King George had actually lodged a protest with the Pope against Breslau's

---

[2] SrS, VIII, 137.

[3] Ibid., 152.

[4] Czech translation of the original message (not preserved) in the Cancellaria regis Georgii, Sternberg Ms, 478–80. Excerpts in Palacký, Dějiny, IV, 2, 243, and Urbánek, Věk, IV, 633.

[5] See Köbner, Widerstand, 107f.

continued defiance, they sent a letter to the Pope which could only be described as a threat with corporative suicide: rather than submit to the heretical King they would put fire to the city and leave it to the last man, woman, and child.[6]

By his time, however, the direct effect of the Emperor's repeated action on behalf of King George had already waned while on the other hand the Czech diplomatic offensive, especially in France, had begun to disturb and annoy Rome. In the early spring of 1463 the two bulls[7] were issued, one of which solemnly declared Breslau to be under papal protection while the other, dated March 29, forbade the city to do homage to George without special permission. In May Jerome of Crete, returned to Breslau from Poland, ordered the bulls to be publicly pronounced in Silesia. But he came up against the resistance of the man who, at this time, can well be considered the spiritual leader of the Czech Catholics: Jost of Rosenberg, Bishop of Breslau. Jost had not been willing to back the King in his attempt to achieve a common front of people of both religions in defense of the Compacts, but neither was he as yet willing to participate in a policy which would clearly jeopardize the political unity and integrity of the Bohemian realm. In a letter to Pope Pius Jost declared that the people of Breslau, whose bishop he was, were neither the only nor necessarily the best Catholic Christians of the Czech realm. He hoped that the Pope would not, for the sake of Breslau, expose all other Catholics under King George's rule to the dangers and sufferings of an open clash. He, together with other good Catholics from all parts of the realm, would see to it that the Christian faith would not suffer.[8] Behind this declaration was a concrete plan for a general conference of Catholic leaders— princes, prelates, nobles, and cities—from Bohemia as well as the dependencies, which would interpose itself between Rome and Prague, forcing the King to give additional guarantees against any further expansion of religious deviation, but at the same time also, by this very policy, disarming the Curia in its attempt to shake and destroy the position of the King as the strict author and representative of domestic union and peace.[9] It is not quite clear why the plan in this form never materialized, even though we know a good deal about the difficulties which Jost encountered especially in his attempt to convince Jerome of

[6] *SrS*, VIII, 180.
[7] *Ibid.*, 183–187.
[8] *FRA*, II, 20, 302ff.
[9] See the various, somewhat confused documentations in Urbánek, *Věk*, IV, 648–650, among them especially *FRA* II, 20, 307–308.

Crete of the correctness of his policy. The two bishops collided, at a Breslau conference in early June, so bitterly that only the presence of the two Dukes of Oels prevented them from resorting to blows.[10] Eventually Jerome, who at this time saw himself almost completely isolated, gave way. He agreed to the temporary suspension of the publication of the bull of March 29 and of any further immediate measures against George. The Catholics should be free to take part in another great peace conference of German princes in Prague.

Jost, at this time, was strongly supported by George with whom, so it seems, he believed himself in full agreement. He had discussed with the King—for a while with the assistance of Tas of Boskovice, the Bishop of Olomouc—the preparation for the great diet, and had succeeded in dissuading George from such aggressive actions as a punitive expedition against Breslau or the public demand for the calling of a church council.[11]

Jost's optimism that the King would now take steps which would satisfy the Curia is as difficult to understand as the optimism of the King that he would now succeed in regaining the support of the Catholics for the maintenance or defense of the Compacts. Jost's hopes, however, are clearly expressed in his correspondence with the Pope[12] and in the reactions of the papal legate at the court of the Emperor, Domenico de' Domenichi, bishop of Torcello, whom George invited to visit him in Prague.[13] The Breslau radicals grew all the more dissatisfied with their bishop. He was, so they wrote the Pope, first of all a Czech baron, of a family that had enriched itself by the acquisition of estates which the heretics had taken from the Church. (As far as this was concerned, they could tell Pius little that he did not know. Indeed he was better informed than most other people about the late Ulrich of Rosenberg and his policy.) In collusion with the King, they continued, Jost actually wanted to prevent the returns of the realm to the Church of Rome.[14] This was probably the low point of the relations between Jost and his cathedral city—though these relations never became really cordial and warm, even at the time when the bishop was forced to come out openly on the side of George's enemies.

---

[10] See Eschenloer, G., I, 212f.

[11] See Bachmann, *Reichsgeschichte*, I 415, with the admission, rather in contradiction to the author's usual judgment, that these were the farthest concessions that, in view of the total situation in Bohemia, could be expected of George.

[12] E.g., *FRA* II 20, 307.

[13] The documentation in Urbánek, *Věk*, IV, 661, n. 214, 215. See esp. *SrS*, VIII, 225, 226.

[14] See Eschenloer, G., I, 213; and *SrS*, VIII, 22ff.

Jost was still a long way from this in the summer of 1463. He was partly responsible for a meeting, in early June, of the leaders of both parties in Prague, which resulted in a letter to the Pope signed, in its majority, by Catholic barons and knights who again urged the Pope to suspend, in the expectation of the impending great diet of Brno, all measures against George.[15] Thus the diet itself began in a general atmosphere of hopeful expectancy—as if it would have been possible for the King, by a sort of magic wand, to solve a crisis which had essentially ceased to be open to solution through the very act of the Holy See—the abrogation of the Compacts.

All such illusions were to fade on the first day, July 18, when the great assembly, with delegates from all the countries of the crown of St. Wenceslas,[16] opened in the castle of Spielberg, where the King had taken residence. The somewhat pathetic character of the meeting is expressed by the close parallels to last year's St. Lawrence Diet even though the most striking event of that meeting—the appearance of Fantino as the grim accuser—was missing.[17]

Again, as then, the first important speech was given by the King. Again he made the most strenuous attempt to convince the Catholics that the Compacts were perpetually valid, and not possibly subject to one-sided cancellation by the Pope, since they had been granted by the Council, which was above the Pope, and confirmed by the Pope's predecessor, Eugene IV. George's own three predecessors had sworn to protect them and had kept this obligation. Could he be expected to act differently? Yet the Pope, believing the mischievous accusations of Breslau, had involved him in the most damaging procedures, thereby gravely endangering the internal peace in the country for which he had worked so hard at the time of his regency as well as his kingship. If the estates wanted to have this peace maintained, then they must not tolerate either the publication or the execution of any papal procedures against him, since their duty toward him as their King was greater and more binding than those to the Pope.

The King had begun and ended his address with the usual request for advice from the estates. Again the estates split into two parties. Again, as in the year before, Zdeněk Kostka, in the name of the Utra-

---

[15] *Ibid.*, 219f.

[16] Markgraf's claim ("Kg. Georg and Papst Pius II, 1462–1464," *HZ*, 1877, p. 244 n.l) that, except for Moravia, none of the dependencies were represented (cautiously taken over also by Bachmann, *Reichsgeschichte*, I, 426) is not quite correct, even though only one of the Silesian princes was present.

[17] The sources are nearly all those of Breslau. See *SrS*, VIII, 258ff., and Eschenloer, G., I 214ff. For interpretive treatment see Palacký, *Dějiny* IV, 2, 247ff.; Markgraf, *op. cit.*, 241ff.; Bachmann, *Reichsgeschichte*, I, 427ff.; and Urbánek, *Věk*, IV, 664ff.

quists presented the enthusiastic declaration of loyalty for the King
and support for the Compacts. The Catholics, however, had at first
some difficulty deciding whether they should be represented by Bishop
Jost at the senior Czech prelate or by Tas, the Bishop of Olomouc,
in whose diocese the diet was being held. The reluctance of both men
to speak up indicates the unhappy position in which they found themselves. In the end it was again Jost who had to try and do the impossible: that it is to combine, in his answer, complete loyalty to the
King with complete loyalty to the Pope. He and his friends, he said,
greatly regretted the papal procedures, but it was to be feared that,
if the King refused to obey the demands of the Pope, the inestimable
achievements of the King's policy of internal peace might get lost.
They wanted to help the King, but not by defying and fighting the
Pope, nor would they like—as the King seems to have demanded—
to wage open war against Breslau, as the city was now under the
Pope's special protection. Whenever the King, Jost said in a later
utterance, were to regain the previous harmony and understanding
with the Pope, Breslau, too, would have to submit to him again.

From the reports—unfortunately preserved only in the Breslau
version, which shows, if no conspicuous distortions, at least rather
obvious ommissions [18]—we can deduct that King George and Bishop
Jost were disappointed with one another. George had expected more
support and less implied criticism from the Bishop and, under his
leadership, also from the Catholics, while Jost had somehow anticipated greater readiness on the part of George to give ground.[19]
George's answer to the Catholics, following a sharp attack on them
by Kostka, sounded rather harsher and less willing to compromise
than his first address. For the first time he spoke, before an important
public audience, like a critic not only of Pope Pius himself but
of the whole Roman establishment, in terms which clearly echoed
the ideas of the living Czech reform movement. The Roman Church,
he said, is far from identical with the Christian Church—the latter
is wider and greater, and represented not by Rome but rather by
ecumenical councils which are above the Pope. This took him back
to the defense of the Compacts, but also forward to the first public
mention—though not the first consideration—of the demand for a new
church council to whom he might have to appeal.

---

[18] See about this Markgraf, *op. cit.*, 243 n.l; also Palacký, *Dějiny*, IV, 2, 247 n. 183.

[19] If, however, Bachmann (*Reichsgeschichte*, I, 419, 430) tries to present Jost as, on the
basis of George's old promises, still expecting the King to drop the Chalice once the time
was ripe, then he clearly neglects the events of the St. Lawrence Diet.

In the course of this concluding speech the King, perhaps realizing how much these last declarations would be resented in Rome, tried to be somewhat more conciliatory. He would, so he said, continue to work for an understanding with the Pope, and he especially emphasized his hopes that the Emperor, as he had promised, would do his utmost to heal the painful breach between Rome and Prague.

During the next few days negotiations took place between the King and his Utraquist friends on the one side and the Catholic prelates and barons on the other. It was a situation which, while foreshadowed by the events of the St. Lawrence Diet, nevertheless went farther in reflecting the widening split in the nation. As often before, the King felt that much of the worst danger arose from the activities of the lower clergy. The year before he had tried to deal with it by addressing and cowing the clergy of both groups. This time, in Moravia where the Utraquist Church had no such strongly developed provincial organization as the Catholics had in their diocese of Olomouc, the King addressed only the representatives of the Roman clergy, with Bishop Tas at their head.[20] He told them that he would not tolerate, in the future, any religious propaganda in forms which attacked Utraquism and its adherents as heresy and heretics, and that any such agitation would in the future be sternly punished. The Bishop of Olomouc, whom George made specifically responsible for the implementation of this order, thus got into a not very enviable position, since he could hardly avoid thereby becoming disobedient either to the King or to the Pope and his legates. He was soon made to feel this through an angry message from Archbishop Jerome of Crete.[21]

Nevertheless the attempt was made, by both sides, to wind up the session of the diet on a note that would not sound too harsh or hopeless. Thus, while no common manifesto could indicate the understanding and agreement that had originally been hoped for, the estates, with prominent participation of the Catholics, did at least send out letters which indicated their willingness to work actively for the maintenance of peace.[22] One, addressed to the Emperor, asked him to renew his efforts for a complete reconciliation between King George and the Pope; the other, directly addressed to Pius II, informed him that

[20] The main source is a letter which the legate Jerome of Crete sent to the bishop. See *SrS*, IX, 1 and 2. I cannot quite see why Urbánek (*Věk*, IV, 668 n. 229) should disagree with Bachmann's assumption (*Reichsgeschichte* I, 432) that this order was given by George during a meeting which he addressed.

[21] *Ibid.*

[22] See *SrS*, VIII, 257, 258.

King George would give the Emperor all the details about his views and intentions so he could negotiate with the Pope on behalf of the King. The estates furthermore begged the Pope to suspend all procedures against the King "to show himself gracious and well inclined to the Kingdom, and by permitting this famous realm, long so lacerated and disturbed by many struggles and wars, to regain its strength in peace and tranquility and thereby to become more useful to God's holy church." Here, at least, if not on the issue of the Compacts itself, we find as yet the two religious parties united: in the consciousness of the immense harm that the country as a whole will suffer if an uncompromising policy pushes her down into the abyss of civil war.

The consciousness of such dangers, if it could be kept fully alert, was bound, for the time being, to strengthen George's and weaken the Pope's position in Bohemia, though it would remain an open question how long George could hold the majority of the Catholics on his side.

At the moment, however, the Pope himself was not unaware of this general mood. In July Emperor Frederick sent his envoy Dr. Hartung Kappel to him to emphasize the King's strength in his own realm and beyond and the degree to which peace in the Empire depended on his good will. Under this impression Pope Pius did agree to suspend the bull of March 29th with it condemnation of George's action, even though the Pope's protection for Breslau and for Duke Balthasar of Sagan was maintained. Archbishop Jerome of Crete, however, was requested to stay in Silesia as papal legate.[23] This welcome news reached the King only after, early in August, he had left Brno for Prague, where several of the delegates of the German princes were waiting for him already.

The chain of events that led to the Prague congress has to be traced back to the Viennese rebellion and its immediate consequences. After the Emperor's liberation he and King George had, as will be remembered, made arrangements intended to achieve a conciliation between the Emperor and Duke Louis through the King's mediation and between the King and Margrave Albert Achilles through the Emperor's mediation. In addition King George had suggested a great peace conference of all parties involved to be held in Prague, to which, at least in principle, Frederick III had also agreed. The way from these arrangements to their implementation was, however, hard to travel

---

[23] Sources for the events reported in this paragraph in *ibid.*, 247–257.

since the distrust of both parties against each other was deep and not easily dispelled. Margrave Albert in particular, while certainly glad to be rid of much if not all of the previous pressure from Prague, was by no means willing to conclude peace simply on the present basis, that is under the unredeemed influence of the battles of Seckenbach and Giengen, with his allies of Württemberg and Baden still captives of the Elector Palatine. He had high hopes that he could induce Duke Philip the Good of Burgundy to enter the field on the imperial side, provided the Emperor would make him some valuable offer, possibly including the title of King.[24]

In view of the key position held by Albert Achilles, peace in Germany might still have been a long way off if George had not taken the initiative. Early in February 1463 he sent one of his diplomats to the margrave, who was just engaged in talks with his Saxon friends, and warmly invited him to come to Prague in person. Albert, encouraged by the Saxon dukes, accepted, and within a few days a complete agreement was reached.[25] It not only implied the end of all hostilities but beyond that the full reinstatement of the old treaty of friendship and alliance concluded in Cheb 1459. All prisoners—not withstanding the larger number in George's hands—were freed without ransom. Albert also agreed to all clauses of the agreements of Korneuburg, including the intended calling of a general peace conference under George's presidency, though he asked—for the time being successfully—that the meeting be held in Nürnberg rather than in Prague. Finally George indicated that, in case Louis should not be willing to negotiate in good faith, he would no longer support him militarily, not even by permitting Czech mercenaries to take service with him, while such permission might well be given for service with Albert.

As far as the place for the final peace conference was concerned, George prevailed in the end. The Nürnberg meeting never materialized, and a meeting in Weiner-Neustadt which, in the Emperor's presence, took place in May, ended without any results, despite the well-meaning but uninformed efforts of two papal legates. The Wittelsbach representatives, among whom Dr. Martin Mair, as usual, took a prominent part, were quite rigid and unwilling to make any substantial concessions, especially in regard to the old struggle over Donauwörth.[26] The only thing on which the two sides could finally

---

[24] See Bachmann, *Reichsgeschichte,* I, 360ff.

[25] See *FRA* II 44, 488; *FRA* II 20, 296ff. Hasselholdt-Stockheim, *Urkunden,* 649ff.

[26] For a detailed account of the spring meeting of Wiener-Neustadt see Bachmann, *Reichsgeschichte,* I, 391–397.

agree was the suggestion of the Czech embassy to adjourn the meeting to Prague, which in practice would give George once more the opportunity to show his ability as the peace-maker of Central Europe, and implemented, on this important point, the arrangements made between him and the Emperor at Korneuburg in December 1462.

This decision for Prague was now made with the full agreement of Margrave Albert Achilles. His confidence in the King seems to have returned to a surprising extent, although the expressions of his friendship—such as the passing on to George of important confidential informations [27]—were probably meant at least as much to strengthen the King's friendly feelings for himself and his brother Frederick of Brandenburg. Perhaps even more characteristic for the whole situation in the Empire was a contribution Albert tried to make to the issue of imperial reform. In a letter—almost a memorandum—directed to the imperial chancery and dated March 16, 1463,[28] he recommended the setting up of two "imperial vicarages," one for the part of the Empire west, the other east of the Rhine. The first one would be under the headship of Duke Philip of Burgundy, the second under King George. The question whether the first appointment would also imply Philip's long desired elevation to kingship remains unanswered. Nor is it clear form the text which powers those two imperial vicars would have. Nevertheless it is interesting to remember that this late revival of the idea of some vice-regal power for George, if not over the whole yet for the greater part of the Empire, should come from that prince who had played such an important role in destroying George's earlier hopes toward this end, and this at a time when the Pope, Margrave Albert's special protector, had long begun to look at George essentially as an enemy. It appears that in Albert's eyes the position of the heretical King was now quite indestructible, for, he writes to the councillors of Frederick III, "thus we should have their (the Burgundian and Czech rulers') help for our whole life, against any enemy, and could always be sure of them, and therefore, if this should come about, His Imperial Grace would remain in the possession of his power to his grave." In the end the margrave even mentions the possibility of marrying the young imperial Prince Maximilian with Princess Mary, Philip of Burgundy's granddaughter, a brilliant idea, as dynastic policy goes, even though the "German Achilles" could not possibly have foreseen the tremendous importance

[27] See his letters to Jost of Einsiedel, reported *ibid.* 371.
[28] *FRA* II 44, 505–507.

that this very marriage would one day have for the splendid rise of Habsburg power and the whole history of Europe.

The Emperor himself, at this time, was very far from dreaming this particular dream, and if he ever connected the famous principle *"Tu, felix Austria, nube!"* with the Burgundian marriage, it was only at a considerably later date. Even less did he give any serious thought to Margrave Albert's suggestion of appointing imperial vicars which would come perilously near to infringing upon his constitutional prerogatives. But he did, now, do his best to hasten the peace negotiations in Prague, in the hope that an early conclusion would leave him more freedom to concentrate on the complicated Austrian situation and to deal decisively with his hated brother. In this regard he had already earlier in 1463 gone so far as to make a high Czech dignitary, Zdeněk of Sternberg, Bohemia's lord high burgrave, his captain general for the whole of the Danube Valley, for the express purpose "that he wage war in the Emperor's place against Archduke Albert of Austria, some of the noblemen of the same principality, the people of Vienna and other enemies of the Emperor to the best of his ability,"[29] using as his basis the town of Weitra, which he had received, probably upon King George's urging, as a reward for his services for the Emperor's liberation from his siege in the Vienna castle. Sternberg's appointment was eventually to cost the Emperor dearly.

The great peace conference in Prague began on August 8th, and as early as August 24th, after little more than two weeks of difficult negotiation conducted under the constant supervision and the equally constant prodding of King George, a number of documents were signed which finally and effectively put an end to the long drawn-out war between the two great princely parties in Germany.[30] The most important treaties were those between Duke Louis of Bavaria-Landshut and the Emperor, and between the same Wittelsbach prince and Margrave Albert Achilles of Brandenburg. For the understanding between the imperial party and Elector Frederick of the Palatinate the road was cleared, too, even though the final acts of peace with him were not signed till six weeks later at Mergentheim.[31]

The details of the arrangements are in most regards of minor interest for us. There was, in almost every case, a compromise. The

[29] Birk, *AÖG*, X, 639–643. See also Urbánek, *Věk*, IV, 670f.
[30] Mainly in *FRA*, II, 44, 538–557. See also, Riezler, *Geschichte Baierns*, III, 425–427, and Urbánek, *Věk*, IV, 678ff.
[31] See Menzel, *Regesten zur Geschichte Friedrichs des Siegreichen*, 406f.

Emperor had the satisfaction that Donauwörth remained an imperial city, while Duke Louis was successful in refusing all the Emperor's demands for admission of guilt and payment of large fines for breach of the peace. In the struggle against Albert Achilles, the duke, ably represented by Dr. Martin Mair, securely and permanently established, through the reconfirmation of the treaty of Roth, his refusal to recognize the competence of Margrave Albert's Nürnberg Landgericht (Court of Appeal) for Wittelsbach territories and subjects. This was, perhaps, the most difficult of all issues, and for a while the margrave's representatives acted as if they would let the whole peace conference be wrecked over it. Finally, however, George's skill and the fact that the margrave's envoys found no support at all on the side of the Emperor's councillors—who were, they reported to Albert, "soft and childish" in their hurry to achieve the peace [32]—induced the Brandenburg-Ansbach delegates to give in. Their tough fight, cautiously supported by King George, did on the other hand yield valuable results to the margrave in almost every other regard. Of the many conquests that Duke Louis had made of castles, towns, and other holdings, he would not retain any, and Albert Achilles could feel that he had emerged from the long struggle, if not victorious, yet far from defeated.

Above all peace had come to large parts of the German countryside after years of ruinous battling. It had come partly because all the princes involved had grown tired, and all of them, even Duke Louis "the Rich," had found it difficult to finance the continuation of the struggle. Yet all this had been true for some time, and so far they had not been ready to make the needed mutual concessions. The almost unexpected success, at this moment, was essentially due to George's direction of the peace conference, the way in which he employed energy and patience, threats and persuasion in just the right measure toward all sides.[33] The words which he had used in his letter to Pope Pius in December 1461, not long before sending his embassy to Rome,[34] and which might have sounded like an empty boast at the time, largely due to the actions of Margrave Albert—these same words would fit exactly if he were to use them now: he had spared no effort to bring

[32] See letter of Albert's envoys to him, *FRA*, II, 44, 543–546.

[33] Even the ever-critical Bachmann gives the King ample credit: "Der König vermittelte mit soviel Geschick und Nachdruck, bewies solche Selbstüberwindung, dass nach langem Streiten und Feilschen...., das schwierige Werk doch endlich gelang" (*Reichsgeschichte*, I, 434f.).

[34] See above chapter XI, pp. 255–256.

about peace in his Central European world, and he had prevailed. What was more, he had prevailed soon after the Pope's legate Domenichi and his assistant Rudolf of Rüdesheim had, at Wiener-Neustadt, remained unsuccessful at the same task. King George's position in the Empire, which might have been considered as weakened when he had suffered defeat in his quest for the Roman kingship, was now stronger than ever before and would remain so, probably, as long as his friendship with the Emperor and the majority of the princes lasted. And it was stronger through a constructive act which, besides the gain of prestige, had brought him little if any direct gain. On the whole the Prague peace conference, then, was another proof of George's unusual ability to identify, in the way which shows the statesman of rank, his own personal and political interests with the true interests of a much wider and more complex community.

It is logical that, in this atmosphere of approaching peace, the idea of a more stable imperial structure—in other words, of a reform of the Empire—should again come to the fore. The thought, of course, was perpetually in the air, and had become somewhat more concrete as soon as the hopes for peace in the Empire began to rise after the Emperor's liberation in Vienna. Discussions of the topic had begun already at the time of Margrave Albert's visit of reconciliation in Prague in February 1463, and were renewed, without making much progress, in Wiener-Neustadt in May.[35] During the peace negotiations of August, the discussions took a more positive turn, since now, beside King George himself, the chief negotiators of at least two other sides became highly interested: the Emperor's counsellor, John of Rorbach, and the Wittelbach's chief diplomat, Martin Mair. With the help of these two men, though perhaps also of one of Albert Achilles' counsellors and, of course, his own advisers, George directed a plan to be worked out[36] which—in contrast to his draft for an international "League of Princes"—is impressive for the sober realism of its basic judgments and the fact that in every respect it appeared far less "utopian" than the league.[37]

[35] For the background, *KBAA*, I, 96–99.

[36] The question of the authorship of the reform plan is treated in great detail by Urbánek, who contributes a greater part to Mair and a smaller to King George than previous historians, especially Bachmann (*Reichsgeschichte*, I, 462). He bases his opinion largely on a memorandum ascribed to Mair. (See *Věk*, IV, 682f. and n. 280.) The memorandum is notable in its prediction that the Emperor's friendship for King George rested on uncertain grounds and that it needed fortifying by arrangements with and between the main imperial princes.

[37] The text, with some additional material, in *FRA*, II, 20, 313–322. A detailed excerpt in Bachmann, *Reichsgeschichte*, I, 463–466.

The basic idea of the new reform plan was a firm alliance between the Emperor and the outstanding princes of the Empire, perhaps somewhat reminiscent of the clause in the Golden Bull of Charles IV, which tried—unsuccessfully—to establish regular meetings between the Emperor and the electors which would result in a closer cooperation of the empire's head with its leading members. The draft which the small committee under George's direction had worked out begins with a general analysis of the situation in the Empire as it appears at the conclusion of the Prague peace conference. It points out that even now the general stability of conditions within the Empire is rather uncertain owing to a number of pending issues such as those between the King of Bohemia and the Roman Curia, between Duke Sigismund of Tyrol and the Cardinal-Bishop of Brixen (Nicholas of Cusa), between the deposed Archbishop Diether of Mainz and his successor Adolph of Nassau. In addition there were still many smaller feuds in the Empire, as well as any number of illegal actions, few of which were properly dealt with by the courts. Very damaging was the plentiful issue, in many places, of illegal or debased coins. If nothing was done about all these calamities it could be foreseen—since some beginnings could already be noticed—that princes and cities would try to deal with them on a purely regional level, by establishing limited leagues and landfrieden unions, with their own courts, armies, and captains. Such a development, however, would completely discredit all imperial institutions as well as the prestige of the Emperor himself. Thus a reform which would reestablish and strengthen imperial authority was an urgent need.

To establish this reform, the draft suggested as a first step a secret meeting to be held in Prague, in November 1463, between the diplomats of the Emperor, the King, the Elector Palatine, Duke Louis of Bavaria, and Margrave Albert of Brandenburg. During this meeting all the open issues between what remained of the two parties in the Empire, in particular those between the Emperor and the Palsgrave, were to be settled and the Emperor's general authority, as well as the Palsgrave's rank as elector, properly recognized. The five princes would then conclude a treaty of close friendship and permanent cooperation for the good of the empire.

The second stage of the reform would be launched by calling, for February 1464, a great reichstag to Cheb. There, the following program should be undertaken: The Emperor should take all necessary steps for a solution of the conflicts pending between temporal rulers (such as King George and Duke Sigismund) and their ecclesiastical foes and between the two competing Electors of Mainz.[38] These and the other princes should furthermore be induced to agree to the following specific measures of reform: the binding acceptance of a general internal peace throughout the Empire and the reorganization and re-staffing of all imperial courts so as to enable them to function properly. There are, in addition, some statements about the competence of the courts and the need of the princes in the union to support them. Considerable attention is given to the financing of this expected reorganization of the imperial judiciary system, especially by a head tax of one groschen to be levied for three consecutive years on every person over fourteen years. From the income of this tax the main part will go to the Emperor, while a smaller percentage will be retained by the main princes participating, including, besides the Wittelsbachs and Hohenzollern, the Saxon rulers. The other princes, however, including obviously the three ecclesiastical electors, would not participate, though the clergy (as well as the Jews) would be taxed more highly than others. The countries of the Bohemian crown would, of course, remain outside the whole scheme, since they could not profit from it, being altogether outside the system of imperial courts and jurisdiction.

The further history of the plan is one of frustration, not too surprising in this age of thwarted reform plans. The plan, taken to the Emperor and the other princes by their representatives at the Prague peace conference, seemed at first to meet nearly everywhere with the strongest approval. Even Frederick III, usually distrustful and overcautious, immediately accepted the suggestion of a Prague conference in November, and positive reaction also came from the other courts in question. Soon, however, the atmosphere of understanding and confidence was dimmed—by actions of the Wittelsbachs.

Duke Louis, for one, could not have been very happy with the recent developments in the Empire. Of the spectacular gains he had made during his long struggle against the imperial party, largely with

---

[38] The way in which the draft, presumably upon the direction of King George, equates King George's struggle against the Pope with that of Diether and Sigismund is strongly disapproved of by Bachmann, who calls it "unjustified and naïve" and claims that the two princes stood "als Verfechter berechtigter staatlicher Interessen und als Widersacher hierarchischer Willkür . . . *moralisch und persönlich hoch über ihm, der doch nur in den Konflikt geraten war, weil er mit allen Mitteln hinterher verweigerte, was er einst willig zugeschworen hatte*" (italics are mine) (*Reichsgeschichte*, I, 466). If anything is naïve here it is the evaluation, as idealistic struggles, of the power conflicts of Sigismund and Diether, while the explanation of how George got into his conflict is even odder than Bachmann's other occasional snap judgments.

the support of King George, much had vanished as a result of the Prague peace conference and of the pressure brought to bear on him by this, his strongest ally. As yet the fiction of the alliance had been maintained, partly, perhaps, because Louis himself wanted it so, but probably even more because his most important and most trusted adviser, Dr. Mair, still believed in King George's strength—or perhaps we might say in his lucky star—and thus tried to maintain, as well as he could, the close ties that once bound him to George. But Mair's existence and personal status—he liked to live rather elegantly—were still more narrowly bound to the Wittelsbachs than to King George. In Landshut, after all, Mair had become something like a permanent civil servant on the highest level, whereas his relation to George was still based on individual and temporary tasks. As long as he had been in Prague and had represented his duke at the peace conference, he had been willing to cooperate with King George rather faithfully on the issue of the imperial reform movement, especially since the whole scope of the plan corresponded so well to his own dreams. But once back in Landshut and engaged in "selling" the plan to Duke Louis, he was faced with the fact that the duke had reservations leading to the demand for very considerable amendments. And at the same time he found that an Emperor strengthened so much by George's recent policy—however much he, Martin Mair, had fought against him previously—was now perhaps worth being wooed directly, both in favor of the Wittelsbach party and of Dr. Mair personally.

On this basis, then, both Duke Louis and his prominent minister engaged in manoeuvres which had little in common with either the spirit or the letter of the recent reform plan.

Duke Louis tried to prepare himself for the tug-of-war that he expected to precede the possible conclusion of the reform agreements by establishing himself a southern regional league to which he invited, besides all the other Wittelsbach rulers and the Dukes of Württemberg, several important ecclesiastical princes such as the Archbishop of Salzburg and the Bishops of Bamberg and Würzburg as well as several Suabian cities. His chancellor, Mair, meanwhile, negotiating at Wiener-Neustadt on behalf of the Palsgrave, presented to the Emperor the amendments by which Louis of Bavaria-Landshut and Frederick I of the Palatinate hoped to make the Prague reform plan more palatable for themselves.[39] They wanted to alter the financial measures in a way which would give the princes a much larger share of the income,

39 See Hasselhold-Stockheim, *Urkunden*, 699; and *FRA*, II 20, 319–321.

which anyhow should be changed from a head tax into a property tax. (Here, incidentally, a modicum of humane thought on the part of Louis might conceivably have entered. He had generally shown a little more understanding of the needs of his people than, say, Albert Achilles. On the other hand he may simply have felt that his own tax scheme would yield a higher income.) The Wittelsbachs, furthermore, wanted to move the great imperial diet from Cheb to Nürnberg or Regensburg. Above all they wanted to increase the number of the original members of the new organization, but at the same time decisively weaken its competence: these princes should not be bound to the Emperor any more firmly than they had been before, there should not be any need to do away with existing alliances (therefore, it would seem, Duke Louis's hurry to increase the number of his allies), and the only function of the new organization would be the pronouncement and possible enforcement of the imperial landfrieden. Yet how could this be enforced with any effectiveness if all the old regional ties and leagues, with all the particularistic interests inherent in them, were to be maintained and even sanctioned by the Emperor himself.

But Dr. Mair, it seems, had at first little difficulty presenting these changes, or at least some of them, to the Emperor and his closest adviser, Bishop Ulrich of Gurk, in a way which seemed attractive enough, particularly since he spiced it with promises for support in the Emperor's recent conflict with Venice concerning the control of Trieste and its Adriatic trade with the Habsburg-owned hinterland— a conflict which, despite the common Turkish danger, had already taken the form of open war.[40]

But above all Mair made strong attempts to procure, for his prince and by implication for himself, the highest permanent influence on the Emperor, by effecting the substitution of Margrave Albert with his long-time foe. Duke Louis was to acquire the dignity of hereditary imperial "Erzhofmeister" (arch-court-master)—a position similar to that promised to him once before, by King George, in the case of his acquisition of the Roman kingship. Dr. Mair himself, however, was to become head of the chancery of the Roman Empire, with an income consisting of one third of all revenues of this office, expected to be large enough to make it profitable for him to pay, merely as a commission, the large annual sum of 9,000 ducats to the Emperor.[41]

[40] See Bachmann, *Reichsgeschichte*, I, 527–531.
[41] *Ibid.*, I, 472, 473.

It is anybody's guess how far the Wittelsbach diplomat and his employers might have had their way with the Emperor had it not been for the watchful and jealous eye of Margrave Albert Achilles. Perhaps Frederick III's consistent policy of caution and procrastination, as well as his notorious parsimony, would have prevented him from making concessions which in the event would have led to a still further weakening of his position. But Albert had his faithful friends and informants at the Emperor's court, and none of Dr. Mair's supposedly secret negotiations remained unknown to him.[42] He sent two of his own envoys to Wiener-Neustadt to inform the Emperor about the scope and success in Duke Louis's search for new allies. Likewise he passed on this news—through George's friend and diplomat, Jost of Einsiedel—to the Czech King. From Jost's answer Albert learned that the King looked at the recent Bavarian activities with considerable displeasure. The way in which the plan, collectively developed and approved, was now to be changed without asking him, the main author, for his agreement or even keeping him informed, annoyed him, and Louis's attempt to develop, before the work got properly started, a firmly organized southern German sphere of influence for himself was bound to appear to George as a sort of sabotage of the whole plan. (It did, indeed, fit rather precisely the description of the dangers for the empire which had been contained in the preamble to the original plan.)

Early in the new year the Emperor, warned already by Albert Achilles, seems to have received a similar warning from George. He had no reason to disregard it, all the less as just at this time George had helped him by directing his friends among the estates of Upper Austria, whose immediate sovereign, Archduke Albert, had died of the plague early in December, to make their peace with Frederick III as their prince.[43] Early in 1464 it was clear that the Wittelsbach attempt at gaining, by diplomacy instead of war, a position of paramount strength in the empire had failed or at least had lost its best chances. On January 26th an imperial order went out to almost fifty southern German imperial cities strictly forbidding any alliance with any prince without the Emperor's express permission.[44]

---

[42] Albert's informant was Dr. Hertnid vom Stein, Dean of the chapter of Bamberg Cathedral. See his report in KBAA, 101–106. For the immediately following events see also FRA, II, 44, 579–582; KBAA, 106–108; and the general account in Bachmann, Reichsgeschichte, I, 474–476.

[43] See Jost of Einsiedel's letter of December 1463, FRA, II 44, 572f.

[44] Ibid., 578f.

Just as Duke Louis had tried to use the idea of imperial reform to replace Albert Achilles' influence on the Emperor with his own and thereby to gain a more secure hegemony for his house in the Empire, so Margrave Albert used the same idea for a reorganization which by its very form would limit Wittelsbach power. Where, so far, the two great Wittelsbach princes (those of the Munich line merely held on to Louis' coat tails) had been strong by bestriding, like the two legs of a giant, all of southern and western Germany (and stood to gain still farther by the inclusion of another Wittelsbach, Elector-Archbishop Rupert of Cologne), Albert tried to limit their role by making all representatives of princely houses enter the new alliance, as it were, like twins: there would be two Habsburgs (Frederick and Sigismund of Tyrol), two Poděbradys (George and Victorin), two Hohenzollerns (Albert and his brother Frederick in Berlin), two Wettins (Elector Frederick of Saxony and his son Albert), possibly two from Suabia (one of the Württemberg dukes, one of the Baden landgraves), and finally, of course, the two Wittelsbachs, Louis and Frederick.[45] This plan, ingenious enough, might on principle have satisfied King George and perhaps even the Emperor, but it is difficult to see how the Wittelsbachs could ever have been induced to accept it. It was, just by its apparent completeness, much less realistic and potentially workable than the original draft. Its main value was, perhaps, that it could be used to counter the Wittelsbach demands.

The fate of the whole reform idea was not yet sealed, but it became more and more doubtful by the various suggestions for change.

As far as the timetable was concerned, the small preparatory meeting of November in Prague seems to have taken place, but we know nothing at all about its outcome. The next step—the great diet of Cheb—never materialized. Nor did the diet meet at any of the other places—Nürnberg or Regensburg—suggested by the Wittelsbachs. Instead the Emperor, with the agreement of George, called a meeting to the one place where he liked to have meetings: his residence at Wiener-Neustadt. The date was changed but little: from Reminiscere (February 26) to Oculi (March 4th) 1464. But instead of being a great diet of all the princes and cities of the Empire the Neustadt meeting turned out to be a rather limited conference. The Brandenburg-Ansbach envoys came fairly early, those of King George rather late, only in the second half of March, while the Wittelsbachs, after

---

[45] See again *KBAA*, 101–106, (especially 101, 102), and much of the other sources mentioned above, n. 42. See also Urbánek, *Věk*, IV, 694.

long delays, decided that they could not send their envoys until much later.[46] Thus the early part of the conference hardly achieved anything even in discussing the reform issue. It was important only in giving an opportunity for the Czech envoys to meet with the papal legates. We shall soon return to their part of the meeting in the context of the struggle between George and Pope Pius.

It was not until June 1464 that the Wittelsbach envoys finally arrived, headed again by Dr. Mair. Margrave Albert's envoys had stayed all through, and now the Czechs also returned to Wiener-Neustadt. The negotiations could start. But all that happened was the burial of the great reform plan. It died because the differences between the parties concerned had become too great, and because no one, especially the strongest potential participants, seemed to have a sufficient interest to push it forward, especially not the Emperor without whose active participation the whole scheme was still-born.

Nor did he really have any urgent reason to work for the scheme. Margrave Albert Achilles, who the year before had tried to make him understand that without an imperial reform of some sort he was bound to lose all the power still left to him, had proved a bad prophet. In the months since Frederick's liberation from the Viennese siege— one of the nadirs of his long reign—his position had improved all the time. The liberation itself, his triumphant emergence from deadly peril, was already a blow to all those who had hoped to see him go under, especially to his brother Albert. The fact that the Emperor could now count on George, the strongest power within the Empire, as his staunch supporter added enormously to his gain, so much, indeed, that there was, especially in Austria, an almost steady defection of former enemies to his side. Already in April 1463 Vienna's burgomaster Wolfgang Holzer—the man who once had been most responsible for turning the people of Vienna against Frederick—tried to gain the Emperor's pardon in exchange for an attempt to deliver to him the city itself and Archduke Albert to boot.[47] Even though Albert made Holzer, and several of his helpers, pay with their lives for this betrayal, the archduke could not thereby stop the wave of defection.[48] While both sides—Emperor and archduke—tried to strengthen them-

[46] About the Czech envoys, see Bachmann, *Reichsgeschichte*, I, 491 n.2, and, partially correcting him, Urbánek, *Věk*, IV, 742 n. 183. On the Wittelsbachs see Bachmann, *Reichsgeschichte*, I, 495.

[47] See *ibid.*, 379–386.

[48] *Ibid.*, 447, 456. For the last phase of Albert's rule in the Austrian duchies see Vancsa, *Geschichte Nieder- und Oberösterreichs*, II, 406–429.

selves by hiring Czech mercenaries, especially the so-called bratříci, now also called "žebráci" ("beggars"),[49] the archduke found it more difficult to find the financial means for such measures than the Emperor, and the pressure which Albert used to get larger tax incomes made him more and more hated, even in Vienna. In October a diet of the estates, meeting at Tulln in Upper Austria, tried to force peace upon the reluctant princes.[50] When this demand was strongly endorsed also by the papal legates, the archduke accepted the majority of the Emperor's demand. Peace seemed finally in view when, on December 2nd, Albert of Habsburg died, probably of the plague, after a sickness of only four days.[51] The course of the illness was similar to that of his cousin Ladislav, six years earlier, and, just as then, now rumors of murder by poison were rampant, with about the same justification—the conclusion from the *"cui bono."* Indeed, by his brother's death, the Emperor was freed from all his worst troubles. In February Vienna did homage and was forgiven.[52] Some time later the Emperor also managed to settle his difficulties with his cousin Sigismund of Tyrol, who acknowledged Frederick as lord of Upper Austria, while Frederick did his best to reconcile Sigismund with the Curia.[53] In this, he was more successful than in the case of King George.

The most important of the Emperor's political gains, however, was his peace treaty with Matthias Corvinus. He had long and stubbornly pursued the goal of his Hungarian kingship—in strange contrast to his indolence in so many other matters. The cautious and respectful warnings and urgings of his friend Pope Pius seemed to have little influence. Finally—perhaps under the threat of the growing Turkish danger—the papal legates, first Jerome of Crete, later Domenico of Torcello, managed in May 1463 to gain his agreement to an ingenious plan which permitted him to save face handsomely while Matthias achieved, at quite a price, the substance of his rights.[54] Frederick, King of Hungary, adopted Matthias as his son. The son, thus, equally King of Hungary, was allowed to rule over the father's realm without the latter's interference. Above all, for a payment of 80,000 ducats, Frederick turned over to Matthias the sacred crown of

[49] Bachmann, *Reichsgeschichte,* I, 388f.
[50] *Ibid.,* I, 449–455.
[51] *Ibid.,* I, 459, 460.
[52] "Anonymus," 303–305.
[53] Bachmann, *Reichsgeschichte,* I, 508–516.
[54] For bibliographical notes on the treaty see *ibid.,* 391 n. 1, and Urbánek, *Věk,* IV, 674 n. 254, 255.

St. Stephen so that finally the young King would have his valid coronation.

At first glance most of the gains seemed to belong to Matthias. But in fact Frederick, too, gained very considerably. The right to call himself King of Hungary, and to be, for himself or his son Maximilian, Matthias' heir in case the young King should die without children, were at best long-term gains, and the few castles and towns now ceded to him by Matthias, and perhaps even the money, were of only secondary importance. But by being at peace now with his great eastern neighbor Frederick gained additional freedom of action. He was now clearly less dependent on any power whose support against Matthias he had previously sought, among them, above all, the King of Bohemia. There is absolutely nothing in our sources to show that George had counteracted or even regretted the conclusion of this peace. But it is obvious nevertheless that from now on he was much less needed by both sides, be it as supporter or as mediator.

It was in George's quest for international support in east and west that it was to become clear how this arrangement at his southern and south-eastern borders had influenced the situation against him. In an age in which dynastic relations were far from insignificant, his own relation to his son-in-law was, as we shall see, bound to suffer even more when, early in 1464, his daughter, the Queen of Hungary, died a very early death in her only childbed. Fate, thereby, cut one of the earliest dynastic threads which George himself had tried to spin, very conscious of its potential significance, at the moment when kingship had first appeared to be in his grasp.

CHAPTER 16

PREPARING FOR THE STORM

IT IS impossible to say whether King George, after five years of his reign, seriously believed that there was still some hope for an understanding with the Curia and Pope Pius II. He tended, it is true, to be an optimist. But he would have been naive and incompetent if he had relied on such a slim chance. His overt policy seems to indicate his willingness to go as far as possible in his attempt to placate Rome. He even continued to try and persuade his Catholic friends and adherents in Bohemia that all would turn out well in the end. Yet at the same time the likelihood of a life and death struggle with the Curia forced him into a policy which would counter that of the Curia especially in two fields: in his relationship with other European powers, and in his dealing with potential dangers and enemies within the realm of the Bohemian crown.

In the field of foreign policy we find him—after the important interlude that culminated in the liberation of the Emperor—once more pursuing a system of international alliances independent from papal interference. In this endeavor the King's main instrument was initially Antoine Marini. But the emphasis, in the process, began to turn from the general ideology that had characterized the original project of the peace league to the seeking of more concrete political cooperation of the powers in question. Among these, in George's view, France was foremost. Also he had reason to feel that, of the courts visited by Marini during his first grand tour, France had yielded the best results, even if they had not been definite. Louis' own feeling at the time had been clearly expressed, both in his communications to Venice [1] and in a letter written to Philip of Burgundy, the latter generally intended to reassure that prince that Louis's intended alliance with the Kings of Bohemia, Poland, and Hungary was not meant as a measure against Burgundy and its present possession of Luxemburg. Apart from that, however, Louis declared his complete readiness to

[1] See *FRA,* II, 20, 290ff.

accept King George's suggestions, since he was happy, for the sake of the defense of the Christian faith and the expulsion of its Turkish enemies, to conclude a full agreement and alliance (bonne intelligence et confédération) with the three Kings as well as all other Christian princes ready to join.[2]

It is obvious that Marini, to whom King Louis clearly had spoken in very similar terms, continued on his tour feeling that he had been successful, and he reported that feeling to King George before, in the late winter of 1463, he first returned to Venice. There, however, in view of the much increased Turkish danger, he now found even less interest in the general scheme of a European alliance and even more desire for immediate military help, and in these terms the Venetians addressed themselves to the Kings of France, Bohemia, and Poland as well as to Duke Louis of Bavaria,[3] while letters urging help also arrived at various courts in Rome from King Matthias, whose realm was threatened by the recent Ottoman invasion of Bosnia.[4] The relationship between King George and Venice, incidentally, remained friendly and cooperative, and George even offered his services in mediating the struggle between the republic and the Emperor in the Trieste struggle—though eventually, here as in other areas of the Italian peninsula, papal diplomacy proved to be nearer and more effective, resulting in the conclusion of peace in November 1463.[5] By this time, indeed, papal diplomacy had also begun to focus much more clearly on George's policy as that of an adversary to be watched and fought.[6] It was remarkably unsuccessful in Poland and had, if any, only a very limited success in France, but a greater one in Hungary.

[2] See *Lettres de Louis XI, Roi de France,* ed. Vaesen and Charavay, II (1461–1465), Paris, 1885, 8off., especially 82, 83. This source has so far escaped the attention of Czech and German historians, including even Urbánek.

[3] See the bibliography in Urbánek, *Věk,* IV, 60⁻ n. 79. There (and later p. 755 n. 233) also the proof that Markgraf ("Über Georgs von Podiebrad Project eines christlichen Fürstenbundes," *HZ,* XXI, 1869, 292–293), and Bachmann (*Reichsgeschichte,* I, 485–487) were quite wrong in assuming that negotiations conducted between George and Louis, according to Lenglet's edition of *Comines,* and belonging to 1467, had already been conducted in 1463 by Marini. The matter would be of secondary importance if it were not for the fact that, out of this (assumed) simultaneity of Marini's French negotiations with George's (real) attempt to further imperial reform and his other German policy, Bachmann concluded, and moralized about, an appalling deceitfulness on the part of the King. Bachmann's slip is the more astonishing as he was familiar with the main source for these negotiations, published by Pažout, "König Georg von Böhmen und die Konzilsfrage im Jahr 1467" *AÖG,* XL, Vienna, 1869, 357–371. (See e.g. *Reichsgeschichte,* II, 86 n. l. where he quotes from an offprint of this publication.)

[4] See Babinger, *Mehmed der Eroberer,* 231ff.

[5] See Bachmann, *Reichsgeschichte,* I, 529–530.

[6] See, especially in relation to France, Urbánek, *Věk,* IV, 604–607.

In Poland the whole issue of the alliance with Bohemia and France became the subject of a debate during the meeting of the national Sejm (diet) in Piotrków in October 1463. Almost certainly it was at this time that Marini, as George's ambassador, visited the Polish court. It seems that even then he was furnished with those documents by which, in the year after, he could present himself to the King of France as an envoy not only of Bohemia but also of Poland—and even of Hungary. Thus the idea of the great alliance as such was still far from dead, in Poland as well as in Bohemia.[7]

But not till half a year later, in March 1464, did those discussions start which, one might think, should have been almost the first ones: the negotiations with Matthias Corvinus, to whom George sent Antoine Marini. In this we recognize in George that penchant for procrastination which harmed the King more than once in his reign. And for a specific explanation we are very largely dependent on deductions and surmises.

One thing, above all else, seems characteristic of George's relationship to his son-in-law: he tended to underrate him. This, at the very beginning of their acquaintance, may have been quite understandable. Then Matthias was still a boy in his late teens, without any experience, let alone any achievements, except that of having survived, by good luck, extreme danger and prolonged imprisonment. It was this youngster, surely full of strongly expressed gratitude and of glowing hope, whom George had liberated and fêted during those fall days of 1457. And it seems that the older man—who had once before had the opportunity to see how quickly a boy can turn into a man—did not find it easy to free himself from the image of 1457. He could rightly feel that without his effective help Matthias would never have become King of Hungary. George thus took him rather for granted, and while it seems extremely unlikely that he ever intended to destroy Matthias' kingship (his actions before and after the Brno treaties of July 1459 tended in effect to safeguard rather than jeopardize Matthias' position), those treaties with the Emperor, if, as has to be assumed, they ever came to Matthias' knowledge, would at least function as a considerable pressure on the young man—a hint of what might happen if, for instance, Matthias should really proceed to that breach of his marriage promise with King George's daughter which at that moment was assumed to be imminent in various court circles of Central Europe. George's wish to be able to exert such pressure may above all have

---

[7] *Ibid.,* 607, 608.

been one of the reasons for his readiness to conclude the Brno agreements, together with his hopes thereby to insure the Emperor's agreement to his quest for the position of King of the Romans. If this is true, then the pressure certainly worked well enough: late in 1460 the marriage agreement was renewed, and only a severe illness of the young ruler—definitely not a "diplomatic illness"—precluded a meeting of the two Kings planned for Olomouc at that time. Finally, in May 1461, the child Kunhuta-Catherine, just 12 years old, was, by the foremost barons of the realm, taken to Trenčín in Slovakia, where she met and was married to Matthias by Archbishop Denis of Esztergom, Primate of Hungary.[8]

The young Queen never had a chance to grow into a woman. When her husband, in mid-February 1464, returned victoriously from his first campaign against the Turks in which he had reconquered most of Bosnia with its capital, Jajce,[9] prospects seemed bright for the young couple. His solemn coronation with the crown of St. Stephen, finally returned to him by Frederick III, was planned for the near future, and there seemed a chance for the early birth of a successor. A few weeks later both the young Queen and the hoped-for heir had died in childbed.[10] By failing to provide him with an heir the dynastic connection with the house of Poděbrady had lost one of its main values for Matthias, even though he continued, in his correspondence, to call George his father. The coronation, nevertheless, took place as scheduled, on March 29th, and for this occasion alone the King of Bohemia was bound to send some representative.

If George now sent Marini to Hungary, his very choice made it clear that he hoped to achieve Matthias' participation in the international alliance, with its implied possibility of checking the papal offensive against him, and this without any prior clearing-up of misunderstandings that had occurred between Prague and Buda. Yet there had been no lack of such friction, even after the marriage of Matthias and Catherine of Poděbrady had overcome most of the earlier difficulties. We have mentioned earlier Matthias' disappointment and anger at the time when he and his allies had been forced, by Bohemian arbitration, into the unwelcome armistice of Laxenburg (September 1461). But probably the greatest cause of trouble was the

---

[8] *Ibid.*, 467, 468.

[9] Babinger, *Mehmed der Eroberer*, 245f.

[10] See the short discussion of the cause of her death and the sources in Palacký, *Dějiny*, IV, 2, 264 n. 196.

existence of reminders, though now considerably weakened, of the Czech and Slovak partisans—the bratříci—in the northern part of the Hungarian kingdom, the present Slovakia.[11] In 1461 and through the beginning of 1462 the bratříci had still shown considerable power of resistance, though their first great leader, John Jiskra, had left the country to serve the Emperor against his brother Albert, and had eventually, after the conclusion of peace between Frederick III and Matthias, become reconciled himself to Matthias' rule. While in the earlier phases of his reign King George had found it advantageous to maintain some influence on these revolutionary soldiers partly because this seemed a possible instrument of pressure, he had by now done his best to dissassociate himself from them. It seems doubtful if this had been recognized and appreciated by Matthias. Yet to make this clear to the Hungarian king would have helped to clear the atmosphere between the two courts, especially if Matthias' support against the Curia was desired, at a time when Matthias was to some extent dependent on papal support, financial and otherwise, and had reason to feel obliged to papal help in his relation with Frederick. If, to all this, is added Matthias' virtual release from any family obligations, it becomes obvious that Marini appeared in Buda at a moment hardly to be called propitious; and one may also doubt whether he was really the right man for the task.[12]

This doubt is strengthened when we hear that Marini told the King, apparently at their first meeting, that in his negotiations with Louis XI of France he had spoken in the name of King Matthias as well as in that of King George. We cannot know whether George had instructed him to emphasize this fact in his negotiations with Matthias. But the very admission expresses, in an awkward way, George's inclination to underrate the young man who had just shown considerable ability to follow in the footsteps of his father, George's old friend, the fighter against the Turks. It is not surprising that Matthias reacted with some asperity to the expression of an attitude which had taken him and his decisions so much for granted.

In his answer to Marini Matthias first praised the idea of a close cooperation of all Christian princes against the Turks, but expressed his astonishment that he had not earlier been approached about its possible realization. Turning to the attempt to negotiate with France

[11] For the following see Urbánek, *Věk*, IV, 491–499, L. Hoffmann, *Bratříci*, 56–63, and J. Spirko, *Husiti, jiskrovci a bratříci*, 109–116.

[12] For Marini's role in Buda see mainly Katona, *Historia critica regum Hungariae*, XIV (VII), 704–712, also Voigt, *Enea Silvio*, III, 490 f., and Urbánek, *Věk*, IV, 752–755.

in his name, too, he said: it was true that he considered George as his father and himself as the son, but the son, too, had his own kingdom, his own councillors and his own requirements and responsibilities, and did not need anybody else to look after his business. He then declared himself in principle ready to renew and strengthen the old friendship with France, which he considered most important; but for that very reason he wanted to discuss the question in some detail not only with his own councillors, but also with those of his allies, such as Venice and—especially—the Emperor and Pope.

Finally the King came out with a strong criticism of the idea of a new church council sponsored by some of the imperial princes (meaning those of the Wittelsbach party, but surely also with a side-glance at George's conflict with the Curia). A council could only be called by the Pope, and in any case little good could be expected from any such assembly, as in the past they had only brought about disunity and schisms. This last statement clearly reveals that the strength of the clerical and specifically curial influence at Matthias' court, at this time, had perhaps reached a high point. Marini himself made it obvious when he later reported that some of the prelates of the Hungarian court even had threatened him with excommunication.

Marini's negotiations dragged far into April. He had begun to negotiate in a somewhat clumsy fashion and committed at least one more *faux-pas* when he offered, only weeks after the death of Queen Catherine, to function as matchmaker for a new royal marriage. The King, with a reference to the needs of propriety, curtly refused. Nevertheless the outcome of Marini's stay in Buda seems to indicate that he operated not entirely without skill. For himself he achieved what he already gained in Poland: his appointment as King Matthias' representative for negotiations with King Louis XI. And while the treaty that he finally managed to conclude on April 14 between Hungary and Bohemia [13] was not of special importance, it did at least regularize the procedures to be taken in order to prevent disturbers of the peace— meaning, of course, those of the bratříci not taken into official service by either side—from crossing the border or settle in strongpoints near it. Some other clauses emphasized the old friendship, yet in the long run the agreement did not lead to any real revival of a close relationship. It did not prevent, above all, Matthias from scenting in the conflict between King George and the Curia some splendid opportunities for his kingdom's and his own aggrandizement. But for this, and thus

13 Katona, *Historia critica*, 712–715.

for the essential failure of his mission, it is hardly possible to make Antoine Marini responsible. A greater, more experienced diplomat than he—Gregory Heimburg—was later to try his hand in the same endeavor and to fail.

If King George was dissatisfied with the report given to him by Marini upon his return to Prague, there is little proof for it. Such dissatisfaction can hardly be discovered in the fact that within the delegation which George now sent to King Louis of France, Marini was not the only fully accredited ambassador.[14] This, after all, was to be more than a tour of exploration. The King of France, for all the difficulties he had encountered, still represented the most formidable single power on the continent, and a closer relationship, especially an official treaty of friendship and alliance with him, would go a long way in countering the policy of Pope Pius aimed at isolating and eventually crushing "the heretic." This would be true even if the hopes for a wider organizational framework for cooperation, such as the league of princes, failed to materialize.

Under these circumstances it was necessary to make the embassy to France representative as well as effective. Thus it had to include, as one of its leaders, a Bohemian nobleman of high status who had King George's confidence and understood his intentions well. George chose Albert Kostka of Postupice, the younger brother of Zdeněk.[15] Albert did not have the long experience nor the deep conviction and strength of character of his older brother, but he seemed more refined, being something of a humanist with a good classical education and a fluent mastery of Latin. He had done well during recent months as the King's governor in Lower Lusatia. The fact that he was much less zealous in his religious views than his father and brother did nothing to disqualify him for his task. George had probably chosen him even before Marini, at the beginning of May, had returned to Prague.

In addition to Lord Kostka and Marini the embassy included another member of the high nobility and six of the gentry. Among the latter the most important was Squire Jaroslav, who had been used before and was to serve later in George's diplomatic service and whose main significance in this case was the very lively, detailed, and informative diary he wrote about the whole undertaking, combining the interest of an old-time travelogue with that of a clear characterization

---

[14] This is Urbánek's guess (*Věk*, IV, 756) which, for the reasons explained in the following sentences, I find unconvincing.

[15] See *ibid.*, 53 n. 164, and in Urbánek's introduction to the publication *Ve službách Jiříka krále*, Prague, 1940, p. XXIV.

of much of the political background against which the story and outcome of the mission has to be understood.[16]

The party, with thirty horsemen, started on May 16th via Nürnberg
(where the pious Utraquist Jaroslav was shocked to see the sacred host
carried on the streets without anybody taking the slightest notice of it)
and Ansbach, where Margrave Albert Achilles received the ambassadors with the greatest honor, taking the leaders on a special hunt. To
shield them from robbers—a danger then vastly greater in Germany
than in Bohemia—the travellers had the protection of princely convoys
throughout, with the margrave providing it as far as Stuttgart, the
Duke of Württemberg as far as Pforzheim, where they were received
and escorted to Baden-Baden. There they were, for several days, the
honored guests of Margrave Charles of Baden and his wife Catherine
of Habsburg, the Emperor's sister. Baden escorts took them on to Strasbourg, while an especially strong convoy of fifty mounted soldiers,
furnished by that great imperial city, took them on difficult and robber-
infested roads across the Vosgues mountains into Lorraine, and thus
finally on into France. During their travels through Germany, much
as they were honored by princes and city magistrates, they found little
sympathy among the common people for whom the Czechs, without
much questioning, quite often were first and foremost heretics.

In France, on the other hand, the embassy was the object of the
greatest curiosity, having come from a country still considered essentially exotic. The good squire himself was not only somewhat annoyed about this but was himself struck by the worldliness and luxury
of the clergy and the large number and lack of modesty of a certain
type of women. The mutual stereotypes would, indeed, retain some
force for a long time to come.

The first meeting of some political importance for the Czechs took
place in mid-June in Bar le Duc, where they were received by Duke
René of Anjou, called King of Sicily. René was the pretender for the
crown of the Regno, which, with Pope Pius' help, had been usurped,
at least according to the French view, by Ferrante of Aragon. The
elderly prince gave the Czech embassy a most friendly welcome based

16 Jaroslav's report has been published repeatedly, first by Palacký in the first issue of *ČČM*,
1827, I, 40-67, again by J. Kalousek in *AČ*, VII, 1887, 429-445, finally and best by Urbánek
in *Ve službách Jiříka krále*. (There, in introduction pp. XXV-XXVI, also material on the
person of Squire Jaroslav.) It is from Jaroslav's report that almost all the information in the
following paragraphs is taken. For modern treatments, all based on the same source, see
Palacký, *Dějiny*, IV, 2, 267-273; Bachmann, *Reichsgeschichte*, I, 542-544; and Urbánek, *Věk*,
IV, 755-765. On Marini's role in this embassy see Ernest Denis, *De Antonio Marini*, 89-101.

clearly on their common antagonism to the Pope,[17] and appointed the two leaders as members of his council. Meanwhile King Louis had gone on a prolonged hunting trip to Normandy, and it was some time before the Czechs, travelling via the impressive city of Rheims, they had made their presence known to him. At first he asked them to come to Abbeville to meet him, but there he kept them waiting for some days, during which they admired the town with its sea traffic and its big ships and were invited by some of its people to their homes. The delay may well have been caused, even then, by those members of the King's retinue who, forewarned by letters from Rome and Breslau (and possibly even from some circles in Bohemia itself), tried to prevent the King from even receiving the "heretics." Marini, however, being a Frenchman and having met the King before, managed to catch up with him on one of his trips, and as a consequence Louis gave the embassy, on June 30, its first official reception at a small castle or hunting lodge near Dompierre, in the presence of the Queen and her brother, the King of Cyprus.

On being admitted to the King's presence Kostka presented his credentials from King George, Marini those of the Kings of Poland and Hungary. The two were then asked to sit down, which they did reluctantly after having been assured that this was in order at the French court for the representatives of Kings. Kostka was then asked by two members of the King's council to speak first but briefly, which he promised to do; then, Jaroslav reports, Lord Albert spoke in Latin "pretty long and much," and this, he reports, was the sense and purpose of his speech: "The Czech King asks and requests the French King, as the most Christian King and one who loves the common welfare of Christendom, to deign and call together a diet of Christian Kings and Princes, so that they themselves or their councillors with full power meet at some place and time, wherever and whenever the French King orders and decides; and that the Czech King requests this for the glory of God and the wellbeing of the general church and the Christian realms; and this he expounded in considerable breadth so it took him an hour or more."

Also, the report goes on to say, Marini spoke about the same matter, in the name of the Polish King in Latin, and of the Hungarian King in French. Marini, apart from supporting the ideas in whose origin he had, after all, had a very considerable part, also spoke of his experiences during his travels in Poland, Hungary, and Venice. He claimed that in Buda, where the bishops threatened to excommunicate him, he

---

[17] See Pastor, II, 267–268.

had also heard about abusive letters written by the Pope about King Louis. He finally stressed how much in the countries he represented, but especially in Bohemia, the people loved France and King Louis.

After the two speeches, the King rose and declared that the ambassadors' requests and proposals were of such high importance that they necessitated a most detailed consideration. He therefore asked the ambassadors to return to Abbeville, where the King would follow them soon.

The next phase of events has almost the quality of fictional intrigue. Clearly the King, while essentially sympathetic to the visitors, did not feel like going rough-shod over the heads of his permanent advisers among whom the prelates were so numerous. Among these was the relatively young cleric who, still in 1464, became Bishop of Evreux, and not much later Cardinal, Jean Balue.[18] It seems that he, particularly, had great influence on the King, at least at this time and for the next few years. Among the others present in Abbeville at the time were the Bishops of Bayeux (Louis de Harancourt), of Evreux (Guillaume de Flogues), as well as the Patriarch of Jerusalem and the chancellor. Before the King's arrival the three last-named as well as Balue [19] invited the two heads of the embassy into the chancellor's house, clearly with the purpose of convincing them that their efforts were hopeless to begin with and would better be given up. This resulted in an open brawl to which, however, Jaroslav with two of his fellow-squires— none of them invited or admitted—could listen through an open window. The French hosts told their guests that the Czech King had no right to suggest or request an international conference. Some of them even claimed that a treaty of friendship and alliance between the two Kings ought not to be concluded without the knowledge and express permission of the, Holy See, for the King of France must not be the friend of someone imprecated by the Pope. At this, Marini got so excited and angry that he exclaimed "The Devil is in that Pope. There is none more mean and narrow-minded in this world, and yet you want that nothing be done without his will." [20] Lord Kostka maintained remarkable calm, declaring that the Czech nation had always

18 His role had found relatively little attention until Urbánek's careful research. See his treatment in *Věk*, IV, 758–763. See also, for the background, Comines' *Memoires* in book II, chapter 15, and book VI, chapter 6, giving details about his relations to Louis XI. On this see also Pastor, II, 372–375.

19 Who at the time in question was not yet, as Palacký assumed, Bishop of Evreux. See Urbánek, *Věk*, IV, 758 n. 238.

20 It is amusing to see how Palacký, still under pressure from the Austrian censor, felt the need to soften this drastic utterance to the point of distorting its sense (see *Dějiny*, IV, 2, 271, in German, 310).

given the Pope as well as the Emperor their due, but adding: "It is still astonishing to hear that you prelates do not want to permit that lay people arrange something good among themselves, but demand that everything always gets done only through the power and influence of the prelates, and that you ecclesiastics always want to take part in all the things that are temporal." People, he added, should be allowed to conclude friendship with one another without having to ask the Pope's permission. Jaroslav concludes this part of his report with a bitter complaint about the irresponsible and vile way in which the accusation of heresy was hurled against his nation.

The King, however, was not so easily subdued by his clerical councillors. His wish to maintain and intensify the contact with Bohemia and King George was not primarily based on any interest on his part in an international organization of princes, nor even on the very real common antagonism to the Pope, but, so it seems, on a scheme of his own which began to occupy his mind just at this time.[21] He considered acquiring for himself the crown of a King of the Romans. This would have made his suzerainty over Burgundy legally more secure, would have gained him stronger footholds in Italy (especially by the confirmation and enfeoffment of the Duke of Milan), and would also have given him opportunities for expansion along France's eastern border, for instance by the acquisition of Metz. While details about all this are missing and our sources are rather indirect, there is no reason to doubt that Louis, well informed about the troubles with which the Emperor had to deal and about some of the older plans for a Roman kingship (especially regarding Duke Philip of Burgundy) gave this tempting scheme some consideration. For any success in this direction, however, King George's support, in view of his position as electoral prince and his influence in the Empire, would have been indispensable.

Thus when Louis came to Abbeville on July 10th he invited the Czech embassy to accompany him to Dieppe, and there or rather in its immediate neighborhood, possibly after some private meetings, he received them again officially at the small castle of Neuville. He bestowed, in a clearly demonstrative gesture, the rank of a French royal councillor upon Lord Kostka, making it more difficult for his own clerical councillors to object to this act when he made the same appointment in writing for Bishop Jost of Rosenberg, the one member

---

21 See the letters of Margrave Albert Achilles in Höfler's *Urkundliche Beiträge zur Geschichte der Häuser Brandenburg und Oesterreich*, AÖG, VII, 37–40, and to it Urbánek, *Věk*, IV, 758–760, and Bachmann *Reichsgeschichte* I, 522.

of the Catholic hierarchy whose relation to King George he knew (or had found out from Kostka) to be closest. He then ordered his councillors to write out a treaty—in the form of a letter of King Louis to King George—in which the two rulers promised one another, for the sake of the well-being and honor of both realms as well as of the Holy Church and the whole of Christendom, to be, and to remain for a future time, brothers, friends, and allies.[22] The King's clerical councillors fought the treaty to the end. The King had to use both energy and persuasion to subdue them. The Czech ambassadors heard him say: "Whether anybody likes it or dislikes it, I want to be on good terms with the Czech King and to conclude with him a treaty of mutual favor and friendship." But the Czechs did not know that the King also gave his clerical friends a special guaranty promising that, while he was resolved to negotiate and have a treaty of friendship with King George, he would not accept any of the errors the existence of which was suspected in the Czech realm or any of its parts.[23] Even so the councillors made a last attempt to sabotage the implementation of the royal order by trying to put into the treaty a special reference to Burgundy's undisturbed possession of the duchy of Luxemburg. This, in fact, would have implied an express renunciation of King George, relating to a country which, at least in theory, had never since the early fourteenth century ceased to belong to the Bohemian crown. The Czech ambassadors could, of course, declare that they had no mandate to negotiate on this issue, and eventually the matter was eliminated. Another dispute arose over the titles used by King George, as the French councillors not only objected to the use of the title "Duke of Luxemburg" but also of those referring to Moravia, Silesia, and Lusatia. Finally an arrangement was made by which both Kings would use only their main titles. Louis' interest in the conclusion of the treaty turned out to be strong enough to enable Lord Kostka to successfully threaten that if the matter were not cleared up soon he would leave without any treaty.

King Louis declared that the plan of the international peace league should be taken up again at a later date, and that for that purpose he would send a French embassy to Prague and other European courts. But in reality he probably never took this plan very seriously, even though, at this time, the league's headship had so clearly been offered to him and to no one else.

[22] For the complex bibliographical history of the treaty, see Urbánek, *Věk,* IV, 763 n. 251.
[23] See Urbánek, *Ve službách Jiříka krále,* 189f.

One might wonder, then, why the French prelates around the King (with whom Pope Pius had reason to be much more satisfied than he ever expressed in his *Commentaries*[24]) should have fought so grimly against the only result that the Czech embassy brought home—the treaty of friendship and alliance. But the very grimness of their fight shows that the treaty was by no means politically insignificant. Especially for King George's position in the Empire, but also in relation to other powers, his alliance with the greatest Catholic power of Europe meant at least a considerable moral strengthening.

One man, however, seems to have doubted whether his achievements had stood up to the promises he had made to King George. Antoine Marini accompanied the other members of the embassy only as far as Rouen. Where he went from there is unknown. He seems to have decided to turn his back on great policy and go back to the more remunerative work of an early capitalist entrepreneur; at least we find him engaged in this activity in Venice in 1468—the last time that we hear of him.[25] The rest of the embassy, leaving Rouen late in July, returned home via Paris, Lyons, Geneva, and Innsbruck. Kostka, who fell ill during the later part of the way, met King George only in mid-September in Brno, where he gave him his report about the journey and its results.

With a very strong position in the Empire, friendship with France and Poland, and an uneasy but by no means critical relationship to Hungary, George could look with some confidence at his international standing at the time when the hopes for a reconciliation with Pope Pius had shrunk to near the vanishing point. But besides the work of minimizing foreign dangers which, in the first half of 1464, had been accomplished with fair success, the Czech King was still faced with domestic dangers which could not be neglected nor taken easy, the less so as the possibility of an openly hostile action by the Pope appeared nearer. By far the strongest and most active enemy he had in any of the lands forming the "Bohemian crown" was still the city of Breslau.

Breslau, as will be recalled, had, in the treaty of January 1460, promised to be obedient to King George and, after three years and one month had passed, to do solemn homage to him "as their true and

[24] See his long tirades, mostly concerned with Jouffroy, in *Commentaries* XII, 830–835.

[25] See N. Jorga, "Antoine Marini," in *Études d'histoire du moyen âge, dediées a G. Monod,* Paris, 1896, 457.

indubitable Catholic and Christian King." But Breslau's opposition to George had already been resumed toward the later part of 1461, especially through its agitation in Rome. This had registered its first striking successes in the fall of 1462 when the Pope suspended the treaty of 1460 and took Breslau under his special protection. Under these circumstances, of course, the date fixed for Breslau's homage, February 1463, passed without any such action.

In King George's eyes Breslau had largely been responsible for the destruction of the pleasant relationship and mutual confidence between himself and Pope Pius. In this, he probably overrated the city's role. It is, after all, doubtful whether the Pope would, in the long run, have been satisfied with George's religious policy of stabilizing the existing relationship between Catholic and Utraquist, stopping, as much as possible, any attempts at mutual aggression and denigration, returning some of the previous Church property to its former owners and suppressing the outbreaks of sectarian radicalism. After the decisions of 1462, made in Rome and Prague, it seems obvious that Pope Pius would not have been willing to accept such an attitude as a full redemption of the famous secret coronation oath.

Yet George was right to the extent that Breslau's agitation had at least contributed strongly to exacerbating the struggle. A report requested from and delivered by Breslau's first procurator, Kitzing, had attempted, if perhaps with only limited success, to destroy in Rome the image of an essentially peaceful religious coexistence which the Czech embassy had painted. It was the work of the later procurators, inspired and directed by Nicholas Tempelfeld, that made George appear, to those who wanted to believe it, not only as a heretic but as a vile and cruel persecutor of the good Christians in his kingdom. As the Breslau agitators knew that their Bishop Jost did not in the least support this vicious distortion, he was, to an increasing extent, accused of being infected by the heretical poison himself. For a while this attempt misfired, and in the second half of 1463 Jost's activity, much strengthened by that of the Emperor, slowed and for a while even stopped the papal action against the King. But one of the conditions under which the Pope had been willing to wait, giving, as it were, King George another, last chance for the demanded anti-Utraquist action, was that the King would do nothing at all against Breslau. This, for George, was obviously hard to take, as it was not only a limitation imposed upon his monarchial rights but a very one-sided armistice which Pius here tried to impose on him. While he had to leave Breslau strictly alone, refraining from even non-military measures against the city, the Breslau agitators, now increasingly in control of the city council and in close cooperation with the papal legate, Jerome of Crete, would be free to continue in their subversive activities and their wild hate-propaganda.

This situation, rather aggravating for any ruler sensitive of the dignity and integrity of his office, became even more unbearable when George learned that the breathing spell granted to him by the Holy See was, nevertheless, used as an opportunity to search for someone to succeed him on his throne. Again Breslau was the first to urge this policy on the Pope, beginning as early as in the spring of 1463. At that time, for instance, an invitation went to King Casimir of Poland from the city council to assume the kingship of Bohemia.[26] That it failed was not Breslau's fault. The further pursuit of this policy emerges from a report which Breslau's latest envoy to the Holy See, Johannes Weinrich, wrote on September 9th concerning his first audience with the Pope.[27] Referring to earlier suggestions Pius told his visitors that he found it difficult to decide on a new King of Bohemia. In particular, he said, he had his doubts about King Casimir, who unfortunately preferred the Prussian sparrow to the Bohemian pigeon. Yet he was willing to consider him. For the time being he had, for the Emperor's sake, delayed his action against George, but always on condition that the King left Breslau alone. Thereby, he said, the city would be protected until a new King was found. Thus the Pope made it very clear that his final intentions were quite what the Breslauers demanded, and that only tactical considerations led him to go slow for a limited time.

The search for a possible successor to George did, indeed, go on. At one stage in the winter of 1463-1464 the Curia, perhaps resigning itself to the present impossibility of finding a suitable candidate, fell back upon a scheme that it had hedged decades earlier, during the Hussite Wars—the suggestion, again, seems to have come from Breslau —to cut Bohemia up into small principalities which then would be less able to maintain themselves as a nation of heretics. This idea was presented to Elector Frederick of Brandenburg during a visit which Archbishop Jerome of Crete paid him, ostensibly in connection with a propaganda tour for the crusade against the Turks. The elector would be able, so he learned from the prelate, to gain much land and money if he lent his strength to the execution of the papal designs

---

[26] See *SrS*, VIII, 235-237.
[27] *Ibid.*, IX, 6-10.

upon Bohemia. The elector, clearly amazed at this program, suggested that Jerome discuss it with his brother Albert, for so long Pope Pius' special protégé. The margrave, to whom the scheme appeared scurrilous, reported it all to his friend, the King of Bohemia, in a letter in which he also discussed, in the most encouraging terms, the latter's plans for an imperial reform.[28] Here his optimism, as we know, was not justified.

King George, thus, was fully aware of the Pope's intentions. Since he was clearly meant to become the victim of false play at the hands of the Pope—the old adage that you need not keep faith with a heretic was still much taken for granted—we can perhaps understand that he now simply played for time, knowing well that collision was as good as inevitable. Nor can we be surprised that he took all the precautions, especially against Breslau, that seemed necessary.

His playing for time appears most obvious in his tactics at Wiener-Neustadt, where his ambassadors, Zdeněk Kostka and Prokop of Rabstein, had arrived in March 1464 with the twofold task of continuing negotiations about imperial reform and of meeting the two papal legates presently dwelling at the Emperor's court. The abortive fate of the reform project has been discussed in the previous chapter. The meeting with the legates, rather naturally, was quite as unprofitable. The gist of the King's message to the legates had been again to ask the Emperor to induce the Pope to send a legate to Bohemia before whom George would justify himself completely regarding all the accusations of his enemies. To him, as well as to the Emperor, he would clarify in detail all his religious convictions, which would confirm his claim to be a true Christian prince.[29]

Domenico Domenichi, Bishop of Torcello, the Pope's main legate—the other was Rudolf of Rüdesheim, recently elevated to the Austrian bishopric of Lavant—had so far been one of the more conciliatory among the important members of the Italian hierarchy, and had even tried to counteract some of Jerome of Crete's wilder outbreaks. Now, however, in his answer to the Czechs,[30] he defended the archbishop—Jerome, he said, had not done anything the Pope had not ordered—and altogether denied any prejudice and misinformation on the side of George's clerical critics, though he admitted the possibility—which he would welcome—that claims of the oppression of Catholics in

---

[28] *Ibid.*, IX, 33–34, Hasselhold-Stockheim, *Urkunden*, 654–655, also *KBAA*, I, 94.
[29] *SrS*, IX, 49–50.
[30] *FRA*, II, 20, 325–328.

Bohemia might conceivably be unjustified. In conclusion, however, he declined to accept the request to send a legate to Bohemia, at least until the King had completely fulfilled his earlier oaths and promises; he threatened that if George failed to do so the Pope would do what he deemed necessary and show to him and to the whole world what power he possessed.

Despite these apparently hopeless results of the meeting the Emperor, through his envoy John of Rorbach—who was also taking to Prague some of the promised money—assured the King that he would not tire in his attempts to bring about peace between the Pope and the King. He did, indeed, immediately send Brother Gabriel Rangoni of Verona to the Pope with the request for a special legate for Bohemia.[31] Gabriel was a Minorite, and his originally rather friendly feelings for the King dated mainly from the fact that the Minorite Monastery of St. Ambrose in Prague had been restored by George's tolerant religious policy. He had, some time earlier, sent letters to the King urging him, in a peculiar mixture of friendliness and almost imperious urgency, to give in and submit humbly to the Pope, who was, after all, talking and acting in God's own name.[32] Yet he continued, in this case, to act on the King's behalf, as did, of course, also the Catholic bishops with whom George just now, early in 1464, held repeated consultations in Olomouc,[33] a city which at the same time renewed its oath of allegiance to him. (His prolonged stay in Moravia

[31] See Höfler in *AöG*, VII, 27–29; *SrS*, IX, 69.

[32] The (Czech) letters in question are to be found in *Cancellaria regis Georgii*, Sternberg collection (XXIII D 172), 468–469 and 494–496. A Latin version of the second one is in Ebendorfer's *Chronicon reg. Rom.*, 209f., there dated May 12, 1463. Palacký attributed the first letter—which, among other things, referred to a "long punishment" of the writer—to Prokop of Rabstein (see his *Dějiny*, IV, 2, 262, in German, 299f.), and Bachmann (*Reichsgeschichte*, I, 494–495) followed and tried to make the most of it (see especially 495 n. 1). Meanwhile Urbánek (*Věk*, IV, 663 n. 217) has presented excellent reasons why Palacký's attribution of the letter to Rabstein is mistaken and why Brother Gabriel should be considered its real author. Thereby, indeed, one of Palacký's conclusions (*ibid.*) in favor of King George also loses its basis: the statement that he who gave his friend and servant the freedom to talk to him in such overly frank terms (as supposed to have been used by Rabstein) can hardly be called a tyrant. In the terms of his time George certainly was no tyrant, yet it seems doubtful whether he would have left Rabstein in his important and influential position as chancellor for the rest of his life (which ended, already at the height of the crisis, in 1468), if the Catholic lord had really taken his stand with such forcefulness on the side of the Pope and his supposed right as George's judge.

[33] See about the Moravian development especially Urbánek, *Věk*, IV, 722–727. The Moravian changes were not only meant to strengthen the King's own political hold over Moravia against crucial attacks but also more specifically to establish his house more securely. Thus he now made his son Victorin governor of Moravia, though he never went as far as giving him the title margrave, which had been born by previous crown princes of Bohemia. This may have been due to his doubts whether the succession should really go to Victorin or rather, instead, to the steadier and more highly gifted Henry.

was also used to change the margraviate's constitutional position within the realm from that of an essentially feudal allegiance to the crown to that of a real union with permanent integration and union.)

The condition under which this continued friendly relationship with Catholic leaders remained possible was George's iron resolve not to recognize the struggle as a fight between two religions, even where the religious element was clearly of the greatest importance. Yet on the other side of the fence only too many purely political or economical ambitions were draped with the coat of deep religious convictions. George saw himself faced with the fact that such larger or smaller rebels had only to appeal to the Curia to find their cause eagerly embraced as truly Catholic and worthy of the strongest support. If there was a question of crediting information coming from Czech officials or even prelates such as Jost of Rosenberg or the Breslau radicals and their new friend and protector Jerome of Crete, it was now always the latter who were believed. The Curia—and this was true under Pius II as well as under his successor—was too glad to find partisans of its own policy within the camp of the enemy not to make the fullest use of them, and it was this practice, on the other hand, that embittered George far more than the ideological struggle in itself.

Besides Breslau and intimately allied with the city, one of the early rebels against George was Duke Balthasar of Sagan. The only one of the considerable number of Silesian princes and dukes who had refused to do homage to the King, he went to the very limit of challenging him when, early in 1460, he was offered the opportunity to be included in the peace arrangement engendered for Breslau by the papal legates, and spurned this chance by not even sending an envoy to Prague. It was only then, having shown patience with him for almost two years, that King George acted decisively: the duke was declared, by his acts, to have forfeited his rights upon Sagan, which was thereupon given to his brother John.[34] Though there was not the slightest suspicion that John was less of a Catholic than his brother, Balthasar immediately assumed the mask of the martyr, as the one Silesian prince who had had the courage to stand up to the heretic. At first his success in this direction was almost nil, but this, too, changed radically after the events of 1462. Balthasar, late in that year, went himself to Rome with a warm recommendation from his friends in Breslau, and by a letter of December 4 the Pope, without the slightest regard to the suzerain position of the King of Bohemia in the

---

[34] See Eschenloer, L., SrS, VII, 99.

Silesian duchies (though his royal position, at that time, as yet had not been questioned by the Curia) announced his decision to take away the duchy of Sagan from its supposed usurper and return it to Balthasar.[35] It was an utterly arbitrary act, worse in principle (if not in significance) than papal support for Breslau, whose earlier peace treaty with George could, after all, be claimed by the Curia to have been due to its effective mediation. By his act against John of Sagan, Pius simply arrogated to himself all the rights of interfering in temporary government ever claimed by the papacy at the time of her greatest power.

The struggle over Sagan took grim forms in 1463, when the Breslau cathedral provost, John Düster, himself an active member of the fanatical circle around Tempelfeld, made use of the special power given to him—strangely enough—by the Pope to excommunicate Duke John.[36] In this case, however, the duke found a defender in Bishop Jost, whose extremely vigorous action resulted in another series of complaints lodged in Rome by Breslau as well as by Archbishop Jerome.[37] Jerome's action, in turn, led in March 1464 to a note of complaint presented by King George's ambassadors in Wiener-Neustadt to the papal legates. For the time being, however, John remained the lord of Sagan, whereas his hostile brother stayed in Breslau and at times served, in the subsequent war, as one of the city's captains.

Beside Balthasar of Sagan two other men played, or tried to play, a comparable role: both members of the Czech high nobility, one in Bohemia, the other in Moravia. Both, Albert Berka of Duba, Lord of Tolstein, and Hynek Bítovský of Lichtenburg, were robber barons almost in the original sense of the word, though already on quite a large scale. Both hated the King whose strong and orderly government had made it much more difficult for them to operate freely. Their victims as well as their enemies were overwhelmingly Catholic. Naturally this did not prevent those noblemen from posing as fighters for Christianity against heresy, nor did it prevent the Curia from accepting, without the slightest attempt at critical examination, the claims of the two men at their face value, and the most intense effort of good Catholics to make themselves heard and to demonstrate the true nature of those men proved unavailing, since Rome was now resolved to see a high virtue in the mere display of hostility against

[35] *SrS*, VIII, 152f.
[36] See Urbánek, *Věk*, IV, 700 n. 16.
[37] *SrS*, IX, 23f.

George. In the summer of 1463 Tolstein castle, Albert Berka's strong-hold in Upper Lusatia, was beleaguered and finally conquered by the royal governor John of Wartenberg and Albert's own cousin, Henry Berka, both good Catholics. Yet this siege figured in one of the Pope's letters to the Emperor as a proof of the intolerable suppression of Catholics by the arch-heretic.[38]

We shall hear more about the equally blatant distortion of all truth in the case of the Moravian Hynek Bítovský of Litchtenburg, member of a Moravian baronial clan that for a long time had been on especially unfriendly terms with the Kunštáts. Hynek himself had—as has been told earlier—allied himself with Archduke Albert during the latter's attempt to gain Moravia soon after George's election. Meanwhile he had, by his depredations in Moravia as well as in neighboring Austria, made a police action against him urgent. He had, however, been shrewd enough, by an early request for instruction from Rome, to procure the information that no man needed to obey anybody who was disobedient to the Papal See.[39] Thus Hynek, too, was able to paint for Rome the picture of the persecuted Catholic, even though in this case George had been careful enough not to take any initiative but to leave the responsibility for all activities against Hynek to the Moravian estates, whose strong Catholic element, especially in the cities, was as eager to get rid of this menace as the Utraquist barons and gentry. This issue, however, did not develop fully until after the death of Pope Pius.

But if George could, at the time at least, leave the issue of Hynek Bítovský to the Moravian estates, no such confidence was possible in the case of his enemies in the north. There, again everything was bound to revolve around Breslau. While the voice of Breslau steadily increased its shrill warnings, in a fierce mixture of fear, defiance, and hatred, the King himself, well informed about these developments by his many friends in Silesia, became slowly convinced that he had to extirpate this thorn in his flank. Thus, from late fall 1463 on, he strengthened his hold over other parts of Silesia, working largely from his city of Glatz, one of his favored residences and, at this time, something like the connecting link between the countries of Bohemia and Silesia. There he received his friends among the Silesian dukes and princes, but also occasionally the leaders of Czech public life, including the bishops Jost of Rosenberg and Protas of Boskovice, despite the angry snarls that arose in Breslau over such intimacy not only from

[38] See *FRA*, II, 20, 323. For the whole struggle of Berka see Urbánek, *Věk*, IV, 701ff.
[39] See Palacký, *Dějiny*, IV, 2, 281ff. and Urbánek, *Věk*, IV, 725ff.

men like Tempelfeld but also Jerome of Crete. From the many complaints of Breslau, telling the Pope how George tried to confine them, we hear of his conquest of Albert Berka's castle of Tolstein (Tollenstein) in October,[40] and some weeks later of his attempt to buy and occupy the powerful castle of Fürstenberg, "key to Silesia" [41]—a situation which gave the papal legate cause to "forbid"—without even consulting Rome, and clearly without the shadow of a legal basis, the sale of any fortresses in Silesia or Lusatia.[42] But there is presumably much justification for the worries of the Breslau merchant princes who, with little enthusiasm but even less courage to resist the popular fury, had been drawn into this life-and-death struggle against the King. For by his possession of Tolstein in the west the King could now threaten their valuable trade with Brabant. Their traffic with Austria and Hungary had already been largely cut off, and now, they report, the heretical King even wants to influence Poland against them.[43]

But the loudest outcry was caused, in March 1464, by the trial of John of Wiesenburg.[44] This man, an impoverished Czech nobleman of northern Bohemia, was accused of having planned the murder, by poison, of King George and his family. He had admitted this intention while under torture but had later revoked this confession. Wiesenburg's interrogation had been conducted by King George's captain in the country of Glatz, Hans Wölfl of Warnsdorf, a Bohemian German and himself a Catholic, but completely devoted to George and thus soon one of the "pet hates" of the Breslau radicals. The unedifying reports about the trial, though rather detailed, do not permit any clear judgment about guilt or innocence of the accused. Admissions of guilt under torture will always remain suspect, though another squire whom Wiesenberg named as an accomplice remained, equally under torture, steadfast in denying any guilt and was released. Wiesenburg was finally declared to have received, in Breslau, 2,000 ducats and two bottles of poison, and was subsequently beheaded and quartered. At one stage even the papal legate, Jerome of Crete, was implicated in

[40] *SrS*, IX, 7.

[41] *Ibid.*, 27.

[42] *Ibid.*, 28f.

[43] *Ibid.*, 17 f.

[44] Wiesenburg's trial seems to have kept its sharp edge to the present. Bachmann (*Reichsgeschichte*, I, 499 f.) is as convinced of his innocence as Urbánek (*Věk*, IV, 711ff.), suspecting the influence of Venetian usage in the case of Archbishop Jerome, is of his guilt. To the present writer neither view seems sufficiently buttressed by the available source material. The main sources are all from Breslau, especially Eschenloer (G., I, 228–234) and *SrS*, IX, 45–49. The rest of the evidence in the detailed bibliographical notes of Urbánek, mainly *Věk*, IV, 712 n. 66, 67, and in Klose, *Dokumentierte Geschichte von Breslau*, III, Breslau, 1782, I, 249ff.

the plot against the King's life, though this specific claim was, perhaps for political reasons, later dropped. The official reaction of the Breslau city council—which was clearly afraid that this procedure might cause a general revulsion against its city—was furious and tried to turn defense into attack. It was, however, not notably successful, except perhaps in Rome where at this moment—in the spring of 1464—King George's credit had anyhow reached the lowest possible point.

For the last time the Bohemian situation was now, in the mind of Pius II, directly connected with the Turkish danger. During the early phase of his pontificate—and of George's kingship—the Pope had hoped to find, in the Czech ruler, a possible fighter against the Turks, and George had done nothing to cast serious doubt in his readiness to be just such a fighter—if and when his domestic problems had all been settled. Now the Pope had begun to regard himself—even though his health and strength was failing rapidly—as the only man able to lead the crusade against the Turks and above all to inspire (and perhaps even more to shame) others into following him. But he, too, wanted to have his "domestic" problems settled—indeed he used the very term [45]—before departing, as he hoped to do, for the eastern side of the Adriatic Sea. Among these problems the Hussite schism was the one great issue on which he had squandered an especially large investment of thought and effort—however faultily conceived—and which had yet come no nearer a solution than it had been five years earlier. He felt betrayed and cheated, not, as he was indeed, by the impossible complexity of the problem and his own inept approach to it, but by the man whose magic powers of healing the breach, of forcing his people back to orthodoxy, he had never ceased to assume and prejudge. He could not admit a deep error of judgment. It was now utterly clear to him that nothing but the King's ill will, his determined treachery, the treachery of the heretic and rebel, had been responsible. And so, finally, before leaving the eternal city on his pathetic trip to Ancona, he resolved upon the last and as he expected, decisive action.

On June 16, 1464, then, a great consistory [46] was held in the presence of hundreds of more or less prominent people, including the ambas-

[45] In his speech preceding George's citation he said: Licet contra Turcos simus profecturi, nichilominus tamen nedum externis sed eciam domesticis providere tenemur, quia parum esset bella externa removere, nisi domestica prius compescantur. (See *SrS*, IX, 81.)

[46] For the largest collection of source material on the consistory see *ibid.*, 77–90. A more complete rendering of the Pope's speech in J. Cugnoni's edition of the "Opera inedita," Rome, 1883, 461–470. See also Voigt, *Enea Silvio*, III, 500; Urbánek, *Věk*, IV, 766–769; and H. Kaminsky, "Pius Aeneas among the Taborites," *Church History*, September 1959, pp. 302–304.

sadors of France (who, however, could not take the news to their King fast enough to influence the simultaneous negotiations between him and the Czech embassy in Normandy). One of the curial officials had to read a speech of indictment, going all the way back to George's supposed early sins, with even the deaths of Menhart of Hradec and Ladislav Posthumus laid at his door. Fantino's imprisonment was much made of, as was the danger threatening the faithful Catholics of Breslau. In his answer, lasting more than an hour, the Pope again presented himself as the incomparable expert in Czech history, which, however, did not prevent him from erring even on some facts of the most recent past.[47] The struggle against the Hussites is presented in terms which tried to prove the essential unity and cohesion of the whole Hussite movement in all its aspects, deriving from Waldensianism and showing little change from its Taborite phase to the Utraquist Church as it existed in the present Bohemia under Rokycana's leadership. While much of this is distorted, it remains, of course, true that this Utraquist Church contained enough of the original concepts and goals of the revolutionary phase to refute George's claim to having always been a true Catholic. In this sense, and by his historical feeling that the Hussite schism carried the danger of permanence, Pius was certainly right to the last. His main error was that he reverted to the earlier illusion, once so convincingly attacked by himself, that this schism could be overcome, if necessary, by a return to the violent forms of "persuasion" which had achieved so little in the twenties and thirties.

In the end of the ceremony, then, the great sinner was solemnly threatened with excommunication and finally summoned to appear before the Pope within one hundred and eighty days to answer for his deeds and to receive his sentence. The citation, thus, remained just one step short of actual excommunication. But by citing him to appear before the Pope, the citation was bound to lose its force as soon as the Pope was no more.

On June 18 Pope Pius II, having himself taken the cross in St. Peter's Cathedral, left Rome [48] to drag his tired and disease-ridden body to Ancona. There, in his somewhat childish and yet perhaps also admirable optimism, instead of those actual straggling hordes of half-

[47] See Palacký, *Dějiny*, IV, 2, 274 n. 200.

[48] See for Pius' last weeks and days the masterly conclusion of G. Voigt's great work *Enea Silvio*, III, 711–724. It is a far more detailed, far more convincing presentation than that given by one of Pius' latest biographers, Paparelli (*Enea Silvio Piccolomini*, Bari, 1950), in his last chapter titled "La bella morte."

starved, down-at-heel would-be crusaders, most of whom were already dispersing, his mind saw strong, fit, well organized armies rearing to throw themselves upon the Turks. By the time of his arrival in Ancona on July 18th, the crusaders had almost all disappeared and, except for his own personal guard of archers, not a single prince had sent even the smallest troop. Yet to the last the Pope hoped to cross the Adriatic to Durazzo and by his appearance near the theater of war to inflame, among the princes of Europe, the old crusading spirit. Throughout late July and early August Pius kept waiting for the promised Venetian fleet. He lived to see their arrival, and thus he could, even on his deathbed, urge the cardinals in his retinue, among them Carvajal and Bessarion, to keep the crusading plan alive. In vain. The Doge who wanted to call on him had to be refused, and was only too glad to be able to return home. On August 14th, 1464, Pius II ended a life which, while full of brilliance and spirit, had yet left his greatest ambitions and designs unfulfilled, nay in a state which did not even permit them ever to be fulfilled.

CHAPTER 17

THE BARONS' REBELLION

THE DEATH of Pope Pius could perhaps give some hope to King George and his adherents that a detente between Prague and Rome might be possible again. Much, of course, would depend on the new Pope. Paul II, the former Cardinal Barbo of San Marco, had none of the intellectual brilliance of his predecessor. The German historian of the Renaissance Popes describes him as a rather narrow man of few deep interests, very proud of his beautiful appearance, generally vain, jealous, and over-devoted to splendor, yet also good-hearted, generous, and rather free of his predecessor's nepotism.[1] It was, thus, perhaps, characteristic that he considered it as an unforgivable sin when King George did not send an ambassador with a congratulatory message to him at the same time as those messages arrived from other rulers.[2] That George did omit sending such a message was clearly a grave diplomatic blunder, hardly sufficiently explainable by the fact that one of George's ambassadors was (later), at the papal court, subjected to insults. On the other hand the further development of the relations between Paul II and George does not give the impression that there would, at this time, have been much chance for a reconciliation, even if the King had avoided that tactical mistake which was bound to play into the hands of his enemies. For the specific issue which soon made the Pope irreconcilable had probably little to do with those formalities, and even less with issues of religion. It was, instead, the struggle between the King and the Moravian estates on the one hand, and Lord Hynek Bítovský of Lichtenburg on the other.

The conflict itself has been discussed before. The legal procedure against this unruly baron had, after long and patient negotiations, been started by the Moravian estates in July 1464, when in particular

---

[1] See Pastor, II, 301–303.

[2] See *FRA*, II 20, 338. The ensuing passage about the Pope's supposed warm feelings for George, taken from the reports of John of Rorbach, should not be taken at face value (as Palacký does, *Dějiny*, 287 [German, 329], or Bachmann in *Reichsgeschichte*, I, 549) but probably was rather intended to prove the effectiveness of the intercession by the Emperor's ambassador.

Hynek's very strong castle of Zornstein was put under siege by an army under the direction, though not under the direct command, of the King's son, Duke Victorin. Among the forces engaged were detachments sent by the Catholic cities of the margraviate as well as by Bishop Tas of Olomouc. This, however, did not prevent Hynek—who had somehow managed to escape from his castle—to find his way to Rome late in 1464 and there to pose as a pious Catholic cruelly persecuted by the arch-heretic George. At the same time he submitted his whole struggle with King George reverently to the Holy Father. This act was quite sufficient to convince Pope Paul of the righteousness of Hynek's cause, and all attempts of King George himself, of the Czech estates, and above all of Bishop Tas, to convince the Pope and his legate Rudolf of Lavant of the true character of the struggle remained unavailing. The Pope not only demanded an immediate end to the siege but even compensation to Hynek for the supposed injustice he had suffered, he threatened all those engaged in the siege with severe ecclesiastical punishment, and considered it an especially impudent affront to his authority when these orders were not obeyed. Zornstein Castle surrendered, after a siege of nine months, in the spring of 1465.[3]

The difficulties that the King encountered in the guise of men such as Albert Berka or Hynek of Lichtenburg were not of immediate significance in regard to the domestic situation in the Bohemia realm. Especially in Moravia the great majority even among the country's Catholics could not help feeling that the King was wholly in the right. Yet there were, among the magnates of the kingdom, many on whom the lesson was not lost that anybody taking a determined stand, on whatever grounds, against the King would find support in the Curia. Thus the small, individual rebellions of the robber barons, and perhaps even more the sustained rebellion of Breslau, were psychologically and politically not unconnected with the great baronial movement which began, seemingly, as a cautious form of political opposition in 1465 and erupted two years later into an open rebellion which threw the country into renewed civil war.[4] But it is difficult to understand motivations which drove such a substantial part of the baronial caste into such action without first gaining a clearer picture of the more

---

[3] For the preceding paragraph, see *FRA*, II, 20, 336–337, 340–353.

[4] The development of this opposition movement among a strong part of the high nobility has, of course, formed an important part of every historical treatment of King George's reign, but perhaps the best and clearest description is still H. Markgraf's article "Die Bildung der katholischen Liga gegen König Georg von Podiebrad," *HZ*, XXXVIII, 1877, 48–82, 251–273.

recent social and political development of the kingdom and of the relation between the different classes and groups to one another, as well as to the King.

We have emphasized that George of Poděbrady, in the beginnings, had stood with both feet in the baronial caste, and that at first he had strengthened it as against the power of the King. True he had always relied on support from the Utraquist knights and cities (especially Prague), even in his original struggles against Ulrich of Rosenberg and the League of Strakonice. Yet in this early time the picture was still that of two factions within the country's high nobility, separated in part by their religion, in part merely by rifts between powerful clans such as the Rosenbergs and the Kunštáts. The support which in early times the Lord of Kunštát-Poděbrady received from Catholic barons such as Zdeněk of Sternberg showed that George himself was, by his enemies as well as his adherents among the high nobility, still considered completely "one of them." This was also shown by his earlier emphasis on the elective character of the Bohemian crown, since the election was essentially in the hands of the high nobility.

But George's attitude, in regard to the role of the baronial caste, began to change (as we saw above, in chapter VI) early in the time of his regency. Already he felt the need to reverse a trend which had tended to weaken the central position of the crown and to strengthen that of the barons. This was, among other ways, expressed by the fact that former ecclesiastical property which was found not to have been acquired in a legal way should fall to the King. It is not surprising to see that George became even more eager to fortify the royal position once he had himself become the bearer of the crown. In general, however, he proceeded with his usual circumspection. During the first years of his reign he had no particular reason to show, in too striking a manner, his preference for the gentry or the cities when he knew that, partly for religious reasons and partly in consequence of the general political situation, these two estates had little choice other than to support him in any case, while this was far less true of the barons. Indeed, as long as he tried—rather successfully—to strengthen his own and his family's economic and political fortunes through the acquisition of new territories in Bohemia as well as in Silesia, he saw to it that some of the other great families had no great reason to begrudge him such acquisitions. We have earlier mentioned the gains which he had permitted the Rosenbergs to make in Silesia. He had tried to do the same for the Sternbergs in Lower Lusatia, especially in Kottbus,

and when the need for reconciliation with the Hohenzollerns resulted
in an end to the specific undertaking against that city he saw to it
that the Emperor added to Zdeněk of Sternberg's holdings by investing him with land in Upper Austria.

At the same time the great offices of the kingdom—those whose
holders were supposed to form the King's Council—were to a large
extent still in the hands of the oldest and greatest families, such as the
Sternbergs, the Zajícs of Hasenburg, the Berkas of Duba. Yet here
we can already discern the King's attempt, by careful shifting, to
strengthen elements on whom he felt he could rely either for personal
reasons or because the new officeholders, many of them coming up
from the gentry or even from lower origins, would have to rely on the
King's good will. Thus after the death of the chief justice of the state
supreme court (velký soud zemský) Zbyněk Zajíc of Hasenburg, in
1463, this position, which had been nearly hereditary in the family of
the Zajíc, was given to the King's brother-in-law, Lev of Rožmitál.[5]
(The King could point out that in the royal court chamber—nejvyšší
soud dvorský—another of the Hasenburgs, John Zajíc, still held the position of chief justice.) The position of chancellor was—and remained to
his death—in the hands of Prokop of Rabstein, who, coming up from the
gentry, had been raised by George to baronial rank. Of very considerable significance was the position of mintmaster of Kutná Hora, which
made its holder a sort of minister of finance. This had been held since
1458 by Zdeněk Kostka of Postupice, another former knight raised
to the peer's rank. But the mintmastership was only one basis from
which this closest of George's friends and supporters was allowed to
operate. We have seen him as head of the most important diplomatic
missions. He was later given the supreme office—that of high burgrave
—when in the civil war its holder, Zdeněk of Sternberg, had become
George's fiercest enemy.

Just as the King could raise knights to the peer's rank, so he could,
of course, make knights from commoners. He used both possibilities
sparingly though effectively. We have noted the Utraquist Kostkas
and Catholic Rabsteins among the first. Examples of the second group
existed especially in the administration of the national capital which,
for the total development of stable conditions in the kingdom, was
of considerable significance.[6] Among these is Vaněk Valečovský of
Kněžmost, who, after the conquest of Prague in 1448, had been ap-

---

[5] See Tomek, Dějepis, IX, 254.
[6] For the following see ibid., 266 and 258.

pointed as mayor of the Old Town—still considered the most important of the city's old, autonomous boroughs. During his regency
George had appointed him royal subchamberlain, an office of far
greater importance than the rather ceremonial one of lord high chamberlain, since the sub-chamberlain (podkomoří královský) was the
King's commissioner for the control and direction of affairs of the
cities. The fact that George appointed, for this job, a man who himself came from burgher rather than noble origin expressed very
clearly his wish to gain a good understanding of city interests and
urban points of view (though, in his eyes, largely identical with the
interests of the city patriciate). This was emphasized again when
in 1468 the King appointed, as Vaněk Valečovský's successor, Samuel
Velvarský of Hradek, who had held the office of Prague mayor for
many years and, much like his predecessor, was raised to knightly
status by King George in 1463. George's lord secretary—an office
which had never become the monopoly of any of the estates—the
faithful Burian Trčka of Lípa, who had served him from the beginning of his kingship, was the member of a knightly family, if an old
and wealthy one. From the lower stratum of the nobility also came
the second man ever to hold the office which had been created by
George during his regency: that of royal procurator, the man responsible for the royal income from fines, escheats, and other rever-
sions: Čeněk of Klinstein. Also, in looking for advisers as well as
for representatives on important diplomatic missions, George made
wide use not only of men of non-baronial origin but even of people
from other countries such as Mair and Marini (and, before long,
of Gregory Heimburg). The leading barons, and especially the older
houses, maintained their hold on the great ceremonial offices such
as high chamberlain, high court master, high marshal, rather than
on those of true substance. Two of the latter, it is true, besides the
less important chamberlain, were, by a custom amounting to law,
reserved to the lords: the offices of high burgrave and of chief justice
of the State Supreme Court. Yet there was little the lords could do
when the King, especially in decisions not directly concerned with
the administration of Bohemia proper, made himself as independent
from their influence as possible. There was, for instance, nothing
that could force him to call the royal or privy council except his own
will, and essentially this was true even for the state council which
included ex officio the great officeholders.

Nevertheless it is rather doubtful whether those historians who speak of George's tendency toward absolutism are quite right.[7] This term should not be used merely to indicate strong kingship as such. It rather presupposes the tendency on the part of the ruler to do away with, or to condemn to complete and permanent impotence, the representative institutions existing in his country. The Tudors in England did not try to destroy Parliament but rather to develop, educate, and use it for their purposes—a process leading, at best, to a sort of dynamic cooperation between the ruler and a considerable part of his people. In a similar way George maintained, though perhaps with less clarity of "educational" purpose than the great Tudors (or the early Vasa in Sweden), a constitutional regime. It is no accident that all the great critical moments of his rule are marked clearly by meetings of the Czech national diet (and less frequently by meetings of the estates of all the countries of the realm). During the last ones—the St. Lawrence Diet of 1462 in Prague and the great diet, this one indeed for the whole realm, convened in Brno in the summer of 1463—it was very clear how much the King relied on the estates as an institution destined, in cooperation with the ruler, to hold the nation together. Unfortunately, and much against George's wishes, a distinct split between two parties had developed. At first it seemed to be based exclusively on religious lines, with a lord—Zdeněk Kostka—always speaking for the Utraquist wing. That he spoke for most of the two other estates—knights and representatives of the cities—as well seemed at the time almost incidental. But now, in 1465, the increasing ferment in circles of the high nobility indicated that dissatisfaction was ripe very clearly on other grounds than religious ones, a fact which, while less obvious, had of course been true before. Only the timing was determined by the fact that now the lords who hoped to resist the King saw chances of support from outside, especially from Rome, which would not have been available at any time before.

That many lords were dissatisfied with the course things had taken cannot surprise us. The barons, or at least most of them, had in 1458 rallied behind George because they considered him as one of them and because they had expected that in the long run, despite his policy as regent, he would identify himself above all with the interests of their own—his own—caste. The wiser and less selfish ones among them did probably expect a further improvement in the economic health and national strength of the kingdom, much

---

[7] See e. g. Urbánek, *Věk*, IV, 186ff.

in line with what had already occurred during George's six years of peaceful regency. But few even among these would have wanted the measure of monarchial centralism and the reduction of baronial influence, and the degree of his independence from the specific baronial image of the good society—the society completely and exclusively ruled by and exploited in the interested of the large baronial landholders —that characterized George's reign.

And into this whole situation, when dissatisfaction had had time to grow among many of the great lords, there now enters a strong personal factor. It is the defection of Zdeněk of Sternberg.

During the period from the beginning of the organized resistance of the barons to the entry of Matthias Corvinus into the open struggle, Zdeněk of Sternberg was undoubtedly George's major antagonist.[8] He was, in many ways, a worthy successor to Ulrich of Rosenberg, the great, proud representative of the baronial caste, at whose court he had spent some of his young years, in the first decade following the end of the Hussite Revolution. Like Ulrich he was proud and reckless, utterly selfish, yet undoubtedly gifted as a diplomat and soldier, not much liked, even by his peers, but generally respected and even feared. He was a very good-looking and very vain man. It may have been due to Ulrich's influence that Zdeněk abandoned, quite early, the Chalice of which his mother, Perchta of Sternberg, had been a zealous and active supporter. Yet before very long—either in 1446 or the year after—in some very unclear connection with an equally unclear crisis of Zdeněk's marriage, we find him in that close friendship and cooperation with George of Poděbrady that characterized their early relation and that certainly helped to determine the successful rise of both men—Zdeněk to the rank of lord high burgrave, the leading office, military and civilian, ordinarily open to any member of the nobility; George to the unusual and dominating position of regency and eventual kingship.

For a considerable time, especially in the period beginning with the conquest of Prague in 1448 and lasting till about 1462, the friendship between both men was, at least by contemporary observers, con-

---

[8] There is no substantial monograph on this important figure. A glorification of his person and role is contained in *Historia Heroum de Stellis*, written by the 17th-century Jesuit Joannes Tanner, Ms dated Olomouc 1674, Prague University Library, XIII, D 160. His career is treated in some detail by Věra Kosinová in the article "Zdeněk ze Sternberka a jeho královské ambice," *Sborník prací věnovaných J. B. Novákovi*, Prague, 1932, pp. 206–218. (see above, chapter III, n.5.) See further Urbánek, *Věk*, I, 186–196, III, 112–113, and *passim* throughout all four volumes.

sidered to have been extremely close. It is described as such in the *Dialogus* written early in 1469 by John of Rabstein, the younger brother of Prokop and one of the finest Humanist minds of his people and time.[9] "One spirit, one hand, one council united Zdeněk and George," he wrote, referring to the conquest of Prague in which Zdeněk helped George to reinstate Rokycana.[10] He strongly underlines Zdeněk's part in George's election and claims that in the following period Zdeněk was present in all the King's councils. "What he affirmed," says Rabstein's friend William of Rabí to the Lord of Sternberg, "you also affirmed, what he negated, you also negated. What he called white, you declared to be like snow; what he called black, you likened to the raven."[11] In reality the relationship was hardly as harmonious, and above all never based on true and steady mutual trust, as that existing, for instance, between George and the other Zdeněk—Lord Kostka of Postupice. George, probably, was quite aware that Sternberg backed him only as long as he could hope that this would lead to solid gains for himself, and there had been periods even during the regency—indeed toward its very end—when there was tension between the two men. Yet in general the lord high burgrave had still seen his best advantage in cooperation with George, and had certainly reaped handsome rewards which Rabstein's *Dialogue* lists in some detail. In the same work, Zdeněk is openly charged with the main motive for the radical change in his attitude toward the King that occurred sometime early in 1465: the Lord of Sternberg has himself the ambition to be King.[12] If this was true, then his action is not difficult to understand. Finding George at this time in real difficulties, he believed that the time had come to turn against him and to put himself at the helm of the movement—as yet incoherent and unsure of itself and its final goals. Sternberg seems to have denied these intentions—this, at least, is how Rabstein quotes him in the *Dialogus*. But that very source indicates that Sternberg was widely believed to have held those ambitions, and there is no question that George himself thought this to be a factor in Lord Zdeněk's betrayal.

It is difficult to decide whether any particular issue brought the break about. Such an issue was hardly necessary, since it is obvious

---

[9] See Jan z Rabštein, *Dialogus,* best and most recent edition by B. Ryba, Orbis, Prague, 1946 (For other editions see bibliographical appendix).
[10] *Ibid.,* p. 20.
[11] *Ibid.,* p. 28.
[12] *Ibid.,* p. 30.

that, since the outbreak of the crisis in George's relationship to the Pope—when Zdeněk of Sternberg, in clear distinction to his earlier attitudes, had already made himself the spokesman of the Catholics—the great lord had lost much of his close contact with the King and could easily feel that his influence upon him was waning if not already gone. (How little this was, as yet, necessitated by the religious development alone could be seen by the continued closeness between King George and the two remaining Catholic bishops among Czech noblemen.) Nevertheless a special issue may well have come between the two men. It was Palacký's guess that it stood in some connection with that great outbreak of the plague, during which the death of a number of noblemen necessitated the appointment, by the King, of other noblemen as wards of their surviving children, which implied administration of their property and the right, if those children should die, of inheriting that property. (This practice had, in times of royal weakness, replaced a more general escheat.) The Lord of Sternberg had, so it seems, in preceding cases taken undue advantage of such wardships, and this was, in Palacký's view, a reason for the King to refuse any further endowments of this kind.[13] If this was really one of the issues, then George's reluctance was probably also motivated by reasons other than essentially moral ones. If he had good reason to sense in the lord high burgrave's recent attitudes the possibility of an impending defection he would not wish to strengthen still further the economic power of this already formidable man. This, in turn, may well have helped to remove any doubts the Zdeněk might have had about his course of action. If he was to maintain his position within his caste and that of this caste itself, if in particular he wanted to retain even the slightest chance of one day gaining the throne now occupied by his old friend and rival, not much time was to be lost, and no other moment might give him the same freedom of action which now would enable him, and no one else, to take over the effective leadership of the nascent movement of baronial revolt.

Zdeněk did, indeed, have a potential competitor of great attraction for the Catholic high nobility. This was, of all people, the Bishop Jost of Breslau. As long as in Bohemia proper no episcopal chairs were occupied by Catholics, Jost, senior to Tas of Olomouc, was the ranking Catholic prelate. At the same time he was a member of the one baronial family that could outshine the Sternbergs and all others by their fame and wealth: the Rosenbergs. The question was whether,

---

[13] See his *Dějiny*, 2nd ed., IV 2, 294 (in German, 336).

in a situation of increasing tension not only between the King and the Curia but also between the King and a large section of the high nobility, Jost could maintain his long held position almost between and above the parties, could still hope to bring the steadily sharpening conflict to a peaceful end. If he lost this hope, then indeed, for all his indubitable patriotism and his personal respect and friendship for the King, his course was rather clearly prescribed. As a bishop of the Roman Church he could not permanently hold out against the pressure exerted upon him by the Curia to join the front against George. And as a Rosenberg, as a member of the greatest of all baronial clans, he would find it difficult to maintain permanently his distance from a movement that would eventually include a majority of the Catholic barons, themselves a majority within the high nobility.

Yet even now in the spring 1465, when the alienation between the King and a slowly growing circle of Catholic barons became ominously noticeable, especially in repeated meetings of small conventicles around Zdeněk of Sternberg, the bishop decided on a last attempt at winning over King George to his own views. He did it in a memorandum that he submitted to Queen Johanna. The Queen, now and in the following years, maintained some contacts with the other side, largely through Catholic relatives such as her brother, Lev of Rožmitál. Of these contacts the King also made occasional use. Her own influence upon George may have been overrated by the Catholics, though there is little question that the King kept her well informed about the course of events and appreciated her good common sense.

Jost's memorandum is of high interest,[14] especially because it indicates that the bishop was fully aware of the sociological background of the struggle and that the relationship between the three main estates—barons, knights, and townsmen—was already under general discussion in connection with the looming crisis. He quotes people—obviously among the King's friends in the gentry—as having said: "Let the barons present themselves on their own, without the knights, and the knights by themselves without the barons, then it will soon become clearly visible who can serve the country better—the lords or the knights." To this the bishop answers: "We know well enough that there are more knights than lords, and more townspeople than knights, and that the peasants are the most numerous. And therefore, whoever wants to install a new order of things, let him first have

[14] See Jos. Truhlář, ed., *Manuálník M. Vácslava Korandy*, Prague, 1888, pp. 203ff. A fairly detailed excerpt from the memorandum is presented by Palacký, *Dějiny*, IV, 2, 297–299 (German, 340–342).

a new world created for himself. If this cannot be done, let us maintain the time-honored order of things, instead of claiming that if we only have the cities and can pull the knights away from them (the lords), then we can knock them down, and those whom among them we can keep on our side, those will be to our advantage."

In answering other arguments that he claimed come from the opposing side, namely that "it was not the princes and the masters who believed in the Lord Christ and obeyed his sacred grace but the simple, common people" (one wonders whether it is King George himself whom he quotes here or rather one of the prominent leaders of Utraquism, perhaps Rokycana, though he, too, was one of the "masters"), the bishop answers: "But who wants to make doctors (masters of theology) out of all those common people?" He goes on to warn that, if over-educated, the common people, instead of strengthened in their religion, will lose it.

Altogether these are the arguments of a shrewd and intelligent conservative politician, warning the King that what he is doing is dangerous because it has true revolutionary implications. Nor was he wrong in drawing such conclusions. King George had at times to brake sharply to prevent the conflict from growing into a revolutionary movement against the lords in general which he would have considered also as a danger to himself.

In these utterances as well as in Jost's references to Wenceslas Křižanovský, the grimly anti-Hussite canon of St. Vitus, whose preachings the bishop promised to try and moderate, we can also recognize some references to a religious disputation which under the King's personal chairmanship had taken place in Prague at a diet in February 1465—a last vain attempt at achieving an understanding between the two religious parties in relation to such issues as the Chalice. It had, of course, not brought the two sides any nearer to each other but had, if anything, sharpened the conflict, so that in the end the King, without any further hope, had closed the meeting.[15] The basic tone of hopelessness in relation to the religious split also dominates the mood of Jost's memorandum, and he sums up his pessimism in the words: "If this kingdom cannot get into the union of the Holy Roman Church, then I fear that the writing will be fulfilled that every kingdom divided against itself will perish. And this would come to pass, unfortunately, if we permitted ourselves to split not merely

---

[15] See Raynaldus-Mansi, *Annales ecclesiastici*, to 1465, §§26–44. A very detailed excerpt, with commentaries, in Jordan, *Das Königthum George's von Poděbrad*, 116–127.

in two but in even more parts, through which the Czech people would wound and destroy themselves. And over such goings-on foreigners might feel much joy and might like to further cripple and tear us apart, which God may prevent. And this will perhaps have an outcome quite different from what anybody may believe today." Jost was clever enough to leave it open who that "anybody" might be.

Surely Jost thought of his own caste first. Yet he was probably also honestly concerned with the fate of his country and of that internal peace for which he had fought with considerable courage and consistency, exposing himself in the process to hostility from both sides. But since in his eyes there was now no longer any solution short of compliance to the papal demands, he did not feel that he had any freedom of action left. Thus we find him, from now on, mostly within the baronial circle that began to take shape, at first, as a still indistinct and, in its methods, undecided opposition movement. To some extent he may even have lent this group of his peers his assistance and presence because he thereby hoped to restrain any tendencies toward hasty or dangerous actions. This, at least, he attempted repeatedly. But in the outcome his presence must also have strengthened the feeling of some of those men who would have liked to remain loyal to King George that there could be no real disloyalty implied in the formation of the baronial group as long as a proven friend of the King's such as Jost gave it his sanction. An especially clear case in point here was Jost's own brother and at present the lay head of his family: John of Rosenberg. It was through Jost that John, a man very unlike his unscrupulous and domineering father, found his way to the barons' league in its early stages. When he realized where its policy was leading, he soon turned his back on it.

The official policy of the league of lords in its early phase, determined in various meetings at Krumlov (the Rosenberg residence) as well as other places in southern and western Bohemia such as Strakonice (seat of Jost's grand-priorate of the Order of the Knights of St. John) and Sternberg's castle of Zelená Hora (near the town of Nepomuk) was not to provoke the King until there was much more support for the baronial cause. Yet the lords also avoided, at this stage, any emphasis on the religious issue, since they did not want to make it too easy for the King to gain the support of all Utraquists in the kingdom. As far as this went, this attitude would be essentially paralleled by that of the King, who was to maintain to the last his standing within the unity of the Christian Church and would never acknowledge that the struggle between himself and part of his Catholic subjects was a religious struggle. This, of course, was exactly the label that George's greatest foreign antagonist, the Roman Curia, would have liked to imprint upon it. Already, on August 2, 1465, Paul II, upon the recommendation of a committee of cardinals, including Carvajal and Bessarion, renewed the summons of George as a relapsed heretic, and four days later he empowered his legate Rudolf of Lavant to declare all oaths of loyalty sworn to George by his subjects as invalid.[16]

Meantime Zdeněk of Sternberg found other ways to damage the King's position, and not without lasting effect.[17] He had done very little in the Emperor's war against his brother, the late Archduke Albert. Yet he made enormous financial demands upon the Emperor, who was already troubled by renewed guerilla actions of some of the Austrian nobles as well as troops of bratříci who had been in Frederick's service and claimed not to have been paid up properly. In relation to Sternberg's claims an arrangement had been made in September 1464 that a committee consisting of three Austrian and three Czech lords should decide, and Sternberg had reluctantly promised to submit to this decision. But, when it was presented, Sternberg, although seemingly agreeable, circumvented it by simply making entirely new demands. Finally in April 1465, Sternberg, with some of his friends, sent a letter of challenge to the Emperor, at the moment when Frederick in Wiener-Neustadt was engaged in a last attempt to mediate between the papal legate Rudolf and King George's ambassador Beneš of Veitmíl. It is difficult to believe that the timing of this declaration of war early May 1465 was accidental, or that Zdeněk did not know how it would impress the Emperor. He was, after all, still the kingdom's highest official, and the Emperor—who bitterly complained in a letter to John of Rosenberg[18]—had had no warning notice that the challenger did this against the wishes of his King. It is perhaps not astonishing that his eagerness to mediate between Prague and Rome and to shield King George against papal attacks decreased considerably, all the more as his influence upon Paul II was anyhow incomparably weaker than it had been on Pius II. The Emperor's now

---

[16] SrS, IX, 135–139 and 143–145.

[17] See the presentation of this somewhat complex issue by Bachmann in Reichsgeschichte, I, 533–535, 553, 561, and the Emperor's letter to King George in A. Chmel, Regesta chronologica diplomatica Friderici III, II, Vienna 1859, 428f.

[18] See FRA II 20, 353–354.

obvious lack of enthusiasm for the continuation of his mediation led in turn to strong resentment by King George, who could not understand how Frederick could ever forget the debt of gratitude that he owed to his liberator of 1462. Zdeněk of Sternberg found that his tricky policy had been highly successful. He now tried to pull Frederick III over to his side by offering him a generous arrangement of the financial issues that had been the central object of the previous struggle. Travelling to Wiener-Neustadt in late August he achieved a complete understanding with the Emperor, who was already softening under the steady pressure from Rome. It was a diplomatic manoeuvre of considerable cleverness, and it certainly helped to strengthen the baronial group in its further policy,[19] since it tended to cause ill feelings in Prague and to spoil the relationship between George and Frederick.

The activities of the baronial group became more conspicuous in the course of the summer of 1465 and made it impossible for George to ignore. Since in unofficial declarations these barons emphasized political requests largely connected with legal and constitutional issues, the King decided to bring all these complaints into the open—and counter them through the support his own policy could be expected to find—at a meeting of the diet of the Czech estates which he called to Prague for September 23. It is clear that he hoped for the presence of the men who were, by this time, known to have formed the opposition: besides the Rosenbergs and Sternbergs, two lords Zajíc of Hasenburg, one Bohuslav of Švamberg (a descendant of a man of the same name once famous as a Taborite revolutionary general), and those of Plauen (Plavno), of Gutstein, and a few more. (Not all families were united. Thus one of the lords of Riesenberg and Rabí stood with the opposition, another one strongly against it, and there was a similar split among the Berka of Dubá. Other Catholic baronial families, such as the lords of Kolovrat, of Lobkovice and others never joined the group.)

But when the diet met in Prague at the appointed date,[20] most of the lords belonging to the opposition had stayed away. Only two of their number appeared on September 25: John Zajíc of Hasenburg, chief justice of the royal court chamber, and Jaroslav of Sternberg, Lord Zdeněk's oldest son.

The two lords called themselves the representatives of the Rosen-

---

[19] See Tomek, *Dějepis*, VII, 104.
[20] The proceedings of the diet, with some background material, in *AČ*, IV, 102ff.

bergs, of Zdeněk of Sternberg, of Ulrich Zajíc, "and other lords who are our friends." When the King asked who those friends were the lords refused to give any further names—an indication that as yet the group, in the lords' own view, was not sufficiently firmly organized. Then they presented their case in a carefully worded message set down in twelve articles:[21] Point 1: The King had not, as supposedly his predecessors, sought advice in the first place from the lords but largely "from some persons who have no competence regarding matters of the land (Bohemia proper) nor regarding the liberties of the lords and knights." Only when the King has made up his mind does he bring these things before the lords and urge acceptance without any changes, getting angry if objections are raised and unwilling to grant much time for deliberations. 2: The King should not use, as they said had been recommended to him, troops of bratříci against Breslau as this would damage the land and the princes of Silesia. 3: The King would like to see one of his sons elected as King. "We have Your Grace for our King and toward Your Grace we have always behaved and shall always behave as to our lord within the frame of our liberties, and while God grants life to Your Grace we shall act as it behooves us. But we do not mean, at this time, to have two lords over us." 4: "Rokycana with his priests still agitates against us and ours, with imagined and groundless complaints, storming and arousing the people, and saying: Oh, why is there no one who avenges these wrongs!" 5: The King is urged, according to his oaths, "to maintain the lords, knights and cities of the Czech Kingdom within their rights, orders, usages and freedoms as Your Grace's predecessors held and kept to our ancestors." 6: Against his original assurances the King is said to have already twice levied the special tax (berna) to the detriment of the country and the poor people. The lords ask for assurances that this will not be repeated and demand that the tax registers be burned, as they are "neither obliged nor willing to submit to any further taxation."[22] 7: The King has repeatedly asked lords and knights for military service without having consulted more than a few people before. He is asked not to do so again in future. 8: The King is supposed, on the basis of the statutes of the land, to give out all goods and lands which escheat to him to people of his choice, but has in fact not always given out all of them but retained some. This should be changed. 9: Some "freelands" which should not have

21 *Ibid.*, 102–105.
22 See about this also K. Krofta, *Začátky české berně*, Prague, 1931, 93–95.

been considered as fiefs had nevertheless, on the basis of "some old registers of light value" been treated as fiefs and had thus escheated to the King. This should not be done any longer. (Actually King George had handled this question as it had been handled by earlier Kings who had used opportunities to create new fiefs, a practice given up only at the time of Wenceslas IV.) 10: The crown jewels and the archives of the country had always, under the King's predecessors, been held by the lords, with the lord in charge obliged by oath to serve the nobility and the whole country. This should be done now again. 11: The King himself had once said that no graver damage could be done to the country than the issue of debased or light-weight coins. This, however, is exactly what has happened and has resulted in a considerable increase in the price of gold and of other prices (the lords claim that they had about doubled). The King is asked to set this right. 12: (This last point is an attempt to justify the whole action and at the same time to give it, on the surface, a slightly more conciliatory tone.) If he now acted "as a wise, gracious and just King" and accepted the lords' demands, this would be rewarded in later times. He had, they go on (and quite correctly) been a vigorous defender of the rights of the estates before he had risen so high in office. Being also a Czech he should not be less concerned with the liberties of the country than his immediate predecessors who had, after all, been foreigners.

After the reading of the baronial memorandum, the King asked whether there was any demand among the present members of the diet to add to the declaration heard. After a period of deliberation the answer was: the estates felt that the absent lords had no right to present these demands without informing and consulting the estates. After that—clearly a considerable time later—the King presented his answer point by point.[23] He tried as much as possible to base his arguments on clearly known facts of the constitutional situation. Thus he declared, to point 1, that everyone in the diet knew how the members of the royal council were selected and received within the royal council and that, in general matters regarding the country of Bohemia, each member was always asked freely to give his view, without any pressure. He also declared that he had not seen any advantage in discussing and voting issues of the common weal by parties or in cliques,[24] since in things of national importance all groups of

---

[23] *AČ*, IV, 105–109.
[24] The term used here by George is *stranně a po rotách*.

the nation ought faithfully and truly to advise and help each other. He regretted the partisan action of the leaguist barons who should instead have come for an open discussion to the meeting of the diet. On point 2 he presented his generally known view on Breslau and expressed his hope that the diet would fully support the needed punitive action against the city, whether or not troops of the bratříci were used or not. To the issue of his succession, point 3, he did not deny that he would like to be followed by one of his sons but declared that very obviously such a decision could only be taken by the free and unfettered choice of the lords, knights, squires, and cities, against whose will he neither could nor wanted to act. On point 4 he pointed out that only recently he had asked Master Rokycana to call together all priests (presumably meaning the Utraquist clergy) and had given them strict orders to avoid, as was necessary within the Compacts, all public attacks on the religious view of others, and this they had promised to keep. He would not tolerate the disturbance of this peace either by one side or the other. Very conciliatory was George's answer to 5. He was not conscious of having impinged on any of the rights of the nation, but, if it could be proved to him that he had ever done so, he would gladly repair the damage. On the other hand he expected the lords to do likewise. To the complaint about taxation (point 6), he remarked that the payment, while originally requested by him, had only been made through the free will of the estates and on the advice of some of the barons, and that it was used, as he was willing to prove, for the common good. To point 7 (the King's request for military service) he asked to which event the lords referred. If it was the campaign to free the Emperor, then, in view of the acute danger, there had not been time enough for any previous consultation, and besides the action had brought much good to the Czech crown and country. About the escheat (point 8), the King declared that he had merely disposed of those estates the settlement of which was clearly within his right, and this always without infringing upon the rights of others, and this had been subject to the investigation of the lords sitting in, ex officio, on the handling of the court and land registers, as everybody knows well. The registers noting the fiefs contested by the lords (point 9) have long been kept at Karlstein castle or in the court register, and their legal character was not decided upon by the King but by the royal chamber or the state supreme court. The King, here, personally addressed Lord Zajíc, who, he said, had as chief justice had ample opportunity to present his

objections but had never done so. In regard to crown and crown jewels
(10), he declared that he had, exactly according to the constitution,
given these precious things to Duke Victorin, to keep them faithfully and truly for the country, and even though his son was now
also elevated to princely rank, nevertheless he still held his Bohemian
peerage and his lands in Bohemia, and was fully able to watch over
those things according to his oath. In relation to the coins (11) the
King claimed that the proportion of good metal in Czech coins compared favorably with that of the neighboring countries, and reminded
his listeners of negotiations he had promised and begun to conduct
with the Emperor and the Saxon princes. (George could have included Poland.) But he did not refer either to the weight or to the
buying power of his coinage.[25] In relation, finally, to the general
rights and freedoms of the Czech estates, the King claimed that it
was due to his own activities that the Czech crown was now no longer
tied to the Austrian princely house but, according to the solemn
recognition by the Emperor, subject only to the free election by
the Czech estates; that furthermore the Emperor, for himself and
his successors, had solemnly renounced all rights of any interference
whatsoever in the government of the countries of the Bohemian crown.
The King then mentioned the other concessions reducing the last,
essentially nominal duties of the Czech kingdom to the Roman Emperor to the very minimum, and claimed in conclusion that he had
done everything possible for the freedom and well-being of the kingdom and would continue to do so.

This detailed account of arguments between the league of the lords
—still in its nascent state—and King George is important since hereby
the two sides choose their position for their future operations. Neither
side can have been under the illusion that this would be anything
but an extended strife. Both sides, obviously, were eager to win over
to their side as large as possible a proportion of the population. It
is for that reason that at this stage the allied barons spoke regularly
of the rights and liberties not only of their own estate but also
of the knights. It is for the same reason that King George described
his position and work as that of a clearly constitutional ruler who
had never trespassed against the accustomed and inherited freedoms
and privileges of the estates and would, if such trespassing could ever

25 Even Palacký (in IV, 2 n. 223 in both Czech and German) admits that here the lords
may have had a point. We shall return to this issue later in connection with the great currency
reform of 1469. See also K. Kastelin, *Česká drobná mince doby předhusitské a husitské, (1300–
1471)*, Prague, 1953, 235-239.

be proved to him, be ready to make amends. Nevertheless a number of issues remained on which the gap between the two sides was obviously so wide as to be virtually unbridgeable. Among these, presumably the most important was the first point: the lords deeply resented the lessening of their influence upon the government which had occurred, to some extent throughout his reign, but to an increasing degree in more recent times, in the King's councils, an influence which, in their own view, should by rights have been far superior to that of the other two estates. For this same reason it is not surprising that the other estates took the King's side in the most vigorous way imaginable. For once the spokesman of the Utraquist side of the diet was not, as he had been so often, Lord Zdeněk Kostka of Postupice, but only representatives of the two lower estates: the kingdom's chief secretary, Burian Trčka of Lípa, spoke for the gentry, while Samuel of Hradek, mayor of the Old Town of Prague, spoke in the name of the cities.[26] Trčka's speech was an especially fervent support of the King's declaration and his whole policy, combined with a sharp denunciation of the baronial complaints, which he called completely unfounded and unjustified. He, as well as the Prague mayor, assured George of the readiness of the two lower estates to stand by the King with all their strength and their lives.

Clearly this was one of the several moments in George's history when some groups among his adherents would have liked to see him make the strongest use of the groundswell of support for himself and of hostility toward the scheming group of Catholic lords.[27] Could he not destroy, by a sort of preventive revolutionary war, the position of this antagonistic group before it had had a chance to gain much support from other quarters?

In fact, this course was not really open to him, not now and not even in the time of his greatest danger. While he had gone remarkably far in freeing himself from the narrow views of the class from which he had emerged, while he could identify himself with a far larger part of the people over whom he ruled, he had never intended to recast society beyond these changes—mainly to strengthen the two lower estates—which, after the destruction of the Left at Lipany in 1434, had remained as the final outcome of the Hussite Revolution. He was still firmly determined to solve that incredibly difficult prob-

[26] *AČ*, IV, 110.

[27] This mood is clearly expressed in popular songs or poems of the time, one of which is, in contemporary translation, published by Bachmann in *FRA*, II, 42, 393f. On the possibility of George's taking the offensive against the lords see also Markgraf, *op. cit.*, 75

lem: to lead Bohemia back, as a member in good standing, into the Catholic comity of European nations without giving up the Compacts and the Chalice. An attack, at this stage, against the Catholic barons as a class would have made this impossible, would have challenged Catholics and baronial classes in other countries. Looked at from the vantage point of his permanent goals and purposes, the mixture of firmness and readiness to be conciliatory made good sense indeed.

We see the conciliatory side of George's policy at work when we hear him declare at the conclusion of the September diet that he was willing to submit the baronial complaints to a serious and detailed discussion if the barons appeared at the next meeting of the estates to be held on and after December 19.

But if some of the lords considered accepting this invitation, their leader Zdeněk of Sternberg was by no means willing to face the King in front of a diet the vast majority of which he knew to stand by the King. He decided to forestall any further action George could take through the diet by calling all his friends to a meeting at his castle of Zelená Hora (in German, "Grünberg," near Nepomuk in western Bohemia). There the group of lords in opposition against King George constituted itself, on November 28, 1465, as an official league (henceforth known as the League of Zelená Hora) by a solemn declaration of protest which, in most parts, was a repetition of the complaints brought forward in Prague a month earlier.[28] This time they put special emphasis on the one issue where the King's position seemed weakest and where they could hope that their complaints would strike a chord also among knights and cities: the lessened value and buying power of the Bohemian coins and the supposed doubling of the price level. But they also demanded again the crown and crown jewels—a possession which in the hands of an opposition would have been a very dangerous weapon. In the end they obliged themselves, for the period of five years, to grant one another all the help and protection in their power if any one of them should meet any untoward experiences. The document was signed by sixteen lords, representing nine different but closely interrelated families, numerically less than half of the Catholic peers of the realm, including, however, some of the richest and most powerful ones.

Their leader, Zdeněk of Sternberg, consistently operated so as to create a situation which would make the break between his clique

[28] *AČ*, IV, 111–115.

and the King as definite and as difficult to heal as possible. This
became especially clear in discussions he and some of his friends held,
during the same meeting, with Bishop Tas of Olomouc, who had
gone to Zelená Hora with the knowledge and agreement of the King,
clearly to find out what game was being played, but also to mediate
if such action was possible without demanding unreasonable concessions from the King.[29] The bishop informed the lords that the King
felt less aggrieved about the demands presented to the diet than by
the information he had had about the intrigues which Sternberg had
spun against him at the Emperor's court in late August—activities,
indeed, which coming from the King's highest official, were bound
to smack of treason. But Lord Zdeněk, far from answering this charge,
immediately went to the offensive, in a particularly shrewd way since
it was made to look as if he merely defended himself against atrocious
attacks. The King, he claimed, had spread the rumor that Zdeněk
and his friends were planning to have him murdered. He had accused
Zdeněk of having arranged with John of Rorbach, the Emperor's
chief adviser, that immediately after the King's death Maximilian, the
Emperor's young son, would be King and Zdeněk his regent in Bohemia. Since this would have been an arrangement closely similar to
the one that had actually existed during George's regency, it seems
not impossible that Sternberg had dreamed of exactly such a repetition of history in his own favor and now tried to project this into
the King's mind. He could then go on to say, with all the indignation of a man whose honor had been deeply offended by vicious
slander, that he had never even contemplated such a crime, but that
the King was clearly trying to build up a case against him and his
friends—a fact which would make it impossible for them to participate
in the December diet. George's subsequent declaration that he had
neither held nor uttered any such suspicion was, under these circumstances, not very effective in bridging the chasm between the parties,
not even when the Bishop of Olomouc confirmed the King's denial.[30]
It may, however, have had an effect on a few of the men who had
originally joined the league. The letters which Lord Zdeněk sent out
not only to the other Czech estates but also to a number of German
princes seem to have made little impression.

At the December diet in Prague, of course, the lords of the league

[29] *Ibid.*, 115ff.

[30] *Ibid.*, 118. The facts seem unmistakable. Yet Bachmann makes it appear as if false accusations by the King, reported to the lords by Bishop Tas of Olomouc, had induced the lords to
conclude the agreement of November 18 (see his *Reichsgeschichte*, I 569).

made no appearance.[31] Messengers whom they sent merely added a few new complaints to the old list: the most important one was directed against the King's order that no purchases of peasant-owned estates by the lords were to be admitted and entered into the land registers without his express permission. This is one of the few instances showing that George realized the grave dangers by which the economic strength and freedom of the Czech peasantry was threatened—under his successor this class was eventually pressed down into serfdom—and that he tried to stop such process of decay by measures effective enough, at least, to provoke the angry protest of the barons.

On this as on all other issues the baronial message completely identified the baronial interests with the liberties and the well-being of the kingdom. The lords, furthermore, demanded that the documents presenting the privileges of the Czech estates—normally kept with the crown jewels on Karlstein castle—be submitted to their scrutiny, to make sure that they were still fully present. The King actually agreed to having all the documents copied and the copies shown to all members of the diet on occasion of the next meeting of the diet scheduled for late February. At the same time the two lower estates, in agreement with the King, resolved to elect a committee to meet with representatives of the League of Zelená Hora sometime in January in Pilsen, Klatovy, or Budweis. While the lords did not refuse outright such negotiations, they asked for their postponement. They were, at this time, still not too sure of the course they should steer.[32]

The uncertainty that reveals itself in the policy of the league at this moment reflected the complex situation: the lords wanted to get more support from the Curia—above all they wanted and demanded

---

[31] See Tomek, *Dějepis*, VII, 114f.

[32] Palacký (IV, 2, n. 225 in Czech, n. 224 in German) believed that December 1465 is the correct date for the mission which took Dobrohost of Ronsperk, one of the Catholic members of the gentry, to Rome and in which he, after previous consultation with the Emperor, requested the Pope, in the name of the league, to give Bohemia another ruler, preferably the King of Poland. The main source for this event is a chronicle called "Relatio historica anonymi ab a. 1458–1469," published in Kaprinai's *Hungaria diplomatica temporibus Mathiae de Hunyad*, II, Vienna, 1767, 591. There, however, the mission is reported to have taken place early in 1467. Palacký, among whose few weaknesses was an inclination for rather light-hearted changes of dates which seemed to him doubtful, was in this case surely wrong, as pointed out already by Markgraf ("Die Bildung der katholischen Liga," *HZ*, 1877, 272). At this stage, certainly, John of Rosenberg and probably even his brother Jost would have opposed such a radical step, and there are no other indications of such a complete reversal, at this time, of the Emperor's policy in relation to George. Even Sternberg was probably not yet ready to ask for another King of Bohemia since at this moment he probably still hoped for the crown himself. The wrong dating made Palacký see a very different course of events —a precipitate rushing of the lords into a civil war for which in reality many of them, above all John of Rosenberg, had little inclination.

money—but, until they were much better prepared, they, or at least most of them, were not yet willing to become slavish instruments of the policy of Rome and to burn all their bridges. At the same time they were by no means united in their views. While Zdeněk of Sternberg was eager for more militant action, expecting that any compromise, even a temporary one, would weaken his position of leadership, Bishop Jost of Breslau was far more cautious, far more conscious of the King's strength and of the dangers involved in a civil war. For his brother John of Rosenberg, the idea of an open and violent rebellion against the King was even more intolerable. Thus it was mainly due to the two Rosenbergs that the open and final break between the barons and the King was once more postponed. It was not the barons but one of Bohemia's cities whose rebellion, inside the kingdom, assumed first a violent form: the western Bohemian metropolis of Pilsen.

The events leading up to this break are not well documented and not very clear.[33] Pilsen's history, indeed, is frequently puzzling and difficult to understand. During the Hussite Revolution, Pilsen had been one of the first to adhere to the radical wing of the movement and had for a while been the headquarters of John Žižka. When he left for Tabor early in 1420, a counterrevolution returned the city to the rule of the strongly anti-Hussite patriciate, and under its influence it remained, in close contact with the Catholic lords of western Bohemia, the most important Catholic center in all Bohemia up to the end of the Hussite Wars. It may well have been the memory of this, but more probably the short and quickly subdued attempt of a former city councillor to organize an opposition to the King in 1458, that determined George in 1462 to give some special power to Pilsen's city judge, a man whom he knew to be a faithful adherent of his, one Andrew Oremus. Under his guidance the city—ethnically mixed, though predominantly Czech, but still overwhelmingly Catholic—had shown no signs of dissatisfaction or unrest, but it is quite understandable that especially in view of its earlier history and its geographic

[33] The Pilsen rebellion is presented rather curtly by Palacký, *Dějiny*, IV, 2, 334f. (in German, 383f.), and in a somewhat distorted way by Bachmann, *Reichsgeschichte*, I, 571, whose "correction" of Palacký is motivated by the not very clarifying words "dessen Darstellung ich aber in obiger Weise modifizieren zu müssen glaubte." The main sources are in *AČ*, IV, 124–127 and in J. Strnad's "Čtyři omluvné listy Plzeňských z r. 1466," *ČČM*, 1884, 102f., while Bachmann seems to rely almost exclusively on the letter from the people of Pilsen sent to Duke William of Saxony, published by him (but without the rest of the material in the Weimar archives, such as King George's letters to Duke William) in *FRA*, II, 44, 610–611. The most detailed and accurate modern account in Tomek, *Dějepis*, VI, 2nd. ed., 117–118.

situation the baronial clique with Zdeněk of Sternberg at the head hoped to gain it for themselves, thus winning a center which would be remarkably like Pilsen's position as center of the "Pilsen Land-frieden" during the Hussite Wars. The pressure of the lords had been increased by messages which Rudolf of Lavant had sent to Pilsen as papal legate.

This pressure caused Oremus and his friends in the city council to send, at the very beginning of 1466, a delegation to the King asking for help, which George promised to grant immediately. When, however, a few weeks later, the royal troops appeared before the gates of the city it turned out that they were no longer welcome. A complete reversal had already taken place in the city, the King's enemies were in charge. Oremus had been banished and some Swiss and German mercenaries had been hired who were now employed in driving the small royal troops away. The whole development must have surprised the King, especially in view of the strong loyalty which most of the other cities of western Bohemia, such as Cheb with its overwhelmingly German and exclusively Catholic population, were to show the King despite the steadily increasing pressures from Rome. The specific reasons for Pilsen's early defection will probably never be fully explained. Militarily the short war that erupted here in the late winter of 1466 had merely the character of an episode. But at the same time it was a most fateful event, for it was the first small act in the bloody civil war that was to shatter the long, blissful peace which Bohemia had enjoyed, thanks to George, for the last fifteen years.

CHAPTER 18

THE MIGHTY PEN: GREGORY HEIMBURG

WHILE THE baronial rebellion in Bohemia slowly, with various starts and stops, got in motion; while King George, very far from considering a preventive war, nevertheless fortified his ties with the lower estates and began strengthening the garrisons in some of his castles, the Curia now stepped up its persecution of the "heretical King." The strongest influence in this direction was exerted by Cardinal Carvajal. The Pope, himself a man of some vigor but of limited insight, might have tried, as he did on other, smaller issues, to change the course laid down by his predecessor, if only in order to prove his independence and originality. But in this cause he felt strongly that he needed guidance. Of the three-man committee of cardinals that he appointed, Carvajal was by far the most highly respected and even feared member. We may wonder whether some of the admiring judgments passed on him by later writers do not go a little far in idealizing this strong and dominating personality.[1] His early dealings with the Bohemian issue, at least, do not betray as much wisdom as he has often been credited with. But there can be no doubt that his part in the powerful recovery of the papal position after the conciliar crisis had been large, at times probably decisive, and that he had generally acted with circumspection and energy during his difficult years as the Curia's representative in Hungary. It is probably also fair to say that his position toward the Bohemian problem, if narrow and in the end fatal to peace, was essentially consistent. And while he was deeply involved in issues of the foreign policy of the Curia, it should still be recognized that religious motivations were dominant in determining his actions, much more so than they had been with Pius II, though, of course, in the great ideological struggles of the time, it is quite impossible neatly to divorce religion and politics.

---

[1] Apart from Gomez Canedo's work quoted earlier (Chapter 2, n. 11) see the evaluation of two historians with such widely diverging views as Pastor (II, 396–404) and Palacký (*Dějiny*, IV, 2, 239f., in German, 372f.). Especially impressed is also Voigt, *Enea Silvio*, III, 511f.

We have already mentioned the steps which, on Carvajal's urging, Pope Paul had taken in August 1465, renewing the summons to King George to appear in Rome within one hundred and eighty days, which had once before been issued by Pius II. King George decided to answer this summons with the help of an experienced international lawyer, and again Dr. Mair was, as it were, lent out to him by Louis of Bavaria. Mair's, as always, well-paid efforts produced a lengthy answer to Pope Paul dated October 21, as well as a number of letters to German and other European princes including the Emperor asking for support in his defense against the Holy See.[2] It can hardly be claimed that the writ contained any new or surprising arguments, but in it George went far in offering to justify himself. The King, so he declared, has not only sworn to the Pope to eradicate heresy from his kingdom, but has, at the same time, sworn to the people worshipping "sub utraque" that he would keep and protect them as this had been done by his predecessors Sigismund, Albert, and Ladislav—that is, within the Compacts. How could those be considered heretics whose character as faithful Christians and true sons of the Church had been acknowledged by the highest authority: The Basel Council? And if this was so, how could he be blamed as having trespassed against the true creed by what he had said at the St. Lawrence Diet in Prague? At the same time the King seemed willing to justify himself before a suitable court—not, however, in Rome, since he could not, as a King, deprive for any time his subjects of his protection and the peace which he alone could safeguard. If however, an assembly of ecclesiastical as well as temporal princes, including the Emperor, were to be appointed either to sit in or near the borders of his country, he would be willing to clear himself of all false accusations and to accept correcting instructions in case any misconceptions could be pointed out to him. Such a tribunal, the King said, could be established, and until it would begin to function, all other procedures against him ought to be stopped.

The King's letter to the Pope, as styled by Mair, was dispatched to Rome by one of the King's trusted younger diplomats, Jaroslav, the knightly member of the great embassy sent to France in 1464. He arrived in Rome in December 1465, but when he tried to present the King's message to the Pope, Paul II, on recognizing the sender, furiously threw the document away—it was later picked up and passed

---

[2] See Palacký, *Dějiny*, IV, 2, 318–319 (German, 365–367). Detailed references to the original (in the "Cancellaria regis Georgis") in n. 234. (German n. 233).

on to Cardinal Carvajal—overwhelmed the helpless envoy with a flood of invective and eventually gave orders for him to leave Rome without any answer.

A somewhat more polite, but in substance not more conciliatory answer received another action ostensibly undertaken in the King's favor, also largely directed by Dr. Mair. This was a diplomatic demarche of Duke Louis, who, for this purpose, sent his councillor Dr. Valentin Bernbeck to the Pope. He arrived in Rome in November 1465 with a long list of suggestions, organized in fifteen points. While we have no actual text of what is purported to be the King's proposals or of Bernbeck's instructions, we have the Pope's answer, which gives us, through its scornful mention of all the various points, an approximate idea of what Dr. Bernbeck had presented to him and to the Cardinals.[3] If we compare it with those documents that bear the King's seal and signature, especially those dispatched at the very same time, we can, with a good deal of confidence, say that quite a number of those points cannot have been fully discussed with and approved by the King. Above all it seems extremely unlikely that he should, as the Pope indicates, have offered to accept, with his whole family, the communion in one kind. There is—despite the contrary claims of some historians—no proof at all that at any time in his life George had made this specific offer with the possible, but still doubtful exception of the negotiations conducted with the papacy early in 1471. Wherever else we find more general promises to act and worship according to the true Christian or Catholic rites they have always, expressly or implicitly, the qualification: "within the framework of the Compacts." The Compacts, indeed, make their appearance in this document, too, for there is mention of a request to the Holy See to send an inquisitor who should have the task and power to persecute all heresy "outside the Compacts," and the Pope immediately saw in this an attempt to obtain thereby an indirect confirmation of the Compacts.

In the center of the whole proposal, as it appears from the papal answer, stands what seems to be a rather detailed offer of military action against the Turks, with every fourtieth male of the Czech kingdom to be mobilized for this purpose; this army, together with all other forces that could be put in the field, should be commanded by George; George, even before any such campaign, should be confirmed by the Pope as Emperor of Constantinople; of his two older sons the oldest, Victorin, should be given the papal approval as successor to the

---

[3] *Ibid.*, Czech, 327ff. and n. 241 (German, 374ff. and n. 240).

Czech throne while his younger, as yet unmarried brother Henry be made Archbishop of Prague.

It was not difficult for the Pope, or for Carvajal if he can be considered the real author of the Pope's letter to Duke Louis, to describe these suggestions as impossible and even ridiculous. But it is almost as easy to show that the suggestions cannot have been George's own demands. George, to give one example, was at this very moment engaged in negotiations, very important to him and in their outcome indeed valuable and consequential, to have his son Henry married to Princess Ursula of Hohenzollern, favorite daughter of Margrave Albert Achilles. George knew well that Margrave Albert had a good chance of becoming, before long, elector and ruler over all the Brandenburg lands. Simultaneous requests for Henry's promotion to Archbishop of Prague would clearly tend to make the desired close tie between Poděbrady and Hohenzollern more difficult or impossible (and this may, indeed, have been the very purpose of Duke Louis' offer, since close ties between his old enemy Albert Achilles and the Czech King was clearly unwelcome to the duke or his chancellor Mair).[4] Less consideration, we may assume, would King George at this stage pay to the elected if not confirmed Archbishop of Prague, Rokycana. But that he would risk alienating this powerful churchman by the doubtful manoeuvre of presenting young Prince Henry as potential archbishop seems rather unlikely, especially in a moment where the King was increasingly dependent on the Utraquist estates. (In addition, while at 17 years amply old enough to marry, Henry seemed, even in the terms of the time, rather too young to be archbishop, though in some cases such appointments had occurred.) It is, of course, possible that, in the course of the previous discussions between George and Dr. Mair, such possibilities had been mentioned and tentatively discussed. But it seems hardly possible that this had been George's matured intention and instruction.

Among other doubtful points to some of which Palacký has already drawn attention [5] is the improbability that Matthias Corvinus—whom George at this time, though wrongly, considered a friend and potential supporter—would have agreed to the Czech King's occupying the throne of a restored Byzantine empire. And though it cannot be denied that at times—and especially as long as Martin Mair had a strong influence on his policy—George's expectations of expanding

[4] See Eschenloer, G., I, 285.
[5] *Dějiny*, IV, 330 (German, 378).

· 411 ·

power were not limited by the borders of the Bohemian crown, it seems still less than likely that he should have let this fantasy range in so uninhibited a way.

Another support for the assumption that the Bavarian intercession in the form in which Dr. Mair had finally directed it was by no means welcome to George, let alone specifically approved by him, might perhaps be seen in the alienation between George and Mair which followed very soon after the demarche in Rome. The reason for this was certainly not the ineffectiveness of this mission. The King had never shown much resentment against his diplomats when some of their efforts failed—he had, indeed, been always willing to give his advisers in the field of foreign policy another chance even after a very obvious failure, and he was to do this also later. But from this date on, as far as we know, direct contacts between him and Dr. Mair ceased, and before long it became obvious that Mair was no longer the King's friend and advocate.

There remains, then, the question how such a strange action could have come about in the first place. But this is not too surprising if we consider Mair's personality and the earlier history of his relation to King George. Mair clearly saw himself not merely as a legal and diplomatic adviser and occasional ambassador for this or that prince, be he one of the Wittelsbachs or even the King of Bohemia. In his view—and at times it seemed not too wrong—he was a great statesman, a maker of top-level policy and shaper of the whole Central European political scene.[6] If his older plans for making George King of the Romans had ever succeeded, Mair would have been the king-maker, as he would, too, in regard to most of the previous candidates for this ever tempting yet never available position. The idea of King George offering himself as generalissimo against the Turks also appears earlier in Mair's thoughts—in the letter he wrote to the King upon his return from Milan in February 1460. Another case of Mair's attempting to direct George, without too much prior consultation, into a course of action thereupon rejected by the King is revealed by the draft for a diplomatic demarche to gain Pope Pius for George's Roman kingship. Now, it seems, Mair, though he had been in personal contact with George only recently and knew what the King wanted, gave his instructions for this new diplomatic demarche quite according to his own lights. Nor can we be quite sure that, even apart from the issue

6 "Ein mächtiger und vielumworbener Staatsmann" he is called by Riezler in his article on Mair in *ADB*, XX, p. 116.

of the Hohenzollern marriage, he was too eager for it to succeed, if success meant to get the King of Bohemia permanently out of his present predicaments. Soon enough we find the great lawyer busily engaged in strengthening those predicaments and increasing the number of George's enemies, as he now felt sure that George was bound to lose out anyhow.

But perhaps we should give Dr. Mair, in his earlier activities, at least some credit for the fact that at the time when he himself was about to turn against the King, an old and at times close friend—indeed in some measure his teacher—joined the ranks of George's legal and diplomatic assistants for the rest of the King's and almost also his own life: Dr. Gregory Heimburg.

Among the great political lawyers of the middle and later fifteenth century Heimburg was surely the greatest, and by far the most famous, although also the most infamous in the eyes of his numerous enemies.[7] Now in his sixties, he had been in the thick of the great ideological struggles of the time for about half his life: A born humanist who had acquired his rich legal knowledge and his degree as *doctor utriusque juris* at the University of Padua, Heimburg threw himself early into the fight for ecclesiastical reform and conciliar supremacy waged at Basel, where he represented Archbishop-Elector Konrad of Mainz. He became, soon afterwards, a strong advocate of the policy of German princely neutrality in the struggle between Pope and Council, later specifically between Eugene IV and Felix V.[8] This policy of neutrality, maintained by Albert II during his short reign, was given up in 1446 by Frederick III—he sold, as Heimburg put it later, his obedience to Rome for 221,000 ducats. It was one of the acts of Frederick III—surely seen in somewhat distorting simplifications—which Heimburg never forgot or forgave.

In his early years Heimburg's relationship with the Roman Church was not yet as bitterly antagonistic as it was to become. He stood in friendly relations with Carvajal and, for a time, even with Aeneas

---

[7] The first monograph on Heimburg, soon out of date, was written by Clemens Brockhaus, *Gregor von Heimburg*, Leipzig, 1861. It made a not always succcessful attempt to do justice to Heimburg's work for King George. Generally far superior is the early work of Paul Joachimsohn (later Joachimsen), *Gregor Heimburg*. While this work gives a good picture of Heimburg's life up and through the struggle for Sigismund of Tyrol, the part on the Bohemian phase is short (only 37 pages) and not as thorough as the general excellence of this brilliant historian of the Reformation would have seemed to promise.

[8] See e.g. Wilhelm Pückert, *Die Kurfürstliche Neutralität während des Basler Konzils*, Leipzig, 1858, 170–172 and *passim*.

Sylvius, who appreciated the German humanist in him more than the lawyer-representative of the anti-imperial and soon also anti-papal reform party.[9] As legal adviser of Nürnberg, Heimburg defended the rights of the great imperial city especially against the dangerous attack of Margrave Albert of Brandenburg (whom nevertheless he admired), and it was during this phase that he met and befriended the far younger Martin Mair.[10]

But the cause célèbre which Heimburg made his own in the late fifties and early sixties was the prolonged and bitter struggle between Duke Sigismund of Tyrol and Cardinal Nicholas of Cusa, Bishop of Brixen.[11] The issue itself was, in its details, complex and of secondary significance. The main actors—the gifted, humanistically inclined but rather temperamental Habsburg prince, and the elderly churchman, great thinker and reformer, philosopher and mathematician, but far too rigid, far too choleric and over-sensitive to make a tolerable politician—both saw those matters in the light of great principles. The cardinal, intending to remove what to him seemed transgressions of worldliness and worldly rule into the ecclesiastical realm, collided with the determination of the lay prince not to permit any encroachment of the bishop into the temporal domain—or what had, by custom and history, become the temporal domain. Thus the episcopal proprietory rights (Vogtrecht) to the Convent of Sonnenburg, together with a radical reform of the nuns' customs and standards, were to be enforced against the vigorous protests of the ladies in question, from the abbess down. But this was only the beginning, since Cusa, contending support from old documents, demanded recognition of his dominion over the entire valleys of the Inn and Eisack Rivers and of his claims to the mining industries of the country. Altogether, the duke had behind him the strong majority of the Tyrolian people, including even a substantial part of the regional clergy, but the cardinal could count upon the support of the Curia, the more decidedly the longer the struggle lasted and the more it became a matter of principle and correspondingly exacerbated. Heimburg was consulted as early as 1457, and the duke, following his advice, appealed in the following year "from the [ill-informed] Pope to the better informed Pope." At Mantua in 1459 Heimburg

9 See e.g. Gerhart Bürck, *Selbstdarstellung und Personenbildnis bei Enea Silvio Piccolomini*, Basel, 1956, pp. 92–95.

10 On Mair and Heimburg's relation to him see Joachimsohn, *Heimburg*, 108–110.

11 There is, on this famous struggle, an extremely detailed monograph by Albert Jaeger, *Der Streit des Cardinals Nikolas von Cusa mit dem Herzoge Sigmund von Oesterreich*, 2 vols., Innsbruck, 1861. Joachimsohn also treats it, as far as Heimburg is concerned, in some detail (*passim* between pp. 173 and 249).

represented the Duke in the proceedings before the new Pope—his old humanist acquaintance, Pius II.[12] When Heimburg declared that the duke would present the issue of territorial rights only to a lay court presided over by the Emperor, he already expressed his opposition against any concessions to the forcefully renewed offensive for the absolute dominance of the papacy. The attempt at an understanding between duke and cardinal, at one moment hoped for by the Pope, quietly failed, and in Heimburg's eyes the whole great congress—the term "council" was carefully shunned—could hardly have a worse finish than the Pope's pronouncement of the bull "Execrabilis," an attempt at barring victims of papal arbitrariness from the one juridical help still open to them—the appeal to a council.[13]

When later Sigismund forced the cardinal, whom he had kidnapped, to sign a compromise agreement, the Pope excommunicated the duke and all his helpers and put the whole country under interdict. As the duke's permanent legal representative, Lawrence Blumenau, had been imprisoned while pleading Sigismund's case before the Pope, the duke again called on Heimburg, who immediately appealed to a future Pope as well as to the Council which, he claimed, was anyhow over-due—a theme to be heard later more frequently from Heimburg. The Pope's answer was to request the cities of Nürnberg and Würzburg, Heimburg's most frequent residences, to confiscate his property and arrest him as a heretic. But the great lawyer-statesman could not be silenced that easily. In a tremendous campaign, culminating in a brilliant pamphlet published early in 1461, he poured scorn on the papal breve, fiercely denounced the Execrabilis, and attacked as heretical the Pope's claim to be above the Council.[14]

At this stage Heimburg's work for Duke Sigismund, a dress rehearsal, as it were, for his later work in Prague, seemed to blend with the general attack which the reform party among the German princes, notably Elector Diether of Mainz and the Wittelsbach princes, directed against both Pope and Emperor, with Dr. Mair attempting to use the widespread feeling against the Emperor to further his scheme of having George of Poděbrady elected as King of the Romans. Heimburg was informed of this plan and thoroughly approved of it.[15] In January 1461 he represented Duke Sigismund at the great assembly of Cheb, where he gained a promise of support from King George. Soon after-

[12] Joachimsohn, *Heimburg,* 162ff.

[13] *Ibid.,* 179f.

[14] *Ibid.,* 197–204.

[15] In a letter from Cheb to John of Rabstein. See Pešina, *Mars Moravicus,* 721f.

wards Heimburg went to France in the hope of finding there support for the idea of a new council, a goal that he was to pursue still later. Meanwhile the Curia proceeded further against Heimburg. Together with his prince, he was, in the great damnation of Maundy Thursday, cursed as a heretic, and some of the best minds of the Curia, especially Theodore Lelli, Bishop of Feltre, were busy answering Heimburg's dangerously effective attacks. Finally, after lengthy mediation attempts on the side of Venice, a successful action was undertaken by Frederick III. It was a remarkable end to a strange struggle. After Duke Sigismund had promised restitution of all clearly episcopal possessions to Cusa, he was absolved from his excommunication, the Emperor having asked forgiveness in the duke's name. None of the ambitious claims of the cardinal survived his death on August 14, 1464. But no attempt was made either by Sigismund or by the Emperor to free from excommunication the man who had been responsible for Sigismund's essential success: Gregory Heimburg continued to be regarded as a damned and condemned heretic. It was not Sigismund but Frederick III whom Heimburg made responsible for this outcome—unfortunate enough, even in view of the very limited troubles which his status imposed upon him—and he never forgave him.[16]

His life, now again in Würzburg, was not too bad—nor had he lost his close contacts with some of the men fairly near the top of the Roman hierarchical pyramid. In September 1465, for instance, he sent a lengthy letter in defense of the King of Bohemia to his old friend, the Cardinal Carvajal. We know its contents—of the letter itself only the enclosed not very short "cedula" has been preserved—partly from Carvajal's detailed answer mailed in the very end of the year.[17] Whether Heimburg's action had been solicited from Prague seems doubtful—in any case the style of the enclosure does not sound like an official or semi-official demarche. He is not even as complimentary in his references to the King as one would expect if this were a job done at George's request and for his reward. But a copy of it may still have served as Heimburg's introduction for entering the King's service.

In his letter Heimburg warned the cardinal to realize the enormous strength of the man who now was the greatest power in the Empire. At the same time he questioned the wisdom of trying to attack as heretical a ruler who had not changed in the least since he had been

---

[16] Joachimsohn, *Heimburg*, 248f.
[17] See *FRA*, II, 20, 336–369, 377–382.

treated with supreme honor and graciousness by Calixtus III and Pius II. The letter made no impression upon the cardinal, whose answer, not unfriendly in its beginning, made the point that, the stronger George was in Germany, the greater the need to eliminate the danger of his infecting other princes with his infidelity.

If George knew of this correspondence, one may wonder if he really hoped that Heimburg, of all people, would be the proper mediator between himself and the Curia. It must have been quite well known to the King that Heimburg's reputation in Rome was not any better than his own. But he also knew that those German circles that counted in the political life of the Empire looked at the great lawyer, pamphleteer, and humanistic polemicist with a respect bordering on awe. When, in June 1466, Heimburg arrived in Prague he could boast two dukes as his escort: Elector Ernest of Saxony and his brother Albert, George's son-in-law. This is of some interest also because it indicates that Heimburg's position in relation to the two princely parties had changed considerably. He was no longer close to the Wittelsbach group but had drawn much nearer to the Wettins and Hohenzollern, including especially also his one-time adversary, Margrave Albert Achilles.

From now on Heimburg belonged to the small circle of George's permanent councillors, the last and greatest of the foreign experts whose advice the king so often asked, mostly appreciated, and rather frequently followed. And for a considerable time some of the most important documents that left the royal chancery of Prague show the mind and style of Gregory Heimburg. The direct diplomatic success of these actions was sometimes limited and doubtful. But the main significance of Heimburg's activity was that he helped the King to clarify and present the real issues: the rights of a lay ruler to maintain his rule against clerical attack. Indeed George's public utterances, supported and often shaped by Heimburg, begin to sound more spirited, more sure of their rightness!

In July 1466 the first of these documents—Heimburg himself called it an "apology" for the King—was, in slightly differing versions, sent to a large number of princes, among them King Matthias of Hungary, King Louis XI of France, the Kings of Poland and Denmark, and all the important German rulers.[18] Heimburg, in George's name, assured the receivers of his messages of his devotion to the person of the Holy

---

[18] See the German version in Müller's *Reichstag-Theatrum*, II, 250–258. For other places see Palacký, *Dějiny*, IV, 2, p. 342 n. 255 (German, 393 n. 254). See also *FRA*, II, 20, 407–409, and Dobner, *Monumenta historica Boemiae*, Prague, 1764 ff., vol. II, 418f.

Father. But immediately he put his finger on the juridically impossible features of the papal summons (for which he does not make the Pope himself but the "Procurator of the Faith," Antonio da Gubbio, responsible). Only when the tribunal before which George is called has spoken, only then should it be possible to consider him either guilty or innocent. Yet the summons itself anticipates a verdict of guilty by depriving the King, without any explanation, of his royal titles. If he, George, were to submit to this dreadful distortion of law he would thereby plead guilty in a cause in which he feels completely innocent. The "apology" vigorously defends the sacred rights of the crowned and anointed King against the illegitimate attack of the Curia in fields which were not hers to decide. With particular energy the apology denies that the King had, at the St. Lawrence Diet, made the heretical statement that there is no salvation for laymen without the Chalice. The addressees are urged to present those arguments with all possible emphasis to the Pope.

Few of the addressees—with the remarkable exception of George's son-in-law Matthias—failed to take the requested steps.[19] There was in Rome itself, however, no palpable success. Yet the intercession with the Holy See was not the only, perhaps not even the most important, goal for the feverish activity that, under Heimburg's guidance, the royal chancery of Prague developed in these weeks and months. Much of it was meant to convince the addressees themselves and to reinforce the links that tied them as princes to the Czech ruler. And in this the action was by no means unsuccessful. Even some of King George's inveterate antagonists showed themselves impressed.[20]

The measure of this success is perhaps most clearly expressed in the efforts the Curia felt it had to make in order to counteract the effect of Heimburg's political propaganda—from the fairly dignified answer of Carvajal [21] to the heated epistle of Bishop Rudolf of Lavant, with its vengeful personal attacks on Gregory Heimburg himself, whose authorship of the "apologies" was no secret anywhere.[22] In a similar vein wrote a cleric who, some years earlier, had counted himself among King George's friends: the Minorite friar Gabriel Rongoni of Verona.[23] But, whereas none of these attacks could have come as a surprise either to the King or his new adviser, the situation was different in the case of the man who now addressed Gregory Heimburg as

---

[19] See *Cancellaria regis Georgii*, D 163, 185-187.
[20] Eschenloer, G., I, 316.
[21] *SrS*, IX, 203-209.
[22] *Ibid.*, 210. Even Pastor (II, 402) treats this answer with some criticism.
[23] *SrS*, IX, 197.

his old, intimate friend and devoted disciple: Dr. Martin Mair.[24] It is a letter of warning, for all the "captatio benevolentiae" contained in its beginning, a warning that Heimburg has just taken over an impossible task—the defense of the heretic against the overwhelming power of the Catholic world. By himself abandoning what he thought a hopeless and probably thankless task, Mair now also gave up many views which figured in his arsenal such a very short time ago. True—Mair had never been a heretic, but neither had George, in Mair's recent views. Now, however, he has discovered that the Compacts have not now and have never had any validity. George's claim that he had to observe them in order to maintain peace in Bohemia is a poor excuse which "does not alleviate but rather augments his crime." For reasons which surely have very little to do with Mair's supposed religious piety, he now, with astonishing completeness, accepts and presents all the familiar arguments of the Curia and ends with sinister prophecies of the King's unavoidable destruction, if he does not utterly and completely submit to the Pope's orders. This, it seems, was hardly the purpose for which Heimburg had been asked to come to Prague or what he would have advised the King to do. The old, close friendship between the two great lawyer-diplomats suffered badly from this letter, and though the contact was not quite broken—Prague's foreign policy was, after all, still interested in retaining some access to the ducal court of Landshut—it never regained the old cordiality.

While the effect of Heimburg's work upon Bohemia's western neighbors was recognizable if limited, it was an outright failure in regard to Bohemia's greatest neighbor to the east. Yet, besides Venice, where his cautious attempts helped to stabilize the friendly but in the long run not especially profitable relationship between Bohemia and the Adriatic Republic,[25] it was Matthias Corvinus upon whom Heimburg settled some of his main expectations.

The correspondence between Prague and Buda contains the sad and tiresome story of a relationship carefully nurtured by one side in the hope of maintaining peace and some degree of friendship, by the other in the clear expectation, occasionally showing all signs of impatience, to get over all the unreal diplomatic preludes to the exhilarating realities of a victorious war.[26] This goal, however, could be reached

---

[24] Printed by Joachimsohn in the documentary appendix, *Heimburg*, 318–324.

[25] *Ibid.*, 274f., also *FRA*, II, 20, 424f.

[26] Most of this correspondence (carried on between the two Kings, Duke Victorin and Matthias, and Heimburg and his friend John Vitéz, Archbishop, later Cardinal of Esztergom) in the documentary volume XI of Count J. Teleki's *Hunyadiak Kora Magyarorszagon*, 206–251.

only when both Hungary's domestic situation and her relation to her dynamic neighbor to the southeast, Sultan Mohammed II, would permit. Till this point was reached, Matthias had to wait longer than he would have liked.

Heimburg might have made less strenuous efforts to gain the friendship and diplomatic help of the King of Hungary if he had been fully aware of an episode that had occurred in the fall of 1465. At that time George had suggested to Matthias a personal meeting at the Moravian-Hungarian border, from which the latter had excused himself because he had to deal with Turkish incursions in Hungarian territory. In his stead, however, Archbishop Vitéz had invited King George to meet him at Trnova in western Slovakia. George, at the time, was tied down by the meeting of the diet in Prague and therefore asked Bishop Tas of Olomouc, who was still considered (even after the loosening of ties with Jost of Rosenberg) as one of the King's faithful friends, to meet the archbishop in Trnava. All we know of these negotiations is that Vitéz considered Tas's suggestions—they were not much different from what George had offered the Curia all along, including the preservation of the essence of the Compacts—as rather hopeful and promised to send them on to Rome.[27] This, apparently, was done, and the letter ended, with the minimal effect that we would expect, in the hands of Cardinal Carvajal. Meanwhile King Matthias had taken a step that went far in showing that the future course of his foreign policy—and of the wars that were to be its continuation by other means—had been largely determined. Reacting to a letter of Pope Paul, he writes on October 2, 1465: "Your Holiness requests that I support with my favor and my power the apostolic proceedings against George, the so-called King of Bohemia, and that I help in the implementation and maintenance of these proceedings in my lands. I have, most Holy Father, dedicated myself and my realm for all times to the service of the Holy Roman Church and of Your Holiness. There is nothing too arduous or too dangerous which, when imposed upon me by the Vicar of God on earth, nay by God himself, I should not regard as a pious and salutary task and which I would not want to take on with intrepid eagerness, especially if it serves to fortify the Catholic faith and to destroy the perfidy of godless men. Nor shall old treaties constrain me since they were concluded only on account of temporary

[27] See Vistéz's letter (from Belgrade) to Bishop Tas in the Gersdorfsche Bibliothek in Bautzen, No 39, fol. 192a-b, as quoted in *RTA*, XXI, further Palacký *Dějiny*, IV, 2, 314 n. 229. Bachmann, *Reichsgeschichte* (I, 573) speaks of the "Tyrnauer Punktationen," without, however, giving any of its substance.

necessity and since I know that they can always easily be dissolved by the apostolic authority; even less shall I be deterred by the power of any human. I have, after all, upon the request of Your Holiness and of your predecessors, opposed enemies of far more weighty power than that of the Czechs. Thus, whether the call is to war against the Czechs or against the Turks—Matthias and his Hungarians will be ready. To the extent of the strength that I and my kingdom possess, we are and will always remain dedicated above all to the Apostolic See and Your Holiness." [28]

Whether or not Palacký was always entirely objective in the position he took toward the struggle between the two Kings, he was certainly in the right when he remarked that Matthias, in this letter, offered far more than had been requested from him: all-out war against the Czechs, possibly in preference to war against the Turks, whereas he had only been asked for support in the implementation, within his own kingdom, of the judicial procedure against George.[29] Indeed his offer, though it pleased the Pope, was at the time not taken too seriously in Rome where it was still presumed, and rightly, that the Hungarian King's task in defending his own realm, and with it all Europe, against Turkish aggression would absorb all his strength, especially if he were to take any drastic steps to weaken or remove this perennial danger. When some news about Matthias' action leaked out it was simply disbelieved, even in Prague. Among those who did not believe it were clearly both King George and Gregory Heimburg. Otherwise the further correspondence between Prague and Buda might well have taken a different turn.

One reason that the Pope did not or not yet react more positively to King Matthias' eager offer was that Rome's strategy was influenced by the hope of finding a strong candidate who would be willing to supplant King George on the throne of Bohemia. The Curia could not, at this stage, consider Matthias, as such, a suitable candidate, not only because a realistic evaluation of the general power situation demanded that Matthias reserve his strength for the unavoidable future struggles with the Turks, but also because it was obvious that there would be considerable resistance to such a policy in the west, especially on the part of the Emperor for whom, in the long run, Matthias was a greater danger than George.

---

[28] The original text printed repeatedly, e.g. in Katona, *Historia critica regum Hungariae,* VIII (ordine XV), 1465-1475, p. 136.

[29] See IV, 2, 315 (in German, 362).

Nor could it be expected that King Casimir of Poland would tolerate such an enormous increase in the political and military power of his great southern neighbor. Casimir, of course, had always considered that he had hereditary claims to both thrones, those of Hungary and Bohemia, though his relation to King George had, at least since the days of Glogau, been one of friendship. It was the hereditary claim, based on Casimir's marriage to a daughter of Albert II and sister of Ladislav Posthumus, which made it rather natural that the hopes of George's enemies soon tended to concentrate on the King of Poland. Suggestions in this direction had, as mentioned before, been made by Breslau at a fairly early date and were seriously considered by Pius II. His successor continued to work toward this goal, and in May 1466 he asked the King of Poland directly to lend his support to the Bohemian Catholic lords and the city of Pilsen.[30]

The Curia held one trump by which it might tempt or force Casimir to support actively the struggle against George: it could try to tie the recognition of Poland's final victory over the Teutonic Knights—after the Thirteen Years' War fought against the Knights in alliance with the Prussian cities—to Casimir's help against the "heretics." Until recently not only the sympathies but also the active help of the Curia had been given to the knights. It was only in the expectation of gaining Casimir's support against George that the Curia—partly through its legate Rudolf of Lavant—gave some help to Poland by taking a more neutral attitude and eventually even expressing some degree of support for the conclusion of a peace which included the cession to Poland of West Prussia and made the remaining territory of the order—East Prussia—into a Polish fief.[31] The Peace of Torun, which was thus concluded in October 1466 with the cautious and conditional blessings of Rome, was therefore expected to free Polish forces and Polish activities for the struggle against the King of Bohemia.

But if this was the view of Rome, it was by no means that of Casimir. He did not intend to follow the long and costly Thirteen Years' War with drawn-out war against the Czech King, with whom he had only recently concluded an alliance and whose military potential he did not underrate. He had, after all, made good use of Czech mercenary troops in the Thirteen Years' War. Nor was he eager to receive the Czech crown as a present from the Pope. There was no

[30] See Zdeněk Tobolka, "Styky krále Jiřího z Poděbrad s králem polským Kazimírem," ČMM, XXII, 7off., specifically this phase of events, 166ff.

[31] See Długosz, V, 467; the text in Dogiel, *Codex diplomaticus regni Poloniae*, IV, Vilna, 163ff. See also Joh. Voigt, *Geschichte Preussens*, VIII, 697–702.

reason to assume that he had any sympathies for Utraquist deviations, and in the policy of consistent benevolent neutrality that he developed toward George, he had to take into account, just as had Louis XI in France, the existence of a not inconsiderable party in his own country which looked with horror at the Czech heresy and would have been willing to go quite far in support of the papacy. Yet he firmly resisted all such attempts, feeling that, far from gaining thereby the Czech crown for his house, he might even risk losing it for good if he were to become the open enemy of the King of Bohemia and of the Utraquist majority of his people. This majority was, as he knew, especially strong among the gentry, and on the basis of his own experience in Poland Casimir would not be inclined to underrate its strength and influence. At the same time he was by no means disinterested—the Czech crown was still an important goal. But he was sober, clear-minded, very patient—and without any penchant for risky adventures. The time, he felt, might come before too long when this crown would be within his grasp without war—at least without war against the very people over whom he would like one of his sons to rule.

Considerations of political principle—or perhaps we might say political philosophy—were also involved in King Casimir's coldness to the papal suggestion. And here we probably have to give some credit to Gregory Heimburg, who had, after all, sent his first great apology, among many other princes, also to the King of Poland. It was somewhat later, 1467, that Casimir declared: "he would not want to believe that an anointed and crowned King could be deposed" [by the Pope], an expression which might well reflect the argumentation of Heimburg.[32] That this was not merely a general expression of King Casimir's political philosophy was revealed when, upon George's request for advice and military help, he gave both—even though, as we shall see, the advice was not always profitable, and the military help moderate in size.[33]

If George's policy and Heimburg's diplomatic correspondence had strengthened Casimir's feeling of solidarity with a fellow-monarch under illegitimate pressure from Rome, the same could be said also in regard to the strongest ruler of Western Europe, Louis XI of France. We have told in some detail the story of the great embassy that George had dispatched to France in 1464 in the expectation that something

[32] See *FRA*, II, 44, 636.
[33] *Ibid.*, 633 ff., also *FRA*, II, 20, 488.

might come out of his proposal for an international peace organization. Even then there had been, in the whole scheme, distinct connections with the older idea of the church council, related to Constance, in terms of its proposed organization in four *"nationes,"* but to Basel by the choice of the first meeting place of the organization. The original scheme seemed no longer hopeful, especially since no support could be expected for it either from Venice or from Hungary, the two powers most exposed to the Turkish threat. A new approach was necessary, and all our circumstantial knowledge of the situation then existing at the Prague court would indicate that it was worked out between the King and Dr. Heimburg—in an exchange in which Heimburg had, from the beginning, felt able to talk to the King not as a servant but as a weighty adviser, almost a friend, and in which, it seems, he also became increasingly able, as had Marini and Mair, to express himself in Czech—or else the King had become increasingly able to absorb all that his diplomatic councillor had to tell him in his own, the German, language. The result, in this case, was a more serious effort to call another church council.

This was not, by any means, a new idea. Marini had mentioned it as a possibility in his discussions with Matthias Corvinus, and Heimburg had once gone to France to gain for this plan the support of Charles VII. The plan had, however, now gained new and greater urgency simply in those terms in which both the Curia and her great enemy, the lawyer-diplomat, were used to think and operate, those of a juridical procedure. The Curia, after all, had thought of her relationship to King George not in terms of mere diplomacy or of a power struggle but in those of putting the King on trial. This point of view was sufficiently accepted in so far as neither George nor his legally trained diplomatic advisers denied that offenses like those for which the Curia, first under Pius and then again under Paul, had summoned him would have justified a trial. The very fact that he considered himself as standing "within the Church" would have made it difficult for him to deny this on principle, though there was, of course, no similarity of views between Rome and Prague on what constituted "the Church." George denied, however, not only his guilt but above all the right of the Curia to try and sentence him, as if he were an ordinary man, by summoning him to Rome, and, in forms which anticipated the sentence, consistently refusing him the sort of hearing which he had all along requested and which would be commensurate with his exalted position. While this alone was, in the eyes of the King and his advisers, a flagrant bending of the law for political ends, the papacy had, at the same time, tried to bar any way out of a situation in which she was and remained both accuser and judge without any court of appeal. This had been the basic purpose of the bull "Execrabilis," which made any attempted appeal to a future council a crime leading to instant excommunication. The "Execrabilis" had immediately found sharp resistance and criticism, especially in the country where it seemed, at the time, especially likely to be applied: in France. It was from France that even now the strongest interest in and the most effective support for the calling of a church council could be hoped for.

On the basis of the decree "Frequens," by which the Council of Constance had established that intervals no larger than ten years should separate one council from the next, a council should have been called by 1459. In a way the Congress of Mantua—called by Pius II in that very year—was a clear challenge to the "Frequens," yet it was never formally declared invalid, and, notwithstanding the "Execrabilis" (which was only concerned with appeals), there was certainly nothing in the demand for a new council to which the Curia could openly object on principle. At the same time it was clear that it would do all in its power to oppose or obstruct such a step, operating simply with the old claim, not recognized during the height of the conciliar movement, that no one but the Pope himself could call a council. If nevertheless there was any hope of calling a council—and for George it began to look like the one practicable way out of his increasing difficulties—then it was necessary to establish a really close contact with all those princes who might see the danger threatening lay rulers if the papacy's overweening claims should be acknowledged by the people of Europe. Among such princes, Louis XI, while not free from troubles himself—he had but recently had to fight the "League of the Public Weal"—would clearly be the strongest and most influential. At the same time he would be unwilling to put up with the weakening of French influence in Italy, a goal which the papal policy had pursued during the reign of Pius II and which it was still pursuing, though in a somewhat changed constellation of alliances, under Paul II. Here the close relationship between the rulers of France and of Milan—at this moment Duke Francesco Sforza's son and successor, Galeazzo Maria—presented an important factor.

It was to King Louis, then, that George's ambassador John Špán of Barnstein came in the early spring of 1467, with fairly precise instructions reflecting both the urgent hopes of the King and some of the

understanding of judicial problems contributed by Gregory Heimburg.[34] The report rendered to King George is not without its amusing
moments. To point out what special feelings of friendship and respect
Louis had for George, the ambassador says that "every time that the
royal name of Bohemia was mentioned, the King of France doffed his
beret." The ambassador had expressed the grief of his King over Louis'
difficulties with the dukes and princes of the league, thereby especially
aiming at the Duke of Burgundy (who, at this time, was also considered one of the potential executioners of the papal sentence against
George). It becomes clear from this report that as yet George, considering himself as the heir of the Luxemburg dynasty, had by no
means put up with the permanent loss of Luxemburg to Burgundy,
especially since the temporary friendship between France and Burgundy, or rather between Louis XI and Philip the Good, with which
the Czech embassy had had to reckon in 1464, was by now, and especially after the accession of Charles the Bold, turning into bitter enmity.
It is on this basis that King George's envoy suggested a common military action against Burgundy, more specifically for the occupation of
Luxemburg.[35]

In the private audience that followed the ambassador's public reception by Louis, he presented the background of hostile alignments
threatening both Bohemia and France. Their leader, the Pope, has concluded a secret compact with the Emperor which, Špán says, is really
no longer secret. Among the other allies of this grouping he mentions
Venice, Burgundy, and Savoy. In Italy this coalition tries to destroy
France's main friend and ally, the Duke of Milan. This goal is brought
in relation with the intended travel of the Emperor to Rome, perhaps
a somewhat dubious interpretation. The Emperor, though this could
not be known in 1467, eventually went on his visit to Rome with the
small retinue of 700 horse,[36] hardly a strong enough force to conquer

---

[34] For the very detailed report see Julius Pažout, "König Georg von Böhmen und die
Councilfrage im Jahre 1467," *AÖG.*, XL, Vienna, 1869, 323–371. The report itself is contained in the documentary appendix VI, pp. 357–371. The actual text of the proposition submitted by Špán to King Louis appears, in Latin, in a document in the Bibliotheque Nationale
in Paris, Ms. fo. 6964, together with a draft in French recommendations of the King's advisers
for an answer to the ambassador. Both are printed, wrongly dated 1481, and even more
wrongly presented as directed against the Emperor Maximilian I, in vol. IV, pp. 78–82, of
Comines, *Memoires,* ed. Godefroy-Lenglet, London, 1747.

[35] See Pažout, "König Georg," 363; and, with more emphasis in the Latin propositions,
clauses XI and XII in Comines, *Memoires,* IV, 79.

[36] See about the Emperor's second journey to Rome in Pastor, II, 420–427. That George
and his diplomats looked rather suspiciously for a good reason for Frederick's long and costly
travel is understandable enough, since to this day a clear explanation has never been presented.

Milan (though he might have liked it if the Venetians had done it for him). Farther north, the ambassador continued, the Duke of Burgundy, besides hoping for a marriage with the Habsburgs, has allied himself with the Electors of the Palatinate, Trier, and Cologne, and with the Bishop of Metz. All these alliances, with Rome holding the threads in her hands, are directed primarily against the two Kings —Louis and George. Thus it is in their interest to strengthen their old alliance and add to this a number of other allies who are, so Prague feels, ready to join in such a system of strategic defense against the war-like plans of the Curia. As additional allies the ambassador names the King of Poland, the three dukes of Saxony (William, Ernest, and Albert), the Margrave of Brandenburg, Duke Sigismund of Tyrol, the Margrave of Baden, the Landgrave of Hessen, the two Counts of Württemberg, Duke Otto of Bavaria, the Archbishop-Elector of Mainz, and the bishops of Würzburg and Bamberg.[37] An especially warm recommendation is devoted to Margrave Albert of Brandenburg. "Master of all organized military movements and well known in all German lands as the most clear-sighted, most spirited of princes." It is for this reason that the Czech ambassador recommends that the King of France cement the friendship with the Hohenzollern prince, following his King's example, by establishing some marital tie.[38]

But the central piece of the whole diplomatic action was the request to King Louis "to call a Concilium of the community of Christian Churches," as the only effective way "to protect Christianity from all such oppressions, wrongdoings and violations." A council alone will be able "to prevent, punish and destroy all such breaches of the peace and arbitrary infringements [of the right of princes] and will enable the Christian communities to live in an orderly, peaceful world pleasing to God." This plan, for the moment to be kept secret, is urged upon the French with the utmost emphasis.[39]

In his answer, King Louis essentially approved of George's suggestion for alliances as well as for the calling of a council. But as the first step Louis suggested a direct French action in Rome by an embassy

---

[37] Pažout's text here (p. 362) contains a somewhat puzzling inconsistency. In the introduction to the passage concerning the allies he states: "So ist die erste pundtnus mit dem Konig zw Beheim: der Konig zw *Hungern*, drey herczogen von Sachsen, zween marggraven von Brandenburg." (Italics mine.) In the following, more detailed list which also gives the names and adds the ecclesiastical and the smaller lay princes, the lead position is given to the Kings of Bohemia and *Poland*, without any mention of the King of Hungary. The latter version seems the more accurate, and corresponds far better to the actual political constellation.

[38] *Ibid.*, 363.

[39] *Ibid.*, 364, 365, and Comines, *Memoires*, IV, 78, clauses III and IV.

to be sent in October, which should urge an end of papal procedures against George, and this in forms which would leave the Compacts of Basel in force. Until then, he suggests the new Franco-Czech alliance should not be announced publicly as this might cause the Curia to claim that France was acting as a party in the conflict. If such a direct demarche should prove unsuccessful the request for the council would be pushed with full vigor.[40]

Louis, in fulfillment of the Czech request, himself sent in the early fall an embassy to Prague, in preparation for the announced demarche in Rome, and among the issues discussed at this opportunity was again the plan to call a council.[41]

The whole action remains an interesting and in a general way successful link in the total policy of George to maintain as positive and cooperative a relationship with France as possible, thereby checking attempts of his enemies, and especially of the Curia, to make use of the stronger principalities in the west of the Empire, such as Burgundy and the Palatinate, which could have resulted in an effective strengthening of the alliance against heretic Bohemia. While not impressive in terms of immediate gains, the resulting maintenance of an active friendship largely based on the logic of political geography should not be underrated.

If, on the other hand, we measure the results of this diplomatic action in terms of what became of George's central demand—the calling of a church council—then, and to that extent, the demarche can hardly be called a success. It is difficult to say whether George and his adviser Heimburg really expected that a council would be called. Both men, and Heimburg especially, must have been aware of the extreme unwillingness of Rome to submit the salvaged power of papal absolutism once more to the dangers of conciliar parliamentarism combined with the demands for reform still growing in so many parts of the Catholic world. They may well have believed that the mere threat of a council would force men such as Paul II and Carvajal to act more cautiously and perhaps to accept the various offers for a compromise (within the frame of the Compacts) that George never tired of presenting. But the actual effect of this policy was probably the very opposite. If a council was feared then the Curia, especially under the leadership of men as hard and determined as Carvajal, would be in-

40 Pažout, "König Georg," 368f. Here Špán's report relates a later stage of the negotiations than Comines, *Memoires*, IV, 80–82.

41 See the final paragraph of Špán's propositions *ibid.*, IV, 80, clause XXI, and for the arrival of the French embassy Palacký, *Dějiny*, IV, 2, 412 n. 319 (in German 474 n. 318).

clined to react not with willingness to compromise but with increased aggressiveness against the main enemy—and this, after all, was George. As yet it was, for his strategic situation in this steadily "warming up" war, of little advantage to him if his enemies feared him, as long as they could still hope to smash him. He had to prove that he could not be smashed, and this would be a hard task. (Nor was it by chance that the Curia did not begin to soften until after Carvajal had died in 1469.)

To return to the negotiations between the Kings of Bohemia and France—the central emphasis on the council is not the only evidence of the important role that Gregory Heimburg had played in its planning and in the directions given to the Czech ambassador. Of equal weight in this regard is the fact that, throughout the Czech presentation of the political constellation in the Europe of the time, the position and policy of the Emperor is completely equated with that of the Pope. This, of course, had been Heimburg's view for a long time.

That King George now shared this attitude was indeed a rather recent development. Earlier, and through the greater part of 1466, George would not have made the Emperor responsible for his growing difficulties with Rome. The events which brought about George's conversion to Heimburg's views were all connected with the great reichstag which met at Nürnberg in November 1466. This meeting was called to organize help against the Turkish danger which, at this time, again began to grow much more threatening. Bosnia, after the temporary successes of Matthias in 1464, had largely been re-conquered by the Ottoman Emperor, and, in 1466, much of the mountain fastness of Albania had been breached, sending its valiant prince Skanderbeg to Rome requesting help. Matthias Corvinus had also urged immediate support. In this situation the Emperor had invited all the princes to send their representatives to Nürnberg, especially also the King of Bohemia.[42]

King George did send an embassy headed by two lords, the Utraquist Albert Kostka and the Catholic Beneš of Veitmil, both among his most experienced diplomats. He clearly expected that the meeting of the reichstag, and especially the general need for concerted action against the Turks, would give him the opportunity to prove that he, as a Christian King, was serious in offering a substantial military contribution to this bitterly needed enterprise. Indeed, there are few instances

---

[42] The events of the Nürnberg reichstag have been reported in considerable detail in Müller's *Reichstag-Theatrum*, II, 211–259. More now in *DRTA*, probably XXI. Some other contributions are listed in Palacký's *Dějiny*, IV, 2, p. 363 n. 271 (in German, 417 n. 270).

which so strongly intimate that the King's offer was made in good faith and was expected to be taken up, even though it is clear that George hoped to achieve, in return, a less hostile treatment by the Holy See.

In this hope he was to be bitterly disappointed. The Curia had made sure that there would be not the slightest chance for a rapprochement— simply by the choice of the papal legate to the diet. It was Fantino de Valle, whose main goal in life, after the events of 1462, was now to contribute as much as possible to the destruction of his one-time employer, the Czech King. He lost no time in making his intentions clear. As soon as the Czech embassy entered the gates of Nürnberg, the legate ordered all divine service in the city to cease, and protested vigorously against admitting the Czech ambassadors, as heretics and accessories of heretics, to the proceedings of the diet. George's friends among the leading men of the reichstag, above all Margrave Albert Achilles, who was personally present, did their best to have the Czech embassy officially accredited and heard. The diet was split.

In this situation the attitude of the Emperor's representatives was of crucial importance. If they had come out in favor of the Czech embassy, it would have been much more difficult for the legate permanently to stop all proceedings—as he tried to do by simply leaving the assembly hall whenever the Czech delegates appeared. The attitude of the imperial ambassadors carried all the more weight as their leader, Ulrich of Grafeneck, was the reichstag's presiding official and had even been nominated as the prospective commander-in-chief of the planned crusade against the Turks, while his chief assistant was the imperial marshall, Lord Henry of Pappenheim. Thus the Czech ambassadors were puzzled and disappointed when the imperial delegation maintained, in the face of Fantino's actions, complete silence, without even the slightest attempt to change the legate's hate-filled attitude. The Czech delegation, in the end, presented to the assembly a detailed memorandum about their King's intentions and offers, together with a sharp attack upon the policy which, by its narrow and vindictive character, destroyed all hopes for a positive outcome of the present discussions.[43] It was surely George's intent—though not necessarily upon his instructions—that the attack was directed not so much against the Pope himself as against Fantino.

Under these circumstances, however, the real purpose of the whole meeting remained unfulfilled. King George's friends among the

43 See *FRA*, II, 20, 415–418, and material in *DRTA*, XXI.

princes, above all Margrave Albert Achilles and the Saxon dukes, tried
to salvage some of it by another common action in Rome. They
planned to have the embassy which they charged with this task stop
over at the Emperor's court in Wiener-Neustadt. To this extent the
plan materialized. There was even some consultation between the
princes and the Prague court, with the result that they received—from
Heimburg as well as from the King—suggestions for the instructions
to be given to the ambassadors.[44]

But the attitude of the Emperor's representatives at Nürnberg left
a deep scar in the relations between King George and the Emperor.
In view of the paucity of more detailed information, it is difficult
now to say whether the lack of support, so crucial at this moment, was
based on a deliberate decision by Frederick to jettison his friendship
with the Czech King. It is not impossible that what looked like a betrayal to George was essentially a result of either the ill will or perhaps even merely the helplessness of the Emperor's representatives in
the face of a development that had not been fully foreseen at Wiener-
Neustadt. This, at least, might conceivably have been the assumption
of Albert Achilles and his friends when they decided for another attempt to gain the Emperor's support for their mission to Rome.[45]

But there are valid arguments against this interpretation which make
it understandable that George now accepted Heimburg's very different
view. It seems unlikely that the Emperor was and remained unaware
of the person (and the policy) of the papal legate until it was too
late to give appropriate instructions to his representatives at the reichstag. Besides, Frederick had long been unhappy about his considerable
financial obligations toward George incurred by his rescue from his
Viennese besiegers four years earlier. In addition he could feel much
less dependent on George's friendship or help since he had made his
peace with Matthias Corvinus. It is not necessary to assume that the
Emperor had, at this stage, already decided for a complete break with
George. This would have been a radical step of the sort which Frederick generally did not like to take if it could be avoided. Nor could he
fail to see that such a policy would tend to make him as dependent on
Matthias as he had previously been on George. But if doing nothing
at all would provide him with the opportunity of getting rid of burdensome and, so it seemed now, unprofitable obligations, then, indeed,

---

[44] *FRA*, II, 42, 363–370.

[45] This, for instance, is Bachmann's assumption. See *Reichsgeschichte*, I, 589–590, n. 4. Cf.
also Markgraf, "Die Bildung der katholischen Liga," in *HZ*, XXXVIII, 1877, 255f.

he might well have chosen this convenient course in preference to one which, while more honorable, might in the long run result in friction between him and the Holy See.

Although, in retrospect, this appears a fair and likely interpretation, not even especially damning in view of the considerable efforts that the Emperor had previously made in Rome on behalf of the Czech King, George himself was not willing to take such a charitable view. For him this was now proof enough that Heimburg was right in his extreme suspicion of Frederick's mentality and policy. This, so he felt, was not only the betrayal of solemn obligations but the worst kind of ingratitude. It was in this vein that, immediately after the return of the Czech ambassadors from Nürnberg, George wrote to the Emperor.[46] That the letter was Heimburg's work is beyond question, but it also clearly expressed George's thoughts. For once, he emphasized, strong hopes had arisen, that led by the three kingdoms of Eastern Europe, Hungary, Bohemia, and Poland, a vigorous and effective military campaign could have smashed the military might of the Turks. He then described the way in which, despite all resistance from secular princes of the empire, the papal legate had destroyed these hopes and prevented acceptance of the offers presented by the Czech ambassadors. He tried to establish the responsibility of the Emperor's servants who, he says, had known well the will of their master. "Is this, o Caesar Augustus, the gratitude for the liberty which was given back to you by our help? . . . This, however, we shall announce to you: that neither food nor drink nor sleep will be welcome to our senses until we have properly revenged the injury which you have so guilefully inflicted upon us." [47] The letter, especially its ending, reads almost like a declaration of war. As yet, however, a direct, all-out conflict between King and Emperor was avoided. Nevertheless, George was determined to show Frederick that it was still in his power to hurt him badly.

For this, there existed ample opportunity through the interior struggles in Austria, which the Emperor, even after the death of Archduke Albert, could not suppress completely. Among a number of potential rebels in Austria, the most important at this moment was George of Stein (Jörg von Stein), once chancellor and diplomatic adviser of Archduke Albert, a wealthy, gifted, versatile, but somewhat unscrupulous baron, long an ally of the Eizinger clan and for years a personal

---

[46] See Pešina, *Mars Moravicus*, 771f.

[47] See for the background of the next paragraph the (detailed but not always very exact) presentation by F. Kurz, *Oesterreich unter Friedrich IV*, II, 66–68, 73–80.

friend of Gregory Heimburg.[48] Some years earlier Stein had received the strong castle and town of Steyr in Upper Austria as a security for the large sum of 14,000 Hungarian ducats which he had lent to the Archduke. After Albert's death an arrangement was made according to which Stein would receive from the Emperor the sum of 6,000 ducats, and would, in return for the difference, retain possession of Steyr with its income for another year. At the end of this year the Emperor demanded Steyr to be returned to him, but Stein refused as he had never received the promised 6,000 ducats. Now, toward the end of 1466, the struggle became critical because Stein was able to make it into an international issue. He had long owned some property in Moravia and now, in conflict with the Emperor, he declared himself King George's subject. His example was followed by Lord William of Puchheim. Around the turn of the year George himself entered the fray. He declared George of Stein as his subject and servant whom he was in honor bound to protect. The town of Steyr, meanwhile, had been gained for the Emperor by a troop under the command of George of Volkensdorf, but Stein, with the help of a fairly strong troop of Czech mercenaries, reconquered it. It was a tense situation.

The Emperor, afraid that this limited conflict might lead to far more extended difficulties and might thoroughly spoil his hopes for a renewed travel to Rome, called a diet of the Austrian estates to Linz, capital of Upper Austria,[49] for which he gave safe conducts to George of Stein as well as to an embassy of King George. For once the Emperor decided to leave his beloved Wiener-Neustadt and went himself to Linz. There, on February 15, 1467, began the discussion with King George's embassy, led by John of Rosenberg, the kingdom's foremost magnate, fully reconciled with the King, further by Apel Vitzthum and Beneš of Veitmil, all Catholic lords. The Czechs demanded that money long owed to their King and overdue for the last three years be finally paid; that George of Stein, as the King's servant, be left in peaceful possession of the town and castle of Steyr as long as he had not been fully paid; and that Czech subjects kept prisoners by one of the Emperor's vassals be released.

The Emperor's answer, a written address to the King presented by the Bishop of Gurk, was as ungracious as possible. King George had

---

[48] For his correspondence with Stein see Höfler's "Böhmische Studien" in *AÖG*, XII, 1854, 336–338.

[49] Main source for the diet of Linz and its direct effects upon the relations between Frederick and George is "Anonymus," 323–334. Some other source contributions listed by Palacký, *Dějiny*, IV, 2, 369 n. 275 (German, 423–424, n. 274).

already received more money than he could fairly ask for. He had not prevented Czech mercenaries—the bratříci—from violating Austrian soil (probably an unfair accusation since the Emperor had himself hired bratříci repeatedly, both in his fights against Matthias of Hungary and against his brother Albert). Now George was also trespassing by taking the Emperor's enemies such as Stefan Eizinger, Puchheim, and Stein under his protection, and making it difficult for the Emperor to leave his country to travel to Rome. Above all—and here, indeed, an entirely new tone becomes audible in Frederick's relation to George—the King was not keeping faith with the Roman Church and was thereby acting against the oath which he had sworn at his coronation.

The Czech ambassadors, greatly irritated, answered immediately. Their ruler, they said, was a free King of the Czech crown and had the right to take as his servants whomever he choose. Having done great services for the Emperor, the King did not deserve nor would he accept an address which went against the King's honor. The King was powerful enough to resist all possible enemies. Finally, the Czech ambassadors referred to the disgraceful and slanderous way in which the papal legate had treated King George's ambassadors at Nürnberg, and to the strange behavior there of the Emperor's representatives.

The Emperor replied that his own councillors had not been guilty of any disgraceful behavior toward the Czech ambassadors. For the papal legate's actions he could not be made responsible, nor could he punish him. In the end, when the Czech ambassadors, having refused to accept the Emperor's written address, left the meeting with all signs of extreme anger, the Emperor rose and, himself highly excited, declared that he was no longer willing to stand the arrogant and offenive attitude of the Czech King, and would call not only upon the Pope but upon the Holy Roman Empire and all Christendom to put an end to this outrage.

There is something strangely unreal in this fierce collision of the two rulers who, while of a very different mettle and very different rank in any possible scale of historical values, shared at least one creditable characteristic: they were both not fond of war and, with few exceptions, would enter it only under compulsion. In retrospect we can easily see that both rulers, by thus working themselves into an ever-growing antagonism, committed grave mistakes. Frederick III, by deciding to abandon his policy of alliance with George and instead challenging this strong neighbor, was not only weakening his position both in his own hereditary lands and in the empire, but also making himself exceedingly and almost fatally dependent on the other great figure of the Central European world, Matthias of Hungary. But in Frederick's case the error of this policy would not become apparent until a good deal later.

This was not true for George. The Czech King, at this moment, had quite enough enemies, led, above all, by as strong and persistent a foe as the Roman Curia. He had no longer any right to think of the young King of Hungary as a friend and ally, even if he could perhaps not clearly recognize him yet as what he was: his most dangerous enemy. While he had made friends of the Kings of Poland and France and, to an almost astonishing extent, of some of the leading German lay princes, his whole position was such that it should have made him beware from acquiring any additional enemies. There is little in the Emperor's policy that would make him appear, until the harsh challenge contained in George's letter and in the action of his embassy at Linz, as totally committed to joining in the alliance against the "heretical King." Indeed there are later phases when it seems clear that this, for Frederick III, was an enterprise for which he had little heart and little real interest. But at this moment George had made it difficult for him not to react strongly.

And if it appears that George's uncompromising attitude toward Frederick III was in itself a blunder, then the specific form of his attack—the use of Austrian rebels against the Emperor—was an even more serious mistake. For the Emperor had no difficulty in answering with a very similar weapon—only in a far more effective form. The Czech ambassadors, upon leaving Linz, met on the way back to Bohemia another Czech ambassador, also a Catholic baron, Burian of Gutstein. Gutstein, however, had come not as spokesman for the King but for the rebellious lords of the League of Zelená Hora. The meeting must have made the royal diplomats wonder.

Gutstein came just at the right time—when the Emperor was in the mood to do whatever would hurt George most. Thus he immediately recognized the league as a belligerent power and gave it the privilege to coin its own money in a mint in Pilsen.[50] These two acts, coming from the head of the Empire—however fictitious most of his ancient power had become by this time—gave this group of rebellious lords an aura of legitimacy and respectability that they had so far never achieved, and they soon expressed their gratification in a solemn decla-

[50] See A. Chmel, *Regesta chronologica diplomatica Friderici III*, II, numbers 4909, 4910.

ration promising to be Frederick's faithful allies and helpers.[51] Gregory Heimburg, who had done so much to clarify the issues and to give George an ideological platform from which to conduct his great defensive struggle, had not counseled wisely when he had urged King George to take the offensive, politically and otherwise, against the Emperor. But the decision, and the responsibility for it, had in the last resort been the King's alone. Here, surely he had himself been too rash and too emotional[52] in following badly considered, emotionally motivated advice. The price he had to pay for it was to be high.

[51] See Kurz, *Oesterreich unter Friedrich IV*, II, 92 note a.

[52] In this case Bachmann—who repeatedly chides George for acting in a rash and "hot-blooded" way—seems quite justified in his criticism. (See *Reichsgeschichte*, II, 32–36). This view, however, seems rather in contradiction to the picture of a cold selfish trickster that dominates and distorts so much of Bachmann's presentation of George's character. George's action is strongly but not convincingly defended by Urbánek in his biographical sketch, *Husitský král*, 222–223.

CHAPTER 19

BUT THE SWORD SEEMS MIGHTIER

TOWARD THE end of the reign of Pius II and during the beginning of the reign of his successor, the Holy See saw its main task in regard to the Bohemian problem as the finding of a new King, a man strong enough not only to defeat the heretical George but also to suppress the heresy itself. Only when such a man was found could one expect the last stroke against George to be fully effective: his solemn deposition and the equally solemn invalidation of all ties binding his subjects to him. A powerful new ruler—acceptable, as Rome hoped, to the Catholics of the Czech realm as well as to the princes of Europe and the Empire—would make the measure effective and assure a tolerably swift take-over, not too painful in its consequences for those whom the Curia hoped to "liberate" from the supposed religious oppression by the heretics. (That this procedure would involve the determined resistance of the majority of a whole nation the Roman Curia had never wanted to believe and to face.)

But when 1466 drew to a close and no strong candidate for the Bohemian throne had come into view, the politicians of the Roman hierarchy began to change their minds. From one of our Roman sources [1] it appears that Cardinal Carvajal—though during most of the fall and winter of 1466 he dwelt in Venice—was strongly in favor of and therefore also partly responsible for this re-orientation. Even if so far no support for the radical step was in view, he is supposed to have said, even if neither the Emperor nor the Kings of Hungary or Poland could undertake the great task, the right path was still for the Pope to do his duty and to leave the rest to God, who would provide what was needed.

This, in any case, was the policy that finally prevailed in Rome. The radical step was to be taken, and the consequences be left to the Lord —that is, ignored. It is one of the basic attitudes which brought about not only what has been called the second sequence of Hussite Wars, but many other religious wars to follow, wars which often were fiercer,

[1] Ammanati, *Commentarii*, 437.

bloodier, and more destructive than most of the military struggles of preceding centuries.

The solemn act took place in Rome two days before Christmas.[2] As it was the most important attempt to destroy a heresy that had been undertaken by Rome for a considerable time, it was staged as dramatically as possible. This was, after all, meant to be the last act of a great trial which had begun with the formal citation of King George to appear and be judged in Rome. In the presence of several thousand people the great consistory first heard the lengthy writs of accusation and statements of proofs for the ready sentence. To preserve the exact form of a trial, one archbishop and three bishops were ordered to call George, or whomever he might have sent to represent him, into the Pope's presence. When, as expected, there was no answer, the Pope himself spoke at some length about the supposed horrors and misdeeds committed by George. He then asked for the reading of the sentence, which said that "George or Jersik of Kunštát and Poděbrady, who has arrogated to himself the Kingship over the realm of Bohemia . . . is pronounced, on the grounds of our true knowledge, as an impudent and obstinate heretic and protector of heretics, protagonist of this cursed heresy, a perjurer and despiser of the Church. Such a one he has been and still is, and therefore he deserves and is subject to all and every sentence, ban and judgment, also excommunication, which, in the law of the Church, is laid down against relapsed heretics, perjurers and patrons and protectors of heretics. Therefore he is deprived and divested of all dignity, dominion and possession, also of all the rights, of a King, margrave, duke and all other such rank; and from all these he shall be dispossessed and expelled. He and all his descendants shall be incapable forever to occupy such dignity. And with this writ we, by virtue of our papal power, find and pronounce through our judgment this man and all his heirs deposed from all dignities and dominions mentioned before, and with this our power we loose and release all barons, all cities, all subjects and all those who had entered into bonds with him, whether resident in the kingdom of Bohemia or wherever else, from all oaths, ties, obedience and all other duties toward him, by none of which they are henceforth or in any later time bound. Therefore everybody beware from breaking or counteracting this our writ of sentence, deposition and invalidation. . . . If, however, anybody were to attempt this, be it known to him

[2] See *SrS*, IX, 210–215, Eschenloer, G., I, 349–352, also Palacký, *Dějiny*, IV, 2, 346–367 (German, 418–421), and Pastor, II, 404 n. 3.

that thereby he will fall into the disgrace of Almighty God and his Apostles Peter and Paul."

This, then, was the decisive step judicially. But also politically. For the Holy See had thus completed that declaration of war which it had first expressed, in a more cautious and conditional form, by tearing up the Compacts in summer 1462. Now the question was how to implement the awesome decision in the absence of any strong foreign power willing to fight the Pope's war. Obviously, much was expected from the Czech baronial opposition. True, until recently King George's domestic enemies had avoided calling their struggle a religious one, since they were rightly afraid that this would turn many of the people of the lower estates against them. The King was even more determined, as far as possible, to limit the struggle with his recalcitrant subjects to the issues of a constitutional and economic character that they had raised themselves. He had, furthermore, shown a great deal of patience in dealing with the League of Zelená Hora, even when he was faced with the increasingly personal, sometimes fierce verbal attacks indulged in by the lay leader of the league, Zdeněk of Sternberg. The negotiations that had taken place, during the spring and summer of 1466, between the King or his friends on the one side and the League of Zelená Hora (meeting at Roudnice) on the other had centered on the great castle of Karlstein and the treasures which, since the time of Charles IV, were always kept there: the crown and the other regalia as well as the basic constitutional documents of the realm.[3] The lords of the league asserted that these treasures had always been under the careful control of a member of the baronial class. King George again pointed out that his son Victorin, who had been put in charge of the Karlstein, was still a baron besides being a prince, and that the second burgrave, Beneš of Veitmil, was a Catholic lord of good standing. The sharpest resistance to these demands of the league came from the Utraquist leaders among the Estates, such as Zdeněk Kostka for the lords and Burian Trčka for the knights. It was obvious enough that if once the regalia came into the hands of the King's enemies, they would gain an immense advantage in legal as well as in psychological and political terms. At this time, however, a provisional understanding was reached that a mixed committee of both parties should investigate the state archives in relation to the rights and privileges of the King and the estates. Meantime Victorin swore solemnly to the estates and the kingdom that he would faithfully look after the regalia till the

[3] See Eschenloer, G., I, 310–312.

questions at issue had been clarified. Finally the King and the lords agreed that no warlike actions would be started for several months.

This arrangement favored the league, which at the time was hardly prepared for war. Yet George still hoped that in the end his patience would be rewarded and that he would gain increasing support among influential Catholics of the kingdom. He relied thereby especially on the support of the Bishop of Olomouc, but also felt confirmed in his optimism by the fact that John of Rosenberg, ever since April 1466, had stood by the King, unmoved by sharp attacks on the part of Sternberg and some of his friends, or by somewhat sentimentally worded entreaties of his brother Jost.[4] Jost, on the other hand, had by this time completely broken contact with the King. He had even been able to convince the people of his Breslau diocese that he was willing to take up their struggle—but not just yet, since under present conditions it could only lead to grave consequences for the party of the lords. This decision to maintain for the time being, if at all possible, this uneasy truce was endorsed by a conference of the league's members held in Zittau (Žitava) in Upper Lusatia in mid-September 1466. On the other hand the meeting tried to strengthen the structure of the league. Zdeněk of Sternberg was officially elected its captain, and the Catholic cities of the realm, notably Breslau and Pilsen, were invited to join the organization, thus for the first time introducing the religious element.[5] If nevertheless the meeting semed to avoid strongly militant tones this was entirely due to the arguments presented by the bishop of Breslau. Whether Jost held to this policy merely in order to gain time which he wanted to use to strengthen the baronial side or whether he still hoped to prevent altogether the outbreak of a bloody civil war is difficult to decide, nor does it seem impossible that both considerations determined his attitude, especially since his realistic mind could hardly see, at this stage, any very sanguine hopes for a quick and easy victory of the baronial side. That Jost had still not given up all hope for an understanding with the King seems to emerge from his suggestion to call a diet for all parts of the realm to Moravia (Brno or Olomouc) to be held sometime in the fall.

The choice of the place indicates that Jost had been in contact with Tas of Boskovice about this question. The Bishop of Olomouc did indeed make a major effort to gain the King's agreement to these

---

[4] See *AČ*, VII, 262–263.
[5] Eschenloer, G., I, 339–340. See also Markgraf, "Die Bildung der katholischen Liga," 259–260.

suggestions.[6] At first the King was unwilling, contending that at most he would submit the issues under dispute to the state supreme court, provided that the lords promised to abide by its decision, with the proper punishment for those refusing to do so. Eventually, however, Bishop Tas succeeded in persuading the King to submit the procedural question to the decision of a board of four arbitrators: the Silesian Duke Conrad "the Black" of Oels, and the Lords Henry of Michalovice, John Zajíc of Hasenburg, and Zdeněk Kostka of Postupice. This board, on October 30, decided that a common meeting of representatives of both parties would meet at Jindřichův Hradec (in German, "Neuhaus") in February, that the truce would be maintained till St. George's day, April 1467, and that at this opportunity the arbitrators would present their findings regarding the constitutional documents.[7]

The meeting at Jindřichův Hradec destroyed all the illusions that King George and his friends may have had about a peaceful solution of the internal conflict. It was decisive also because it was the first confrontation of George's policy of compromise with the die-hard attitudes of his foes after the lightning of Rome's deposition act had struck. In essence the act tended to separate the partisans of the two camps, even though many of the prominent Catholics maintained, some temporarily, others permanently, a policy of neutrality, and though there was, in the long run, also an extremely small number of turncoats among Utraquists.

It was characteristic of George's tactics, and his resolve to be and remain "the King of both Kinds of people," that a large number of Catholics were among his representatives—he himself was not present —at the meeting in Jindřichův Hradec. Indeed the only prominent Utraquist of whose presence we hear was Zdeněk Kostka, while the other delegates who openly represented the King's cause were John of Rosenberg, the Lord High Chamberlain Henry of Michalovice, the Lord Chancellor Prokop of Rabstein, and William of Riesenberg and Rabí, all of these belonging to the "barones sub una." (This list by no means exhausts the list of Catholic barons, who, except for Rosenberg, never wavered in their loyalty to George. It also includes the lords of Rožmitál, of Chlum and Košmberg, at least the majority of the great house of Kolovrat and many others.)[8] Duke Conrad "the Black" of

---

[6] *AČ,* IV, 121–122.

[7] *Ibid.,* 131–132. About the meeting itself, see Palacký, *Dějiny,* IV, 370–372, and F. Teplý, *Dějiny města Jindřichova Hradce, J.* Hradec, 1927, pp. 23 ff.

[8] See e.g. Pešina, *Phosphorus septicornis,* 285f.

Oels, though a friend of the King, considered himself a neutral mediator, and the same seemed essentially true of Bishop Tas of Olomouc. On the other side all the prominent members of the League of Zelená Hora were present, with the only, and rather conspicuous, exception of Jost of Rosenberg, who may have wanted to avoid responsibility for what he knew to be impending and beyond his strength to avert.

During the negotiations the arbitrators presented copies of all the documents referring to the rights and freedoms of the estates, which had been kept in the Archives of Karlstein Castle, and assured the members of the League of Zelená Hora that the King was willing to make amends wherever it could be shown to him that he had in any way infringed upon his constitutional obligations or limitations. The argumentation of the arbitrators was supported by John of Rosenberg, who presented to the assembly copies of constitutional documents from the famous family archives of the baronial house of Rosenberg.[9]

But all those attempts were in vain. The leadership of the League at this meeting was firmly in the hands of Zdeněk of Sternberg, who had not the slightest intention of considering a compromise which might have weakened his position. It seems that he was able to terrorize his own allies into a policy of unmitigated militancy. He began by declaring that he simply did not believe the arbitrators' assurance that all documents at the Karlstein had been presented to them, and that anyhow the copies shown "were not worth a penny." He refused even to discuss the issues, as nothing short of the full acceptance of the original baronial demands could be considered. And he finally declared that he would not be satisfied with any concessions made by the King unless these were confirmed by guarantees given by the Emperor, because the King was the Emperor's vassal. This last assertion seems to have shocked even his own partisans, since patriotic Czechs were not generally willing to admit that there was such a relationship. But for Zdeněk, at this stage, anything that in his view might damage or humiliate the King was welcome. Indeed one of our most valuable sources shows that he was already completely under the sway of that fierce hatred that remained his dominant driving force for years to come.[10]

It soon became clear to everybody that, however far the King's representatives were willing to go, no compromise would be reached

---

[9] See *ibid.*, 134, also Rabstein, *Dialogus,* 32–34; further Tomek, *Dějepis,* VII, 139–140; Bachmann, *Reichsgeschichte,* I, 594–595.

[10] Rabstein, *loc.cit.*

with the leader of the league and thus with the league itself. Yet when Sternberg was asked whether his intention was to wage war for the Catholic faith against the Hussite heresy he sharply denied this, claiming that the defense of the faith was the task of the supreme pontiff, that the Czech schism was an old national disease, and that, if previous generations had not been able to destroy this heresy, he himself could not hope to do it. His concern, he claimed, was merely with the freedoms and rights and with the monetary order in the kingdom.[11] This denial, in the light of Sternberg's policy and propaganda very soon after this meeting, seems somewhat puzzling. But the instructions which he had so far received, especially from the papal legate Rudolf of Lavant, had only directed him not to accept any compromise, without as yet authorizing him to present himself as acting upon the orders of the Holy See. While it is certain that, during the day at Jindřichův Hradec, Sternberg was informed, in general terms, about what had occurred in Rome during the Christmas season, the details about it were only made known to him some time later. Only then had Rome developed, politically even more than militarily, the over-all strategy in which Sternberg was to play a highly important role, yet by no means that of a supreme leader.

For the other side there was now little freedom of action. A national diet had been called to Prague for the last days of February, presumably in the hope that, if any compromise should have been reached in Jindřichův Hradec, implementing legislation could now be passed. Such hopes had been destroyed. Nevertheless the diet, meeting under the King's personal chairmanship,[12] still discussed possibilities of appeasing the Holy See. The overwhelming motive—even among those Utraquists who approved of such policy—was to maintain the good will of the many Catholics faithful to the King, especially by giving them as clean a conscience as was possible under the circumstances. A good example for this need is the case of Lord Lev of Rožmitál, Queen Johanna's brother, who had just returned from a long trip through the countries of Western Europe. Lev declared that further attempts for a reconciliation both with Rome and with the league were necessary and offered his own services for this undertaking. (A last attempt at a personal understanding with Sternberg was indeed, at this time, undertaken by the Queen.)[13] Similarly it was decided

---

11 *Ibid.*
12 About the diet, see *FRA*, II, 20, 428–434.
13 See the references in Tomek, *Dějepis*, VII, 150 n. 88.

that the Catholic lords loyal to the King should send another embassy to Rome, via Venice, where some supporting action was hoped for.

A considerable portion of the meeting was taken up with discussions of the recent behavior of Zdeněk of Sternberg and the lords of his league. The stiffening of the mood against them was shown when the assembly refused to admit an envoy of the league (his person is unknown), supposedly because he was not properly accredited. The King readily fulfilled the demand of the Utraquists in the diet to promise them the continued defense of the Compacts. He also agreed to a reconfirmation of a number of constitutional and economic privileges and guarantees relating to taxation, military service, coinage, estate inheritance and escheat and some others, all of them essentially as they had been found during the recent research and thus corresponding to the old laws of the kingdom. There was only one major change, one that cannot do much credit to King George: by it he permitted the lords and the gentry to purchase free estates belonging either to townspeople or peasants and to have those purchases entered into the land register without special permission by the King. He thereby renounced an important piece of his own legislation that had been designed especially to protect the peasantry against the progressive alienation of the remaining allodial land often achieved by illicit pressure. It is perhaps understandable that in the difficult position in which the King now found himself he sought to avoid any friction arising from the vested interests of the nobility, even if he was aware that they were in conflict with the best interests of the nation as a whole. It is yet part of the tragic element in George's reign that the specific and largely extraneous pressure to which he was increasingly subjected throughout the later part of his reign made him more ready for such concessions and weakened his ability to check, as a strong ruler, the greed of the high nobility in both religious camps.

While officially the negotiations of the diet ended on the line of continued efforts for peace, the chief actors—above all King George himself and his closest advisers such as Zdeněk Kostka or Gregory Heimburg—were quite aware now that the civil war, urgently desired by the Curia as well as by the league's leadership, had become inescapable. Thus George no longer hesitated to prepare himself actively for the impending collision, both within the Bohemian realm and in his relations to foreign powers. The King was confident that his foreign policy had resulted in immunizing his neighbors—with the exception of the Emperor—against the subversive policy of Rome. His enemies, on the other hand, clearly hoped that it would be possible before long to organize a powerful international coalition against the King of the heretics. As it happened both were right; neither, however, to the extent they had hoped.

King George, for instance, expected that especially those German rulers with whom he had concluded those life-long "Einungen" (unions, alliances) would now support him by military means. This would be especially true in relation to Albert Achilles. And indeed this relationship did prove of great help and significance to George during the years to follow. The margrave had just a few weeks earlier shown that he was—for a good Catholic—surprisingly independent from even the strongest Roman pressure. Ever since 1465 had Paul II tried to dissuade the influential prince and old friend of the Emperor's from going through with his promise to give the hand of his daughter Ursula—generally considered the best-loved of his children—to Henry, Duke of Münsterberg, King George's younger son. He must not, so the margrave was told, corrupt the clean blood of his good Christian house with the poisonous blood of the arch-heretic.[14] In spite of this angry and unremitting pressure the wedding was performed in Cheb in the presence of the princely parents from both houses, early in February 1467, at a time when Albert was already fully informed about George's "deposition" by Rome and about the break between him and the League that had occurred at Jindřichův Hradec. By thus defying Rome the margrave risked excommunication for being a friend and protector of heretics. When it came, he took it calmly, and while he had never deviated in the least from orthodox Catholicism and was quite determined not to do so in the future, he did not seem to be any the worse for it.

This policy in the following period reflects his clear judgment. There was no sentimentality in it, yet he felt that consistent loyalty to the ties that bound him to the King of Bohemia was the right course not only, and not in the first place, for moral as much as for practical reasons. Thus all attempts to gain his cooperation against George, even in purely diplomatic terms, regularly met with a firm refusal, whether the temptation came from the Pope, the Emperor, or even from his own brother, the Elector. Surely he was not happy that his policy led to a strong alienation between him (as well as his Saxon friends) and

---

[14] See e.g. Riedel, *Codex*, III, 1, 405, and *FRA*, II, 44, 617f. See further George's letter, promising support to Margrave Albert in case the marriage should cause any trouble to him, in the Bamberg St. Arch. C 17, 3, nr. 85. Related documents quoted also in *DRTA*, XXI.

the Emperor, who now, in the late sixties, was much closer to the Wittelsbachs than to their old antagonists of Hohenzollern and Wettin. But Albert persisted in what he himself called a policy of "essential neutrality." [15]

There is little question that such a "neutrality" on the side of his Brandenburg and Saxon allies and relatives was somewhat less than what King George had hoped for when, immediately after the end of the diet (and at about the same time as his ambassador urged the King of France to go all out for the calling of a new church council), he asked the allied German princes to come to his aid against the Czech baronial rebels.[16] Neither the Brandenburg margraves nor the Saxon dukes went so far in their support. If George was disappointed, however, he did not show it. Before long he must have realized how very useful this neutrality was for him. It was through these friendly German neighbors, above all, that even in the worst times of the war his country was never without contact with the outer world. It was their resistance, in many forms, which helped to vitiate or at least to blunt the attempt of George's enemies to destroy him by the means of an economic blockade; without their resistance the crusading furor among some part of the German population, though perhaps never too effective as a military threat, might have been more dangerous and would not have lost, before long, so much of its strength and persistence. And above all their continued political, economic, and social intercourse with George's Bohemia, together with similar support from Poland, prevented the papacy from effectively reducing the country to a hopelessly isolated, thoroughly despised outlaw—a status which would have made it impossible for such a relatively large part of the Catholic population to remain faithful to King George and withstand the steadily increased propagandistic pressure of his enemies.

Of George's friends among the German princes, Margrave Albert was clearly the most active and the most influential, the one also with whose views and whose policy, owing to his lively and informative correspondence, we are most familiar. (His brother Elector Frederick II, whose political judgment was shallower and who was more easily influenced, had his moments of weakness and temptation when only Albert's urgent warnings prevented him from sliding into the other camp.) But the contributions of the Saxon dukes to George's political

[15] Riedel, *Codex,* 434.
[16] *FRA,* II, 20, 454.

struggle were also of great value for him, and the effort behind their policy has to be measured against the considerable opposition which they met at home as well as from Rome.

The relation between the Saxon dukes and King George had, indeed, only recently been cemented by one of the King's truly ingenious political moves. It was related to the city and district of Plauen.[17]

The lords of Plauen were among the wealthiest barons of the kingdom, but much of their holdings, though fiefs of the Bohemian crown, were situated outside the traditional borders of the kingdom. This was true of the town and district of Plauen itself (which was eventually to become the main urban center of the southwestern region of Saxony). Early in King George's reign, there had been some friction between the King and Lord Henry of Plauen when Henry had started a feud with the city of Cheb, which the King protected. But things came to a head when the lord, during the development of the League of Zelená Hora, had begun an unpleasant struggle with his own vassals, the local gentry of Plauen. When those men appealed to the King, he summoned the lord, but Henry immediately appealed to the papal legate Rudolf of Lavant, thereby challenging the King's right to have any jurisdiction in this case. The King thereupon fined him in absentia and, when Henry still refused to take any cognizance of the sentence, deprived him, as a faithless vassal, of the town and region of Plauen, investing his son-in-law Albert of Saxony with this important possession.

George's action did little to increase the resistance of the hostile barons against him—this movement, for the reasons discussed before, took its course, and by his appeal to Rudolf of Lavant the Lord of Plauen had already made his choice in a rather irrevocable manner.[18] But Albert's enfeoffment and the immediate occupation of the town and region of Plauen by the two dukes forged a new and strong link between them and King George. It did not force them to support, at length, the Czech ruler by military means (though there was some military help in the earlier phase of the war). But as they were determined to hold on to this substantial gain—and this, they did, with permanent consequences for Plauen and Saxony—they could not pos-

---

17 For the most detailed and best documented presentation of the Plauen issue see H. Ermisch "Studien zur Geschichte der sächsisch—böhmischen Beziehungen, 1464–1471," *Neues Archiv für Sächsische Geschichte,* I, 218–223. The transfer of Plauen to Albert in Dresden, H.St. Archiv Urk. 7936–37, as quoted in *RTA,* XXI.

18 But Bachmann, as so often, sees in George's policy here only lack of consistency and inability to master his emotional hatred of the great lords. See *Reichsgeschichte* I, 577.

sibly take a stand against George, that is as against a lawless usurper of the Bohemian throne. For their own right to Plauen stood or lapsed entirely with their enfeoffment by George as the true and rightful lord over this dominion. If this was disputed, their occupation and possession of this region was the merest robbery, a view which was indeed held by the papacy and which the Saxon dukes would never acknowledge.[19] The Saxon-Bohemian friendship, in the period to follow, had its ups and down, it strengths and weaknesses, according to the situation of the moment and the changing expectations for the outcome of the war. Yet throughout this time the Saxon dukes, much like their friend and adviser Margrave Albert, essentially kept the friendship alive, were generally successful in preventing their vassals from serving against the King, tried and eventually succeeded in dampening the "crusading spirit" of the anti-Hussite hotheads among the common people of their territories, frequently disregarded or even sabotaged, and eventually achieved much easing and limitation in regard to, the economic blockade of Bohemia decreed by the papel legate, and in the end were the most active and most nearly successful mediators working toward an understanding between Rome and Prague.[20]

What, at this decisive moment, was the situation in the realm? In Bohemia the overwhelming number of cities as well as rural districts were firmly in the hands of the King and his party. Only one city of importance, Pilsen, had so far joined the baronial organization which now openly claimed to be a league in defense of the Catholic faith. It is, incidentally, remarkable how relatively little influence, in this situation, was sometime exerted by nationality. Pilsen was substantially Czech, though with a long anti-Hussite tradition. The city which was the most German in western Bohemia, Cheb, resisted with remarkable determination the threats and blandishments of the barons and the papal legate.[21] The lords of the league owned, of course, a considerable number of strong castles, especially in the west and southwest of the country, but also some in the center and the east.

In Moravia the situation was less clear. The gentry, as in Bohemia, mostly belonged to the Utraquist faith, and in addition the Catholic wing of the high nobility was relatively weaker than in Bohemia. It

[19] See *SrS*, VIII, 168–169.

[20] A characteristic example is the correspondence between Pope Paul and Bishop Dietrich of Meissen, in Dresden H.St.A.W.A. Böhm. Sachen Kapsel V, fol. 293, as quoted in *DRTA*, XXI.

[21] See Tomek, "Chování měšťanů Chebských v rozepři králů Jiřího a Vladislava a papežským dvorem," *ČČM*, XXIII, IV, 74–102, especially 76–91. See also the corresponding passages in Heribert Sturm, *Eger, Geschichte einer Reichsstadt*, Augsburg, 1951.

might be said that they were as much in a minority as the Utraquist barons were in Bohemia. But, on the other hand, militant Catholicism in Moravia had, in the cities, a strength which it did not possess in Bohemia.

True, in population and economic strength, the Moravian cities did not, at the time, reach the level of their sisters in Bohemia. Above all a large number of them had, by previous rulers, especially by Sigismund and Albert, been pledged and in fact sold to affluent members of the high nobility. Of originally twenty-seven royal (or more precisely "margravial") cities, only eleven were left at the beginning of the Hussite wars, only six in King George's time.[22] Of these only two, Uničov in the north and Hradiště in the south (on the Morava river, later usually called Uherské Hradiště) were strongly Czech and just as strongly Hussite. The other four, larger than the first-named: Olomouc, Brno, Jihlava, and Znojmo, were still dominated by the German patriciate and had retained their solid Catholicism.

We have earlier dealt with the relation of these cities to the King: with Jihlava's rebellion and the recognition tendered somewhat hesitantly by the other three. Since then their attitude, especially that of their leading families and their governing councils, to George had been always correct and often cordial, a fact expressed also in the rather frequent visits the King had paid especially to Olomouc and to Brno, where he owned a handsome if not palatial residence, still standing today. During the conflict between Hynek Bítovský of Lichtenburg and the King, the cities, despite the urgings of the Pope, had supported the King both politically and militarily.

Nevertheless, as the pressure grew, its effect began to be perceivable also in Moravia's four Catholic royal cities, especially, presumably, in Jihlava, where the lower strata of the population had, in 1458, made their peace with the King only when military pressure had become irresistible. Yet as long as there seemed any hope for a peaceful settlement, and above all as long as Bishop Tas of Olomouc stood by King George, the four cities, too, tried to resist the papal pressure. When, in the summer of 1466, Pope Paul urged the four cities to abstain from any help for the King, especially against Pilsen, they answered him, on September 14th, in a letter[23] which seems especially remarkable since, more than perhaps any other, it shows the falseness of many of the papal accusations against George, but also the severe inner conflict

---

[22] See F. Matějek, *Feudální velkostatek a poddaný na Moravě*, Prague, 1959, 31ff.
[23] See *FRA*, II, 46, 38–39.

into which the policy of Rome had forced the King's Catholic subjects. The Pope, so the message says, was badly informed. Under King George's rule Moravia had experienced an era of peace the like of which had not existed in the land within human memory. Nor had they ever experienced from him any disturbance or infringement of their Catholic faith and ritual. This was true not only in Moravia, but, as they well knew, just as much in Pilsen. The people there had no right to claim that their rebellion had anything to do with their religion. If anybody who thought he had complaints against the King could, by starting a rebellion, justify himself with his dedication to the Holy See, how could peace in the land possibly be maintained? Clearly, if the King should ever attempt to pull them away from their careful religious obedience to the Roman Church and to the Catholic faith, then they had every reason to resist him and cease their obedience toward him. But he had never in the least tried this. In regard to temporal things, however, it was proper for the Moravian cities to obey the King and to keep the fealty they had sworn, as it was said in the Scripture: "Render unto Caesar the things which are Caesar's and unto God the things that are God's."

The Pope, of course, was not impressed by the argument that the policy demanded by him would destroy the country's peace. And perhaps the four cities would not have emphasized it if they had not, at the time, felt sure of support from their nearest ecclesiastical authority, the Bishop of Olomouc. Yet the days of his steadfastness, too, were coming to an end.

The young prelate, so long a devoted friend of the King whose influence upon George, in the last years, had seemed to be steadily growing,[24] did indeed find himself in an impossible position. At about the same time that the Moravian cities had tried to justify their loyalty to King George before the Pope, the bishop had written to Paul II in a similar vein,[25] still trying to emphasize the need of Czech arms for the defeat of the "most cruel Turks." But he probably irked the Pope and his advisers by calling the arch-heretic *"serenissimus Bohemie rex."* The answer, in any case, was not merely another letter but a bull depriving the bishop of his income from the estates belonging to the episcopate of Olomouc, with the threats of far harder punishment if the bishop should stick to his disobedient policy.[26] Much as he

---

[24] See e.g. his activities in relation to Breslau, as discussed in Koebner, *Der Widerstand Breslaus*, 118–122.
[25] *FRA,* II, 44, 614–616.
[26] *AČ,* IV, 133–134.

clearly regretted it, Tas could not permanently defy the Pope's orders without risking his whole future as a Catholic prelate, especially after the official act of deposition had followed. At Jindřichův Hradec he had still presented the King's case, but at the subsequent Prague diet his absence—though not necessarily suspicious since only few representatives of the dependencies were present—seemed to indicate the beginning of the end of Tas's loyalty to the King.

For some time the break did not become open. But in April 1467 the bishop and councillors of the cities came together to consider what steps to take in concord "upon the request of the most gracious lord the King." [27] It seems that the outcome was a decision to cooperate with the Catholic league in Bohemia. On May 22nd, in any case, the cities asked the Emperor to protect them against possible countermeasures from the King, and on June 4th they abrogated their obedience.[28] By that time, however, the war was already in progress. And it was, to a considerable extent, the early development of this war which led to the defection of the Moravian cities as well as other fence-sitters.

That the civil war—so far limited to the skirmishes with Pilsen—would now spread all over the realm was simply a consequence of the political and religious geography of the kingdom and its dependencies. It was initiated by a whole series of letters.[29] Zdeněk of Sternberg wrote the King, renouncing all obedience, as early as March 2nd, a step which the King answered with his letter of challenge on April 20th.[30] These letters were also pieces of propaganda, and in regard to this the Catholic side, with its widespread apparatus, had clearly an easier time than the King, all the more as George was handicapped by his determination never to attack the Catholic Church as such. His difficulties, in this regard, are highlighted by the great appeal action which he staged in Prague on April 14th.[31]

The King had asked a large number of prominent people to join him at court on this day, among them almost all the great barons and dignitaries of the kingdom now in Prague. Most of the Utraquist lords were absent, including the most politically important of them, Zdeněk Kostka, whom the King at this very time had, in place of the rebellious Lord of Sternberg, entrusted with the highest state office,

[27] *FRA*, II, 20, 453.

[28] See Palacký, *Dějiny*, IV, 385–386 (in German, 442–443).

[29] See *AČ*, IV, 139–141.

[30] Palacký, *Dějiny*, IV, 2, 380 (German, 436).

[31] Eschenloer, G., II, 12–16; Pešina, *Mars Moravicus* 799–800 (not, as Palacký quotes erroneously, 779); and above all *FRA*, II 20, 454–458.

that of lord high burgrave of Prague. Yet several other Utraquist officials attended.[32] Besides these prominent laymen there were the two leading Catholic clerics of Prague: the dean of the Prague cathedral chapter, Hilarius of Litoměřice, and his chief assistant, the canon Wenceslas Křižanovský, as well as some abbots, vicar generals, and canons of monasteries and churches of the Prague region. Before this remarkable and overwhelmingly Catholic assembly the King now read the text of his solemn appeal against the Pope's deposition, a document that in its detail shows the helping hand of Gregory Heimburg.

The Pope, he said, had tried to deprive him of his royal title even before beginning the judicial procedures. He appealed, therefore, with all due reverence for the Papal See, to the Pope himself to let off his ire and hate and give him, as a crowned and anointed King, a hearing proper in form and place. If, however, the Pope were to persevere in his hate-driven prejudgment, then he, the King, appealed to the universal council as the great synod of Constance had determined and as, but for the Pope's negligence, it should long have been called. He further appealed to a future Pope, and to the whole Christian congregation wherever it loved right and justice. The King ended by asking all those present to do their best to keep the peace, while he promised them that he would, as he had always done, protect them and preserve carefully their religious freedom.

The appeal, with its concluding promise, may have fortified the devotion of most of the noblemen present. But to the ecclesiastical dignitaries, the situation seemed embarassing. They could hardly refuse to notarize, as did all others present, the fact of the appeal. But their spokesman, Hilarius of Litoměřice, immediately arose to protest the appeal, with reference to Pope Pius' bull "Execrabilis," which had outlawed just such appeals. The King's answer was that he could only defend himself and his honor by following the advice of his faithful friends and his experienced legal advisers. Hilarius and Wenceslas Křižanovský, nevertheless, left Prague at the earliest opportunity. They

---

[32] The Catholic lords present are of some interest. They include Lev of Rožmitál, master of the royal court; Henry of Michalovice, lord chamberlain; Prokop of Rabstein, lord chancellor; William of Riesenberg and Rabí, best known from his role in John of Rabstein's *Dialogus* as King George's faithful and vigorous defender; three members of the great house of Kolovrat, of whom only one, John, subsequently turned against the King; Ješek of Boskovice, a brother of the Bishop of Olomouc; one of the Kunštát's and four or five others, less well known, altogether a substantial number which contradict the impression that nearly the whole of Bohemia's Catholic high nobility had turned or was turning against him. The Utraquists present were mostly knights, some of townsmen's origin, such as Vaněk Valečovský of Kněž-most, sub-chamberlain, or Samuel of Hradek, mayor of Prague's Old Town.

went to Pilsen and there soon turned into the most active and un-inhibited propagandists of the rebel league. The King had let them go freely because he still wanted to avoid anything that could be inter-preted as an act infringing upon the freedom of his Catholic subjects. The same motive is clearly expressed in an event which an early chronicler [33] reports in the following words: "When the masters and priests of Prague with Master Rokycana became aware [of the flight of the Catholic clerics] they went to King George and said: 'Look, here you have a good opportunity. Since the doctors of the castle have fled from the castle and have gone over to the enemies, thereby betraying their King, appoint in their place Utraquist masters and priests, and there will be unity below and above.' But this request did not seem proper to the King, though he could well have done it. Thus a man, when he can do something, does not want to do it. Then later, when he would like to do it, he can no longer do it. The King an-swered Master Rokycana: 'Master, you have mastered long enough. Now let me be the master for a change.' And immediately great troubles began to befall him. And Master Rokycana did not go to him as freely any more."

The passage, clearly written by a good Utraquist, shows the resent-ment and frustration that took hold of a good many people with a strongly Hussite ideology, men who, as repeatedly in the past, had hoped that the fierce attack loosened upon the King in the name of Catholic orthodoxy would now finally induce him to take the counter-offensive under the sign of the Chalice. For Rokycana in particular there was the distinct disappointment that the King still reserved the great church of St. Vitus, the traditional seat of the Archbishop of Prague, to the orthodox Roman clergy though their Prague represen-tatives had just turned against him. Thereby he, Rokycana, the elected Archbishop of Prague, lost what must have seemed an unexpected last chance to take possession of what should in his view have been his own cathedral. We probably have to believe the chronicler's report about the alienation between the two men. It was not the first one, after all, but neither does it seem to have been a lasting one. And it must be admitted that the King—who sometimes must have been sorely tempted to follow such an emotionally satisfying course—knew well enough what he was doing when, in this situation, he curbed the aggressive enthusiasm of his fellow-Utraquists. It was only thus that he could retain a following among loyal Catholics. The number of

[33] *SLČP*, 164.

Catholic clerics who, in areas where the papal legate had ordered the interdict to be kept, defied this order and continued offering the sacraments to their flocks was large beyond all expectation, and especially the monasteries in Bohemia and Moravia remained faithful to the King, most of them to the extent of actively supporting his war effort.[34]

King George had, as already reported, answered Zdeněk of Sternberg's declaration of disobedience with his own letter of challenge on April 20th, and on May 1st a number of the members of the league sent their own letter of challenge to "George, formerly King of Bohemia." [35] They felt free to act this way since the embassy which, under the leadership of Dobrohost of Ronšperk, had been sent to Rome by the league after the break-down of the negotiations at Jindřichův Hradec, had brought back not only the official papal confirmation of Zdeněk's position as captain general of the league but above all—what had been requested most urgently—a substantial monetary subsidy and the promise of more to come.[36] This, indeed, had been bitterly necessary if the league was to achieve any successes against the King's economic and military strength. It was not long till it became clear that even this help was utterly inadequate.

With the open outbreak of the bloody struggle the limelight fell again upon another participant, one that had long craved just this role as the savior of Christianity from heretical corruption and destruction: the city of Breslau. All through 1466 Breslau had been the residence of Rudolf of Lavant, the papal legate. Quite in harmony with the wishes of the city (and especially with its crafts guilds) the legate had constantly favored the most uncompromising policy against George. While essentially this was also the policy of the Curia, it is nevertheless clear that the promises made to him by Breslau and the whole hate-filled atmosphere there confirmed him in his ideas about the need and the feasibility of a well-planned military enterprise that would destroy the heretic with one fast, powerful stroke. Rudolf himself, a passionate, energetic, capable man and an excellent organizer,

---

[34] See *FRA,* II, 20, 458–459, and Eschenloer, G., II, 72; further Palacký, *Dějiny,* IV, 2, 395 n.305 (in German, 454 n.304).

[35] See *AČ,* VI, 267–277.

[36] This embassy had, following a mistaken sentence in Eschenloer's chronicle, been moved by Palacký (*Dějiny,* IV, 2, 309 n. 225 and German, 354, n. 224) back to 1465, in supposed correction of other contemporary sources, especially Kaprinai's *Hungaria diplomatica,* II, 577ff. and Ammanati, *Commentarii,* 436. In his article "Die Bildung der katholischen Liga," *HZ,* XXXVIII, 1877, 79, 266, 272–273, Markgraf has shown that Palacký's dating was wrong, with considerable consequences for the understanding of the sequence of events.

certainly did his utmost to strengthen the front against George, to add new allies, discourage would-be helpers of the King, shake neutrals out of what he considered their indecision.[37] That Breslau was to play an important role in the war was taken for granted by him and even more by the majority of the people of the city. The city council would have liked to gain time so as to increase its strength economically (by waiting for the impending spring fair with its tax and toll income) and thereby also militarily. But as before the old radical leaders—the city preachers with Nicholas Tempelfeld in the lead—thwarted any rationally cautious policy, telling the people that, in this great religious war, miracles would happen and that one good Christian would easily slay ten heretics. Nothing was needed but Breslau's participation to ensure the quick victory of the Catholic front. This participation, so the rumors went, would amount, with militia and mercenaries hired by Breslau, to no less than ten thousand men.[38]

The army that actually took the field in the middle of May consisted, including the troops of the bishop, of somewhere near 3,000 men, about 400 of them a militia of Breslau citizens levied by the guilds. This first major campaign was directed against the principality of Münsterberg, an object of importance not only because of its strategic situation but also for political reasons, since the principality belonged directly to the royal house of Poděbrady. And in this first enterprise of the war Breslau seemed to show that it was indeed a sort of David in the struggle against the Prague Goliath. In short sequence the Breslau troops took first the town and castle of Münsterberg, then the monastery of Kamenz and finally, soon afterwards, the stronger town of Frankenstein. All surrendered without much resistance when Breslau's siege guns began to shell the walls. Before the end of May the principality of Münsterberg was mostly in the hands of the Breslau forces.

This easy victory did considerable harm to King George. Not only did it make the people in Breslau jubilant and extremely confident but it was quickly reported to all parts of the Bohemian realm together with rumors which increased the strength of the Breslau army to not less than 20,000 men.[39] As a result, wherever there was a strong

---

[37] Main source is *SrS*, IX. See there among many others: 129f., 135, 143–145, 166f., 218f., 221, 223–225, 228, 236–240.

[38] For the best treatment of this phase of events see Koebner, *Der Widerstand Breslaus*, 123–128. There also, on pp. 124 and 125, are listed the sources, the most important and most detailed of which is Eschenloer G., II, 33ff. See also *SLČP*, 165, and Długosz, *Opera omnia*, XIV, 482–483.

[39] Eschenloer, G., II, 33–34.

party against the King, it tended to receive considerable, in some cases decisive, additional support. Thus the final decision of the Moravian cities to join the league was, by one of the best observers of the time, credited to the Breslau victory of Münsterberg.[40] The same was true for the development in Lustia, where the Sixtowns, until recently considered quite safe by the King's party, abrogated their allegiance to George on June 8th, and even accepted Jaroslav of Sternberg, Zdeněk's son, as governor, though as yet they refused to participate in the war against the King.[41] A rebellion also broke out in the ethnically mixed city of Budweis in southern Bohemia, where the Czech Mayor Andrew Puklice, a Catholic but a faithful adherent of King George, was killed by adherents of the Catholic league. There, however, the loyalists soon regained the upper hand and the city very quickly returned to the King's fold.[42]

That there had been no effective royalist forces to defend this Silesian principality was essentially due to the King's decision to make sure first of the great bulk of the territory of Bohemia proper. This was basically a correct decision. As long as Bohemia was firmly in his hands nothing was permanently lost. If, on the other hand, his control over Bohemia should ever be shaken, he would have little chance to recoup his fortunes. This was as true in this war as it had been during the Hussite wars, and the King faced this simple truth with great clarity and decision—his whole strategy, in the years to come, was based on this understanding. In order to safeguard Bohemia and to eliminate, as soon as possible, all those positions from which his domestic baronial enemies could have tried to strike against him and to disrupt trade and travel within the country, he decided to besiege and conquer the main castles which, inside Bohemia, were in the possession of his enemies.

As early as June 28th attacks were made on no less than six of the strong castles belonging to Zdeněk of Sternberg, among them the strategically important Roudnice, which the Sternbergs, at the time of extreme Catholic weakness, had taken over from its original owner, the archiepiscopal see of Prague. Zdeněk's two main residences, the palatial castles of Sternberg and Konopiště, were also put under siege, as were the castles of the Hasenburgs and several other leaguists.[43]

[40] *Ibid.*, 35.

[41] See the reports of the royal governor, Beneš Kolovrat, and the activity of Rudolf of Lavant in *FRA*, II, 20, 445–452, 459–465.

[42] See K. J. Erben, "Ondrej Puklice ze Vstuh, meštěnin Budějovický," *ČČM*, X, 1846, 163–211.

[43] See *SLČP*, 164, 165.

When, however, the news about the defections in Moravia and Lusatia reached Prague, it became clear that quick action was also needed outside Bohemia. It was already too late to regain positive control over the deserting cities in Moravia or Lusatia, though it is, of course, doubtful whether in any case their defection could have been permanently prevented. But the impression that George's rule could be easily toppled, which the Breslau propagandists and other members now tried to create and half believed themselves, had to be stopped at all costs, even if it meant weakening or slowing down, for a time, the action against enemy castles in Bohemia. This, however, was made easier by the fact that, after the first successes of the King, the Lords Zajíc of Hasenburg showed willingness to negotiate.

The King ordered his oldest son, Prince Victorin, until now engaged in the siege of Sternberg Castle, to meet with other forces in Glatz, from where a counterattack was to be made against Breslau. Another royal army, commanded by the Moravian lord Ctibor Tova-čovský of Cimburg, marched into Silesia from the southeast and destroyed, on June 11th, a small army of the bishop of Breslau. The main army, which had only recently gained the capitulation of the castle of Frankenstein, found itself, in this place, suddenly encircled by Victorin's army.[44] An attempt was made to relieve the besieged force by troops led by Duke Balthasar of Sagan, but he failed to arrive in time. When the Breslau army, in the night of June 15th, tried to battle its way through the circle, only part of them succeeded. In the early morning the Czechs penetrated the city, where they captured not only a substantial part of the Breslau troops but the complete military materiel, including, it seems, scores of guns of various caliber, ammunition, horses, war waggons, and other equipment. For Breslau this defeat was felt, not without justification, to be a real catastrophe, destroying completely the image of the city as a potent military ally of the Curia and the rebellious barons. King George, in order to make sure that the lesson was not lost on either friend or foe, had several hundreds of prisoners as well as many guns (the chronicler reports 400) and battle waggons brought to Prague to show them there to the people. The prisoners were finally released for a substantial ransom so they would report at home in Silesia about the power of the King and the reserves at his disposal.

That these reserves were indeed far stronger than anticipated by George's enemies becomes especially clear from two pieces of evidence

---

[44] For the following see *ibid.*, and Eschenloer, G., II, 36–47.

coming from different sides that supplement each other especially
well. One is a letter written by King George to a Polish nobleman
at the court of Cracow, undated but clearly belonging to the very
end of July or the beginning of August.[45] "You know," he says therein,
"already about our great victory near Münsterberg (meaning Frankenstein), since a good many Poles took part in the fighting on our side.
Meanwhile we have taken the castle of Roudnice—there was nothing
stronger in all Bohemia—from the Lord of Sternberg." The King follows this up with a list of eight other castles and strongholds that
have been conquered from Sternberg, John Zajíc of Hasenburg, and
others. His son Henry, Duke of Münsterberg, has surrounded Jindřichův Hradec, powerfully helped by John of Rosenberg. One great
member of the league, Burian Lazanský of Bechyně, has returned
to the King's side. And at the Reichstag of Nürnberg the German
lay princes have categorically refused any help to the King's enemies.

What might have seemed like too much boasting on the part of
the King was fully confirmed by the other side, in a letter sent by
Jost of Breslau to Rudolf of Lavant, who at the time of the writing—
August 7th—dwelled in Cracow at the court of King Casimir.[46] Indeed, so he says, Sternberg has (in addition to Roudnice) already lost
the castles of Kostelec, Lesno, and Mladějovice, and what is worse,
his greatest and most important castle, Konopiště, in the very heart
of Bohemia, is in grave danger, since the King has sent heavy artillery
and other siege machinery there. Jost's castellan in Strakonice, one
of his main residences in southwest Bohemia, has told him: "You cannot hope to hold what you have in Bohemia. Our neighbors will not
give us a single horse or man." Furthermore the Lords of Hasenburg,
Ulrich and John, have entered into an armistice with the King's party,
since the mercenaries they had hired—who were vassals of Meissen—
had all been called back by the Saxon dukes. King George, he continues, seems to glory in the certainty that the King of Poland has
promised him not to assume against him the Czech kingship offered
to him by the Pope. But George's information, according to his,
Jost's, latest informations, is correct. Two postscripts say: "Too bad,
Budweis has reconciled itself with George, Kadaň has fully submitted
to Duke Henry who had occupied the castle, Upper and Lower
Lusatia have become useless to us since they have lost their previous
good government. In Moravia the royalists have occupied a monastery

[45] *FRA*, II, 20, 476–477.
[46] *Ibid.*, 477–479.

near Brno and are now firmly holding the great fortress of Spielberg against the men of Brno."

The messenger carrying Jost's deeply pessimistic letter also took with him a letter which one of Bohemia's greatest Catholic lords, William the younger of Riesenberg and Rabí, addressed to the legate in answer to Rudolf's sharp and urgent order to give up his support for George if he wanted to avoid the most severe ecclesiastical punishment.[47] William's letter, while surely making use of some arguments which he found in Gregory Heimburg's arsenal, is still a most remarkable document, emphasizing his willingness to obey the Pope in all matters concerning the faith, but absolutely unwilling to obey the order to break his oath to the King, as this would destroy his personal honor, which he could not subject to anybody's arbitrary judgment. If this decision of his should lead to punishment he would have to put up with it and meanwhile join the appeal launched by the King.

Bishop Jost forwarded this remarkable letter to Rudolf after having intercepted William's messenger and prevented him from going on through Silesia to Poland, supposedly because he was afraid that the man might act there as a spy for William and the King. Yet one may well wonder why the bishop was so eager to make sure that the letter reached the addressee. There is always the suspicion that the bishop, while surely, at this time, not happy about his own and his friends' military setbacks, had his doubts about the immense eagerness and confidence with which Rudolf of Lavant went on organizing the war effort of his party. He was surely as aware as his friend and admirer, Breslau's town secretary Eschenloer, that there were strong currents, especially in the Empire, against the policy which the Roman Curia tried to force upon Catholics everywhere.

"The princes of Meissen and Brandenburg with their bishops and especially the archbishops in Germany were worried about this matter and did not approve of the Pope's policy. In their lands and cities you could hear cursing and scolding against the Pope and especially against the people of Breslau. The Pope, so these people grumbled, wanted to awaken the Bohemians—who had wanted nothing but live in peace and have friendly trading with all countries—to war, and force them to go to battle; since once before, when also all Christendom had been against them, their military prowess had steadily prevailed and had destroyed countries and people. Those lordships

[47] See Palacký, *Dějiny*, IV. 2. 396–398 (in German, 454–459).

thereupon had asked the professors of the Universities at Leipzig and Erfurt whether it was needful to wage against the Czechs who, after all, wanted peace; whether it was permissible to have peace with heretics; or whether it was required to murder them and thus to force them to return to the Faith . . . and by masters in those schools much was said and written claiming that Papal Holiness should not deal so harshly with the Czech people since they wanted to live in peace, but should guide them gently with fatherly teaching and advice, and through sending a legate such as Girzik had asked for. . . ."

Eschenloer's story about the popular mood in the German principalities continues in the same vein, with more details,[48] and he can certainly not be reproached for being partial to the King, whose downfall he would have welcomed if only it could have been brought about with less bloodshed and suffering—above all with less loss of trade and prestige for his city of Breslau. Yet we cannot claim that his report contains the whole story. Beside the sober and serious elements who wanted peace, there were still sufficient numbers of adventurers in Germany who were attracted by the old idea of "washing their hands in the blood of heretics," of making booty, giving a free rein to their aggressive instincts, and being rewarded for all this with the promise of speedy salvation. Some students fell for this attractive offer, but the majority came from the flotsam of German society, people especially whose economic roots had been loosened or destroyed by prolonged periods of civil wars and feuds. For a while the Curia hoped that it would be possible to recruit a large army from this source, and so a whole, fairly strong organization was created to preach the cross against the heretics. The enterprise was organized and headed by the new papal legate in Germany, Lorenzo Roverella, Bishop of Ferrara,[49] whose zeal for the speedy and utter destruction of the heretics was, if possible, even greater and less inhibited than that of Rudolf of Lavant, which was why he had been given this task. For a while this drive was, indeed, very successful, at least as far as mere numbers were concerned, and especially in territories such as Bavaria, where the ducal government freely permitted the preaching of the cross.

Like all wars where religious hatred played a role, this one was cruel, but no other group became so notorious for its beastly cruelty as did the German "Kreuzer" (crusaders). Czech-Utraquist sources

[48] Eschenloer, G., II, 17–20.
[49] See details in *DRTA*, XXII.

which give horrible details [50] might be considered prejudiced, yet they are fully confirmed by reports from the Catholic side which speak of massive destruction of whole villages, Catholic as well as others, of the destruction of nunneries and the humiliation of their inmates, of the mutilation and murder of women, children, and infants.[51] Understandably this was paid back, to the limited extent possible, by the Czechs who got hold of "crusaders." Thus we have no reason to doubt the Catholic source which reports that in one day some two hundred crusaders, caught and made prisoners in an ambush near Olomouc, were all killed.[52] Before long it seems to have become known in Bavaria and elsewhere that participation in this "crusade" was not exactly a safe and pleasant sort of adventure, and the rush to join abated. By October we hear, in a note sent from Znojmo to Brno, that all the "Kreuzer" which Zdeněk of Sternberg had used to strengthen his forces, as a type of mercenaries that could be hired for very little money if any, had now left him.[53]

The two papal legates, Rudolf of Lavant and Lorenzo Roverella, had, during this first summer of the war, made other efforts to improve the situation and the chances of George's enemies. The search for a ruler to take the Czech crown from the hands of the Pope went on, and special efforts were made to find, in Germany, princes ready to fight the Pope's war in Bohemia, mainly during another reichstag held in Nürnberg during the second half of July and the first of August.[54]

The diet, to which the Emperor had been invited but to which, as usual, he did not come himself, was officially presented as one in the long row of Reichstag sessions which were to prepare effective measures against the Turkish danger. That the number of important figures of the empire taking part was rather large did not indicate optimism that, for once, energetic and successful measures would be devised and taken. The presence of two Dukes of Saxony, two of

---

[50] See *SLČV*, 142–145. Part of this report was also contained in Palacký's edition as republished by J. Charvat in 1941 (quoted here always as *SLČP*), but the German censor ordered it to be stricken. It was later published in the pamphlet, distributed after the war, called *Censura a dílo F. Palackého*, Prague, 1945, pp. 17–19.

[51] See Rabstein, *Dialogus*, 44–46. Eschenloer, G., II, 77, 120–130.

[52] *FRA*, II, 20, 489.

[53] *Ibid.*, 481.

[54] About the Nürnberg Reichstag see first Kluckhohn, 267–272, with documentary material in Excurse 10, pp. 376–379, further Bachmann, *Reichsgeschichte*, II, 90–98, both with sources. Kluckhohn does not see the somewhat ambiguous character of Louis' (or Mair's) policy but still considers him a sincere friend of King George. See however Riezler, *Geschichte Baierns*, 435f. Of the sources see esp. Müller, *Reichstag-Theatrum*, II, 262ff.; further *FRA*, II, 20, 472–474; *ibid.*, 44, 642, 643; finally *DRTA*, XXII.

Bavaria, of Duke Sigismund of Austria, the Margraves of Brandenburg and of Baden, nine archbishops and bishops, was perhaps less
significant than the presence of Lorenzo Roverella, of the Bishop of
Passau and of Ulrich of Grafeneck, Frederick III's captain general, as
representatives of the Emperor, of Hilarius of Litoměřice and two
barons representing the Bohemian rebels, and last but not least of
two ambassadors from Hungary, among them John Vitéz, Archbishop
of Esztergom. These men came not with a strong hope for or vision
of fighting the Turks, since they knew as well as anybody else that
such an enterprise was completely impossible as long as there was
a bloody war in Bohemia. This, indeed, was an inescapable alternative which had not only been presented by King George, in some
essentially identical memoranda, to friends and allies,[55] but which
was stated most emphatically by several of the German princes or
their representatives. In essence the papal party, too, saw and half
admitted that the two tasks excluded one another. They could not
well acknowledge that, by pushing the Bohemian adventure, they
decisively helped the Ottoman Empire to dig itself in as a huge and
increasingly invincible power in southeastern and south-central
Europe. Thus they merely declared that the destruction of the heretics
had to come first, clinging to the fiction that this would be a quick
and relatively easy task. In reality it was at this time that, by putting
the Bohemian business ahead of the Turkish one, the Curia in fact
relegated the great hope of liberating the Christians of the Balkan
region and removing the steady Turkish pressure in the realm of
vague dreams. It was a sad and final write-off of Pope Pius' greatest
and most fervent plan, and though he himself had contributed much
to the outcome of this fatal course, one may well be reluctant to
believe that he would have gone quite as far in burying his crusading
hopes in favor of the desperate Bohemian enterprise.

No such sober considerations had any place in the thoughts and
actions of Legate Roverella. When the German princes, in the discussions about securing domestic peace as a basis for proceeding
against the Turks, tried to include the King of Bohemia as one of
the electoral princes of the Empire, the legate sharply protested, and
with him the Bishop of Passau, chief ambassador of the Emperor.
Both prelates then tried, in cooperation with the delegates of the
Czech rebels, to persuade as many of the princes as possible to join
in the war against George, supporting this demand with the publica-

[55] See an example (with wrong date) in Höfler, "Fränkische Studien IV," *AÖG*, VII, 1851,
44–46. Also Gemeiner, *Regensburgische Chronik*, III, Regensburg, 1821, 459 n. 890.

tion of a papal bull which, in accord with the ceremony of December 23, declared all alliances concluded with the heretic ruler as null and void. But this whole attempt was a failure. The King's friends made it clear that, even if they could not openly side with George against the Curia, they would even less take the Curia's side against George, and that their aim was to put an end to the whole unfortunate war, much of which was still, in their eyes, a baronial rebellion for reasons other than those of religion.[56] This resistance greatly annoyed the legate. But the friction increased. Upon the order of Elector Ernest of Saxony, the Meissen lord marshal read some papers relating to the conflict. In the process he committed, in the legate's eyes, the double crime of submitting, for the reichstag's consideration, the suggestion of calling a church council and of giving George of Poděbrady—from whom the demand for the council had emanated —the title "King of Bohemia." Repeatedly, with a loud and angry voice, the legate told the lord marshal to be quiet, and when his order was not obeyed he stalked out of the assembly, followed by most of the prelates present.[57]

If the resistance of the princes to papal threats and entreaties was clearly a success for which Margrave Albert Achilles—he himself had in vain tried to get rid of the papal ban—could and did congratulate King George,[58] the action of the German princes which emerged from the reichstag was less pleasing and useful to King George than he had hoped. The main reason for this was the participation, in the basic negotiations, of the Bavarians led not so much by Duke Louis as by his chancellor, Dr. Martin Mair. Mair's turn away from and against King George has been discussed. In his correspondence with Gregory Heimburg early in 1467 he had tried to soften this nasty impression by an appeal to what appeared to him a realistic and sober attitude, which would acknowledge the hopelessness of resisting, in a matter of principle, the decisions of Rome. But his realism, it seems, still made him ready to cooperate in a scheme which might conceivably lead to an understanding between Prague and Rome, and at the time the Saxon and Brandenburg princes, not exactly eager to challenge outright the papal-imperial party, seem to have welcomed the cooperation of this clever man. The result was a memorandum,

---

[56] See the letter of Albert Achilles to George, *AÖG*, VII, 49. In a way this was an answer to a message sent to the princes by Zdeněk of Sternberg, who claimed that nothing but the religious issue stood in the way of Bohemia's internal peace. See Cancellaria regis Georgii, Ms XXIII, D 163, 130.

[57] *FRA*, II, 20, 474.

[58] See above, n. 56.

the first in a series of schemes which at this time were still utterly unacceptable to Rome. Yet, a few years later, they were to form the basis of an arrangement considered fully acceptable.[59]

According to this first plan, the King and his family would oblige themselves to take, for the rest of their lives, the communion in one kind only. A papal legate and inquisitor would be sent to some German city where, in the presence of all parties to the dispute, the legate, after careful investigation of the articles on which the Czech deviation is based, would decide whether the Czech people were obedient to the Holy Church. The King, meanwhile, will take care not to take a stand separate from that of the Pope, the Emperor, and the other Christian princes. Especially he will clarify his declaration, supposedly made in public at the diet in Prague, that he believed the communion in both kinds to be needful for salvation, by "giving this declaration a Christian understanding and interpretation, making it clear that he had not made this in any sense other than for the well-being of Christendom and his Kingdom."[60] This understanding ought to be followed by a reconciliation between the King and his enemies, leading to full recognition of his restored kingdom, as well as by his substantial participation in the hoped-for crusade against the Turks under one of his sons or another strong military leader. The memorandum ends with a lively and frightening warning of the dangers that may beset the Empire and the German people if this war is allowed to continue and spread, and especially emphasizes that "obviously a war like this prevents the campaign against the Turks." These people, the memorandum concludes in an almost prophetic sentence, "learning that there will be no help for the Hungarians, will make an even stronger effort, will penetrate more deeply in Hungary and will eventually bring misery also to the Germans. Thus the heresy in Bohemia would not be eradicated, yet at the same time Christianity be harmed so badly by the Turks that it is more than hard even to think of such misery."

It is almost possible to discern, from an analysis of this interesting

[59] The scheme itself in the form of a draft or memorandum is given in *KBAA*, I, 135–147. Reference to some lesser sources in Ermisch, "Studien zur Geschichte der sächsisch-böhmischen Beziehungen," *NASG*, I, 245 n. 84.

[60] This part of the draft—and it should not be forgotten that what we have is merely a draft—is quite contradictory, in that at first it seems to assume that George had really made the heretical utterance, while immediately afterwards it takes it for granted that George will, without any difficulty, be able to give this same declaration a "Christian"—meaning "orthodox" —interpretation. For Bachmann, however, this very ambiguous statement is a rather conclusive proof that the princes had no doubt of George's guilt in this matter, with the further implication that therefore he must indeed have been guilty. (See his *Reichsgeschichte*, II, 107 n. 1.)

and impressive yet at the time rather useless document, which parts were shaped especially under the guidance of Dr. Mair and where the influence of Margrave Albert or the Saxon dukes prevailed. We cannot be sure at which stage of diplomacy it arrived in this form. The representatives of the Curia could hardly like it since, on the face of it, it seemed designed to save George and since it bared so pitilessly the enormous dangers to which the policy of Rome and her allies exposed all those whom supposedly it was going to protect: the Christian community of Europe. Yet, because the scheme went so far in burying the Compacts, they could not too easily veto it, and above all they could count on George himself to block its implementation. If all those years he had so stubbornly adhered to the "invalid" Compacts, it did not seem likely that he would now, in a military situation which seemed far from bad, be ready to give up.

They were not mistaken. While George, too, had to avoid a peremptory refusal, his answer to the princely embassy that informed him about the new plan seems to have contained enough "buts" to stop the enterprise in its tracks.[61] He was willing to negotiate on the basis of the scheme, but clearly without accepting in advance any obligations and any final decisions to be made by a papal "legate and inquisitor," especially concerning the Compacts. This decision was taken, in September, to a meeting of the princes at Landshut,[62] and there the scheme was buried by Dr. Mair's attempt to substitute for it a new alliance of the three princely houses with the Emperor and by the Emperor's own veto of any further steps in George's favor. When, however, the Saxon and Brandenburg princes strictly refused to join any alliance directed against the King of Bohemia, this phase of the diplomatic game, as far as the Empire was concerned, came to its usual abortive conclusion. No action was taken against the Turks, but also no action of any alliance of imperial princes against the heretics. In addition the Wittelsbachs, still cleverly albeit cautiously advised by Martin Mair, decided that, with the two other princely houses determined to keep out of any combination against George, they too would avoid, for the time being, close identification with the Emperor's position and policy.[63]

---

[61] The answer itself is not preserved but in essence Bachmann's reading of the sources (see e.g. *KBAA* I, 153–156 and *FRA*, II, 44, 642–643, 646) seems correct. (See *Reichsgeschichte*, II, 108.) What is not correct is his moralizing interpretation, claiming that George had merely been expected to fulfill his old pledge and had, again, reneged on it.

[62] See Kluckhohn, 272. A rather optimistic report by Margrave Albert to his brother in Riedel, Codex III, 1, 446. See also *KBAA*, I, 147.

[63] Kluckhohn, 273.

The Emperor made a last, almost desperate, attempt to convince the German princes of the need to present a united front against George: at a meeting at Regensburg called for October but not beginning its work till November 1467. Not even Dr. Mair took those efforts very seriously, and the envoys of Margrave Albert declared expressly that "we shall in no way conclude an alliance against the King and Crown of Bohemia." [64] At a moment when the old rebellion of Austrian lords against Frederick, though as yet hardly supported from Bohemia, grew in strength, and another rebellion broke out in Styria, Frederick III found reason to feel unhappy. Yet this time he did not go the way that in earlier times had seemed the easiest way out of troubles, especially the troubles with his own subjects—a direct appeal to the King of Bohemia. He had by now become a prisoner of the Curia, which, for all the burdensome demands it made on him, seemed the only effective power that could give him reliable backing and hope for the future. Soon he was going to solidify these ties still further by his long-planned journey to Rome.

In Rome itself, despite all the disappointments suffered recently in the struggle against the Czech heresy, there was still hope that the Czech problem could be solved by finding a capable and powerful candidate for the Bohemian throne who, lured by the handsome prize, would throw all his strength into this fight. And since legitimacy still seemed an important element it seemed almost a matter of course that the papacy as well as the Czech rebels would turn to Poland, to King Casimir IV whose consort was a daughter and sister of former Kings of Bohemia and whose realm was, for such a long stretch, contiguous with that of the Czech crown. So far, as we have seen, all attempts to win Casimir over had failed, even when the Curia made its recognition of the treaty of Toruń with the Prussian order dependent on such an act. But neither the rebel lords nor the papacy gave up hope. Whether it is true, as one chronicler claims, that early in May a meeting of the lords in Jihlava actually "elected" King Casimir as King of Bohemia is rather dubious,[65] rather can we assume the collective expression of a wish. However, an elec-

[64] See above all *KBAA*, I, 167f., 169f., 171ff. A draft for a defense pact (*ibid.*, 178–182) never even became the subject of serious consideration. See also Bachmann, *Reichsgeschichte*, II, 116f.

[65] The election is claimed by Długosz, *Opera omnia*, XIV, 485. See, however, against this Papée, "Polityka polska w czasie upadku Jerzego z Podiebradu," in *Rozprawy . . . akademii umiejętności*, VIII, Cracow, 1878, 345–454, with a special discussion of the topic on pp. 363ff., and the same author's *Studya i szkice z czasów Kazimierza Jagiellończyka*, Warsaw, 1907, pp. 67–69.

tion might well have taken place if the Polish King had given it the slightest encouragement. During July George's enemies made an extra effort to overcome Casimir's reluctance. Following one of Zdeněk of Sternberg's envoys, there arrived in Casimir's capital of Cracow the Minorite brother Gabriel of Verona, together with the papal diplomat, Peter Erclens. As they had little success they finally asked, toward the end of the month, the papal legate Rudolf of Lavant to come and assist them.[66] The negotiations, even after Rudolf's arrival, lasted for a full month, and the papal party conducted it without any scruples. Characteristic is a letter which Rudolf wrote to the Queen, asking her to avenge her brother's death by helping to destroy his murderer, George of Poděbrady.[67] Yet all this was of no avail.

In his final answer,[68] given to the papal envoys on August 28th, after the King had also consulted the estates of the provinces of Little Poland and Great Poland, he gave his thanks to the representatives of the Pope and the Catholic league for the honor expressed in their requests to assume the Czech crown. But this was, he said, too serious and consequential a step to be taken without the most careful consideration and advice of all estates of the realm, including especially also those of Lithuania. He could, therefore, give no definite answer until the matter had been discussed by the diet of the whole realm due to assemble some time in the summer of 1468. Meanwhile Casimir offered to send an embassy of prominent envoys to Bohemia, which would contribute to the conclusion of peace in the Czech kingdom and induce King George to return fully to the unity of the Christian church. (It was in this context that the King was heard to remark that he did not believe a crowned and anointed King could be deposed by papal decision.)[69] In the meantime the Curia should stop the procedure against George as well as the preaching of a crusade against him.

---

[66] See Długosz, *Opera omnia*, XIV, 484–486, and Eschenloer G., II, 60–64. See further Tobolka in *ČMM*, XXII, 173–175; Papée in *Rozprawy*, VIII, 366ff., and in *Studya i szkice*, 66ff., also Caro, *Geschichte Polens*, V, Gotha, 278ff.

[67] To this phase belongs the truly poisonous letter or pamphlet in *SrS*, IX, 209–210, though the copy preserved was directed to Matthias Corvinus. The pamphlet makes one wonder about Rudolf of Lavant, who is generally depicted as a man of basic decency if something of a zealot. (See e.g. Markgraf, "Rudolf von Rüdeshiem, Bishof von Breslau," in *Allg. Deutsche Biographie*, XXIX, 529–534.) Here he reports that Hynek Bítovský of Lichtenburg (the worst of Moravia's robber barons) had said he himself had heard George declare that he intended to kill King Ladislav! The poison used by George was, Rudolf has heard, mixed and provided to him by the Jews. It is John of Capistrano all over again, and we can see that Rudolf's long stay in Breslau had had its effect on the prelate.

[68] Długosz, *Opera omnia*, XIV, 486.

[69] Müller, *Reichstag-Theatrum*, II, 266.

There was hardly any doubt in the minds of Rudolf of Lavant and his baronial allies that this answer was essentially a "No," even though it was put in the form of a deferred decision which, Casimir might feel, would leave George under some degree of pressure and would thus make him more dependent on his Polish friends.

The reaction of George's enemies to this decision was not unanimous. The Czech rebel lords were deeply disappointed, actually felt cheated and made no secret of it, hinting that they might now have to turn to another protector.[70] This, indeed, was also the legate's intention, but in his case the disappointment, if there was any, was quickly overcome. Being a good German he seems to have had his doubts, from the beginning, whether the establishment of a great Slavic empire of Poles and Czechs, based upon personal union under a Jagiellon King, was really desirable. In addition his somewhat prolonged stay at the Polish court had made him doubt whether the Jagiellon state was really as strictly Roman Catholic as it was eager to appear. He cannot have been, or cannot have remained, unaware that there were under Casimir's rule millions of "Utraquists"—particularly those subjects in the Grand Duchy of Lithuania who worshipped according to the Eastern ritual and thus accepted the Chalice for laymen as a matter of course.[71] Casimir, as Grand Duke, had been their ruler ever since 1440 without this deviation in the ritual ever having been a point of concern. In addition Hussite teachings which had penetrated into Poland earlier in the century, while perhaps not very prominently in evidence, were yet far from having been suppressed. This, indeed, was the impression which Rudolf of Lavant himself carried away from his visit to Cracow and which made him "worry lest, if the Czech realm got into the hands of the Poles, its heresy would be thereby not destroyed but rather strengthened . . . since it is obvious that for many years the Polish priests have favored and still favor the heresy in Bohemia, since many a priest whom the heretics have is not a Czech but a Pole, and unfortunately there are not a few among the lords and the gentry in Poland who are poisoned by the heresy."

This characterization of the religious situation in Poland occurred in a message sent, in 1468, to Elector Frederick II of Brandenburg, with the precise purpose of offering the Bohemian crown to the Hohenzollern prince.[72] It was not the beginning of this action. The first,

---

[70] Palacký, *Dějiny,* IV, 2, 407 (German, 467).
[71] See about this e.g. Caro, *Geschichte Polens,* V, 267–268.
[72] Riedel, *Codex,* III, 1, 456; see also Eschenloer, G., II, 89.

as yet less distinct and detailed offer had been made to the elector as early as November 1467. And between the failure of the Polish negotiations in August and the wooing of the Brandenburg ruler other attempts had been made to find a willing candidate for this not-so-vacant throne: the Emperor, in particular, seems to have sounded out Duke Charles the Bold of Burgundy.[73] Of this Burgundian attempt we know very little, all the more of the action intended to tempt Frederick of Brandenburg and its further development.[74]

In the outcome this appears merely as an episode, but in a symptomatic way it is of considerable interest. One may ask why the legate, surely not without papal permission, should have selected just this elderly German prince whose economic as well as military power, while not insignificant, was also far from imposing, as the German civil war of the earlier sixties had clearly shown. To some extent it does indicate that the papal party began to get rather desperate in view of the strong position in which King George found himself after the war had lasted throughout much of 1467. But there was also some shrewd calculation in the choice of Elector Frederick. If he could have been won over for this role it would have been a highly dangerous blow to George's diplomatic position in Germany. It would have made it next to impossible for the elector's brother and prospective successor, Margrave Albert Achilles, to maintain his safe and advantageous position of a neutrality favorable for and friendly to the Czech King. Once the Hohenzollerns had broken with George and thereby renewed their old intimacy with the Emperor, the Saxon dukes could not have held out either. (Albert Achilles anyhow suspected them of flirting with the other side.) Thus, even with all the resources at his disposal, George would have had a much harder task, and this might have led to increased difficulties also on the domestic front.

The offer was made as urgent, but also as tempting, and its refusal as difficult as possible.[75] If the elector declined, he would not only lose the warm friendship of Pope and Emperor—this is essentially implied —but a Czech-Polish personal union, which might well be the only

[73] Eschenloer, G. II, 53f., also the treatment in M. Jordan, *Das Königsthum Georg's von Podiebrad,* 297–298, and Palacký, *Dĕjiny,* IV, 2, 427f. (German, 491f).
[74] The first to publish part of this material was Minutoli in *KBAA,* II, 453ff. More complete was Droysen's version, in *Verhandlungen der k. sächs. Gesellsch. d. Wissensch.,* IX, Leipzig, 1857, 146–190, under the ponderous title shown in our bibliography. Its interpretive introduction is still valuable, but the documentary part is presented better by Riedel, *Codex,* III, 1, where the whole "Böhmische Handel" occupies pp. 455–478. See also Droysen's treatment in his *Geschichte der preussischen Politik,* II, 341–349.
[75] Riedel, *Codex,* 455–458.

alternative, would endanger, in a most serious way, the life and future of the Brandenburg state, especially considering Poland's interest in the Neumark and, as may be added, the uncertainty of the future of eastern Pomerania. Against those dangers and possible losses the elector would, if he accepted, immediately obtain ample political and financial help from the Pope as well as from the Emperor with the right to receive, from the German clergy, the "decima," a tithe still augmented by the income from a new campaign of indulgence. It was hardly necessary to underline the weighty addition of power in the Empire if the house of Hohenzollern, following the example of Charles IV, were to combine the two electorates of Bohemia and Brandenburg. No wonder that Frederick's appetite was whetted, and that his first re-action was excitement and day dreams of royalty.[76]

That there were many aspects to the proposal, Frederick was quite aware. What were the chances? Old memories of early Hussite days should have been reawakened. Another Frederick of Hohenzollern, the present elector's father, had stood on Bohemian soil as the Empire's and the papacy's generalissimo in supreme command of a crusade against the Czech heretics. He had, in the end, been forced to leave without any positive results and any glory.[77] It was not Frederick II but Albert Achilles who remembered this first. Frederick, on the contrary, claimed that his father, faced with so glittering a prize, would not have hesitated. His letter in which he tried, though in an uncertain and somewhat worried way, to obtain Albert's blessing, shows clearly how inferior his judgment was to that of his younger brother. But at least he was conscious of it to the extent of not daring to take the plunge without Albert's agreement. This, however, he could not obtain.

The letter, or rather the sequence of letters and "cedulas" which the valiant margrave and heir apparent to the rulership of Brandenburg sent to his brother, is a most interesting document.[78] It shows that Albert was about as excited as his brother, but excited with an almost desperate sense of the extreme dangers inherent in an acceptance of the offer. He does not want to say outright that he is unwilling to help his brother should he persist in his wish to accept the offer. But he presents a sort of balance sheet of assets and liabilities arising from such an acceptance, and in it the liabilities loom threateningly large

[76] *Ibid.*, 460–464. These daydreams went far enough that the elector worried about the regalia, now in the possession of "the heretics," and their replacement by new ones to be consecrated by the Pope.

[77] *Ibid.*, 472. For the background, see Heymann, *Žižka*, 344, 348–353.

[78] Riedel, *Codex*, 470–482.

against the assets. Above all he sees in the plan something very much like a trick, a deliberate attempt of the Wittelsbachs and other enemies to make Brandenburg bear all the burden of a Bohemian war without real hopes for gain.[79] He emphatically reminds Frederick of the elective character of the Bohemian crown. Even if he should gain it—and then (an almost impossible condition) have children born after his elevation—they would not inherit automatically, and at best the Czech estates would choose among them. In this connection he claims (not quite justifiedly) that all Czech rulers had to "buy themselves in." [80] He emphasizes that no King could be safe there without a strong backing from the majority of the people which however could not be expected since, as people say, "there is no faith in a Bohemian." [81] He indeed goes as far as may appear plausible in making this whole Bohemian kingship appear to his brother as unattractive as he can paint it (even dropping a hint which seems to leave doubt in the natural death of King Ladislav) for fear that Frederick may still fall for the mere lure of the title. Finally he warns the elector to be extremely careful in whatever news he would permit to get through to the Czech barons, for, as he says, probably with good reason: "they have just as many spies . . . on both sides as we have in German countries, and I'll be willing to bet a horse, whatever Sternberg and the Czech barons learn, Girsick (George) will know it before eight or ten days have passed." [82] Finally, to leave a little comfort to his presumably badly disappointed brother he reminds him that, if and when King George should die, it might conceivably be much easier to gain this kingdom by negotiation than by war.

Margrave Albert's warning was accepted, and Elector Frederick decided to put up with the displeasure of Pope and Emperor rather than risk the dangers of a head-on challenge of George's power. He also heeded his brother's warning not to let his considerations become public. His diplomatic correspondence with the Czech ruler remained normal and even cordial.

Meanwhile King Casimir had continued with great circumspection his difficult policy of making King George his creditor and yet keeping

79 *Ibid.,* 472f.
80 *Ibid.,* 474. Palacký pointed out that Albert of Bavaria had been elected but declined, a fact which in this case clearly excluded bribing of the estates. See *Dějiny,* IV, 2, 429 n. 330 (in German, 494 n. 329).
81 "Non est fides in Bohemo." See Riedel, *Codex,* 478.
82 *Ibid.,* 476.

on tolerably good terms with Rome. He showed George his friendship by a modest degree of military help. In the early fall of 1467 he sent a small corps of cavalry, it seems 600 men, to join the Czech army in Silesia.[83] At the same time he dispatched the embassy which, as he had already announced in Cracow, was to try to mediate between George and his enemies within and outside his realm. It consisted of Stanislaw Ostrorog, burgrave of Kalisz; Jacob of Dębno, starosta (lord mayor) of Cracow; and the Cracow canon and famous chronicler, John Długosz.[84] The latter, a zealously orthodox Catholic and grim hater of Hussitism, soon made himself not only the spokesman but also the spiritus rector of the activities of the embassy. This resulted in a "mediation" which in many ways favored the papal-baronial party far more than King George.

The first and in many ways most important task that the Polish delegation set itself was to arrange for an armistice. The assumption was that during such an armistice it might be possible to negotiate the outstanding issues and points of conflicts. This might have been true if a will toward such a settlement had really been present on both sides. King George seems still to have thought that there was such a possibility, provided his friend Casimir were to establish direct contact between himself and the Pope, whom he thought to be ill-informed about the whole matter. Yet it is more than obvious that this was not, or not yet, a realistic appraisal; the goal of the papacy, and of course also of Zdeněk of Sternberg and his friends, was not peace on the basis of any conceivable compromise but the complete annihilation of the heretical King and his followers. If the leaguists, nevertheless, eventually accepted an armistice the reason was that in military terms their situation had, since the spring and early summer of 1467, substantially deteriorated. This is clearly shown in all contemporary reports, whether they come from the King's side or that of his enemies.[85] It is also reflected in the fact that several members of the league had separately offered to quit fighting against the King.[86] The most important of these was the bishop of Breslau, Jost of Rosenberg, who concluded a "permanent" peace arrangement with King George on September 22 and indeed, from that moment on, took no further part

---

[83] See *FRA*, II, 20, 488; *FRA*, II, 44, 633, 636; *SrS*, VII, 176.

[84] Długosz, understandably is therefore also one of the main sources. See *Opera omnia*, XIV, 489–492, and later passages. Further Eschenloer, G., II, 83–107, and L. (*SrS*, VII) 148–157, and *AČ*, IV, 147–160.

[85] See e.g. *FRA*, II, 20, 489; Eschenloer, G., II, 71; *FRA*, II, 42, 438–440, *FRA*, II, 44, 632f. and others.

[86] See e.g. *FRA*, II, 20, 489; Eschenloer G., II, 65.

in the war. Whether an illness to which he succumbed a few months later had anything to do with his withdrawal may be doubted. On the whole it can be said that his view of the war had, from the beginning, been one of strong dislike and skepticism, though he had tried to do what he had considered his duty as a prince of the Church—as long as he saw any chance of victory. This was no longer the case. For the radicals in the Catholic camp who had been angered by his peace move, his death was rather an advantage: his successor as Bishop of Breslau was Rudolf of Lavant, still a determined representative of the "tough line," who would have many bitter experiences before he, too, finally came to understand and appreciate his predecessor's deep loathing for this unholy struggle.[87]

Among the barons, the two Lords of Hasenburg had been the first to ask for and obtain an armistice. But the King, too, lost a valuable supporter. John of Rosenberg, Jost's brother, had at first taken a notable part in the war in southern Bohemia, especially by his participation in the siege of Jindřichův Hradec. While he was engaged in this enterprise—not an easy one in view of the strength of town and castle—his own possessions became, for a while, the chief object of the war effort of Zdeněk of Sternberg for whom the loyalism of this great and influential Catholic lord was especially hard to bear as it made his own position appear so much less a matter of high principles and so much more as an expression of material interests and personal ambition. But the double-pronged attack upon Rosenberg—waged militarily by Sternberg and "morally" by the papal legate Lorenzo Roverella—finally had at least a partial success. Lord John complained about insufficient support from the King. Also he may have felt that by retiring from the war (he concluded an armistice on October 9th) and taking a "neutral" stand, he was not unduly harming King George, especially since this was just what his brother Jost had recently done from the other side. The league, however, experienced a lessening of military pressure in southern Bohemia and could still hope eventually to pull Rosenberg over fully to its side.[88]

As far as the Polish embassy is concerned, it is hardly necessary to follow each of its movements between the political centers of the two sides, or rather between Prague, on the one hand, and the place where

---

[87] See Jost's letter of the last period before his conclusion of peace in *FRA*, II, 20, 477–479, and *FRA*, II, 44, 631–632. His enemies especially resented his order to imprison the Breslau canon Düster, one of the most fanatic war lovers, see *SrS*, IX, 244–248.

[88] The correspondence between John of Rosenberg and King George is in *AČ*, VII, 287–298; that between Rosenberg and the league, *ibid.*, 299–304.

Zdeněk of Sternberg happened to be at any given moment. This, throughout much of the fall, was still Jihlava, in Moravia but so near the Bohemian border that he could at least try to maintain some contact with his main position in Bohemia: Konopiště. This great castle had been besieged from the beginning, but it was fairly amply supplied and strongly defended so that it had still been able to hold out when nearly all other Sternberg castles had succumbed. It was now to play a role in the negotiations. King George was willing, so he told his Polish visitors late in October, to grant an armistice and concede to King Casimir the right to arbitrate all issues pending between himself and the rebellious barons, provided they, too, were to recognize in advance such an arbitration sentence and to surrender Konopiště.[89] This demand, presented to Lord Zdeněk early in November, made the proud lord quite furious. If, he declared, Konopiště should ever come into George's hands, he would not talk again of peace or armistice.[90] Eventually, however, the Poles mediated an agreement whereby Konopiště—as well as the royal fortress of Hoyerswerda in Lusatia, which had held out equally bravely against all attacks from the papal side—were to be supplied only on a day-to-day basis with an armistice to last from November 29th to January 25th.[91] Meanwhile the papal side would be permitted to arrange for a meeting of all its important representatives in Brieg in Silesia—later Breslau was substituted—where the possibilities of a more lasting agreement should, with Polish help, be investigated.

In reality the heads of the papal party—especially Rudolf of Lavant, Zdeněk of Sternberg, and his peers, some Silesian princes, and finally the representatives of Breslau, Pilsen, and the four anti-royalist Moravian cities—used the Breslau conference most effectively, but by no means in the search for peace.[92] Palacký—writing about these events almost with the anxiety and inner participation that would have been expected in the case of a contemporary Czech patriot—was nevertheless quite right when he criticized King George's readiness to permit, by armistice and safe-conduct passages, his enemies to arrange this great congress which, as we shall see, helped them organize for a new

---

[89] *FRA*, II, 20, 500–502.

[90] *Ibid.*, and Eschenloer G., II, 89f.

[91] *FRA*, II, 20, 496–499.

[92] The Breslau day—of which more later—is of course treated in detail by the eye-witness Eschenloer. See G., II, 96–105; *SrS*, VII, 163–173. Another eye-witness report by J. Frauenburg, town secretary of Görlitz, in *FRA*, II, 20, 503–512. About this source see Palacký, *Dějiny*, IV, 2, 389 n. 297 (in German, 446 n. 296). A report by Rudolf of Lavant to Frederick of Brandenburg in Riedel, *Codex*, 450–452.

offensive phase under far more suspicious conditions.[93] It is clear that George's main reason for this "soft" attitude was his belief that it was necessary for, or at least helpful in, keeping Casimir's friendship and support. Yet it is just as clear that he could never have gone as far as he went in his concessions if his intelligence had been working well and fast enough, if, in other words, he had been fully aware of the game that, with much skill and not a little treachery, was being played in Breslau. He was, indeed, at this moment facing, as it were, the wrong way, partly influenced by Gregory of Heimburg, who saw the Emperor as the enemy who above all must be beaten. And to at least the same extent it was Heimburg who had confirmed him in that wishful thinking which would not quite acknowledge, despite many telltale signs, that the great and dangerous enemy was already crouching for the deadly jump—not in the Austrian south but in the east, in Hungary.

[93] See *Dějiny*, IV, 2, 418–419 (in German, 481).

CHAPTER 20

MARS HUNGARICUS

As early as October 1465 King Matthias of Hungary had offered his military services to Pope Paul, "whether against the Czechs or against the Turks," with the implication that he would probably enjoy an enterprise in the west a good deal more than one in the east. The Curia had, at that time, not taken the offer seriously, noting, realistically, that Hungary was in the first line of assaults coming from the Ottomans, and as yet had not won more than a few tactical battles. Matthias could thus ill afford a full scale engagement against this strong western neighbor without endangering the safety of his own realm as well as all the chances—however uncertain they may have appeared—of organizing a great counteroffensive against the fatal Turkish westward expansion. This view was reasonable, and was widely shared by the temporal rulers of Central Europe as well as of Italy, especially of Venice. But by late 1467 or the beginning of 1468 this was no longer the firm and clearly understood policy of the Curia in relation to Hungary's task. Pope Paul, it is true, was still far from ready to enclose King Matthias in the circle of those rulers to whom, more or less officially, the Czech crown was to be offered. But while attempts at wooing men like Charles of Burgundy, Frederick of Brandenburg, and, most tenaciously, Casimir of Poland went on, the war against the great heretic took a course so unsatisfactory that the makers of the papal strategy, above all the two papal legates Lorenzo Roverella and Rudolf of Lavant, felt that they could not overlook any possible military support. Obviously no one else could, in such terms, provide as effective a strengthening of the papal cause as the King of Hungary, at least as long the Turks left him alone.

Matthias himself, in this phase, became more and more attracted by the Bohemian lure. There had been a time when his position in regard to his former father-in-law had been one of clearly inferior strength. In the early sixties the Czech throne had seemed solid and unshakable, while his own was still under attack from without—especially by the Emperor—and from influential baronial circles within. King

George's attitude at that time had been ambiguous. He himself had declined baronial offers from Hungary, but, hopeful that the Emperor would support the scheme of his own elevation to Roman kingship, he had, at one stage, promised to support the Emperor's claims to the Hungarian throne. Far from keeping this promise, however, he had effectively mediated between Frederick and Matthias. At the same time he maintained contacts within Hungary which would give him a degree of influence in that country, a policy quite parallel (though somewhat more cautiously conducted) to what he had done in relation to part of Austria's ever-dissatisfied high nobility. This indeed was, to a considerable extent, international practice at the time, and in the second half of the decade George himself became its victim to the highest degree. But as King Matthias felt his own position becoming stronger and George's less solid, he increasingly resented whatever lines of communication still went from Prague to some of his (real or suspected) adversaries, and he increasingly permitted himself to get publicly angry about them.

The actual substance behind Matthias' suspicions and complaints is, in many cases, difficult to determine. Some of it relates to issues in which Czech policy, George's policy, plays a secondary role, while the real antagonists are Hungary and Poland. This was especially true in relation to Moldavia, the land between the Carpathians and the Dnjestr River, which was claimed as a vassal principality by both the Polish and the Hungarian crowns. That Stephen, the Vojvoda (duke) of Moldavia, was in contact with Poland is certainly true.[1] Whether he also had contacts with Bohemia and if so, of what character, is still unclear. But at a time when Matthias' intentions regarding George were anything but friendly, he may well have assumed or taken for granted that George, too, had hostile intentions. Meanwhile the diplomatic correspondence between the two courts, as mentioned before, showed especially during 1466 and 1467 a strong tendency on the part of King Matthias to seek a quarrel and to blow up existing issues far beyond their normal significance. This, in any case, was true in relation to Matthew Lukovský of Sternberg, one of those Moravian noblemen with whom some feuding, especially in the border areas of Austria and Hungary, seemed a way of life. King George had several times proceeded against him, but not in a way that seemed sufficiently radical and effective to Matthias. It was in the lengthy correspondence about

---

[1] For Matthias' attitudes toward Moldavia, in connection also with his Transylvanian policy, see E. Horvath, *Geschichte Siebenbürgens*, Budapest, s.d., pp. 44–48.

this man that Matthias began to use an outright threatening tone.[2]

More complex was the issue of the bratříci. It was already loaded with emotional undertones, and this has been true again ever since the rise of a modern Czech and Hungarian historiography. Nor are our sources ample enough to guide us safely away from emotional prejudgments and value judgments onto the safer ground of hard facts. Rather naturally the existence of a strong element of mostly Czech partisans in northern Hungary, in a region that had been part of the Greater Moravian Empire in the ninth century and had belonged to the early realm of the Přemyslides in the tenth and eleventh centuries, strengthened the idea of a close relationship between the Czechs of Bohemia and Moravia with the Slovaks. Especially those decades when, partly owing to the political weakness of Hungarian central power, the Czech condottiere John Jiskra had ruled all Slovakia in successful challenge to the Hunyadis, indicated an earlier precedent to a Czechoslovak political union. Thus it seems natural enough that even today the episode of the bratříci in Slovakia's mid-fifteenth-century history is considered far more important, and as carrying far more positive historical values, in the eyes of Czechoslovak than of Hungarian historians. But once we get to the later phase of events, when Jiskra had ceased to be a central figure and had, in concord with the Emperor, made his peace with King Matthias, the difference of value judgments becomes visible even within Czechoslovak historiography. For Palacký, for instance, the bratříci of the 1460's have little in common with the Hussite "warriors of God" but are "the dregs of many nations," and their downfall, at least as an almost independent power, is hardly a tragic event though perhaps pitiable in the case of individuals. For present day Czech and Slovak historiography, on the other hand, it is just the bratříci and their movement, independent from the influence or direction of Jiskra (himself eventually a great feudal lord) which deserves admiration as the true continuation of the Hussite revolutionary struggle against feudalism.[3] While probably not without idealizing exaggeration, the modern more sociological interpretation seems to contain a fair deal of truth.

Whatever the proper interpretation, it is clear that by 1467 the bratříci in Slovakia had largely lost their strength as an important regional power, and that Palacký was right in emphasizing the exist-

[2] See J. Teleki, *Hunyadiak Kora Magyarorszagon*, XI, 179–216. Matthew, incidentally, was no relation to the great Sternberg clan of Bohemia.

[3] See Palacký, *Dějiny*, IV, 2, 356–358 (in German, 409–411), and on the other hand Hoffmann, *Bratříci, passim*.

ence of some non-Czech elements within the remaining groups, not a few of them Poles and even Germans.[4] Many of these groups, mostly still under Czech leaders, had so long been dependent on any employment to be found in wars that they offered their services wherever they would be accepted. While they would generally prefer, if they could, to fight for the King of Bohemia they could not be too choosy. Indeed we have found them repeatedly in the Emperor's service, and it was partly as former, not fully paid-off mercenaries of the Emperor that they now began to cause much trouble to the border regions of Austria and Moravia.

It is an open question how much concentration of autonomous "bratříci" in Slovakia came, as Palacký thinks, from those troops that, having been subject to military measures in both Austria and Moravia, sought a refuge in Hungary. There is good reason to assume that the movement had never been completely suppressed within the Hungarian realm, and that the fairly substantial concentration of armed strength in the fortress-town of Kostolany, in the Váh Valley north of Trnava, presented their last important stronghold. There, then, the hard pressed troops in Austria and Moravia could find a refuge.

It was there, too, that the autonomous bratříci movement was finally liquidated by a strong Hungarian army. After a siege lasting two months and an only partially successful sortie, the greater part of the enclosed partisan army surrendered in late January 1467, and in a bloody afterlude their chief leader Jan Švehla with 150 others was hanged, while according to some reports 300 more, including women, were drowned.[5] Matthias reported this success to Duke Victorin quite belligerently, demanding action against other enemies of his kingdom supposedly still existing in Moravia, and threatening that otherwise he would take action himself.[6] An answer, though still a cautious one, came in a letter from Gregory Heimburg to the Archbishop of Esztergom, warning his Hungarian friends not to overrate the significance of this "little victory" (victoriola) as a triumph of Huns over Slavs, and above all not to forget that it could hardly have been achieved without the willing cooperation of King George.[7]

This, certainly, was true, since George had refused all help to the beleaguered troops. But the destruction of the movement as such was

---

[4] loc. cit. (see note 2 above).
[5] See FRA, II, 20, 184f.; and Bonfini, Rerum hungaricarum decades, IV, Budapest, 1941, part 1, 5–8. See also Vancsa, Geschichte Nieder- und Oberösterreichs, II, 475–478.
[6] Teleki, Hunyadiak Kora Magyarorszagon, XI, 241.
[7] Ibid., 245f.

not achieved through the physical extermination of these men—at most a few hundred of them. A much larger number of those who had previously belonged to the bratříci, whether under Jiskra or under such men as Aksamit, Talafús, and Švehla, survived and found their way into the armies of the belligerents of the time. The largest and most important military body formed largely out of former bratříci, many of them "Czech heretics," was the so-called "black legion" (fekete sereg) of Matthias of Hungary. It was to play a notable role in his future wars, including, ironically, his struggle against the Czech heretics.[8] Czech condottieri—who had previously been in command of bratříci—were also among some of Matthias' prominent generals, foremost among them Francis of Hag (František z Háje), a Czech squire from Moravia who became, before long, one of King Matthias' favorites. (These facts show, incidentally, that Matthias, notwithstanding the warning remarks of Heimburg, was as free of any narrow nationalism as George. It is ironic that both of them, and Matthias far more than George, later became the symbols of such nationalism, often in its most fervent form.)

King George meanwhile continued, in agreement with the general political line favored by Heimburg, to work for a rapprochement with Matthias. He sent Lord Albert Kostka of Postupice to Buda, who not only tried to remove all supposed misunderstandings over the issue of the bratříci, but also to justify King George's attitude toward the Emperor. Matthias, at first, remained rather cool and justified his position with the half-joking remark that, of his "two fathers," the one (George) had always tried to discipline him by keeping the threat of the whip or rod over him, while the other (Emperor Frederick) had always treated him with kindness and never tried to punish him. Thus he, as all children, was inclined to hold with the loving rather than the stern father. The remark was immediately repeated to the Emperor's court, where it caused much satisfaction.[9]

But this was not the end of these discussions. It seems that unpleasant news from Hungary's southern borders, which were again threatened by Turkish raids, helped to make Matthias more cautious. It would be wiser, for the time being, to give Kostka and with him King George the impression that the old friendship was still, or again, fully established, and that Bohemia had nothing to fear from Hungary.

[8] See Z. Toth, *Matyas kiraly idegen zsoldosserege* (King Matthias' foreign mercenary troops), with German summary, Budapest, 1925, *passim* and especially pp. 366–368. See also B. Homan and G. Szekfu, *Magyar történet*, II, Budapest, 1936, 497–498.

[9] See Pažout, "König Georg und die Konzilsfrage, 1467," *AÖG*, XL, 350f.

Albert Kostka's final report was answered by King George in late February with a letter full of praise for a diplomatic job well done. Especially pleasing to George was Lord Albert's report that Matthias still felt like a close friend and near relative of George, and that there was hope for an early meeting of both rulers.[10]

It seems that George, here, became (and remained too long) the victim of his own and Dr. Heimburg's wishful thinking (and perhaps also of Kostka's naïveté in having to face this superior diplomat). That Matthias in reality only hoped to get into the act as fast as possible soon became obvious. In the spring of 1467 the Moravian rebels began to receive active support from across the Hungarian border. In July or early August one of the King's captains, again of Czech or Slovak origin, named Blasius or Blažek Podmanický, crossed over into Moravia with a fairly strong troop and did considerable damage before being called back.[11] It seems most unlikely that this was done without Matthias' knowledge and agreement, but the Turks again gave him urgent reasons to call off this adventure at the time, and therefore, in a long letter, he apologized to King George. In the same letter he asked George not to support Count Sigismund of Pösing, brother of the governor of Transylvania, who had become involved in a widespread conspiracy which led to open rebellions in Transylvania, Moldavia, Croatia, and some border districts of Hungary proper. It sounds likely enough that there had been contact between Pösing and King George, even though, except for this one letter, our sources are silent about it. George was, of course, in no position to support, in an effective military way, the rebellions in Hungary's eastern dependencies, for geographic reasons and also because of his own difficulties. But it seems natural that he was eager to be informed about events in Hungary's eastern flank and perhaps willing to support morally and financially a development that would make it more difficult for Matthias to go over to the attack in the west. Matthias, on the other hand, tried to buy off any such policy with the promise to abide faithfully by the treaty of friendship and cooperation solemnly renewed in 1464.[12] We

---

[10] See George's letter in the Moravian State Archives, Brno, Cerroni Sb. II, 251, 46/240.

[11] There were at least two men of the same or almost the same name involved in these struggles, one a mere mercenary captain, the other a nobleman of some standing who played the far greater part. Palacký, it seems, confused the two. See about this V. Chaloupecký, *Středověké listy ze Slovenska*, 114–115, and Urbánek, "K historii doby Jiskrovy na Slovensku," 76–79.

[12] See Matthias' letter to Albert Kostka of Postupice in Teleki, *Hunyadiak Kora Magyarorszagon*, XI, 339, and for the general background. W. Fraknói, *Matthias Corvinus*, 122ff. Fraknói's statements and interpretations, invariably glorifying Matthias and imputing improper

know that he did not for a moment intend to keep such promise, but
in Prague hopes rose again that Matthias, if treated with the greatest
care and the warmest friendship, might be induced at least to keep
neutral. This, indeed, remained the keynote of George's diplomacy,
and Heimburg's correspondence in relation to Matthias all through
the fall and winter of 1467. Far from making any active use of the
severe predicament in which Matthias found himself, Duke Victorin
even offered him military help.

At the time the offer was made—and this makes it perhaps appear
a little less generous than it might have been otherwise—Matthias had
already weathered the worst part of the storm that had broken loose.
In a way his long and careful preparation for a major war—publicly
declared to be meant against the Turks but in fact intended for use
against Bohemia—helped him now, especially in financial terms. With
the agreement of the diet he had increased, but also improved the distribution of the taxes and was now better able than before to keep
large bodies of mercenaries under arms.[13] In Transylvania he had
quickly reestablished his rule. Later in the year, in his march farther
east into Moldavia, he had suffered a critical defeat at Moldvabanya,
being himself seriously wounded in the battle.[14] Yet he ended up as
master of the situation, thereby also inducing Duke Stephen of Moldavia, who had in vain asked for Polish help, to come to terms. Early in
the new year, at a meeting in Nagyvarád (Oradea, Grosswardein) he
also obtained, on fairly moderate terms, the submission of the two
Zapolyai brothers, Stephen and Imre, men of great influence in Transylvania as well as in the Tatra region who were, together with
Matthias' own mother and a strong part of the gentry, the most consistent adversaries of the planned western adventure.

Matthias was lucky enough to receive, at Nagyvarád, an embassy
from the Porte, which arrived with 400 horses and offered, so it was
said, peace for three years. The story that there had never been a
genuine Turkish embassy but only a fake one, put up by George's
former friend and now chief enemy, Ujlaki, is certainly wrong,[15] but
it contains one element of truth: there was no generous long-term offer
and indeed no peace with the Turks, as Matthias tried to make his
estates believe. There was, at best, an unwritten arrangement for a short

---

motives to his adversaries, must, here as everywhere, be taken with the greatest caution
and skepticism.

[13] See Franknói, *Matthias Corvinus*, 120, 121.

[14] *Ibid.*, 126.

[15] See Palacký (who seems half to believe it) *Dějiny*, IV, 2, 439.

armistice which another embassy, led by John Jiskra to the court of the
Ottoman Emperor, was supposed to transform into peace, but which
in fact did not outlast the year 1468.[16] Yet the King had to make the
representatives of the estates believe, in sharp contrast to what he had
declared so loudly and frequently in the past, that there was not really
any danger from the Turks, at least not for a long time to come.

The effort thus to convince even the skeptics of the necessity, the
profit, and, above all, the relative safety of a Bohemian war was made
by Matthias at a great diet held at the city of Eger, in the very beginning of March 1468. The text of the long speech he made there, as
preserved by his court historiographer Bonfini, seems fairly authentic.[17]
After reading several letters which, since 1466, he had received from
Pope Paul, urging him to enter the war on the side of the Emperor and
the Catholic grandees of Bohemia, he painted in more than vivid
colors the terrible dangers deriving from the Czech heresy which had
already infected the lands of Moravia and Silesia and now threatened
Hungary. It meant an end to all religion, reckless spoliation of churches
and monasteries, even total moral corruption (such as the shameless
practices of the Adamites).[18] No other war could bring more honor
and glory than the fight to destroy this pest. War, in any case, was
good, leisure, bad for the Hungarians who are born for the bearing
of hardship. The King then went on to talk of the impudent challenge
of the bratříci, which he identified with official Bohemian policy.
Though the movement as such had ceased to exist, he asked: "How
long, noblemen, will you tolerate such insults?" He then proceeded to
argue that the Czechs, though strong, handsome, warlike, and contemptuous of death, have recently become enervated by the debauch-
eries of mind and body. Also, not all Czechs would have to be fought
since many of their best were already on the side of the Pope and
Emperor. The Turks, on the other hand, are not a danger: they are
tied down by their eastern wars in Syria and Egypt, and there is
hope for a long period of peace with them.

Under the deep impression of this speech, we hear, as well as the

---

16 See among others Babinger, *Mehmed der Eroberer*, 284, 285.

17 *Rerum hungaricarum decades* IV, part 2, 20–25. The city of Eger (German "Erlau")
in Hungary, northeast of Budapest, must not be confused with the western Bohemian
city of Cheb, in German, "Eger."

18 The mention of this very special movement that had been destroyed by Žižka in 1422
(see Heymann, *Žižka*, 261–264) makes it appear likely that Matthias or rather one of his
advisers, presumably Johannes Pannonius, had Aeneas Sylvius' *Historia Bohemica* at his
disposal. It contains a whole chapter (41) on the Adamites, based, as Aeneas says, on informations given to him by Ulrich of Rosenberg.

impact of *"Turcorum honesta lagatio,"* the diet decided unanimously to obey the Pope and fulfill the request of the Emperor. That this unanimity was not originally present and not quite genuine is clear enough from our other sources, but the King's political victory, after his recent hair-breadth escape from disaster, is an imposing expression of his nerveless strength in all imaginable situations. He was indeed a formidable foe.

Perhaps, at this juncture, we might try to understand Matthias' motives. It is hardly correct to say, as does a recent short history of Hungary,[19] that "to his subjects [Matthias] justified these campaigns, and the taxes which he levied to finance them, by the argument that Hungary alone was no match for the Turks; that the sovereign princes of Austria and Bohemia would not help him and could not be trusted not to stab him in the back; and that he could therefore only organize the great crusade if he had at his disposal the resources of the Bohemian and imperial crowns." He personally never argued in these terms, but this, indeed, is an explanation very near to the one which Hungarian historians, especially in the nineteenth century, manufactured for Matthias' fateful decision. They felt that, thereby, it would become understandable why, for the time being (and in the outcome permanently), Matthias gave up all thoughts of the great crusade against the Turks, all hope of finishing the work begun by his great father, the only hope that could be cherished for making Hungary's future safe. This explanation, simply, was that Matthias had not in fact given up those thoughts and hopes but had merely postponed their enormous task. But this interpretation collapses in the face of the historical facts.[20] They show that at no time after 1468, down to his death twenty-two years later, did Matthias attempt to use what strength he had gained in the west for a turn eastward; that, instead, he let himself become permanently embroiled in war in the west, war not only against the Czechs but, eventually, also against the Emperor and Poland; that he answered the repeated Turkish invasions in Hungary, e.g. in 1469, 1474 and 1476, with what amounted strategically to purely defensive moves on a local level; that he—as indeed also Venice and other western powers—left completely unused the one great opportunity when Mohammed, in 1473, was engaged in a life-and-death struggle with the greatest potential ally the European powers ever found in

[19] See C. A. Macartney, *Hungary, a Short History* (in general an excellent little work), Edinburgh, 1962, p. 58.

[20] Bachmann's arguments (*Reichsgeschichte*, II, 146) seem justified. See also L. Kuppelwieser, *Die Kämpfe Ungarns mit den Osmanen*, 2nd ed. Vienna 1899, 136–185.

Asia, Usum Hasan, Sultan of the Turkomans of the White Ram, during which time all European regions under Ottoman rule were completely bared of all effective defensive forces.[21] (This in spite of the Sultan's urgent entreaties to move against the Ottomans.) Nor was there any thought of action when, in 1481, the great conqueror died, or when, in 1487, peace had been concluded between Matthias and George's successor Vladislav II. There is just no doubt possible: Matthias had really turned his back to the Turkish danger and was only interested in the West, in what to him was really Europe. It was in the West (seen from Hungary), in Central Europe, that he wanted to be a great King, that he wanted to enter the halls of fame that meant much to him. The East was, despite all Byzantine traditions, dark, barbaric, hopeless. In the West alone was, to him, light, greatness, beauty, the whole hope of the budding rinascimento.[22] But the terrible East, the ever growing Ottoman expansion could not be wished away, could not be eliminated by disregarding it. Nobody can say for sure whether Matthias, at any time, would have been able, with or without allies, to push the Turks far back (as he had done, within narrower limits, when he temporarily reconquered Bosnia in 1464). His greatness and the strength he gave, for a while, to Hungary is expressed by the acknowledgement that in the era following the Turks' great failure before Belgrade in 1456 no one but he, or a coalition in which he was prominent, could conceivably have done it. The fact that it was never attempted gave the Ottomans an extraordinary good chance to fortify themselves in the whole Balkan peninsula, including their northern and western fringes, in a way which, from the end of the fifteenth century, made the very idea of throwing them back quite hopeless. It would be wrong and unhistorical to make Matthias alone or even essentially responsible for this European debacle. There are many factors, many institutions, many people that have a share in this, not least the Curia, who in her preoccupation with the Czech heresy forgot or abandoned her own clear insight of earlier years. It

---

[21] See Babinger, *Mehmed der Eroberer*, 325–353.

[22] Professor Peter Sugar, in a personal discussion, has drawn my attention to the probability that, for many of the people (and especially condottieri) fighting for Matthias, any conquests in the east, e.g. in the Balkans, would have appeared far less tempting and profitable than those in the west, and that it would not have been easy for the King to overcome their resistance. I am grateful to him for this suggestion which seems to provide an additional motivation for Matthias' decision, without however invalidating the basic criticism of his policy, which now begins to be acknowledged as correct also by contemporary Hungarian historiography (see especially the treatment by L. Elekes, *Matyas es kora*, Budapest, 1959, e.g. p. 113).

would be just as wrong to insist, especially in view of the serious misgivings shown in 1468 by responsible people in Hungary and elsewhere, e.g. in Venice, that the decisions of Nagyvárad and Eger, and
the long-term policy they implied, had nothing at all to do with the
fatal trend of events that followed.

In the negotiations about the armistice which King Casimir's ambassadors had arranged between King George and his leaguist enemies,
the Czech King had demanded and obtained one important clause:
neither party was prevented from giving military help to an ally outside the borders of the Bohemian realm. It was soon clear where the
King expected to give such help: to his friends and allies among the
Austrian nobility. This, however, meant military action against the
Emperor.[23] Why was George so eager to strike in Austria, at a time
when the situation in his own realm was still full of dangers, even if
the rather obvious danger from the east was neglected? Heimburg's
influence, his old hatred of the Emperor, explains much but hardly
everything. In political terms George's decision, made in November
1467, changed very little. Ever since his formal recognition of the
League of Zelená Hora as a belligerent party with sovereign rights,
Frederick III had, not only de facto but also de jure, been at war with
George. Nor was this merely a paper war. The Emperor freely permitted the preaching of the crusade in his lands. And he received permission from the papal legate to use such forces, whether they came
from Austria or Bavaria, in his own territory, for the struggle against
those barons who had put themselves under King George's protection,[24] particularly George of Stein, Stephen and Oswald Eizinger, and
William of Puchheim. When in November 1467 the Emperor gave to
his captain general, Count Ulrich of Grafeneck, the order to attack
and suppress the rebels, they naturally appealed to King George for
help. The King promised support, especially to George of Stein, in the
meantime asking the Eizingers to give George what help they could.[25]
He then tried to have his Austrian partisans included in the armistice
arranged by the Poles. To this, however, the Emperor was unwilling
to agree at a moment when his arms seemed rather successful.

In this situation the King was not only sensitive to his honor and
prestige but also saw a direct military danger in case the Emperor

[23] See Bachmann, *Reichsgeschichte*, II, 134.
[24] See the letter from Breslau to Görlitz in *FRA*, II, 20, 489, and Frederick's letter in
SrS, IX, 249–250.
[25] See *ibid.*, 248, 249.

should be able to eliminate all domestic resistance and thus be free to concentrate against Bohemia. To relieve his Austrian adherents, a small body of infantry was sent south across the Bohemian border in the direction of Linz, while larger preparations were made in the south of Moravia.[26] But these measures, for once, did not cool the Emperor's readiness to fight. With a determination unusual for him he further increased his army, without much regard to the costs involved, and the course of the Austrian war—as yet limited in scope— went clearly in his favor. But now George, too, felt obliged to act with vigor. On December 29th Duke Victorin, from southern Moravia, wrote a threatening letter to the Emperor: without any further delay the Emperor was to pay the old debt which, in recognition of his liberation, he still owed to his father the King, and leave George of Stein not only in peace but indemnify him fully for the damage caused to him.[27] It was hardly a message meant to lead to negotiations, rather an ultimatum which was not expected to be accepted at any date. Indeed we do not know of any answer, but ten days later, on January 8th, 1468, the duke followed up his earlier message with a declaration of war directed to "Frederick, Prince in Austria, Styria, Carinthia, Carniola etc., without touching the Roman Empire." [28] And now a powerful Czech army crossed the Moravian border into Lower Austria, commanded by Victorin, to whom his father had, in the person of Wenceslas Vlček of Čenov, given an old, experienced professional condottiere as adviser. February and early March saw the Czechs pushing relentlessly forward toward Vienna. By March 14th the Emperor, himself safely south in Gratz, sent out anxious calls for help, asking, for instance, the Silesians and Lusatians who had concluded the armistice with George to reenter the war immediately.[29] But it was not from that side that Frederick's Austria was saved. The savior—and he would never let the Emperor forget this any more than George had permitted him to forget his help after 1462—was Matthias of Hungary.

Was George's action against Frederick III a mistake? Was it, above all, his "most fatal mistake"? The second judgment at least, is hardly a correct evaluation. Matthias, it is true, used the attack upon "his father Frederick" as an excuse for his own declaration of war. But we know that he had decided to enter the war as chief executor of the papal sentences long before the invasion of Austria. The claim, above all,

[26] *FRA*, II, 20, 518–519.
[27] *SrS*, IX, 252–253.
[28] *Ibid.*, 253–254.
[29] *Ibid.*, 261–262.

that, without this attack, "the fire of war in the Bohemian countries might have died away," is, of course, utterly wrong in view of all that our sources tell us.[30] At no time in 1467 or 1468 did either the papacy or the leadership of the Catholic league allow this fire to die out, as this would have been identical with the survival of the great heretic and his heresy, and, in the eyes of the lords, the unwanted survival of a strong monarchial state. The armistice which George's enemies had accepted and, indeed, desired was never considered by them as a prelude to peace, as an opportunity for genuine negotiations, but only as a breathing space in which to gain or regain strength and to let new forces, especially those of Hungary, join the fray.

If, then, there is still some justification in considering George's policy in the fall and winter of 1467 as one of doubtful wisdom, it is not because, if conducted differently, it could have decisively changed the course of the war. It is rather based on the impression that, in relation to the Emperor, the King, who had long taken him too much for granted, now, under Heimburg's influence, tended to overrate his ill-will, the depth and consistency of his antagonism, and therewith also the danger implied in his support of papacy and league. It is true that Frederick could be headstrong, especially in what he considered the defense of his basic positions. He was far from being a generally aggressive character, but he resented being pushed around (as his adversaries did so frequently). Prague's policy, now as earlier at the diet of Linz, tended to confirm his hostility against George rather than to weaken, let alone eliminate, him as an enemy. And just as George had overrated the danger emanating from the Emperor, he had tended to underrate the danger threatening him from Hungary. Here, too, Heimburg's influence played a role. But in addition it appears that George truly found it difficult to think of Matthias, a young man for whom he always had a strong liking, as a dangerous enemy seriously bent on his destruction. Not even Matthias' entry into the war quite convinced George of this danger. Wars, after all, could be fought for limited purposes, and often ended quickly with the foes turning into good friends, even close friends again, which had occurred in his relationship with Albert Achilles. For a long time George would have liked to think that somewhere in Matthias' breast, too, the spark of friendship and understanding had not become quite extinguished. Nor

---

[30] The preceding sentences refer to Bachmann who, in his *Reichsgeschichte* simply calls it a "grossen Fehler," but goes far beyond this general statement in a later publication: His article "König Georg und Gregor Heimburg," in *MVGDB*, vol. 35, 1897, pp. 149–150.

was he convinced of the contrary by the underhanded way in which
Hungary's sudden entry into the war had been arranged in detail between Matthias and the Catholic allies, whose chief representatives
were, in the early weeks of 1468, still assembled in Breslau under a
state of truce.

The armistice agreement which had originally been concluded only
till January 25th had in the meantime, despite George's hesitation, been
extended till Ascension Day (May 26th) upon the repeated and earnest
urging of the Polish mediators.[31] Again it must be said that this was of
far greater value to the papal party than to King George. Without this
truce, the King, it is true, could not easily have deployed so considerable an army against the Emperor, but this was to be of little if any
use to him. His enemies, on the other hand, were free to organize
themselves effectively under the papal legate who, on January 20th,
was elected Bishop of Breslau.[32] Above all they could, from this vantage ground, put increasing pressure upon the Silesian dukes, some
of whom now joined the league (though their actual contribution to
the war remained insignificant).[33] At the same time the congress sent
out ambassadors to ask for stronger and speedier help. The Minorite
friar Gabriel of Verona, together with Hilarius of Litoměřice, went to
Rome, with a long report, complaining about the great difficulties the
league was meeting, such as the stubborn attitude of the German
princes and King Casimir's armed help for the heretic.[34]

More important, however, was the mission of Tas of Boskovice. As
the only remaining Czech holding a Roman bishop's crosier, as well
as the one who had hesitated longest to take a stand against the King,
he was now asked to undertake a task which, if successful, was bound
to be especially harmful to King George. In George's service he had
repeatedly acted as ambassador to the Hungarian court, negotiating
with Archbishop Vitéz as well as with King Matthias. Thus he had
indeed, as Lord Ctibor Tovačovský of Cimburg reminded him in a
long letter written in the summer of 1467, been privy to his King's
most secret thought and plans. The Lord, a close relative and old
friend of the bishop, implored him to throw off the degrading com-

---

[31] For the various sources of these (in the outcome quite unprofitable) negotiations and
agreements see Palacký, *Dějiny*, IV, 2, 427, n. 329 (in German, 491 n. 328). See also *SLČP*,
166 for the prolonged armistice.

[32] See *SrS*, IX, 250–251, 257–259, 271–272, and for the general course of events at Breslau
FRA, II, 20, 503–512.

[33] See e.g. *ibid.*, 509–510.

[34] See Eschenloer, G., II, 104.

munity with those "who, like treacherous Judasses, plan to betray the King their lord and forget their sacred oaths to him." When Bishop Tas answered that all this bloodshed would never have occurred if George had followed his, the bishop's, advice instead of that of the "bloodthirsty" Rokycana, Tovačovský could answer that Tas, as he himself well knew, had always been truly close to King George, closer indeed than Rokycana; that Tas, not Rokycana, had been the one whose advice the King had sought first. The lord's two letters, moving documents written by one of the impressive figures of early Czech humanism, had no effect.[35] On the contrary, if Tas and his new friends were indeed conscious of that close friendship which had so long bound him to his King, then, once Tas had deserted the King, this knowledge could only strengthen the feeling that now he must go as far as possible to wash away that painful memory of his personal ties with the great heretic. It was in this frame of mind that Tas now went to Hungary, where he met King Matthias soon after his return from Transylvania. If, against all expectations, there was any need to convince the King of his duty as a good Christian, the bishop surely would do his best. After having spent some time in Matthias' headquarters in Trnova, where he was also joined by Zdeněk of Sternberg, both men could inform their friends in Breslau of the firm promise of Matthias to enter the war at an early time—indeed long before the envisaged end of the armistice which the Poles had arranged with George upon the leaguists's request.[36]

Now things occurred with great speed. On March 31, 1467, Matthias sent his letter of challenge to Victorin, as the commander of the Czech army which had invaded the territory of his "father, friend, and ally," the Emperor.[37] A week later, from his headquarters in Pozsony (Bratislava), Matthias explained his decision with the need to protect the faithful Christians of Bohemia and its dependencies against the severe sufferings they had to undergo at the hands of the heretics, a need which, he said, had been presented to him most movingly through their ambassador, Bishop Tas of Olomouc. He considered this undertaking no less pleasing to God than his long struggle against the Turks. He was, he asserted "not driven by ambition nor by the hope of any

[35] The correspondence in *AČ*, 141–146, with considerable excerpts in Palacký, *Dějiny*, IV, 2, 399–403 (in German, 458–463).

[36] See *SrS*, IX, 262–264; *FRA*, II, 20, 522.

[37] "The King's letter," Bachmann says somewhat astonishingly "seems lost." Yet all he had to do to find it in an only slightly shortened version was to open Palacký, *Dějiny*, IV, 2, 441–442, or in German, 508–509.

worldly gains but only by the compassion with those unjustly op-
pressed, the obedience to the papal See, and the urge to defend the
true faith." [38] It was not the first, nor was it to be the last, time in
history that a war motivated by sheer lust for conquest was presented
as a selfless and holy struggle.

The contest into which King George was forced by Matthias' entry
into the war seemed, and indeed was in many ways, an unequal struggle. To some extent this was even true in personal terms. George, by
now, was forty-eight years old, which, in terms of the time and its
average life expectancy, was far from young and even beyond middle
age. After a strenuous life—his first war experiences dated thirty-four
years back—he now possessed little of the militant vigor that, though
tempered by caution and wisdom, had once been one of his characteristics. Indeed (though on the surface this seems contradicted by his
willingness to take on the Emperor) he had long been thoroughly sick
of war (at least of any serious war that was more than an angry
gesture). His often proclaimed love of peace was genuine and his
"soft" attitude during the recent negotiations with the league had
shown it to his disadvantage. Nor was his health good. He had gained
much weight and had become short of breath.

King Matthias, on the other hand, was now at the height of his
strength. No longer the inexperienced youth who had taken over the
reins of government, just over ten years ago, he was still, at twenty-
eight, full of the aggressiveness and the nearly inexhaustible strength
that made the comparison with Alexander the Great, occasionally used
by admirers, something more than mere flattery. His liking for war as
an art was supplemented by an elementary understanding of military
problems and by just enough experience to caution him most of the
time, though not always, against rash enterprises. In this regard he
was superior to Prince Victorin, whom King George had put in charge
of the Czech offensive against Austria and whom he left in command
of strong armies during many months of this new phase of the war.
Victorin had as much energy and dash as Matthias but had neither his
experience nor his caution. He hardly ever saw beyond the immediate
moves he intended to make, while Matthias had, in general, a far
greater, more comprehensive strategic conception.

The Hungarian army, compared to the Bohemian, consisted to a
greater extent of seasoned veterans of earlier wars serving under ex-

---

[38] See Katona, *Historia critica regum Hungariae*, XV, 294–297.

perienced officers. Both they and the ranks contained large numbers of Czechs (former bratříci); they also contained more freely mobile units, especially of light cavalry. In many cases King George's forces proved to be stronger in infantry and artillery, especially also in battle wagons. The Hungarians were almost always superior in cavalry, which, through short hit-and-run attacks as well as scouting and coverage of troops on the march, proved of great value to Matthias.

But the greatest advantage enjoyed by the Hungarian King was related to the financial strength of the two kingdoms. Regrettably we have no precise basis for a comparison of the incomes of the two kings. Hungary with her dependencies was vastly larger than Bohemia with her dependencies, but this did not in itself signify greater wealth or a larger royal income. However, in both kingdoms, the most important source of money was the royal claim to the income from the mining of precious metals. This, indeed, was very great in both countries. In the fourteenth century, under the Anjous and Luxemburgs, their combined extraction had produced more than half of all the silver and more than 90 percent of all the gold produced in Europe.[39] At this time, the percentage had fallen, but was still very high. In Bohemia the silver mines of Kutná Hora were still, or again, a most important source. Under King George they had recovered much of their once great productivity, which had suffered from destruction during the Hussite wars.[40] Further sources of silver existed in Bohemia at or near Stříbro, Příbram, Jachymov, and in Moravia at Jihlava, which, however, had now fallen to George's enemies. While Hungary's silver production was smaller than Bohemia's, perhaps only about half as large, gold production, quite insignificant in Bohemia, was huge in Hungary, especially in Transylvania and Slovakia. From it the King's revenue rose at times to 800,000 Hungarian gold ducats annually, an amount probably never reached in Bohemia. In addition Matthias, feeling politically stronger and more secure than his former father-in-law, could more freely make use of the tax income of the kingdom, especially on the basis of the newly raised tax on individual peasant holdings called the gate tax (porta) gathered for the King through the landlords. This was not all. Matthias could count on, and had actually received, sizable subsidies from Rome, based on the alum finds in the papal states. (That these had originally been intended for

[39] See B. Homan, *Geschichte des ungarischen Mittelalters*, II, 349–350.
[40] See Castelin, *Česká drobná mince*, 212–223; and Palacký, *Dějiny*, IV, 2, 453–455 (in German, 522–523).

the long-planned general crusade against the Turks did not bother Matthias, nor, for that matter, the Curia which had begun to look at the Bohemian heresy as the greater evil.) Matthias, furthermore, could expect contributions in men, money, and material from his allies, while George (if we disregard the small and temporary help from Poland) had no such sources of support from outside.

Above all, however, Matthias had the tremendous advantage of being the aggressor, able to combine his forces with those of his allies for an unremitting attack from many sides against the same object. This, again, had implications not only for the strategy but also for the economy of the war. Matthias, who could hope to fight on foreign soil, did not have to think of his war effort as a life-and-death struggle where any false step might lead to disaster. (After the first year, in a diet at Pozsony-Bratislava, the estates again were ready to vote him new taxes.) He could therefore dare occasionally to go to the very limit of his resources, and indeed kept a strong army of mercenaries under arms for far longer times than George ever could. He did, eventually, run considerable risks doing so, both in military terms and, even more so, by challenging domestic resistance to what, in the long run, was felt to be a highly oppressive taxation. But in general his luck did not forsake him.

King George could permit himself no such luxury. His revenue, smaller than that of Matthias to begin with, could hardly be supplemented from any other sources. As long as the war was waged on his own territory he could, it is true, call a levy of all able-bodied men, most of whom had had some training and were fairly well armed. If he could combine his mercenaries with such a levy he would be able to muster what was, in the terms of the time, a large army, perhaps up to 20,000 men, about a quarter mercenaries, the rest citizen-soldiers. But such a levy, according to the laws of the land, was always based on the assumption that the men were needed only in an emergency, that is up to six weeks. If the King intended to keep them under arms beyond this period, he had to pay them as he would pay his mercenaries, in the case of a mounted soldier, a ducat per week. Under these circumstances the king had to be very careful never to come near exhausting his resources. He could not know how long this war would last, could not be sure whether and how many additional enemies the papal propaganda might still arouse against him. He had never had the inclinations of a spendthrift, but in general he had rewarded handsomely those of his friends and servants who, he felt, had been deserving.[41] Now he became so anxious about money that even Gregory Heimburg complained about his niggardly ways.[42] This attitude was bound to have an important impact upon the way he waged this war. More than once he would break off a campaign at what seemed to be a crucial moment, leaving the enemy in control of positions which had been valuable and could not easily be regained. The suggestion has been made that he also became more and more doubtful whether he would be able to pass on his crown to one of his sons and that at least he wanted to make sure that after his death they would not lose, for financial reasons, the substance of their princely position.

Neither King George nor his enemies could have had any doubt that Matthias' entry into the war resulted in an enormous shift in the balance of military strength, and, thereby, in the chances for the outcome of the war. In Prague, it seems, there was at first some reluctance to belive the somber news, and the first reaction was to attempt a last-minute settlement by diplomatic correspondence, but, of course, with no success.[43] George's enemies, on the other hand, indulged in triumphal happiness. In Rome one of the cardinals wrote to the Pope and to Carvajal, jubilantly thanking God, who had, it seemed, awoken from a long sleep, and praying to Him to let consuming fire rain down upon the Czech criminals. The Pope himself, on the occasion of the solemn Maunday Thursday cursings, not only added a few names from George's family to that of the King himself but enclosed all Catholics still helping the heretic.[44] Of two bulls issued at this effective moment, the more important one promised far-reaching indulgences to people helping the war effort even if only by money, while forgiveness of the gravest sins was asured to those ready to serve with arms.[45] It did result in a second wave of crusading volunteers strengthening especially the lords of the league. They, including the new Bishop of Breslau, who enthusiastically thanked King Matthias for his "sacred resolve," took it for granted that now they themselves were no longer bound by the armistice concluded with the heretics. They would, of

---

[41] See e.g. the case of Zdeněk Kostka, those holdings in Moravia turned over to him as listed in F. Matějek, *Feudální velkostatek a poddaný na Moravě*, 33–34.

[42] However, the tight-fisted George rewarded Heimburg quite handsomely with the large estate of Chvatěruby.

[43] See Teleki, *Hunyadiak Kora Magyarorszagon*, 330–340.

[44] See Raynaldus-Mansi, *Annales ecclesiastici*, X, ad a. 1468.

[45] *SrS*, IX, 265–270. See also Paul's letters to German ecclesiastical and lay princes of April 20, 1468, as quoted in *DRTA*, XXII (and shortened in Lichnowsky, *Habsburg*, VII, reg. 1260); further, in the same collection, Roverella's letter to the Archbishop of Trier of July 11, Koblenz Staats-Archiv I C nr. 16292 fol. 76 a – 77 b, cop. chart.

course, immediately take the field again to support the Hungarian invasion.

Of the size and strength of Matthias' army, Zdeněk of Sternberg, who had seen it at Trnava, gave accounts indicating that fast and decisive victory could not possibly escape this magnificent assembly of man and horses, wagons, and guns.[46] "His Royal Grace," he says "has over 12,000 fine troops, as good as the Czechs [was he not one of them?] could ever have." Two weeks later he elaborates: there are, among those 12,000, no less than 8,000 cavalry, and at least 50 heavy guns, such as howitzers and tarras cannon. He has never seen such an army, and would not believe it had he not seen it himself. Further 3,000 cavalry and a few thousand infantry was added to Matthias' army from the Emperor's Austrian levy and from German mercenaries hired by Sternberg.

The allied army that now moved, partly from Hungary and partly from Austria, across the border into southern Moravia, by this very move, forced the Czech army to evacuate most of the northern part of Lower Austria, though it seems that Victorin himself, with part of his troops, held on to Stockerau for some time. As the situation appeared critical, King George himself, with fresh forces partly from Moravia, marched south to oppose the Hungarians. While Matthias' army was, with its allies, probably about 20,000 strong, the Czech army was hardly much inferior, containing fewer cavalry but larger contingents of infantry and battle wagons.[47] The two main bodies came in contact near Znojmo and, after some skirmishes, the Hungarians retreated southwest across the border, toward the small Austrian town of Laa, leaving a limited body of troops under the command of Francis of Haj, the former bratříci captain, to occupy the castle of Martinice near Znojmo. The Czech army followed the Hungarians and offered battle, but Matthias, well aware of the risk involved, refused and remained in his fortified camp. Perhaps in the hope that this would lure Matthias out of his firm position, George ordered the castle of Martinice to be attacked and stormed, and after some time and having suffered considerable loss Francis of Haj capitulated and was taken prisoner with about one hundred and fifty men.[48] (He was, before long, ransomed by Matthias.) Apart from this minor victory for the Czechs and some local skirmishes along the Moravian-Hun-

---

[46] *FRA*, II, 20, 522–524.
[47] *Ibid.*, 524–525.
[48] *Ibid.*, 526–527.

garian border, no military events of any significance occurred in April or early May.

Since so little seemed to have occurred, King George decided once more to approach his former son-in-law with the suggestion for a peaceful understanding. There was a meeting between some of the leading noblemen of both sides, finally even between the two Kings themselves. It seemed as if an understanding was nearly achieved, on the basis of an international conference to be held in Venice with both rulers present. There an attempt would be made to reconcile the Czechs with the Pope and enable them to give him unconditional obedience. If no agreement could be achieved there, arbitrators, chosen by both sides, would decide. A new archbishop would be appointed and to him former church estates should be restituted. The Emperor would be left in peace, and the Hungarians be indemnified for the cost of their short campaign. As a security, the Spielberg—the great fortress dominating Brno—was to be turned over to Matthias. To give a chance to this whole attempt at general pacification a three-year armistice was to be concluded between George and his foes.[49]

It appears that George, for all the difficulties which such an arrangement would present to him, considered acceptance. However, Matthias had not had any serious intention of making peace with so little gained for himself. (He would, of course, also have had trouble convincing the papal legates of the necessity of such an early compromise with the heretics.) Therefore, just as it looked as if everything had been settled, he suddenly presented a set of additional demands. Besides the Spielberg George should also turn over to Matthias the great Hradčany Castle in Prague, Karlstein Castle with the regalia of the kingdom, and several other securities. The result was what Matthias undoubtedly had foreseen and intended: George angrily refused even to consider such absurd demands. Thus the negotiations were broken off, and the war went on. Matthias, indeed, had profited by this period. The Czech army had, meantime, run short of supplies and could no longer stay in its encampment. Hoping to get the Hungarians to join battle, George, on May 4th, broke camp and marched northward. When the Hungarians followed, he turned around, and again Matthias retreated. George could not catch up with him until the Hungarians, near Znojmo, had crossed the Dyje River. There was an artillery duel across

---

[49] See Matthias' reports to the papal legate in Katona's *Historia critica*, XV, 307, 312ff. Bachmann's documentation (*Reichsgeschichte*, II, 155 n. 1) contains several errors. It is also a distortion or at least a misunderstanding when he claims, on the same page, that George had offered complete and unconditional submission to papal demands.

the river in which the Czechs caused considerable damage to the Hungarians, who thereupon pulled back behind the protecting walls of the city of Znojmo.[50] Since there was little hope of luring out the Hungarians and the King had maintained the general levy for more than a month, he decided to break off the campaign. On May 10th, having ordered Victorin with a few thousand of his permanent troops—mostly mercenaries—to occupy the city and the strong monastery-fortress of Třebíč as a point from which to wage a guerilla war against the Hungarians, he himself with the greater part of his forces returned to Prague, releasing on the way the Moravians and the other temporary levies.[51] He may also have felt that his presence farther north was needed to deal with the renewed activities of his enemies in Silesia.

There was justification for this. Matthias had just asked for their more active participation. This was not a single act. Throughout the war he made repeatedly strong efforts to get his allies in the north and west to join him in a powerful, fully coordinated thrust which would place the allied arms into the center of the kingdom, threaten Prague, discourage or neutralize the Utraquist leadership and the Catholics still faithful to George, and push the "neutral" Catholics, some of them neutral mainly because of their exposed geographic position, into a more active cooperation with the papal party.

It was only natural that Matthias wanted to make the fullest, the most tightly coordinated use of all the forces, monies, weapons, and manpower available. And George, on his part, was right in considering this a danger which he had to watch and to which he had to take preventive action. This, actually, was often not too difficult to achieve. Even considering the relatively long time it took to march an army, say, from southern Moravia directly or through eastern Bohemia to central or western Silesia, King George had the advantage of the "interior line," an advantage which years before had helped Žižka in his defense strategy. To some extent the news of a Czech move northward was sufficient to frighten the Silesian cities (and the Bishop of Breslau) into a purely defensive attitude. They would not dare, unless quite sure of George's whereabouts, to expose themselves to an attack while their own relatively small mercenary forces (militias, of course, could hardly be used for anything but immediate home defense) had joined the King of Hungary or were elsewhere on some undertaking over which they, the smaller allies, no longer had any control. The

50 See Eschenloer, G., II, 115.
51 Ibid., 128.

same was true for the Pilseners and their baronial friends. Thus Matthias' strategy suffered from one of the basic difficulties that has beset wars of coalition throughout the centuries: the difficulty of getting the allies to achieve full cooperation and coordination, especially if this pre-supposed the effective control of all the movements by one commander-in-chief.

While, from this point of view, George's northward retreat was not entirely without its rewards, and while financial considerations could not fail to play an important role in his over-all conduct of the war, the decisions he had made regarding his position in southern and western Moravia were nevertheless, in their immediate impact, most damaging to the Czech cause. Matthias, always well informed about the movement of his enemies, knew that the previously formidable army which he had so consistently refused to battle had by now melted to a fraction with which he could deal without much risk. He made use of his speed in catching up with Victorin's small army, hardly much more than 2,000 men, even before it had been able fully to establish itself in Třebíč and to put the city into a satisfactory state of preparedness. In a battle fought outside Třebíč Matthias' enormous majority forced the Czechs to seek refuge in the town, but there were not even defenders behind all parts of the walls when the Hungarians struck with all they had, including incendiary missiles which were effective enough, together with a strong wind, to let the whole town go up in flames. Victorin, with his troops, was forced to retire into the monastery, one of those monastic fortresses that took, here as in many other towns, the place of the castle and that were sometimes as strong and firm as the greatest castles. The people of Třebíč, too, sought refuge in the monastery to escape from the enemies and the flames, but as supplies were extremely limited, the Prince was forced to evict them and thus to expose them to the dangers of the open land roved over by hordes of enemy soldiers or to the sufferings of imprisonment. Třebíč itself, until then one of the wealthiest and strongest of Moravia's towns, was completely destroyed and never quite recovered its previous prosperity.[52]

Even with the townspeople evicted from the monastery, the danger had not passed. Negotiations conducted between Matthias and Victorin personally on granting the latter free egress broke down. The siege went on, and supplies dwindled. George at first sent a relief army under Prince Henry, but his attempt to batter his way through the en-

---

[52] See for this and the following paragraph Eschenloer, G., II, 128–129; *SrS*, 277–279; Długosz, *Opera omnia*, XIV, 507; *SLČP*, 167–169; *FRA*, II, 20, 529–531, 535.

circling Hungarian army failed, causing him some losses, though in the skirmish King Matthias himself was wounded. Henry then established a wagon fortress in the neighborhood of Třebíč, hoping for another opportunity. Finally King George himself, having collected another levy, largely from Prague and other royal cities, marched south to Polna, on the Moravian border, and hence sent part of his troops, under two experienced captains, Hrabaně of Vlkanov and Jeníc of Mečkov, to join the troops of Prince Henry, who meanwhile maintained contact with his brother's army by letters fixed to arrows which were shot over the heads of the besiegers. It was arranged that on June 6 the enclosed Czech troops, divided into three parts, would try to batter their way through the Hungarians while one part of the Czech army in the neighborhood would be used for a diversionary manoeuvre and another for direct help at the place of the sortie. The enterprise was essentially successful, the two princes with their troops joined forces and, ineffectually pursued by Hungarian cavalry, soon afterwards met their father at Polna. From our somewhat confused sources it is not quite clear whether it had originally been planned to leave one part of the Czech garrison of Třebíč, amounting to about 500 men under Vlček of Čenov, in occupation of the fortress, or whether they had not succeeded in getting through the Hungarian lines. They were in a perilous position, suffering from hunger, but in the Hungarian camp supplies were also low, and eventually, on June 15, Vlček's troops were granted free withdrawal on condition that for the next four weeks they would not fight against the Hungarian King.

Of the other military developments of the time by far the most substantial was the invasion of an army of mercenaries from Silesia and Lusatia, reinforced by a large number of newly hired "crusaders," altogether about 9,000 men under the leadership of one of the Silesian princes, Henry of Glogau, and of Zdeněk's son Jaroslav of Sternberg whom his father, in the name of the league, had appointed governor of Upper Lusatia. From Zittau the army struck and marched under unspeakable devastations and cruelties—even Eschenloer was horror-stricken [53]—about thirty miles toward Turnov. There they met a much smaller Czech army led by two Catholic barons faithful to King George: Henry of Michalovice, and Šťastný of Waldstein. The Czechs occupied a waggon fortress in an elevated place above the Jizera River, their enemies another one in a lower position by the river. Lord Henry had the ingenious idea of destroying the dams of two large fish ponds

[53] German version, II, 126–127, which is the main source for the whole campaign.

nearby. The escaping waters formed a huge wave in the river which flooded the whole enemy camp, drowning many men and causing a panic among the others. In this situation the small Czech army attacked and caused great losses among the Lusatians and Silesians, taking from them all their booty. But Henry of Michalovice himself, since 1455 lord high chamberlain, received during the pursuit a wound which, while not immediately fatal, eventually led to his death.

Just as unsuccessful was another attempt to invade Bohemia, this one coming from southern Germany. The invaders were mostly "crusaders," but their leader was the only German prince ever to take an active part in the war against George: the Wittelsbach Duke Otto of Bavaria-Mosbach.

The defeat of the northern invasion made, for the time being, further large-scale attempts at invading Bohemia less attractive to George's enemies in the two northern dependencies. But they had still some scope for activity left in their own countries. In Lusatia the siege of the great fortress of Hoyerswerda went on (just like in central Bohemia that of Sternberg's Konopiště), and in Silesia the troops of the bishop of Breslau and his allies besieged and eventually gained town and castle of Bolkenhain, while Münsterberg had already been evacuated previously by the Czechs.[54]

None of the setbacks of King George, however, was as severe as the one he had suffered in Moravia. Until now, and especially before Matthias' entry into the war, by far the greatest part of the country had stood reliably behind King George, and the four German-Catholic cities had been islands of rebellion, themselves under constant pressure and frequent attack from royal strongpoints in their immediate neighborhood, Brno, for instance, from Spielberg Castle, Olomouc from the great monastery-fortress of Hradiště. Besides these strongpoints King George had been able to count on many towns and castles all over the margraviate, and on the loyalty of the overwhelming number of lords and gentry, so that he had been able to move at will and with complete freedom through this most important and most Czech of Bohemian dependencies. But as a result of Matthias' impressive successes, particularly of the conquest and destruction of Třebíč, the situation in the country underwent a far-reaching change. The Utraquist nobility of the country, while far from welcoming the invader, became less eager to fight him and endanger their lives and possessions by military resistance, after having seen their King, twice within a quarter of a

---

[54] See Palacký, *Dějiny*, IV, 2, 465 n. 358 (in German, 535, 536 n. 357).

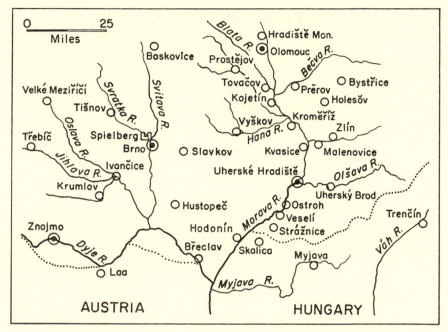

The Theater of War in Southern Moravia, 1468–1470

year, practically abandon them to the invader. Clearly the feeling that, in comparison to Bohemia, Moravia was merely a secondary concern to George, must have been widespread and does occasionally find expression. The disappointment about this led quite a few Utraquist members of the Moravian nobility to make arrangements with Matthias which gave them a measure of security against attack in return for the mere promise not to take an active part in the war against the King of Hungary. Such a decision would be still easier as, before long, it became clear that Matthias was not the zealous Catholic he pretended to be, and in fact cared little about the ritual followed by the people he hoped to gain as subjects.

As a result, the situation in Moravia became essentially the reverse of what it had been. There were now, and remained, islands of resistance against King Matthias, such as the smaller royal cities of Uničov in the north and Uherské Hradiště in the south, some dependent cities like Sternberg and Přerov, as well as a number of strong castles belonging either to the King himself (like Spielberg or Hradiště) or to such men who remained unshaken in their loyalty to George as Zdeněk Kostka of Postupice (previously rewarded for his unusually great services with some Moravian possessions), the Lords Tovačovský of Cimburg

(Ctibor and John), of Pernstein, (John and Sigismund), one or two members of the house of Boskovice, George's own cousins of Kunštát and some others. These castles and few towns, then, presented at best a hope for George some day to regain control of the margraviate. Not even all of these could be held in the months to follow. In any case the greater part of the land itself was, for the time being, lost to him.

Besides the military means to be used, the papal party, now so enormously strengthened, also continued its efforts to isolate George diplomatically. In the foreground of the foreign powers that had kept friendly relations with the Czech King stood Poland. It was, therefore, only natural that attempts were made again to win King Casimir over to the papal cause. In its service Bishop Tas of Olomouc, who seemed to have been so successful in his Hungarian mission, was now sent to Poland. The only difference was that Matthias, far from needing to be convinced, had eagerly waited for the invitation, while Casimir had so far seemed determined not to take the Czech crown out of the hands of the Pope. The question was whether now, after Matthias' entry into the war and the corresponding weakening of George's position, Casimir might not be won over if given some specific guarantees. The message, taken in May to Cracow by Bishop Tas, contained not only the repetition of the offer of the Czech crown but also the suggestion of marrying one of his daughters to Matthias. It was received with extreme coolness. The Polish court, annoyed by King Matthias' intervention and distrustful of his ulterior motives, was now even less willing to take the part of the Czech barons and the Pope than ever before. Above all, the King declared in his answer to the Moravian prelate, if anyone should, disregarding his rights and those of his sons, try to get hold of the Czech kingdom he would find him a determined and persistent enemy. He concluded that an improvement in the relations between Poland and Hungary—so frequently disturbed and spoiled by Matthias—could perhaps be achieved through a meeting of their councillors.[55]

Far friendlier was the reception of King George's ambassador, who arrived immediately after Bishop Tas's departure.[56] Lord Albert Kostka of Postupice, whose family since the days of the great war of 1410 had had close relations with Poland, presented King George's complaints that the baronial league had broken the armistice concluded under the

[55] Długosz, *Opera omnia*, XIV, 500–502.
[56] *Ibid.*, 503–504.

sponsorship of King Casimir and his ambassadors, and asked the Polish ruler to try and continue his attempts at a mediation between George and the Curia. The Czech King was very conscious of the fact that at this stage the Polish friendship must under no circumstance be lost or weakened. This is expressed in a step which must have been a most difficult decision for George to make: for the first time we find him make the promise that, at a future diet, he would support the election of one of Casimir's sons as his successor.[57] This is not a final decision and there are later moments when George's old hope of having one of his own sons follow him on the throne are revived. From now on, however, he was clearly conscious that in the interest of the nation this hope might have to be buried and that all he could still expect with some confidence was to ensure for his country a Slavic ruler, more importantly one who, as his predecessors, would be willing to maintain and defend the Compacts and thus restore and maintain domestic peace.

The Polish court agreed to Kostka's request for a new mediatory action. It was not quite without significance that in the new embassy Jan Długosz was no longer a member but had been replaced by Nicholas Skop, Burgrave of Oświęcim.[58] The activities of the embassy which spent several weeks with King George and then, in the late summer, joined King Matthias' headquarters at Olomouc, had, indeed, very little if any success, since their suggestion for a renewed and prolonged armistice, to be used for negotiations with the Holy See, was countered by the papal legates Roverella and Rudolf of Breslau with conditions which came rather near to a complete military surrender and thus could not be taken seriously. Thus also evaporated the hopes, apparently indulged in by the Polish negotiators, that a long armistice—a year and a half was suggested—would let the warlike spirit subside and give a chance to real negotiations between Prague and Rome. That all this was not as chimerical as it might appear is shown by the fact that two years later these negotiations did take place and were largely successful on the basis of a true compromise, that is a solution in which the Curia gave up its aim of smashing by force Czech Utraquism. But these two years would bring very important changes in the military

[57] Długosz, *op.cit.*, 500ff., gave the offer, if such it can be called, a far more definite character than, considering the later stages of its development, it could possibly have had at the time.

[58] His own way of reporting this (on p. 504) is not without significance. At the same time it can probably be said that, from the entrance of Matthias into the war (whom he clearly considered an upstart standing in the way of proper Jagiellon claims) his attitude to the Bohemian war becomes somewhat more neutral and less prejudiced.

as well as in the political conjunction of Europe. At the moment George's enemies did not see any reason for compromise.

Indeed no phase of the war seemed as hopeful for them, and as hopeless for the King of the Heretics, as the late summer and early fall of 1468. Palacký, echoing earlier similar judgments,[59] speaks of the "eight weeks of disaster," but "eight weeks" might well be considered an understatement, since the unfortunate sequence of losses of important positions, but also of important men in his services, began in late August, and since there were hardly any Czech successes of significance until November, perhaps even December 1468. A decisive turning of the tide had, indeed, to wait until early 1469.

Of the graver losses, the first was the fortress of Hoyerswerda, until now the one strong royalist position in Upper Lusatia. George's hope that the place would eventually be relieved by his Saxon relatives proved to be mistaken. The fortress, having withstood a siege of almost a year, surrendered on August 27.[60] At almost the same time the King suffered a serious loss when John of Rosenberg, who had lately maintained an uncertain neutrality, yielded to the strong pressure exerted upon him, especially by the papal legate Roverella, and obliged himself, in an agreement signed on August 31, openly to join the rank of the King's enemies within two weeks.[61] The great baron's desertion weakened considerably the King's position in southern Bohemia, particularly as he was almost immediately joined by the city of Budweis. This, it is true, did not mean that the King's party had been eliminated in the south. John of Rosenberg soon complained as bitterly over the attacks and damages inflicted upon his holdings there by the King's partisans as he had formerly complained about those he had suffered from the King's enemies.[62] Yet for the time being such limited actions did not alleviate the steadily worsening situation especially in the dependencies. Frankenstein town and castle, place of Breslau's first great defeat by the King's troops, was gained by the Silesians on September 17, just a few days before a relief army, dispatched by King George and led by Prince Henry, could reach the place.[63]

Of greater importance for the whole conduct of the war were the strongpoints held by the Czech royalists in Moravia, among them the

---

[59] See e.g. Eschenloer, G., II, 140: "Die Ketzer hatten dise Zeit gross Unglück, dass man hoffete, ir Ende würde kürzlich sein müssen."

[60] *FRA*, II, 20, 553–556.

[61] *Ibid.*, 557, 560.

[62] See V. Březan, "Rosenberské kroniky krátký výtah," in *ČČM*, IV, 1828, 64.

[63] Eschenloer, L., (*SrS* VII) 192; *SrS*, IX, 296.

great monastery of Hradiště near Olomouc (not to be confused with the southern Moravian city of Uherské Hradiště). It had been remarkable that, despite the pressure from Rome, the abbot and the monks of the monastery had so long maintained their loyalty to George. Without their willing cooperation the monastery would have been difficult to defend. Hradiště monastery was especially valuable as it denied the Hungarians the full and free use of Olomouc—considered Moravia's second capital as well as the center of the Roman Church in the margraviate. For this reason both sides made strenuous attempts to secure or, in the case of the Czechs, to maintain possession of the great fortress. How important King George deemed the place is shown by the fact that, to secure its relief, he sent his closest friend and confidant, Zdeněk Kostka of Postupice, with a fairly strong army. Kostka had reached the upper Morava River at the Castle of Zvole, south of the town of Zábřeh, when he was, in a night battle (the details are rather obscure) badly beaten by a Hungarian army led by the Czech-born condottiere Francis of Háj. The Czech troops had to flee back to Zábřeh, but what was perhaps worse than the defeat itself, worse also then the following capitulation of Hradiště monastery, was the fact that Kostka was severely wounded in the battle and died the day after, October 2, in Zábřeh.[64]

Zdeněk Kostka's loss was the gravest of the many personal losses that King George suffered at this time. Kostka had been his friend long before his own steep rise to power, and it was to George that he and his brother Albert owed their rise into the rank of the barons. In the baronial Curia Zdeněk had soon been the leading representative of the Utraquists, whose position and policy he had defined and defended with clarity, moderation, and determination, in a way which was bound to have considerable influence upon King George. He had often acted as one of Bohemia's chief diplomats—for instance, as the leader of the great embassy to Rome in 1462. But perhaps of even greater importance was his activity as mint-master of Kutná Hora, where he had a decisive part in strengthening and reforming the silver production and the minting of silver coinage which had suffered severely during the Hussite wars. By doing this he had also aided King George's policy of a strong monarchy which would not be exclusively dependent on the largesse and the whims of the estates and especially of the baronial class. It seemed only natural that, upon Zdeněk of Sternberg's open rebellion in 1467, the King transferred the country's highest office,

[64] See Eschenloer, G., II, 139; SrS, IX, 297–298; SLČP, 170, 403–404.

that of lord high burgrave of Prague, from his chief enemy to his main friend and supporter, Zdeněk Kostka. He did not hold it for long. (His successor became Jan Jenec of Janovice, a far lesser man who was yet to remain lord high burgrave for the rest of the century, even though his position was at first not recognized by Zdeněk of Sternberg and his friends.)

Kostka's death had been preceded by that of John Michalec of Michalovice, lord chamberlain, who succumbed to the wounds he had received in the struggle near Turnov. For him, one of his faithful Catholic adherents, George found a worthy successor in Lord William of Riesenberg and Rabí, who, despite his sincere Catholicism, never wavered in his devotion to King George and whose manful defense of his king is impressibly depicted in the *Dialogus* of John of Rabstein.

Besides the direct victims of the war, George lost, just at this time, several valuable friends and servants through illness. His long-time chancellor, Prokop of Rabstein, at one time the common friend of King George and Pope Pius, who for health reasons had already been unable to finish a last and hopeless diplomatic mission to Matthias just before the latter's entry into the war, now succumbed to this prolonged ailment. His role during the last years was perforce a limited one, yet despite his really intense Catholic piety he had never turned away from the King. A faster illness felled one of the most important leaders of the Utraquist gentry and its frequent speaker at the diets, Burian Trčka of Lípa—since 1457 the country's lord secretary. Thus George must have felt a good deal lonelier in those later war years, and the fate of his country and his people as well as of his family must have weighed on him increasingly. On occasion, it appears, he more frequently sought advice and support from the Queen, whose strong and reliable personality may have been an increasing help in those trying times. Of the two sons to whom he had assigned important political and above all—against the advice of some of his friends and advisers— military roles, Victorin, for all his dash and courage, had not proved himself as a soldier of great gifts and above all of sufficient circumspection. (He had just recently lost another fight near Brno.) George, here as in other cases, would not withdraw his confidence on the grounds of a single if even a signal failure. Yet it appears that gradually he began to trust Henry, the younger son, more than Victorin, and though in these weeks Henry, too, seems to have missed an opportunity when he did not prove fast enough to save Frankenstein, the day was

to come when his father's favorable judgment was strongly vindi-
cated.[65]

On the whole, of course, all the responsibilities rested on George,
and while there is no question that many of the recent misfortunes,
and above all the loss of Kostka, must have shocked and pained him,
the news from his court (such as the occasional but always extremely
lively reports from Gregory Heimburg) made it clear that, at least in
front of others, he maintained his confidence, even his certainty of
ultimate success. And he was not the only one who, in the face of those
severe setbacks, still trusted to the strength left for the defense of the
core of the realm. The arguments underpinning such trusts are perhaps best expressed in the famous *Dialogus* of John of Rabstein, the
late Prokop's younger brother and, like him, a Catholic dignitary—he
was provost and thereby head of the chapter of the great church of the
Vyšehrad in Prague.[66] The *Dialogus,* as rather clearly appears from its
content, was written, or at least finished, quite early in 1469, following
the phase of Czech defeats and probably contemporaneously with the
earlier part of the great diet of Regensburg. In this publication we hear
John of Rabstein—he always speaks as the voice of cool, almost neutral
reason—answer Zdeněk's predictions of a huge, many-sided attack on
Bohemia by Matthias, the Emperor, and all the German princes with
an expression of extreme skepticism. If the attempt were made, so he
says, to put such gigantic armies into Bohemia, they could not sustain
themselves there for lack of provision, since the countryside was robbed
out and burned down and all substantial food reserves had long been
taken into the firm places which were at the King's disposal. Above all,
however, "George has, in Bohemia alone, beside the royal city of
Prague, still forty-six well fortified towns in his hands, beside the great
castle of Prague he owns seventy-two supremely strong mountain
castles, not even counting the numerous other strongpoints fortified by
walls, trenches, and water. Such strength, you think, can be broken in
one year? Not even in many years, as anybody should realize who
knows well enough the spirit, the robust hardiness and fortitude of the
Czech people."[67] It is perhaps interesting that the Catholic Rabstein, in
talking about a great war which at least to some extent was a civil war

---

[65] See *KBAA,* I, 215–218.
[66] See Bohumil Ryba's biographical sketch of him in the same author's edition of the
Dialogus, Prague, 1949, pp. 5–12.
[67] *Ibid.,* 58–60.

within Bohemia, identifies "the Czech people" quite unmistakably with those who, at this time, rallied around King George.

That there was, indeed, such a rallying process is evinced in the long and fiery declaration or manifesto which was published in the beginning of 1469 by a group of some three thousand men from both Czech countries who had gathered for a sort of general demonstration for the defense of their nation and their creed.[68] They called this "the letter of old Czechs, true lovers and defenders of the truth of Christ, also of the Czech language (meaning nation)." In a fierce attack against the Pope as well as the Hungarian King (some bitter anti-Hungarian remarks can, incidentally, even be found in Rabstein *Dialogus*) [69] the authors of the proclamation revive both the style and the spirit of the Hussite Wars. Now as then the Czechs will conquer, remembering that "then a small number of faithful Czechs, led by brother Žižka of glorious memory, with little arms and almost naked, armored only by their faith in Christ and strengthened by heavenly help and His sacred blood, put to flight and destroyed such large armies." The nationalism as well as the special emphasis on the Chalice forms the basis for a wider movement toward a popular national activity of which the assembly of the three thousand was but an impressive symptom. Perhaps the temporary elimination of a large proportion of the high nobility had erected a sociological atmosphere somewhat nearer to that of the Hussite Revolution.

Yet it would probably be a deception to think that the dynamic tide of the 1420's with its mighty sources flowing in town and country was returning in its full scope. In general Utraquism had long ceased to be a freely growing movement and had become a well-organized national church, still quite conscious of its glorious past and its reforming task and independent enough to irritate and provoke all the conformist and anti-heretical instincts of Rome, yet generally dependent on a leadership which would not want to let it get out of hand. We have no knowledge of John Rokycana's attitude toward this manifesto except that his name seems in no way connected with it. Nor does its terminology quite sound like the one which Rokycana would have chosen. Rather does it sound like the spirit of Martin Lupáč speaking out of his fresh grave—the Hussite suffragan bishop had died, an old man, in April 1468.

[68] See "Tři vášnivé projevy z války za krále Jiřího," ed. F. Dvorský, part III, *AČ* XX, 557–563.
[69] In Ryba's edition, Prague, 1946, pp. 56–58.

One thing, however, is clear: to the extent that the militant religious attitude would implicitly deny the character of "good Czechs" to anyone not an adherent of the Chalice, especially to all Roman Catholics, however loyal to King George, it would not be acceptable to the King. He, whose whole understanding of the Compacts was based on mutual tolerance and who had just appointed a Catholic, William of Rabí, as lord chamberlain of the kingdom, would continue to be, as the late Prokop of Rabstein had once formulated in Rome, "the King of both kinds of people." Nevertheless the ground swell of popular fighting spirit must have had its welcome effect when, soon after, the King had to call again for a great levy of defense.

The plans of his enemies, indeed, were still based on the optimistic assumption that he and his military and governmental power were about to collapse. Neither the influential papal legates nor Zdeněk of Sternberg was willing to face the facts that John of Rabstein so clearly presented, at just this time, in his dramatic pamphlet, the *Dialogus,* although Sternberg, at least, might have learned a lesson from the experience of his attempt to relieve the castle of Konopiště. Twice in the course of November, with the support of Hungarian troops, he made a valiant attempt to get through with troops and above all with the badly needed food supplies to Konopiště. Twice he was beaten back with very heavy losses in men and material.[70] Finally, sometime in December, the great castle, the only enemy strongpoint in the very center of the kingdom and Zdeněk of Sternberg's most important holding, had to capitulate, thereby freeing considerable forces for other purposes.

But seen from farther afield this seemed a minor affair, easily compensated for by the capitulation of the Spielberg to the Hungarians.[71] King Matthias, having gone back to Hungary to obtain from a meeting of his estates in Bratislava additional means for waging this long and costly war, was extremely eager to gain also support from the west, specifically from the Empire. At a meeting of representatives of German princes in Landshut called late in November by Duke Louis—whose attitude, as that of Martin Mair, could no longer be called neutral—Matthias' ambassador in the Empire, George Provost of Bratislava, tried to prepare the ground for a great anti-Bohemian alliance and seemed to have made progress.[72] Details were beginning to

---

[70] See *SLČP,* 404. (Rhymed chronicle on the war with the Hungarians.)
[71] See Eschenloer, G., II, 145.
[72] See Bachmann, *Reichsgeschichte,* II, 198, 199.

be determined at a reichstag which was called for February 17, 1460, to Regensburg.

This meeting, as inconsequential as those before, still throws an interesting light upon the situation in the early months of 1469.[73] One of the first issues to come up at least behind the scenes was the partial drying up of the previous sources of "crusaders," despite the loudly proclaimed expectation of an early collapse of Hussite Bohemia. Rover-ella was very angry that none of the German princes had appeared personally, but he had, so he reported, supremely good news from the field: the King of Hungary has occupied Kutná Hora, Bohemia's second city and the main source of King George's regular income.[74]

After the official opening, the Hungarian ambassador, Provost George, maintained this hopeful note. He did not exactly claim Kutná Hora any longer, but another important Bohemian city on the way there from Moravia: Německý Brod.[75]

Indeed Matthias—and this was the only truth in these wild claims—had decided to invade Bohemia, and this would soon lead to a decisive encounter. Matthias, Provost George added, had not the faintest intention of acquiring himself the kingdom of Bohemia, since by right he could claim seven kingdoms all belonging to the Hungarian crown, each of them richer in income than Bohemia, and if he wanted to increase his power he would rather secure what belonged to him by right than a strange land.[76]

It seems doubtful whether these Hungarian assurances were fully believed by the representatives of the German princes. In any case the negotiations had hardly started in earnest when it became clear that no understanding on a common front against Bohemia (as supposedly prepared at Landshut) was possibly forthcoming. While some epis-copal and city representatives together with all the Wittelsbach princes promised the legate that their employers would give help against the heretics to the best of their ability, the ambassadors of Brandenburg and Saxony bluntly declared that their functions at this meeting were to inform themselves on the plans afoot, to report these back to their princely employers, "and nothing else."[77] They added that their princes would, on March 15th, meet with those of Hessen and decide together what answer to give to the Emperor and the papal legate.

[73] For the Regensburg Reichstag of 1469, see the rich material collected in vol. XX of the DRTA, about to be published; furthermore FRA, II, 46, pp. 78ff.

[74] FRA, II, 46, pp. 78–80.

[75] Ibid., 85.

[76] Ibid., 83–84.

[77] FRA, II, 42, pp. 460–462.

There is proof that Bishop Roverella was disappointed about this turn of events, and made Margrave Albert Achilles, particularly, responsible for the lack of unity which was bound to diminish the zeal of others in investing money, arms, and men in the Bohemian adventure.[78] Yet, hard and devoted man that he was, he did not give up in his attempt at salvaging as much as possible of the great plan for a truly international military alliance against the King of Heretics. That, nevertheless, he felt suddenly forced to break off all such attempts and merely to ask for an adjournment of the reichstag by two months, indicates that the cause must have been really extraordinary.

It was indeed. On March 10 Bishop Roverella informed the meeting, with a voice expressing deep shock, that he had just received letters from King Matthias saying that he had concluded a provisional peace till Easter with "Jirsick." [79] The legate was, as he explained, still doubtful whether these letters were really authentic, not only because their content was so unbelievable but also because the writing was not proper chancery style and because never before had the King written to him in such a way. But soon he had to admit that the letters were quite authentic; that something had gone wrong with the Hungarian invasion in Bohemia; and that the best he could do was to accept the invitation to join in the further negotiations between the two Kings, in or near Olomouc. For the time being the war, so it appeared, was over. So, at least, did King Matthias seem to look at things. It would be no easy matter to prevent this "peace," which in the nature of things could only be an armistice, from becoming a real peace. To prevent this, indeed, would now be Roverella's task as well as that of his friends and of all obedient servants of the papal cause.[80] Above all he would have to go to Moravia (he left on March 12) to see what could possibly have induced the Hungarian King, the certain victor of a few days earlier, to give up, with such apparent ease of conscience, his self-chosen, yet sacred task of destroying the heretical ruler of Bohemia.

[78] *Ibid.*, 464.

[79] *FRA*, II, 46, pp. 91–92.

[80] The reichstag of Regensburg did not end with the legate's departure. In particular Dr. Mair was, throughout the following days, still active in trying to prepare the soil at least for a defensive alliance of all German princes with the Emperor against the "heretics" which seemed possibly to have become even more necessary in view of the contingency that George needed no longer to regard Matthias as his main enemy. See Bachmann, *Reichsgeschichte*, II, 213–215, and soon also the material in *DRTA*, vol. XXII.

CHAPTER 21

THE TURNING OF THE TIDE

IN JANUARY 1469 King Matthias had returned from Hungary with new troops, some of them derived from additional feudal levies—the results of having convinced reluctant barons of the correctness of his predictions—the great majority mercenaries hired with the money voted to the King by the estates in Bratislava. Back in Moravia he had good reason to feel satisfied by the general war situation. By far the greater part of Moravia was firmly in his hands, and in Silesia and Lusatia the majority of his allies were strong, many of George's weak or inactive. Even in Bohemia itself his side had at least begun to "nibble off" some far from negligible corners, such as the cities of Pilsen and Budweis. In the southeast he held the smaller town of Polna, a personal holding of the house of Poděbrady, just across the Moravian border not far from Jihlava, which in October had fallen to a sudden assault by one of Zdeněk of Sternberg's sons. There had, it is true, been some recent setbacks after the series of successes all through the fall, including the conquest, by Duke Victorin, of the strategically important town of Ostroh, on the Morava in southern Moravia, and the reprovisioning, from there, of the city of Uherské Hradiště.[1] Yet there was surely no justification at the time for looking at all this as a decisive change in the fortunes of war.[2] Even the limited local strengthening of the Czech position in southern Moravia did not really give Matthias any cause to worry seriously for his freedom of movement in what had to be the basis for further offensive actions. The margraviate, in most of its parts, had remained quite safely at his disposal.

But now, for the first time, he decided to challenge the Czech lion in his den. It seems most unlikely that he, generally a clever and unemotional judge of his military chances, really dreamed at this time (as was claimed for propaganda reasons) that he could conquer Prague. The wars of the time show with few exceptions (such as Con-

---

[1] See *KBAA*, I, 198.
[2] As e.g. Palacký does. See his *Dějiny*, IV, 2, 479, in German 552.

stantinople) that great cities—and in the standards of the times Prague
was a great city indeed—were practically unconquerable as long as
their provisions lasted and they were held by resolute defenders.
Matthias was not going to repeat, at least not at so premature a
moment, the attempt of his predecessor, the Hungarian King Sigismund, by trying to gain the capital with inadequate means. Yet in
another way he followed Sigismund's example, doubtlessly aware of
the history of a great (if not lasting) success: Matthias set, quite clearly,
Kutná Hora as his direct goal. This city, especially as Bohemia's great
center of silver mining and coining, had in wartime always attracted
would-be conquerors, and its loss would indeed have been a well-nigh
fatal blow to the Czechs. It is certainly not surprising that, as soon as
the news of Matthias' new enterprise was received, King George (just
as Žižka had done in December 1421), anticipating the enemy's intention, called a strong levy into being and based it on Kutná Hora.[3]

Matthias, in the meantime, marching straight north from Brno and
crossing the Bohemian border in mid-February near Svitavy, now
turned in a northwesterly direction, keeping near the old road across
eastern Bohemia via Litomyšl and Vysoké Mýto. His army, at this
moment, counted about 9,000 men, among then 4,000 cavalry. Perhaps
because he wanted to be sure of reinforcements but also because he did
not want to be held up by secondary enterprises, the Hungarians went
around the fortified cities but burned, plundered, and destroyed a wide
swath of the countryside along their way. Around February 20th they
arrived at Hrochův Týnec, where they were joined by a few thousand
troops of the Czech league of lords, led, it seems, by Zdeněk of Sternberg himself. Their number had now increased to somewhere around
12,000 men. Against them King George had mobilized an army slightly
superior in total numbers though, as always, much inferior in cavalry.

In the days following February 20th, George, alone in full command, slowly moved his army eastward, basing the main body on
Čáslav. Meanwhile Matthias' army had moved a few miles farther west
and laid itself before the strong town of Chrudim, apparently hoping
for quick conquest and the chance to use the city as basis of his
further operations. However the one assault attempted was a failure.
Eschenloer, generally a good and detailed source about this campaign,
tells us that, reconnoitering around the city with a small troop of

<hr />

[3] On the history of the Hungarian invasion of Bohemia and the ensuing events see all
contemporary sources, mainly Eschenloer, G., II, 146–149; Długosz, *Opera omnia*, XIV,
520–521, *SLČP*, 171, 405, 406.

horsemen, Matthias was taken prisoner by the city's militia but was not recognized; that, owing to his simple clothing and to his good command of the language, he was believed when he claimed to be merely a stable boy and was subsequently released.[4] But this description does not sound very believable. It has too much in common with other stories showing Matthias as a master of appearing here and there in disguise, a sort of fifteenth-century Harun-al-Rashid. Its origin may well be Hungarian (from Matthias' own court) and would have had time enough to travel to Breslau later when that city became for a while Matthias' headquarters. It would just prove once more to all contemporaries that the young King was, by divine providence, safe in all dangers.

Military Moves Leading up to the Treaty of Vilémov

The real danger was still imminent. After the unsuccessful attack on Chrudim, Matthias, without long delay, moved a little farther west, in the direction of his goal, but also of the Czech army. The little town of Ronov, only seven or eight miles east of Čáslav, was the westernmost point which he reached in this whole campaign. By then he must have suspected that his situation was becoming increasingly difficult. Our sources do not permit us to describe the Czech counter-moves with any degree of geographic clarity or accuracy. So much,

4 Eschenloer, G., II, 147.

however, is clear: King George had planned a great encircling movement, making full use of the mountainous terrain which gave little chance for free-wheeling movements to Matthias' cavalry; he barred some of the easier openings by quickly erected earth works and felled trees and occupied them by his troops which he constantly reinforced by local levies. Matthias' must have been increasingly aware of this danger which, if he tried to press on in the direction of Kutná Hora, would have forced him to attack not only superior numbers but also difficult positions, and this without any chance to get provisions from the largely destroyed countryside. It was clearly this awareness that induced Matthias, at this moment (about February 23rd) to make a sharp turn almost exactly due south, hoping thus to escape from the closing ring of the Czech forces. But it was already too late.

Matthias' army stood now in the vicinity of the town of Vilémov, but, far from having escaped the dangerous trap, he was more thoroughly caught. A free exit to the south was largely barred by a number of hills called the "Iron Mountains" (Železné hory). The wintry weather had become more severe and must have especially bothered those of his troops coming from the milder Adriatic regions. At the same time the Czech regular forces continued to receive reinforcements from the peasantry of the region, many of them obviously eager to revenge the damage that had been done to them by the marauding hordes of the enemy.

In this nearly desperate position, King Matthias decided to parley. Some short time ago, presumably on his return from Poland, Lord Albert Kostka had been taken prisoner by the Hungarians. Matthias had treated him well and now sent him, as an experienced diplomat and former friend of both Kings, under a flag of truce to George, asking for a personal meeting in which, he promised, all pending question would be quickly and safely solved. George, to the amazement and intense anger of his own people, including many of his foremost advisers, accepted Matthias' offer in principle, refusing permission to start an attack at a moment when his troops burned for action. Now, if at any time, superior in numbers as it clearly was, the Czech army would probably have had an excellent chance of annihilating the enemy, perhaps even of taking its main leaders, the Hungarian King and the Lord of Sternberg, prisoners. But George remained firm. The two Kings met, on the morning of February 27, in a half-burned peasant hut in the village of Ouhrov, where they conferred without any witnesses. After a few hours they had reached complete agreement. Or so, at least, thought the Czech King.[5]

It is indeed astonishing that George was ready to sell, for any price, the extraordinary opportunity which Matthias' over-bold offensive, his own wise strategic answer, the generous response of the Czech people of the region, and finally the weather had played into his hands. In particular it seems strange that he was willing to sell this opportunity for promises which were never set down in writing. It has been surmised that the reason for this omission was George's insistence at being given the title of Czech King and that Matthias, after the act of curial deposition, felt that he could not grant it any longer. But it has been pointed out that, even if such reluctance on the part of Matthias, in his present predicament, can be taken as an acceptable excuse, there would have remained other ways for George to make sure that Matthias' promises, in the end, would not remain mere promises.[6]

Before probing George's motives, we have to know more about the agreement concluded at Vilémov. Despite the lack of written contracts or notes about the agreement, we are not entirely in the dark about its content, even though our knowledge comes through indirect sources —the informations to their attendants given by the Kings themselves after the event. Some of these are certain beyond any dispute. There was to be an armistice, beginning immediately and lasting at least till April 3rd. Meanwhile a final peace was to be concluded. If the period of five weeks was not sufficient, the armistice would be prolonged. Immediate negotiations with the legates were envisaged—they actually did take place. As to the other two main clauses—and they seem to present the essential quid pro quo of the treaty—we are in the dark at least about some very important circumstantial points. The first is George's demand that Matthias do his utmost to mediate between him

[5] The sources on the meeting in Vilémov are essentially those quoted above (n. 3) but with considerable additions. The most important is probably the report to the city council of Görlitz in *FRA*, II, 20, 564–566. See also the report from the Regensburg reichstag in *FRA*, II, 44, 654–660 and the account in *SLČV* (ed. Šimek, Prague, 1937), 139–140. The meeting is, of course, treated in some detail by Palacký, IV, 2, 487–490, in German 561–565, by Bachmann, *Reichsgeschichte*, II, 206–210, and by Tomek, *Dějepis*, VII, 2nd ed., 235–237. A monographic article on the subject was published by Bachmann in *MVGDB*, vol. 31, 1893, pp. 342–358. It is one of his least valuable productions, highly opinionated as well as carelessly and hurriedly written. Even the title "Der Vertrag von Wilemov (25. Februar 1469) und seine Bedeutung" is wrong, since the agreement was concluded only on February 27th. For the main points he is trying to make, see below.

[6] He might, for instance, have demanded, as a condition for the cessation of hostilities, that fortresses now occupied by Matthias such as the Spielberg, Frankenstein, or Hoyerswerda be put as securities in the hands of King Casimir. See e.g. Urbánek, *Husitský král*, 254, also Bachmann in the middle paragraph on p. 347 of his article in *MVGDB*, 31.

and the Holy See and thereby also to bring domestic peace to Bohemia. Here is the main request—or, perhaps, we might say, the main condition—put forward by George. But there are considerable differences in the presentation of the way in which this request or condition was presented by George and accepted by Matthias. The sources depending on information from the Czech King say that he demanded religious peace and unity within the framework of the Compacts. These depending on information from Matthias say he demanded religious pacification on the basis of complete obedience to the demands imposed by the Holy See.

Logically and perhaps theologically the two ideas seem in complete contradiction. Historically, that is, in terms of the history of George's thought and policy, there is no contradiction, or at least not a striking one. Only within the Compacts, George felt, could any religious peace, any reestablishment of religious unity, be achieved. This and only this is what he has always wanted and promised: Allow us and confirm us the Compacts, and within this framework we shall be completely obedient to the Holy See. True, in the long run this proved to be an illusion because the gap had become too deep. Yet war could not close it, and late in the following year, in 1470, the Curia began to think more seriously about a compromise encompassing some form of a recognition of the Compacts. Clearly, therefore, in historical terms George's demand, and its acceptance, under the present circumstances, by Matthias, are neither overly unrealistic nor a sign of George's supposed duplicity and insincerity in his dealing with Rome. That, for instance, he really meant to fulfill his famous and no longer secret coronation oath is (regrettably) shown in that just at this time, in the fall of 1468, he had started a new persecution of the one sect which openly advocated a full break with Rome: the Czech Brethren.

The assumption, occurring especially in modern Hungarian historiography, that George had promised unconditional obedience (thus abandoning the Compacts) is based on Eschenloer.[7] This author, of course, always depicted George as perjurer who, without inhibitions, made promises he never intended to keep. We have emphasized earlier that there is no proof for George's ever having declared himself ready to sacrifice the Compacts and especially not the Chalice. There is, however, another argument: Matthias could not hold out promises for a reconciliation between George and the Holy See, for he knew that he

---

[7] II, 148. See, on the other hand, Špán of Barnstein's report in *FRA*, II, 42, 485–487, Riedel, *Cod. dipl. Brand.*, III, 1, 500–501, and *FRA*, II, 20, 568–569.

could never achieve such an agreement. This, at first glance, sounds plausible and seems to make George's readiness to accept the "peace" of Vilémov even more astonishing. But, on closer scrutiny, this argument loses much of its force. Such an agreement with the Compacts essentially intact was, in 1470, seriously considered and in 1471 eventually granted by Paul II, even though George did not live to see the consummation of this act of religious peace. The decisions of the papacy around this time were to such a large extent political rather than religious that nothing was as "impossible" as it might have seemed from a purely religious or theological point of view. True, a good deal of pressure would have been needed to induce the papacy to such a change of policy, a pressure that came about later through the unexpected military successes of the Czechs and the whole, rather radical change of the political line-up in central and east-central Europe. However it would be difficult to imagine a more effective pressure than a decision of King Matthias to quit the war, whatever cries of anguish might have come from George's enemies. This would have immediately destroyed all hope for a victory over the Czechs, and a peace between Rome and Prague might then have been the best, perhaps the only, insurance for a survival of Catholic strength in Bohemia. How strong a pressure was contained in the possibility of Matthias' quitting the war is revealed very clearly in the weeks to follow. It is inconceivable that George could have expected any other outcome, and we still have to ask why he should have permitted himself to be deceived in so painful a way.

There is no doubt that this whole demand for mediation between Prague and Rome had been George's demand, request, and condition. But what about the other important clause in the treaty about which there can be some doubt? We know that George undertook to work for Matthias' elevation to the same rank which he himself had coveted some years ago, the position of King of the Romans. Our Czech sources indicate that he declared himself to be ready for such work upon the urgent request of Matthias, who, himself, promised his effective intercession in Rome as his reward for George's efforts.[8] They also quote Matthias as having claimed that the Emperor (and also the Pope) had already held out prospects to him in this direction. What, then, could be expected from George on the basis of a reestablished friendship

---

[8] See Margrave Albert on the report of George's ambassador Špán of Barnstein, Riedel, *op.cit.*, III, 1, 500–501, the same in *FRA*, II, 20, 568–569. Also George's later letter to the Hungarian nobility, in *AČ, I,* 490–491.

was that he would lend the Hungarian King his own vote as an elector, and would try to influence the two other electors who were still known as his friends: those of Saxony and Brandenburg. The assumption that this whole idea issued from Matthias' side has in modern times been vigorously contested, and in its stead the claim was made that this could only have been George's own idea.[9] One of the main arguments for this theory—doubtful even on the basis that there is absolutely nothing in any of our sources to support it—is that the Emperor had never in the past made binding promises (as Matthias seems to have claimed) for his support of a Roman kingship to be established at his own side, nor was he to do so in the future. This, of course, is true, but it is also true that his shrewd policy of hints and vague (though not binding) promises made many a man in a long line of princes hopeful that he would be the one to reach this shimmering goal. Of all these princes Matthias was the strongest and the most ambitious one. His disappointment over the Emperor's unwillingness later contributed to the break between the two allies, followed by a hostility lasting many years. There is, indeed, no good reason at all to doubt that this demand came from Matthias and was merely accepted, within the frame of what appeared as political possibilities, by George. (Nor did Matthias now leave all the work for his desired elevation to George. On the contrary he himself began immediately to work very actively for it.) [10]

But even this leaves us wondering. Why should George in his present strong position agree to steps apt to add considerably to the permanent greatness of a man who, in the last year, had done him more harm than anyone else throughout his life? Clearly, in the parley between the two Kings, Matthias proved to be more skillful and clever, a more effective diplomat than George. And in the case of George this inferiority must have been based on a faulty judgment of his adversary, possibly also on a lack of sufficient confidence in himself and his military potential at this moment.

But this last conjecture must be qualified. One of the characteristics

9 See Bachmann's article quoted in n. 5., pp. 349–351, and *Reichsgeschichte*, II, 208–209. In both passages, and especially in his great book, Bachmann presents the issue as if he had solid proof for his claim that the Roman kingship for Matthias was not his but George's brain child, when in reality he has no proof at all and not even a good case of plausible conjecture. The presentation of what, on such a basis, happened in the private and totally unwitnessed discussion between the two kings (*Reichsgeschichte*, II, 209) is pure fiction, a transgression of which Bachmann, with less justification, accused Palacký in his treatment of George of Poděbrady.

10 See the mission of Jerome Beckensloer, sent in March to Elector Frederick of Brandenburg. (Merseburg Zentral-Archiv, Akten des Brandenburg-Preuss. Haus-Archivs Rep. XXVI Ia, 41 fol. 8, as quoted in *DRTA*, XXII.)

that gives us the right to call George a great figure in the history of his country and people is just his steadfastness, his staunch confidence in himself, but also in the righteousness of his cause—the cause of a Bohemia free to live out her political and religious life within that measure of freedom and mutual understanding that the Compacts had offered. George never was a timid or weak man, never easily disheartened, and in the situation in which he found himself at Vilémov in late February 1469 he certainly had less reason for disheartenment than for some time before. The man who overcame the "eight disastrous weeks" with their terrible military and personal losses and then was able cooly to direct the operations leading to the encirclement of Matthias and his army can well be counted among the great indomitables who, in military as well as in political terms, retained the vision of victory even in their darkest hours.

Yet it is not impossible that at this stage of his life, and conscious of the bitter lessons it had taught him, George felt that he must not tempt fate. He may have believed that his former son-in-law's promise of peace would be preferable to the slaughter of thousands—even were the battle to end in victory—which seemed to be the great alternative, all the more as victory in war, as he had said before, could never be completely certain.

But there remains the fact that George misjudged his opponent. He did not believe that there was any personal hatred between him and his former son-in-law, and in this he was surely right. Matthias, who later occasionally showed real hatred of the Emperor,[11] never expressed himself in any such an emotional way about George. But neither was there (as George seems to have believed), any feeling of kinship. And while, in the next few weeks, at the repeated meetings during the armistice, Matthias treated George and his sons with all those forms of respect and cordial friendship that sent shivers down the spines of his smaller allies, it was precisely these allies—his future subjects—whom he wanted to impress. One wonders also whether at the bottom of it there was not some light contempt for the man who had allowed himself to be duped so quickly by his promises, by his easily turned on charm and the emphasis that his royal word must not be doubted.

Nevertheless it is impossible to say with any degree of certainty whether the game that Matthias was to play so brilliantly in Olomouc,

---

[11] See e.g. F. C. von Scheyb, *Historische Abhandlung zur Bestimmung der Oesterreichischen Gränzen gegen Ungarn*, Ms 1754, No. 290, in *HHSA* Vienna, Appendix on "Ursachen des Kriegs 1477–1485," pp. 357ff.

with his foes as well as with his allies, was already planned when he tried and succeeded to "promise his way out" of all military difficulties during the discussions in Vilémov.[12] It is not inconceivable that, at least for a short while, he seriously considered getting out of this war. Sometime he must have truly worried how he could fight it through successfully if the Turkish attack was resumed in strength and if he could not finish the Bohemian business before too long. And the belief, so lively a few weeks earlier, that George and his "heretic" Bohemia would not last long must have received a severe shock in those days of late February 1469. But once Matthias was free again and his army safely out of Bohemia, these doubts, we can assume, did not last long. After all he had taken his choice for expansion westward, he must have been aware of the difficulties of gaining the Roman before the Bohemian throne, and if his seeming friendship with the enemy did indeed, as George had hoped, put pressure on the leaguist party and the papal legates, it was soon used not for reconciliation with Rome but for an entirely different purpose.

Among the Czechs in King George's entourage the arrangements of Vilémov caused at first much disappointment and criticism. It was said that if only Duke Victorin had been there he would never have permitted a compromise so favorable for Matthias.[13] Yet after the first sobering, the Czech mood recovered quickly. The general feeling was that, as the result of a Czech military success, the Hungarian King had given up and that there would be no more war, since the armistice was supposed to bind not only Matthias and his Hungarians but also all his allies.[14] The impression of an enormous success for the "heretics" was clearly shared by many people who had, more or less under duress, joined George's enemies. Thus, for instance, the people of Schweidnitz and Jauer in Silesia hurried to declare themselves again faithful subjects of King George, and, though an immediate, sharp intervention of Bishop Rudolf prevented them from publicizing this action, they

[12] AČ, I, 490f.

[13] SLČP, 171, 172. Bachmann's angry remarks about what he calls the "Declamationen des heimischen Berichterstatters" (quoted, of course, after Palacký's original edition, the only one then in existence) in MVGDB, XXXI, 346, are strangely out of place. These reports, while not sophisticated, are just in this case probably reflections of good observation and faithful chronicling rather than "a low social status and low intelligence, of a man who completely lacks political understanding." Much of the criticism of the King's policy shown in the writings of the "Old Annalists" do, however, betray the strongly Utraquist background of the writer or writers, which explains part of their unhappiness in the face of a royal compromise with the other, the militant Catholic side.

[14] Eschenloer, G., II, 148.

nevertheless began serious negotiations to reestablish friendly relations with George's governor in Glatz, Hans Wölfl of Warnsdorf.[15] Those, on the other hand, who had fervently hoped for George's fast destruction were at first as unwilling to believe that the whole story of the Vilémov "peace" was true as Bishop Rovarella had been in Regensburg.[16]

King George's own judgment about the situation was revealed when as early as March 1st he released his army and returned to Prague. In addition he immediately set to work to fulfill his part of the bargain: to strengthen Matthias' chances for the Roman kingship. Indeed it is through activities of his envoy, John Špán of Barnstein, that we hear most clearly George's own version of the arrangements made at Vilémov. The King's ambassador contacted the Saxon dukes and tried to see Margrave Albert Achilles at Kulmbach, where however, since the margrave was absent, he left a lengthy memorandum instead.[17] From there he went on to the French court, since King Louis had asked George to send him one of his reliable diplomats for, as he said, top-secret negotiations. Their precise purpose remains unknown, except perhaps for the fact that in consequence of Louis' break with his long-time adviser Cardinal Jean Balue (who shortly before had been deprived of his offices and imprisoned) the old resistance of court circles against a more active cooperation between France and Bohemia had been largely removed. Yet our sources do not tell us of any new or influential act of cooperation resulting from the visit, and before too long the only change in the relations between Bohemia and the great western power was a rapprochement between George and the man who had long been his and Louis' common enemy: the Duke of Burgundy.

Clearly negative, on the other hand, was the reaction of the German princes. Margrave Albert—the decisive political figure at least for the Hohenzollern—declared he did not believe that the Emperor would give up the Empire or that the electors would want a non-German as King of the Romans.[18] But he was also distrustful of his Saxon friends who may, he thought, have an arrangement with George for which they alone hope to receive some reward. The Saxons, on their part, were equally distrustful and emphasized their willingness to cooperate closely with the Emperor, if absolutely necessary even against

[15] *Ibid.*
[16] *FRA*, II, 20, 565.
[17] See the sources quoted above, n. 8.
[18] See his letter to Frederick II in Riedel, *Codex*, III, 1, 500f.

George. It is a moment when the long friendship between Wettin and
Poděbrady seems no longer very solid.[19]

But this negative attitude was not limited to George's old allies in
Germany nor to his gravely endangered Czech foes. The apparent
switch to sudden amity and something potentially like a close alliance
between the two Kings was bound to cause distrust in almost all
quarters. Even when George had tried to get the Roman kingship for
himself, it was probably his not being a German rather than the suspicion of heresy which had been decisive for all those acts blocking his
rise. The same would be true to an even greater extent of a Hungarian
trying to become the actual ruler of Germany with the help of a Czech.
The Emperor himself, for all the half-promises he had made (and was
still going to make) to Matthias was not seriously willing to cede the
substance of whatever imperial power he possessed to his "beloved son
Matthias," and the fact that just in those days one of Matthias prominent vassals from the Burgenland region, Frederick's once so faithful
courtier Andrew Baumkircher, had resumed a rebellion against the
Emperor without being called to order by the Hungarian King,
strengthened the Emperor's old distrust of Matthias. The alliance between the two rulers, always a matter of expediency rather than of
inclination, experienced in these days its first serious crack.[20]

The royal court of Poland was no happier about the new situation.
So far Poland had tried to mediate between the two enemies, hoping
to gain in the end, at least after George's death, the crown of St.
Wenceslas for one of her princes as a reward for the support given
to the Czechs within the limits of political possibilities. If now the
two enemies became friends again, if George was beholden to Matthias
rather than to Casimir for restored peace (and vice versa), why, then,
should anybody have to pay any price or reward to Poland? The
Polish King, therefore, decided to send another embassy, consisting of
Jacob of Dębno and the Cracow canon, Paul of Glownia, to the two
Kings, with the purpose of strengthening George's position against

---

[19] This development is shown in its right dimensions by Ermisch, "Studien zur Geschichte
der sächsisch-böhmischen Beziehungen," II, 26–29. Bachmann goes too far when he describes
the Wettin attitude (in *Reichsgeschichte*, II, 238) as a complete and definite change-over
from the alignment with the Hohenzollerns to one with the Wittelsbachs. It is certainly
true that there was a notable rapprochement between the Saxon dukes and the Emperor. But
already the Emperor himself had begun to waver in his antagonism toward George.

[20] For this sequence of events see Bachmann in *Reichsgeschichte*, II, 235–236. As for
sources on the Baumkircher affair, see Unrest's *Oesterreichische Chronik*, Weimar, 1957,
pp. 23ff. Somewhat doubtful is F. Kurz's presentation (*Oesterreich unter Friedrich IV*,
II, 102–104).

claims which might endanger the future succession of one of his sons in Bohemia. The envoys were eventually to go on to Rome.[21]

The great meeting near Olomouc at which, according to the agreement of Vilémov, the final peace between the Kings of Bohemia and Hungary (including, of course, the latter's allies) was to be contracted, was one of the most remarkable instances of play-acting—we may almost say of comedy-acting—that ever occurred in diplomatic history. It is the more remarkable as only one man directed the play, the same who also did most of the acting: King Matthias of Hungary. If a modern historian [22] presents this development as if Matthias, originally resolved to fulfill all his promises given at Vilémov, was only slowly and with great effort prevailed upon by Roverella and the heads of the Catholic league not to conclude this peace and not to abandon his allies, then he was taken in almost five hundred years later to the same extent that Matthias' allies—and, of course, also King George— were taken in at the time. Matthias, in fact, was not easily influenced, even by the representatives of the Curia, one way or another. He weighed very coolly his advantages. At an early time—we have no means of knowing exactly when, and the thought may have been in the back of his mind years earlier—he decided that the Bohemian venture was worth all troubles and costs if it brought him the crown of Bohemia. Palacký was right when he assumed that behind this goal there still beckoned the hope for the Roman kingship, yet for Matthias a combined Hungaro-Bohemian kingship was—and not only because of the Bohemian electoral position—a far stronger basis for reaching this distant goal than the Hungarian kingship alone.

The great peace conference itself began only on April 7, which necessitated a repeated renewal of the armistice.[23] Matthias and his allies had in the meantime held preliminary meetings at Brno, George and his advisers in the faithfully Utraquist Moravian city of Uničov. On the first day the two Kings met in a tent erected on open ground half-way between Olomouc, where Matthias was staying and the town of Sternberg where George had taken residence. In Matthias' retinue

---

[21] See F. Papee, *Studya i szkice z czasów Kazimierza Jagiellończyka*, 95–97.

[22] Bachmann, *Reichsgeschichte*, II, 220. In his immediately following treatment of the peace congress of Olomouc, he judges Matthias' role more realistically.

[23] There is a wealth of material on the congress. See the long and especially informative report from Olomouc to Görlitz in *FRA*, II, 20, 570–582; to Cheb, *ibid.*, 44, 661; Eschenloer, G., II, 155–161; Długosz, *Opera omnia*, XIV, 521–522; *SrS*, XIII, 3–4. For modern treatments see Palacký, *Dějiny*, IV, 2, 495–510 (German 571–589); Tomek, *Dějepis*, VII, 239–247; Bachmann, *Reichsgeschichte*, II, 220–227.

were the two legates Lorenzo Roverella and Rudolf of Breslau; the Minorite inquisitor Gabriel Rongoni; John Beckensloer, a German born in Breslau but now bishop of the Hungarian city of Eger and one of Matthias' favorites. As representatives of the Emperor came the new bishop of Lavant, John Roth, once King Ladislav's secretary, and the Count of Sulz. Among the Bohemian lords were Zdeněk of Sternberg, John of Rosenberg, John and Ulrich Zajíc of Hasenburg, Bohuslav of Švamberg, Henry of Plauen, and others. In King George's retinue were his sons Victorin and Henry, the two Silesian dukes Conrad the Black of Oels and Přemek of Těšín, Albert Kostka, the two Moravian barons Ctibor and John Tovačovský of Cimburg (both of whom, especially after the death of Zdeněk Kostka, played an increasingly important role in King George's councils), and, among his regular diplomatic advisers, Beneš of Veitmil and Peter Kdulinec of Ostromíř, the latter one of George's "court masters" and also a capable military leader, as well as other less well known figures among his helpers and advisers. Thus, for the first time since the outbreak of the civil war in 1467, all the important leaders of both sides had what seemed a solid chance to meet and to try to overcome their difficulties and misunderstandings in the service of peace. But in fact nothing of the sort happened.

A real effort in this direction was made only by King George. On the first day he had a long private talk with Matthias which seemed to continue the friendly atmosphere that had prevailed at Vilémov. To demonstrate his good will Matthias, in a further step, took George's sons and advisers with him to Olomouc to give them a chance of meeting with the papal legates. Bishop Roverella, however, far from being ready to listen to the Czech negotiators, put the whole city under interdict as long as the heretics were there. Yet Matthias did not make it that easy to the prelates. He was determined to show to everybody, friends, as well as foes, how eager he was to achieve peace, nay how utterly fed up he was with the war and how happy to get out of it. And to some extent he succeeded. Our Breslau observer, at least, felt that his intentions were completely obscure. Matthias' attitude to the heretics—whom he treated repeatedly as dear and honored guests—looked overly and dangerously friendly to Eschenloer.[24]

It was probably the degree of trust which Matthias thus nourished that caused King George to take a step which was surely an unusually strong proof of his will for peace. He sent two of his principal servants,

[24] See Eschenloer, G., II, 156.

the Catholic Lord Beneš of Veitmil, and the Utraquist knight Peter Kdulinec of Ostromíř, to Lord Zdeněk of Sternberg to find out whether some rapprochement was possible.[25] It clearly was not. The noble lord overwhelmed his guests—who cautiously tried to probe their way toward some understanding—with a stream of abuse and wild cursing relating to them as well as to King George whom he now brazenly accused of having killed King Ladislav. The whole performance, fairly bursting with poisonous hate, was not only a complete confirmation of the utterances related by John of Rabstein in his *Dialogus* but also of a wildly abusive letter which sometime earlier, in 1468, he had written to Duke Victorin.[26] Nevertheless the negotiations between the principals went on, with Matthias suggesting that the Czechs should present all their offers and requests regarding the Holy See in writing.

Yet in this "peace conference" between the two warring parties, the actual negotiations between them were never for a moment taken seriously by King Matthias, but simply used, and used most skillfully, as an effective background for another series of negotiations that took place between himself and the multitude of his allies, above all the leaders of the league and the papal legates. The men of the league, specially, had been warned very early, presumably already in Brno, by people claiming to know the King's mind, that he would quite definitely get out of the war and leave the leaguists to their presumably sorry fate (destruction by or capitulation to George) unless much firmer ties could be established between them and the Hungarian ruler.[27] In other words: "I shall quit the war, unless you make me King of Bohemia."

One might ask why, with his Czech allies as dependent on him as they were, so much pressure had to be applied at all. But in this case—as it was highly uncertain when Matthias could hope to achieve a valid coronation—much of the substance of this new kingship would depend on its international recognition. Matthias was well aware that not only Casimir of Poland and some German princes but also the

---

[25] A very detailed report on this discussion, most likely based on information from a participant or at least eye witness, in *FRA*, II, 20, 573–574. Much of it also quoted verbatim by Palacký, *Dějiny*, IV, 2, 499–501 (in German, 573–575).

[26] See "Tři vášnivé projevy z války za krále Jiřího," ed Dvorský, in *AČ*, XX, Prague, 1902, 553–557. Victorin, in addressing Zdeněk, had called him traitor. He answered by calling Victorin a dishonorable, impudent liar and treacherous heretic of bastardly birth, and imputed not only regicide to his father but also incest to his dead mother, incidentally his own (Sternberg's) near relative.

[27] See Palacký, IV, 2, 496 n. 388 (in German, 572 n. 387).

Emperor were by no means willing to agree to his assuming the Czech crown. He could not even be sure of the support of the Curia, since until now it had been papal policy to accept happily Matthias' military help against George but not to consider him, mainly because of the potential Turkish danger, as a suitable candidate for the Czech throne. In addition, Paul II, just at this time, seems again to have considered a "solution of the Czech problem" which would abolish the royal power of the Bohemian territories altogether and instead—an idea once vented already during the Hussite Wars—have partitioned the country into a number of small duchies and countries.[28] What Matthias needed was, therefore, a very strong action by his allies which would overcome all possible resistance or even reluctance on the part of the representatives of the Roman Curia. Once he had the support of Rome, he could also hope to overcome difficulties made by the Emperor.

After the preliminary contacts between the Hungarian court and the allies in Brno—several of which, surely, went on unnoticed—the first meeting relating to Matthias' elevation of which we have substantial knowledge took place on April 7, the very day which also brought the first official meeting between the two Kings. The invitation to the Olomouc conference had come from Bishop Rudolf of Breslau, and Zdeněk of Sternberg immediately took the lead. There is a strange repetition in the position of this ambitious man. Again, as in 1458 (after the severe losses he had suffered and his corresponding military and economic weakening which he now discussed quite openly), his old ambition to become himself King of Bohemia had to be put aside and he had to be satisfied with the second-best: to play the role of king-maker, with a chance to remain the first man under the new King. At this first opportunity Zdeněk declared that no victory could be achieved, nor could there be any hope for economic recovery, unless the Czech lords and the dependencies had a King again, hinting that there was now only one possible choice. Bishop Rudolf, at this stage, suggested delaying any decisions until the present discussion with the heretics was finished. The majority of the people present agreed.

This meeting, as well as the next one held on April 12, was kept strictly secret. At the second meeting Zdeněk expressed himself much more clearly. Again he discursed on the need to have a real authority for the struggle against George; but the one man, he said, who could

---

[28] See Heimburg's letter in *KBAA*, I, 215.

serve in this capacity, King Matthias, might be tempted by circumstances to return into his own kingdom and to abandon his Czech allies. There was only one way to make sure this would not happen, and also to express the deep gratitude which the true Christians of the Bohemian realm owed to their protector: to elect him King of Bohemia in place of the deposed George, an act which should be performed as soon as possible.

Zdeněk's speech was supported first by the two Bishops of Breslau and Olomouc, then by lords, prelates, representatives of the cities (with Breslau in the lead, the Moravians following and the two Bohemian cities, Pilsen and Budweis, in the end). It was finally resolved to ask King Matthias on the following day to assume the Bohemia kingship. This was done by Lord Zdeněk and the bishops. The answer was only that he would talk it over with his councillors.

On April 14th the King again received Zdeněk and the bishops and declared that for many reasons he could not accept their offer, much as he appreciated it. He explained that, if he assumed the Bohemian kingship this implied the obligation to conquer the country and eradicate Czech heresy. They all knew how his predecessor Sigismund, together with other princes, had made this very effort and had failed. He had to beware the same fate. How could he know that, as King of Bohemia, he would even continue to receive the inadequate support he had received so far from Pope, Emperor, and princes. Thus he could certainly not shoulder this burden unless they and the legates guaranteed that he would receive the equivalent of an imperial army of 12,000 horse for half a year, which would amount to about 250,000 ducats. When Lord Zdeněk, rather despairing, declared that this sum was entirely beyond reach, the King promised that, if the legates would firmly promise him subsidies of 200,000 ducats from all countries in question, including the Holy See, he would take over the Czech kingdom, eradicate the heresy, and not ask for another penny from the Holy Father. The discussion ended with agreement that such an approach should be made to the legates.

Matthias had tried to convey the impression that he was extremely reluctant to become King of Bohemia and would do so only upon the desperate wishes of all his allies, and only on the condition of ample military and financial help from Rome and the Empire. But as soon as strong resistance appeared, especially against those financial conditions, it turned out that he could be bargained down rather easily—in other words, that he was really enormously eager to assume this position, and had played "hard to get" in order to make sure that the offer would be made, and made as favorably as possible.

The difficulties arose from a quarter where they might least have been expected: legate Lorenzo Roverella, though he ardently desired to save the alliance and continue the war, declared to the Hungarian King that he had no orders from the Pope regarding the election of a new King of Bohemia, and later both legates referred Matthias to the difficulties made by the electors of the Empire in regard to any money contributions to the war (certainly an understatement). Finally, on April 17th, Matthias had at least one considerable success: not only the Bohemian allies, led by Zdeněk of Sternberg, but also both legates, Rudolf and Lorenzo, visited him and entreated him to assume the Czech crown, in return for which they would do their best to get support and contributions from the west. This step, Matthias could trust, anticipated and to some extent advanced papal recognition. After a personal discussion between Zdeněk and Matthias, the general assumption was (rightly) that the King had obliged himself, without any large monetary commitments on the side of his allies, to accept the crown if he was elected.

Even though by this tacit agreement the question of Matthias' elevation and thereby also the question of the continuation of the war had substantially been decided—Matthias himself had admitted in his first pretended refusal the implication that this act meant continuing the war—he continued his play-acting. It appears that he particularly enjoyed teasing friends and foes, and this—based on a strong sense of sarcastic humor that occasionally appears also in his correspondence —was probably the main motive for his last actions at Olomouc. On April 20 he once more invited George and his retinue to an official negotiation which was staged in the same way and at the same place as the first one held two weeks earlier. At his arrival he seemed to snub the Czech King, who had waited for him, by not dismounting and greeting him, but when this led to expressions of delight among his people he completely changed his manner, treated his guests with the greatest friendship and civility and even declared that he would still find a way to bring "those of the chalice and those of the wafer" together in friendship. The matter became slightly ludicrous when, upon his suggestion, the court jesters of the two Kings were ordered to fight one another, an episode that at one moment seemed almost to lead to a free-for-all. Real negotiations, however, hardly got off the ground, since the main action was the reading by a Hungarian official of those conditions which Matthias and the legates had laid down as answer to the recently submitted (and to us unknown) written suggestions and demands of King George. The list of demands then put before George reads as follows: [29]

If George wants to die as a King and have peace in his land he must:
1. himself, with his whole family, return to the Catholic faith and church and let go of all articles disapproved by the Church (i.e. the Compacts);
2. return all church estates, put them into their previous state, and if any of them had been pawned away (as many had, especially to leading Catholic grandees like the Rosenbergs and Sternbergs) to redeem them by full payment to the present occupants;
3. enable the King of Hungary to install, in Prague, an archbishop, abbots, provosts, and servants of God to extirpate all heresy there;
4. support the King of Hungary in the reconversion of the people who had been seduced and fallen in error;
5. seize and deliver the arch-heretic Rokycana into the hands of the legates;
6. adopt the King of Hungary as his son (a point which could have many implications for the settlement of the crown after his death);
7. agree to allow the King of Hungary to keep and permanently protect all the territories of the Bohemian crown that he has now in his hands or that adhere to him;
8. command all his subjects to swear an oath to the King of Hungary that they will keep all these conditions;
9. keep the title of King of Bohemia and an appropriate income as long as he lives;
10. conclude peace with the Emperor; and
11. return all possessions which the Catholic barons lost to George during the war.

One may wonder whether any of George's adversaries, especially Roverella, thought it possible that George, in return for the permission to retain the mere title and income of a King of Bohemia, would let go of all the substance, all the power, all the popular support he had, and in addition commit an act as dishonorable as the demanded sur-

---

[29] *FRA*, II, 20, 569–570, also in Palacký, *Dějiny*, IV, 2, 498–499 (in German, 574–575, where, however, it is presented at a wrong date [between April 12th and 15th]).

render of Rokycana. Matthias, who knew his former father-in-law better, surely had little fear that he would accept these humiliating and in every way impossible terms. However, in case he was mistaken, he had assured himself, by the demand for adoption, of his chance eventually to acquire the whole Kingdom.

King George's immediate reaction has not been recorded. We know, of course, that the list of demands was not even considered by George. Even so, with his enormous patience and his determination never to give up hope, he did nothing that would, on his side, have appeared to put an end to the great action for peace which he had tried so hard to bring about. Seeing, however, that there was little or no hope of coming to any understanding with the present papal legates (and especially Roverella), whom he made primarily responsible for the difficulties, he decided to limit his efforts for the moment to a continuation of the present state, meant to be a preliminary peace (beyfrieden) rather than a mere armistice. He himself left, on April 22, for Uničov and entrusted the Lords Albert Kostka and Beneš of Veitmil with the negotiations in question. They offered to Matthias, in George's name, maintenance of the peace till Whitsun 1470. In the meantime they requested that the legates remove the ban from Catholic lords and towns loyal to King George as well as the general excommunication of all Utraquists, and give safe conduct for a new embassy to be sent from Prague to Rome. Furthermore they asked King Matthias (as he had promised at Vilémov) to take all needed steps to obtain a gracious and willing hearing from the Pope for George's ambassadors. The Abbot of Hradiště monastery who had been punished for keeping faith with George should receive back his estates. Finally all prisoners made so far in the war should be freed.[30]

In view of the definite decisions already made behind the scenes, it seems rather strange that for four days the Czech demands caused [31] a good deal of angry debate and discord in Matthias' camp. It shows the confusion in those people's minds. Eventually all that the legates were willing to accept was an armistice prolonged to New Year 1470, and the release of the prisoners. The Czech negotiators agreed to this arrangement as the best they could get under the circumstances. On May 1st, at a meeting with his allies, Matthias informed them of this, and told them they should not take the peace arrangement too much to heart. He had been forced to do this by very important reasons. Also

30 The demands in FRA, II, 20, 580.
31 Ibid., 580–581.

they should not be impatient as to the question of the kingship. They would have good news by Wednesday (May 3rd).

On that day, indeed, all the Bohemian delegates of Matthias' party met in the cathedral of Olomouc. After mass they organized themselves under Zdeněk of Sternberg's leadership as an electorial diet which immediately proceeded to elect the Hungarian King as King of Bohemia. Following this, Matthias was conducted by the leaders and legates into the cathedral where, being informed about his election, he declared his acceptance. He swore the usual oath of Czech Kings into the hands of the Archbishop of Esztergom and the Bishop of Breslau and received the homage of the barons present.[32] He then immediately distributed among them the main court offices. Sternberg's old position as high burgrave was confirmed, John of Rosenberg became lord chamberlain, John Zajíc of Hasenburg lord chancellor, his brother Ulrich chief justice, Bohuslav of Švamberg lord master of the court and so on.[33] These men, however, had little or no chance to administer their high offices in Bohemia, where alone they could have been valid, since there all the offices were in the hands of men appointed by George, most of them (with the exception of the lord chancellor and the sub-chamberlain) Catholics. There were also serious flaws in the election as such, the most important being that besides the incompleteness and one-sidedness of the representation of the high nobility the Czech gentry was hardly represented at all, and none of the Czech cities except Budweis and Pilsen. The absence, above all, of Prague, the *caput regni,* was, on the basis of fourteenth- and fifteenth-century traditions, by itself almost a sufficient reason to consider the election illegal and invalid.

For Matthias such legalistic considerations had little weight. He had been a fairly strong King of Hungary years before his coronation with the crown of St. Stephen. What really mattered to him now was that, instead of being merely an ally and "protector," he could henceforth act as lord and master in all those territories of the Bohemian realm where his military power reached and that the Czech lords who had elected him were bound to obey his commands. When one considers that so much of their revolt against George had been an attempt to free themselves from what they considered an overly oppressive—we should call it an absolutist—rule, the change that they had brought about for themselves soon turned out to be of doubtful value. While some of them felt obliged to maintain the fiction that their fight was

---

[32] *Ibid.,* 581–582; Eschenloer, G., II, 159–161.
[33] Eschenloer, G., II, 160.

for religion, and thus had to continue at all costs, not a few of them sooner or later felt and even admitted that they had jumped from the frying pan into the fire. This was to have consequences also for their participation in the war.

What was King George's reaction to the news about Matthias' election? He had been warned about this possibility and had replied that if a King of Bohemia was made in Olomouc, he would make four such Kings in Prague, and then there would be six of them.[34] But in truth this was no joke for him. We have no direct information on what he said or did immediately upon receiving the news. By then he had probably left Moravia and had returned to Prague. But he soon showed by his actions that he regarded Matthias' election as a betrayal, as a breach of solemn promises which could never be forgiven or forgotten. It is only now that Matthias, the young man for whom he had never quite lost his feeling of amity and kinship, became truly his enemy, *the* enemy whom he had to beat at all costs, even at the cost of his dearest dream: the establishment of the house of Poděbrady as another national dynasty of the Czech kingdom.

The one effective diplomatic counter-blow to Matthias' usurped Bohemian kingship would be to activate Polish policy, which presupposed, of course, recognition of the Jagiellon dynasty's claims (if not de jure as a hereditary right, at least de facto by the firm promise of certain election). Matthias was aware of this danger. From Breslau, where he had gone late in May, he sent John of Hasenburg, his newly appointed Bohemian lord chancellor, and Bishop Tas's brother Dobeš of Boskovice to Cracow. Arriving there on June 16th, they excused Matthias' election with the great difficulties to which they had been exposed by Casimir's refusal to accept the Czech crown out of their hands. At the same time they asked, in Matthias' name, for the hand of one of Casimir's daughters. Thus, in all probability, the Polish King's grandson would one day rule over both Hungary and Bohemia.[35] (This, actually, was to come about, though in a way very different from the one now expected by Matthias.)

Casimir's answer was essentially negative and cool, but at the same time cautious and non-belligerent. A marriage between Matthias and Poland's ruling house was out of the question. But for the time being he was not going to do anything drastic in relation to Matthias' election.

This somewhat irresolute and cautious character of Casimir's policy

---

[34] *Ibid.*, 157.
[35] Długosz, XIV, 523–524.

was also reflected in his reaction to the approach that came from the other side. King George, had, at a diet held in Prague,[36] expressly asked for and received the power to negotiate with the Polish court about the succession. While his own kingship would be guaranteed for his life and his sons would be indemnified, mainly by additions to their Silesian holdings, King Casimir's oldest son would be selected as George's successor. As King he would do his best to bring about the full reconciliation with the Church of Rome, and besides he would be married to King George's youngest daughter Ludmila. The whole offer was, of course, made on the supposition that Poland would help to defend this future heritage.

The Czech ambassadors, arriving at Radom early in July, presented these suggestions to the Polish court.[37] They added the request that the Polish court refuse any acknowledgment of those high offices that Matthias of Hungary had had no right to confer upon Czech nobles.

Clearly this was, in general, good news for Casimir and his court, but from some sides—especially clerical ones, such as the Archbishop of Gniezno, but also the Habsburg Queen Elizabeth—strong objections were made to the demand for the marriage between the royal children. Having refused marriage with the upstart Matthias they would no more favor marriage with the offspring of a heretical marriage. It seems doubtful whether Casimir himself was similarly impressed by this argument, though he seems to have gone along with it, and the issue eventually tended to become so important that the plan of the succession of Prince Władysław to the Czech throne occasionally appeared to be in danger of foundering over it. At the time, however, it was probably a welcome screen behind which the King could hide his reluctance to pledge himself in too binding a manner to military participation in the war, especially as long as thereby he seemed to challenge not only the King of Hungary but also Pope and Emperor. Even so some indirect support for George was provided when Casimir, at this time, began to make military preparations such as hiring new troops, which would especially tend to reduce any hopes for strong efforts on the part of Silesian enemies of George. Matthias, who thereupon enquired about the purpose of these preparations, received the ice-cold answer that the King of Poland did not need to account to anyone for his actions.[38] It seemed obvious enough that Casimir only

---

[36] See *AČ*, IV, 437; and Palacký, IV, 2, 514–516 (in German, 593–596).
[37] Długosz, XIV, 526–527.
[38] These are Heimburg's informations, but they sound quite true. See *KBAA*, I, 203–204.

waited for a more favorable turn of the general situation to shed his "neutrality" more effectively.

If Matthias and his allies—now largely his subjects—failed to gain or at least to mollify Casimir, they were luckier in other attempts to strengthen, by diplomatic means, the King's rather uncertain position. At first he seemed least successful with the Pope, who, at this moment, and with the Polish embassy in Rome vigorously protesting against papal recognition of Matthias as King of Bohemia, was quite reluctant to take sides and, indeed, did not give his official sanction to the act of Olomouc for about two years. But Matthias could feel fairly sure that eventually he would win over the Holy See, especially since at this time Turkish activities became again much more dangerous and destructive, especially in the regions west of Bosnia. No one but Matthias was able to do much about this.

But his aim was still, beyond the Czech crown, the position of King of the Romans, and for this he needed the German princes. Among them he had, as might have been expected, most success with the Wittelsbachs, as their chief diplomatic adviser, Martin Mair, had now for quite some time considered George's downfall as unavoidable. The negotiations conducted between Matthias and the Wittelsbach dukes led to a regular alliance between Louis of Landshut and Matthias in which, it seems, Albert of Munich and the Palsgrave also joined.[39] Though it never resulted in any active help given to Matthias it recognized his Bohemian kingship. Only one of these princes, however, had any direct influence upon the college of electors, and it was the electors who were most important to him, by their recognition of Matthias' own rank as one of the electors, and their willingness to vote for him when the time was ripe to elect a King of the Romans.

To the great festivities held in Breslau in June Matthias had invited the electors and princes of the leading north-German houses, and one of them, Frederick of Brandenburg (accompanied by his young nephew John) had appeared, while the Saxon dukes had merely sent some of their councillors. Frederick, who on this whole issue was certainly more "neutral" than his brother Albert and would hardly have been willing to face excommunication for the sake of his friendship with and relation to "the heretic," had gone to Breslau in the

---

[39] There had already been a defensive treaty between the Wittelsbachs and the Saxon dukes on July 8th. (see *FRA*, I, 44, 664–667). Bachmann, quoting it (*Reichsgeschichte*, II, 237) as a symptom of the supposed radical turn of Saxon politics, omits to mention that among potential enemies the Saxons exempted King George. For the agreement between the Wittelsbachs and Matthias we have a draft of July 21st in *FRA*, II, 20, 600–601. The final treaty was signed in Bratislava on September 1st.

vague hope that this might lead to a royal marriage for his daughter. Upon his arrival he became immediately the object of Matthias' very special attention. At the great Corpus Christi procession that followed the homage of the Silesian—dire threats were necessary to get some of the dukes to attend—Elector Frederick walked on Matthias' left, with Roverella on the right. From his long letter to his brother Albert, it is clear how much Frederick enjoyed all the honors which were heaped upon him. He had just enough pride to refuse a permanent rent, to be paid to him for good advice, to the amount of 2,000 Hungarian ducats. When, however, after he had already left, an express messenger caught up with him, bringing him a special letter of friendship with 1,000 ducats, he did not return them, comforting himself with the old saying that one should not look a gift horse in the mouth. For all this, he refused the King what he wanted most, a "permanent alliance," declaring that he could not conclude any such contract without the agreement of his brother and of his Saxon and Hessian friends. What remained was that the old man, about to step down from his position in favor of his younger, cleverer, and far more vigorous brother, had had "a good time" in Breslau. Matthias could have saved those 1,000 ducats.[40]

It appears that Matthias, in his hope for a rapid acquisition of the Roman kingship, had been far too optimistic. Like George at an earlier time, he had believed that he could operate by a combination of pressure on the Emperor and friendship (combined with promises) with the electors. But Matthias soon saw that the Emperor's position, weak though it was in Austria, especially in view of the still active rebellion of the group around Baumkircher, maintained considerable strength in its relation to some of the princely houses of Germany, including at least the Bavarian Wittelsbachs and the Saxon princes who had recently strengthened their ties with the Emperor. Too much pressure, in this situation, might antagonize the Emperor and bar Matthias' elevation to the Roman kingship permanently. In addition the Turkish attack was dangerous to both rulers, to Matthias in Croatia, to the Emperor in Carniola, Carinthia, and even Styria. Under these circumstances Matthias tried to achieve a reconciliation with Frederick III, especially by arranging, through the mediation of the Archbishop of Esztergom, an armistice between Baumkircher and the Emperor.[41] And Matthias began to woo his "father" Frederick much more assidu-

---

[40] See Frederick's detailed, rather naïve-sounding report to his brother Albert Achilles in *KBAA*, I, 191–193.

[41] See the material (incl. sources) on the background of this development in Bachmann, *Reichsgeschichte*, II, 233–237.

ously when he realized, early in July, that his clever play in Olomouc, with its triumphant finale, resulted in the premature end of his armistice with King George.

Did Matthias really think it possible that George would consider the "peace" agreements of May 1st as valid and inviolable when two days later he had himself broken all previous promises to George by his assumption of the Czech throne? Did he expect that George would keep still and peaceful till he, Matthias, had made all arrangements to give him the death blow and thus to fulfill his promises to George's most irreconcilable enemies? It seems astonishing, and his evident outrage at George's resumption of military activity ("God will revenge this perfidy") could as well have been some more play-acting.[42] Yet the fact that he and his allies were caught quite unprepared indicates that he had really thought George harmless and naïve. The only explanation seems to be that George, during their negotiations at Vilémov and Olomouc, had shown him his personally warm feelings, and at the same time his love for peace, so strongly that Matthias felt he could rely on the effectiveness of these two emotions even after what, in the end, he had done to George.

But here he was really mistaken. George now bore a personal feeling of enmity against Matthias, and he showed it not only by his recent diplomacy. His whole mood, which led to a considerably changed way of waging his war against Matthias, is expressed rather well in a long letter which just at this time, on July 4th, 1469, Gregory Heimburg wrote to Margrave Albert Achilles. The beginning of the letter, at least, deserves quotation. "Your Grace," he says, "should not doubt that the cause of my lord the King stands as well as it has ever stood before. He had wanted to believe the words of the Hungarian King against the wishes of all his faithful advisers. Thereby he had deceived himself. He still ought to get over the damage. If only His Grace had had as much confidence and trust in me as has now been established between us, I should have opposed the arrangement more effectively, but as it stood I had to beware lest people would decry me as one who wanted to prevent peace. I have never seen a man of great courage long more for peace, but now he has learned that he must fight for it and will not achieve it by patience and kindness." [43]

[42] See his letter to Bishop Rudolf of Breslau in *FRA*, II, 20, 599–600.

[43] See *KBAA*, I, 202. The letter also contains some rather optimistic remarks about the Emperor, for whom, he says, "the cause of this war has lost its significance and has become quite strange" and who receives advice, even from some of his clerical councillors, to seek restoration of his friendship with King George, as "the Czechs are more humane than the

Heimburg was right. The road to peace was not a defensively conducted war. This was true now as it had been true at the time of the Hussite Wars, when only the great offensives of the brotherhood armies into the Empire and Hungary had induced the other side to consider compromise and peace. And Heimburg was also right that the King had now fully understood this truth. His policy, and specifically his strategy, now became far more enterprising and aggressive. At the same time he showed his wisdom by one great act of reform which in a remarkable way contributed to a stabilization of conditions in the domestic field. This was his great "coin reform," which should better be called the currency reform of 1469.

George's monetary policy throughout his reign had, until now, been far from exemplary. Rather had he followed the poor examples of some other princes. During his regency and at the beginning of his kingship, the very fact of internal peace and security had nevertheless resulted in a lowering of prices which was much appreciated. But then the age-old practice of coin-debasement made itself felt. True, George never went to the length of inflationary coin policy that the Emperor had practiced, yet he had had trouble preventing those "black shinderlings" from entering Bohemia. The protest on this account that had come from the League of Zelená Hora at the time of its formation was the one important complaint against which George had had difficulty defending himself and to which he could only answer that he had done no worse but rather better than most of his neighbors. In fact while early in his regency, 31½ Prague silver groschen had been enough to buy one gold ducat (normally of Hungarian provenience), the number of groschen needed during the early sixties increased to 42 and, toward the middle of the decade, to 48.[44] During the early years of the war there was some improvement (to 40), but this probably meant merely that, with much of the production of the Kutná Hora mint going into direct war expenses, less was left for general circulation. In addition, this was not the only source of money supply since the League of Zelená Hora coined its own money in Pilsen;[45] after his election at Olomouc Matthias lost no time in coining inferior Czech pennies in the dependencies,[46] sometime later also at Budweis.[47]

Hungarians." At the time this letter was written the situation had not yet matured to this point, but the trend was already visible.

[44] See K. Castelin, *Česká drobná mince doby předhusitské a husitské*, 232–233, 258.

[45] *Ibid.*, 240–243.

[46] See *FRA*, II, 20, 592.

[47] Castelin, *op.cit.*, 244–249.

It was partly this action which prompted George to answer it with a truly effective monetary reform.

It was perhaps the outstanding event of the Prague diet of June 1469. The law presented to the diet and immediately enacted [48] raised the quality of the silver groschen to one twenty-fourth of a ducat, the level that had existed prior to the Hussite revolution; the value of small coinage (which had suffered even slightly more than the silver groschen) was raised to twelve pennies for one groschen. George, at the same time, strictly forbade accepting any foreign currency with the one exception of Saxon groschen (two of them to be worth one Prague silver groschen). This attempt to prevent Gresham's Law from operating might have been less successful if the war and the partially successful blockade of Bohemia had not reduced the country's foreign trade to much smaller proportions than normal. The Saxon exemption reflects the fact that there the blockade was never fully enforced, since, apart from the friendship of the Saxon princes, it tended to hurt their own lands as much if not more than Bohemia.

The effectiveness of the reform appears in several ways, not the least of which was that in many parts of Bohemia, including those border regions acknowledging Matthias' kingship, people tended to refuse acceptance of his inferior coins.[49] Altogether it was surely a remarkable achievement to stabilize Bohemia's currency, based on the silver groschen, at the very height of a devastating combination of foreign and civil war, in a way which made it possible to keep this currency stable for another eighty years.[50]

The Prague diet of early June was important in that it gave a strong backing to George's policy in the diplomatic and the monetary fields. It seems, on the other hand, that George tried not to make his military preparations too manifest, but aimed rather at achieving a measure of surprise. The angry and bitter letter of protest that the diet in Prague, as the representative institution of the estates of the kingdom of Bohemia, wrote to the King and the estates of Hungary, may have been considered a letter of challenge, but was probably not taken as such by the recipients.[51] In any case George's enemies in Silesia and Moravia were as unprepared as they were in Bohemia herself. In Bohemia some

---

[48] See *AČ* IV, 437–440, and Emler, *Reliquiae tabularum terrae regni Bohemiae,* II, Prague, 1872, 355–357. On the whole legislation see the treatment in Castelin, *op.cit.,* 249–257.

[49] *Ibid.,* 246.

[50] *Ibid.,* 257.

[51] See Palacký, *Dějiny,* IV, 2, 523 n. 414, (German, 602).

most energetic attacks were directed against the possessions and castles of members of the baronial class who had accepted the appointment to high state offices from Matthias. Lord John Zajíc of Hasenburg, once one of George's appointees for a high judicial position and now Matthias' lord chancellor, underwent especially heavy losses in several of his castles and estates in the northwest corner of the country and himself barely escaped being taken prisoner.[52]

But perhaps the change brought about by Czech campaigns in the dependencies was more startling. Eschenloer reports from Silesia: "From Glatz [the Czechs] invaded the territories of the [Breslau] episcopate, and attacked the monastery of Heinrichau. This they thoroughly destroyed, and everywhere all over Silesia they burned, killed and robbed cruelly. Great grief thereupon arose again in Silesia. King Matthias, who had recently been greeted with joy and consolation, was now cursed; and against the people of Breslau there arose, all through the land, the old vilification. No one wanted to fight against the heretics, all waited to see what the King [Matthias] would do. This permitted the heretics to gain a very powerful upper hand. Many people in Silesia, and especially in the duchies of Schweidnitz and Jauer, abandoned the cross and secretly concluded agreements with the heretics, without regard to the oath they had sworn to King Matthias. . . . All these began quickly to doubt, all wavered. O, what weak faith there was among all these, even among the Breslauers. . . . From St. Kilian to St. James the heretics could do pretty much everything as they liked it . . . it was truly frightening, this sudden great good luck of the heretics." [53]

Thus in Silesia. But in Moravia, too, the situation changed rapidly, and many of the Utraquist nobles who had tried to keep out of what had seemed a hopeless struggle rejoined the cause of their old King and margrave. Here, again, the war was conducted in a more aggressive way than before, and special efforts were made to strengthen the Czech holdings on the lower Morava River, which controlled one of Matthias' main routes of access and could now be used as bases for an invasion of Hungary. But in one of these strategically very sound offensive undertakings the Czechs suffered a setback which, especially in terms of usable propaganda, appeared a great victory for the Hungarians.

The man responsible for this debacle was Duke Victorin, to whom

---

[52] See Długosz, *Opera omnia*, XIV, 528, who assumes that the Czechs hoped to exchange the baron for Duke Victorin (see below).

[53] German edition, II, 177.

King George, as repeatedly before, had entrusted the command-in-chief in Moravia. Unfortunately the young man had learned little from previous experiences. With a small troop of only 600 cavalry, he occupied the town of Veselí, on the Morava south of Uherské Hradiště and only a few miles from the Hungarian border. While some details, as usual in this war, remain obscure, it is obvious that he had omitted the careful reconnoitering that would otherwise have made him aware of the presence, in the neighborhood, of vastly superior Hungarian forces, under Matthias' own command which (on July 27th) immediately enclosed him in the little town.[54] What then occurred was much like what had happened at Třebíč early in the Hungarian war: again Matthias managed to set fire to the town by bombarding it with incendiary missiles, and again the small troop of defenders, led by the man whose "knightly-heroic courage" even his enemy Eschenloer admires, tried to batter their way through the besieging Hungarians. But this time Victorin, though already some distance away from the town, was surrounded by a troop of Serbian cavalry. Matthias, Eschenloer tells us, "received this Victorin with joyous laughter as his dear brother-in-law and capital enemy." It is true that the duke, in his imprisonment, was treated with all imaginable courtesy—perhaps not so much in recognition of his heroic qualities but rather because Matthias guessed (rightly) that this prisoner, if treated handsomely, might one day become an asset for his (Matthias') own plans and intentions.

What was the real significance of Victorin's capture, apart from the undeniable propaganda success and the loss, by the Czechs, of 600 good horsemen? Eschenloer (writing several years after the event) claims: "This was a loss which Girsike never overcame to his end. This defeat killed him, though he acted as if it did not matter much."[55] And Pešina, writing two centuries later, says that the loss "affected George with incredible pain."[56] There is only one source from George's immediate surroundings: Gregory Heimburg. The diplomat (who believes that treason was involved in the whole matter) says: "Our King

---

[54] See Eschenloer, G., II, 178–179, and SLČP, 173, 407. Heimburg (KBAA, I, 213–214) claims that the duke was betrayed by his brother-in-law Henry of Lipé (who, like Victorin in his first marriage, seems to have been wedded to a daughter of Ptáček of Pirkstein) and who supposedly had a secret understanding with Matthias. Pešina (Mars Moravicus, 845–847) defends the baron, Bohemia's hereditary lord marshal, against this reproach, without, however, finding any credence with Palacký, Dějiny, IV, 2, 525–527, n. 418 (German, 605–607 n. 417). For the relation between Henry and Victorin, see also Balbinus, Liber curialis, Prague, 1793, pp. 100–101.

[55] German, II, 179.

[56] Mars Moravicus, 846.

is as serene as before and quite unchanged, as is proper,"[57] and in
another letter, written a week later: "Duke Victorin's capture means
no greater harm than the weight attributed to it by the father. He,
however, is quite unmoved and unchanged. There may even be some
advantage to it, for if our King had given command all through three
years of war only to experienced captains, things might have turned
out better." Heimburg continues with a scathing criticism of Victorin's
mistakes which would never have occurred under a "serious and circumspect captain."[58] It was, so he says, "not enough that Duke Victorin
was courageous, a commander has to have other qualities as well."
Clearly Heimburg thought of a pamphlet on the art of war which he
had once written especially for the benefit of Duke Victorin.[59] It had
been a fruitless effort.

Victorin's capture, however, did not induce King George to remove
responsibility from his younger son. Duke Henry, indeed, even before
his brother's capture, had begun to impress not only his father but
the King's advisers, among them Heimburg, by his mature judgment,
his seriousness, and his wide knowledge in many fields, including
languages.[60] It was Henry who, together with his father, was before
long given the chance to wipe out, by a truly impressive military success, the sad impression created by the events of Veselí.

Henry's main task during the summer of 1469, that is after the resumption of hostilities, had been to regain some strength—and to
weaken the position of Matthias and his allies—in Silesia and Lusatia.
Against him, Matthias had sent his cleverest and most experienced
general, the Moravian-Czech condottiere Francis of Háj, who did his
best to organize the resistance of George's enemies in Silesia while the
same task, for Lusatia, was given to Zdeněk of Sternberg's son Jaroslav.
But in these struggles which lasted into October, including a battle
of some importance near Zittau,[61] it was the Czechs who in most cases
were the victors. They waged the usual war of general destruction
against many of those cities and nobles considered rebels, and Eschenloer had good reason to utter still more lamentations of the sort we have
quoted above.

In Moravia, on the other hand, the events of Veselí seemed for a
while to have destroyed all chances for the continuation of an offensive

---

[57] *KBAA,* I, 214.
[58] *Ibid.,* 216–217.
[59] See Cancellaria regis Georgio, Ms XXIII D163, 270–274.
[60] *KBAA* I, 203, 214.
[61] See Eschenloer, L., *SrS,* VII, 212–213.

strategy by the Czechs, since their main basis, the positions along the lower Morava River near the Hungarian border, seemed in great danger of being lost altogether. Of these positions, the city of Hradiště was by far the strongest and most important. So far all attempts of Matthias to eliminate this thorn in his side had failed. But the Hungarians had, already in 1468, begun to besiege the city and, to do this effectively, had erected a number of strong bastions all around the walls to prevent any supplies from reaching the defenders. During the armistice, in the spring and early summer, normal food supplies had been allowed in, but the bastions had not been removed. Now Matthias, who understandably paid special attention to this theater of war, had strengthened his siege army around Hradiště, especially the forces occupying the bastions. When in October King George, aware of the danger, tried to supply the city by sending trains of food convoyed by small forces (300 horse and 600 infantry), the Czechs were attacked just outside the city by a greatly superior force. They managed to fight their way into the city but had to abandon their supply train, which made the situation in Hradiště worse instead of better. The defenders thereupon made an arrangement with the Hungarian besiegers that they would surrender within six weeks if meanwhile no relieving army had arrived from Bohemia. They also informed King George of this arrangement.[62]

The King decided to send Henry with strong forces to relieve Hradiště. Henry arrived there in ample time at the end of October and without leaving the Hungarians any chance for counter-measures immediately stormed one of the bastions. He killed or captured some two hundred Hungarians and opened the way for ample supplies to reach the hungry defenders. Matthias, informed about this mishap at his headquarters in Uherský Brod, immediately approached with an army which he thought to be considerably stronger than that of the Czechs. He was confirmed in this conviction when Henry gave the order to retreat, as if he wanted to evade a battle and return northward. Henry had not used all his forces but seems to have kept some of them hidden—another reason for Matthias to underrate the strength of his

[62] Most details about this development in Eschenloer, G., II, 188–189. See also Długosz, *Opera omnia* XIV, 529–530; *SLČP*, 173–174; and Pešina, *Mars Moravicus*, 849–851. The latter, though not very clear and reliable, probably does not deserve the scathing treatment given him by Palacký in his own report on the great fight (*Dějiny*, IV, 2, 530ff., n. 423, in German 611ff., n. 422). It is characteristic of the idealization of Matthias by Hungarian historians of all times that this painful defeat of the great King is generally passed over in silence. Katona, however, who generally bases much of his story on what he finds in Długosz, declares (XV, 401) that he simply does not believe the Polish chronicler's account about the Czech victory.

foe. Thus, for the first time, the Czechs drew Matthias into an encounter in which he could not make use of a strong protecting position. What seemed like a pursuit first—in the course of which the Hungarian troops partly lost their cohesion—quickly became an open battle when the Czechs turned around.

Henry's army inflicted, in this battle of November 2, a heavy defeat on the Hungarians, destroying separately two of the five approaching columns until the remainder, realizing what was happening, fled eastward at top speed. Yet their losses were high. The only source that gives us any figures claims that Matthias, on this day, November 2nd, lost 1,100 dead and large numbers of wounded and prisoners, while of the Czech army, apart from a considerable number of wounded, only ninety were killed.[63] Whether these figures are correct or not—the measure of the Hungarian defeat is shown not only by the headlong flight but also by the fact that some of the leading noblemen of the other side were taken prisoners by the Czechs, among them the Hungarian grandee John Count of Pösing—ironically one of those who at an earlier time had opposed the war against Bohemia—further, Bishop Tas' brother Dobeš of Boskovice, and George of Sternberg, one of Zdeněk's sons.[64]

Matthias made strong efforts to stop the flight and to make a stand at Uherský Brod, to which place the Czechs now pursued him. But he was not successful, and so decided to retire farther south across the Hungarian border to the town of Skalica, where he seems to have felt safer. Thus, for the time being, the lower Morava Valley region in Moravia, from Hodonín northward to near Kroměříž, was free of enemy troops, and Henry used this situation for several raids into Hungarian territory, especially the Váh valley, which suffered the usual depredations.

If there was in this war a military event which had decisive significance, it was the battle of Hradiště. Far from ensuring an over-all victory to George, it nevertheless established a new basic pattern for the further conduct of the war. It made it clear that this war was no longer a one-sided affair, no longer merely a struggle of self-preservation of the King of Bohemia against Matthias and the Czech rebels. Hradiště, both the battle and the successful holding of the city, also shows that Moravia had by no means been given up for lost by George

---

[63] Pešina, *Mars Moravicus*, 851.

[64] Thus state Długosz and Pešina. Eschenloer, G., II, 189, claims that one of the Czech nobles, the Moravian baron of Pernstein, was captured and later exchanged against Dobeš. This, however, probably occurred at a different time.

and that, apart from its value as a country nationally and otherwise intimately tied to Bohemia, its strategic value as the potential offensive basis against Hungary herself was not forgotten. King George did, indeed, now become very conscious of the possibility of carrying the war, on a large scale, into Hungarian soil, and did not give up this plan to the end.

The impression made by the Czech victory was deep. This was true even in the case of Matthias, who asked Duke Henry for an armistice. The answer, given after consultation with King George, declared that the Czechs were ready to cease hostilities if Matthias desisted from using the title of King of Bohemia; if he released Duke Victorin; if he evacuated Olomouc, Brno, and other localities in Moravia and Silesia; if he stopped the plundering and burning in the lands of the Bohemian crown, and returned all his troops peacefully to Hungary.[65] It was hardly likely that, at this stage, Matthias would acknowledge the defeat of all his plans and intentions in such terms. In any case we do not know of his response. (But it seems that when the Czech army returned to Bohemia in the winter—it was an unusually early and severe one—Matthias tried to have the siege of Hradiště renewed and the bastions rebuilt and reoccupied.)

That the general mood among the rest of George's enemies was far from hopeful emerges from Eschenloer's report. "From all this," he says, "there arose in our party great sadness and worry, since it was seriously to be feared that Matthias would just never return from Hungary. The heretics let loose with great shouting about this battle, and in Poland, too, there was great joy."[66] That the impression this Czech success made in Poland was strong is confirmed by Długosz, who also went farther in tracing the consequences of the battle than other sources. "From this time," he says, "the Bohemians, with their spirits rebounding, began also to be superior in their success. A large part of the Catholic barons of Bohemia, such as Burian of Gutstein and Svantoslav (meaning Bohuslav) of Švamberg, deserted the King of Hungary and joined up with Girzik."[67] In reality the majority of the lords formerly belonging to the League of Zelená Hora did not, as Długosz makes it appear, officially change over from Matthias to George but, as the two lords mentioned above, received permission from George to maintain a position of neutrality in the military strug-

---

[65] The source, this time given credit even by the cautious Palacký, is Pešina, *loc.cit.*
[66] German, II, 189.
[67] *Op. cit.* 530.

gle. This, of course, presupposed that they would divest themselves of the high state offices which they had accepted from Matthias as King of Bohemia. Other important members of the baronial side asked for and achieved armistice agreements for one year.[68]

Despite the disappointments George had suffered in the negotiations at Vilémov and Olomouc it can be said that his military, and with it his political, situation at the close of 1469 had enormously improved compared to what it had been twelve months earlier. No one dared to predict any longer that the end of the heretics was only a matter of a few months. In large parts of the enemy camp disheartenment, even hopelessness, had begun to spread. The year 1470 was not going to bring about any further radical changes in the military picture—on the contrary, many of the military events of that year had a curiously repetitive character. But the indomitable spirit of resistance that had been shown, despite all difficulties and sacrifices, by the King himself, his foremost advisers, and indeed by the masses of the Czech people was, in this thirteenth year of his kingship, going to have its impact above all in the diplomatic field. The great coalition that seemed to have been forged so firmly against the King of the Heretics between Pope and Emperor, King Matthias and the baronial rebels, some hostile cities and a few German princes, began to break up. 1470, indeed, was to be a year of strong hopes for Bohemia's embattled ruler.

[68] John of Rosenberg and the brothers Zajíc of Hasenburg. See Palacký, *Dějiny*, IV, 2, 533 (German, 614).

CHAPTER 22

CLEARER SKIES AND THE END OF THE ROAD

AT THE beginning of 1469 King George and his Utraquist Bohemia
had appeared to be almost completely isolated. The expectation, after
Vilémov, that there might be peace and renewed friendship between
George and Matthias, did not, as we have seen, at first improve
George's international position. It simply caused distrust everywhere,
in Poland, in Germany, and at the Emperor's court, against both
rulers. In view of Matthias' strength at the time, and his ability to
obtain backing for any policy (except peace with the heretics) from
the Holy See, he could afford to face this distrust much better than
the Czech King. The coolness which at this time seemed to develop
between George and the two princely German houses whom inter-
marriage, treaties, and common interests had throughout the crisis
kept from joining the rank of his enemies—this coolness was still
largely the effect of the period immediately after Vilémov. Paradoxically Matthias' election in Olomouc—despite the "defensive treaty"
of the Wittelsbachs with Matthias and Frederick of Brandenburg's
visit to Breslau—had tended to improve George's standing at least with
some of those princes whose defection would have been a heavy blow
for him.

The changing mood that followed the usurpation of Olomouc is
perhaps best expressed in a letter written to King George by Margrave
Albert Achilles late in July 1469. In it he first expresses his impression
that Matthias would never have entered the war against George if he
had not all along nourished the hope of making himself King of
Bohemia. But, he continues, "there is no doubt that his chance for receiving help has, in many parts of Germany, grown worse now rather
than better. For now that he claims this kingdom as his own, whoever
will want to help him gain it?[1] And so people in the German lands
would rather have a Bohemian for a King than have a Hungarian King

---

[1] "So hat man in teutschen landen lieber einen Beheim zu einem konig, dan das man ein
ungerisch konig zu einem konig von Beheim auch haben solt; das seyt on zweyfel." See
KBAA, I, 205, 206.

to also be King of Bohemia; have no doubt about this!" The last sentence, in its German original, is quite as ambiguous as in this translation. Did Albert actually mean "have a Bohemian for *their* King," or merely have a Bohemian rule Bohemia? If the first meaning had been intended it would reflect an astonishing change of mind, for no one had been more effective in blocking George's Roman kingship than he. In view of the general situation, the second version seems by far the more likely, and also fits the margrave's whole policy much better. He had been remarkably firm and steadfast in maintaining, against all papal and imperial pressure, against the wavering inclination of his brother the elector, and in view of at least some rather doubtful moves of the Saxons, his personal and political ties with "the heretic," chafing occasionally under the excommunication, and clearly somewhat angry when George, of all people, advocated a Roman kingship for Matthias. In this, as in any potentially overwhelming central power in the Empire, he saw a real danger; and in this, at least as far as Matthias' candidacy was concerned, he and George had now no longer the slightest disagreement. The margrave's constancy was not a matter of sentiment; he had been a friend, but never to the detriment of what he thought were his own legitimate interests. But his was not a cold, calculating mind; rather it was one combining shrewd judgment with a strong instinct, and in the main he turned out to be right. (He could be sure of this only some time later, when the unwelcome barrier between himself and the Emperor was raised.)

For the further course of events the policy of the Emperor would be of crucial importance. He had, so far, countered all attempts to create a second (and, in influence, probably first) King of the Romans with a mixture of passive resistance and a generally clever evasive diplomacy. All the various candidates put forward by Martin Mair had had to give up. But this, perhaps, was a different situation. Matthias, after all, could make claims which none of the prior candidates could have made. By entering the war, he had relieved the Emperor from the dangers and burdens of a Czech invasion. Without his effective help some of the Emperor's crown lands were exposed to Turkish attacks. On the other hand he could (and did) wield internal pressure, whenever he chose, by supporting Austrian rebel barons such as Baumkircher in exactly the same way in which George had done before.[2] In addition, he could count at least upon toleration and friendly under-

[2] See Krones, "Beiträge zur Geschichte der Baumkircherfehde 1469–1470," *AÖG*, LXXXIX, Vienna, 1901.

standing from the Roman Curia. Would the Emperor be able to shake off Matthias' powerful offensive for the conquest of the Roman kingship with the same comparative ease with which the earlier candidates had been thwarted?

King George had his doubts about this. He had certainly believed Matthias when, in the negotiations at Vilémov, the latter had claimed that the Emperor had given him strong assurances in this direction. His ambassador Špán had quoted this directly in his memorandum submitted to Margrave Albert. As late as December 1469 rumors were current in Prague court circles [3] that the Emperor's promises were still upheld, that at least three electors—Mainz, Trier, and even Saxony— had given their consent, that the Emperor had spoken to Matthias of his intention to retire to a high church position after which he would give his children and his lands into Matthias' trust. The question whether the Emperor had ever hinted at any such prospects may be left open. But rumors like this, even though merely reflecting wishful thinking, may have had their origin in Hungary. There was, at least, no question that Matthias was determined to reach this goal by all means at his disposal. George, on the other hand, was now just as determined to keep him from reaching it as he had some months earlier been willing to help him toward it. Yet he was not sure that the Emperor would not give way. He had, after what he called the "Easter play of Olomouc," still suspected the Emperor of complicity in this game, and had little confidence in Frederick's strength and steadfastness in defending his own position. In this situation there seemed to him only one way of preventing Matthias from acquiring the power he sought: to find someone else who could be expected to gain and occupy the position of King of the Romans with sufficient strength so as to bar the way to this throne to anyone else. His candidate was, not too astonishingly, Charles the Bold of Burgundy.

The young duke had followed his father, Philip the Good, in 1467. He had, as it were, inherited from him the dream of kingship, the only thing, as it seemed then, that his powerful position and his rich and splendid court still needed to be reckoned among the greatest European powers. Charles, building on the strong foundations laid by his father, was at this moment at the pinnacle of his might. He had only recently beaten and humiliated Louis XI, and after negotiations with Duke Sigismund of Tyrol he had acquired some considerable Habsburg possessions on the left bank of the Rhine. This seemed to bring a step

---

[3] *KBAA*, I, 218, Gregory Heimburg to his brother-in-law.

nearer the fulfillment of the hope for a unified Burgundian territory from the North Sea to the Franche Comté, a revival of the old Lotharingia. The idea of an intimate liaison between him and the house of Habsburg—eventually the one great success to be gained by the imperial dynasty during Frederick's rule—was already considered and talked about. Thus George's choice seemed a natural one. In addition the embassy sent in the spring, with Špán of Barnstein in the lead, to Louis XI may after the rather unprofitable completion of its mission [4] have reported on the special strength recently gained by the duke. In any case George, in July 1469, sent George of Stein, now one of his frequent diplomatic servants, to Burgundy, where he concluded a provisional agreement with the duke. In it Charles declared himself ready to accept the Roman royal crown and pay 900,000 ducats for it, while George promised to procure for him the support of the Electors of Mainz, Saxony and Brandenburg and, of course, give him his own vote. The duke felt that he would have no difficulty in obtaining the support of the Palatinate in view of his good relations with Palsgrave Frederick.[5]

This time George made, it seems, a rather strong effort to gain the help of the German princes in question, going so far as to mention (in a message passed on through George of Stein) [6] the possibility of ceding to Margrave Albert some important territory in Lusatia or around Cheb or to pay him 60,000 ducats—which would have come out of the supposed Burgundian payment. "On this undertaking," says Stein, "the King has set his heart more than on any other and will spare no effort to bring it about, since without a change in the Empire he does not believe he can trust that his sons will maintain their princely honor and dignity." The "change in the Empire" was just one which would make Matthias' Roman kingship definitely impossible.

When this message was sent, presumably in October 1469,[7] it was still assumed in Prague that the step would have to be taken in opposition to the Emperor. Yet the whole enterprise had the curious effect of making the rapprochement between George and Frederick III easier rather than more difficult. One step in this direction had already been taken when Charles the Bold authorized George of Stein to func-

---

[4] *FRA*, II, 618.

[5] See Comines, *Memoires*, III, Preuves, 116–118, and IV, 378–381.

[6] *FRA*, II, 20, 616–619.

[7] It is undated. Palacký's assumption (January 1470) is only a guess and seems, in view of the background, too late, as already pointed out by Bachmann, *Reichsgeschichte*, II, 282 n. 1.

tion, upon his return, as his own ambassador to Duke Sigismund of Tyrol, whose main task it would have to be to inform and, if possible, win over the Emperor.

Meanwhile Frederick's interest in the war, as Heimburg had rightly remarked, had greatly cooled. His Roman visit may well have contributed to this change, since it must have proved to him the cynical way in which many of the Curial officials looked at this affair.[8] Matthias' assumption of the title of King of Bohemia—without the Emperor's prior agreement—surely was a further step in this alienation. But above all there was the Hungarian ruler's demand to be made King of the Romans. There can be little doubt that the possibility had already been under discussion, in terms which probably would have made use of the old treaty of 1462 by which Matthias had become the Emperor's son, but also by mentioning the possibility of Matthias marriage with the Emperor's daughter. By acting as he usually did, that is with evasion and procrastination, Frederick III could not fail to exasperate Matthias. But Frederick himself was equally sure to feel gravely endangered by Matthias' urging. He was fully aware that his savior, ally, and "son" was a man of fierce ambition and complete recklessness who would not be satisfied with the title of King of the Romans but would expect real power, substantial enough to reduce him, Frederick, to a mere shadow. Thus the Emperor never would—indeed never did—give in to Matthias' demands. Yet it was difficult for him to confront Matthias, in the present situation, with a brusk refusal.

There was one way which would probably make it easier and less dangerous for the Emperor to pursue a policy which might lead to an open clash between him and Matthias: a rapprochement with George leading to the liquidation of the war between them and thus also lightening the great financial burden which the struggle had imposed upon the Emperor. Thus suggestions which had been submitted to Frederick III in the summer of 1469 by his nephew (and George's son-in-law), Duke Albert of Saxony, were now, in the later fall, taken up more seriously. On the other hand, the Emperor cancelled a personal meeting with Matthias originally planned for October 4, and an embassy which the King sent in November to Frederick's residence in Wiener-Neustadt, presenting rather stiff demands, was left waiting till nearly the end of the year. Finally, having shown their intention

---

[8] About this see J. Toews, "Emperor Frederick III and the Holy See," University of Colorado dissertation, 1962.

to depart, they were coolly informed that the Emperor was willing to
to meet the King, but without the rather unusual guarantees he had
demanded for his safety.[9] If a complete break did not occur at this
stage it was largely due to the special efforts of Bishop Roverella, who
began to play a role similar to that played in previous years by Cardinal
Juan Carvajal. (The great Spanish cleric, incidentally, died just at this
time, on December 6th, 1469).[10] But it was also due to the Hungarian
defeat at Hradiště which Roverella lamented[11] and which made it
appear unwise for Matthias to break with his imperial ally at this
particular moment.

The negotiations between King George and the Emperor were in
the meantime taken up in earnest, though at first, it seems, in secret.
While much of the rapprochement seems to have been due to Duke
Albert of Saxony, who was now much more successful than in his first
attempts during the summer, the specific agreements were concluded
by one of the Vitzthum brothers, who had served the King in several
diplomatic missions before.[12] Though details about the results are
missing, it is clear that the Emperor promised to recognize not Matthias but George as King of Bohemia and to resume his earlier attempts at bringing about the needed reconciliation with Rome. To
strengthen his position against possible attacks by Matthias, the Emperor also began negotiations with Poland, sending there one of his
diplomats of Polish origin, Raphael Leszczyński, a move which may
have been suggested and was certainly approved of by Prague.[13]

In supporting this move King George could feel that Poland's
policy, for all her seeming caution and indecision, was bound to support him if Casimir did not want to lose all chances for the Czech
succession. If this issue nevertheless had in the meantime made little
progress, it was not because the Czechs had not tried. A diet meeting
in Prague in October had dispatched to the Polish diet meeting in
November in Piotrków an embassy[14] meant to impress the Poles by
its size and brilliance. The ambassadors, hoping to get a stronger en-

---

[9] See *Monumenta Hungariae historica*, Acta extera, Matyas, II, Budapest, 1875, 204–206.

[10] Palacký, trusting Lopez de Barrera's old biography, puts it a year later. See however
Gomez Canedo, *Don Juan de Carvajal*, 250–251.

[11] See *FRA*, II, 42, 481–482.

[12] *Ibid.*, 46, 114–115. About the Vitzthums (this is the spelling which the family used down
into modern times while the Czech spelling is "Fictum"), see Urbánek, *Věk*, IV, 328.

[13] See Papée, *Studya i Szkice*, 114–115.

[14] For details see Tobolka, "Styky krále Jiřího s králem Kazimírem," *ČMM*, XXII, 376–377.
For the sources for this and the following paragraph see Długosz, *Opera omnia*, XIV, 533–534;
FRA, II, 42, 475, and Eschenloer, L., 217.

dorsement of the Czech side, also in military terms, upon George's instructions agreed to the Polish request that Prince Władysław be crowned during King George's lifetime, but they also insisted that in this case Princess Ludmila, as his bride, be crowned simultaneously. The suggestion made before by the Poles that King George, before his death, might step down in favor of the Polish prince was, of course, never seriously considered.

The Czech position led to considerable differences of opinion among King Casimir's advisers, and the King finally gave the not very satisfactory answer that the question could be finally decided only after the arrival of a papal legate. This visit, however, did not take place until next summer. Yet, Casimir, in view of George's better military position, had to be careful not to antagonize the Prague court to an extent which might jeopardize the chances for the Polish succession altogether. Thus, to prove to George his undiminished value as an ally, Casimir gave some help by permitting considerable numbers of Polish mercenaries to enter George's service, and at the same time threatening Breslau, as the real author of all present troubles, with the stoppage of all her trade with Poland, a measure apt to reduce her willingness to invest still more—in money or men—in the fight against George.[15] Of the answer that Leszczyński brought to the Emperor we have no specific news, but from now on the contact between Casimir and Frederick III, which for a long time had been as good as nonexistent, was firmly maintained and became an important factor in this phase of central European diplomatic history.

Lord Vitzthum, who had, in these last weeks, represented King George at the Emperor's court was soon afterwards, at the very beginning of 1470, sent to Burgundy, with full authorization from both the Emperor and the King of Bohemia. What he could now suggest to Duke Charles—the offer was later made in a more official form—was the hope for a royal crown, hardly, however, the Roman one. Rather was it the elevation of the Burgundian lands to the rank of a kingdom.[16] This, in contrast to the royal marriage, never came about. But in the present connection the important thing was the complete understanding that on this issue had been reached between King George and the Emperor.

Hand in hand with the rapprochement between these two went a cooling off between the Emperor and the Wittelsbachs. An exception

---

[15] *SrS*, XIII, 14, and Eschenloer, G., II, 191f.
[16] See Bachmann, *Reichsgeschichte*, II, 284–288.

was Duke Otto of Bavaria, the only German prince who, for a short time, had fought against George on Czech soil. Whether it was this very unpleasant experience or his personal friendship with Albert of Saxony—in any case he changed sides and even offered, toward the end of 1469, to accompany Albert on a special mission to Rome in favor of King George's rehabilitation.[17]

But the situation in the Empire was, at the beginning of 1470, by no means clarified. Until very recently Duke Louis of Landshut, or one might better say Dr. Martin Mair, had pursued his plan for a combined alliance of the four dynasties—Habsburg, Wittelsbach, Wettin, and Hohenzollern—with the King of Hungary. And there had been moments when at least one or the other of the Saxon dukes—and possibly, in the last instance, even the Hohenzollerns—was not sure how long to hold out if the pressure from Pope and Emperor should become stronger. The Emperor, at this time, was no longer a real threat, though he was careful not to let the news of his reconciliation with George become known prematurely, especially not in Hungary. But George now felt strong enough to attempt an action which should reverse the political trend in the Empire and regain as much as possible of the political strength that he had enjoyed there for so long, thereby also undermining the German policy of Matthias Corvinus.

This effort was made in an appeal or memorandum directed to the German princes and cities [18] on January 1, 1470. While the wording of the document shows, at least in part, Heimburg's diction,[19] it nevertheless is valuable for revealing King George's own understanding of Bohemia's relationship to the Empire, and indeed of the status of this issue at the time. The document begins by accusing the rebel barons of trying to stage, for purely selfish purposes, a general revolt against George. When the leaders of the rebellion realized that they could not succeed in subverting the loyalty of the common people of the realm, they invented lies. They spread the word that at the Court Day in Prague George had publicly uttered such heretical opinions as

17 *KBAA*, I, 219.

18 *FRA*, II, 20, 610–615. See also C. T. Gemeiner, *Regensburgische Chronik*, III, 460–461, and George's letter to Albert Achilles in F. Priebatsch, ed., *Politische Correspondenz des Kurfürsten Albrecht Achilles*, I, Leipzig, 1894, 102–103 (cited later as "Priebatsch"), with the King's request for further distribution of the appeal.

19 This shows again that Bachmann was wrong in claiming that after the election of Olomouc "Heimburg's prestige was hopelessly lost through this second Hungarian failure," especially in view of the fact that George had attempted the understanding of Vilémov against Heimburg's advice. His position in the center of things in Prague down to the death of King George clearly emerges from his correspondence with Albert Achilles. (See Bachmann's "König Georg and Gregor Heimburg," in *MVGDB*, 35, 1897, 152, and *Reichsgeschichte*, II, 229–230.)

that there was no salvation for anyone not taking the communion in both kinds. Yet there were many witnesses who had then been present who could testify that he had never said this. The manifesto also accuses the Pope of having denied George justice and the right of a proper hearing. Then it emphasized that Bohemia was the only kingdom that had not turned away from the Holy Roman Empire, as all other Christian kingdoms had done in order to indulge in complete freedom from all ties and connections with the Empire. By maintaining such ties, the Czech kingdom had done great service to the Empire. Now, however, it was high time for the electors and princes to see to it that the kingdom of Bohemia not be alienated from the Empire. For this it was necessary for them to stand up for the kingdom and make sure that a fair hearing was given to the King as God himself does not condemn anyone unheard. Otherwise, nothing was left to the kingdom but to take those steps by which, with God's help, she could defend herself and her honor against such violent insults and attacks. "But if this should lead to the cutting of all ties between the noble crown of Bohemia and the Roman Empire, which we would deeply regret, then at least you ought to remember that we have been abandoned by you and other imperial princes and forced to such an action by the Holy Father without any guilt of our own."

While the immediate reaction to this appeal is not known, it is nevertheless obvious that the activities which, in 1469, supported the recognition of Matthias as King of Bohemia and elector of the Empire ceased almost completely in 1470, and that, for and during those imperial meetings that took place in 1470, the dominating issue became again the defense against the Turks rather than the destruction of the Czech heretics.[20]

But this very fact was bound to remind princes and Emperor of the degree to which they still depended on the King of Hungary. True, it was in Matthias' own interest to keep the Turks from invading central Europe, as they could not possibly do it without harming territory belonging to and claimed by the crown of St. Stephen such as Croatia. Yet it was not only possible but almost normal in the terms of the political morals of the time for a prince—in this case Matthias— to permit such harm to be done to one's own subjects provided it led to even greater harm inflicted upon the subjects of a hostile prince, in this case the Emperor. And above all it was quite impossible to plan (as was being done so regularly and so inconsequentially) for a great

[20] E.g. the reichstag of Nürnberg in the early fall of 1470. (See *ibid.*, 304–308).

anti-Turkish crusade without, for reasons of geography and power resources, expecting Matthias to play a leading role in it. Thus it is certainly understandable that the Emperor, resolved though he was not to yield to Matthias' aspiration to the Roman crown and also to liquidate the fruitless and dangerous struggle with the Czechs, was not eager to come to a complete break with Matthias. The latter, on the other hand, surely had information enough to realize that he was in some danger of diplomatic isolation. Thus, encouraged also by Rover-ella, he again suggested a personal meeting to Frederick, and the Em-peror agreed.[21] On February 10th, accompanied by a brilliant retinue of bishops and noblemen, the King rode into Vienna, and there began a long period of negotiations, with Matthias, in the most courteous forms, wooing the Emperor.[22] Having been refused a Polish marriage Matthias now asked officially for the hand of the Emperor's daughter Kunigunda. As a future son-in-law, however, he requested also eleva-tion to the rank of King of the Romans. If the Emperor was ready to support him he believed that a good majority among the electoral princes—he himself would hold the Bohemian vote—should be easy to obtain.

The Emperor tried hard to maintain the cordial atmosphere by ex-ternal means, and for a while it looked as if Emperor and King were the closest of friends who demonstrated their father-son intimacy even by publicly embracing while being driven through the streets of Vienna. (Like a pair of love-birds, said the people.)

In the actual negotiations the request for the hand of the arch-duchess was not refused, but the King's attention was drawn to the fact that she was a child of five, too young to marry for the next ten years. The Emperor seems also to have been ready to concede that, in case his son Maximilian should die without descendants, Matthias, as son-in-law, would be his heir. In the essential question, however, that of his early accession to the Roman kingship, the Emperor proved as eva-sive as before. And this, after all, had been the real aim of this whole effort. When Matthias felt that he was not making any progress by suave diplomacy, he tried harsh and threatening tones, repeating in the main his older requests for high payments, for stronger participa-

[21] See Kurz, *Oesterreich unter Friedrich IV,* II, 246. A curious declaration of Matthias' advisers, pledging, as it were, their word for the King's good behavior, *ibid.,* 247.

[22] The most detailed description of the Vienna meeting in Fraknói, *Matthias Corvinus,* 149–151. For the sources see there, 151 n. 1, and Bachmann, *Reichsgeschichte,* II, 288–291, and especially also in the forthcoming vol. 22 of *DRTA,* which will have all the material in better detail than *Mon. Hung. Hist.,* Acta Extera, II. (Much of these are reports of the Milanese Ambassador, Christoforo Bullati, to his duke.)

tion of Emperor and Empire in the war against George, and for the
Emperor's renunciation of his title as King of Hungary conceded to
him in 1462. But this very method brought out the stubborn determination of which Frederick III was capable in a struggle for his
imperial prerogatives. After the first three weeks, the negotiations had
again become completely deadlocked. Matthias was ready to leave, and
though for a short time the Archbishop of Esztergom, a friend and
confidant of both rulers, managed to calm him down, he soon lost all
patience and on March 11th, without even taking leave from his host, he
left by boat for Bratislava. For the moment the break seemed complete, and Frederick's re-orientation, which had already gone quite far
before the Vienna meeting, proved to be all the more necessary.

Among the people most unhappy about this development were several leaders of the Czech rebels who had been present in Vienna.
Their situation in the war was becoming more and more difficult, and
did not show much hope for brightening up. For under the determined leadership of her king, now much more hopeful not only of
survival but of victory, the Czech nation was willing to flex her mus-
cles. At a diet of the estates held in Prague in March 1470 the King
submitted a law creating a permanent defense force, independent from
either the general levy, which could be called up in times of danger,
or from whatever mercenary troops the King would hire. The law was
accepted, in a spirit of vigorous concord, by all three estates.[23] According to it, all the districts or provinces represented at the diet, altogether
ten out of the thirteen in which the country was divided, were supposed to maintain a permanent striking force, liable to fight anywhere,
at any time and for any period. For each of the ten the commanding
officers and their deputies were named, or rather elected by the individual districts, about six of them barons, most of the others knights,
but also some burghers. The commander-in-chief was to be appointed
by the King.

The actual numbers were determined, at this stage, for only eight of
the districts, those of the other two apparently to be decided later. The
numbers ranged from slightly over 1,000 for the more populous to
about 350 for the smaller districts, adding up to a little over 5,000 or,
with the addition of the remaining two, probably 6,000 men. About
one-tenth of these troops were to be cavalry, the great majority infantry, a small number especially named as lance carriers. For each 18 to

[23] See *AČ*, IV, 441–444.

20 men there was to be one battle waggon, amounting in all to about 250 waggons.

This was, of course, a striking force of limited size, but in addition to George's other manpower resources it was of considerable value. Among these additions were mercenaries hired by the King also from other countries (such as Poland, a reversal of the "normal" situation when the King of Poland made ample use of Czech mercenaries). George, it is obvious, no longer worried that a long exhausting defensive war would dangerously drain his resources, especially since his income from the silver mines had lately risen to a very respectable level.[24] Therefore he was now willing to spend more of this income for military purposes than he had before. But he became all the more careful about all expenses not geared to the war effort, thereby eliciting the unhappy complaint of Heimburg that he was becoming stingier, having, like other princes, learned the art of parsimony from the Emperor.[25]

King Matthias, since his entry into the war, had spent very large sums which, for the pay to mercenary troops alone had by the fall of 1469 already amounted to 400,000 ducats. Now, at a diet held in Buda, he approached his estates for a third extraordinary tax and, overcoming considerable resistance, was finally voted one ducat for each "porta," altogether about 800,000—a heavy burden for the population.

Around Easter, late in April, both sides started to renew the struggle. Matthias entered eastern Moravia from Trenčín, at the head of an army which was only 4,000 men strong but consisted entirely of cavalry. He intended to march north toward Silesia. There things had begun to develop, from Matthias' point of view, in a rather disquieting way. He could no longer count on the support of all those princes and cities who had, a year earlier, been awed into doing homage to him. The first of the princes to openly challenge him was Duke John of Ratibor, who, already in January 1470, had again declared himself for King George. Soon afterwards several Silesian and Lusatian cities complained bitterly to Bishop Rudolf of Breslau and to Matthias' military governor Francis of Háj about the lack of protection from the invasion of Czech raiding parties. Matthias' intended march was meant to restore his political and military position in the two northern depend-

24 See *KBAA*, I, 219.
25 *Ibid.*

encies.[26] At the same time he had strengthened the siege troops beleaguering Hradiště.

But before Matthias had moved far from the region of the lower Morava River, he heard that a Czech army of about 5,000 infantry and 1,000 horse had entered Moravia. Thereupon Matthias retreated into Hungary to mobilize stronger forces.[27] Meanwhile, about the middle of May, the Czechs, led by Hrabaně of Vlkanov and John Chotěřinský, conquered two of the Hungarian bastions, captured or killed their defenders, and brought new provisions into Hradiště. From the region around Hradiště they undertook several raids across the Hungarian border into the valleys of the Váh and Mijava Rivers. It seems that they also intended to conquer the remaining bastions around Hradiště. In one of these attempts Hrabaně was himself captured.

But in June Matthias returned to Moravia, this time at the head of a much stronger army, estimated at 10,000 to 12,000 men, no less than two-thirds of them cavalry. It was now the turn of the Czechs to retreat from their position before Hradiště, and they established themselves in an encampment farther south near the border city of Hodonín, from where they undertook repeated raids across the river into Hungarian territory. It was near Hodonín, however, that one of the main horrors of this war was committed. A troop of Hungarian-Serb cavalry (called Raci or Rajci) had succeeded in capturing a convoy with provisions destined for the Czech troops at Hodonín. They killed all the men—585 of them—and presented their heads to Matthias who had promised them one ducat for each head. Matthias then ordered all these heads to be, by a catapult, shot into the Czech encampment. The report about this comes from Eschenloer who called it, perhaps with a grain of irony, a "grande spectaculum."[28]

For George the campaign of this summer had still to begin. Starting on July 6th from the region of Kutná Hora-Čáslav, he led an army of 8,000 infantry and 1,000 horse into Moravia. At the same time the smaller Czech army at Hodonín was ordered to march northward so as to join George's troops somewhere in central Moravia. Matthias, informed of this, sent out a strong force of cavalry to intercept the

---

[26] Tomek, *Dějepis*, VII, 270.

[27] For the following see mainly *SLČP*, 409; *FRA* II, 20, 631–633; and among secondary sources Tomek, *Dějepis*, VII, 271–272.

[28] Palacký (*Dějiny*, IV, 2, 548, German, 632) and Urbánek (*Husitský král*, 267) both take Eschenloer's exclamation as an expression of pure delight, but, in view of his earlier protests against barbarous deeds of his own party, I have doubts about this.

troops before they could effect the junction. The Hungarians caught up with the Czechs while the latter were crossing a tributary river of the Morava near the town of Tovačov, and threw themselves upon the rear guard. Czech losses from this action are listed by Hungarian sources as many hundreds of men taken prisoner or killed; by Czech sources as a total loss of 13 waggons and 200 men.[29] The news about this, like those of some later skirmishes, was reported to Silesia as a huge victory over the heretics and celebrated with the singing of the Tedeum all over, so as to raise the low morale of George's enemies in the country. In fact, however, the main purpose of the Czech move could not be thwarted. The two armies eventually joined up and thus formed a military body which, while not nearly as fast and mobile as that of Matthias, with its large cavalry forces, was superior to it in massive strength and fire power and which Matthias could hardly hope to defeat in an open battle.

This junction, however, did not occur till early August. Four weeks before that date the two great armies, moving about cautiously, stood opposite each other near Brno, where Matthias made full use of the protection presented by the city and Spielberg Castle, while George had established an encampment in the open, some distance away. There he had been joined by many of the leading men of the kingdom. At this moment George hoped that, in one way or another, he could force a decision. Soon, however, it became obvious to him that, as in earlier, similar situations, Matthias was not willing to risk the danger of an open clash with the Czech army which, even before the junction with the other force, was numerically somewhat superior to his own. In order, however, to break this deadlock, George asked some of his leading barons to present to Matthias, under a flag of truce, a series of demands and suggestions.[30] The first was an offer of peace, made to avoid any more spilling of blood, provided Matthias stay his aggression, leave with his troops the countries of the crown of St. Wenceslas, and agree to submitting the question of damage done to the decision of the electors of the Empire. This, in the main, was a repetition of the demands made upon Matthias' request for an armistice after his defeat at Hradiště. If, as was to be feared, the Hungarian King would not accept this, King George offered to let a personal duel between the two Kings decide the outcome. If this, too, was refused Matthias should at least agree that the two armies meet in open battle. Both

---

[29] See *FRA*, II, 20, 632, and Duke Henry's report to Albert Achilles, *ibid.*, 636.
[30] See *AČ*, I, 485–487. For the whole development see also Eschenloer, G., II, 202–209.

parts should have a chance to wait four days for whatever reinforcements they could add to their present strength.

The whole offer seems, at first glance, strange, unrealistic, even absurd. It is hardly surprising that Matthias did not, in substance, accept any of the three alternatives. George's initiative, however, is apt to remind us that this ruler, for all the "modern" aspects of much of his thinking and policy, was still in other ways a man of the Middle Ages, willing to submit his own fate and that of his country and his people to the judgment of God. For what, if not the trust in a true judgment of God, could give this middle-aged man, already gravely hampered in his movements by an obesity based on chronic dropsy,[31] the confidence that he could prevail in single combat over a vigorous man hardly more than half his age? This astonishing confidence in the divine judgment also shows how wrong are those historians who have claimed that George was a man without real religion. In fact he was, in his religious principles—including a measure of tolerance—far more sincere than Matthias, who, some years later, had no religious qualms (to the great advantage of the country) about leaving the governorship of Moravia to a great Utraquist baron,[32] yet presented himself as the pious crusader defending good Christians who had suffered great harm from vile heretics. In this answer (of July 24th) directed to the Czech noblemen [33] and containing many cleverly formulated barbs, Matthias denied that he or his people were shedding Christian blood. They were shedding only heretical and heathen blood as was their duty and as they would keep doing. He then declared himself ready for peace, provided that George defer the fate of the kingdom under his rule to the judicial decision of Pope and Emperor; accepted (but only on paper) George's offer of a duel; and claimed that, so far, George had always fled in the face of the Hungarian army and would, if he could, certainly do so again.

Six days later, on July 30th, George replied,[34] not however to Matthias but to the Transylvanian vojvoda (governor), Nicholas Čupor of Monoslo, and other lords and knights in the Hungarian army. In his note he presents his case, that of the true King of his country, against the man who imagines, without any right, himself to be

31 In his offer George demands expressly that, in view of the heaviness of his body, which hampers him, the space used for the combat be properly limited. But even this, of course, would not have given him an even chance.

32 See e.g. R. Dvořák, *Dějiny markrabství moravského*, Brno, 1906, 187–188.

33 *AČ,* I, 487–489.

34 *Ibid.,* 490–491.

Czech King and calls himself so although he has never been, is not, and never will be King of Bohemia. Then, however, George's letter answers Matthias' (indeed rather absurd) claim that George had fled in the face of the Hungarian army. He goes into considerable historical detail, giving a whole list of opportunities for battles carefully evaded by Matthias, from the early maneuverings near Laa to the most recent occurrences. "It is also well known," he wrote, "whether, near Vilémov, he dared to stand up to us in open battle. Rather, when he saw his predicament, he got out of it by promises that he made to us, so that trusting his promises, we released, as it were, him and his army out of our hands. After that he did not keep any of the promises he had made. But this you know well, that he ran away before the illustrious Prince Henry, our dear son, from Hradiště to Uherský Brod and beyond."

On the same day a letter was also sent by the Czech lords in George's retinue to Matthias himself[35] in which they protested his claim to Czech kingship since King George was properly elected, crowned, and accepted and was already in the thirteenth year of ruling the kingdom and since they, the lords, have not nor want to have any other King. Matthias was neither regularly elected nor accepted. Finally they protested with special vehemence the mendacious distortion in his calling them heretics.

That George, in his reply of July 30th, addressed himself to prominent members of the Hungarian nobility was not merely a reflection of his unwillingness to talk any longer to Matthias directly. It also showed his expectation that Matthias would find effective resistance to his policy among a growing number of his magnates and other people.[36] Some symptoms of considerable dissatisfaction had become visible in the summer and fall of 1469, but were still essentially limited to groups that had been considered doubtful supporters of Matthias, and especially of his western adventures, such as Nicholas Vardai and the counts of Pösing-St. Georgen. Now, however, the dissatisfaction, with forms bordering on conspiracy, reached circles much nearer the throne, such as the primate of Hungary, Archbishop Vitéz of Esztergom, who until then had backed Matthias faithfully, and John Pannonius, the Bishop of Pécs, long one of Matthias' most intimate helpers, from whose elegant Latin pen most of the King's important diplomatic and pro-

[35] *Ibid.*, 491–492.
[36] See for the following Heimburg's information in *KBAA*, I, 203, 210, 215; Długosz, XIV 549; and Fraknói, *Matthias Corvinus*, 148.

grammatic pronouncements had flown. However these conspiracies were more symptomatic (especially in relation to the heavy taxation imposed by Matthias on all parts of the people) than consequential. Matthias' would-be rebels, many of them reacting to the King's strong hand much as the Czech rebel barons had reacted to George's policy, had not, as had their Czech peers, the advantage of the religious pretense and the papal support.

But King George kept the possibility of a more effective invasion of Hungary well in mind, thinking that this might result in a strengthening of oppositional elements in the country. Therefore, once his hope for an immediate decision—by single combat or an openly arranged battle between the armies—had in fact been dashed, his strategy focused again upon the Moravian-Hungarian border region. Thus, while Matthias with his army remained in his position near Brno, George marched east again, and there, in the vicinity of Kroměříž, the planned joining with the other army, meanwhile led by Prince Henry and Wenceslas Vlček of Čenov, took place as arranged.

From Kroměříž the Czech army—now one of the strongest that had yet taken the field—marched south [37] and in an operation that recalled Prince Henry's triumph of the year before attacked and destroyed the Hungarian siege forces around Hradiště. This done, all the bastions around the city were demolished and the city was given ample provisions in case new attempts should be made against her. (She did, indeed, prove truly unconquerable, even long beyond the lifetime of King George). To celebrate this success the King entered the city, where he was greeted by the brave defenders with the greatest enthusiasm. Also some towns and castles along the lower course of the river, down to Hodonín, were freed from Hungarian occupation and received new stocks of provisions. In addition to these southern enterprises a new invasion of Hungary took place, by cavalry and infantry, which seems to have penetrated southeast as far as Trnava [38] and which waged the usual war of destruction, confiscating goods and burning houses. But this, for once, was not the only purpose of these invasions. King George himself took part in some of them, in order to see, as he wrote to the people of Kutná Hora, whether the people across the border would not want to join him against Matthias.[39]

The people in this northwestern region of the Hungarian kingdom

[37] See FRA, II, 20, 636, and Eschenloer, G., II, 201.
[38] FRA, II, 46, 120–121.
[39] See Palacký, Dějiny, IV, 2, 556 (in German, 641).

were, of course, Slovaks, at least in the rural areas, and this may have had something to do with George's hope for a movement there in his favor and against Matthias. The memory of Jiskra's rule in northern Hungary and of the struggle of the bratříci must still have been very much alive in people's minds, and Hussite ideas, regarding both religion and social changes, may also have survived to some extent. George's wish to explore possibilities for support within Hungary— not only among dissatisfied magnates but also among the common people of closely related ethnic stock and language—thus made good sense. Yet it seems doubtful whether we should go along with a modern interpretation [40] which sees in this step George's thought "that it would be possible not only to pull Slovakia into this great struggle but perhaps to add it directly to the Czech state." This would, in his present situation, probably have been an unwise ambition. But this interpretation also transfers, in an anachronistic way, the modern conception of Czechoslovak statehood into a historical situation in which nationalism, while far from absent, had very different shapes and goals.

King George did not further press his attack upon Hungary. It seems that he decided to postpone this enterprise for the following year when he could hope that his general political situation, already so distinctly improved, would leave him more freedom of action militarily. Meanwhile he had not given up hope of meeting the Hungarian forces where they were now, in Moravia, and doing battle with them.

Since early July when the two armies had faced one another near Brno, Matthias had kept strangely inactive. Perhaps he was still waiting for reinforcements from Silesia. A small army of about 2,000 men —far less than he had demanded—had tried to join him but had so far been prevented from doing this by Czech forces in the Morava valley. Finally, in the second half of August, he moved from Brno to Olomouc, where he camped for several days, thereby making the junction with the Silesians easier. After a short move south toward Kroměříž, he returned to Olomouc. The Czech army was very near—King George had his headquarters in mid-August at Malenovice near Zlin, where he received, among others, a Polish embassy. Nothing seemed to point to any major enterprise of the Hungarians which would have restored to them the lost initiative. Yet Matthias was aware of the considerable loss of prestige and morale, especially among his allies or

---

[40] Urbánek, *Husitský král*, 268.

subjects in the Bohemian dependencies, which the unfavorable military development in Moravia—and corresponding troubles in Silesia—had brought about. Something had to be done, and fast.[41]

An unusual turn of the weather gave him his chance. All through the summer there had been much rain, but in the second half of August this took on torrential proportions, with the result that all over Moravia rivers and brooks had flooded the countryside and had become difficult or impossible to bridge or ford. This, of course, made the Czech army, with its large numbers of battle waggons, even slower and less mobile than normally. Matthias decided to make the best of this opportunity, trusting that anyhow the main part of the forces available to George had been committed to the campaign in Moravia. About or immediately after August 20th he led the main part of his cavalry, nearly 8,000 men, without any other elements, into Bohemia. With lightning speed he moved westward along the same road that had once taken him to Chrudim and Vilémov, but this time he went farther, even penetrating the region of Kutná Hora, in which he camped on August 25th. He had given the strictest orders not to stop anywhere, not to try to make any conquests, not even to enter houses for booty, but merely to burn all the villages within the reach of his troops. In this he was successful enough, even though Eschenloer's triumphant announcement that 1,500 villages were burnt by him was absurd. There was probably not one half of that number of villages within the path of the raiding troops.

Upon the news of this unexpected raid, the Czechs themselves reacted with a speed apparently not anticipated by Matthias. Above all the newly organized permanent defense forces of the kingdom were called to arms and Queen Johanna—functioning as regent in the absence of her husband—took command of them, moving quickly east from Prague toward Kolín and Kutná Hora. At the same time the main Czech army in Moravia entered Bohemia in the hope of intercepting the raiders. Matthias, upon receiving this information, again made a sharp turn south, in time to avoid another trap like that which had caught him at Vilémov. Within a couple of days his army was back in Moravia, resting shortly behind the strong walls of Jihlava, and then went on via Telč to Znojmo. According to the most neutral source available—Długosz—the Hungarians suffered heavy losses on

---

[41] For the following see Długosz, *Opera omnia*, XIV, 540–541; Eschenloer, G., II, 202; *SLČP*, 410; and *FRA*, II 20, 637. For some minor additions see Palacký, *Dějiny*, IV, 2, 558 n. 443 (German, 643 n. 442).

the breathlessly fast retreat, since all those whose horses could not keep up with the main body were pitilessly abandoned to the not so tender graces of the infuriated Czech peasantry.

There is hardly any justification for moral indignation about this large-scale raid.[42] Burning villages in enemy country was surely a usual form of the warfare of the time, and was used also by the Czech armies, not only during their own small raids into Hungary but just as much in Silesia and Lusatia, and also on the estates of prominent rebel lords in Bohemia. A more important question is how useful this "blitz" invasion was to Matthias. It was, of course, used to the limit for propaganda purposes, especially in Silesia, where, at the time, such a propaganda was especially necessary. But this certainly did not have a very lasting effect. It was clear that by such raids the Hungarian King could not possibly win his war. Yet he apparently felt that this was all he could do for the remainder of the year. (It turned out to be his last military enterprise of any significance in his personal struggle against his former father-in-law.) Throughout September he stayed in Znojmo. Then, having left some 2,000 of his mercenaries at the disposal of Zdeněk of Sternberg and some others as reinforcements for the defense of the major Moravian cities occupied by him, he returned with the remainder of his army to Hungary. Financial limitations may have played as important a role for this unpromising conduct of the war as the need to be present in Hungary and watch out for renewed domestic attempts at subverting his rule, especially since these had begun to receive strong support from Poland.

In Silesia it had been seriously feared that after Matthias' return to Hungary and the dissolution of his forces in Moravia—including the Silesian corps, which had been dismissed in September—the armies of King George would now invade Silesia in strength.[43] This, indeed, George intended to do. But his governor in Glatz, Hans Wölfl of Warnsdorf, asked him for the moment to refrain from such a step. He was hopeful for the success of negotiations which he had been conducting for some time with representatives of the duchies of Schweidnitz and Jauer as well as with Duke Conrad the Black of Oels, who, following the example of Duke John of Ratibor, intended to return to full obedience to King George. There were other symptoms indicating that Matthias' position in Silesia had become shaky. At a meeting of representatives of princes and cities which Bishop Rudolf had called

---

[42] As Palacký does (*ibid.*).
[43] Eschenloer, G., II, 209–210. For the following, see Tomek, *Dějepis*, VII, 282–283.

to Breslau late in October, plans were discussed for a delegation to be sent to Matthias asking for permission—in view of the weak protection they had received from him—to seek peace with King George. What had probably made the strongest impression in Silesia was the fact that the small Silesian auxiliary corps which had joined Matthias in Moravia had suffered heavy losses—not necessarily from enemy action but frequently from illness and lack of food—and that the reports of those who had returned were anything but hopeful. The defeatist mood dominating even Breslau is described vividly by Eschenloer.[44] It included the masses of craftsmen and other little people—just the ones who in previous times could not get quickly enough into the war against the heretic. Now they demanded that peace be concluded immediately and at any price, and it was up to the councillors to keep their heads—seeing the grave dislocation and destruction of the city's trade and the pressure exerted by all three Kings, George, Matthias, and Casimir. But the defeatism went up to the highest circles, and even included Bishop Rudolf, another one of those who had once been utterly irreconcilable and had attacked his predecessor Jost of Rosenberg for his softness.[45] Now he admitted, most unhappily, that the Pope had been badly advised, that the whole war was a terrible mistake since the real strength of the heretics had never been taken into proper account, and that it would be far better to live in peace with them. And even Dr. Tempelfeld no longer dared to contradict.

This mood had already shown itself during the preceding winter, and the return—or failure to return—of the members of the Silesian troops had intensified it. For the leaders of Matthias' party, the King himself, Zdeněk of Sternberg, and Francis of Háj, the one way to restore confidence was to boost successes in small skirmishes into great victories or sometimes to invent those altogether. The city of Kutná Hora, for instance, was "conquered" by this propaganda more than once.

A manoeuvre of this sort succeeded, for the time being, in counter-acting the desintegration of Matthias' political front in Silesia. He himself wrote from Bratislava that he intended soon to return to Olo-mouc with his troops, whereas in truth he was about to leave for Buda,

---

[44] Eschenloer, L., 229–230 (German, II, 209–212).

[45] Eschenloer, G., II, 194–196. For a similar expression of defeatism in Bohemia see the letter of the administrator of the Catholic archiepiscopal chapter of Prague, Hanuš of Kolovrat, to Rudolf of Breslau, in which he describes how the Catholics of Moravia are demoralized by the hopelessness of the war and the absence of Catholic services, and begin the waver in their loyalty; *FRA*, II, 608–609.

where he spent all winter. At the same time Zdeněk of Sternberg reported a great victory over the people of several Bohemian cities—with 1,000 heretics killed—which, at most, was a small skirmish not mentioned in any other source.[46] This propaganda, however, momentarily had the desired effect of stemming the threatening wave of defections. Thereupon the planned campaign into Silesia was indeed undertaken by the Czechs.[47] The major thrust went into the duchy of Opole (Oppeln), where an army of 4,000, under Wenceslas Vlček of Čenov, established a strongpoint on both sides of the Oder River, which was then used for raids in many directions, while Wölfl of Warnsdorf undertook a similar action, though with smaller forces, in the region of Brzeg (Brieg). In many parts of Silesia—as once during the Hussite Wars—people now tried to buy themselves free from the threatened destruction by large money payments.[48] In general the Silesian princes and cities, even if most of them did not dare to openly renounce their loyalty to Matthias, tried at this time to slip out of any commitments into a position of neutrality.

This, as was mentioned before, was also the policy of a growing number among those Catholic lords who had once joined the League of Zelená Hora. It had become more widespread early in 1470, in a rather unexpected way, which was intimately connected with events in Bavaria.[49]

For some time there had been a conflict between the two Dukes of Bavaria-Munich, Albert and Otto. Albert had dismissed the hereditary marshal of the duchy, Hans of Degenberg and Nussberg, and had driven him out of the country. Hans had found refuge with King George, and when the struggle between the dukes intensified he had asked the King's permission to use the services of several western Bohemian barons, all so far members of the league, in waging war against Duke Albert. Albert was rather close to Duke Louis and his chancellor Martin Mair, who had become such a determined enemy of George. He had in 1469, together with Louis, signed the treaty of alliance with Matthias, and the latter had even mentioned the possibility of making him governor of Bohemia. Thus a war against Duke Albert would weaken the whole Wittelsbachs party and would help to punish a man whom George had reason to consider dangerous. It

[46] *Ibid.*, 212.
[47] Długosz, *Opera omnia*, XIV, 541.
[48] Eschenloer, G., II, 194–196.
[49] Palacký, *Dějiny*, IV, 2, 545–546, and n. 435 (in German, 629–630, n. 434). Among other sources, see Gemeiner, *Regensburgische Chronik*, III, 461–463.

was therefore in George's interest to permit the shift of forces. The ten or twelve lords in question—we do not know their names—not only left the league and promised neutrality but strengthened the front of those princes—now also including Duke Otto of Bavaria—who wanted to liquidate the war and to preserve George's position on the throne of Bohemia.

Whereas the understanding about this quiet arrangement had largely gone through the mediation of the Bavarian lord marshal, direct negotiations followed shortly. In November 1470 a meeting between some of the King's councillors and a number of leaguist barons took place in the town of Rokycany in the Pilsen district.[50] In Pilsen, at the same time, Zdeněk of Sternberg was present, surely to watch carefully for what was going to come out, yet without taking any part in the negotiations. But at this meeting, in any case around this time, another of the earliest, most prominent and most energetic leaders of the League of Zelená Hora, Lord Burian of Gutstein, made his peace with George and acknowledged him again as his King.[51] Gutstein had been among a small number of barons who had shown some oppositional tendencies back in 1461, had helped to found the league in 1465, and had, at Matthias' election at Olomouc, accepted from him the office of chief justice of the royal court chamber. His change of sides was probably based on his feeling that Matthias' attitude toward the high nobility was more arbitrary and absolutist than had been George's. He remained on George's side and was, after his death, a vigorous supporter of his successor, Vladislav II, against Matthias.[52]

Burian of Gutstein was only one of several. But there was also one prominent servant of King George who, sometime in 1470, changed sides. This was Albert Kostka of Postupice. His role during the negotiations at Vilémov and Olomouc seems to have been considered rather ambiguous by King George's other advisers. Whether they had good reasons to suspect him, or whether he merely resented their suspicion—in any case we soon find him among Matthias' Czech courtiers. He also accepted the full Catholic ritual—the only important Utraquist leader to do so all through these years.[53] The great Utraquist tradition of this family was maintained by his younger brother, John Kostka of Postupice, and some of his nephews.

[50] *AČ*, I, 326, and *FRA*, II 46, 139.
[51] See about him in some detail, Urbánek, *Věk*, IV, 469.
[52] Tomek, *Dějepis*, VII, 395.
[53] See Palacký, *Dějiny*, IV, 2, 550 n. 440 (in German, 634 n. 439).

Another loss for George which was, however, more apparent than real, was the town of Cheb. This ethnically German city, center of a district which had always had close ties to the Franconian regions west of Bohemia, had yet been one of King George's favored places. Several of the most important congresses and conferences had taken place there, and until now the city had steadfastly refused to abandon the King and withstood even a lengthy period of excommunication for this sake. Finally, finding further resistance too difficult and costly, she gave in, but in a purely formal way, and at the same time tried to get special protection from a man who, at this time, showed himself again as one of George's most active and effective friends among the German princes: Albert Achilles.[54]

The Brandenburg margrave, who for so many years had, in the politics of the Empire, played a role far superior to the small Franconian territory he could call his own, had recently acquired much additional strength. His brother Frederick II, who had no sons, had abdicated on April 2, 1470, for reasons of age and poor health after a reign of 30 years, and Albert now became the ruler of all Hohenzollern lands and one of the seven electors.[55] The recent rapprochement between King George and the Emperor, together with his own increased strength, would clearly make it desirable for the Emperor to regain Albert's friendship. It would be all the more valuable for him as his own relations to the most powerful member of the house of Wittelsbach, Elector Frederick of the Palatinate, had during the last few months drastically deteriorated.[56] Disregarding warnings of the Emperor, the Palsgrave had attacked the imperial city of Weissenburg in Alsace. The Emperor answered with the imperial ban and categorically refused all attempts at mediation made by the Bavarian Wittelsbach and some other princes. The stage seemed set for restoring the old, intimate friendship between the Emperor and the new head of the house of Hohenzollern, whose relation to the Palsgrave had never been good. Albert's rehabilitation in the eyes of the Emperor had already been well prepared for by another Albert, the young Duke of Saxony, the Emperor's nephew and King George's son-in-law.

The Emperor, since late summer, had resided in the Carinthian town of Villach, which, for a while, had become an important diplo-

---

[54] See *FRA*, II, 20, 603–604, 631; *ibid.*, 42, 418–420, 494–499, 509. See also the detailed narrative in H. Sturm, *Eger, Geschichte einer Reichsstadt*, I, 109–114, and II, 234–235.

[55] Regarding the transfer of power from Frederick to Albert see Gundling, *Leben und Thaten Friderichs des Andern*, pp. 615–620.

[56] For the background see Bachmann, *Reichsgeschichte*, II, 300–304.

matic center. There he invited the Elector of Brandenburg, who, in October, followed the call and spent the later fall and early winter at the Emperor's court. He was, as he reported, received with unusual honors, was solemnly enfeoffed with the electoral dignity and the office of imperial chamberlain, and received the long-coveted acknowledgment of Brandenburg claims to the duchies of Pomerania. He also received the assurance that the Emperor would work for the withdrawal of his excommunication. It was only natural that this would presuppose a settlement of the Czech question out of which Rome's dissatisfaction with Albert had grown. From Albert's accounts it emerges very clearly that this settlement between Prague and Rome —long considered an utter impossibility except on the basis of total subjection—was now, at least by the Emperor, considered a virtual certainty, and one which would come about in the very near future.[57]

The official pronouncements of the Curia did not show much change, and, among the papal legates, Lorenzo Roverella, at least, would have been utterly averse to any compromise. But his word had only limited influence, and his far more powerful predecessor, Cardinal Carvajal, was no longer living. When Matthias, well aware of the weakness of his Bohemian kingship without a valid coronation, asked to be sent a crown especially consecrated by the Holy Father, as a true Bohemian royal crown, Paul II instead sent him, with his blessings, a precious hat and a consecrated sword, together with a moderate sum of money. It was an honor, if taken as such, but it did not strengthen Matthias' claim. It still seemed an open question whether the Pope, in the end, would come out in favor of Matthias or Casimir.[58] Yet for the first time it was possible for representatives of Czech Catholics faithful to King George to dwell in Rome and to begin unofficial negotiations. And these negotiations found active support now from the Emperor and the rulers of Poland and Saxony.

None of these acted without strong motivation. Frederick III had realized, after Vilémov, the danger in which he would be if ever

[57] See his report, of late December or early January, to William of Saxony, in *FRA*, II, 44, 668–675, with the remark on George: "Des Girsiken sach wirdet gericht, das bit seine lieb [the Emperor] in gehaym zu halten." (p. 669). For the background see also Bachmann, *Reichsgeschichte*, II, 309–310. Specifically for the reconciliation of Albert and Frederick III, and its implications upon Brandenburg's rights to Pomerania, see Felix Rachfahl, *Der Stettiner Erbfolgesstreit, 1464–1472*, Breslau, 1890, pp. 267–274.

[58] For Paul's attempt to leave the issue open between the two main contenders (perhaps because a reconciliation with George was now no longer considered quite impossible), see Długosz, *Opera omnia*, XIV, 537–538. For other sources see Palacký, *Dějiny*, IV, 2, 572 n. 454 (in German, 659 n. 453).

George and Matthias were his joint enemies, and he had no longer any doubts about which of the two was, for him, the more dangerous. The King of Poland was aware that his hopes for a Jagiellon on the Czech (and possibly also on the Hungarian) throne could now be achieved only with, not against, George's good will and that one way to achieve this good will might be to bring about an understanding between Prague and Rome. For the Saxon princes—among whom, after some considerable time, we find also Duke William of Weimar— one of the main impulses was the economic needs of their countries. The attempt made by the papal legates to enforce a complete blockade of Bohemia, while never fully successful and never willingly enforced by the Saxon dukes, had nevertheless done much more harm to Saxony than to Bohemia.[59] There had recently been a relaxation of the pressure exerted especially by the Bishop of Breslau, but this in itself indicated that renewed activity in Rome by a Saxon embassy might have far better chances now than at any time before. While not free of wavering, the Wettin princes had, by and large, felt that they had done for their kinsman across the border all that had been in their power. But he was important enough for them so that now, conditions having improved so much, they would willingly make a far greater effort. (This all the more as the Saxon princes, as intimate with the Emperor as possible, had recently begun also to develop closer ties with Casimir of Poland,[60] who requested their support for papal confirmation of the Peace of Torun.) As a specially impressive token of this fully restored close friendship, Duke William of Saxony agreed, sometime in the second half of 1470, that his daughter Catherine, affianced earlier to Duke Hynek (Ignatius) of Münsterberg, King George's youngest son, should now actually be married to the Czech prince. It was an act which, not long before, would surely have led to Duke William's excommunication, as had happened, for the same reason, to Margrave Albert Achilles. Now "the mixing of good-Christian and heretical blood" caused hardly a ripple.[61] The atmosphere had indeed changed.

[59] There is a good deal of material on this in the Saxon sources, some of it not yet published. See e.g. the references in Ermish, "Studien z. Gesch. d. sächs.-böhm. Beziehungen," II, 1881, 36-37, 41-42.

[60] Possibly in agreement with George. See Ermisch, *"Studien z. Gesch.,"* 44.

[61] See the mildly head-shaking expression of the dean of the Prague Cathedral chapter, John of Krumlov, in his letter to Roverella in *FRA,* II, 20, 646. There also appears information that the blockade was breaking down everywhere and that not only the Saxons but also Nürnberg and Regensburg were openly trading again with Bohemia, presumably sending their goods through the Franconian territories of Elector Albert Achilles.

Matthias Corvinus was very much aware of this change of atmosphere. What probably bothered him most was the suspicion that he had no longer the full backing of the Holy See, and that Rome was actually considering a compromise solution. Late in 1470 he sent a message to the Pope (with strong support also from Lorenzo Roverella), complaining that the leaders of the Polish embassy which had visited the Czech encampment in Moravia (in Malenovice) had promised the heretics that King Casimir, in union with other princes, would achieve for them the confirmation of the Compacts. The Pope's answer, of December 1470, criticized such promises which dared to anticipate the decisions of the Holy See, and soon afterwards he also urged the Emperor not to abandon his alliance with the King of Hungary. But Matthias was shrewd enough (and sufficiently used to employ duplicity himself) to smell an ambiguous attitude when he came across it.[62] His isolation had proceeded at an alarming rate, and he was not going to look on quietly, without a serious attempt to regain for himself the political initiative.

Sometime toward the end of the year, probably shortly before Christmas, Matthias submitted far-reaching peace proposals to George. He was ready to guarantee him the rule over the whole of the kingdom of Bohemia proper for the rest of his life. He would release Duke Victorin from his imprisonment and would agree to his elevation to the rank of Margrave of Moravia.[63] (This, presumably, would imply Victorin's functioning in the margraviate as his, Matthias', governor, since he did not intend to give up either his title or his rights of rulership either to the dependencies or, after George's death, to the kingdom itself.) If he, Matthias, should eventually die without male offspring, Victorin and his brothers would be the heirs of the whole realm. Matthias suggested that King George send negotiators to meet with his own representatives at the town of Polna, near the Moravian-Bohemian border.

Matthias' offer was clearly interesting enough for George to find out

[62] See above, n. 58.
[63] Our only source is Długosz (*Opera omnia*, XIV, 549–550), whose overly terse language tends to cause differences in interpretation. Thus Tomek, for instance (*Dějepis*, VII, 287), assumes that the elevation of Victorin to the rank of margrave would only take place when, at George's death, Matthias became actual ruler of Bohemia proper. There is however, nothing in Długosz's wording to support this assumption. Długosz, incidentally, speaks of an elevation to Margrave of Moravia *"or Silesia,"* which seems unlikely, as there had never been such a title. The elevation to "Margrave of Moravia," on the other hand, would seem most appropriate for the King's son, who had, for some time before the war, been in fact the governor of the margraviate, and it might even have been part of Matthias' rather successful effort to gain or regain the friendship of his honorably imprisoned brother-in-law.

as much as he could about it. He sent three of his chief advisers: William of Rabí and Riesenberg, Peter Kdulinec of Ostromíř, and Beneš of Veitmil. Matthias' representatives were Zdeněk of Sternberg, Albert Kostka, and Bishop Tas of Olomouc. It is a pity that we know so little about these intriguing negotiations. From this little, however, we can conclude that Sternberg, this time, had strict orders to behave in a way very different from that in which he had seen fit to treat two of George's three ambassadors, Veitmil and Kdulinec, when they had approached him in their King's service at Olomouc in 1469. They, on their part, must have found it strange to be addressed by three men, all members of the high nobility of their own country, each of them at one time a close friend of their King but now, in the eyes of George's representatives, traitors to their King. Yet it was these men, according to the report we have,[64] who now tried to speak the language of patriots. They asked George's ambassadors (and through them the Czech people) to weigh the welfare of the common fatherland. If they persisted in accepting the King of Poland's oldest son, Władysław, as their future King, they would expose this country to prolonged and still more fatally devastating war. If, on the other hand, Matthias followed upon George's death, then they would gain a powerful, wise, and rich King who, besides, would be able to regain for the Czech people, far more easily than the King of Poland, the good graces of the Pope and his permission to retain the Basel Compacts. George's ambassadors agreed to present these offers to a diet of the Czech estates to be called to Prague for February 14th, and, at that diet, Matthias' offer was discussed at some length. But in this situation King George, too, had a very powerful and indeed the decisive voice.

It was not in George's character to drop an offer like Matthias' without looking at it carefully. It did, after all, have considerable attractions. In fact the arguments brought forward by Matthias' ambassadors all sounded perfectly plausible and convincing. If Matthias could be trusted, his offer, and his offer alone, could immediately end the war, save many lives, preserve towns and villages—considerations which weighed heavily with George. If Matthias could be trusted, then indeed it should be easier for him than for almost anybody else, including King Casimir, to regain for George the favor of the Pope and some form of a recognition of the Compacts. If Matthias could be trusted, then George's sons would, under the proposed treaty, have a better, securer position than under the conditions so far proposed from

---

[64] Again Długosz, *Opera omnia*, XIV, 549–550.

Cracow. And if Matthias died without heir (as indeed he was going to do), the way would be open for the house of Poděbrady to retain the throne and firmly to establish a national dynasty. These should have been truly powerful inducements.

If only Matthias could be trusted. But was it not obvious that he could not be trusted? Had he not broken his royal word of honor, solemnly pledged at Vilémov? Had he made the slightest attempt to work for the reconciliation between Prague and Rome, as he had then promised?

George had already expressed the answer in his message to the Hungarian noblemen of July 30, 1470: "He did not keep any of the promises he had made." Matthias' cynical policy now caught up with him, to the great disadvantage, as we may say with the wisdom of hindsight, of both realms. For there is no question that, whatever his faults, Matthias would have been a vastly better King of Bohemia than the weak teenager who followed George. Indeed the whole development of Central Europe might have been different and probably better, if Matthias' offer could have been accepted, that is, if he could have been trusted.

Yet for George, it seems, there was no longer any possibility of trusting him. He had gone much too far in doing just that. He could not repeat this. He would not again act with that almost naïve gullibility which he had permitted himself at Vilémov. If he now engaged in any negotiations, if he allowed any serious discussions of Matthias's proposal also at the February diet, then the purpose was not to give the scheme any real chance. As long as he could maintain the impression that he took it very seriously, the offer could yet be useful. It enabled him to put greater pressure on King Casimir to accept the conditions under which the young prince had been designated as his successor.[65] At the earliest moment, perhaps still before the end of the year, and apparently in some secrecy, he sent one of his most trusted friends among the Catholic clergy, Paul, Provost of Zderaz, to King Casimir, who then dwelled in Lithuania.[66]

The Polish King, clearly shocked, reacted with great speed. It was

---

[65] This is also the interpretation given to George's attitude at this time by Papée, *Studya i szkice,* 124.

[66] Not in Cracow, as Bachmann (*Reichsgeschichte,* II, 321) says. The greater distance has some significance for the dating of the whole affair, as we know that Jacob of Dębno, with instructions based on the provost's message to King Casimir, arrived in Prague latest in mid-February, a fact not mentioned by Bachmann. We must therefore assume that Matthias' action was started still in December 1470, in spite of his simultaneous protests to Rome.

again Jacob of Dębno, repeatedly Casimir's chief negotiator in Prague as well as in Rome, who was sent to save the situation. In Prague he found his task none too easy.[67] What exactly were his promises we do not know, but they must have been far-reaching, and he considered it a great success when the diet, with George's assent, agreed to postpone any final decision on the issue till he had concluded negotiations with the Holy See. And indeed it was a success for Poland, though one which George had intended all along. As the trip to Rome would, of course, take considerable time—he did not cross the Alps until the end of March[68]—it did in itself come near enough to destroying any chance for the Hungarian offer. Matthias was not a patient man and would not wait very long.

It was not Jacob of Dębno and his embassy who successfully overcame most of the resistance that still survived in Rome against a modus vivendi with King George. It is certain that King George had had someone whom he personally trusted at work in Rome for some time, though we have no details about this.[69] But progress had also been made during the last few months by the Saxon dukes and their representatives in Rome. Prominent among them was the Meissen chancellor Hermann of Weissenbach, who spent a considerable time of the fall of 1470 and the following winter in Rome for this purpose,[70] supported in increasing measure by the Emperor's permanent representative Cilly. Another Saxon legation was already on its way to Rome before the Polish mission had even reached Prague, and arrived in the Holy City on March 20, 1471. It carried with it a series of suggestions organized in ten clauses which, at least in several of its main points, had obviously received the approval of King George, though we cannot be sure whether the final formulation had been seen by

[67] When Długosz (*Opera omnia*, XIV, 550) claims that without his arrival and his great speech before the Czech diet Matthias' offer would certainly have been accepted, then this is probably based on the somewhat self-congratulatory report of the ambassador who wanted to put his diplomatic merits in this important question in the brightest possible light.

[68] Papée, *Studya i szkice*, 140.

[69] This secret emissary seems to have succeeded in gaining very fully the confidence and friendship of at least one Cardinal, whose name is also unknown. (See Palacký, IV, 2, 571, in German, 657). We have, however, a letter of George's to this Cardinal in which, probably sometime in the course of 1470, he emphasized his deep conviction that he had never thought of himself as standing outside the Church Catholic, nor believed that there was any salvation "*extra* ecclesiam." See FRA, 20, 639, as well as Raynaldus-mansi, *Annales Ecclesiastici*, X, 502. See furthermore the valuable material presented by J. Hamršmid, "Co věřil král Jiří o přijímání pod obojí způsobou," in *Sborník historického kroužku*, Prague, 1893, I. 36–39.

[70] See Ermisch, "Studien z. Gesch.," II, 47, also for the following lines.

him.[71] The whole diction of the document seems to indicate that proposals on these lines had been characterized as probably acceptable by representatives of the Curia before. The proposals immediately underwent a serious and, it seems, relatively open-minded study by a committee of the Sacred College—men who no longer had to tremble before the wrath of Carvajal—as well as by Pope Paul himself. The committee then turned them over, it seems for further, direct negotiations, to Cardinal Francesco Piccolomini of Siena. In the accompanying directives the maintenance of strict secrecy was requested, but Legate Roverella, Bishop of Ferrara, was to be informed.

Among the main points of this series of suggestions the first one was King George's public declaration that he did not believe nor had he ever thought or said that there was no salvation for those not taking the communion in both kinds. This, of course, the King had repeatedly declared before, the last time in his public pronouncement to the German princes and cities at New Year 1470, and he was certainly willing to repeat it as often as necessary. Another group of clauses (2, 3, and 5) referred to the appointment of a capable Catholic cleric as Archbishop of Prague. He would head the Bohemian Church in the normal way, would direct the elimination of errors or misdeeds among the clergy (presumably including the Utraquist priests), and would receive the King's protection as well as the possession and full use of castle and town of Roudnice. (Roudnice, of course, was an old possession of the archbishopric of Prague, but had, with other church estates, been acquired cheaply by the Sternbergs. It had been lost by Zdeněk of Sternberg early in the war, and it is ironical that just this loss, and this gain by the heretics, should now help the Church to regain possessions which otherwise the great lords were never willing to let go.) King George would furthermore (point 6) do his best to facilitate the return of other former ecclesiastical estates to the church.

The central issue among the proposals as well as the negotiations which developed around them was, of course, the question of the Eucharist (points 4 and especially 8). One of the main difficulties here was the widespread usage, backed by the Utraquist Church, of giving

---

71 Raynaldus-Mansi, *Annales Ecclesiastici,* 503–505. Strangely, neither Palacký nor Bachmann paid any attention to this highly interesting document. Only Tomek gives an adequate excerpt of it and of the commentaries added by the committee of cardinals (*Dějepis,* VII, 291–292). A Ms dated April 8, which must have been, directly or indirectly, the basis of Raynaldi's publication, is contained in the Secret Vatican Archives, under A r m XXXIX 12, fol. 130–133. A photostat of this was kindly put at my disposal by Prof. Josef Macek, in Prague. There are no deviations in the text, but it contains the directive demanding complete secrecy, only Roverella to be informed about this state of affairs.

the communion in both kinds to children and infants. This usage had never been permitted, owing to Czech resistance at the time, nor specifically forbidden by the Basel Compacts, and it tended to make people believe more firmly in the absolute need of the Chalice for salvation. This child communion should be stopped. If, however, the proposal said, the archbishop and his helpers could not convince people that this custom was wrong, he would refer the issue to the Pope, whose decision would then be upheld by the King. It seems doubtful if this formula had been endorsed by George. If it had, then it is clear that he would encounter considerable resistance from the Utraquist Church in any attempt to enforce it.

As far as adults were concerned, the situation, originally created by the Compacts, would essentially be reinstated. People personally used to having the communion in two kinds and desiring it "out of the zeal of their religious devotion" should be permitted to retain it. They should, however, not take it daily but be led, as to the frequency of their communion, by the advice of their confessor. There should be no arrangement which would, in specific towns or villages, make the communion in the two kinds obligatory—a policy which had been favored by Rokycana. This paragraph concludes with the hope (similar to that contained in early Catholic commentaries to the Compacts) that, since permission is only given to living adults, the deviation would not survive very long—a hope surely not shared by King George. The preserved marginal comment from the cardinals says: "This chapter is of great importance, and needs careful consideration. It is not easy to concede so much even to adults, since the Compacts have already expired." This is a rather revealing utterance coming from the Curia at this moment, for it indicates the position taken in the midst of serious negotiations. As such this position, the expression of reluctance but by no means a refusal, had little in common with the bitter and vengeful utterances about Utraquist communion coming from the same circles for so many years, and still audible, like a late, hollow echo, in the actions and words of the zealous and not yet fully informed Legate Roverella.

We cannot, on the other hand, wonder that there should be the demand for such careful consideration. Where hostility and distrust had dominated so long, it was difficult to assume suddenly a complete absence of such feelings. And, after all, the Curia was expected, besides the rather cautious and limited concession of the Chalice, to retract completely all the punitive measures taken against George. He would, so clause 10 says, "be restituted in his royal dignity, would be addressed with his royal title, and would be considered, treated and presented as the King of Bohemia by the Apostolic See." In return the King would offer his full obedience to the Apostolic See. Again the commentary of the cardinals is noteworthy. It merely asks whether it might not be wise to see for a limited period how things work out before so complete a rehabilitation is granted. But there is no outright demand for such a postponement.

There was one man who, being rather impulsive, seems to have been ready to go farther than the cardinals: Pope Paul himself. It seems that he had finally come to the conclusion which Rudolf of Breslau had expressed some time before: that he had been badly informed about the whole struggle.[72] We have a report from one of the Saxon ambassadors, Nicholas of Köckeritz, who describes in detail the discussion he had with the Pope.[73] In this interview he had summed up and added some details to several of the points contained in the Saxon proposals. Indeed it almost looks as if here we have to do with a second, parallel group of proposals, largely but not wholly identical and more specifically endorsed by George. He emphasized especially the fact that the King was ready to leave the appointment of a new Archbishop of Prague to the Pope; that the archbishop was to supervise all priests in Bohemia, opening the way to proper ordination to those who had not received but deserved it; finally that all people demanding the communion in the two kinds after consultation with their confessors should be entitled to it, while the issue of child-communion should be examined anew regarding its possible validity. (Here we encounter a noticeable difference, as in the ten points child-communion had already been considered inadmissible.) The ambassador, in this audience, showed the Pope a document of accreditation, signed by King George.

After prolonged secret negotiations the Pope told the Saxon ambassadors that, if the King of Bohemia was willing to fulfill what he had offered to do, then he would, on coming to Rome, "receive such honors and be shown such reverence as in the time of our lives had never yet been offered to any King of Bohemia . . . and we shall not

---

[72] See also Heimburg: "Der heilig vater hat nit gevallens daran, das man im sodche mere anbracht hat von kung and von kungreich," in his letter to Elector Albert Achilles of February 27th, in Priebatsch, I, 216.

[73] For the following see the important article by Otto Eduard Schmidt: "Des Böhmenkönigs Georg von Podiebrad Lösung vom Kirchenbann und sein Tod," *Neues Archiv für sächsische Geschichte*, LIX, Dresden, 1938, 39–65.

only meet him on his way but shall carry him on our own arms toward and through the gates of the city of Christ. When, however, one of the witnesses remarked to this declaration of his Holiness that for this the King of Bohemia was too heavy, so much so that he had difficulty carrying himself, the Pope answered: Well, perhaps not a long way but at least for a short distance we will carry him." There is, in this amusing utterance, some melancholy irony. For the unusual heaviness of King George was a symptom of his ebbing health, and the Pope, who wanted to meet him and to carry him in his arms, if only for a short distance, was himself fated to survive the King of Bohemia only by a few months.

All these negotiations were conducted in complete secrecy. It would not do at this moment to alarm Matthias. Thus care was taken not to let the legates know what was being considered.[74] But the secrecy had another advantage: if the negotiations should not have a positive outcome, the Curia could later deny that they had gone on. George's descendants, on the other hand, considered the reports of the Saxon ambassadors (which have only recently come to light again) as a proof that the King's excommunication had actually been lifted before his death.[75] For this, however, our reports give hardly any adequate proof, as at the time of his death the negotiations had not yet been concluded.

The question should still be asked whether it is likely that George had been willing to accept at least the bulk of the concessions contained in the Saxon proposals, and whether, if so, he had not conceded more than the Utraquist clergy and the more ritually and theologically conscious among his subjects would have been willing to accept. Perhaps the answer to both questions ought to be in the affirmative. It is clear that King George was eager to be recognized again as "a true Christian King." There was a time when he would have defended John Rokycana's position as the Archbishop of Prague. But now, early in 1471, Rokycana was a very old man, far beyond his three score and ten, and, it seems, suffering from the effects of a light

---

[74] See again Heimburg: "Das wirdt auch so still gehandelt, daz die legaten, die im Land umlaufen, nit ervarn bis all ding ergeet." (Priebatsch 216). This was, however, not true, as we have seen earlier, in relation to Roverella who presumably had to be warned in order not to make further promises to Matthias.

[75] See the detailed discussion of this aspect in Schmidt, *op.cit.*, Pastor (II, 408–409) is probably right in pointing out that Paul's later reference to George as "damnate memorie" shows that the absolution had not been given, clearly owing to the King's premature death. It is strange, on the other hand, that Pastor does not mention with one word the course of the negotiations which was already clearly reflected in Raynaldi's publication.

stroke. He would not, one could assume, be at the head of his church for long [76] and his claims had not been actively upheld for some time even by the Utraquist estates. It would be unrealistic to let his position, so doubtful in terms of church law and church politics, stand in the way of a possible settlement. Above all, of course, Rokycana himself had been worried by the absence of a bishop able to ordain priests.

There can be little doubt that the literal and complete acceptance of the Saxon proposals, especially of such clauses as the abolition of child-communion, would cause resistance among some of the Utraquist clergy and laity. Yet George, though a religious man, had never been deeply concerned with liturgical detail and had probably never fully understood some of the implications of the independent theological development of Utraquism. For him there was one great issue at stake: would it be possible again, in Bohemia, for adult laymen to take the Chalice without being called "heretics," thus restoring internal peace. True, as earlier, the Church clearly would not consider this a permanent solution. But on the basis of a similar non-permanent settlement—the Compacts—there had, after all, been religious peace, or at least the absence of bloody religious struggle, for several decades. King George would probably be satisfied with a similar solution which would enable him, as he could hope, to reunite the realm and lead it to a new period of strength and health. For this, surely, he could expect to gain the support of a substantial majority of his war-weary people.

There was still another reason why, for George, the direct understanding with the Curia may, in his present situation, have been of higher value than ever before. He had decided against Matthias' peace offer. He was half bound to the offer made by the Czech estates to the King of Poland. But only half-bound. So far Casimir had not accepted and, as things turned out, never accepted a condition which George was not willing to sacrifice: the marriage of Prince Władysław with his daughter Ludmila, which would make their descendants at least half-Czech and would safeguard the position of his sons as the new King's brothers-in-law. As long as this was not accepted by Casimir, George had not lost his freedom of action. He knew that the Curia (though in earlier times it had offered the Czech crown to Casimir) was now no longer eager to support the Jagiellon claim. If full peace with Rome was restored without any effective help from Poland, then

---

[76] That his death was, at this time, thought of as likely to occur soon seems to emerge from the last letter the Brethren wrote him. See Müller, *Geschichte der böhmischen Brüder* I, 162–163 (in Bartoš's Czech edition 100–102).

perhaps the old hope for a succession of one of his sons—preferably Prince Henry—could be revived and Bohemia would retain a Czech national monarchy. The chances for reaching this goal did not look bad in these early months of 1471.

In Prague, as the winter began to turn toward spring, the general mood at the King's court continued to rise. The Emperor had meanwhile concluded an alliance with King Casimir which could only be directed against Matthias.[77] Frederick's attitude toward the King of Bohemia was now friendly and full of promise, especially since, upon the King's order, George of Stein had, in October 1470, given up all his claims against the Emperor.[78] In February Frederick III wrote a cordial letter to George, informing him that he was calling to Regensburg a great diet devoted to the war against the Turks, but that all outstanding questions, also in regard to Bohemia, would be fully solved at that time.[79] The same information came from Elector Albert Achilles, who could not speak strongly enough about the good will of the Emperor.[80] He also knew and informed Heimburg that now the Bavarian dukes, through the mediation of Saxony, were trying to reestablish their friendship with Bohemia, which had been so completely abandoned. But the elector was confident that King George was too well informed about Dr. Mair's intrigues at all meetings of the reichstag, and of Bavarian support for the "crusaders," to let the Wittelsbachs get off that lightly.[81]

Among those recently irreconcilable enemies who in these weeks groped for a way toward reconciliation was even the grimmest of them all: Zdeněk of Sternberg. The great baron had always wanted to be on the winning side, and now, for the first time, it looked decidedly as if this was to be George. In addition Zdeněk had had serious troubles with Matthias.[82] His son Jaroslav, for some time governor of the Lusatian Sixtowns, had been considered incompetent by Matthias. The King had therefore removed him, without even informing the father, and had put a Silesian prince in his place. Soon afterwards, in late January, the Bishop of Breslau reported at a meeting in Görlitz that Matthias was very annoyed with Zdeněk, who had made arrogant

[77] On October 20, 1470. See the treaty in Dogiel, *Codex diplomaticus regni Poloniae* I, 163.
[78] See Bachmann, *Reichsgeschichte*, II, 318.
[79] See Priebatsch, I, 219; the same in *FRA*, II, 20, 512.
[80] Priebatsch, I, 222–223.
[81] *Ibid.*, 229.
[82] For the following see *FRA*, II, 20, 640–642; also Eschenloer, G., II, 215–216.

claims for cities and estates in Moravia for himself and his sons. Even at that time it seems that the King had heard rumors about Zdeněk's attempts to regain contact with King George for his own sake. Matthias declared that he did not care in the least what Zdeněk did, and if he should decide to revert again to "Girsik," this would mean as much to him, Matthias, as if one of his dogs died.

In a position as unpleasant as this, Zdeněk did indeed try to regain access to George, using, "in a subtle way," as Heimburg reported, the mediation of the estates. He had more sponsors among the lords around King George than could have been expected, not because of his "virtues" but because even these lords were quite willing to gain some additional strength as a counterweight against too much power in the hands of a victorious King. In the end, however, they were unsuccessful, and Zdeněk had to stay where he had been for so long.[83]

There had once been a time when George had occasionally supported Matthias against rebellious or recalcitrant lords. But there had rarely been true solidarity among Kings. As things were now, and after what Matthias had done to him, King George received with real pleasure the news of Matthias' troubles with his own high nobility, including the leading prelates. He expected, as he wrote to Elector Albert Achilles on March 9th, further news about these developments in Hungary, and would hasten to pass them on to his old friend.[84] His mind, however, was already on the Moravian-Hungarian border, where, by now, the snow had begun to melt. "For we have the strong hope," he continued, "just as he has drunk with us of the Bohemian beer, so we shall, with God's help, all the more certainly drink with him of the Hungarian wine." It was the word of a man who felt strong enough to undertake, in the near future, a strenuous military campaign which would take him deep into enemy country and would force the King of Hungary to give up all his conquests and claims.

Other news from Prague generally gives the impression that the King, despite his corpulence, was in good shape. His mood, as nearly always, reflected his indestructible optimism. February had been a happy time, the King and Queen had celebrated with some zest both the Lenten time and the marriage of Prince Hynek with Princess Catherine of Saxony.[85]

---

[83] See Heimburg's report to Elector Albert, Priebatsch, I, 216.

[84] See his letter to Elector Albert Achilles of March 9, *FRA*, II, 42, 511–512, and Priebatsch, I, 218–219.

[85] See Duke Henry's slightly earlier letter to Albert, *FRA*, II, 42, 510–511.

On February 22nd, however, an event occurred which was bound to throw a shadow on this pleasant mood. It was the death of Master John Rokycana, the first and only Utraquist archbishop,[86] in many ways the restorer and preserver of Utraquism as a living religious community. No one except George himself had, in the Poděbradian era, been as influential as he. To the more intolerant among the Catholics he was the devil himself. To the Utraquist masses in Prague and in other parts of Bohemia he was a prophet who could not err. Yet, being a strong and masterful personality who did not easily suffer opposition, he had also made some powerful enemies in his own camp, and there were periods when there was tension between him and King George. This, it seems, had not been true for the last two or three years when the King bitterly needed and obtained the backing of this powerful man with his vast influence over the minds of the majority of the Czech people.

King George is reported to have visited Rokycana during his last illness. But when he was buried in the Týn Church which, mainly through him, had become the great cathedral of Hussite Prague, we hear that among the people present were Queen Johanna, the royal princes, and many lords and knights; only the King himself did not come.[87] The presence of the Queen shows clearly that the King's absence was not meant to express lack of feeling over the passing of the great churchman. King George, indeed, had become so heavy, his feet so swollen that he could no longer walk (as he would have to do in the church) on his own legs.[88] It was a somber sign which could not be quite forgotten when all those optimistic reports came out of Prague even in March.

We do not know of any lengthy period during which the illness—dropsy, itself only a symptom of malfunctioning inner organs—would have made the people of Prague aware that their King was dying. Death, it appears, came very suddenly, during the night preceeding March 23rd, just two weeks before George's 51st birthday. Something may have occurred that led to such a quick and unforeseen end—a brain stroke, perhaps, or a heart attack. The King's death at this critical moment stunned not only his friends but the masses of the Czech people in Prague and all over the country. Mourning was deep and

[86] *SLČP*, 175.
[87] *Ibid.*
[88] See Długosz, *Opera omnia*, XIV, 550.

strong, not only among Utraquists but also Catholics.[89] For two days the body laid in state in the town palace where thousands could pay him their last respects. On the 25th of March he was buried, beside the tomb of King Ladislav, in the cathedral of St. Vitus up on Hradčany hill, where his remains still rest. But his intestines, with his heart, were buried in the Týn Church by Rokycana's grave.

The feelings of the Utraquist people about their dead King speak with the voice of the Old Annalist.[90] King George, so he says, "died soon after Master Rokycana, within four weeks. One defended with his word, the other with his sword the Chalice of Christ. . . . He was always found constant in receiving Christ's most precious blood to the day of his death. He died in the midst of this great war. Have mercy, O Lord God, on his dear soul!"

[89] See the letter of Jacob Heimburg, Gregory's son: "mit grossen eren und clage aller leut alhie, *beides wesens*." (Italics are mine.) Priebatsch, I, 230.
[90] *SLČP*, 175.

CHAPTER 23

THE PODĚBRADIAN PHASE OF HISTORY

THE DEATH of King George, at the very moment when he seemed to have achieved the near-miracle of emerging victoriously from his long ordeal, has especially impressed Czech authors as the tragic outcome of a great historical drama. Palacký has perhaps given this feeling its most passionate expression.[1] "Nothing was further needed," he says, not without oversimplifying matters, "than to continue on the course recently begun, in order to make reappear the days of prosperity and blessing. But there interfered from above a will that knows neither barriers nor rules, and called away the distinguished hero in the very moment when, having drunk the cup of suffering to the bitter end, he should finally have been able to create and enjoy renewed public welfare and new glory. Fate, so it seems, has wanted the Czech to be not so much victor as martyr." George's last Czech biographer, Rudolf Urbánek, expressed the idea of an event of tragic dimensions in a less emotional and historically more pertinent way when he wrote: "In few occasions of our history has the death of an individual had such far-reaching consequences for our destiny: George was the pillar on which the vault of the Czech nation rested. His personal rise and fall only summed up the development of the Czech nation. . . . His death shook all of Central Europe, shook, above all, the foundations of Czech national life to their very depths."[2]

There is a good deal of truth in this. It might perhaps be said that not only in Czech history but in all of history the enormous impact of the death of a single man, though not infrequently paralleled, has rarely been surpassed. The Czech people had, at this moment, arrived at a crossroads. Was there any hope that the Czechs, under the leadership of a strong monarchial personality, would go a way not too unlike that which was taken at this time (though with considerable differences from one country to the other) in France and Spain, in Tudor England and soon after in Vasa Sweden? Or, after the recovery

---

[1] *Dějiny*, IV, 2, 5, 75 (in German, 661).
[2] Urbánek, *Husitský král*, 274.

from the shock of the Hussite Revolution, was the Czech high nobility bound to gain the upper hand and finally and lastingly to establish that type of society for which the German term "ständesstaat"
(state dominated by the estates) has no good equivalent in English?

If George had survived, even for a period of ten or fifteen years, and
had been succeeded by one of his sons (presumably Henry), this
might, it seems to us, conceivably have left a chance for the first alternative. His death at this time, when the succession was bound to go
tional way, made the second alternative unavoidable. We shall have to
to the young Polish prince, already elected in a tentative and condi-
discuss what this decision meant for Czech history.

At the moment one of the immediate consequences was the total
collapse of the secret negotiations with the Curia. Francis Cardinal
Piccolomini, new papal legate for the Empire, had, as a result of the
discussions held in Rome, especially with the Saxon legation, received
instructions from the cardinal's committee and the Pope which, if our
meager sources are any guide at all, aimed at a solution acceptable to
both sides, including, above all, a qualified permission to take the communion in both kinds.[3] Whether this understanding, in view of the
difficulties still existing on both sides, would then have come about
cannot be known. But it is obvious that, as long as George was present,
powerful, and surrounded by an increasing number of friends and
allies, among them the Emperor, pressure on the Holy See for a compromise would have continued to grow, especially in view of the Turkish danger which, beginning in the eighth decade, had become steadily
more threatening and acute.

It is perhaps for this reason that the attitude of the Holy See, once
it had been informed about George's death, becomes better understandable. It is certain that all further negotiations now ceased and the papal
legate received new, very different instructions. The Curia now acted
as if there had never been anything like serious negotiations, and Paul
II, only so recently willing to carry King George in his own arms across
the threshold of the Holy City, now referred to him, in a letter to
Legate Roverella in Hungary, as *"Georgius. . . . damnate memorie."* [4]

This seems, at first glance, like a nasty sort of political opportunism.
But under the circumstances it should not be surprising. Paul II was
neither one of the best nor one of the worst Popes, as far as political

---

3 See the sources quoted at the end of the preceding chapter.
4 See Aug. Theiner, *Vetera Monumenta Historica Hungariam sacram illustrantia*, II, Rome,
1860, 425.

opportunism was concerned. And, in purely political terms, his change of attitude makes some sense. To grant concessions to the living George would, from the curial point of view, have been wise if it was repaid by an arrangement which could be presented to the world as the final return of the Czech deviationists into the union of Catholic Christianity. It might lead to an end of the long and costly war and would thereby free forces badly needed against the Turkish threat. But once the great man—he who alone, in the long-held view of the Church, had the power to end the deviation—had died, no such hopes could be entertained with equal confidence in regard to any potential successor.

The secondary candidates who made their appearance soon after King George's death—his son-in-law Albert of Saxony[5] and his son Henry of Münsterberg—were never taken seriously in Rome. The Curia, rightly, took it for granted that the succession would be decided between two men only, Vladislav II, as he was now called, and the King of Hungary. It was Vladislav who, by a great diet held in May at Kutná Hora (where Matthias sought recognition and thereby acknowledged implicitly the doubtful legality of the "Easter game of Olomouc") was elected King. The legality of his kingship was reconfirmed by a solemn coronation with the true Bohemian regalia by Roman Catholic bishops in August.[6] To gain the election he had had to promise to keep and protect the Compacts, and during the earlier part of his reign he was too dependent on the Utraquist nobility and gentry to openly challenge this obligation.

As a presumed protector of heretics—the famous aspersion never ceased—young Vladislav was, of course, not persona grata with Rome.[7] For a while the Curia held back, especially as, in the summer of 1471, it looked as if the King of Hungary might succumb to a simultaneous attack of his domestic enemies and a Polish invasion army. But with his usual mixture of energy, speed, and diplomatic skill, Matthias again weathered the storm, drove the Poles back, punished severely the leaders (but not the backers) of the domestic opposition, and was soon

---

[5] Albert was strongly encouraged to take the initiative by Heimburg. (See *FRA*, II, 42, 514–516, and II, 46, 143.) The duke trusted Heimburg's position, which, however, turned out to be quite weak as soon as the basis of its former strength had gone with the death of George. The Czech estates behaved rather ungratefully and deprived the German lawyer-diplomat of his Bohemian estate. On his last period of life—already a septuagenarian, he survived his royal master only by a year and a quarter—and on the revocation of his excommunication see Joachimsohn, *Heimburg*, 286–287.

[6] See about this phase of events Tomek, *Dějepis*, VII, 305–321.

[7] Sixtus IV, elected later in 1471 at Pope Paul's death, also recognized Matthias as King of Bohemia.

master of the situation. From now on he enjoyed the unwavering support of Rome against Vladislav. When, nevertheless, his renewed attacks on Bohemia had no substantial success it was due neither to Vladislav's allies—his father Casimir and the Emperor—nor to the young King's non-existent military prowess, but rather to the tepid support of the Catholic barons who had been on Matthias' side. They grew steadily less active, and it was the estates on both sides of the battle line who tried to bring about an end to a war which could do nothing but harm to their holdings and in which a total victory of Matthias would merely subject them to a determined and often brutal absolutism.

Those attempts of the estates of both sides—with the high nobility leading—had a first success at a meeting in Německý Brod in 1472,[8] and, though the peace concluded there did not last, similar efforts eventually helped bring about the peace of Olomouc of 1478. In it the Bohemian realm was divided between both Kings, with Vladislav retaining Bohemia proper, Matthias the dependencies, and both rulers acknowledging each other's title.[9] At Matthias' death in 1490, Vladislav was elected King of Hungary as well, and thus the lands of the crown of St. Wenceslas were reunited.

Ladislav's election in Hungary in 1490 did the same thing to that country that it had already done to Bohemia: it permitted the nobility, long tired of having been led by the nose, to throw off such unpleasant tutelage and to have, instead, a king whom they in turn could lead by the nose (or, as they put it themselves, by his plaits). That Vladislav would be this type of ruler could not possibly have been known when the Czechs elected him—first, in 1469 (when he was thirteen, and again in 1471. It was very clear to the Hungarians in 1490 when he had been Bohemia's unkingly king for nineteen years. In the total result the "ständesstaat" triumphed in both Bohemia and Hungary (as it also was to triumph before long, with more strength remaining to the gentry, in Poland, whence Vladislav had come).

The rule of the estates, that is, in fact, the rule of the nobility thus emerged victoriously all over eastern Europe, the area between the slowly disintegrating Holy Roman Empire, the slowly awakening Muscovite giant, and the still furiously expanding military state of the Ottomans. It was an enormous region, reaching from the Baltic to the Black Sea, from the headwaters of Main and Saale in the west to

---

[8] Tomek, *Dějepis*, VII, 329ff.
[9] *Ibid.*, VII, 404–406.

the eastern fringe of the Dniepr valley, huge in size and large in population and all of it ruled over, in the late fifteenth and early sixteenth centuries, by brothers—sons of King Casimir IV.

But the prominence of the nobility did not make for strength. The great "Jagiellon System" collapsed in 1526, when at Mohács the Turks won that battle which led to the destruction and partition of Hungary. (It had been largely Matthias' fault that all chances of throwing the Turks back had been passed up when it might still have been possible. But the desperately poor state of Hungary's defenses in the 1520's was due to the irresponsible selfishness of Hungary's nobility in the years after his death.) For Poland the sixteenth century was, in many regards, still a time of greatness. But there, too, under the particular structure of her "royal republicanism" and parliamentarism, her strength began to wane. And in Bohemia, the rule of the estates, especially under the Jagiellon Kings (who after 1490 were largely absentee rulers) helped, as in the other two kingdoms, to bring about unhealthy changes in the socio-economic structure which were, in the last instance, fatal. The final catastrophe occurred for the Czechs a century later than for the Hungarians, but in both cases it was a single battle which decided the fate of the nation because it revealed the inner weakness of state and society and crippled the will to resist.

What were these unhappy changes? Probably, one of the most crucial was the destruction of the freedom of the peasantry. Here, again, is a remarkable similarity between the developments in all three kingdoms (and we could, here, add large parts of Germany as well). In Bohemia the attack of the baronial class (already supported in this endeavor to some extent by the gentry) began in earnest in 1479 and was continued throughout the following decades.[10] The attack was directed against the freedom of the peasantry to move, especially to migrate into the cities which attracted them much. Legislation of this kind was, for a while, successfully opposed by the cities. Indeed we frequently find, in the later years of Vladislav's reign as well as during the short reign of his son Louis (1416-1426), the cities in a well-organized and centrally led political and at times even military opposition against the nobility. (No urban opposition of such strength or significance existed in Poland or Hungary.) The Czech cities fought against the attempts of the barons to dominate completely and without any checks the government of the country, in particular to exclude

10 See *AČ*, IV, 444ff.

the cities from the general participation in the work of the diets, in legislation and jurisdiction, rights which they had partly gained and partly successfully defended during and after the Hussite Revolution. Their eventual defeat (it did not become final and obvious till the time of the early Habsburgs) had some economic causes. But it was also due to the lack of support by the King (with the exception only, in 1523, of a very short-lived attempt of King Louis to back the cities) and to the alliance which the knights, rather unwisely, concluded with the barons.

In the end not only was the peasantry reduced to unmitigated serfdom, tied to the soil, and burdened with steadily heavier work loads but the cities had lost most of their strength and with it the capacity to form a sound balancing element in the total framework of Bohemia's society and state. During the Hussite Revolution, and also during the great defensive war which King George had had to wage during the last years of his life and reign, the great majority of the Czech people, including the peasants, had been ready to fight because they knew what they had to defend: not only the Chalice, important as this was to them, but also the cities whose people governed themselves and helped to make laws for the nation, and the villages where even with its limited freedoms the peasantry felt at home. All this had radically changed by 1620. By then there were still many people ready to die for their religion, or even to preserve it by emigration. But the masses of the Czech people in town and country had long lost the belief in their ability to defend themselves and their land with arms in hands, as had the masses of the people in most countries of Central and Eastern Europe. Victory, now, simply went to that side which had the stronger and better-paid mercenary armies.

The Czech nobility, in Bohemia and Moravia, was not "all bad," either in the fifteenth, sixteenth, or seventeenth centuries. We have only to think of men such as Zdeněk Kostka, the Rabsteins, the brothers Tovačovský of Cimburg or, at a late time, the Žerotíns of Moravia, who were among the most important patrons and protectors of the Czech and Moravian Brethren. The Czech nobility, going over to Protestantism in growing numbers, soon identified, in agreement with other groups of the population, the religious reform movement, now far broader and more varied, with the idea of national independence to be defended against the alliance of Habsburg absolutism and the Counter-Reformation. There were some dedicated idealists among the men involved in the Czech rebellion of 1618, men noble in spirit as well as in name or rank. But they could not give the needed uplift to a nation in peril because, under the long-time rule of their class, too large a part of this nation had been pressed down into sullen passivity regarding the country's political development and destiny.

The mere fact that this was the course of history, and a course not limited to Bohemia but in so many ways equalled in Hungary and Poland, may tempt us to conclude that this was the only possible course. If this is accepted, then the Poděbradian era appears merely as the prelude to the Jagiellon age and to the national weakening which it implied. It is easy to think of some factors which might support such a view. There is the obvious fact that Bohemia's neighbors travelled the same or a very similar road. But this in itself proves very little. Eastern (or East-Central) Europe was not really as homogeneous a unit as it might appear at first glance. Also the closest of neighbors, with nearly identical historical backgrounds, have frequently taken different courses. (Take the two parts of the Netherlands at the time of the Dutch rebellion, or the separate historical road travelled by Switzerland in comparison to Western Austria or the Upper Rhine region of Germany.) Yet the three kingdoms of the East were not only neighbors. Their fate was interconnected in other ways, such as the common dynasty and its ways and weaknesses.

More support for the assumption that Bohemia's course was unavoidable can perhaps be found in the fact that the struggle between the central power of the king and the divisive and often anarchic power of the high nobility had been an old feature of Czech history even at the time of George, and that there had been various periods when the royal power had been weakened to the point where its chances of recovery became slim. There had not been one of the last Přemyslide rulers—from Přemysl I Otakar down, nearly all of them men with a fair degree of willpower, strength, shrewdness, and competence —who did not collide, sooner or later, with the barons, and in the case of the most impressive among them, Přemysl II Otakar, the opposition of the feudal lords significantly contributed to his tragic end. Of the Luxemburgs, John had had trouble enough, his domestic power was weak, and it was only his son, Charles IV, who again had established a strong central power. Even he did not succeed in having his great work of unifying law reform, the Maiestas Carolina, accepted by the estates. Under Wenceslas IV much of Charles' centralizing work had been undone, and the high nobility seemed to have everything under control until the Hussite Revolution—which part of the lords joined, others opposed—temporarily gave the cities and the great broth-

erhoods, supported by parts of the gentry, the decisive role in the conduct of national affairs. In the interregnum and the period of virtual
anarchy that filled especially the fifth decade of the fifteenth century,
the barons regained a great deal of their strength, economically as well
as politically, though they were as yet unable to deprive the other two
estates of their co-determining role in the national diets. This phase,
finally, was followed by another one of centralized power—the Poděbradian one. It was to be the last one, at least in the framework of an
independent Czech state. And the question now is whether "historical
fate," as it were, or, better, an irreversible historical trend had ordained
that this had to be the last one; that the strong kingship which might
—as it did in Western Europe—have maintained a healthier social
structure and a healthier development never returned, that instead
eventually a different absolutism appeared, coming from without,
hand in hand with the Roman Counter-Reformation, opposed alone
by the "ständesstaat," which now was to become the only visible form
of Czech national strength and independence. In particular we may
ask what factors we can detect in the political and social climate, as
it appeared in this third quarter of the fifteenth century, which should
either have helped or hindered the survival of a stronger kingship.
Some comparison with other European states in a similar stage of
development would perhaps be helpful. (It is obvious, for instance,
that similar ups and downs of royal power can be found also in Western, especially in French history.) And in the framework of this consideration the role and significance of George of Poděbrady himself
may appear in clearer light.

In our search for such factors we have to return to the specific position of the cities. In this regard Bohemia differed very significantly
from the other two kingdoms of Eastern Europe as well as from Germany, and was probably nearest to Western Europe. To begin with,
the number of important royal towns directly under the King and
entitled to representation in diets was larger than in either Hungary
or Poland—far larger in proportionate terms, since Bohemia was the
smallest of the three, but larger even in absolute figures. In addition,
their historical role had been vastly greater. This role, considerable
even throughout most of the fourteenth century, had become truly
crucial and largely dominant during the Hussite Revolution.[11] This was
true for Prague especially during the early phases, and later just as
true for Tabor and her sisters cities and for the member-cities of the

---

[11] See for this Heymann, "The Role of the Towns in the Bohemia of the Later Middle
Ages," *Journal of World History*, II, 2, Paris, 1954, 326–346.

Orebite brotherhood. In Hungary and Poland, the cities, in the same periods, never rose to a leading position on the national scene and were above all still largely dominated by a German patriciate, thus marking them as foreign elements, not fully assimilated and not fully recognized. The great majority of the cities in Bohemia (but far less so in Moravia) had been thoroughly czechized during the Hussite Revolution, and even their dominant upper class, the city patriciate, had, with few exceptions, become mainly Czech. This urban middle class could thus claim to be a substantial part of the Czech nation, now represented in every meeting of the estates through its own curia.

Even though after the battle of Lipany (1434) the baronial class had recovered much of its power and influence, it had not succeeded in reestablishing a monopolistic position in the diets whose decisions—especially between 1439 and 1450—were for a while the only valid authority in the land. Together with the cities the gentry had gained much economic strength and political power. For a while it even looked as if, in order to retain their position, the cities would have to oppose the rise to the power of regency by the young leader of the Utraquists, the Lord of Poděbrady. This, however, proved to be a misapprehension.

The relationship of George of Poděbrady to the cities is one of the central factors concerning the significance of the Poděbradian phase of Czech history. If he wanted to cease being essentially an instrument of his own class, if he wanted to represent and govern the nation as a whole such as he saw and understood it, then he was bound to strengthen, and draw strength from, the other two classes or estates with any influence, the gentry and the cities. With the gentry as a class he rarely if ever had any difficulties, in part because they had become so largely, almost uniformly, Utraquist and were bound to support the lay leader of their religious community. But in regard to the cities, the situation was somewhat more complex. Here original prejudices had to be overcome, and in some cases this was never fully achieved, especially where, as in Breslau or Pilsen, they were fortified by strong religious antipathies. And the prejudices were not quite one-sided. George, it could be said, wanted a society with some sort of balance, one not dominated by any single group or caste, not even by one of the two churches. But if this excluded an over-powerful baronial caste, and if George, for its sake, had to grow above his original, class-bound ideas and goals, it proscribed in his mind even more radically any freedom of action, especially revolutionary action, by the lower classes in the cities. We have seen some examples of this attitude in Tabor, in Jihlava, and in Vienna. We ought to remember that the most determined opposition against George, though presented in religious terms, came from the lower classes of Breslau and Jihlava, not from the patriciate, who took up the struggle much more reluctantly. In most cities the patricians, whether the Czechs in Prague, Kutná Hora, and Hradec Králové or the Germans in Cheb, were the King's good friends. This did not exclude his being generally popular with the masses as well, and, while in his policy we find much to remind us of Charles IV, George never copied his great predecessor's hostile policy toward the craft guilds. On the whole, George's relation to the cities clearly reflects his wish to strengthen them—and within them the conservative, patrician element—as a needed counterweight to the power of the high nobility, but also as an important source of economic and financial strength for the crown—which again, in critical times, could serve him against the baronial rebellion.[12]

George's use of Czech people of burgher origin (such men as Vaněk Valečovský of Kněžmost and Samuel of Hradek) in positions of high influence goes hand in hand with his employment of foreigners of urban middle class origin, men such as Mair, Marini, and Heimburg, especially for diplomatic services.[13] It was a method widely used at this time and soon after by strong monarchs in other countries, such as Louis XI of France, Ferdinand II of Aragon, Henry VII of England, and, just a few decades later, Gustavus I Vasa. In Hungary similar methods were tried by Matthias, but there was less of this in Jagiellon Poland.

Are we justified then in calling George's ideas and methods of government "absolutist"? [14] I have earlier expressed my doubts in this interpretation. It seems to me that what George aimed at was as near to the idea of a strong but constitutional monarchy as we can find it in this age of transition from medieval feudalism to more modern forms of government. We should not talk of absolutism unless there was, as in France (and some time later in Spain) an attempt by the King to get rid of the nation's representative body or at least to deprive it

---

[12] The various town histories of the time give details about the ways on which George, not unlike some of his royal predecessors, strengthened the towns by giving them economic privileges. Good examples can be found, for instance, in the work done by Jos. Dobiáš, *Dějiny královského města Pelhřimova*, Pelhřimov, 1936, II, 1. See also Urbánek, *Věk*, IV, 185ff.

[13] Another man of urban background, a German from Cheb in whom George had great confidence and whom, for his diplomatic services, he raised to knightly rank was Jost of Einsiedel. For bibliographical notes on him see *ibid.*, 28 n. 62.

[14] As Urbánek does, just in relation to his attitudes toward the cities, *ibid.*, 186f.

substantially of its rights and functions. This can hardly be said of George. His goal, in relation to the estates, was not to remove them or to deprive them of their participation, especially in the legislative field, but rather to gain and retain as much influence within their ranks as possible. This he tried to do—and largely succeeded —by raising men whom he could fully trust to the highest position within the royal council. They, in turn, would become spokesmen of the King's policy in the nation's diet. Among these men Zdeněk Kostka was the most important and by all odds the greatest statesman who worked under and for George. He thereby took a notable part in the activity which might well be called, after the English example, the "education of parliament by the King." (In the Curia of the knights, Burian Trčka of Lípa played a similar role.)

It is clear that men such as Zdeněk of Sternberg or even John of Rosenberg did not enjoy or appreciate this sort of "education," of which we have a short but vivid description in the contemporary work of Master Paul Žídek.[15] To some extent the fatal decision for rebellion taken by the league of lords may have been based on the very feeling that, if not more effectively opposed, this policy might before long be too successful and inaugurate a period in which the backing of the estates would give the King a well-nigh unassailable position.

This backing—with the subtraction of the rebels—the King retained. But he was careful throughout to take no important, consequential legislative steps without the agreement of the estates, except, to some extent, in foreign policy which, of course, had always been and would remain the prerogative of the crown. At the same time, by Kostka's improved management of the Kutná Hora mint, by taking up long term loans—some of which were eventually repaid by the sale of crown holdings—and by generally strict and even tight-fisted economizing, the King managed to remain rather independent from the estates in financial terms—an attitude again somewhat reminiscent of that of Henry VII. It is nevertheless true that, in his relation with the estates, especially after the outbreak of the civil war in Bohemia, the King had to watch his step. We have seen that, having attempted to protect by law peasant-freeholders from being pushed into selling their land to members of the nobility, George was eventually forced to retreat, pressured, probably, by the common front of all three curias

---

15 "I have seen with my own eyes the Lord of Rosenberg sitting in the royal council far below the Lord Zdeněk Kostka, and the Lord Kostka was directing the proceedings all the time, and the High Lords all said Amen, with the sweat running down their faces." See Pavel Žídek, *Spravovna*, ed. Zdeněk Tobolka, Prague, 1908, p. 12.

—barons, knights, and cities. The peasantry, then as before or after, had no strong spokesman and no protector if the King did not assume this role. Yet, in a time when enemies rose everywhere inside and outside the kingdom, we can perhaps understand that he was reluctant to expose himself to additional attacks for the sake of the peasantry. Even so, after all, it was due to him that there was no substantial change in the status of the peasantry during his own reign (or soon after). It seems doubtful whether he would ever have yielded to baronial pressure on the issue of peasant freedom of movement in quite the spineless way in which his successor acted or failed to act. The same goes for many other issues.

By discussing what George would have done had he lived longer, or what his successor would or would not have done had he been a different man, we do indeed cross the border from historical findings to historical speculation. Whatever may be our philosophy, we must admit that the discussion of the great "ifs" can never prove anything. On the other hand we cannot admit that, in that day and age, the personal qualities of a man like Vladislav II could have been of secondary importance. There are no "ifs" involved in stating that Vladislav's unusual weakness, consistently displayed during a reign of forty-five years, did give the forces of the nobility, and especially of the baronial class, an unusually good chance to operate freely, never hindered but usually supported by the king, and thereby constantly to gain strength and to weaken all potential or real powers opposed to them. It may still be speculation to say that a less weak-kneed king, a man less deserving of Vladislav's famous nickname "Rex Bene" or "Král Dobře," would, throughout those forty-five years, have left a different imprint upon the development of Czech social and political structure. But there is little speculation in calling it inconceivable that a man of George of Poděbrady's mettle, or even a less powerful yet generally energetic and purposive personality, would have permitted any of the following developments to take place: the almost complete elimination of the royal influence from the workings of the State Supreme Court; the practical elimination of the Royal Court, the one judicial body that had always been essentially the King's own domain; the complete abolition of the King's right to dispose of escheated estates, severely diminishing both his political influence and his money income (through the possible sale of escheated property); practices leading to the far-reaching limitation, if not elimination, of the King's direct income from silver-mining, especially in Kutná Hora; and finally changes in the structure and personal composition of the King's council, which made this body, under George clearly a royal privy council, into an institution directed by and serving the interests of the estates, primarily, of course, of the high nobility.[16]

In the long run it was especially King Vladislav's financial impotence and dependence which, originally due to his lack of personal strength, compounded that political and personal weakness. Finally his preference for his Hungarian residence after 1490, with all the disadvantages of absentee-rulership, contributed to make Vladislav into a mere puppet of the high nobility to an extent which had no parallel at any previous time of Czech history, not even under Wenceslas IV. In this way, then, George's work of consolidating a constitutional but basically strong and sound monarchy was sabotaged and destroyed with a vengeance. From the early sixteenth century on, any chance for a development that might be called "Tudorism" was, in the Bohemian realm, out of the question. It was only by way of a catastrophic collision with an essentially foreign power, the Habsburgs, that Bohemia eventually, like all or almost all other nations on the continent of Europe, entered the age of Absolutism, to the great disadvantage of the Czech people as a whole.

Seen in this context it could perhaps be said that King George's whole reign was a great but tragic episode, tragic in the sense that, due to his early death and the extraordinary weakness of his successor, none of the political and constitutional achievements and trends of his reign could be salvaged, let alone developed any further. But his reign assumes a different aspect, one far less liable to be considered as an episode and a failure, when we include in our discussion the religious element. It is largely on this basis, that is through the appreciation of his defensive but essentially successful struggle against Rome, that George has achieved his fame as a historical figure.

It is as the "Hussite King" that George has mostly been described, especially by Czech historians of the nineteenth century, thus putting the emphasis on his role as the defender of this first national church in Europe which deviated substantially from the Roman ritual and even some of the Roman creed. In recent times this claim has been challenged, on the basis that George cannot possibly be considered

---

[16] For these developments see, apart from the 19th-century standard works such as Palacký's and Tomek's, K. Krofta's *Dějiny československé,* Prague, 1946, 283–289, 306–307, and still more recently *Přehled československých dějin,* I, Prague, 1958, 287–290 (this part by J. Macek).

as a representative of the great revolutionary tradition of Hussitism.[17] If, indeed, the term "Hussite" is limited to the revolution as such, this is true enough. Neither in his temperament nor in his political philosophy was George a revolutionary, perhaps not even in that limited sense in which Napoleon could think of himself as a child of the French Revolution. Though faithful to the Compacts and the Chalice, George clearly conceived of himself as a Christian King in the terms in which the later Middle Ages had developed the understanding of this office. If he looked to any model in Czech history it was not John Žižka, the great Hussite commander who, according to a doubtful tradition, had been his godfather, but rather Charles IV, regarded as a strong and enlightened ruler and father of his people but also as a pious son of the Church, reform of which he sought only on clearly orthodox lines.

George's perhaps hardly conscious identification with the great King-Emperor may have contributed to his decision to reach for the crown of King of the Romans. And both the lofty model and the attempt to combine the two crowns show that George, though not without awareness of some of his limitations, had a very high opinion of his royal office as well as of his own ability to administer this office. When he repeatedly expressed the belief that he had been raised to this place by God, then he was not merely using a common enough formula but expressed his serious belief in having been called to kingship. He had very little difficulty, from the moment of his election and coronation, in regarding himself not as a baron gone a step higher, not as a primus inter pares, but as the bearer of the old, sacred crown, high above anyone else, however affably he might treat his subjects. Some of his sharp reactions against clerical attacks were based on his resentment when he felt that his kingship was not properly respected. A notable example was the arrest, diplomatically rather unwise, of Fantino de Valle in 1462. It was followed by many energetic protests against the Pope's unwarranted and therefore invalid attempts to depose him, as a punishment inflicted without proper hearing for the accused who was a crowned and anointed king.

In his long struggle with Pius II and Paul II, George was essentially on the defensive. He had, from the beginning of his regency (and even before, at his meeting with Aeneas Sylvius in Benešov in 1451), come out for a more solid understanding between his people and the Curia than had so far been achieved. If he could not always prevent the more

---

[17] *Ibid.*, 277–278.

active leaders of the Utraquist Church from trying to gain new territory or establishing a stronger, more monopolistic position in territory
where it was already dominant, he never encouraged them in this
direction but rather tried to restrain them, just as he tried to restrain
the Catholic side from parallel actions. Conscious that expansion from
either side would tend to disturb the domestic peace he was above all
eager to maintain the status quo as closely as possible. And maintenance of the status quo was, in essence, all that was implied in the demand for the confirmation of the Compacts. It might even be said that
this basic idea—the maintenance of a tolerable status quo—was the
guiding light of much if not most of George's domestic policy and not
a little of his foreign policy.

This guiding principle does not seem, at first glance, to be a very imposing conception. Seen, especially, against the tremendous background
of the Hussite Revolution—by all odds one of the greatest dynamic
movements for socio-political and spiritual freedom in all history—the
essentially static conception of maintaining conditions and preventing
disturbances may seem, as it were, philistine, uninspiring, and non-
creative. Yet what George tried to maintain was, after all, not a rigid
structure, either nationally or internationally. It was rather the idea
of a balance—balance of living forces internally, balance of viable
powers or nations internationally. In this sense, however, human progress, whatever our standards may be in specific terms, has depended
on that rhythm in which revolutionary outbreaks, piercing constrain-
ing and outdated crusts of material and spiritual domination and
freeing newly rising forces, were followed by periods characterized by
some form of constructive stabilization. (The historian for whom the
belief in the possibility of progress in history is merely a sort of
superstition will disagree.)

But while it is certainly true that George was, in the usual sense of
the word, not a revolutionary either in thought or action, but a man
trying to create conditions of stability based on internal and international balance, his historical role was nevertheless not merely stabilizing, let alone static. Induced not by his temperament or his
weltanschauung but rather by circumstances and by the forces fighting
against him—especially, of course, the Roman Church—George did
eventually assume a position which can, in terms of effective action as
well as symbolic significance, be called revolutionary. This was the
area of the development of the lay state, fully independent from any
church domination, and of a lay-dominated European state system.

This fact has sometimes been introduced with rather exaggerated claims for George of Poděbrady. He was not an epoch-making pioneer in this field.[18] Important precedents (such as the Statute of Praemunire or the Declaration of Rense) had resulted, in the fourteenth century, from the hostility which the French-dominated Avignon papacy had caused in many quarters, espcially in England and the empire, and the crisis of the papacy had, in turn, led to the conciliar movement with its Gallican product: the Pragmatic Sanction of Bourges. George's struggle came, as it were, at the tail end of that great movement, and his efforts—in cooperation with Louis XI—for a new council were as unsuccessful as his appeals to such a council or to "a better informed Pope."

George, therefore, has no claim to having initiated the struggle against the obsolete claims of the papacy to wield suzerain power, all over Europe, in relation to non-religious issues. Yet, having become a victim to what even many Czech Catholics considered as an especially outrageous interference in the conduct of non-religious public affairs of the Bohemian realm, he went new ways in his defense, ways which raised this struggle to an ideological level which it had not reached before. In this context we have to think above all of the great scheme of the League of Princes, in which the Pope was given no more than an auxiliary role. No less significant was George's choice of his political and legal advisers in this struggle, first Marini and (despite his later shift) Mair, later Gregory Heimburg. Heimburg's appointment was made in the full knowledge that it would greatly antagonize the Curia. Whatever criticism could be directed against the German lawyer for some of his advice to George, especially regarding his relation to the Emperor, Heimburg's "apologies" and a vast part of his official correspondence gave, as it was supposed to give, a high degree of decision and clarity to the King's struggle for freedom from ecclesiastical interference, and thus supports substantially the King's claim to historical greatness. The international echo of this brilliant propaganda in the field of political philosophy was considerable, not only in the Empire, but also in France and especially in Poland, whose King used Heimburg's very diction in disputing the Pope's right to depose a crowned and anointed King.

---

[18] It was a German, a Prussian historian, Gustav Droysen, who in his *Geschichte der preussischen Politik* (II), emphasized and probably somewhat over-emphasized this aspect of George's work. One of Droysen's students, the Lusatian Sorb Max Jordan, went still farther and even called his book *Das Königthum Georgs von Poděbrad. Ein Beitrag zur Geschichte der Entwicklung des Staates gegenüber der katholischen Kirche* (Leipzig, 1861).

George's struggle for the right of the lay ruler and the lay state to exist and develop without ecclesiastical interference is, in historical perspective, the only basis for finding revolutionary impact in his work. But does this imply that we cannot therefore call him the "Hussite King"? Such a denial, as said before, presupposes the complete identification of Hussitism and the Hussite Revolution. The Hussite Revolution, essentially, died at Lipany in 1434, but Hussitism as a religious development survived throughout and beyond the fifteenth century, taking shape in the two great branches, the Utraquist Church and the Unity of the Brethren. In both these churches a vast part of what, in the sixteenth century, became the spiritual content of the Protestant Reformation was anticipated, in forms which made it possible for the leading reformers of the sixteenth century to look at the Czech reformed church largely as related and brotherly movements. In our attempt at a summarizing evaluation of the historical significance of George of Poděbrady and the Poděbradian age a word must therefore be said about their direct impact upon the religious development.

There is little we could add to our previous discussions of George's personal attitude to religion. He had taken his devotion seriously, both in his regular attendance of occasions of worship and in his belief that he was acting as closely as he could according to what God demanded of him. Another, not unimportant basis for his refusal to make himself the instrument of papal plans for destroying Utraquism was his understanding that, since the Hussite Revolution, the masses in town and country had ceased to be mere objects of the decision of princes and prelates and thus could not have been forcibly converted even if he should have made a strong effort. With this understanding he was far superior to his critics and enemies in Rome.

George had never been narrow-minded. His Utraquism had never meant to him any radical separation from the masses of his Catholic subjects, and had not prevented him from occasionally taking part in Catholic religious celebrations "up at the castle." This tolerance had made it possible for the two religious groups to live, if not without friction, at least without serious internal struggles, throughout George's regency and the first ten years of his kingship. It was just the strength of George's kingship which gave the overwhelming majority of the people, both in the Hussite majority and the Catholic minority, a security which had been absent during the interregnum (as it had, of course, been absent during the revolutionary period). Without this feeling that there was security of religious freedom for Catholics as well as Utraquists it would be impossible to explain why, at the height of the war and of papal intransigence and persecution, a large proportion of Catholics of all classes through Bohemia, including most of the monastic clergy, faithfully, we may even say stubbornly and often at considerable sacrifice, preserved their loyalty to George. George's humaneness as well as his political intelligence induced him to remain adamant in refusing to make this war, on his side, into a religious, an anti-Catholic war. He was, for this reason, repeatedly attacked and criticized by zealous Utraquists.

Yet a case can be made for the assumption that by that very policy, in preference to any alternative, George saved the Utraquist Church. The survival of a strongly Hussite Bohemia in what has, with limited justification, been called the second Hussite War, was largely due to the fact that at no time was George's kingdom, in political, military, and even economic terms, completely isolated. Such an isolation was one of the main strategic goals of the Curia and her legates. The attempt was defeated by George's diplomatic skill, the successes of his defensive and eventually also offensive military strategy, but above all by the fact that his (Catholic) friends in Poland, in the Empire, in France could not be persuaded by papal propaganda that Czech Utraquism, as led by George, was a real danger to Catholic Europe.

Under these circumstances the second great offensive of Rome against the heretical Czechs had failed. By 1471 it had largely been given up as a doubtful, even hopeless enterprise. The later papal backing for Matthias against Vladislav, while still, on the surface, using the old anti-heretical slogans, cannot be compared with the passionate and vigorous war effort made by the papal party during 1468-1470. Luckily for Bohemia and the Utraquist Church this energy had largely been spent and exhausted while George was still alive. From now on for the next 150 years no power outside or in Bohemia was strong and determined enough to attempt another all-out assault on the reformed Church of the Czechs. True, Vladislav, especially after the peace of Olomouc of 1478, made some attempts at weakening the Utraquist clergy, even to the point of martyring one of their most popular priests.[19] But resistance to this move was too strong. Finally the fate of the Utraquist Church was safeguarded by the Statutes of Kutná Hora of 1485 in which both religious groups, Catholics and Utraquists, rep-

---

[19] The priest Michael Polák, who was, as the name shows, a man of Polish origin. See *SLČP*, 415–420.

resented in the diet of the kingdom, guaranteed each other, on the basis of the Compacts, mutual tolerance and freedom of worship, remarkably to the extent that even subject persons had the free choice of worship without regard to the religion of their lords.[20] It was a splendid victory for King George's religious policy—fourteen years after his death, yet largely due to his policy and his unshakable faith in the idea of religious peace and mutual respect.

Yet the same King George who, under his Jagiellon successors and down into the earlier Habsburg period, remained in the minds of the Czech people, Utraquists as well as most Catholics, a great king and a great prince of peace, became in the historiography of the other Hussite Church, the Unity of Brethren, a harsh persecutor, assisted in this evil work by none other than John Rokycana, the head of the Utraquist Church.[21]

Rokycana, in truth, had come out publicly against some of the teachings of the Brethren, especially during the period from 1468 to 1470, sometimes called the phase of the second persecution.[22] Originating from Rokycana's own teaching as well as that of Peter Chelčický, the Brethren had, by the late sixties, developed thoughts which increasingly deviated from those of the Utraquist clergy and seemed to justify the suspicion that they had embraced Taborite-Pikhart ideas. This seemed especially true in regard to the Eucharist, since they doubted the real presence of Christ, refused to worship the host, and sharply criticized the habit of giving communion to unworthy people. They demanded that people joining their community undergo a second baptism. They had cut completely all their ties with the Roman episcopal tradition and had elected their own priests without any ordination on the basis of Apostolic succession. Their attitude to wordly as well as ecclesiastical authorities reflected their wish to escape completely from "the world" with all its sinful corruption. They had repeatedly asked Rokycana to join them and had, when he declined, reproached him for his supposed inconsistency and lack of courage. Rokycana, as head of a large, essentially all-inclusive national church, could not possibly follow this request. Yet throughout the last decade of his life, while

---

[20] See *AČ*, V, 418ff. and F. M. Bartoš, *Bojovníci a mučedníci*, Prague, 1939, pp. 56–62.

[21] See e.g. Tůma Přeloučský, *O původu Jednoty Bratrské a o chudých lidech*, ed. V. Sokol, Prague, 1947, pp. 50–56.

[22] The literature on the problems touched on most sketchily in the following paragraphs is enormous. See e.g. the (careful yet not completely unbiased) treatment in J. Th. Müller's *Geschichte der Böhmischen Brüder*, I, 149–164 (in Bartoš's Czech edition, Prague, 1923, pp. 91–102.)

publicly dissociating himself from such teachings,[23] he had at least tried to soften the antagonism and to protect the leaders of the small but growing religious community from too much suffering. He was only partially successful, but this was hardly his fault. If we compare his attitude with that of the great reformers of the sixteenth century toward the sectarian developments of the Radical Reformation, for instance Zwingli's treatment of the Anabaptists (who had been his, Zwingli's disciples as the Brethren had been Rokycana's), then, though he could not prevent the harsh treatment of a number of Brethren who became martyrs of their faith, Rokycana's behavior appears remarkably patient, cautious, and humane.

But what about King George? Does not the persecution of the Brethren deprive him of any right to be called humane or tolerant? We have discussed earlier the motivations for his proceeding against the Brethren in 1461. It was at the height of his country's military and political crisis that the leaders of the Unity of Brethren tried, by a special petition,[24] to convince King George that their religious policy was in conformity with the country's needs. They wanted to prove, before a council of all Christian nations, that it was not only permissible but necessary to cut all ties with Rome since the office of the papacy was not carried by the power of the divine spirit and neither its blessing nor its cursing flowed out of the strength of the word of Christ. They seem to have believed, somewhat naïvely, that, himself persecuted by papal intransigence, the King would welcome such an argumentation and therefore at least tolerate their own attitude which they felt was the only clear and consistent one. So they begged him to give them a place where they could quietly and modestly live and work as good Christians and obedient subjects.

They understood King George as little as the King could possibly understand them. For him they were those very sectarians and deviationists whom he had promised, in his coronation oath, to lead back, by whatever means he had, to the proper faith. He was willing to defend, against Rome, that religious freedom which was based on the Compacts. But the teachings and the organization of this new sect had no place whatsoever within the Compacts. In addition it looked to him, now more than ever, like a revival of Old Tabor, even if its pro-

---

[23] See his declaration "against the Pikharts" in Bidlo, *Akty Jednoty bratrské*, I, Brno 1915, 488–491. About the claim that the King had acted against the Brethren upon Rokycana's instigation see also F. M. Bartoš, "Rokycana za t.zv. druhého pronásledování Jednoty bratrské," in *ČČM*. XCIX Prague, 1925, 72ff. and Urbánek, *Věk*, IV, 450 n. 175.

[24] See Bidlo, *Akty Jednoty bratrské*, II, 7, also Müller, *op.cit.*, 157–158 (in Czech 97–98).

gram disowned any militancy. He could not possibly, in his day, look at this whole problem as a purely religious issue. The fast growth of this sect seemed highly dangerous to his own attempt, maintained with so much effort, to fight the image of the Czech national church as a heretical outlaw in a Catholic Europe. Any permission for the Brethren to go their own "narrow path" would strengthen this dangerous image.

It is a sad fact that this "second persecution" cost seven human lives. Perhaps it is a blot on George's record of humaneness and tolerance. But it is very clear that this was not a religious persecution. Throughout his whole reign the reproach the King had to defend himself against, and not only from one side, was that of being not sufficiently dedicated to the victory of one religious cause. And even after his death this image—that of a man not devoted enough to the destruction of heresy—determined the attitude of his family, especially of Queen Johanna, toward the Church of the Brethren.[25]

In the last instance it could be argued that the survival of the Church of the Brethren—and with it of one of the greatest, purest, and most lasting contributions of the Czech spirit arising out of its heroic Hussite phase—was dependent upon the survival of Utraquism and was thus indirectly due to the consolidating work of George of Podĕbrady. While, in some ways, the Brethren were closer to the revolutionary ideas of dynamic Hussitism at the time of the revolution, the unconditional pacifism which they professed and practiced in their early history would not have enabled them to stand up by themselves to a systematic policy of persecution and eradication, and their fate would have been more closely similar to that of the majority of Anabaptist groups in the sixteenth century. What saved the Brethren from such extermination and enabled them to grow, throughout the sixteenth century, into a strong, flourishing, influential and culturally highly productive church was, in their critical earlier period, the protection which they received from influential members of the Utraquist Church. While the Utraquist consistory itself was generally unfriendly, the very existence of a multi-religious society in the country, such as it had survived thanks to George of Podĕbrady, made possible also the survival of the Brethren.

But this statement, claiming, as it were, an indirect and unintentional merit of George's for the survival of the Brethren, has immediately to be hedged rather severely. For this survival was not only unintentional. It could almost be said that, if it had depended, to some extent, on

[25] See, for the whole question, Urbánek's chapter in *Vĕk*, IV, 399–463.

George's kingship while he lived, it depended just as much on his disappearance at the time he died. The great baronial protectors of the Brethren at the time of King Vladislav II had all been faithful adherents and supporters of King George, but if they were now able to thwart all efforts of the Jagiellon King to exterminate the heresy of the Brethren, then this was largely due to the degree in which the power of the crown had decreased, and that of the baronial class had grown. Those great protectors were humane and liberal in their religious attitude, but they also saw their economic advantage in having, on their estates, people as serious, hard-working and intelligent as the majority of the Czech Brethren in Bohemia and Moravia. And eventually the Brethren ceased to be a church of the little people and began to contain in their ranks a growing number of members of the nobility. Thus the great age of the Unity of the Brethren, not in terms of the purity of their teachings and ethics but of their strength, general appeal and national importance, was precisely the age of the "ständesstaat." Their church was destroyed, at least in Bohemia, together with all other Protestant churches, at the very time when Habsburg absolutism, after 1620, smashed and degraded the proud and rebellious Bohemian nobility and largely replaced it by a court aristocracy of mixed national origin. What survived, in any form, of the Church of the Brethren had to go either underground or to emigrate, like her last bishop who was also the greatest Czech mind of the seventeenth century: John Amos Comenius. It is this common fate of Czech Protestantism, Czech religious freedom and Czech political independence with the great days of the Czech "ständesstaat" which has colored and, to some extent, confused the general attitude and the value judgments of Czech historiography in relation to those last one and a half centuries of Bohemian independence before the deluge of the Thirty Years War.

We have earlier objected to considering King George's reign merely as a prelude to this long but distinct period of slow political decadence under the Jagiellons and early Habsburgs. But in the cultural field it was indeed a prelude to that same period, without being a prelude to decadence.

To some extent, indeed, the cultural development was a continuation of trends which had started already during—and partly even before—the Hussite Revolution. This was especially true of the development of the Czech language as an instrument not only of religious communication but of thought and expression in almost any field and on any level. During the revolution itself the Czechization of the vast majority of Czech cities had contributed to this process, but in the Poděbradian age it became even more widespread and regular. (And this without any attempt at forcible Czechization at the hand of King George.) The complete victory of the vernacular over Latin (and, of course, German) in all public documents anteceded by far developments of a similar character in neighboring Poland, let alone in Hungary. Practically all communications emerging from the royal chancery, except those meant for international intercourse, were written in Czech. So were (as already during the Hussite Revolution) the official and semi-official pronouncements coming from the meetings of the diets, but now also from the city halls of most cities and from the administrations and courts of all levels.[26] The same period, largely because of Jiskra's prolonged governing position in northern Hungary and the activities of the bratříci, saw a notable strengthening of the Czech language in Slovakia, where it became a vehicle of expression in private letters as well as in a good many official communications at least on a local level.[27] But the Czech language was also paid an impressive compliment by the King of Hungary. Besides Latin and occasional German letters a great many Czech letters left Matthias' chancery, in which, as in the leadership of his army, there were a number of Czech officials. But not a single letter of the great King and brilliant humanist is preserved that was written in Magyar.

In Bohemia the Poděbradian period brought a remarkable continuation of Czech literary production. Much of this was still devoted to religious issues and came from both Catholics and Hussites. The Catholics, men like Hilarius of Litoměřice, used, Latin for their religious disputations, but from the greatest minds of this later period of Hussitism, Peter Chelčický and John Rokycana, we have an ample literary heritage, written, in both cases, in a strong and colorful Czech, which enriched the language and, together with the heritage of Hus himself, inspired later generations at the time of the Czech cultural renaissance in the early nineteenth century. There is also a not inconsiderable

26 Among many sources evincing this change a very striking one is the *Kniha svědomí města Nového Bydžova*, ed. J. Kapras, Nový Bydžov, 1907, in which all decisions of this city's courts are at first in Latin, begin to be mixed with Latin and Czech in the late 1440's and early 1450's, and after that are exclusively given in Czech. For the Czechization of the cities of Bohemia see Jos. Klik, *Národnostní poměry v Čechách od válek husitských do bitvy bělohorské, ČČH*, 27, 28, and book edition, Prague, 1922. There also (pp. 37–43) material on Humanism and the successes of the Czech language.

27 See Václav Chaloupecký, ed., *Středověké listy ze Slovenska, (1426–1490)*.

amount of writings of some other leaders of the Utraquist Church such as Martin Lupáč and of Rokycana's friend and successor, Wenceslas Koranda the Younger, while the great literary period of the Church of the Brethren did not begin until later.

The Poděbradian age, however, marks also the beginning of Czech humanism as an intellectual and literary movement.[28] Among its representatives was John of Rabstein, the author of the impressive *Dialogus,* which, meant to influence also people outside Bohemia, was written in Latin. Of one of the more important humanist literary productions Simon of Slaný's main works, a *Panegyricus,* devoted to King George, and his *Chronicae annotationes,* were unfortunately lost, but at least one among the King's faithful friends and defenders, Ctibor Tovačovský of Cimburg, left a literary heritage which is remarkable both in its literary form and its political content. Of lesser rank, in literary terms, but of great historical interest, is Paul Židek's Czech *Spravovna,* a sort of program of good government devoted to (and intended for) King George by this intelligent, alert, and well-meaning but somewhat unstable Catholic master of Jewish origin, who was also the author of a Latin-written encyclopedia. Of considerable interest finally are some travelogues, two of them reflecting closely King George's foreign policy.[29] Rather poor, on the other hand, was the period's contribution to historiography.[30]

The Poděbradian age, incidentally, also saw the introduction of the art of printing into Bohemia.[31] The first printed Czech book, interestingly, was a Czech edition of the same (or a very similar) Chronicle of Troy which was printed by Caxton in 1474, but the Czech book (by an unknown printer) appeared six year earlier, in 1468. It was published, however, not in Prague but Pilsen, the center, in those years, of militant Czech Catholicism. Soon afterwards, but already after George's death, we also find incunabula printed in Prague and Kutná Hora.

A field in which we find renewed flowering in the Poděbradian

---

[28] See J. Truhlář, "Počátky humanismu v Čechách," *Rozpravy česke akademie,* Ročník I, tř. III, No. 3.

[29] See Urbánek, *Ve službách Jiříka krále,* Prague, 1940, which contains the report of Squire Jaroslav about the trip to France (quoted in detail above, chapter 16), and of Václav Šašek of Bírkov about the much longer travel of Lord Lev of Rožmitál through all countries of western Europe, including England. Of the latter, several editions exist in different languages, including a recent one in English by M. Letts, in the Hakluyt Series II, 108, Cambridge, 1957.

[30] See my introduction to the bibliography of this book, pp. 612–620.

[31] See Josef Volf, *Geschichte des Buchdrucks in Böhmen und Mähren bis 1848,* Weimar, 1928, pp. 11–17, 21–27.

period is painting.[32] This art had suffered during the Hussite Revolution as a result of the war itself and of the Puritan hostility of the Taborite movement to the magnificence of church buildings and their decoration. But with the recovery of domestic peace and economic health under George, the cities as patrons of art became active again, and a trend toward a more realistic late-Gothic style, showing strong traces of characteristic Renaissance qualities, gave new impulses to Czech painting. There are, in this period (around 1460) again some remarkable altar pieces of the Virgin in southern Bohemian cities, and in Prague there appears, by 1470, for the first time the work of a painter who ranks with the great Czech painters of the late fourteenth and the beginning of the fifteenth centuries: the Master of the St. George Altarpieces who, it seems, had at that time a large and highly appreciated workshop in Prague. Less conspicuous was the recovery of architecture. But there, too, some activity reappears, making it possible at least to go beyond mere repair and soon to resume work on such monumental buildings as the great Church of St. Barbara in Kutná Hora, one of the most magnificent works of Central European late Gothic. In the field of music, on the other hand, the flowering especially of the choral song in the times of the Hussite Revolution did begin to let off, with little to replace it until the time when, in the sixteenth century, the Church of the Brethren began to develop its rich cultural activity.

King George's role in Czech history was great enough to make him an important subject of the arts. In modern times Alois Jirásek made him the hero of one of his great historical novels, titled "The Hussite King." Among the numerous modern likenesses— and in view of the many existing contemporary or near-contemporary drawings and woodcuts we can feel, in contrast to the many modern "Žižka" statues and paintings, that these are really likenesses—those of Mikulas Aleš are the most popular and have contributed greatly to the fact that the figure of the stout man on horseback, with his moustache and his long, flowing hair, has long been an extremely familiar symbol for kingly strength and national greatness. Significant moments of his life—such as his coronation or the meeting with Matthias Corvinus in the burnt-out hut near Vilémov—have become subjects of historical paintings. But it is perhaps more significant that even during his life-

---

32 See Jaroslav Pešina, "Studie k malířství poděbradské doby," in *Umění*, ročník VII, 3, Prague, 1959, and the same author's *Painting of the Gothic and Renaissance Periods 1450–1550*, Prague, 1960, 7–9, 14–19.

time, and immediately thereafter, George was presented in works of art by his admirers as well as, occasionally, by his enemies. The latter, naturally, depicted him as the great heretic, and we have a rather amusing story about one of these presentations from Eschenloer. The Abbot of the Monastery of the Virgin in Breslau had, some time after the King's death, built a new chapel in the vicinity, and in it he had ordered a mural to be painted presenting the last judgment. It showed, among those sent to hell, the figure of King George carried downward by two devils. When Duke Henry of Münsterberg heard of this, he sent a message to the abbot telling him that, unless this shameful presentation of his father was quickly removed, he would burn down every single of the villages belonging to the monastery. The abbot, frightened, immediately complied and King George, at least in effigy, was saved from hell.

A number of likenesses of George were created in his time and soon after by and for his friends and adherents, several of them sculptures erected in Utraquist cities like Prague, Kutná Hora, Hradec Králové and Slaný.[33] The most significant of these, in historical terms, was the one which Rokycana had ordered to be put into a large niche in the central gable of the great Týn Church in Prague where it was visible, for a long time, to the crowds which used to assemble on the wide square in the center of the Old Town. It was made of marble and depicted the King, with the crown on his head, holding in his right hand an unsheathed sword, in his left the Chalice, the great symbol of Hussitism which the King, for all his devotion to peace, had defended so effectively.[34] After all the storms that have swept through the old city, the marble statue has disappeared long ago, but the niche high up in the gable is visible as it was then, and history-conscious people will point it out to you, seeing with their mind's eye the figure of George of Poděbrady looking across the Vltava valley, the last great son of his nation who wore the ancient crown of St. Wenceslas, and wore it with dignity, strength, and consistent dedication to his difficult task.

[33] See e.g. on George's statue in Slaný, the report by Zacharias Theobald, *Hussiten-Krieg*, III, Nürnberg, 1621, 117–118.
[34] See Urbánek, *Věk*, IV, 183–185, esp. n. 115.

A WORD ON THE HISTORIOGRAPHY AND
BIBLIOGRAPHY OF THE PODĚBRADIAN AGE

THE KING of Heretics who so badly wanted to be a right Christian King could not help being, all through his years of power and responsibility, a controversial figure, probably more so than the majority of the "great men" of his time. The wildly contradictory value judgments of his contemporaries were bound to influence all the sources dependent on them, and all the later historians dependent on those sources. If this, in itself, tended to make it more difficult to do justice to George's historical role in the form of a well balanced judgment, the difficulty was increased by the fact that in the Poděbradian period the Czech people did not produce any real historian who would have given us a detailed, thoughtful, and intelligent consideration and representation of the events observed. Earlier in the century, during the Hussite Revolution, Lawrence of Březová, while far from "objective" in his treatment of his (Catholic or Taborite) enemies, did at least give wealth of detail and color to his "Hussite Chronicle." For the Poděbradian age we have three men who can probably claim to be historians: the Italian Renaissance writer (and later Pope) Aeneas Sylvius, whose changing evaluations of the Czech King (from his earlier writings down to the *Commentaries*) have been discussed in the text of this book; the Polish cleric and diplomat John Długosz, whose intense hatred for all "heretics" made him distort, to some extent, the policy of George as well as of his own King, who generally was much more on George's side than on that of his enemies; and finally Breslau's town secretary Peter Eschenloer. While the last of the three was probably the most hostile of all, he was also the most lively of them, with the strongest sense of the substance of history, and the critical reader has little difficulty in pealing off the prejudices and thereby baring the flesh of historical facts. Yet he, just as the other two, observes and writes not only with a prejudiced eye but from an outside position. Hence he cannot be a substitute for a presentation that might have come from the center of the Czech state, from Prague, from some place near the court of King George. The only important contemporary Czech source, the "Old Annalists" (Staři letopisové), are highly useful, but on the whole this is an uneven and often overly summary collection of chronicles, generally rather reliable but rarely containing sufficient detail. During the later years of George's reign we have, as a (so far underrated) source, of the greatest value because of its nearness to the centers of decision, the letters written from Prague by Gregory Heimburg, especially those to Margrave Albert Achilles. They give us glimpses into George's attitudes and motivations that we find in no other source, and again we can only regret that there are not more of them, and that nobody has taken the trouble to collect them—as yet not all are even published—and to publish and evaluate them in a special study. One might expect that a good deal of material on the war years should come from Hungarian sources. King Matthias, after all, had what King George had never acquired: his court historian, Bonfini. Yet his writings as well as those of his successors are not only, as must be expected, written "ad majorem regis gloriam" but their yield is, as far as the history of the great war between the two kings is concerned, surprisingly meager. This lack of historical detail and substance, incidentally, persists in most Hungarian historiography also of later times in regard to the Hungaro-Bohemian struggle of this time. Even the important collection of documents arranged in the mid-nineteenth century by Count Teleki was, regarding this topic, largely dependent on material sent to Teleki by Palacký. But in this category —the unearthing of hitherto unknown documents and other pertinent sources—publications of some value can perhaps still be hoped for from future Hungarian historiography.

Just as the Poděbradian age, so the Jagiellon era failed to produce a truly significant Czech historian (perhaps with the exception of Bartoš Písař, whose work, however, does not go back to Poděbradian times). One has to go to the second quarter of the sixteenth century, and thus to the early Habsburgs on Bohemia's throne, in order to find again some literature aspiring to be true historiography. It is a claim which, in the case of writers such as Kuthen, Dubravius, and above all the famous (but long ago exposed "Bohemian Livy," Václav Hajek of Libočany, can be maintained only if a rather generous view is taken about the latitude that on the basis of personal, especially religious, prejudice (and in Hajek's case of a position approximating that of Ferdinand I's court historiographer) should be granted to the historical writer of those times. As both Dubravius and Hajek were Catholic churchmen we cannot, perhaps, be astonished that, in relation to George of Poděbrady, the curial view is at least partly maintained.

It is all the more remarkable that in the seventeenth century, at a time when Habsburg reaction was at its worst, two Catholic clerics turned historians do more justice to the figure and history of the "Hussite King." They are the Jesuit scholar Bohuslav Balbín (Balbinus) and his friend the canon, later bishop, Thomas Pešina of Čechorod (Pessina de Czechorod). Both of them deviated from the older pattern of simply writing the chronological story of the country from mythical origins to the present. Instead they began to specialize, Balbín, for instance, by his emphasis upon intellectual developments and upon genealogy, Pešina, on the other hand, by concentrating, in his most important work, on the regional and the military history of the margraviate of Moravia. Balbín was the greater and more reliable of the two, a man with a more independent judgment and a strong pride in his nation which he could not suppress, at considerable cost to himself, even when writing about the great heresies and heretics of the fifteenth century. Balbín's protestation (in his *Epitome*) that there was no justification for calling King George a heretic may have contributed to the difficulties he had with his superiors. Both he and Pešina were still far too dependent on Hajek, yet both of them are of importance today as they knew and used contemporary sources which have since been lost. From their works, however great their weaknesses, emerges a picture of King George that seems nearer the truth than much that was written later by such modern spokesmen of the old curial point of view as, for instance, the semi-official German nineteenth-century historian of the papacy Ludwig Pastor (*Geschichte der Päpste*).

One thing, incidentally, can be said about all the more important historians of the sixteenth and seventeenth centuries: none of them succumbed to the attempt made by George's passionate enemies (contemporaries as well as later ones) to charge him with the terrible guilt of having poisoned his predecessor. This was just as true for the German-Moravian historian of Hussitism, Zacharias Theobald (d. 1627).

The eighteenth century, toward the end of which we witness the beginning of the cultural renaissance of the Czech nation, produced some Czech historians who began to use more critical methods of work. With it King George begins to emerge somewhat more clearly from the fog in which he seemed to have been wrapped for so long. The most important among those were the Jesuit Frantisek Pubička (Pubitschka) and the man who, with some qualifications, can be regarded as the last and almost only precursor of Palacký: František Martin Pelcl (Pelzel). In contrast to the majority of seventeenth-century historians who wrote in Latin, those of the eighteenth century mostly wrote in German.

In was František Palacký who, starting in the late twenties of the nineteenth century, brought truly modern research methods into Czech historiography. His main work (started in German but continued in Czech and published in both languages) though containing quite a few factual errors or misinterpretations, remains to this day a work of importance to the student of Czech history. Above all, however, it was Palacký who made a systematic beginning with the publications of those sources which alone could provide background and substance to the study of the late medieval history of the Czech nation and kingdom: the enormous wealth of official documents, diplomatic and domestic, acts of diets, private letters, and messages etc. which, despite the large number of destroyed sources, survived in the archives of the princes, the great baronial houses, the episcopal and other chapters and the cities. And perhaps the study of no other age, not even that of the Hussite Revolution, owes so much to Palacký's work as researcher, paleographer, and editor of those sources as the Poděbradian phase. No one can hope successfully to approach this age even now without thorough study of the early volumes of *Archiv český,* in which Palacký published the enormous material in Czech of that age, or the *"Urkundliche Beiträge zur Geschichte Böhmens . . . im Zeitalter Georgs von Podiebrad,"* which contains similar material in German and Latin. If those editions fall somewhat short of the strictest standards of critical source-edition expected today, we must remember the gigantic quantity of largely unorganized and unexplored material he had to wade through, and the limitations imposed on him in terms of time and of assistance for his work.

It is generally agreed that Palacký's evaluation of George's personality and historical role contains an element of idealization (though it would be wrong to claim that he was completely uncritical toward him). But Palacký was by no means alone in following Pelcl's judgment that George was "probably the greatest King of his time." One of the most respected German historians of Palacký's generation, Gustav Droysen, the author of the great *"History of Prussian Politics,"* went surely farther than Palacký in the idealization of George, and it was one of his students, Max Jordan, who in the mid-nineteenth century wrote a nearly dithyrambic monograph about George, extolling him especially as the great protagonist of the modern lay state against Roman presumption.

It was only natural that in the further development of the historical treatment of Poděbradian Bohemia there would be a tendency toward more critical and soberer judgments. It began in 1861 with a long review article by the German Renaissance historian and biographer of Aeneas Sylvius, George Voigt, discussing in detail both Palacký's work, generally giving it the praise it certainly deserved, and Jordan's monograph, whose considerable weaknesses he exposed. While Voigt's was merely a single critical contribution, the following decades of the nineteenth century saw two German-writing historians, the Sudeten-German Adolf Bachmann and the Silesian Hermann Markgraf, both men of great erudition and enjoying a deservedly high reputation, proceed in the exploration of the Poděbradian age, thereby adding more to new knowledge and new understanding of George and his time than can probably be said of their Czech contemporary, V. V. Tomek, the author of the monumental history of the city of Prague and the only one of Palacký's immediate successors who devoted a major part of his work also to this phase of Czech history.

Of the two German historians in question the somewhat older Markgraf's work was smaller in quantity, nor did it attempt any radical reevaluation. It was, on the other hand, extremely careful and solid. Markgraf was, first of all, a historian of Silesia, and his interest in George of Poděbrady was essentially based on his profound studies in the history of that country and especially of Breslau in the fifteenth century. We owe to him the first publication of the early Latin version of Peter Eschenloer's history of Breslau, as well as two great volumes containing the major part of Breslau's political correspondence in the Poděbradian age. These highly valuable source publications, which, among other things, are especially rich in material on papal policy, surpass most other comparable publications of the nineteenth century by their systematic thoroughness and accuracy. But besides this work of editing and publishing, in an exemplary manner, those chronicles and documents, Markgraf also was the author of a number of monographs dealing with such central topics of George's reign as his relationship to Pope Pius II, his plans for a League of Princes, and the organized opposition and eventual rebellion of the Catholic lords against the King. All of these stand out by the careful, sober, and unprejudiced way in which he approached his controversial subject. It is a pity that he did not build, on so much valuable groundwork, a more comprehensive treatment of the Poděbradian age.

Markgraf's work, substantial as it was, still looks small in size when compared to the production of Adolf Bachmann. (See on him the recent biography, valuable also as a contribution to the intellectual life of that time, by Harald Bachmann, Munich, 1962.) Throughout the last quarter of the nineteenth and into the earliest years of the twentieth century this gifted son of a German family from the Egerland in western Bohemia poured out an impressive number of publications. To the one volume of documents in German and Latin published by Palacký in the *Fontes rerum Austriacarum* Bachmann added three more—true, not limited to Bohemia but extending over the whole of the Empire for the period in question and put together in a rather unsystematic way. A large number of monographs, ranging in size from short articles to books, partly preceded and partly accompanied the author's work on two larger undertakings, each of them a "magnum opus" in its own right: the *History of the German Empire in the age of Frederick III and Max I* (2 vols., 1884, 1894), and his *History of Bohemia* (2 vols., 1899, 1905). While in the second work (which, like Palacký's, goes to 1526) the Poděbradian age covers only some 330 of over 1,700 pages, the proportion of the Bohemian story in the earlier *Reichsgeschichte* is far greater. This, indeed, is his most important work, since it not only gives the history of Bohemia in those years but the whole extremely complex and often quite confusing background of the imperial court and its Austrian lands, the papacy, the main events and developments in and between the German principalities, and the foreign relations of all of these, e.g. to France, Burgundy, Poland, Hungary, and the states of the Italian peninsula. It will probably be a long time before this work can be adequately replaced by something better and more up-to-date. Accordingly Bachmann's prestige and his influence on the following generations of historians—not only in Germany and Austria but also in Hungary and in the West— has been great. Yet while Bachmann's achievement was astonishing and in many ways brilliant, it also has considerable weaknesses. In the *Reichsgeschichte* the material itself, with its very vastness and lack of a natural center of gravity, often defeats all attempts to organize it in a way which would permit a proper focus and with it a tolerably coherent narrative. It would, however, be hardly fair to hold this against the author. The frequent presence of a sharply polemical note (directed mostly against Palacký) can perhaps be called characteristic of much that was written in those days including that of Palacký's, who, for instance, was often too harsh in his criticism of Bachmann's teacher, Constantin Höfler.

But there are more serious flaws in Bachmann's work which should be recognized so as to avoid acceptance of some of his faulty judgments and conclusions. He had a penchant for purely deductive assumptions and, once conceived, he would stick to them even if the sources should have given him second thoughts. In one case especially this tendency resulted in presenting what seems to me a total misinterpretation of King George's religious policy. It is his assumption that George's secret coronation oath meant, even in his own eyes, a regular conversion from Utraquism to orthodox Catholicism; that he fully intended to implement all promises supposedly implied in this conversion, including especially the abolition of the Compacts and of the communion *sub utraque;* that only political considerations blocked this step; and that therefore, when he failed to do so, the position of the Church in accusing him of having broken his word and having perjured himself was fully justified. In order to strengthen this interpretation (and with it his strong disapproval of George's basic policy) Bachmann then read repeatedly the offer to drop Compacts and Chalice into George's diplomatic activities which, on the basis of the sources, never contained so far-reaching an offer. There are several, similar, though not nearly so consequential misinterpretations on issues such as the rebellion of Pilsen, the war situation at the beginning of 1468, the conference of the Kings at Vilémov, and the role of Gregory Heimburg which was the subject of a polemical discussion between Bachmann and Heimburg's biographer Joachimsohn in which the latter's position was the sounder one.

Thus, while Bachmann's work will continue to be one of the most important secondary sources to the Poděbradian age, he should not be taken as a dependable authority, especially not in his value judgments which, apart from their underlying prejudice, are all too often based on doubtful assumptions, occasionally even on mere errors in dating.

After Palacký and Tomek, Markgraf and Bachmann, and the Frenchman Ernest Denis, little of any importance on the Poděbradian age was published anywhere. Not till 1915 did a book appear in which a Czech historian tried to present, on the basis of all the material that had become accessible or was about to be collected, a more precise, more complete, and more colorful historical portrait of the great King and the age to which he gave his name. This was Rudolf Urbánek's *Věk podebradský* (The Poděbradian Age), itself the third part of the *České dějiny* (Czech history), a grandiose work launched only three years earlier by Václav Novotný. And while Urbánek's "magnum opus" came out with steadily growing intervals—volume 2 came in 1918, volume 3 in 1930, and volume 4 (whose fate had already become highly doubtful) not until 1962—there flowed, in the years following 1915, a steady stream of important contributions to varying aspects of the Poděbradian age from Urbánek's pen, interrupted only by the historian's active participation in the Žižka quincentennial publications of 1924 and later by the difficulties arising during the German occupation. Unlike his predecessors, Urbánek did not publish any additional source works, with the exception of two small volumes which were reissues or translations of primary sources that had appeared in print before. Yet an enormous contribution to the organization and evaluation of sources, printed and unprinted, is contained in the footnotes to all his publications, the *Věk poděbradský* as well as his many other books and articles.

The *Věk poděbradský* is, truly, an imposing work. Its weakness, if such it can be called, is its very vastness and attempted completeness. It goes into far greater detail than any of the preceding volumes of the *České dějiny*. In consequence, the first three volumes, each of about 1,000 pages, carried the narrative only as far as 1460, still a very early moment in the history of George's kingship. With volume 4, which appeared only a few months before Urbánek's death, he pushed forward to the summer of 1464, ending with the death of Pius II. There were still left those seven years which included the King's great struggles—the domestic one against the rebellious League of Lords, and the great war against Matthias of Hungary and his allies. While we know from his more popular biographic sketch published in 1926 (*Husitský král*) Urbánek's general ideas about this last important phase of George's reign, it will ever be deeply regretted that his great work will remain incomplete.

Urbánek's *Věk poděbradský* clearly aspired to becoming the "definitive treatment" of the Poděbradian age in Czech historiography. And in many ways it will probably remain just that, at least for the period covered by it. Yet it will by no means obviate further research and further interpretative discussion of this highly interesting phase of Czech history. During Urbánek's life, it is true, there was little room for substantial work by other scholars in what had been, as it were, his very special domain. (Among the few exceptions is F. M. Bartoš, whose enormous fertilizing influence upon the whole huge field of Hussite studies entered the Poděbradian age with a number of valuable monographic contributions.) Now, however, we can even get a strong impulse for additional production from Urbánek's heritage. In the foreword to volume 4 he says that, if he should be given the chance to finish the work, the last (fifth) volume would, apart from the actual history of George's last years (which he called the Second Hussite War), contain a "synthetic part" called "Poděbradian Bohemia," discussing the conditions of the country in the fields of literature and art, of constitutional development, administration, law, the social, economic, and military development. This, indeed, is in itself an enormous program and one wonders how Urbánek, had he lived long enough and had he continued his extremely detailed analysis and narrative, could have packed this huge material into a single volume, even one of 1,000 pages. Perhaps a partial answer to this question is that the material available in some of these fields, especially in the socio-economic sphere, is still rather scanty. Here, surely, are tasks for the younger generations of Czech and, to some extent, non-Czech historians which would make it possible to put a firmer basis of understanding and interpretation under the future discussion of the Poděbradian age.

The following bibliography, while certainly not exhaustive, attempts to be fairly comprehensive and above all to contain all those titles that have been, wholly or partially, of any significance as sources for the writing of this book. There is, I believe, only one field in which there are considerable gaps, if we think of the Poděbradian age merely in chronological terms: the early history of the Czech Brethren. This was a development with strong and most important beginnings during the years of King George's reign, but since by far the more important part of its history belongs to later times it has, in this book, been touched upon only in a rather slight way. I hope to return to it in a later publication.

Not all the material listed here can be found in libraries in the western hemisphere, and it has been necessary for me to use, as in previous publications, many libraries in America as well as libraries and archives in Czechoslovakia, Germany, Austria, and Italy.

BIBLIOGRAPHY

I. WORKS ON HISTORIOGRAPHICAL, BIBLIOGRAPHICAL AND ARCHIVAL MATERIAL.

Bachmann, Harald, *Adolf Bachmann, Ein österreichischer Historiker*. Munich, 1962.

Bartoš, F. M., *Soupis rukopisu Národní musea v Praze*. 2 volumes, Prague 1926, 1927.

——, *Literární činnost M. Jana Rokycana, M. Jana Přibrama, M. Petra Engliše*. Prague, 1928.

——, "Husitika a bohemika několika knihoven německých a švýcařských," *Věstnik k. české společnosti nauk*, tř. I, 1931, Prague, 1932.

——, "Nová postila M. J. Rokycana," *Reformační Sborník*, VII, Prague 1939, 158–160.

Heymann, Frederick G., "R. Urbánek, Věk poděbradský," *Jahrbücher für Geschichte Osteuropas*, XI, 1, Munich, 1963, 142–145.

Kraus, A., *Husitství ve literatuře, zejména německé*. 3 vols., Prague, 1914–1927.

Krofta, Kamil, "K literárni činností J. Pribrama a J. Rokycany," *ČČM*, vol. 77, Prague, 1903, pp. 425–434.

——, "N. V. Jastrebova Studie o Petru Chelčickém a jeho době," *ČČH*, XV, Prague, 1909, 59–72, 152–172.

——, "O spisech Václava Korandy mladšího z Nové Plzně," *LF* XXXIV, 1912, 122–128, 215–232.

——, *O bratrském dějepisectví*. Prague, 1949.

Krones, F., "Die erzählenden Quellen der Geschichte Mährens im 15. Jahrhundert," *Zeitschrift d. Vereins für Geschichte Mährens und Schlesiens*, IV, Brno, 1900, 1–105.

Lhotsky, Alphons, *Österreichische Historiographie* (Österreich-Archiv). Munich, 1962.

Macůrek, Josef, "Rozwój czeskich badań w zakresie stosunków polsko-czechoslowackich," *Kwartalnik Historyczni*, XLII, Lwow, 1928, 246–275.

Markgraf, Hermann, *Magister Peter Eschenloer, Verfasser der Geschichte der Stadt Breslau*. (Programm des K. Friedrich Gymnasiums), Breslau, 1865.

——, "Die 'Kanzlei' des Königs Georg von Böhmen," *Neues Lausitzisches Magazin*, vol. 48, 1870, pp. 214–238.

Novák, Arne, *Dějiny českého písemnictví*. Prague, 1946.

Odložilík, Otakar, "Životopisec husitského krále," *Křesťanské Listy a Husův Lid*, vol. 64 (23), Chicago, 1962, pp. 161–165.

Palacký, F., *Würdigung der alten böhmischen Geschichtschreiber*. Prague, 1830.

Also re-edited in Czech and with additional footnotes by J. Charvát, in *Dílo F. Palackého,* I, Prague, 1941.

Petrů, Eduard, *Soupis díla Petra Chelčického a literatury o něm,* Prague, 1957.

Pettenegg, E. G. v., *Die Urkunden des Deutsch-Ordens-Zentralarchivs zu Wien.* I, Prague and Leipzig, 1887.

Prochaska, Faustin F., *Miscellaneen der böhmischen und mährischen Litteratur.* Prague, 1784–1785.

Truhlář, Joseph, *Catalogus codicum manuscriptorum, qui in c.r. bibliotheca publica atque universitatis Pragensis asservantur,* 2 vols; Prague, 1905, 1906.

Urbánek, Rudolf, " 'Kancelář' krále Jiřího," *ČČH,* 1911, pp. 13–27. (Also in *Z husitského věku,* Prague, 1957, pp. 216–229.)

Weber, Jaroslav and others, *Soupis rukopisu v Třeboňi a v českém Krumlově.* Prague, 1958.

Vlček, Jaroslav, *Dějiny české literatury.* new edition, Prague, 1951.

Zeman, J. K., "Nové publikace o Jednotě bratrské," XIX, *Husův lid,* Chicago, 1958, 37ff.

Zíbrt, Čeněk, *Bibliografie česke historie,* part III, vol. 1, Prague, 1904, especially 110–186.

F. Hrejsa and others, "Literární přehled spisů z oboru českých náboženských dějin" (1927–1940), *Reformační Sborník* vol. II–VIII, Prague 1928 ff.

Bibliographical Surveys in *ČČH* and *ČSČH.*

II. UNPRINTED SOURCE MATERIAL

Archives used:

Prague: National Museum
   University Library, Manuscript Collection
   Czechoslovak State Archives
Brno: Czechoslovak State Archives
Olomouc: Czechoslovak State Archives
Kroměříž: Czechoslovak State Archives
Munich: Main State Archives
   Secret State Archives
   Secret (Wittelsbach) House Archives.
Bamberg: State Archives
Vienna: University Library, Ms. Collection
   Haus-, Hof- und Staats-Archiv.
   Central Archives of Order of Teutonic Knights.
Weimar: Thüringisches Landeshauptarchiv (through microfilms).

III. OTHER PRIMARY SOURCES, MOSTLY PRINTED

Note: A very small number of works (such as those by Balbinus, Katona, Klose, Thomas Pešina, Zacharias Theobald) were inclosed among primary sources even though they are not properly contemporary sources. This has been done with works whose actual value consisted not in their general narrative or interpretive parts but only in the specific historical facts (mostly in the form of documents) transmitted by them on the basis of contemporary sources available to their authors, some of them since lost.

Achery, Luc d', *Spicilegium sive collectio veterum aliquot scriptorum qui in Galliae bibliothecis delituerant.* Paris, 1723.

Acta Sanctorum Octobris, X., Paris 1869.

Aeneas Sylvius (Pope Pius II), *Opera.* Basel, 1551.

——, *Pii II, P. M., Orationes politicae et ecclesiasticae,* ed. Mansi. 3 vols., Lucca 1745.

——, *Historia Bohemica.* Edition used here: J. G. Steck, Frankfurt, 1687.

——, *Commentarii rerum memorabilium.* Frankfurt, 1614.

——, *The Commentaries of Pius II,* ed. F. Gragg and L. Gabel. Smith College Studies in History, vol. XXII, 1, 2, XXV, 1–4, XXXX, XXXV, Northampton, 1937–51.

——, *Der Briefwechsel des Eneas Silvius Piccolomini,* ed. Wolkan. Fontes rerum Austriacarum, vol. 67, Vienna, 1912, vol. 68, 1918.

——, ed. Voigt, G., "Die Briefe des Aeneas Silvius vor seiner Erhebung auf den päpstlichen Stuhl," *AÖG,* XVI, Vienna, 1858, 333ff.

——, *Historia rerum Friderici III imperatoris.* in A. F. Kollar, *Analecta,* II, Vienna, 1762.

——, *Die Geschichte Kaiser Friedrichs III,* transl. and ed. by Th. Ilgen. (Geschichtsschreiber der deutschen Vorzeit, XV, Jahrhundert, Vol. II), Leipzig, 1900.

——, *Aeneae Sylvii opera inedita,* ed. J. Cugnoni. Rome, 1883.

——, *De viris illustribus.* Bibliothek des literarischen Vereins, vol. I. part 3, Stuttgart, 1843.

——, *Ausgewählte Texte* (Festgabe an die Universität Basel), ed. Berthe Widmer. Basel, 1960.

Albert Achilles, *Das Kaiserliche Buch; Politische Korrespondenz;* see Höfler and Minutoli, ed., and F. Priebatsch, ed.

Ammanati, Jacob, *Commentarii Iacobi Piccolomini.* Frankfurt, 1614 (bound together with Aeneas Sylvius, *Commentarii*).

Arras, Paul, "Regestenbeiträge zur Geschichte des Matthias I Corvinus," *Ungarische Jahrbücher,* vol. IV, 2, Berlin, 1924, 186–213.

Bachmann, A., ed., *Urkunden und Aktenstücke zur österreichischen Geschichte im Zeitalter Kaiser Friedrichs III und König Georgs von Böhmen. FRA,* II, 42, 1879.

——, *Briefe und Akten zur österreichisch-deutschen Geschichte im Zeitalter Kaiser Friedrichs III. FRA,* II, 44, Vienna 1885.

——, *Urkundliche Nachträge zur österreichisch-deutschen Geschichte im Zeitalter Kaiser Friedrichs III. FRA,* II, 46, 1892.

Balbinus, Bohuslav, *Epitome historica rerum bohemicarum.* Prague, 1777.

——, *Syntagma illustrissimae familiae comitum de Kolowrat.* Prague, 1770.

——, *Tabularium Bohemo-Genealogicum.* Prague, 1770.

————, *Epitome historica rerum bohemicarum*. Prague, 1777.

————, *Liber curialis (seu de magistratibus et officiis curialibus Regni Bohemiae)*. Prague, 1793.

Beheim, Michael (Michel Beheimb), "Ein Buch von den Wienern," Hormayer's *Taschenbuch für die vaterländische Geschichte*, vols. 6, 7, 8, Vienna 1826 ff.

————, *Das Buch von den Wienern, 1462–1465*, ed. Th.G. von Karajan. Vienna, 1843.

————, "Zehn Gedichte Michael Beheims zur Geschichte Oesterreichs," *Quellen und Forschungen zur vaterländischen Geschichte*, Vienna, 1849.

————, "Die historischen und politischen Gedichte Michael Beheims," ed. Gille, *Palaestra*. vol. 96, Berlin, 1910, 4–8.

Bidlo, Jaroslav, ed., *Akty Jednoty Bratrské*. (Prameny dějin moravských, III), 2 vols., Brno, 1915, 1923.

Birk, Ernst, "Beiträge zur Geschichte der Königin Elisabeth und des Königs Ladislaus," *Quellen und Forschungen zur vaterländischen Geschichte*, Vienna, 1849.

————, "Urkunden-Auszüge zur Geschichte Kaiser Friedrichs III in den Jahren 1452–1467," *AÖG*, 10, 11, Vienna, 1853.

Bonfini, Antonio (Antonius de Bonfinis), *Ungerische Chronika*. Frankfurt, 1581.

————, *Rerum ungaricarum decades*, ed. Juhász. (Bibliotheca scriptorum medii recentisque aevorum; Saeculum XV) III, Leipzig, 1936, IV, Budapest, 1941.

Burkhardt, C. A. H., *Correcturen und Zusätze zu Höflers Kaiserlichem Buch*. Jena, 1861.

————, *Das Funfft Merckisch Buech des Churfuersten Albrecht Achilles*. (Quellensammlung zur Geschichte des Hauses Hohenzollern, I, Jena, 1857.)

Březan, Václav, "Rosenberské kroniky krátký výtah," *ČČM*, 1828, part IV.

Celtes, Conradus, *Fünf Bücher Epigramme*, ed. Karl Hartfelder. Berlin, 1881.

Chaloupecký, Václav, ed., *Středověké listy ze Slovenska, 1426-1490*. (Slovenský archiv, vol. I), Prague-Bratislava, 1937.

Chelčický, Peter, "Rozpravy Chelčikého v rkp. Pařižském" (letter to Rokycana), ed. K. Černý, *Listy filologické*, vol. 25, Prague, 1898, 259–280, 284–404, 453–478.

————, *Das Netz des Glaubens*, Trans. C. Vogl, German translation of *Sít' víry*, Dachau, 1923.

Chmel, Joseph, *Regesta chronologica diplomatica Friderici III*. Vienna, 1838.

————, *Materialien zur österreichischen Geschichte*. Vienna, 1838.

————, *Diplomatarium Habsburgense Seculi XV. (1443–1473)*. *FRA*, II, 2, Vienna, 1850.

————, "Handschriftenauszüge aus der K. Hof und Staatsbibliothek zu München," *Sitzungsberichte der Kaiserlichen Akademie der Wissenschaften*, V, Vienna, 1850, 591–728.

————, *Monumenta Habsburgica*. I, Vienna, 1854.

Chronica der edlen Grafen von Cilli, see S. F. Hahn. Collectio monumentarum veterum et recentium, II, Braunschweig, 1726.

Cochlaeus, Joannes, *Historiae Hussitarum libri duodecim*. Mainz, 1549.

Comenius, see Komenský.

Comines, Philippe de, *Memoires,* ed. Godefroy, with additions by Lenglet du Fresnoy. vols. II, III, and IV, London, 1747.

Cusa, Nicholas of, "De Pace Fidei," ed. and transl. by J. P. Dolan, in *Unity and Reform,* Notre Dame, Indiana, 1962.

Deutsche Reichstagsakten, ält. Reihe. Several volumes (18, I, ed. H. Quirin and H. Boockmann, 19, I, ed. H. Weigel and H. Grüneisen) are nearing publication, vol. 21 and 22 (ed. I. Most) will follow soon.

Długosz, Joannes, Sr., *Opera omnia,* ed. Alexander Przezdziecki. vol. XIII and XIV, Cracow, 1877, 1878.

Dobner, Gelasius, *Monumenta historica Boemiae nusquam antehac edita*. 6 vols., Prague, 1764–85 (esp. vol. II).

Doering, Matthias, *Continuatio chronici Theodorici Engelhusii,* ed. I. B. Mencken (*Scriptores rerum Germanicarum, praecipue Saxonicarum,* vol. III), Leipzig, 1730.

Dogiel, Matthias, *Codex Diplomaticus regni Poloniae*. Vilna, 1758–1764.

Döllinger, Ignaz von, *Beiträge zur Sektengeschichte des Mittelalters,* II, Dokumente, München, 1890.

Dubravius, Joannes, *Historia Bohemica*. Edition used: J. G. Steck, Frankfurt, 1687.

Ebendorffer von Haselbach, Th., *Chronicon Austriacum,* ed. H. Pez, *Scriptores rerum Austriacarum,* II Leipzig, 1725, 682–986.

——, *Chronica regum Romanorum*. Mitteilungen des Instituts für österreichische Geschichtsforschung, Ergänzungsband III, Vienna, 1890.

Emler, J. ed., *Reliquiae tabularum terrae regni Bohemiae a. 1541 igne consumptarum*. II, Prague, 1872.

Eschenloer, Peter, *Geschichten der Stadt Breslau, 1440–1479,* ed. J. G. Kunisch, 2 vols. Breslau, 1827–1828.

——, *Historia Wratislaviensis,* ed. Markgraf, *SrS,* VII, Breslau 1872.

Flacius Illyricus, Mathias, *Catalogus Testium Veritatis*. Basel, 1556, and later editions.

Freher-Struve, M., *Germanicarum rerum scriptores aliquot insignes,* II, Strasbourg, 1717.

Gaspare de Verona, "Vita Pauli II," in Muratori, *Rerum Italicarum scriptores praecipui*. III, 2, Milan, 1734.

Gaspare de Verona e Michele Canensius, "Vite de Paolo II," ed. Muratori, New Edition: *Raccolta degli Storici Italiani,* III, 16, Cita di Castello 1904–1911.

Gemeiner, Carl Theodor, *Regensburgische Chronik, 1430–1496,* III, Regensburg, 1821.

Gersdorf, Ed. v., *Codex diplomaticus Saxoniae Regiae,* II, 3, Leipzig, 1867.

Gindely, A., *Quellen zur Geschichte der böhmischen Brüder*. *FRA,* II, vol. XIX, Vienna, 1859.

Goldast, Melchior, *Monarchia S. R. Imperii*. 3 vols. Hanover-Frankfurt, 1611–1613.

——, *Commentarii de Bohemiae regni incorporatarumque provinciarum iuribus ac privilegiis*. Frankfurt, 1627, later edition 1719.

——, *Appendix privilegiorum Bohemiae*. Frankfurt, 1714.

Grotefend, H., *Quellen zur Frankfurter Geschichte*. I, Frankfurt, 1884.

Grünhagen, C. and Markgraf, H. ed., *Lehns- und Besitzurkunden Schlesiens und seiner Fürstentümer* (Publikationen aus preuss. Staatsarchiven VII and XVI), Leipzig, 1881–83.

Grünpeck, Joseph, *Geschichte Friedrichs III und Max I*, transl. by Th. Ilgen (Geschichtsschreiber der deutschen Vorzeit, 15. Jahrhundert, vol. 3), Leipzig, 1891.

Hahn, Simon Friedrich, ed., *Collectio monumentorum recentium et veterum*, 2 vols., Braunschweig, 1724–1726.

Haller, J., *Concilium Basiliense*. 3 vols., 1896.

Hasselholdt-Stockheim, Gustav v., *Herzog Albrecht IV von Baiern und seine Zeit*. Documentary volume, Leipzig, 1865.

Hegel, C., ed., *Chroniken der deutschen Städte*. (Esp. Augsburg, Nürnberg, V, X, XI, XXII, XXIII), Leipzig, 1866–1894.

Hieke, W. und Horčička, A., ed., *Urkundenbuch der Stadt Aussig*. (Städte und Urkundenbücher aus Böhmen, III), Prague, 1896.

Hilarius of Litoměřice, "Hilaria Litoměřického traktát k panu Janovi z Rosenberka," ed. Zd. Tobolka, *Historický archiv české akademie*, No. 13, Prague, 1898.

Hilarius of Litoměřice, *Hilarii Litomericensis disputatio cum Johanne Rokyczana coram Georgio, rege Bohemiae, per 5 dies habita a. 1465*, ed. B. V. Strahl. Prague, 1775.

Hinderbach, Joannes, *Historiae Austriacae Aeneae Silvii continuatio*, in A. F. Kollar, *Analecta*, II, Vienna, 1762.

Höfler, C., "Urkundliche Beiträge zur Geschichte der Häuser Brandenburg und Österreich, der Länder Ungarn und Böhmen" (Fränkische Studien IV), *AÖG* 7, 1851, pp. 25–46.

——, "Böhmische Studien: Gregor Heimburg, Georg Podiebrad und Ludwig XI von Frankreich," *AÖG*, 12, 1854, pp. 317–355.

——, *Geschichtschreiber der husitischen Bewegung in Böhmen*, 3 vols. (*FRA*, Series I, vols. II, VI, VII), Vienna, 1856, 1865 and 1866.

——, *Urkunden zur Beleuchtung der Geschichte Böhmens im 15. Jahrhundert*. Prague, 1865.

Höfler, Constantin and Minutoli, Julius v. ed. *Das Kaiserliche Buch des Markgrafen Albrecht Achilles*. 2 vols. (1440–1470, 1470–1486), Bayreuth and Berlin, 1850.

Jaroslav, Squire, see Kalousek, J., and Urbánek, R., ed.

Joachim, E. and Hubatsch, W. eds. *Regesta historico-diplomatica Ordinis S. Mariae Theutonicorum.* I, 2, 1455–1510, Göttingen, 1950.

Johnsdorf, Benedict, "Böhmische Chronik," ed. Franz Wachter, *SrS.*, vol. 12, 109–123 Breslau, 1883.

Kalousek, J. ed., "Denník Českého poselstva ku králi Francouskému, roku 1464," *AČ,* VII, 427–445. (See also English translation by Wratislaw.)

Kaňák, M. and Šimek, F., eds., *Staré letopisy české z rukopisu křižovnického* (cited as *SLČK*). Prague, 1959.

Kapras, Jan, *Kniha svědomí města Nového Bydžova z l. 1311–1470.* Novy Bydžov, 1907.

Kaprinai, Isztvan, *Hungaria Diplomatica temporibus Mathiae de Hunyad.* Vienna, 1767.

Karajan, Th. G. von, *Kleinere Quellen zur Geschichte Oesterreichs.* Vienna, 1859.

Katona, Stephanus, *Historia critica regum Hungariae (stirpis mixtae).* Vols. VII, VIII, ordine XIV, XV (1458–1464, 1465–1475) Cluj ("Colotzae") 1792.

Kętrzyński, Wojciech, ed., "De persecutione Iudaeorum Vratislaviensium a. 1453," *Monumenta Poloniae Historica,* IV, Lwów, 1884.

Klose, Samuel Benjamin, *Darstellung der inneren Verhältnisse der Stadt Breslau 1458 bis 1526,* ed. Stenzel, *SrS,* III, Breslau, 1847.

——, *Dokumentierte Geschichte und Beschreibung von Breslau.* Vol. III, part 1, Breslau, 1782.

Kniezsa, Štefan, ed., *Stredoveké české listiny* (Slovanské jazykové pamiatky z Maďarska, vol. I), Budapest, 1952.

Knothe, H., "Eine auf Wilhelm von Sachsen bezügliche Urkunde Georg Podiebrads," *Festschrift zum 75. Jubilaeum des. k. sächs. Alterthumsvereins,* Dresden, 1900, pp. 197ff.

Kollar, Adam Franciscus, ed. *Analecta Monumentorum omnis aevi Vindobonensia,* 2 vols. Vienna, 1761, 1762.

Komenský, Jan Amos (Comenius), *Historia persecutionum Ecclesiae Bohemiae ab Anno 894 ad Annum 1632.* Leiden, 1648 also in English, London, 1650.

——, *Historie o těžkých protivenstvích církve české,* ed. F. Šimek and M. Kaňák, Prague, 1952. (Critical edition of above title in Czech)

——, *Historia Fratrum Bohemorum.* Halle, 1702.

König von Königsthal, Gustav Georg, *Nachlese ungedruckter Reichstags- und reichsstädtischer Collegialhandlungen unter Kaiser Friederich III.* Frankfurt, 1759.

Koranda, Václav, Jr., *Manuálník M. Vásclava Korandy,* ed. Jos Truhlář. Prague, 1888.

——, "Poselství krále Jiřího do Říma k papeži r. 1462," ed. A. Patera, *AČ,* VIII, 321–364.

Kremer, Christoph Jakob, ed., *Urkunden zur Geschichte das Kurfürsten Friedrichs I von der Pfalz,* Frankfurt and Leipzig, 1765.

Kronthal, Berthold und Wendt, Heinrich, ed., *Politische Correspondenz Breslaus im Zeitalter des Königs Matthias Corvinus, 1469–1479, SrS,* XXXIII, Breslau 1893.

Kürschner, F., ed., "Jobst von Einsiedel und seine Correspondenz mit der Stadt Eger," *AÖG,* XXXIX, Vienna 1868, 245–292.

Kut, Bohumil, *Československé dějiny v archívních dokumentech.* I, Feudalismus, Prague, 1961.

Lewicki, E. M., *Codex epistolarius saeculi decimi quinti.* III Cracow 1894.

Loserth, J., ed., "De factis regni Bohemie; ein Gesandtschaftsbericht von Prag v. J. 1454." *MVGDB,* vol. 18, pp. 229–306.

———, "Die Denkschrift des Breslauer Domherrn Nicholas Tempelfeld," *AÖG,* LXI, 1889, 109 ff.

———, "Regesten zur Geschichte der mährisch-ungarischen Beziehungen vornehmlich in der Zeit der hussitischen Söldnerbanden," *ZVGMS,* vol. 22, Brno, 1918, pp. 59–73.

Louis XI of France, *Lettres de Louis XI, Roi de France,* ed. J. Vaesen and E. Charavay. II (1461–1465), Paris, 1885.

Lünig, Johann Christian, *Teutsches Reichs-Archiv, Pars Specialis.* VI, Leipzig, 1711.

Lupáč, Martin, *Hádání o kompaktátech,* ed. A. Císařová-Kolářová, Prague, 1953.

Mansi, J. D., *Sacrorum Conciliorum nova et amplissima collectio,* vols. 29 and 30, Venice, 1788 and 1792 (Facsimile reproduction Paris 1904).

Marini, Antonius, "Rada králi Jiřímu o zlepšení kupectví v Čechách," ed. Palacký, *ČČM,* 1828, part 3, pp. 1–20.

Markgraf, H., ed., *Politische Correspondenz Breslaus im Zeitalter Georgs von Podiebrad, SrS* VIII and IX, Breslau, 1873, 1874.

———, *Annales Glogovienses bis 1493, SrS,* X, Breslau 1877.

———, *Breslauer Stadtbuch.* (Codex Diplomaticus Silesiae XI), Breslau, 1882.

Matthias Corvinus, *Epistolae Matthiae Corvini regis ad pontifices, imperatores, etc.,* ed. E. Keltz. I and II, Kaschau-Košice, 1743, 1744.

———, *Epistolae ad Romanos Pontifices datae et ab eis acceptae,* ed. J. Decsenyi-Schönherr. (Monumenta Vaticana Historiam Regni Hungariae Illustrantia, Series I, vol. 6), Budapest, 1891.

Mencke, Johann B., *Scriptores rerum Germanicarum praecipue Saxonicarum.* III, Leipzig 1730.

Menzel, Karl, *Regesten zur Geschichte Friedrichs des Siegreichen.* (Quellen und Erörterungen zur bayerischen und deutschen Geschichte, vol. II, part 2), Munich, 1862.

Müller, Johann Joachim, *Des heiligen Römischen Reiches Teutscher Nation Reichstags-Theatrum unter Keyser Friedrich V.* Jena, 1713 (cited as "Müller, *Reichstags-Theatrum*").

Nagy, I., and Nyari, A., eds. *Monumenta Hungariae Historica, Acta Extera,*

(Magyar diplomacziai emlékek, Mátyás király korából, 1458–1490) I and II, Budapest 1875–1877.

Nebeský, Václav, ed., "Cantio de Rokycano et suis sectariis," *ČČM*. vol. 26, III Prague, 1852, pp. 44ff.

Neumann, A., *Nové prameny k dějinám husitství na Moravě*. Olomouc, 1930.

Oelsner, L., "Schlesische Urkunden zur Geschichte der Juden im Mittelalter," *AÖG*, 31, Vienna, 1864, 57–144.

Palacký, F., and Birk, E., ed., *Monumenta Conciliarum generalium seculi decimi quinti, Concilium Basiliense*, I and II, Vienna, 1857 and 1873.

Palacký, F., "Český denník poselstva do Francii," *ČČM*, I, 1827, 40–67, also ed. Kalousek, *AČ*, 1887.

———, ed., *Staří letopisové čeští, 1378–1527, Scriptores rerum Bohemicarum III*, Prague, 1829, same reedited by J. Charvát in *Dílo F. Palackého*, II, Prague, 1941, (but watch for deletions by German censor during World War II).

———, ed., *Archiv český*, 37 vols., Prague, 1840ff. (later volumes by other editors).

———, ed., *Urkundliche Beiträge zur Geschichte Böhmens und seiner Nachbarländer im Zeitalter Georgs von Podiebrad, FRA*, II, 20, Vienna, 1860.

———, ed., *Urkundliche Beiträge zur Geschichte des Hussitenkrieges*, II (1429–1436), Prague, 1873.

Pastor, L., *Acta inedita historiam pontificum Romanorum praesertim saeculi XV illustrantia*. Freiburg, 1904.

Pelikán, Josef, *Rožmberské dluhopisy 1454–1481*, Prague, 1953.

Peschke, Erhard, *Die Theologie der Böhmischen Brüder in ihrer Frühzeit* (Documents, in vol. II: Forschungen zur Kirchen- und Geistesgeschichte, vol. XX). Stuttgart, 1940.

Pešina, Tomáš (Thomas Joannes Pessina de Czechorod) *Phosphorus Septicornis* (*Divi Viti Ecclesiae Pragensis Majestas et Gloria*). Prague, 1673.

———, *Mars Moravicus*. Prague, 1677.

Pez, H., ed., "Anonymi synchronii lessus in obitum Ladislai Posthumi," *Scriptores rerum Austriacarum*. II, Leipzig, 1725, 679ff.

Pray, Georg, *Annales regum Hungariae*, Vienna, 1763–1770.

———, *Historia regum Hungariae*, II, Buda, 1801.

Přeloučský, Tůma, *O původu Jednoty bratrské a o chudých lidech*, ed. V. Sokol. Prague, 1947.

Priebatsch, Felix, *Die politische Korrespondenz des Kurfürsten Albrecht Achilles, 1470–1474*, Leipzig, 1894.

Quellen und Forschungen zur vaterländischen Geschichte, Literatur und Kunst, Vienna, 1849.

Quirinus, Augustus Marcia, *Pauli II, Veneti Pont. Max. Vita*. Rome, 1740.

Rabstein, Jan of, "Johannis Rabensteinensis Dialogus," ed. Adolf Bachmann, with German introduction, *AÖG*, vol. 54, Vienna, 1876, 351–402.

————, *Dialogus* (with Palacký's Czech translation) ed. and introduced by B. Ryba, Matice česká, Prague, 1946.

Raynaldus, Odoricus, *Annales ecclesiastici,* ed. J. D. Mansi. vols. 9 and 10, Lucca, 1752, 1753.

Riedel, Adolf Friedrich, ed., *Codex Diplomaticus Brandenburgensis.* Part II, vol. 5, part III, vol. 1, and supplement volume, Berlin, 1848, 1859, and 1865.

Rokycana, Joannes, "Tractatus de septem sacramentis ecclesiae," ed. Cochlaeus in appendix to his *Historia Hussitarum,* Mainz, 1549.

Rokycana, John, *Postilla,* ed. Frant. Šimek. 2 vols. (Sbirka pramenů českéhu hnutí náboženského ve století XIV. a XV., No. 16 and 17), Prague, 1928, 1929.

————, *Traktát o přijímání krve,* ed. F. Šimek. (Věstník k. české spol. nauk. tř. fil. 1940, II) Prague, 1941.

————, *M. Jan Rokycana, obránce pravdy a zákona božího,* (a selection from his sermons, writings and letters), ed. F. Šimek. Prague, 1949.

Rosicz, Sigismund, *Chronica gesta diversa et historia de miserabili morte regis Ladislai,* ed. Franz Wachter, (S.r.S.XII), Breslau, 1883.

Rožmitál, Lev of, His Travels, described by Šašek of Bířkov: in Latin: (ed. K. Hrdina) *Commentarius itineris atque peregrinationis,* Prague, 1951. In Czech: (ed. Urbánek) *Ve službách Jiříka krále,* Prague, 1940, pp. 31–184. In German: (ed. Schmeller) *Des Leo von Rosenthal Ritter-, Hof- und Pilgerreise,* Stuttgart, 1844. In English: (ed. M. Letts) *The Travels of Lev of Rožmitál,* Hakluyt Series, II, 108, Cambridge, 1957.

Rynešová, B., and Pelikán, *Listář a listinář Oldřicha z Rožmberka,* vol. III and IV, Prague, 1937, 1954.

Rzyszczewski and A. Muczkowski, eds., *Codex diplomaticus Poloniae.* vols. 2 and 3, Warsaw, 1847–58.

Schlesinger, Ludwig, ed., *Stadtbuch von Brüx.* (Beiträge zur Geschichte Böhmens, IV, 1.), Prague, 1876.

————, *Urkundenbuch der Stadt Saaz.* (Städte- und Urkundenbücher aus Böhmen II), Prague, 1892.

Schmidt, Valentin and Alois Picha, eds., *Urkundenbuch der Stadt Krummau in Böhmen.* II (Städte- und Urkundenbücher aus Böhmen, VI, 2) Prague, 1910.

Schwandtner, J. G., *Scriptores rerum Hungaricarum veteres ac genuini.* I-III, Vienna, 1746–48.

Senckenberg, Heinrich Christian, ed., "Anonymi Chronicon Austriacarum" in *Selecta iuris et historiarum,* V, Frankfurt, 1739.

Šimek, František, ed., *Staré letopisy české z vratislavského rukopisu.* With introduction by F. M. Bartoš, Prague, 1937 (cited as *SLČV*).

Šimek, F. and M. Kaňak, ed., *Staré letopisy české z rukopisu křižovnického.* Prague, 1959 (cited as *SLČK*).

Stránský, Pavel, *O státě českém.* Czech translation by E. Tonner of Stránský's *Respublica Bojema,* 2nd ed., Prague, 1913.

Strnad, J., ed., "Ctyři omluvné listy Plzeňských z r. 1466 proč odpadli od krále Jiřího," *ČČM.,* 1885, pp. 102–107.

Szujski, I., ed., *Codex epistolaris saeculi decimi quinti.* II, 1444–1492 (Monumenta med. aevi hist. res gest. Poloniae illustrantia), Cracow, 1876.

Teleki, Count József, *Hunyadiak Kora Magyarországon.* X and XI, Documents to 1476, Budapest, 1855.

Tempelfeld, Nicholas, "Tractatus, utrum liceat electo in regem Bohemiae dare obedienciam," ed. J. Loserth, *AÖG.* LXI, 89–187, and separate print, Vienna, 1880.

Theiner, Augustin, *Vetera Monumenta Historica Hungariam sacram illustrantia.* II, Rome, 1860.

——, *Vetera Monumenta Poloniae et Lithuaniae gentiumque finitimarum historiam illustrantia.* II, Rome, 1861.

——, *Codex Diplomaticus dominii temporalis S. Sedis.* III, Rome, 1862.

Theobald, Zacharias, *Hussitenkrieg.* III, Nürnberg, 1621.

Tobolka, Zd. V., ed., *Hilaria Leitmeritzkého traktát k p. Janovi z Rosenberka.* (Hist. Archiv č. akademie, XIII), Prague, 1898.

Toeppen, M., ed., *Acten der Ständetage Preussens unter der Herrschaft des Deutschen Ordens.* V, Leipzig, 1886.

Tovačovský z Cimburka, Ctibor, *Hádání Pravdy a Lži o kněžské zboží a panování jich.* Prague, 1539.

——, *Kniha Tovačovská,* ed. V. Brandl. Prague, 1868.

Unrest, Jacob, *Oesterreichische Chronik,* ed. K. Grossmann. Weimar, 1957. (See also older edition listed above, Hahn, *Collectio Monumentorum.*)

Urbánek, R., ed. *Ve službách Jiříka krále* (Národní klenotnice, vol. 5) Prague, 1940. (See also Lev of Rožmitál).

——, ed. *O volbě Jiřího z Poděbrad za krále českého.* Prague, 1958.

Václavek, Bedřich, ed., *Český listář.* Prague, 1949.

Valečovský of Kněžmost, Vaněk, "Traktát podkomořího Vaňka Valečovského proti panování kněžskému," ed. J. Čelakovský, *Zprávy o zasedání k. č. spol. nauk,* Prague, 1881, pp. 325–345.

Volkmer and Hohaus, eds., *Urkunden und Regesten zur Geschichte der Grafschaft Glatz.* (Glatzer Geschichtsquellen II), Habelschwerdt, 1888.

Wachter, Franz, ed., *Liegnitzer Chronik (Geschichtsschreiber Schlesiens des 15. Jahrhunderts) SrS,* XII, Breslau 1883.

Wadding, L., *Annales Minorum seu trium ordinum a S. Francisco institutorum.* 2nd ed., vol. 12 and 13, Rome 1735. (3rd. edition Quaracchi, 1934).

Wagner, F., "Zusätze und Korrekturen zu Höflers Kaiserlichem Buch," *Zeitschrift f. preuss. Geschichte und Landeskunde,* XVIII, Berlin, 1881, 304–350.

Weizsäcker, Wilhelm, ed., *Quellenbuch zur Geschichte der Sudetenländer,* I, Munich, 1960.

Wratislaw, A. H. transl. and ed. *Diary of an Embassy from King George of*

Bohemia to King Louis XI of France, 1464. London, 1871. (See also Kalousek.)

Zeibig, H. J., ed., *Copey-Buch der gemeinen stat Wienn, 1454–1464. FRA,* II, 7, 1853.

Zeumer, Karl, *Quellensammlung zur Geschichte der Deutschen Reichsverfassung in Mittelalter und Neuzeit.* 2nd ed., I, Tübingen, 1913.

Žídek, Pavel, *Spravovna,* ed. Zd. Tobolka (Historický Archiv České Akademie Cís. Frant. Josefa No. 33), Prague, 1908.

IV. PRINTED WORKS: SECONDARY SOURCES AND INTERPRETIVE WRITINGS

Titles marked with an asterisk (*) are secondary works which also contain, in an appendix or otherwise, substantial primary source material. A small number of unprinted doctoral dissertations are included.

Ady, Cecilia, Pius II, London, 1913.

Andreas, Willy, *Deutschland vor der Reformation.* 5th ed. Stuttgart, 1958.

Angermeier, Heinz, "Das Reich und der Konziliarismus," *HZ,* vol. 192, III, 1961, 529–583.

Aschbach, Joseph, *Geschichte Kaiser Sigmund's.* IV, Hamburg, 1845.

Aubenas, Roger, and Robert Richard, *L'Église et la Renaissance (1449–1517).* vol. 15 of Fliche and Martin, *Histoire de l'Église,* Paris, 1951.

Aubin, Hermann, *Geschichte Schlesiens.* I, Breslau, 1938.

Babinger, Franz, *Mehmed der Eroberer und seine Zeit.* Munich, 1953.

Bachmann, Adolf, "Ein Jahr böhmischer Geschichte: Georg von Podiebrads Wahl, Krönung und Anerkennung," *AÖG,* vol. 54, Vienna, 1876, 37–174.

————, *Zur Krönung Georgs von Podiebrad.* (Program des deutschen Staats-Realgymnasiums), Prague, 1876.

————, "Die ersten Versuche zu einer römischen Königswahl unter Friedrich III," *Forschungen zur Deutschen Geschichte,* vol. 17, Göttingen, 1877.

————, "Die ungarische Krone und König Georg von Böhmen," in *Zeitschrift für die österreichischen Gymnasien,* No. 28, Vienna, 1877, pp. 320–336.

————, "Bemerkungen zu Johann's von Rabenstein *Dialogus,*" *Jahresbericht über das deutsche Staats-Realgymnasium in Prag,* Prague, 1877.

————, Die ungarische Krone und König Georg von Böhmen," *Zeitschrift für die österreichichen Gymnasien,* Vienna, 1877, pp. 321–336.

————, *Böhmen und seine Nachbarländer unter Georg von Podiebrad, 1458–1461.* Prague, 1878.

————, "Georg von Podiebrad," *ADB,* vol. 8, 1878, 602–611.

————, "Herzog Wilhelm von Sachsen und sein böhmisches Söldnerheer auf dem Zuge vor Soest," *N. Archiv f. Sächs. Geschichte,* II, 1881, 97–128.

——, "Die Wiedervereinigung der Lausitz mit Böhmen," *AÖG*, vol. 64, Vienna, 1883, 249–351.

——, *Deutsche Reichsgeschichte im Zeitalter Friedrichs III und Max I*, 2 vols. Leipzig, 1884 and 1894.

——, "Die deutschen Könige und die kurfürstliche Neutralität," *AÖG*, 75, 1889, 1–236.*

——, "Der Vertrag von Wilemow (25. Februar 1469) und seine Bedeutung," *MVGDB*, 31, 1893, 342–358.

——, "Neues über die Wahl König Georgs von Böhmen," *MVGDB*, 33, Prague, 1895, 1–16.

——, "Über König Georg von Böhmen und Gregor Heimburg," *MVGDB*, 35, Prague, 1897, 144–152.

——, *Beiträge zur Kunde böhmischer Geschichtsquellen des XIV. und XV. Jahrhunderts*. (V: "Die Series rerum gestarum etc., first in *MVGDB* vol. 36, then separately published in Prague 1898).*

——, *Geschichte Böhmens*. II, Gotha, 1905.

Balcar, Anton, *Die Politik Königs Georg von Poděbrad*. Teschen, 1876–77.

Banlaky, Josef, *A Magyar nemzet hadtörtenelme*. Budapest, 1937.

Bartoš, F. M., "K počátkům Petra Chelčického," *ČČM*, 88, Prague, 1914, 27–35; 149–160; 303–314.

——, K traktátovým cyclům Jana Příbrama proti Petru Payneovi a Táborům," *LF*, vol. 41, Prague, 1914, 112–121.

——, "Valdenský biskup Štěpán z Basileje a jeho účast v ustavení Jednoty bratrské," *ČČM*, 90, Prague, 1916, 273–277.

——, "Chelčický a Rokycana," *LF*, 48, Prague, 1921, 30–40, 118–135.

——, "Z počátku Jednoty bratrské," *ČČM*, 95, Prague, 1921, 30–43, 127–139, 203–218.

——, "Mládí Jana Rokycany," *ČČM*, 96, Prague, 1922, 76ff.

——, *Bratr Řehoř, tvůrce Jednoty bratrské*. Prague, 1924.

——, "Žižka a Rokycana" (Studie o Žižkovi a jeho době I), *ČČM*, 98 1924, 2–15.

——, "M. Jan Hus v bohoslužbě a úctě církve pod obojí," *Národopisný věstník českoslovanský*, XVII, Prague, 1924, 20–38.

——, "Rokycana za t. zv. druhého pronásledování Jednoty bratrské," *ČČM*, 1925, 72–75.

——, *Z husových a žižkových časů*. Prague, 1925.

——, *Lipany*. (Knihovna Svazu Národního Osvobození 92), Prague, 1934.

——, "Jihlavská Kompaktata," *Český bratr*, Prague, 1936, pp. 12ff.

——, *Bojovníci a mučedníci, obrázky z dějin české reformace*. Prague, 1939.

——, "Martin Lupáč a jeho spisovatelské dílo," *Reformační sborník*, VII, Prague, 1939, 115–140.

——, "Návrh krále Jiřího na utvoření svazu evropských států," *JČSH*, XII, 1939, 65–82; also separate edition, 1940.

——, "Dva němečtí státníci na dvoře husitského krále," in *Nové obrázky z naších dějin* (Knihovna pokroku sv. 167), Prague, 1940.

——, "Kdo byl Petr Chelčický?" *JČSH*, XV, 1946, 1–8.

——, *Světci a kacíři*. Prague, 1949.

——, *Dvě studie o husitských postilách*, *RČSAV*, 65, part 4.

——, "Jesuitský obránce husitského krále," *Křesťanská revue*, XXIII, Prague, 1956, 184–186.

——, *Ze zápasů české reformace*, Prague, 1959.

——, "Husitšti kazatele a postily věku poděbradského," *Teologická přiloha křesťanské revue*, XXVIII, No. 10, 1961.

——, "Cusanus and the Hussite Bishop M. Lupáč," *Communio viatorum*, No. 5, Prague, 1962, 35–46.

——, "A Delegate of the Hussite Church to Constantinople in 1451–1452," *Byzantinoslavica*, XXIV, 2, Prague, 1963, 287–292.

——, "Jiří Poděbradský a J. A. Komenský v zápase o mir světa," *Křesťanské Listy a Husův Lid*. Chicago, April 1964, pp. 50f., 59f.

Basin, Thomas, *Histoire des règnes de Charles VII et de Louis XI,* ed. Quicherat. 4 vols., Paris, 1855–1859.

Bayer, V., *Die Historia Friderici III*. Prague, 1872.

Beck J. v. and J. Loserth, eds., "Urkundliche Beiträge zur Geschichte der hussitischen Bewegung und der Hussitenkriege mit besonderer Berücksichtigung Mährens und der Mährisch-Hussitischen Söldner," *Notizenblatt des Vereins für Geschichte Mährens und Schlesiens,* Brno, 1896.

Berzeviczy, Albert v., "König Matthias Corvinus and Königin Beatrix in Wien und Oesterreich," *Ungarische Jahrbücher*, XII, Berlin, 1932, 205–214.

Betts, R. R., "The Place of the Czech Reform Movement in the History of Europe," *Slavonic and East European Review,* vol. 25, London, 1947, 373–390.

——, "Social and Constitutional Development in Bohemia in the Hussite Period," *Past and Present,* No. 7, April, 1955, 37–54.

Bittner, Konrad, *Deutsche und Tschechen*. Brno, 1936.

Bondy, G. and F. Dworsky, *Zur Geschichte der Juden in Böhmen, Mähren und Schlesien*. 2 vols., Prague, 1906.

Böttiger, C. W., *Geschichte des Kurstaates und Königreiches Sachsen*. 2nd ed., I, Gotha, 1867.

Boulting, William, *Aeneas Sylvius*. London, 1908.

Bretholz, Berthold, *Geschichte Böhmens und Mährens*. II, Reichenbach (Liberec) 1922.

——, *Brünn, Geschichte und Kultur*. Brno, 1938.

Brock, Peter, *The Political and Social Doctrines of the Unity of Czech Brethren in the Fifteenth and Early Sixteenth Centuries*. The Hague, 1957.

Brockhaus, Clemens, *Gregor von Heimburg*. Leipzig, 1861.

Brunner, Otto, "Beiträge zur Geschichte des Fehdewesens im spätmittelalterlichen Oesterreich," *Jahrbuch für Landeskunde von Niederösterreich,*

XXII, Vienna, 1929, 431–504.

——, "Oesterreich, das Reich und der Osten im späteren Mittelalter," in Nadler und Srbik, *Oesterreich, Erbe und Sendung im deutschen Raum,* Vienna, 1937.

——, *Land und Herrschaft, Grundfragen der territorialen Verfassungs-geschichte Oesterreichs im Mittelalter.* 4th ed., Vienna, 1959.

Bürck, Gerhart, *Selbstdarstellung und Personenbildnis bei Enea Silvio Picco-lomini.* (Basler Beiträge zur Geschichtswissenschaft vol. 56), Basel, 1956.

Calmette, Joseph, *L'Élaboration du Monde Moderne.* Paris, 1934.

——, *Le grand règne de Louis XI.* Paris, 1938.

Čapek, Jan. B., "Husitský král v očích současníků," *Záření ducha a slova,* Prague, 1948, pp. 51–59.

Caro, Jacob, *Geschichte Polens.* V, part I and II, Gotha, 1886, 1888.

Castelin, Karel, *Česká drobna mince doby předhusitské a husitské 1300–1471.* Prague, 1953.

Cedlová, Marie, "Náboženské názory Petra Chelčikého i bratra Řehoře i jejich vzájemny poměr," *ČČM,* 106, Prague, 1932, 63–115, 278–322.

    Československá vlastivěda. IV, Dějiny; and vol. VII, Písemnictví, Prague 1932, f.

Chaloupecký, V., "Selská otázka v husitství," *Sbírka přednašek University Komenského,* vol. I, Bratislava, 1926, pp. 41–47.

——, "Jiskra z Brandýsa," *Tvůrcové dějin,* II, Prague, 1934, 534–544.

Champion, Pierre H. J. B., *Louis XI.* 2 vols., Paris, 1927 (also in English, London and New York 1929).

Charvát, Ed. J., *Censura a dílo Františka Palackého.* Prague, 1945.*

Chassin, Charles-Louis, *Jean de Hunyad.* (La Hongrie, II), Paris, 1856.

Chmel, Joseph, *Geschichte Friedrichs IV.* II, Hamburg, 1843.

——, "Zur Geschichte des österreichischen Freiherrngeschlechtes der Eizinger von Eizing," *AÖG,* I, 1848.

——, *Beiträge zur Geschichte des Königs Ladislaus des Nachgeborenen,* Sitz.-Ber. d. Wiener Akademie d. Wiss. XXV and XXVIII, and separate edition, Vienna, 1858 and 1859.*

Choc, Pavel, *Boje o Prahu za feudalismu.* Prague, 1957.

Chylík, Jindřich, "Nejstarší český spis národohospodářský," *Sborník věd právních a státních,* XXXII, Prague, 1932, 406–415.

Cibulka, J., *Český řád korunovační a jeho původ.* Prague, 1934.

Císařová-Kolářová, A., "Návštěva Eney Silvia v Táboře," *JČSH,* No. 20, 1951. 61ff.

Combet, J., *Louis XI et le Saint Siège.* Paris, 1903.

Coxe, William, *History of the House of Austria.* 3rd ed., I, London, 1847.

Creighton, Mandell, *A History of the Papacy from the Great Schism to the Sack of Rome.* 2nd ed., II, III, and IV, London, 1899–1903.

Csuday, Jenö, *Geschichte der Ungarn.* 2nd ed., I, Vienna, 1900.

Czerwenka, Bernhard, *Geschichte der Evangelischen Kirche in Böhmen.* 2 vols., Bielefeld-Leipzig, 1869, 1870.

Danou, Pierre, *Essai historique sur la puissance temporelle des papes,* 4th ed., I, Paris, 1818.

Demel, Jaroslav, *Geschichte des Fiskalamtes in den böhmischen Ländern.* (Forschungen z. inner. Gesch. Österr., ed. Dopsch, 5, I), Innsbruck, 1909.

Daenell, E., *Die Blütezeit der deutschen Hanse.* II, Berlin, 1906.

D'Elvert, Christian, *Geschichte der Bergstadt Iglau.* Brünn, 1850.

Dempf, Alois, *Sacrum Imperium.* Munich and Berlin, 1929.

Denis, Ernest, *De Antonio Marini,* Latin thesis printed for the Faculty of Letters in Paris, 1878.

———, *Georges de Podiébrad, Les Jagellons.* (Fin de l'indépendence Bohème, I), Paris, 1890.

———, *Konec samostatnosti české, Vol. I: Jiří z Poděbrad, Jagielovci.* (Same work in Czech but of some importance because of the documentary and critical apparatus added by the translator Jindřich Vančura.) 3rd ed., Prague, 1921.

Dersch, Wilhelm, "Schlesien am Vorabend der Reformation," *Zeitschrift des Vereins für Geschichte Schlesiens,* Vol. 68, Breslau, 1934, 69–94.

Długoborski, W., and others, *Dzieje Wrocłavia.* Warsaw, 1958.

Dobiáš, F. M., *Učení Jednoty bratrské o večeři páně.* Prague, 1940.

Dobiáš, Josef, *Dějiny královského města Pelhřimova.* II, 1, Pelhřimov, 1936.

Drivok, P., *Aeltere Geschichte der deutschen Reichsstadt Eger.* Leipzig, 1874.

Droysen, Gustav, "Ein von Albrecht Achilles an Friedrich Churfürsten von Brandenburg gerichtetes Gutachten betreffend die Krone Böhmen," *Verhandlungen d. kgl. sächs. Gesellsch. d. Wissenschaften,* Phil. hist. Classe, IX, 146–190 Leipzig, 1857. (146–173, interpretation; 176–190, document).*

———, *Geschichte der preussischen Politik.* 2nd ed., II, Leipzig, 1868.

Dudík, Beda, *Forschungen in Schweden für Mährens Geschichte.* Brno, 1852.*

———, *Iter Romanum.* 2 vols., Vienna, 1855.*

Düx, Joh. Martin, *Der deutsche Cardinal Nicolaus von Cusa und die Kirche seiner Zeit.* mit dokumentarischen Beilagen, 2 vols., Regensburg, 1847.*

Dvořák, Rudolf, *Dějiny Moravy.* (Vlastivěda moravská I), Brno, 1899.

———, *Dějiny markrabství moravského.* (stručné vydání), Brno, 1906.

Eberlein, Helmut, *Schlesische Kirchengeschichte.* 3rd ed., Goslar, 1952 (1st ed., Breslau, 1932).

Elekes, Lajos, *Mátyás és kora.* Budapest, 1956.

Erben, K. J., "Ondřej Puklice z Vstuh, měštěnín Budějovický," *ČČM,* X, Prague, 1846. 163–211.

Ermisch, Hubert, Mittel- und Niederschlesien während der königlosen Zeit 1440–1452," *ZVGAS,* 13, II, 1877.

———, "Studien zur Geschichte der sächsisch-böhmischen Beziehungen in den

Jahren 1464–1471," *Neues Archiv für Sächsische Geschichte und Alterthums-kunde,* I, 1880, 209–266; II, 1881, 1–49.

———, "Die Erwerbung des Herzogtums Sagan durch Kurfürst Ernst und Herzog Albrecht," *Neues Archiv f. sächs. Geschichte.* XIX, 1899.

Eubel, C., *Hierarchia catholica medii aevi.* II, 1431–1503, Münster, 1901.

Feeser, N., *Friedrich der Siegreiche von der Pfalz, 1449–1476.* Neuburg, 1880.

Fessler, Ignaz, *Mathias Corvinus,* Karlsruhe, 1809.

———, *Geschichte von Ungarn,* ed. E. Klein. II and III, Leipzig, 1869.

Figgis, John Neville, *From Gerson to Grotius 1414–1625.* Cambridge, 1907.

Fink, Karl August, "Der Kreuzablass gegen Georg Podiebrad in Süd- und Westdeutschland," *Quellen und Forschungen vom Preussischen Historischen Institut in Rom,* XXIV, Rome, 1932–1933, 207–243.

Fischer, I. W., *Geschichte der kgl. Stadt und Gränzfestung Olmütz.* Olomouc, 1808.

Flaišhans, V., "Postilla Jana Rokycany" (review of Šimek's edition), *ČČH,* 35, 1929, 618–629.

Fousek, Marianka S., "The Pastoral Office in the Early Unitas Fratrum," *The Slavonic and East European Review,* London, June 1962, pp. 444–457.

Foustka, Radim, "Petra Chelčického názory na stát a právo," *Acta Universitatis Carolinae,* I, Iuridica, Prague, 1955.

Fraknói, Wil., "Die Anfänge der europäischen Politik des Königs Mathias von Ungarn 1464–1470," *Oesterreichisch-Ungarische Revue,* X, 65ff., 71ff.

———, "Cardinal Carvajal's Legationen in Ungarn," *Ungarische Revue,* X, 1890, 1–18, 124–143, 399–425.

———, "König Matthias erste Versuche zur Erwerbung des deutschen Thrones 1468–70," *Ungarische Revue,* X, 1890, 501ff.

———, *Mathias Corvinus, König von Ungarn 1458–1490.* Freiburg Br. 1891.

———, *Matyás király levelei.* Budapest, 1893.

———, *Die Hohenzollern und Matthias Corvinus.* Munich, 1916.

———, "La Politica europea di Re Mattia," *Corvina,* Budapest, 1921.

Frauenholz, Eugen v., *Das Heerwesen in der Zeit des freien Söldnertums.* 2 vols., Munich, 1936–1937.

Franklin, O., *Albrecht Achilles und die Nürnberger.* Berlin, 1866.

Friedberg, J., "Polityka Kazimierza Jagiellońzyka wobec papieza Piusa II," *Mitteilungen des Gymnasiums in Przemysl,* Przemysl 1901.

Frind, Anton, *Die Kirchengeschichte Böhmens.* III and IV, Prague, 1872, 1878.

Gade, John A., *Luxemburg in the Middle Ages.* Leiden, 1951.

Gebhardt, B., *Die gravamina der deutschen Nation gegen den römischen Hof, Ein Beitrag zur Vorgeschichte der Reformation.* 2nd ed., Breslau, 1895.

Gellner, G., "Nemoc Ladislava Pohrobka," *ČČH,* 1934.

Genzsch, Hans A., "Die Anlage der ältesten Sammlung von Briefen Enea Silvios," *MIÖG,* 46, 1932, 372–464.

Gill, Joseph, *Eugenius IV, Pope of Christian Union. (The Popes' Strange History,* I) Westminster, Maryland, 1961.

Gindely, Anton, *Geschichte der Böhmischen Brüder.* Prague, 1861.

Goll, Jaroslav, *Quellen und Untersuchungen zur Geschichte der Böhmischen Brüder.* 2 vols. Prague, 1878, 1882.*

———, "Rokycanova Postilla," *ČČM,* LIII, 1879, 59–70, 199–211.

———, "Jednota bratrská v. 15 století," *ČČM,* LVIII, 1884, 37–53, 157–173, 447–471.

———, *Čechy a Prusy ve středověku.* Prague, 1896.

———, *Chelčický a Jednota v XV. stoleti,* ed. Krofta. Prague, 1916.

———, *Vybrané spisy drobné.* 2 vols., Prague, 1929.

Gomez Canedo, Lino, *Don Juan de Carvajal, Un espanol al servicio de la Santa Sede.* Madrid, 1945.*

Gotheim, Eberhard, *Politische und religiöse Volksbewegungen vor der Reformation.* Breslau, 1878.

Gradl, Heinrich, "Eger und Heinrich von Plauen 1451–1454," *MVGDB,* XIX, Prague, 1881, 198–214.

———, "Die Irrlehre der Wirsperger," *MVGDB,* XIX, 1881, 270–279.

———, *Geschichte der Stadt Eger.* (Deutsche Chroniken aus Böhmen), III, Brno, 1884.

Gregorovius, Ferdinand, *Geschichte der Stadt Rom im Mittelalter.* 5th ed., VII, Stuttgart, 1908.

Grüneisen, Henny, "Die westlichen Reichstände in der Auseinandersetzung zwischen dem Reich, Burgund und Frankreich bis 1473," *Rheinische Vierteljahrsblätter,* 26, Bonn, 1961, 22–77.

———, "Friedrich I, der Siegreiche," *NDB,* V, Berlin, 1961, 526–528.

Grünhagen, Colmar, *Geschichte Schlesiens.* I, Gotha, 1885.

———, "Breslau und die Landesfürsten während des Mittelalters," *ZfGS,* XXXVI, 1901, 1–28.

Gumpelzhaimer, Christian G., *Regensburg's Geschichte.* I, Regensburg, 1830.

Gundling, J. P., *Leben und Thaten Friderichs des Anderen, Churfürsten zu Brandenburg.* Potsdam, 1725.*

Gutkas, Karl, *Geschichte des Landes Niederösterreich.* I, St. Pölten, 1957.

Guttenberg, Erich v., "Albrecht Achilles," *NDB,* I, 1952, 161–163.

Haller, J., "Pius II, ein Papst der Renaissance," *Reden und Aufsätze zur Geschichte und Politik* (also in Deutsche Rundschau, 1912), Stuttgart, 1934.

Hamršmid, Jos., *Jošt z Rožmberka a jeho doba.* Prague, 1892.

———, "Co veřil král Jiří o prijímání pod obojí způsobou," *Sborník historického kroužku,* I, Prague, 1893, 36–39.*

Hantsch, Hugo, *Die Geschichte Österreichs.* 3rd ed., I, Graz, 1951.

Hanuš, Ignaz Johann, "Ctibor von Cimburk's Werk: 'Hádáni Pravdy a Lžy'," *Sitzungsberichte d.k. böhm. Ges. d. Wiss.* Prague, 1862, 35–39.

Haselbach, K., *Die Türkennot im 15. Jahrhundert*. Vienna, 1864.

Hashagen, Justus, *Staat und Kirche vor der Reformation*. Essen, 1931.

Haškovec, Prokop, "Rukopis Rokycanova výkladu na evangelium sv. Jana," *LF*, XXIX, Prague, 1902, 62–66, 150–157.

———, "Rokycanův výklad evangelia Janova," *Program real. gymnasia*, Pardubice, 1903.

Haupt, Hermann, *Die religiösen Sekten in Franken vor der Reformation*. Würzburg, 1882.

Heck, Roman, and Maleczyńska, Ewa, *Ruch husycki w Polsce*. Wrocław, 1953.

Heck, Roman, "Czeski plan związku wladców europejskich z lat 1462–1464 i Polska," *Studia z dziejów polskich i czeskoslowackich I*, Wrocław, 1960.

Hefele, K. J., *Konziliengeschichte*, ed. Hergenröther. VIII, Freiburg, 1887.

Heimpel, Hermann, "Karl der Kühne und Deutschland," *Elsass-lothringische Jahrbücher*, 21, 1941.

———, *Deutschland im späten Mittelalter*. (Vol. I, part 5, of Brand-Meyer-Just, *Handbuch der deutschen Geschichte*), Konstanz, 1957.

Helbig, Herbert, "Reich, Territorialstaaten und deutsche Einheit im Spätmittelalter," *Die Deutsche Einheit als Problem der europäischen Geschichte*, ed. Hinrichs and Berges, Stuttgart, 1960.

Hemleben, Sylvester, J., *Plans for World Peace through Six Centuries*. Chicago, 1943.

Herben, Jan., *Husitství a bratrství*. Prague, 1926.

Hermann, Amandus, *Capistranus triumphans*. Cologne, 1700.*

Heš, G., "O působení Jana Vitěze ze Zredna a Jiříka z Poděbrad ve volbě Matyáše Korvina za krále uherského," *Program českého gymnasia v Jindřichském Hradce*, 1893.

Heymann, Frederick G., "The Role of the Towns in the Bohemia of the Later Middle Ages," *Journal of World History*, II. Paris, 1954, 326–346.

———, *John Žižka and the Hussite Revolution*. Princeton, 1955.

———, "John Rokycana—Church Reformer between Hus and Luther," *Church History*, 28, Chicago, 1959, 240–280.

———, "The Hussite-Utraquist Church in the Fifteenth and Sixteenth Centuries," *Archiv für Reformationsgeschichte*, 52, 1961, 1–16.

———, "The Death of King Ladislav: Historiographical Echoes of a Suspected Crime," *The Canadian Historical Association Report*, 1961, pp. 96–111.

———, "City Rebellions in 15th Century Bohemia and their Ideological and Sociological Background," *Slavonic and East European Review*, 40, No. 95, June 1962, 324–340.

Heyne, Johann, *Dokumentierte Geschichte des Bisthums und Hochstifts Breslau*. III, Breslau, 1868.*

Hocks, Else, "Idee und Leben," in Peter Mennicken, *Nicholaus von Kues*, Leipzig, 1932.

——, *Pius II und der Halbmond*. Freiburg 1941.

Hofer, Johannes, *Johannes von Capestrano*. Innsbruck, 1936.*

Höfler, Constantin, "Urkundliche Nachrichten über König Georg Podiebrad's von Böhmen Versuch die deutsche Reichskrone an sich zu reissen," *Münchner Gelehrte Anzeigen, 1849*, 4ff.*

——, *Über die politische Reformbewegung in Deutschland im 15. Jahrhunderte*. Munich, 1850.

——, "Neueste Studien zu München, insbesondere über Georg von Poděbrad," *Sitzungsberichte der K. böhm. Ges. der Wiss.*, Part 2, Prague, 1862, 39–65.

——, *Kaiserthum und Papstthum*. Prague, 1862.

Hoffmann, A., *Kaiser Friedrichs III Beziehungen zu Ungarn in den Jahren 1458–1464*. Breslau, 1887. Same published by: *Program des Gymnasiums im Glogau*, 1901, 1902.

Hoffmann, Ladislav, *Bratříci, protifeudalní bojovníci 15. století*. Prague, 1959.

Holeček, Josef, *Česká šlechta, základy časové i historické*. 2nd ed., Prague, 1918.

Hóman, Bálint, and Szekfü, Gyula., *Magyar történet*. II, Budapest, 1936.

Horčička, Adolf, "Die Erhebung von Neumarkt zur Stadt, 1459," *MVGDB*, XXXVII, 1899, 211–213.

Hormayer, J., *Der Oesterreichische Plutarch*. XVIII, Vienna, 1812, 1–109.

——, "Georg von Podiebrad," *Böhmische Regenten*, Vienna, 1857, pp. 88–117.

Hosák, Ladislav, "Středověké vyprávěcí prameny k dějinám Moravy," II and III, *Sborník vysoké školy pedagogické*, Olomouc, 1956–57.

——, "Učast českých žoldnéřů na bojích v Rakousích 1439–1460," *Sborník vysoké školy pedagogické, Historie V*, Olomouc, 1958.

——, "Olomoucký patriciát v boji proti husitskému revolučnímu hnutí," *Acta Universitatis Palackianae Olomucensis*, Historica I, Prague, 1960.

Hrejsa, Ferdinand, *Zásady Jednoty českých bratří*. Prague, 1939.

——, "Psání mistra Rokycána Petrovi Chelčickému," *Reformační Sborník*, VIII, Prague, 1941, 39–44.

——, *Dějiny křesťanství v Československu*. III, Prague, 1948.

Hrubý, František, "Z hospodářských převratů českých století XV. a XVI.," XXX, *ČČH*, Prague, 1924.

——, *Severní Morava v dějinách*, Brno, 1947.

Hrubý, Hynek, *České postilly*. Prague, 1901.

Huber, A., *Geschichte Oesterreichs*. Gotha, 1888.

Jacob, E. F., *Essays in the Conciliar Epoch*. London, 1943.

——, "The Bohemians at the Council of Basel, 1433," *Prague Essays*, ed. R. W. Seton-Watson, Oxford, 1949, pp. 81–123.

Jacob, Eugen, *Johannes von Capistrano*. 4 vols., Breslau, 1903–1911.

Jaeger, Albrecht, *Der Streit des Cardinals Nikolas von Cusa mit dem Herzoge Sigmund von Oesterreich*. 2 vols., Innsbruck, 1861.

Janner, Ferdinand, *Geschichte der Bischöfe von Regensburg*. III, Regensburg and New York, 1885.

Janssen, Johannes, *History of the German People*, II, St. Louis, 1896.

Jireček, H., "Jan Jiskra z Brandýsa," *Slovesnost*, p. 185.

Jireček, J., "Über die culturellen Beziehungen der Ungarn und Böhmen im XIV. und XV. Jahrhunderte und über die ungarischen Hussiten," *Sitzungsberichte der Kgl.böhm. Gesellschaft der Wissenschaften*. Prague, 1885, 101–113.

Joachimsohn, Paul, *Gregor Heimburg*. (Historische Abhandlungen aus dem Münchner Seminar, I) Bamberg, 1891.*

——, "Die Streitschrift des Minoriten Gabriel von Verona gegen den Böhmenkönig Georg von Podiebrad v. J. 1467," *Program des Realgymnasiums*, Augsburg, 1896.*

——, "Zu Gregor Heimburg," *Historisches Jahrbuch der Goerres-Gesellschaft zur Pflege der Wissenschaft im katholischen Deutschland*, vol. 18, pp. 554–559.

Jordan, Max, *Das Königthum Georgs von Poděbrad*. Leipzig, 1861.*

Jorga, Nicola, "Antoine Marini," *Études d'histoire du Moyen Age, dédiées à G. Monod*, Paris, 1896, pp. 445ff.

——, *Geschichte des Osmanischen Reiches*. II, Gotha, 1909.

Kalina, Tomáš, "Hilarius Litoměrický," *ČČH*, V, 1899, 311–321.

——, "Václav Křižanovský," *ČČH*, V, 1899. 333–359.

Kallen G., *Aeneas Silvius Piccolomini als Publizist*. Cologne, 1939.

Kaminsky, Howard, "Pius Aeneas among the Taborites," *Church History*, 28, September 1959, 281–309.

Kanter, Ehrhard Waldemar, *Die Ermordung König Ladislavs, 1457*. Munich, 1906.

——, *Markgraf Albrecht Achilles von Brandenburg*, Berlin 1911.

Kapras, Jan, *Národnostní poměry v české koruně od válek husitských do bitvy bělohorské*, Prague, 1912.

——, *Prawne stawizny Hornjeje a Delnjeje Łužicy*. Budyšin (Bautzen), 1916.

——, *Právní dějiny zemí koruny české*. Prague, 1913–1920.

——, *The Peace League of George Poděbrad, King of Bohemia*. (The Czechoslovak Republic, II, 5), Prague, 1919. (Also in Czech in *Právnické Rozhledy*, XIX, 1918–19, 177–185.)

——, *České Slezsko v historickým vývoji*. Prague, 1933.

——, *Přehled právních dějin zemí koruny české*. 5th ed., Prague, 1935.

Kavka, František, *Husitská revoluční tradice*. Prague, 1954.

——, "Majetková, sociální a třídní struktura českých měst v první polovině 16. století," *Sborník historický*, 6, Prague, 1959, pp. 253–294.

Kejř, Jiří, *Dvě studie o husitském právnictví*. (Rozpravy čs. Ak. Věd, vol. 64, part 5), Prague, 1954.

——, *Boj o státní formu v husitském revolučním hnutí*. (Právněhistorické studie II), Prague, 1956.

——, *Počátky dvorského soudu*. Rozpravy čsl. akademie věd, vol. 66, IV, Prague, 1956.

————, *Právní život v husitské Kutné Hoře.* Prague, 1958.

Kern, Th. v., "Der Kampf der Fürsten gegen die Städte 1449 und 1450," *Raumer's Historisches Taschenbuch,* 1866.

Kestenberg-Gladstein, Ruth, "The Third Reich" (especially "Bohemia, and the Taborites and Wirsbergers"), *Journal of the Warburg and Courtauld Institutes,* vol. 18, London, 1955, 245ff.

Klick, Josef, *Národnostní poměry v Čechách od válek husitských do bitvy bělohorské,* Prague, 1922 (also publ. in *ČČH,* XXVII, XXVIII).

Kliment, Josef, *Svaz národů Jiřího z Poděbrad a idea jediné světovlady.* Prague, 1935.

Kluckhohn, August, *Ludwig der Reiche, Herzog von Bayern.* Nördlingen, 1865.

Kneschke, R., "Georg von Stein," dissertation, University of Leipzig, 1913.

Koch, Josef, "Nikolaus von Kues," *Die grossen Deutschen,* ed. Heimpel, Heuss, Reifenberg, I, Berlin, 1956, 275–287.

Koebner, Richard, *Der Widerstand Breslaus gegen Georg von Podiebrad.* (Darstellungen und Quellen zur schlesischen Geschichte, XII), Breslau, 1916.*

Köhler (General), "Über den Feldzug 1468 in Mähren," *Jahresbericht für 1875 der Schlesischen Gesellschaft für Vaterländische Kultur,* Breslau, 1876, pp. 260 f.

Koller, Johann, "Worin äusserte sich am deutlichsten das Wesen des Husitismus, und wie verhielten sich die Deutschstädte Mährens zu demselben?" *Programme des deutschen Gymnasiums in Olmütz,* Olomouc, 1883, 1884.

Konrad, Paul, *Die Einführung der Reformation in Breslau und Schlesien.* (Darstellungen und Quellen zur Schlesischen Geschichte 24) Breslau, 1917.

Kop, František, and others, *Praha 600 let církevní metropoli.* Prague, 1944.

Koser, Reinhold, *Geschichte der brandenburgisch-preussischen Politik.* I, Stuttgart, 1913.

————, "Die Politik der Kurfürsten Friedrich II und Albrecht von Brandenburg," *Hohenzollern-Jahrbuch,* No. 13.

Kosinová, Věra, "Zdeněk ze Šternberka a jeho královské ambice," in *K dějinám československým v období humanismu; sborník prací věnovaných J. B. Novákovi,* Prague, 1932, pp. 206–218.

Kovacs, Endre, *Magyar-cseh törtenelmi kapczolatock.* Budapest, 1952.

Kralik R. and Schlitter, H. *Geschichte der Stadt Wien.* 2nd ed., Vienna, 1927.

Kramer, H., "Die Grundlagen der Aussenpolitik Herzog Sigmunds von Tirol," *Tiroler Heimat,* vol. 11, 1947, 67–80, and vol. 12, 1948, 79–92.

Kraus, Victor von, *Deutsche Geschichte im Ausgange des Mittelalters (1438–1519).* I, *Deutsche Geschichte zur Zeit Albrechts II und Friedrichs III.,* Stuttgart and Berlin, 1905.

Kremer, Christoph Jakob, *Geschichte des Kurfürsten Friedrichs I von der Pfalz.* Frankfurt and Leipzig, 1765.

Kretzschmar, Hellmut, "Die Beziehungen zwischen Brandenburg und den wettinischen Landen unter Kurfürst Albrecht Achilles und Herzog Ernst, 1464–1486," *Forschungen zur brandenburgischen und preussischen Geschichte,* 35, 1923, 21ff; 37, 1925, 204ff.

——, *Sächsische Geschichte.* I, Dresden, 1935.

Krofta Kamil, *Stará ústava česká a uherská.* Prague, 1931.

——, *Začátky české berně.* Prague, 1931.

——, "My a Maďaři v minulosti," *Časopis svob. školy polit. nauk,* V, 1, Prague, 1932, pp. 2ff.

——, "My a Maďaři v bojích s Turky," *ibid.,* VI, Prague, 1934, 97ff.

——, "La France et le mouvement religieux tchèque," *Le Monde Slave,* III, Paris, 1935, 161–185, 321–360.

——, *Listy z náboženských dějin českých.* Prague, 1936.

——, *Čechy v době husitské (1419–1526).* Prague, 1938.

——, *Dějiny československé.* Prague, 1946.

——, *Duchovní odkaz husitství.* Prague, 1946.

Krones, Franz, *Oesterreichische Geschichte für das Volk.* IV: Die österreichischen, böhmischen und ungarischen Länder 1437–1526, Vienna, 1864.

——, *Die zeitgenössischen Quellen zur Geschichte der Grafen von Cilli.* Graz 1871 (Also in *Beiträge zur Kunde steiermärkischer Geschichtsquellen*), vol. 8.

——, "Die österreichische Chronik J. Unrests," *AÖG,* XLVIII, Vienna, 1872.

——, *Handbuch der Geschichte Oesterreichs.* II, Berlin, 1880.

——, *Grundriss der österreichischen Geschichte.* Vienna, 1882.

——, "Beiträge zur Geschichte der Baumkircherfehde 1469–1470," *AÖG,* LXXXIX, Vienna, 1901.

Krummel, Leopold, *Geschichte der böhmischen Reformation.* Gotha, 1866.

Kupelwieser, L., *Die Kämpfe Ungarns mit den Osmanen bis 1526,* 2. ed., Vienna 1899.

Kurfürst, František, *Válečné dějiny československé.* Prague, 1937.

Kürschner, F., "Nachrichten über die Vorgänge in Schlesien unter den Königen Georg und Matthias," *ZfGS,* VIII, 1867, 403–413.[*]

Kurz, Franz, *Oesterreich unter Kaiser Friedrich IV,* 2 vols., Vienna, 1812.[*]

——, *Oesterreichs Militärverfassung in älteren Zeiten.* Linz, 1825.[*]

Lánczy, Julius, "Beziehungen zwischen Ungarn und Siena" (Pius II und Johann von Capistrano), *Ungarische Revue,* XV, Leipzig, 1895, 145–164.

Langenn, F. A. v., *Herzog Albrecht der Beherzte.* Leipzig, 1838.

Lasek, F., *Bratrský hejtman Jan Talafús.* Litomyšl, 1946.

Laslowski, Ernst, "Beiträge zur Geschichte des spätmittelalterlichem Ablasswesens," *Breslauer Studien zur historischen Theologie,* XI, Breslau, 1929.

Lazarus, P., *Das Basler Conzil.* Berlin, 1912.

Ledermann, László, *Les précurseurs de l'organisation internationale.* Neuchâtel, 1945.

Lehr-Spławiński, Tadeusz, and others, *Polska-Czechy, Dziesięć wieków sasiedztwa*. (Pamiętnik Instytutu sląskiego, Seria II, 7), Katowice, 1947.

Leminger, Emil, *Královská mincovna v Kutné Hoře*. (Rozpravy české akademie věd, Tř. 1, čis. 48, 1912, č. 70, 1924).

Lhotsky, Alphons, *Thomas Ebendorfer*. (Schriften der Monumenta Germaniae historica, vol. 15), Stuttgart, 1957.

Lichnovsky, Prince E. M., *Geschichte des Hauses Habsburg*, VI, VII, Vienna 1842, 1843.

Looshorn, Johann, *Geschichte des Bisthums Bamberg*. IV, 1400–1556, Munich, 1900.

Lopez de Barrera, Domenicus, *De rebus gestis Joannis cardinalis Carvajalis Commentarius*. Rome, 1752.

Loserth, J., "Die Krönungsordnung der Könige von Böhmen," *AÖG*, LIV, 11–36.

———, *Geschichte des späteren Mittelalters*. Munich, Berlin, 1903.

Lucius, Chr., *Pius II und Ludwig XI von Frankreich 1461–1462*. (Heidelberger Abhandlungen z. mittleren und neueren Geschichte, vol. 41) Heidelberg, 1913.

Lug, V., *Das Verhältnis des Grafen Ulrich II von Cilli zu König Ladislaw Posthumus*. Liberec (Reichenberg), 1904.

Lupínek, F., *Jan Roháč z Dubé*. Kutná Hora, 1930.

Macek, Josef, "Třidní struktura Loun v. r. 1460," *Časopis společnosti přatel starožitností*, vol. 58, Prague, 1950, pp. 157–170, 220–229.

———, *Husitské revoluční hnutí*. Prague, 1952 (also in English translation).

———, Narodnostní otázka v husitském revolučním hnutí," *ČSČH*, III, 1955, 4–30.

———, *Tábor v husitském revolučním hnutí*. I, 2nd ed., Prague, 1956; II, Prague, 1955.

Machovec, Mílan, *Husovo učení a význam v tradici českého národa*. Prague, 1953.

MacKinnon, James, *The Origins of the Reformation*. London, 1939.

Macůrek, Josef, *Dějiny Maďarů a uherského státu*. Prague, 1934.

———, *Dějiny polského národa*. Prague, 1948.

———, "Slezsko a jeho úloha ve vývoji česko-polských vztahů na přelomu 15. a 16. století," *Česko-Polský sborník vědeckých praci*, I, Prague, 1955.

Maetschke, E., *Die Grafschaft Glatz*. Glatz, 1932.

Mailath, Johannes, Count of, *Geschichte der Magyaren*. II, Regensburg, 1852.

Maleczyńska, Ewa and others, *Beiträge zur Geschichte Schlesiens*. Berlin, 1958.

Maleczyński, Karel, *Dzieje Wrocławia I*. Do roku 1526, Katowice-Wrocław, 1948.

Mandrot, B. de, "Dépèches d'ambassadeurs Milanais en France durant les premières années du règne de Louis XI," *Annuaire bulletin de la Societé de l'Histoire de France*, Paris, 1910, pp. 114–140.

Marek, Jaroslav, *Společenská struktura moravských kralovských měst v 15. a 16. stol*. Prague or Brno, probably 1964 or 1965, (read in MS.).

Markgraf, H., *Das Verhältnis des Königs Georg von Böhmen zu Papst Pius II,*
1458–1462. Jahresbericht des K. Friedrich Gymnasiums, also published as
book, Breslau, 1867.

———, "Das Verhältnis des Königs Georg von Böhmen zu Papst Pius II, 1462–
1464," *Forschungen zur deutschen Geschichte,* IX, Göttingen, 1869, pp.
217–258.

———, "Über Georgs von Podiebrad Project eines christlichen Fürstenbundes,"
HZ, XXII, Munich, 1869, 257–304.

———, "Geschichte Schlesiens und besonders Breslaus unter König Ladislaus
Posthumus," *ZVGAS,* XI, Breslau, 1872, 235–274.

———, "Über den böhmischen Herrenbund i. J. 1465," *Jahresbericht der*
Schlesischen Gesellschaft für vaterländische Kultur, Breslau, 1875.

———, "Die Bildung der Katholischen Liga gegen König Georg von Podiebrad," *HZ,* XXXVIII, 1877.

———, "Jost, Bischof von Breslau," *ADB,* XIV, 570ff.

———, "Rudolf von Rüdesheim, Bischof von Breslau," *ADB,* XXIX, 529ff.

Maršan, Robert, *Jiří z Poděbrad, tvůrce spořadaného státu.* Jičín, 1937.

Martinů, Johann, *Die Waldesier und die husitische Reformation in Böhmen.*
Vienna & Leipzig, 1910.

Matějek, Fr., *Feudální velkostatek a poddaný na Moravě v druhé polovině 15.*
a v prvné polovině 16. století. Prague, 1959.

Menčík, Ferdinand, ed., "Písen o přijímání kalicha," *ČČM,* No. 53, Prague, 1879,
153–157.*

Mendl, Bedřich, *Z hospodářských dějin středověké Prahy.* Prague, 1925.

Mennicken, Peter, *Nikolaus von Kues.* Leipzig, 1932.

Menzel, Karl, *Kurfürst Friedrich der Siegreiche von der Pfalz.* Munich, 1861.

———, *Diether von Isenburg, Erzbischof von Mainz, 1459–1463.* Erlangen,
1868.

Meuthen, Erich, *Die letzten Jahre des Nikolaus von Kues.* (Wissensch. Abhandlung d. Arbeitsgemeinsch. für Forschung des Landes Nordrhein-Westfalen,
Vol. III) Köln, 1958.

Meyer, Chr., "Zur Geschichte des Krieges zwischen Albrecht Achilles und
Herzog Ludwig von Baiern 1460," *Hohenzollernsche Forschungen,* I, Berlin, 1892.

Meyer, Arnold Oskar, *Studien zur Vorgeschichte der Reformation, aus Schlesischen Quellen.* (Historische Bibliothek XIV) Munich and Berlin, 1903.

Meynert, Hermann, *Geschichte des sächsischen Volkes.* Leipzig, 1835.

Mika, Alois, "Feudální velkostatek v jižních Čechách (XIV–XVII. stol.),"
Sborník historický, I, Prague, 1952, 122–213.

———, "Problem počátku nevolnictví v Čechách," *ČSČH,* V, 1957, 226–248.

Mitchell, Rosamund J., *The Laurels and the Tiara, Pope Pius II 1458–1464.*
London, 1962.

Mohler, Ludwig, *Kardinal Bessarion als Theologe, Humanist und Staatsmann.* (Quellen und Forschungen der Görres-Gesellschaft XX), Vol. 1, Paderborn, 1923.

Molitor, Erich, *Die Reichsreformbestrebungen des 15. Jahrhunderts.* (Untersuchungen z. dt. Staats-und Rechtsgeschichte, ed. Gierke, vol. 132), Breslau, 1921.

Molnar, Amedeo (and others.) *Od reformace k zitřku.* Prague, 1956.

———, "L'évolution de la théologie hussite," *Revue d'Histoire et de Philosophie Religieuses,* No. 2, Paris, 1963, 133–171.

Morgenbesser, M., *Geschichte von Schlesien,* 4th ed., Breslau, 1908.

Most, Ingeborg, "Der Reichslandfriede vom 20, August 1467," in *Syntagma Friburgense* (Festschrift f. H. Aubin), pp. 191–233.

Mrázek, Jan, *Die königliche Stadt Ungarisch-Hradisch.* Uherské Hradiště s.d.

Müller, Johann Sebastian, *Des Chur- und Fürstlichen Hauses Sachsen Ernestin- und Albertinischer Linien Annales.* Leipzig, 1700.

Müller, Joseph Th., *Geschichte der Böhmischen Brüder, 1400–1528.* I, Hernhut, 1922, also in Czech, transl. and ed. Bartoš, *Dějiny Jednoty Bratrské,* Prague, 1923.

Müller, Karl, *Kirchengeschichte.* II, part I, Tübingen, 1902.

Müller, V., *Svobodníci. Pokus o monografii ze sociálních dějin českých z 15. a. 16. stoleti.* Prague, 1905.

Müller, Willibald, *Geschichte der Hauptstadt Olmütz.* Olomouc, 1895.

Nejedlý, Zdeněk, "Mládí M. Jana z Rokycan," *ČČM,* LXXIII, Prague, 1899. pp. 517–534.

———, "Česká missie Jana Kapistrana," *ČČM,* LXXIV, Prague, 1900, 57–72, 220–242, 334–352, 447–464.

Nejedlý, Zdeněk, *Prameny k synodám strany pražské a táborské v letech 1441–1444.* Prague, 1900.*

———, *Dějiny husitského zpěvu.* 2nd ed., Spisy (collected works), vols. 40–45, Prague, 1954–56.

Neumann, Augustin, *České sekty ve stoleti XIV–XV.* Prague, 1920.

Nováková, Julie, "K polemice Hilaria Litoměřického s Rokycanou," *LF,* 66, Prague, 1939, 365.

Novotný, V., *Über den Tod des Königs Ladislaus Posthumus* (Věstnik k. č. společnosti nauk, No. X for 1906), Prague, 1907.

———, *Husitská kázání z konce XV. stoleti* (Věstník k. č. společností nauk, No. IV for 1930) Prague 1931.

Nuhliček, Josef, "Kutná Hora v době Jiříkově," *Středočeský sborník historický,* 1960. (read in MS.)

Obermann, K., and J. Polišenský, eds., *Aus 500 Jahren deutsch-tschechoslowakischer Geschichte.* Berlin, 1958.

Odložilík, Otakar, "Petr Chelčický," *Tvůrcové dějin.* II, Prague, 1934, 528–536.

———, "George of Poděbrady and Bohemia to the Pacification of Silesia 1459,"

University of Colorado Studies, Series B. vol. I, No. 3, Boulder, 1941, pp. 265–288.

———, "Problems of the Reign of George of Poděbrady," *Slavonic and Eastern European Review*, XX, 1941, 206–222.

———, "Pán obého lida," *Husův Lid*, XIX, No. 3, Chicago, 1958, 35ff.

———, "Záběry zblízka i zdálky," *Křesťanské Listy a Husův Lid*, Vol. 63, Chicago, Nov. 1961, 164–168.

Palacký, F., *Dějiny národu českého v Čechách a v Moravě*, several editions. Used here: 2nd ed., Vol. IV, 1 and 2, Prague, 1877. Same in German: *Geschichte von Böhmen*, IV, 1 and 2, Prague, 1857–1860.

———, *Zeugenverhör über den Tod König Ladislaws*. Abhandlungen der K. böhm. Gesellschaft d. Wissenschaften V. Folge, vol. 9, Prague, 1856.*

———, "O válečnému umění Čechů v XV století," *ČČM*, II, 1838, 3–11; *Radhost*, II, Prague, 1872, 70–76; *Spisý drobné* ed. Nováček, II, Prague, 1901, 11–16; *Dílo F. Palackého*, ed. Charvát, III, 1941, 161–168.

———, "Rodopis někdy panův z Cimburka," *Slovník naúčný*, II, 1861, 122–124; *Radhost*, II, 1872, 414–423, *Spisy drobné*, II, 324–331.

———, "Přehled současný nejvyšších důstojníků a úředníků," doplnil J. Charvát, in *Dílo F. Palackého*, I, Prague, 1941, 321ff.

Paparelli, Gioacchino, *Enea Silvio Piccolomini*. Bari, 1950.

Papee, Fryderyk, "Polityka polska w czasie upadku Jerzego z Podiebradu wobec kwestii następstwa w Czechach, 1466–1471," *Rozpravi z posiedzeń wydziału historyczno-filozoficznego Akademii Umiejetności*, VIII, Cracow, 1878, 345–454.

———, "Zabiegi o czeska koronę (1466–1471)," *Studya i szkice z czasów Kazimierza Jagiellończyka*, Warsaw, 1907, 51–140.

Pastor, Ludwig von, *Geschichte der Päpste seit dem Ausgang des Mittelalters*.* I and II, Freiburg i.B., many editions after 1885, (edition used here 4th, 1904). (Also in English translation, with differently numbered volumes, e.g. much of the content of II in III of English edition.)

Paulová, Milada, "Styky českých Husitů s Cařihradskou církví," *ČČM*, XCII, 1918, 1–20, 111–121, 215–228, 306–319.

———, "L'Empire byzantin et les Tchèques avant la chute de Constantinople," *Byzantinoslavica*, XIV, Prague, 1953, 158–225.

Pažout, Julius, "König Georg von Böhmen und die Konzilsfrage im Jahr 1467," *AÖG*, XL, Vienna, 1869, 323–371.*

Pelzel (Pelcl), F. M., *Geschichte der Böhmen*. I, Prague, 1817.

Peřinka, F. W., *Dějiny města Kroměříže*. I, Kroměříž, 1913.

Pervolf, J., "Čechové a Poláci v XV. a XVI. století," *Osvěta*, III, Prague, 1873, 774ff.

Peschek, Chr. A., *Handbuch der Geschichte von Zittau*. Zittau, 1837.

Peschke, Erhard, *Die Theologie der Böhmischen Brüder in ihrer Frühzeit*. (Forschungen zur Kirchen- und Geistesgeschichte, Vol V) Stuttgart, 1936.

Pešina, Jaroslav, "Studie k malířství poděbradské doby," *Umění*, r. VII, 3 Prague, 1959.

———, *Painting of the Gothic and Renaissance Periods, 1450–1550*. Prague, 1960.

Pfeiffer, Gerhard, *Das Breslauer Patriziat im Mittelalter*. (Darstellungen und Quellen zur schlesischen Geschichte, vol. 30), Breslau, 1929.

Pinkava, Viktor, "O rodišti krále Jiřího Poděbradského," *ČMM*, XXIX, Brno, 1905, 392–397.

Pogonowski, J., *Projekt związku władców króla Jerzego z Podiebrad*. Warsaw, 1932.

Polišenský, Josef V., *Doba Jiřího z Poděbrad*. Prague, 1940.

———, "Bohemia, the Turk and the Christian Commonwealth," *Byzantinoslavica*, XIV, Prague, 1953, 82–108.

———, "Problémy zahraniční politiky Jiřího z Poděbrad," *Acta Universitatis Palackianae Olomucensis*, 1960, pp. 107–125.

Pošvář, Jaroslav, "Slezsko v česko-polských politických vztazích v první polovině 15. století," *Slezský Sborník*, 1959, pp. 74–87.

———, "Poznámky k politickému postavení Slezska v III. čtvrtině 15. století," *Slezský Sborník*, I, 1960, 39–60.

Preidel, H., *Die Deutschen in Böhmen und Mähren, ein historischer Rückblick*. 2nd ed., Gräfeling, 1952.

Prochaska, Ant., "Jerzyk król Czechów," *Przegląd Powszechny*, XV, 11, Cracow, 1898.

Prokeš, Jaroslav, *M. Prokop z Plzně, Příspěvek k vývoji konservativní strany husitské* (Husitský Archiv, vol. III), Prague, 1927.

———, "K počátkům M. Jana Rokycany," *Věstník k. č. spol. nauk*, 1927, No. VI, Prague, 1928.

Pückert, Wilhelm, *Die kurfürstliche Neutralität während des Basler Konzils 1438–1448*. Leipzig, 1858.

Rachfahl, Felix, *Der Stettiner Erbfolgestreit, 1464–1472*. Breslau, 1890.

Ranke, Leopold, *Die Römischen Päpste in den letzten vier Jahrhunderten*. Many editions, e.g. Ranke's Meisterwerke, vol. VI, 1, Munich, 1915.

Rautenberg, Wilhelm, "Böhmische Söldner im Ordensland Preussen, 1454–1466." Dissertation, University of Hamburg, 1953.

Reuther, Hans, "Znaim und König Georg Podiebrad," *ZVGMS*, XXX, Brno, 1928, 173–187.

Říčan, Rudolf, *Dějiny Jednoty bratrské*. Prague, 1957.

———, *Die Böhmischen Brüder*. (German transl. of *Dejiny*) Berlin, 1961.

———, and others (ed. Hromádka), *Jednota Bratrska 1457–1957*. Prague 1956.

Richter, Heinrich M., *Georg von Poděbrad's Bestrebungen um Erlangung der deutschen Kaiserkrone und seine Beziehungen zu den deutschen Reichsfürsten*. Vienna, 1863.

Riedel, Adolf Friedrich, "Die Stellung Kurfürst Friedrichs II zu den von Georg

Podiebrad angeregten deutschen Fragen," *Märkische Forschungen,* VIII, Berlin, 1863.

———, "Zur Beurteilung des Aeneas Sylvius als Geschichtschreiber nach seinen Berichten über den Markgrafen Albrecht," *Monatsberichte der k. preuss. Akademie der Wissensch,* Berlin, 1867, 549–571.

Riezler, Sigmund, *Geschichte Baierns.* III, Gotha, 1889.

———, "Martin Mair," *ADB,* XX, 113–120.

Rocquain, Félix, *La cour de Rome et l'esprit de réforme avant Luther.* III, Paris, 1897.

Ropp, Goswin von der, "Zur Charakteristik des Kurfürsten Albrecht Achilles von Brandenburg," *Hohenzollern-Jahrbuch,* II, Berlin, 1808, 79ff.

Rowe, John Gordon, "The Tragedy of Aeneas Sylvius Piccolomini: an Interpretation," *Church History,* September 1961, 3, 288–313.

Ryba, K., "K biografii humanisty Jana z Rabštejna," *ČČH,* XLVI, 1940, 260–272.

Rynešová, Blažena, "O účasti Oldřicha z Rožmberka na jednání o mír mezi Táborskými a Rakousi," *ČČM,* CVII, Prague, 1933, 55–75.

Rýšavý, Richard, "Die erste Hussitenmission des hl. Johannes von Capestrano in Mähren," *Franziskanische Studien,* vol. 19, 1932, 224–255.

Salaba, Josef, "Jiří z Poděbrad a Oldřich z Rožmberka r. 1450," *Zvon,* Prague, 1903, pp. 113ff.

Šašková, G., *Jednota bratrská a konsistoř podoboji v době administrátorství M. Václava Korandy.* (Věstník k. č. společností nauk 1925, I) Prague, 1926.

Schalk, K., *Aus der Geschichte des österreichischen Faustrechts 1440–1463.* (Abhandl. z. Geschichte u. Quellenkunde d. Stadt Wien III), Vienna, 1919.*

Scharpff, Franz Anton, *Der Cardinal und Bischof Nicolaus von Cusa.* Mainz, 1843, and later edition: Tübingen, 1871.*

Schelz, T., "Gesamtgeschichte der Ober- und Niederlausitz," *Neues Lausitzisches Magazin,* vol. 58, Görlitz, 1882.

Schieche, E., "Schlesiens Kampf gegen Böhmen, 1460–1474," in *Geschichte Schlesiens,* II, Breslau, 1938.

Schlesinger, Ludwig, "Die Apologie der Kaadner gegen Georg von Podiebrad," *MVGDB,* XIII, Prague, 1875, 126–143.*

Schmidt, Otto Eduard, *Gregor von Heimburgs Kampf und Vermächtnis.* (Schriften zur Grenzlandkunde vol. XII), Dresden, 1937.

———, "Des Böhmenkönigs Georg von Podiebrad Lösung vom Kirchenbann und sein Tod," *Neues Archiv für sächsische Geschichte,* vol. 59, Dresden, 1938, 39–65.

Schmidt, Valentin, Die Fälschung von Kaiser- und Königskunden durch Ulrich von Rosenberg," *MVGDB,* XXXII, 317ff; 33, pp. 181ff., Prague, 1894, 1895.

———, Das Rosenberger Dominium und dessen Umgebung 1457–1460," *MVGDB,* XXXVII, Prague, 1898, 287–308.

Schmidt, Walter E., "Das religiöse Leben in den ersten Zeiten der Brüderunität," *Zeitschrift für Brüdergeschichte,* I, 1907.

Schrötter, G., "Dr. Martin Mair, ein biographischer Beitrag zur Geschichte der Reformation des XV. Jhds." Dissertation, University of München, 1896.

Schulz, N. (?), "Versuch einer Ehrenrettung Georg Podiebrads, Königs in Böhmen und Marggrafens der Lausitz, von dem Verdacht des Königsmordes," *Neue Lausitzische Monatsschrift,* VII, Görlitz, 1806, 294–345.

Schürer, Oskar, *Prag, Kultur, Kunst, Geschichte.* Munich, 1930. (Also later editions.)

——, *Geschichte von Burg und Pfalz Eger.* Munich, 1934.

Schürmeyer, W., *Das Kardinalskollegium unter Pius II.* Marburg, 1914.

Schwarzenberg, Prince Karl, *Die Sankt Wenzels-Krone und die böhmischen Insignien.* Vienna, 1960.

Schwarzer, Otfried, "Stadt und Fürstentum Breslau in ihrer politischen Umwelt im Mittelalter," *ZVGS,* LXV, Breslau, 1931, pp. 54–90.

Schwitzky, Ernst, *Der europäische Fürstenbund Georgs von Poděbrad.* Marburg, 1907.

Sedláček, Augustin, *Děje města Čáslavě.* Prague, 1874.

——, "Ještě o rodišti Jiříka z Kunštátu. O mateři Jiříka," *ČMM,* XXX, Brno, 1906, 54–63.

Sedlák, Jan, *Studie a texty k náboženským dějinám českým.* 2 vols. Olomouc, 1914, 1915.

Seibt, Ferdinand, "Gutsherrschaft und Grunduntertanen im böhmischen Ständestaat," *Bohemia, Jahrbuch des Collegium Carolinum,* Munich, 1962, pp. 225–238.

Seppelt, Franz Xaver, *Geschichte des Bistums Breslau.* Breslau 1929; republished in 1948 as *Das Bistum Breslau im Wandel der Jahrhunderte.*

——, *Das Papsttum im Spätmittelalter.* Leipzig, 1941 (Geschichte der Päpste, vol. IV) also 2nd ed., revised by G. Schwaiger, Munich, 1957.

Seton-Watson, R. W., ed., *Prague Essays.* (To the 600th anniversary of the University of Prague), Oxford, 1949.

Siegl, Dr. Karl, "Zeugnisse für die Rechtgläubigkeit der Stadt Eger vor Verhängung des Interdikts 1467," *MVGDB,* XLII, 1904.

——, "Zur Geschichte der Fürstentage Georgs von Podiebrad in Eger in den Jahren 1459, 1461 und 1467," *MVGDB,* XLII, 1904.

Sigmund, Paul E., *Nicholas of Cusa and Medieval Political Thought.* Cambridge, Mass., 1963.

Šimek, František, "Ukázky kazatelské činností neznámého husitského kněže," *ČČM,* CVII, 1933, 183–205.

——, *Učení M. Jana Rokycany.* (Rozpravy české akademie věd a umění, class III, No. 77) Prague, 1938.

——, "M. Jan Rokycana," *Hrdinové a věštci českéko národa,* Přerov, 1948, pp. 246–268.

————, *O životě a díle Petra Chelčického.* Prague, 1950.

Šimek, Joseph, *Kutná Hora v XV. a XVI. stoleti.* Kutná Hora, 1907.

Šmahel, František, "Počátky humanismu na pražské universitě v době poděbradské," *Acta Univ. Carol., Historia,* Prague, 1960, pp. 55–90.

Smirin, M. M., *Deutschland vor der Reformation.* Berlin, 1955.

Sommerfeld, Gustav, "Aus Dr. Gregor Heimburgs letzten Lebensjahren," *MVGDB,* LXIX, 1931, 46ff.

Špirko, Jozef, *Husiti, jiskrovci a bratríci v dejinách Spiša.* Levoča, 1937.

Stachon, B., *Polityka Polski wobec Turcyi i akcji antytureckiej w wieku XV.* Lwów, 1930.

Stědry, F., *Dějiny města Louny.* Louny, 1930.

Stein, Walter, "Über den angeblichen Plan eines Bündnisses der Hansestädte mit König Georg von Böhmen 1458," *Hansische Geschichtsblätter,* Leipzig, 1897, 239ff.

Steinmetz, Max, ed., *Die frühbürgerliche Revolution in Deutschland.* (Sektion Mediävistik der Deutschen Historiker-Gesellschaft, Vol. II), Berlin, 1960.

Sternberg, K., *Umrisse einer Geschichte des Böhmischen Bergbaues.* Prague, 1837.

Stieber, Miloslav, *Böhmische Staatsverträge.* (Forsch. z. inn. Gesch. Österr., ed. Dopsch, vol. 8) I (Seit Přemysl Ottokar II bis zur Gründung des habsburgischen Reiches). Innsbruck, 1912.*

Stloukal, Karel, "Z diplomatických styků mezi Francii a Čechami před Bílou Horou," *ČČH,* XXXII, 1926, 473–496.

Sturm, Heribert, *Eger, Geschichte einer Reichsstadt.* 2 vols., Augsburg, 1951, 1952.

Supan, A. G., *Die vier letzten Lebensjahre des Grafen Ulrich II von Cilli.* Vienna, 1868.

Sutowicz, J., *Walka Kazimierza Jagiellończyka z Maciejem Korwinem.* Cracow, 1877.

Szécsen, Count A., "Gedächtnisrede auf König Mathias vor der Historischen Gesellschaft Budapest," *Ungarische Revue,* X, 1890, 503ff.

Tadra, Ferdinand, "K pobytu Jana Kapistrána v zemích českých," *Věstník k. č. spol. nauk,* 1889, 31–48.*

Taillandier, Saint-René, *Bohème et Hongrie.* Paris, 1862.

————, "Le roi Georges de Podiébrad, épisode de l'histoire de Bohème," *Revue des deux mondes,* XL, 605–650, 915–956, XLI, 118–163, Paris, 1862.

Tapié, Victor L., *Une église tschèque au XVe siècle: L'unité des frères.* Paris, 1934.

Tenora, Jan, "Z mladých let pana Jiřího z Kunštátu a z Poděbrad," *ČČM,* LXIX, Prague, 1895, 290–297.

Teplý, František, *Dějiny města Jindřichova Hradce.* J. Hradec, 1927.

Ter Meulen, Jacob, *Der Gedanke der internationalen Organisation in seiner Entwickelung 1300–1800.* The Hague, 1917.

Thudichum, Friedrich, *Papsttum und Reformation im Mittelalter, 1143–1517*. Leipzig, 1903.

Titz, Karel, *Ohlasy husitského válečnictví v Evropě*. Prague, 1922.

Tobolka, Zdeněk, "Byl Jiří z Poděbrad přitomen bitvě u Lipan?" *ČČM*, 1896, 260–261.

——, *O volbě a korunování Jiřího z Poděbrad*. Prague, 1896.

——, *O životě a spisech Hilaria Litoměřického*. (Hist. Archiv české akademie věd, XIII) Prague, 1898.

——, "Styky krále Jiřího z Poděbrad s králem polským Kazimírem," *ČMM*, XX, Brno, 1898, 70–76, 163–175, 300–310, 373–384.

Toews, John B., "Emperor Frederick III and the Papacy." Dissertation, University of Colorado, Boulder, 1962.

——, "Dream and Reality in the Imperial Ideology of Pope Pius II," Medievalia et Humanistica, 16, Boulder 1964, pp. 77–93.

Tomaschek, J. A., *Recht und Verfassung der Markgrafschaft Mähren im XV. Jahrhundert*. Brno, 1863.

Tomek, Ernst, *Kirchengeschichte Österreichs*. II, Innsbruck-Vienna, 1948.

Tomek, Václav Vladivoj, *Dějepis města Prahy*. 2nd ed. (ed. Novotný) VI and VII, Prague, 1906; 1st ed., VIII and IX, Prague, 1893.

——, *Geschichte der Prager Universität*. Prague, 1849.

——, "Chování měšťanů Chebských v rozepří králů Jiřího a Vladislava s papežským dvorem a Matiášem králem uherským," *ČČM*, XXIII, part IV, Prague, 1849, 74–102. Same in German: *Abhdl. d. K. Böhm. Gesellschaft d. Wissensch.*, v. Folge, 6, 1849, 36ff.

Toth, Zoltan, *Matyás király idegen zsoldosserege*, Budapest, 1925.

Toth-Szabo, P., *A cseh huszita mozgalmak es uralom törtenete Magyarorszagon*. Budapest, 1917.

Trnka, František, *Náboženské poměry při kutnohorské konsistoři r. 1464–1574*. (Vestník K. č. spol. nauk), Prague, 1932.

Truhlár, Josef, *Počátky humanismu v Čechách*. (Rozpravy české akademie, Ročník I, tř. III, No. 3) Prague, 1892.

——, "Snahy o nástupce Rokycanova v hodnosti arcibiskupské," *Věstník české akademie*, Prague, 1901, pp. 100ff.

Uhlirz, Karl and Mathilde, *Handbuch der Geschichte Oesterreichs und seiner Nachbarländer Böhmen und Ungarn*. 4 vols., 1927–1944. New ed., Graz 1963.

Ullmann, C., *Reformatoren vor der Reformation*. Gotha, 1866.

Urbánek, Rudolf, "Kancelář krále Jiřího," *ČČH*, XVII, Prague, 1911, 13–27.

——, "K české pověsti královské," *Časopis společnosti přatel starožitnosti*, XXIII, 1915.

——, *Věk Poděbradský* (*České Dějiny*, ed. Novotný etc., part III) 4 vols., Prague, 1915 to 1962.

——, *Jiří z Poděbrad a česká národní království*. Prague, 1920.

——, *Jednota Bratrská a vyšší vzděláni až do doby Blahoslavovy*. (Spisy filos. fakulty Masarykovy university, No. 1) Brno, 1923.

——, *Konec Ladislava Pohrobka*. (Rozpravy české akademie věd a uměni, Class I, No. 67) Prague, 1924.

——, *Žižka v památkách a úctě lidu českého*. (Spisy filos. fakulty Masarykovy university 10), Brno, 1924.

——, *Táborství po Žižkovi*. (Žizkova doba, Vol. 5) Prague, 1924.

——, *Husitský král*. Prague, 1926.

——, *Dvě studie o době poděbradské*. (Spisy filos. fakulty Masarykovy university v Brno No. 27), Brno, 1929.

——, "Doba poděbradská," *Československá vlastivěda*, IV, *Dějiny*, Prague, 1932, 226–269.

——, *Volba Jiřího z Poděbrad za krále Českého*. (Sborník přispěvku k dějinám hlavního města Prahy díl V), Prague, 1932.

——, *Lipany a konec polních vojsk*. Prague, 1934.

——, "K 500 výročí českých polních rot na Slovensku," *Vojensko-historický sborník*, V, 1, Prague, 1936.

——, "Idea českého státu za Jiřího z Poděbrad," *Idea československého státu*, Prague, 1936. (Also in German "Die böhmische Staatsidee unter Georg von Podiebrad," in *Die Tschechoslowakische Republik*: Prague, 1937.)

——, "První utrakvistický humanista Šimon ze Slaného," *LF*, LXV, Prague, 1938, 220–228, 335–347.

——, Contributions on the Poděbradian Age in V. Mathesius, ed., *Co daly naše země Evropě a lidstvu*, Prague, 1939, pp. 102–107, 111–123.

——, "Tři Janové z Rabštejna," *Sborník filologický*, XI, Prague, 1939, 199–238.

——, "K historii doby Jiskrovy na Slovensku a ve východní Moravě," *Věstník české spol. nauk.*, tř. fil. 1939, No. II, Prague, 1940.

——, "Ženy husitského krále: Kunhuta ze Šternberka a Johana z Rožmitálu," *Královny, kněžny a velké ženy české*, Prague, 1940, 175–186.

——, "K ikonografii Jiřího krále," *Věstník české akademie věd* No. 61, Prague, 1952, pp. 50–62.

——, "Humanistický novoutrakvista M. Matouš Kollin z Choteřiny a starší tradice husitská," *Časopis společnosti přatel starožitnosti*, vol. 64, Prague, 1956.

——, *Z husitského věku, Výbor historických uváh a studii*. Prague, 1957. (With complete bibliography of U.'s works).

——, "Jan Paleček, šašek krále Jiřího, a jeho předchůdci v zemích českých," *Přispěvky k dějinám starší české literatury*, Prague, 1958.

——, "K pětistému vyroči královské volby Jiřího z Poděbrad," *Věstník čsl. akademie věd*, 1959.

Valois, Noel, *Le Pape et le Concile, 1418–1450*. Paris, 1909.

——, *La crise réligieuse du XVe. siècle*. Paris, 1909.

Vancsa, Max, *Geschichte Nieder- und Oberösterreichs* (Allgemeine Staaten-geschichte III, 6). II, Stuttgart, 1927.

Valouch, see Walouch.

Vaněček, Václav, "Zapomenutá česká vizitka," *Literární Noviny*, No. 31, Prague, August 1963.

———, "Eine Weltfriedensorganisation nach den Vorschlägen Georgs von Podiebrad und des J. A. Comenius," *Sitzungsberichte der d. Akademie der Wissensch. zu Berlin*, Kl. für Philosophie, 1962, No. 3, Berlin, 1963.

Vansteenberghe, Edmond, *Le Cardinal Nicholas de Cues, 1401–1464*. Paris, 1920.

Varillas, Antoine, *Histoire de Louis XI*. 4 vols., Paris, 1689.

Varsick, Branislav, "Husitské posadky na Slovensku a ich vplyv na svoje okolie" (Husiti na Slovensku III). *Sborník filozofickej fakulty University Komenského*, XI, Historica, Bratislava 1960, pp. 3–77.

Vast, H., *Le Cardinal Bessarion (1403–1472)*. Paris, 1878.

Vogl, Carl, *Peter Cheltschizki, ein Prophet an der Wende der Zeiten*. Zürich and Leipzig, 1926.

Voigt, Friedrich, *Geschichte des brandenburgisch-preussischen Staates*. 2nd ed., I, Berlin, 1867.

Voigt, Georg, *Enea Silvio de' Piccolomini, als Papst Pius II, und sein Zeitalter*. 3 vols. Berlin, 1856, 1863.

———, "Georg von Böhmen, der Hussitenkönig," *HZ*, 1861.

———, "Johannes von Capistrano, ein Heiliger des 15. Jahrhunderts," *HZ*, X, 1863, 19–96.

———, "Friedrich III," *ADB*, VII, 1878, 448–452.

Voigt, Johannes, *Geschichte Preussens*. 9 vols. Königsberg, 1827—, (mainly VIII and IX, 1838, 1839).

Vojtíšek, Václav, "Na Táboře v letech 1432–1450," *Sborník Žižkův*, ed. Urbánek, Prague, 1924, pp. 134–148.

Volf, Josef, "Rokycanův traktát proti Hilariovu Lucisti pekelnému," *ČČM*, LXXXIII, Prague, 1909, 226–233.*

———, "Hilaria z Litoměřic Traktát Arcus gehennalis," *ČČM*, 1911, 33–68.*

———, "Jafetův 'druhý traktát' Hilaria z Litoměřic," *ČČM*, 1911, 305–317.*

———, "Mikulas Jaquerius a jeho dialog s Rokycanou," *ČČM*, No. 87, Prague, 1913.*

———, *Geschichte des Buchdrucks in Böhmen und Mähren*. Transl. J. Langer, Weimar, 1928.

Volkmer, F., "Georg Podiebrad und die Ereignisse seiner Zeit im Glatzer Lande," *Glatzer Vierteljahrschrift VI*, 1886–1887, pp. 177–207.

Wallner, J., "Iglaus Widerstand gegen die Anerkennung Georgs von Podiebrad," *MVGDB*, XX, Prague, 1884, 103–120.

Walouch (Valouch) František, *Žiwotopis swatého Jana Kapistrána*. Brno, 1858.

Wandruszka, Adam, *Das Haus Habsburg*. 2nd ed., Stuttgart, 1959

Weigel, H. "Kaiser, Kurfürst und Jurist," from *Aus Reichstagen des 15. und 16. Jahrhunderts* (Schriftenreihe d. hist. Kommission b. d. bayer. Ak. d. Wiss. No. 5), Göttingen, 1958.

Weiss, Adolf, *Chronik der Stadt Breslau*. Breslau, 1888.

Weiss, Anton, *Aeneas Sylvius, als Papst Pius II,* mit 149 bisher ungedruckten Briefen, Graz, 1897.*

Weizsäcker, Wilhelm, "Über die Nationalitätenverhältnisse in Böhmen von den Hussitenkriegen bis zur Schlacht am Weissen Berge," *MVGDB*, XLI, 1924, 117ff.

——, "Fürstenbund und Völkerbund," *Prager juristische Zeitschrift*, X, 1930, 234–245.

Wendt, H., "Die Stände des Fürstentums Breslau im Kampfe mit König Mathias Corvinus 1469–1490," *ZVGAS*, V 1. 32.

Werner, Ernst, ed., *Städtische Volksbewegungen im 14. Jahrhundert.* (Sektion Mediävistik der Deutschen Historiker-Gesellschaft Vol. I), Berlin, 1960.

Widmer, Berthe, *Enea Silvio Piccolomini.* Biographie und ausgewählte Texte, Basel, 1960.*

Winter, Zikmund, *Dějiny řemesel a obchodu v Čechách v XIV. a v XV. století.* Prague, 1906.

Wostry, W., *König Albrecht II.* (Prager Studien aus dem Gebiet der Geschichtswissenschaften), Prague, 1906, 1907.

Wurscher, A., *Die Beziehung des Königs Mathias von Ungarn zu Georg von Podiebrad und Wladislaw von Böhmen.* Vienna, 1885.

Zaun, J., *Rudolf von Rüdesheim, Fürstbischof von Breslau.* Frankfurt, 1881.

Zeissberg, H. R. von, "Der österreichische Erbfolgestreit nach dem Tode des Königs Ladislaus Postumus," *AÖG*, LVIII, 1–170, and book edition, Vienna, 1879.

Zellmer, W., *Zur polnischen Politik des Kurfürsten Friedrich II von Brandenburg.* Berlin, 1883.

Ziehen, Edward, *Mittelrhein und Reich im Zeitalter der Reichsreform.* 1934.

Zimmermann, A., *Die kirchlichen Verfassungskämpfe im 15. Jahrhundert.* Breslau, 1882.

Zinkeisen, Joh. Wilh., *Geschichte des osmanischen Reiches in Europa.* II, Gotha, 1854.

Zöllner, Erich, *Geschichte Oesterreichs.* 2nd ed., Munich, 1961.

Zucker, A., "Jiří z Poděbrad a české mezinárodní otázky v XV. století," *Česká Revue*, vol. 4, 1901, 129–136.

INDEX

INDEX

Wenceslas of Krumlov, Catholic Prelate, 64, 182–83
Westphalia, 35
West-Prussia, 422
Weissenbach, Hermann of, Saxon chancellor, 576
Weissenburg, city of, 570
Wettin, dynasty of, 116, 162, 186–89, 193, 214, 417, 554
Wiener-Neustadt, 49, 59, 128–30, 165, 195, 201, 209, 215, 321, 324, 327, 346, 350, 353, 355, 357, 375, 378, 396–97, 431, 433, 551
Wiesenburg, John of, 380–81
Wildstein, castle of, 47, 49, 96
William, Duke of Saxony (Weimar), 35–36, 47, 131, 204, 219, 346, 427, 572; his claim for the Bohemian throne, 154, 156, 158–62, 186–87, 295; his arrangement with King George, 188–92
William II, German Emperor, 126
Witold, Grand Duke of Lithuania, 155
Wittelsbach, dynasty of, 122, 186, 187, 214, 217, 349, 417, 471, 510, 547, 554, 582
Władysław III, King of Poland and Hungary, 12, 125, 296
Wölfl (Welfl) of Warnsdorf, Bohemian captain, 380, 522, 566, 568
Worms, Bishopric of, 213
Wunsiedel, town of, 188, 189
Württemberg, principality of, 187
Würzburg, city of, 415–16
Wyclyf, John, 245, 270

Zábřeh, town of, 505
Zajíc of Hasenburg, John, Chief Justice of the Royal Court Chamber, 387, 397, 441, 458, 525, 532–33, 540
Zajíc of Hasenburg, barons of, 20, 387, 397, 456–58, 473
Zajíc of Hasenburg, Nicholas, 102
Zajíc of Hasenburg, Ulrich of, 398, 525, 532
Zajíc of Hasenburg, Zbyněk of, Chief Justice of the State Supreme Court, 48, 188 225, 387
Zapolyai, Imre, 482
Zapolyai, Stephen, 482
Žatec, city of, 62, 296
Zator, duchy of, 297
Zelená Hora (Grünberg), castle of, 395; League of (Union of rebellious Catholic lords), 43, 335, 400, 403–5, 435, 439, 442–44, 447, 451, 453, 456–57, 486, 488–89, 524, 538, 545, 568–69, 619
Želiv, monastery of, 175
Želivský, John, 175
Zemské desky (Court registers), 100–1, 400
Žerotín, Lords of, 591
Žídek, Paul, Czech Catholic master and author, 596, 609
Zittau (Žitava), city of, 440, 499, 542
Žižka, Jan, Hussite general, 5, 14, 16–17, 21, 23, 26, 60, 65, 106, 138, 164, 271, 406, 497, 508, 513, 599, 610, 619
Zlin, town of, 564
Znojmo, city of, 19, 127, 133, 140, 161, 173–74, 176, 206, 209, 257, 449, 495–97, 565–66
Zornstein, castle of, 385
Zvole, castle of, 505
Zwingli, Huldreich, 25, 605